AT THE HEART OF REASON

Northwestern University
Studies in Phenomenology
and
Existential Philosophy

AT THE HEART OF REASON

Claude Romano

Translated from the French by Michael B. Smith
and Claude Romano

Northwestern University Press
Evanston, Illinois

Northwestern University Press
www.nupress.northwestern.edu

Printed in the United States of America

10 9 8 7 6 5 4 3 2 1

Library of Congress Cataloging-in-Publication Data

Romano, Claude, 1967– author.
[Au coeur de la raison, la phénoménologie. English]
At the heart of reason / Claude Romano ; translated from the French by Michael B. Smith and Claude Romano.
pages cm. — (Northwestern University studies in phenomenology and existential philosophy)
"Originally published in French as Au coeur de la raison, la phénoménologie by Editions Gallimard, Paris, 2010."
ISBN 978-0-8101-3137-8 (pbk. : alk. paper) — ISBN 978-0-8101-3138-5 (cloth : alk. paper)
1. Phenomenology. I. Title. II. Series: Northwestern University studies in phenomenology & existential philosophy.
B2433.R663A813 2015
142'.7—dc23

2015011487

For I am not of the same opinion as an excellent man who recommends that when one has once convinced himself of something one should afterward not doubt it any more. In pure philosophy that will not do. . . . One must rather weigh the propositions in all sorts of applications . . . try out the opposite, and postpone decision until the truth is illuminated from all sides.

—Immanuel Kant

The test of a first-rate intelligence is the ability to hold two opposed ideas in the mind at the same time, and still retain the ability to function. One should, for example, be able to see that things are hopeless and yet be determined to make them otherwise.

—F. Scott Fitzgerald

Contents

Preface

This work, like all philosophical works, has more than one goal. To simplify, it pursues three main objectives.

First, it attempts to formulate as clearly as possible what I will call *the phenomenological problem.* Does our experience possess immanent structures, and if so, what is their status? Are they contingent or necessary? Are they autonomous—and to what point—with respect to the instituted rules of language and the conceptual schemes by means of which they can be expressed and thought? To address this problem, to take it as the guideline for a philosophical investigation cannot obviously constitute a neutral attitude with respect to what was called, at the end of the 1960s, the "linguistic turn," and what has given "analytic" philosophy its present form. To maintain that the phenomenological problem continues to be relevant today amounts to implying that the *linguistic turn,* whatever its merits may otherwise be, has not made a philosophy of experience superfluous; nor has it cast any decisive light on the relationship between experience and language. Far from having brought us an answer to this problem, it has made it more acute.

Secondly, this book defends, in all of its ramifications, what might be called a *phenomenological thesis*: there is indeed an autonomy of the prelinguistic order, of "prepredicative" experience, as Husserl would have said, with respect to the higher forms of thought, and to language. Experience possesses an immanent logos, and it is precisely this logos that phenomenology intends to bring to light. Furthermore, language itself only becomes fully intelligible once it has been re-situated in its relation to a prelinguistic intelligence—which is one with our being-in-the-world—that constitutes its soil, its germinative ground.

The intelligence of language is in close continuity with a prelinguistic intelligence inherent in our *experience* of the world itself, of others, of ourselves, to which it is connected by an umbilical tie. This is why the analysis of language cannot constitute the exclusive methodological organon of philosophy. If language is not an empire within an empire, if it prolongs and modifies a prelinguistic intelligence that possesses its inalienable right, the *linguistic turn* can be nothing but an impasse.

Finally, this phenomenological thesis, to be understood and pursued in all its consequences, calls for a critical deconstruction of the received concept of experience—a deconstruction which will be undertaken in part 2 of the present work. The defining trait of historical phenomenology is to have conceived of experience in a profoundly original way that does not enter into the coordinates of the empiricism versus Kantianism debate. The necessity with which we will be faced of transforming the Husserlian concept of experience will not lead us to renounce this originality, but rather to deepen it. I will challenge what I call the "Kantian framework" (or better, the empiricist-Kantian framework) that prescribes its limits to much of contemporary philosophy—not only "continental" but "analytic" as well. This framework essentially consists in a view of experience that conceives all its order and structuring as alien to it, as stemming from language, culture, and their schemes. A certain linguistic philosophy, realizing Hamann's hope,[1] has in fact installed language in the position of the Kantian categories. In this view, the senses have no sense besides the one language bestows on them; the sensible dimension of an aesthetic has no autonomy with respect to a "pure logic." Analytic philosophy in some of its contemporary versions thus rehabilitates the "constructions" of neo-Kantianism "that come from on high," as Husserl used to call them. Experience, in this view, is considered as *conceptual* through and through. The critique of this Kantian framework is the third objective of this book.

It suffices to express these objectives to see the importance of the problems raised. What is at stake in phenomenology is not only the status of experience as such, nor the status of language and its meanings, but their problematic unity and, through it, the problem of reason itself. Phenomenology did not invent the idea of descriptive philosophy; it cannot be reduced to a new Cartesianism; it does not necessarily end up being a thought of Being; nor does it exhaust itself in a renewed characterization of the world, the subject, or experience. What it attempts to elaborate first and foremost is *a new image of reason.*

Husserl was perfectly aware of this. In his view, beyond reason that is restricted to logic, beyond a theory of the proposition, of its relations of valid inference and its truth conditions, beyond mathematics and the natural sciences in general—or rather *below* them—there exists a "logic of the world," grasped in its sensible epiphany, in its primordial appearance, a *Weltlogik,* or, as he also says, "a logos of the aesthetic world"[2] that we can—that we must—try to bring to light. In order to speak of a "logic" of the world or a logos that is immanent in sensibility, the concept of logos must first be extricated from a theory of the psychological faculties. "The word reason," Husserl writes, "is not meant here in the sense of a faculty of the human soul."[3] Thus experience, the infra-rational, is not irrational: it is neither the pure raw datum to which the empiricists have acclimatized us, nor that same datum completed and shaped by concepts or categories, as in the picture given by the neo-Kantians, which ends up reducing the "given" itself to the infinite progress of reason. In opposition to this concept of reason, which Husserl characterizes as "narrow-hearted," in contrast with an *engherzige Vernunft*,[4] we should set a reason that is broadened to include its other, namely sensibility, experience, the prepredicative: a big-hearted reason that rehabilitates the sensible world as being necessary to its very existence. As Heidegger will say, freely interpreting Aristotle's famous formula, *oudepote noei aneu phantasmatos ē psukhē* (the soul never thinks without an image),[5] and in fact paraphrasing the *Logical Investigations*, "A thought without a founding sensuousness is absurd."[6] Husserl continued in the passage to which this sentence implicitly refers: "*The idea of a 'pure intellect,'* interpreted as a 'faculty' of pure thought (here, of categorical action) and *totally isolated* from any 'faculty of sensibility' could only be conceived of *prior to* an elementary analysis of knowledge in its obviously irreducible components." It is too soon to examine whether this affirmation is warranted. The fact remains: it is to an enlarged reason that Husserl intends to lead us back, by bringing us back to the "things themselves." It is this big-hearted reason, which situates the heart of reason in the relationship between thought and the sensible world, which is the main object of his research. Phenomenology, even when focusing on history and culture, even when devoted to describing logical and mathematical idealities, does not abandon that enlarged reason (as opposed to an autarchic and self-sufficient one) that is its telos and raison d'être. It is not an infra-rationalism, but a "super-rationalism," to borrow an expression that Husserl used one day in a letter to Lévy-Bruhl.[7]

Since this book is concerned first of all with reason, it will come as no surprise that it is also a book about method. In our day, it is as if an embarrassed silence surrounded questions of method in phenomenology—a silence that has become almost deafening in contemporary French phenomenology. It is as if to go into methodological questions were tantamount to preferring sterile preliminaries to "the things themselves." As if phenomenology were less a "*methodological conception*" (*Methodenbegriff*),[8] as Heidegger said in 1927, than the discovery of "a new style in philosophy" (Levinas).[9] Along these same lines, a recent commentator has argued that it is "the most grievous misinterpretation to make it [phenomenology] into a method,"[10] adding, in passing, that phenomenology "is less the name of a domain of objects, a method or a philosophical tradition than a quality or virtue. . . . In other words, a work of phenomenology works similarly to the way a beautiful picture does: it allows us to see, without our always being able to say why."[11]

As may have become apparent, nothing could be further from the perspective taken up by the present book than this landscape-painter conception or practice of phenomenology. Quite to the contrary, I will take seriously the numerous and extremely difficult problems raised by the very idea of *phenomenological description.* The painter is not called upon to justify his or her artistic activity: the justification for such activity lies in the quality of the paintings produced thereby. But such a justification *is* required of the phenomenologist, because phenomenology is a *philosophical* undertaking and philosophy cannot be sundered from the *logon didonai,* from the necessity of "giving one's reasons," or, to translate the Platonic formula in a different way, from the need for "justifying what you advance." The following pages are, for the most part, devoted to such a justification. As for those readers who may feel so comfortable within phenomenology as it stands that it would not even occur to them to question its validity—this book is not for them. It will not attempt to disturb their philosophical peace of mind.

There is a certain misunderstanding, at times willfully maintained, surrounding the problem of method. If Husserl has taught us anything, it is that method is not introduced into philosophy from the outside, that it does not consist in a set of empty precepts decreed in the abstract,[12] that is, independently of the objects upon which this discipline bears; rather, the method in this case is inseparable from the philosophical approach itself, and from the "thing," or "subject matter" (*Sache*) to which it purports to lead us back. A method is not only an approach, a way of proceeding. It has a *normative* function. To know how to get to the truth is to know what justifications can be given for one's assertions, and it is to know thereby *what is true.* Truth and method cannot be sundered. Even if philosophical activity is taken to be purely descriptive, the issue of how to describe is but one with that of what justification can be given for the rightness, the relevance, the "truth" of a description. In phenomenology, as in philosophy, method is the thing itself.

If we must not underestimate the importance of method, neither must we overestimate it. Precisely because there is, in philosophy, no universal agreement on the method to be followed, the latter only manifests itself generally through actual philosophical practice; it is less a "methodology," that is, a body of abstract rules defined in advance, than an attempt to justify conclusions after the fact. This is why method is also philosophy itself. But a philosophy cannot be reduced to a method: it draws most of its strength from the radicalness and novelty of its questioning. In this sense, as Heidegger insisted, "there is no such thing as *the one* phenomenology, and if there could be such a thing it would never become anything like a philosophical technique. . . . The only thing that is truly new in science and in philosophy is the genuine questioning and struggle with things which is at the service of this questioning."[13] Everything is controversial in a great philosophy, except the depth of the questioning from which it is drawn.

If we agree to these two claims—the internal link between method and justification, and the view according to which any philosophy worthy of the name advances by the questions it raises beyond what it is capable of justifying when it formulates its own method—then we must conclude that the truth of a philosophy (or of a philosophical trend) that goes beyond what it can justify corresponds rather to what it *could ideally justify* concerning its assertions. This is why the present work is both an introduction to phenomenology (in the sense of an introduction *into* phenomenology, a self-presentation of this approach), and a transformation of phenomenology: the attempt at a better justification of its fundamental theses—a self-presentation of phenomenology *as* its own transformation.

There is no other justification in philosophy than that which can be given by a convincing argumentation. Argumentation is the life of all thought aspiring to some rigor. Contrary to a widespread misconception, phenomenology is no exception to this rule, even if certain of its main arguments are sometimes elliptic, implicit, or just barely sketched out. The style of this book will, accordingly, be mainly argumentative. Here again, it is important to avoid both underestimating and overestimating the power of argumentation in philosophy. Every reasoning proceeds from premises, which can always be subjected to further questioning. Furthermore, many philosophical arguments are not conclusive, in the sense that there is no genuine contradiction in accepting their premises and denying their conclusion—especially in the cases in which those premises or that conclusion contain ambiguities and can be interpreted in several different ways. But even when arguments are conclusive, it remains to be determined whether their premises are of any interest. Even the greatest formal rigor does not guarantee that a particular argument will have philosophical significance and "weight." Conversely, the most important philosophers are not always those who are "technically" the most irreproachable: we may find many contradictions and questionable conclusions among the greatest of them. It is the radicalness of his or her questions that distinguishes the true philosopher, and not mere considerations of coherence.

At once a retrospective and a prospective work, this volume attempts to clarify problems through history and history through problems. It never considers phenomenology as a fixed set of doctrines, and even less as an available collection of already settled claims that it would suffice to welcome and take for granted. "In every serious philosophical question," said Wittgenstein, "uncertainty extends to the very roots of the problem,"[14] and it is at the roots of this uncertainty, that is, at the roots of the *phenomenological problem*, that I have tried to situate myself. My purpose is to recapture the living movement of a genesis: the one phenomenology brings along itself, when it proposes new problems even more than new solutions. But this movement will be approached *through its contrast with other trends of contemporary philosophy and in a permanent dialogue with them.* Hence it will come as no surprise that "analytic" philosophy is almost as present in these pages as so-called "continental" philosophy. To bring these two traditions, which have so long ignored each other or only perceived the most superficial aspects of each other, into a mutual dialogue often requires a return to what is the most simple—and which, as we know, is always the most difficult—by examining elementary examples chosen for that very reason: among others, the spatial object, sound, or color. Here, the greatest conceptual sophistication rejoins the most basic, the most fundamental. Some of our analyses, especially at the beginning of the volume, will have something of the phenomenological kindergarten and of the object lesson about them.

To those who may wonder at the omnipresence of Husserl, the importance given to Heidegger and Merleau-Ponty, and the relative absence of other well-known figures in phenomenology, let me say that this is not a history book; my purpose is not to furnish an exhaustive ledger of phenomenological "doctrines," but only to sketch out the fundamental questions underlying them. When we try to delve more deeply into this matter, sooner or later we come up against Husserl. Not that the answers he brings us are always uncontroversial, but it is not rare that he has formulated the right questions.

The purpose of this book, then, may be stated as an attempt to elaborate the problems underlying historical phenomenology, or, better yet, as the elevation of phenomenology itself to the status of a problem. If, in philosophy, asking the right questions is far more important than being able to give the right answers; if, behind every assertion, a question lies hidden that must often be uncovered, then lifting phenomenology to the level of a question is not as easy a task as may be commonly supposed. At every moment, at every stage, I have tried not only to reconstruct what phenomenology has been, but to ask myself what it should be. This is why this book is also a personal work of phenomenology, the limitations and impasses of which are my own responsibility. It calls for a certain degree of endurance on the part of the reader, even though it is addressed to the philosophically minded reader in general, without expecting on his or her part a mastery of the basic phenomenological concepts. It sometimes takes the liberty to move through certain byways, excursus, and digressions—but only apparently so. For here it is not the trip that is worth the detour, but rather "the detour that is worth the trip."[15]

A French author, quoted by Conrad, used to say that the novel was "*trop difficile!*" If so, what of philosophy? But Conrad concluded: "It is indeed *too* arduous in the sense that the effort must be invariably so much greater than the possible achievement. In that sort of foredoomed task which is in its nature very lonely also, sympathy is a precious thing."[16]

Paris, June 2009

AT THE HEART OF REASON

Part 1

Confrontations

> Think in order to escape—first from their dead-end thoughts, then from your dead-end thoughts.
>
> —Henri Michaux

Introduction

Methodological Questions

"Describe" enjoins phenomenology. But describe to what purpose? What does "to describe" mean? What is a description? It would be premature to attempt to answer these questions at this stage. It will take no less than the first part of this book for me to try to give them form and substance.

This makes the issue of determining where to begin our inquiry all the more delicate. After all, what gives us an assurance that there is such a thing as the one "phenomenology" to be found behind the rich variety of philosophical undertakings that can be labeled as "phenomenological"? The idea of a descriptive philosophy seems to be their lowest common denominator. But description can be understood in so many ways that it alone can hardly provide us with the requisite guideline for such a task. Simone de Beauvoir speaks in her memoirs of the emotion Sartre felt one day when, as he was sitting next to Raymond Aron before an apricot cocktail, the latter told him: "You see, my dear fellow, if you are a phenomenologist, you can talk about this cocktail and make philosophy out of it!"[1] But it is not very enlightening to say that it "suffices" to describe an apricot cocktail to do phenomenology, or even philosophy—let alone in a humorous vein. Husserl, a great cigar lover, wrote a short essay for fun with his student Daubert on tobaccology.[2] In that case, the phenomenologist could scarcely be differentiated from a good novelist or poet. And since, in contrast with the latter, he claims to furnish, not contingent descriptions of certain facts, but *necessary* descriptions, he might be arguably compared with that Chekhov character who "said nothing but things everybody knew"—for example: "Man cannot live without food."[3] Could really the "science of the trivial"[4] that Husserl strove to achieve be itself a trivial science?

Moreover, the phenomenological tradition is not the only one to have claimed the title of "descriptive philosophy." This idea, deeply rooted in Austro-German philosophy, especially in Brentano's psychology, has fared variously in different philosophical "schools," from the direct heirs of Brentano (Stumpf, Twardowski) to Gestalt psychology (Ehrenfels, Wertheimer, Köhler, Koffka, Lewin), linguistics (Marty, Bühler), and Wittgenstein's grammatical philosophy.[5] When Wittgenstein proclaims: "And we may not advance any sort of theory. . . . We must do away with all *explanation*, and description alone must take its place," specifying that "this description gets its light, that is to say its purpose, from the philosophical problems,"[6] he continues to follow that same Austrian tradition that he shares with Husserl and his successors. Thus, by itself, and without qualification, the idea of a descriptive philosophy is not *strictly* phenomenological.

Perhaps it will be objected that phenomenology stands out within the complex web of conceptions to which it belongs in one respect at least: the *object* of its descriptions. While the descriptions of Wittgenstein, in keeping with that philosopher's conception of philosophical activity, are concerned exclusively with the grammar of our language,[7] that is to say, with the rules governing the use of expressions, the subject matter, the *Sache* of phenomenological description is neither mainly nor exclusively linguistic. Very well, but how may it be characterized positively? The issue about what the primary object of phenomenological description should be remains unsolved. On closer examination, there is no agreement on this point among phenomenologists. The "descriptive" watchword refers to a description sometimes focused on the psyche (the early Husserl), at other times on an "I" having a transcendental status (the late Husserl); sometimes on Being in contrast with beings (Heidegger), or on the body-subject and its modalities of experience (Merleau-Ponty), and at other times on a supposedly "absolute" life (Michel Henry), on a givenness that operates beyond Being (Jean-Luc Marion), or on the event as opposed to the fact, and so on. To decide what the subject matter of phenomenology is is never a neutral operation with respect to the content of a given phenomenology and its presuppositions. This is why the concept of description is above all a negative concept, acting as a foil, so to speak, against a conception of philosophy taken to be inadequate. Husserl, opposing what he qualifies as "metaphysics," that is, a dogmatic system claiming to explain phenomena by leading them back to principles, champions his descriptive method by proclaiming: "*Doch genug der verkehrten Theorien!*" ("Enough now of absurd theories").[8] Description, in phenomenology as well as in Wittgenstein, is nothing but the positive counterpart of this rejection: "I seek not to instruct but only to lead, to point out and describe what I see."[9]

This explains in part at least the heterogeneity of the philosophical movement founded by Husserl. Already in 1925 Heidegger remarked that "there is no phenomenological school"[10] and it is difficult not to agree. What indeed is there in common on the doctrinal level, or even on that of description, in undertakings as varied as those of Heidegger, Max Scheler, Eugen Fink, Roman Ingarden, Oskar Becker, Jan Patočka, Maurice Merleau-Ponty, Jean-Paul Sartre, Aron Gurwitsch, Alfred Schütz, Erwin Strauss, Emmanuel Levinas, Ludwig Binswanger, Michel Henry,

Edward Casey, and Henri Maldiney? Even more serious, a number of decisive fault lines of twentieth-century philosophy are to be found less between phenomenology and other movements or trends than within phenomenology itself. Anti-psychologism and its conterpart, the Platonism of universals, represent a unifying thread connecting Husserl's work with those of Gottlob Frege, Alexius Meinong, Bertrand Russell, and even Charles Sanders Peirce, more clearly than with those of many of his heirs. The adoption or refusal of transcendental idealism marks a deep divide between Husserl and Fink, on the one hand, and the phenomenologists of realist inspiration—Ingarden, Adolf Reinach, Johannes Daubert, Alexander Pfänder, Hedwig Conrad-Martius, and Edith Stein—on the other. The reference to Descartes allows us to set in diametrical opposition a phenomenology of Cartesian inspiration (pursued with varying degrees of faithfulness to Husserl by Sartre, Levinas, and Henry) and a radically anti-Cartesian phenomenology, inaugurated by *Being and Time* (*Sein und Zeit*), in which the critique of the cogito is not far from many of Wittgenstein's "grammatical" remarks. The Husserlian method of the intuition of essences is accepted by Reinach, Scheler, Ingarden, and Gurwitsch, but rejected by Heidegger and the hermeneutic trend. The question of whether phenomenology can, in any sense, claim the status of a "science" is answered in the affirmative by Husserl and the early Heidegger (with a few minor reservations), but staunchly rejected by the later Heidegger, Merleau-Ponty, Levinas, and Hans-Georg Gadamer. On this point, it is not absurd to draw a parallel between Husserl's ideal of a scientific philosophy, which will prompt him to say "we are true positivists," and the same ideal in the Vienna Circle, while the anti-positivism of the late Heidegger and his successors should be rather compared to the positions of the late Wittgenstein, John Austin, and Peter Strawson. But this classification would still require further nuance. Indeed, if we define positivism in philosophy by what Georg Henrik von Wright calls a "methodological monism,"[11] that is, by the idea that there is a unity of the scientific method, the model of which is given by the natural sciences, so that the human sciences (*Geisteswissenschaften*) are assumed to be completely reducible to the sort of explanation prevalent in the natural ones, then Husserl's phenomenology is categorically opposed to that thesis (with which the logical positivists are in agreement), and Husserl stands, with Wilhelm Dilthey, Heidegger, Gadamer, and the later Wittgenstein on the same side of a dividing line separating them from John Stuart Mill, the logical empiricists,[12] and Willard Van Orman Quine. For the former, philosophy has its own area of competency, which is called "description of the life-world," "understanding in its historical dimension," or "grammatical analysis." For the latter, philosophy is limited to clarifying and systematizing the statements of science; it even develops in close "continuity" with science.[13]

The intent of these classifications is not to outline a historical picture of phenomenology and its situation within the philosophy of the twentieth century—that would require another book—but only to afford a glimpse of some of the difficulties that lie in our path. They might suggest not only that there is no phenomenological school, but that there is, strictly speaking, no genuine unity in phenomenology as such; there would then no longer be any justification for speaking of *the one* phenomenology. This finding, if true, would put an end to this book even before it starts.

But is the situation that hopeless? To use an exhortation of Merleau-Ponty—which could serve us along these pages as a *protreptikos*: "It is within ourselves that we will find the unity of phenomenology and its true meaning."[14] This means that the question of whether or not a philosophical movement possesses a unity is always a philosophical question, and not a historical one. My aim is to show that the phenomenological method is consistent and productive if we are prepared to rethink it from the start; that it is a method no less rigorous than those that prevailed in other philosophical trends of the twentieth century, and that, though not superior, it is not inferior to them. This entails the adoption of a skeptical attitude toward divisions that have been presented as settled, but that are less certain today than ever.

In philosophy, as in other fields, labels become fixed only when they are outdated. We read everywhere that philosophy in the twentieth century underwent a schism similar to the one that previously separated the Christian church into East and West. According to this narrative, philosophy lives split into two rival schools, the one "continental," because emanating from Old Europe, the other "analytic," rooted in the Anglo-Saxon world. This is largely a fiction that rests on misunderstandings: not only because these two philosophical traditions have a common origin, but more fundamentally because the division, which had some relevance fifty years ago, no longer corresponds to much today. There was probably a time when, on both sides of the Atlantic or the English Channel, philosophers were so certain of the validity of their method that they could pretend not to know what was going on elsewhere: analytic authors could invest all their efforts in the minute problems of linguistic philosophy, persuaded that they were participating in the "collective division of labor" of a scientific movement in all respects comparable to those existing in the hard sciences, while continental authors could devote most of their energies to the learned exegesis of some aspect of Heidegger's doctrine, in response to the "history of metaphysics." On both sides, things have changed. Analytic philosophy has to a large extent turned away from its initial problems, and many of its prominent representatives—Putnam, Rorty, Evans, Brandom, McDowell—practice a philosophy in which it is not so easy to determine what remains "analytic." On the old continent, the dividing lines also appear less obvious. It is not clear, for example, that the "analytic" interpretation of Wittgenstein alone does justice to a thinker deeply rooted in the German and Austrian traditions. On the one hand, the phenomenological trend has experienced countless vicissitudes; on the other, post-positivist analytic philosophy has abandoned not only the principles of positivism, but the principles of *analysis itself.* Since Quine, the meaning of this term has become increasingly unclear.

Indeed, a large part of the most interesting productions in the analytic tradition has consisted in a systematic critique of its main premises. As Hilary Putnam notes: "Analytic philosophy has great accomplishments, to be sure; but those accomplishments are negative. Like logical positivism (itself just one species of analytic philosophy), analytic philosophy has succeeded in destroying the very problem with which it started." But, he concludes, "this 'deconstruction' is no mean intellectual accomplishment."[15] Alas, it is not clear that phenomenology has made comparable progress in the systematic questioning of its own premises and method—in that enterprise of self-destruction—even though it has taken some significant steps in that direction. It is not clear that continental philosophy, and more specifically, phenomenology, has reached the kind of "intellectual accomplishment" referred to by Putnam. One of the goals of the present work is to fill this gap in part.

Now, in a time when boundaries are blurred, when problematics intersect and coincide on many points, when Donald Davidson can confess—not without some irony toward his colleagues—that he has learned a lot from reading Gadamer, that he regrets not having read him earlier, and even that Gadamer "sensed from the start the goal he [Gadamer] would pursue, and [that he had] pursued it with brilliant success" and that he himself—Davidson—setting out from a completely different context and with great effort, ended up "in Gadamer's intellectual neighborhood";[16] in a time when Rorty praises Heidegger, when Brandom writes about *Being and Time,* and Putnam devotes whole pages to Foucault and Derrida, it seems that the moment is particularly appropriate to ask ourselves without dogmatism, and by integrating into our reflection elements coming from both trends, what the identity of one of them, namely phenomenology, is—or can be. "The philosopher is not a citizen of any community of ideas," Wittgenstein warned: "That is what makes him into a philosopher."[17]

The problem that arises is what method to adopt. Like Descartes and Kant before him, Husserl's ambition was to propose a *new* method in philosophy that could reorient metaphysics away from its endless quarrels and place it on the sure path of science. This method, in his view, is *without presuppositions.* Wittgenstein, in both the early and the later phase of his thought, had a similar purpose. To borrow his later formulations, to bring words back from their metaphysical to their everyday use *is* at the same time to show, through a grammatical analysis, that metaphysical statements are meaningless, not because they violate established and sacred rules, but because the metaphysician *has conferred no meaning on them*—which he must be brought to recognize for himself. According to this conception, there is something like an absolute method in philosophy, a presuppositionless method which can lead to "*complete* clarity" (vollkommene *Klarheit*), that is to say to the point at which philosophical problems should "*completely* disappear."[18] The trouble with these palace revolutions that philosophy regularly undergoes is that they are only apparently neutral, and that the idea of a presuppositionless method—and its corollary, the view it would be possible in philosophy to advance no *claim* at all—are mere illusions.

No, the idea of grammatical analysis is not presuppositionless, as I will establish later, and the project of bringing words back from their metaphysical to their everyday use is based on a set of questionable premises: to name just one, the view that there is an ordinary use of language sufficiently distinct and free from any contamination by its "extraordinary" (namely metaphysical) use to serve as a guideline in this endeavor. No, the idea of an intuition of essences in Husserl's sense is not without prejudices. It does not enable us to return to an Adamic state of philosophical reflection from which this reflection could expand infinitely, unhindered by any obstacles.

Methodological revolutions in philosophy are always based on unexamined claims, debatable and controversial premises and presuppositions that have not been made explicit, so that the alleged "new" method can only be adopted in all sincerity—or all naïveté—by a philosopher who has already accepted a number of underlying assumptions. In other words, since there is no universally accepted method in philosophy—in contrast to what happens in astronomy for example, where there is no controversy on the object of that science nor on its way to proceed—and since the adoption of a particular method already raises philosophical problems, the idea of a philosophically neutral method makes no sense.

The bitter experience of the Vienna Circle is a case in point. Again in this instance, we were told, the idea was to practice a scientific philosophy based on nothing other than a logical analysis of language. But what is a logical analysis? That is the whole question. The logical empiricists attempted to answer it by providing a *logical analysis* of the notion of meaning and related concepts: synonymy, convention, and so on, thus already exposing themselves by this very fact to the objection of circularity. A proposition has a meaning, they argued, if and only if it is either (a) analytic *a priori*, that is, a tautology or derivable from one, or (b) synthetic *a posteriori*, that is, deducible from observational statements (or protocol statements). Now, first of all, it is hard to see how this theory of meaning, which underlies what must be considered a logical analysis, could itself derive from a logical analysis and not involve a substantial claim on *the nature* of meaning; second, the statement that "every meaningful statement is either derivable from analytic truths (therefore itself analytic), or derivable from empirical statements" *itself violates the meaning criterion it advances*, since it is neither analytic (tautological) nor synthetic (based on experience).

If revolutions of method in philosophy are doomed sooner or later to stumble on their presuppositions, phenomenology can hardly escape the same consequences. If we want to answer the question of the validity of the phenomenological method, we obviously cannot, on pain of circularity, take for granted any of the methodological precepts phenomenology advances. We cannot appeal to a method borrowed from phenomenology in order to evaluate the success and limitations of this philosophical project. Husserl is probably right to think, as we noted earlier, that *if* phenomenology is possible, the method cannot be imported into its field from outside. But this statement does not apply to an inquiry into the foundations of phenomenology itself. To say the truth, we know what phenomenology is not by some "special insight" that it would afford us, but by historical examination. And we can only address the issue of its philosophical relevance by confronting the philosophical claims it has endorsed to potential criticisms. In short, the only method that is practicable is "dialectical" in an Aristotelian sense. When no method specific to a given science (in this case, to a given philosophy) is available, where we cannot build on any consensus about principles, we can only argue case by case, setting out from objections. When what we need to do is provide a justification for a particular philosophy—or a particular trend in philosophy—we cannot avail ourselves of premises taken for granted by representatives of this trend, but only set out from *critiques* to develop a plea in its favor.

This is why, in the entire first part of this book, the argumentative method will prevail, and it is only once certain problems are solved that a more phenomenological approach will replace it to be applied to new problems. Hence this book begins as a "transcendental dialectic" and will end as an "analytics of principles," which will take as its guiding thread the problem of experience. The first part, "Confrontations," will set in opposition, without pretending to completeness, phenomenology and its detractors, mainly from the analytic school. The second part, "Transformations," will constitute a meditation more internal to the phenomenological field; it will try to deepen the description of this field by proposing an alternative conception of experience to those advanced historically by phenomenology. Just as Croce asked at the beginning of the twentieth century what is alive and what is dead in Hegelianism,[19] I will ask, at the beginning of the twenty-first, a similar question regarding one of the most significant traditions of the past century.

As I have stressed, my task will be that of bringing to light the "foundations" of phenomenology, not only as it was, but also, and primarily, as it should be. Here I am not using "foundation" in its traditional (Aristotelian or Cartesian) metaphysical sense—the sense of a first principle (ἀρχή) of being, which would also be a supreme being, or that of a first truth providing an ultimate foundation for knowledge. To inquire into its foundations means only to question the premises that govern the phenomenological method, that give this movement its unity and specificity—to *argue* in their favor. Philosophy may abandon the idea of ultimate, self-evident, and self-warranted justifications—and probably it should do so. But it cannot abandon the inquiry into reasons, at least as long as it remains philosophy.

1

The Return to Experience

But experience with its demands precedes conceptual thinking and its demands.
—Edmund Husserl

Phenomenology has probably endorsed only one claim: the description of the structures of experience is not reducible to bringing to light the linguistic resources through which that description is carried out. Or more simply: the structures of experience are not conferred on it by the language through which it is described. This claim is as simple in its formulation as it is complex and rich in its consequences; we will only be able to appreciate its importance in the course of the investigations that follow (chapters 2 to 12).

We have already seen Husserl's formula to rule out all speculative—metaphysical—approaches in philosophy: "Back to the things themselves!" The *Sache*, the thing that will become an issue for thought, is the "still dumb" experience as it unfolds below the level of our linguistic intelligence. We open our eyes, we make a gesture, a move, and this move seems already endowed with an immemorial "wisdom" that has nothing to do with a knowledge that could be formulated in beliefs or judgments—a bodily gnosis by virtue of which we have a purchase on the world, we are anchored in it, and inversely, the world gives itself to us, unfolding around us with a recognizable order and salience, providing landmarks for our orientation and exploration. This world, subjacent to language, subtending discursive knowledge, and which is to geometric space as landscape is to geography, is what the phenomenologist is involved with; it is his "thing," his subject matter. Not, let it be noted, that phenomenology limits itself exclusively to the analysis of the *sensible* world. In addition to perception, it deals with complex forms of experience in which language plays an essential role, and which involve history, society, art, and culture. But even in these cases, it proclaims the priority of a prelinguistic order by virtue of which history and society, for example, are not merely objects of discourse, but sustain our lives at every moment as the very ground of our most basic practices. To understand Husserl's injunction, we must therefore read it in full: "*von den bloßen Worten . . . zu den Sachen selbst*"—"from mere words to the things themselves."[1]

This return from opinions and speeches to *things* is actually a return to the experience that we have of them. But what does "to return to experience" mean? This formula can be understood in several ways. First, it may mean returning to the *subjectivity* of which that experience is the experience. But, second, it can also mean to analyze experience in its own right in a rigorously immanent way. In Husserl, these two senses of the formula are closely connected. But since the present task is not to initiate ourselves into Husserlian phenomenology, but into phenomenology without further qualification, the first interpretation is still too ambiguous to serve as a starting point. At this stage, we have no idea of what is meant by "subject." Phenomenology gives us many descriptions of the subject, all different, and often incompatible. Patočka has developed a phenomenology which he described as "asubjective." Others, such as Heidegger and Merleau-Ponty, refused to consider the subject/object distinction as a good starting point and subjected it to a radical critique. If we want to be able to orient ourselves in the maze of phenomenology, we cannot rely uncritically on any concept of the subject. We must therefore adopt the second reading of the formula, in order to explore its meaning and presuppositions.

What does it mean to return to experience under the constructions of language and theory, to allow the experience to unfold of its own accord, and to analyze it as it presents itself, as it is at its own level? What does it mean to leave out theories, opinions, and even speech, to "give voice" to our experience, however "dumb" it may be? And first of all, is there really such a thing as an experience that rustles with silence prior to our articulating a word about it? Here a clarification is in order. Regardless of whether it is right in what it affirms and even more in what it denies, phenomenology speaks only of "prelinguistic" experience—or as Husserl liked to say, of "prepredicative" experience—in a very specific and delimited sense. The question raised here is one of principle and not of fact. In fact, we never cease categorizing the world through linguistic concepts; we perceive the table *as* a table and the candlestick *as* a candlestick because once we learned to use those terms. There is no temptation in phenomenology to return to a mysterious origin, free from language, from the viewpoint of which experience would be described. The prelinguistic world is *not* the mute world of the infant, assuming such a thing exists. The relevant sense of priority here is not chronological but logical. The question raised by phenomenology, and which is therefore a question of principle, is whether everything in experience that has meaning and structure draws this meaning and structure from language and from language alone. And the answer is no. There is even less a temptation, in phenomenology, to conceptualize experience as ineffable in any sense whatsoever. For Husserl, as for most of his heirs, everything that is experienceable is in principle expressible.[2] Hence the "prelinguistic" with which phenomenology is concerned is one that can be recognized as such only by a being who is able to speak, and which remains always expressible in principle *without remainder* by such a being.

Once we have cleared up this misunderstanding, it becomes possible to reformulate our problem. What is that "experience" of which phenomenology speaks, and to which we should return? Is there a specifically *phenomenological* conception of experience, and if so, what is it? To understand this, a historical survey may be helpful. Phenomenology was born at the beginning of the twentieth century out of a galaxy of other philosophical trends that tended, each in its own way, in the direction of a *descriptive* philosophy, and that aspired to break the spell of metaphysics. Breaking the magic circle of a thought that could not extricate itself from problems of its own making as a result of its having produced systems not directly related to experience, William James in the United States, Brentano and his students in Austria (Meinong, Stumpf, and Ehrenfels, soon followed by Gestalt psychology) distinguished a *descriptive* psychology, which is not concerned with explanation, and a *genetic* psychology, which conducts experiments to provide a causal account, but needs, in order to examine the physiological basis of mental phenomena, a correct description of what it has undertaken to explain. In their view, as well as that of Dilthey and Bergson, experience has to be described as it presents itself to a reflective or introspective analysis. But what experience? Despite their differences, these philosophers belong to a movement challenging the dominant empiricist model, which intends to construct experience out of separate pieces, on the basis of "ideas" conceived as indivisible atoms, and their principles of association. They are at the same time opposed to Kantianism, which they consider a specious alternative to that empiricism. James and Bergson, the former by the concept of "stream," and the latter by that of "duration" (*durée*), challenged the psychological atomism of sense data and insisted that lived experience was only meaningful in the context of psychic life taken as a whole—that is, seen in the light of its temporality. In *An Introduction to Metaphysics,* Bergson defines his intuitive method as "a true empiricism";[3] James, in turn, lays claim to a "radical empiricism" which differs from classical empiricism by its refusal to derive the flow of experience from elementary processes—from a "complex of sensations,"[4] in the words of Ernst Mach. Already in *Principles of Psychology*, James lists among the sources of error in psychology the idea that the perception of multiplicity has its origin in a multiplicity of perceptions, and the perception of succession in a succession of perceptions. Such a "multiplicity of building blocks,"[5] out of which consciousness is supposed to be constructed, lacks all reliable introspective foundation. In the rest of his work, James goes even further, considering "pure experience" as a single "primal stuff . . . of which everything is composed"—the subject no less than the object.[6] A similar stance in favor of a holistic psychology which opposes both the associationism of John Stuart Mill and the mental mechanism (*Vorstellungsmechanik*) of Johann Friedrich Herbart can be found in Dilthey—in "Experiencing and Thinking" ["Erfahren und Denken"] (1892), for example—in the statement according to which there is an order immanent in sensibility. "'Somewhere in sensations there must also at the same time be immediately given their order as an inherent property.' We are thus led through the facts themselves [*durch die Tatsachen selbst*] to the postulation of an immanence of order or form in the very stuff of our experiences."[7] But in Husserl's view what is still lacking in these undertakings is a rigorous method. Not sharing Bergson's ineffabilism, probably considering James's radical empiricism as a relapse into metaphysics, Husserl finds his starting point in Brentano's "descriptive psychology," which he claims to elevate to the rank of rigorous science. But among the philosophers and psychologists of his time, the one who had the most lasting influence on him was Carl Stumpf, to whom he dedicated his *Logical Investigations.* Stumpf adopts Brentano's idea of "descriptive psychology," renaming it "phenomenology" in memory of Hegel and of Johann Heinrich Lambert's *Neues Organon* (*Neues Organon oder Gedanken über die Erforschung und Bezeichnung des Wahren und dessen Unterscheidung vom Irrthum und Schein,* 1764), the work in which that term appears for the first time. Understood as a "descriptive theory of phenomena,"[8] phenomenology is possible by virtue of the fact that "everywhere within the domain of phenomena, there are . . . immanent laws of structure."[9] These "structural laws of phenomena"[10] as Stumpf also calls them, are not derived from the higher functions of thought, such as the act of counting, comparison, or judgment, but are immanent to the sphere of experience. Relations of similarity between colors are not the result of an act of comparison; they mobilize no judgment; they are seen directly. The same goes for the relationship between the parts and the whole. I see a tree-lined walk, a flight of birds, a string of twinkling lights, all at once. I do not, after the fact, reconstruct their unity on the basis of elementary sensations. Here we have what von Ehrenfels called "qualities of form,"[11] which are given along with perception. Similarly, I see *three* balls at once at the center of a pool table; I did not count them, because they are given to me with a typical configuration. In the field of hearing, Stumpf analyzes, in his *Tonpsychologie,* the fusion (*Verschmelzung*) that occurs between simultaneous tones and makes possible the musical phenomenon of the chord. In all these cases, the necessary relationships between phenomena "though not themselves phenomena, are nevertheless given by and in the same phenomena and are essential to any description."[12] The typical example of a structural law inherent in the order of experience is the necessary dependence of color on spatial extension. "Even within the realm of phenomena . . . color and extension form a unified whole in which they can be distinguished only by abstraction."[13] This is the prototype of a lawfulness that it is phenomenology's task to uncover. Stumpf makes use of the imagination to bring out the objective possibilities and impossibilities grounded in the very nature of phenomenal contents, thus anticipating Husserl's "eidetic variation." He stresses that the necessary nature of these structural laws is in the precinct of an entirely *a priori* knowledge, and is therefore irreducible to an empirical generalization. The necessary relationship between color and extension, the "geometry of colors" developed by Meinong,[14] as well as the universal principles valid in hearing, such as: "All tone has pitch, timbre, and intensity" and "Given three tones of different pitch, one of them must necessarily lie between the other two" are neither empirical truths nor axioms in the field of logic: they are analytic, Stumpf says, but not in the sense of the formal analytic.[15]

Husserl's phenomenology will also undertake to describe these structural laws of experience, whose necessity is neither the conjectural one belonging to truths derived from empirical generalizations, nor the entirely formal, and hence strictly independent of experience, necessity attaching to logical truths. The investigation of the "invariable general style of experience," as Husserl sometimes calls it, will be carried out by means of a grasping of essences and essential relationships that govern the domain of experience as such, calling into question the inherited oppositions between empiricism and Kantianism, and paving the way for an entirely new approach to the relationship between the *a priori* and the empirical.

To understand this, it is necessary to see what distinguishes Husserl from both the empiricist and the Kantian tradition. Hume, whom Husserl recognizes as having anticipated the phenomenological approach in many respects,[16] contrasts two sorts of sciences: those that are concerned with matters of fact, and are not demonstrative, and those that are demonstrative, but do not relate to any fact and do not depend "on what is any where existent in the universe,"[17] because they link ideas to one another independently of all experience. Geometry and algebra belong to the latter category. They are based solely on relations of ideas. A proposition such as: "The sum of the angles of a triangle is equal to two right angles" is not dependent on any fact of the world. This dichotomy between two realms of truth leads to the idea that the empirical sciences, those relating to *matters of fact*, are not able to establish anything necessary. They are limited to the identification of empirical and therefore contingent links between our "ideas" (themselves derived from our impressions). These links are ultimately based on "human nature" alone. Nothing guarantees that the sun will rise tomorrow, beyond the subjective (anthropological-factual) principle of custom, which enables us to associate these ideas in a constant way. Thus, all links formed in experience are nothing but *fictions*. Experience is merely a mosaic of sensations held together by habit; all knowledge of necessary laws is denied to the sciences dealing with it. Empiricism in its most extreme form leads to two consequences that Husserl will criticize. 1. A phenomenalism—like the one defended in his day by Mach—according to which we cannot escape the circle of our sense data, and consequently cannot be sure that an object corresponding to the way we associate these data—and that would be accessible to other minds—actually exists. 2. A radical skepticism that results from the view that our sensations present no order other than a contingent one, that is, relative to *our* nature. Such a skepticism, Husserl tells us, is not only fatal to the very possibility of a science of nature: it is in itself an absurdity (*Widersinn*). Indeed, on the one hand, the concepts of cause and effect have no other legitimacy or validity than the one conferred on them by a psychological genesis based on the subjective principle of habit. On the other hand, the very idea of a *psychological genesis* is grounded on the concepts of cause and effect, and presupposes their validity. "Obviously, if the judgments of experience do not grant any legitimacy, they do not grant any psychological explanation either. If our convictions derived from the sciences of experience are illusions, psychology cannot give us the satisfaction of showing the source of these illusions, or even help us label them as illusions. For psychology is itself a science of experience."[18] Thus Hume and the "extreme empiricist school, until this present day," remain trapped in a vicious circle.

Unfortunately, the critical philosophy of Kant, which presents itself as an antidote to Humean skepticism, is unsuccessful in breaking away from it entirely. "Kant, though he attacks empiricism, still remains dependent upon this very empiricism."[19] Indeed, the *Critique of Pure Reason* adopts the empiricist starting point, the "raw material of our sensuous impressions,"[20] which in Kant's view needs to be shaped in a second moment by the human *Gemüt* [mind]. According to the "Copernican revolution," all order and all lawfulness in phenomena originate not in these phenomena themselves, but solely in the nature of our minds, that is, in sensibility and its pure *a priori* forms (space and time) on the one hand, and understanding as the "*faculty of rules*"[21] on the other. All we know *a priori* of things is what we ourselves have put into them, so that any *necessary* connection between the phenomena by virtue of which they are constituted in a regulated and ordered experience comes from the pure understanding and its *a priori* concepts. The understanding is "through these concepts . . . the author of that experience in which its objects are found,"[22] and since the concepts of the understanding derive from the forms of judgment, any synthesis of phenomena can only be an intellectual synthesis.[23] Have we thus overcome Humean skepticism? Far from it. Indeed, Husserl contends, the view according to which order and structure are introduced into phenomena from the forms of sensibility and concepts contained *a priori* in the human *Gemüt* only postpones the difficulty somewhat. For now the question arises as to whether the constitution of the human *Gemüt* is not in turn *contingent.* If all necessity arises from our minds and if not only the existence of such a mind, but its very constitution, are contingent facts, then the "necessity" that this mind may introduce into phenomena to constitute them into an experience is a mere matter of fact, a pseudo-necessity. In short, the whole difficulty here lies in Kantianism's continually maintaining the reference to *our* nature as factual *human* nature. "It is we therefore," writes Kant, "who carry into the phenomena which we call nature, order and regularity, nay, we should never find them in nature, if we ourselves, or the nature of our mind, had not originally placed them there."[24] What exactly is the status of this "we"? If it refers to the empirical human being, Husserl argues, that is, to our contingent nature, we have not advanced one step in overcoming Humean skepticism, for if all necessity in experience depends on *our* nature, and if that nature is contingent, *that "necessity" is itself contingent*—which is exactly Hume's claim.[25]

Thus, despite his precautions, Kant falls back into both a "psychologism" and an "anthropologism," that is to say, into a doctrine that relativizes the universality of the *a priori* by restricting its validity first to the psyche and second to the *human* psyche.

> Kant abhorred the founding of the theory of knowledge on psychology as a purely empirical science of the activities of the soul. This point is quite correct. But a kind of psychology does seem to be present in his doctrine of forms. To the nature of the human intellect—certainly not of the individual man or the people or race, but of man in general—

> there belong certain functional forms whose lawfulness is such that it possesses a universal validity and belongs to every man as such. Hume would say, in exactly the same way: the laws of habit belong to the essence of human nature, and they are the sources of the sciences of fact. Man forms necessary and universal habits because he is man, and thus the unity of the world of experience and empirical science arises. While Kant introduces, in place of the principle of habit, other—but just as subjective and, more generally, human—experience-shaping principles, does it really make such a fundamental difference? Isn't the Copernican revolution also present in Hume's doctrine according to which all the units of experience conform to thought?[26]

The *a priori* principles of understanding are hardly better than habit as the "principle of human nature," because they are rooted just as much in a mere psychological, and ultimately anthropological, fact. In short, Kant overcame skepticism only verbally, because he refused to admit that there may be *a priori* laws governing experience in the same sense that there are in the field of mathematics or logic, that is to say, *a priori* laws such that they do not depend *in any way* on the contingent constitution of our minds.

In a word, what must be understood is that experience is a domain in which matters of fact always present themselves in conformity with invariable universal laws, that is, exemplify relations of ideas in the Humean sense. All in all, Hume was closer to the truth than Kant,[27] since he did not make relations of ideas depend on the contingent nature of our minds; but he failed to see that the domain of these relations of ideas, that is, the domain of the *a priori* in its true phenomenological sense—the possibility of which he glimpsed[28]—goes far beyond the domain of mathematics, extending actually to the entire field of experience, which leads to a reassessment of the whole question of the articulation of the empirical with the *a priori.* The contents of experience, material things, sounds and colors, for example, also have their *quid,* their *essence*; and for every essence we can also find laws of essence that are true *a priori,* that possess an absolutely universal validity. These essences and these laws of essence belong to what Husserl calls "a material *a priori,*" that is to say, an *a priori* that is grounded *in the very nature of the contents of experience* which exemplify it, in the very nature of space, sound, and color, for example. If the colors of objects may vary arbitrarily, some relationships between colors, or the dependence of color with respect to extension, are true *ne varietur* for any possible experience, including the experience of beings with a psychic constitution different from ours. It is an *a posteriori* truth that a given sound has resounded; but it is an *a priori* truth that a sound must have a timbre, pitch, and intensity, and that given three sounds of different pitch, one of them is always between the other two, because

> sounds for which that did not hold would just not be sounds. . . . I am of course the one who sees and says that. But, the law says nothing about me and does not presuppose my existence, is not asserted and based upon any hypothesizing of that existence. The law does not belong, say perhaps, to me as a specimen of the species *homo, animal,* and so on, but belongs to sounds as such and to nothing else. . . . Wherever living beings, beings with minds, may be found, whether on earth or in heaven, whether in empirical reality or in a make-believe, possible reality, they can only judge correctly if they judge sounds the way I judge. Sounds cannot occur to them that do not exhibit that without which sounds would just not be sounds."[29]

The material *a priori* is grounded in the very nature of the contents of experience. It is independent of the subject—objective—to the precise extent that it depends on these contents. The *a priori* laws that are true of colors define what color *is* for any consciousness capable of experiencing it. Similarly, the fact that all spatial things can be seen only through changing silhouettes or adumbrations (*Abschattungen*) defines what a spatial thing *is* and is valid in all possible worlds, for any possible consciousness. Even God, as Husserl's *Ideas I* emphasizes, could not perceive such a thing otherwise.[30] The mistake that we often make—and that was already made by Hume, as we have seen—is to restrict this kind of truth to the domain of mathematics and geometry.[31] We readily admit that the Pythagorean theorem is true *a priori,* that it does not rely on any experience of the right-angled triangle, but that it is rather the other way round: any experience of a given figure will be the experience of a right-angled triangle only if the perceived figure satisfies the Pythagorean theorem (and this is true, even though no experience of a "perfect" triangle would ever be possible). But it will be more difficult for us to recognize that a proposition such as "Every sound has duration" presents a necessity of the same sort.[32] It belongs to the essence of sound *necessarily* to have duration (but not spatial extension), and this is true whatever sounds may have resounded since the beginning of time, and even if there had never been a single sound in the world. However, this necessary truth does not follow (no more than does the Pythagorean theorem, for that matter) from the laws of logic alone, since logic says nothing about the properties that a sound (or a triangle) must possess necessarily. "This sound has no duration" is not a formal contradiction; it is a materially false *a priori* proposition.

Thus Husserl's answer to Hume and Kant is basically as follows.

1. Experience is not structured only by contingent synthetic links; it possesses necessary characteristics.
2. These necessary characteristics are not subjective but objective. They depend on the very nature of the phenomena that possess them; they apply to all possible experience, and are not tributary to the contingent particularities of the human psyche.

Therefore we must criticize two aspects of Kant's doctrine of the *a priori* that make the latter into a "half-mythical" *a priori*:[33] (a) the identification of the *a priori* with the subjective, and (b) its identification with the formal. First, *a priori*, as Reinach points out, involves necessity, but "the necessity is not one of thought. Rather it is a necessity of being."[34] The impossibility of my representing a color without lightness or without saturation, for example, is not the result of a subjective incapacity, an accidental failure of my faculty of imagination, but it is an objective impossibility that concerns the essence of color as such. The possibilities and impossibilities that appear in the domain of essences (material *a priori*) exemplify the axiom formulated by *Logical Investigations*: "What cannot be thought, cannot be, and what cannot be, cannot be thought."[35] The invoking of "God" or of "angels" has no other purpose, in Husserl's view, than to stress this point. The material *a priori*, because it is dependent on the very nature of the content that illustrates it, reveals a perfectly objective necessity, a state of affairs independent of the subject who may eventually grasp it. As Heidegger will rephrase it, "The *a priori* in Kant's sense is a feature of the subjective sphere. . . . Against this, phenomenology has shown that the *a priori* is not limited to subjectivity, indeed that in the first instance it has primarily nothing at all to do with subjectivity."[36] Second, the Kantian distinction between a matter of experience, necessarily *a posteriori*, that is to say, a sensory datum, and *a priori* forms, rooted in the human *Gemüt*—forms of receptivity and forms of spontaneity—is no longer valid. A truth can be both *a priori* and material; that is to say, it can depend on a content of experience, the content *color*, for example.

But, it will probably be objected, since this content is itself a content *of experience*, isn't the idea of an *a priori* content a contradiction in terms? Doesn't "*a priori*" mean "prior to all experience"? But then, how can the *a priori* be at once *about* experience and *prior* to experience? How can our experience be permeated by laws that are "prior to experience" or be structured by them? This is the dilemma.

This dilemma is only apparent if we understand the precise meaning of "*a priori*" in the phenomenological perspective. To speak of the *a priori* of experience, for Husserl, amounts to speaking about the essence or *eidos* (these terms are interchangeable)[37] of experience. In Husserl's view, essence is a universal that can be "grasped" and intuited in specific acts of consciousness. This Platonism, purified from any "metaphysical hypostatization" and from the mythology of a "heaven of ideas" is, according to him, strictly phenomenological. We begin to see the role assumed by imagination in the grasping of essences, of the necessary relations between essences, and of essential laws. An essence is an invariant, that is to say a property (or set of properties) common to everything that falls under it. Similarly, a law of essence is a structural invariant which can be expressed by a proposition that is true "in the totality of the universe and in every possible universe."[38] To capture an essence or a law of essence, it suffices to go freely in imagination through a multitude of variables, in order to apprehend through them what remains invariant, what is essential to all those instances. To discern the *eidos* of color, for example, it suffices to run through a multiplicity of fictive specimens of color in order to grasp the identical element that is present in them, the *hen epi pollōn* (unity of a multiplicity), as Plato used to say.[39] Similarly, to grasp the essential dependence of every color with respect to extension, one has to notice that a color without extension is quite simply unimaginable, whatever color one represents to oneself. Husserl uses the expression "eidetic variation" to refer to this free perusal of imaginary variables in order to grasp the invariant *eidos* that sets its limits to this variation.[40] The possibilities and impossibilities highlighted by this process are not only, as we have seen, possibilities and impossibilities of thought, but of being: the impossibility of thinking or imagining things differently means an impossibility of things *being* otherwise.

We are now in a position to be able to address the difficulty raised above. There is no contradiction in the laws of essence sought after by phenomenology being both *about* experience and *prior* to experience. They are about experience in that the *a priori* is synonymous with *eidos* and *eidos* is always *eidos* of a fact or a manifold of facts that exemplify it.[41] They are independent of experience in that they are valid not only for our factual experience as it has unfolded thus far, but for *any possible experience* (in all possible worlds); thus insofar as their generality is an "unrestricted" generality for which it is impossible to imagine even one single counter-example. Whatever melody I could possibly imagine in any possible world, I could never imagine sounds that do not possess the three properties that define the essence of all sound as such. Thus, we understand in what sense the essence of sound can be said to be, or not to be, *a priori*: it is *not a priori* if by that we mean that it has no relation to our experience, since we must have perceived sounds in order to be able to grasp their eidetic invariants. One who was born deaf is unable to do this. But it is *a priori* in the sense that its generality is "unrestricted," that is, valid in all possible worlds for any possible experience, in such a way that no counter-example is thinkable (imaginable) here. The "*prius*" of the *a priori*, its priority, *is ontological before being epistemological*. The *a priori* is first a characteristic of objects (their essence) and only through this a feature of our knowledge. We must perceive colors to capture the essence of color, but that essence does not depend on our grasping it, and it is not at all limited to our factual past or present experience. "*A priori*" means, therefore, in this context: *preceding in principle all factual experience by virtue of its unconditional validity*. As Husserl says, "The universal truths in which we merely explicate what belongs to pure essential universalities, precede in their validity all questions concerning facts and their factual truths. For that reason the essential truths are called *a priori*, preceding in their validity all facts, all findings drawn from experience."[42] The *a priori* is therefore that which has a validity that cannot be restricted by any fact because this validity is not based on experience; thus the *a priori* is the *absolutely* necessary; but it is by no means the *innate*, and consequently the various *a priori* of experience must be *discovered*, exactly as in the case of the Pythagorean theorem.

Why, it may be asked, do the *a priori*, in the sense of the absolutely general, and the necessary coincide? Husserl's implicit modal reasoning is the following. "*A priori*" means "which can be known independently of experience" (in the sense I have just specified); therefore *a priori* is what cannot be invalidated by any experience (here a counter-example is not even *conceivable*); therefore *a priori* is what possesses an unrestricted generality (what is valid in all possible worlds); hence *a priori* is what is unconditionally necessary, since the necessary is equated with what is the case in all possible worlds. As Husserl writes, "any eidetic particularization and singularization of an eidetically universal predicatively formed affair-complex, *in so far as* it is that, is called an *eidetic necessity*. *Eidetic universality and eidetic necessity are therefore correlates*."[43]

This unrestricted generality and this validity in all possible worlds bring closer together *a priori* material truths and *a priori* formal truths, which are also called "analytic." The essential truths, Husserl specifies, "have a value and validity analogous to purely analytic truths."[44] But Husserl, unlike Stumpf, does not call these material truths "analytic" (distinguishing two senses of "analytic"—formal and material), but "synthetic *a priori*." However it may be with this terminological issue, to which we will have to return, the idea of a pure morphology of experience, with its immanent forms of organization and structuration, raises two possible objections. It can be denied that there are such material *a priori*, either because it is assumed that these alleged *a priori* are not *a priori* and that they can be reduced to empirical generalizations, or alternatively, because it is assumed that they are not material and are taken to be reducible to analytic, and therefore formal, truths. The first objection would be that of classical empiricism, the second, as we will see later (chapter 6), is that of logical empiricism. Therefore we must clarify (1) what distinguishes the laws of essence and propositions of essence from empirical generalizations, and (2) what distinguishes them from formal laws, laws of logic.

First of all, what allows Husserl to think that generalities of essence are not inferred from experience, that they are not merely inductive generalizations, or hypotheses conceived on the basis of such generalizations? "The unrestricted universality of natural laws must not be mistaken for eidetic universality,"[45] he points out. Why not? The answer, which is only implicit in his texts, seems to be the following. In the case of an empirical regularity such as "Water boils at 100° C" (under normal pressure conditions), it is always conceivable that in the future this regularity may no longer be verified. Then we would have to change physics. The situation is entirely different for material eidetic generalities. If I wanted to imagine a tone that did not have pitch, a color without saturation, or an orange that was not intermediate between red and yellow, not only could I not imagine them, but *I would not even know what to imagine.* This point is important because it shows that we are not dealing here with a mere subjective inability, attributable to my contingent human constitution. This sort of inability exists: for example, I can imagine two sheep, but not 123 sheep. This is a *factual* inability, because if I were not affected by it, I would know perfectly well what to imagine. In the case of a material eidetic impossibility, by contrast, the impossibility to imagine means an impossibility for the state of affairs to be imagined. What distinguishes a material eidetic law from an empirical law such as those set out by a physical theory is the impossibility to imagine the least counter-example. When I cannot even conceive what might constitute a counter-example, I am no longer dealing with an empirical law, but with a "pure" law, possessing a *truly* unrestricted generality, that is, valid in all possible worlds—and thus with an *absolutely* necessary state of affairs.

Consequently, unlike the empirical generalizations that always remain hypothetical, the generalities of essence that phenomenology attempts to describe are free from any dependence on the contingent peculiarities of *this* world. "Every eidetic science is *necessarily* independent from any science of matters of fact."[46] Not only are material necessities not obtained by induction or generalization, but there is nothing hypothetical about them: *they underlie the possibility of any discovery of contingent empirical laws.* If there were no internal, necessary relations between phenomena, such as temporal and spatial relations, we could never discover any external, contingent relations either, such as causal relationships. In order for event A to cause event B, they must follow each other in a certain order and bear specific spatial relationships between them. Hence the causal relationships revealed by induction presuppose an immutable spatiotemporal form of experience, and thus a form determined *a priori.*[47] In short, as Wittgenstein will put it, "if there were only an external connection, no connection could be described at all, since we only describe the external connection by means of the internal one."[48] But while these internal relationships are conceived of by Wittgenstein, in his later philosophy, as grammatical conventions, to Husserl they are structural laws immanent in the phenomenal order; they are precisely *a priori* of experience as such.

We now understand what separates the eidetic laws from the laws of nature, and what gives phenomenology its inherent priority with respect to all empirical investigation. But what about the objection that would consist in denying, not that the necessities mentioned by Husserl are *a priori,* but that their apriority has a different status from that of the analytic "truths"? Later on, I will carefully examine (see chapter 6) this objection raised by the Vienna Circle, but I can already sketch the main lines of a response. What makes the option of equating the status of phenomenological truths with that of logical ones tempting is the impossibility, in both cases, to think the opposite state of affairs. "All sounds have duration" is a proposition such that *I cannot even conceive what would obtain if that proposition were false.* Does this not make it into a mere tautology, whose negation would be a formal contradiction? Husserl's answer is no. If the statement "this sound is without duration" were a logical contradiction, it should be able to be fully formalized, so that by a substitution of variables (*x, y*) to the material terms ("sound," "duration"), that is, by their replacement with the pure form of "something," the falsity of that proposition would become obvious by virtue of its form alone. Now, this is not the case. The necessary falsity of the assertion depends on the content of the terms of which it is composed. Although it is false in all possible worlds, this proposition is not a formal, analytic contradiction. In other words, it is not logic that arbitrarily fixes the meaning of the word "sound" in such a way that for sound the property of possessing duration would follow from that initial convention. In order to understand the truth of "all sound has duration," I must have some experience, however minimal, of sound, even if the truth of that proposition is not of an empirical nature. The proposition is true *for any possible experience of sound*, and not only for my actual experience up to the present time.

The doctrine of material *a priori* nonetheless raises serious difficulties. In conclusion, I will mention three of them.

First, is it true that the unrestricted validity of material *a priori* is the strict *analogon* of that of the formal *a priori*, so that eidetic phenomenology is *nowise* a factual science? Is it true that eidetic truths have "a value and validity analogous to purely analytic truths"?[49] It depends on the meaning of "analogous" in this instance. That all spatial things must necessarily be perceived by adumbrations is only true *for a world in which spatial objects exist*. In a world made up solely of emptiness, or only of gas, such a material proposition is neither true nor false, for nothing in it would correspond to the expression "spatial thing." Similarly, that all color is extended or that orange is intermediary between yellow and red—these statements are only true in a universe in which colors exist (if we define color by reference to the chromatic spectrum, excluding white and black, a universe without colors is perfectly conceivable), or to put it differently, in a universe in which an *experience* of colors takes place. Thus, we should specify the nature of synthetic, *a priori* truths as follows. Such truths are necessary in all possible worlds *in which the objects they are about exist*. On the contrary, analytic truths are valid for all possible worlds *without restriction of any kind*: "2 + 2 = 4" is true even in a world consisting in a vacuum, in which no object whatsoever could be counted. We should not say that "2 + 2 = 4" is true *on the condition that numbers exist*, because there is no requirement for numbers to "exist" as entities of some kind for this arithmetic operation to be true, and necessarily so. But then it is not at all clear that material necessary truths are "necessary" in the same sense as analytic truths. If material truths depend on the nature of their objects, but also on *the nature of the experience of these objects*, then the connection between these truths and experience may well be extremely tenuous, but it is not nonexistent. A man blind from birth cannot know *a priori* that all color has lightness, hue, and saturation, since this proposition is not related for him to any experience of color whatsoever. Therefore we must recognize that material idealities, unlike the formal idealities of logic and arithmetic, remain somehow "chained" to a fact, that of the experience of a world of a specific sort,[50] and this despite their *a priori* character. As *a priori*, they are indeed valid unconditionally, that is to say, in all possible worlds, but—as paradoxical as this formulation may be—they are unconditionally valid *on the condition* of the existence of a specific sort of experience, that is to say, on the condition that men exist, or more generally living beings having an experience of the world of this sort.

But then these *a priori* material necessities, while not becoming hypothetical necessities, are no longer *entirely unconditioned.* Are not the propositions on colors valid solely for animals having a physiological constitution such as to allow them to perceive such a thing as color? Husserl will be forced to recognize more and more openly the indispensable character of what he will call "arch-facticity"—but under these conditions it is not at all obvious that the propositions of the phenomenologist would be valid for angels and even gods. Rather we should distinguish not two, but three kinds of necessities: hypothetical necessities of the laws of nature; non-hypothetical and unconditional necessities of logic; necessities that are non-hypothetical, yet conditional, because relative to the existence of an experience of a certain sort (and of a subjective constitution of a certain sort that makes that experience possible), which are explored by phenomenology. But then it becomes difficult to free the third type of necessity from all dependence with respect to an anthropological fact, and "anthropologism" is partially restored. As Husserl will be forced to admit, a facticity seems included *a priori* in the very makeup of material *a priori,* and this also renders increasingly aporetic the idea of a *pure eidetics,* of a method similar to those of mathematics that phenomenology could use for its own purposes.[51] "*Fact,* with its *irrationality,*" Husserl confessed later, "is itself a *structural concept within the system of the concrete a priori.*"[52]

A second major difficulty is the question of the limits of the eidetic method in phenomenology. Are *all* phenomenological descriptions descriptions of essence in the sense I have just specified? Most of the time, Husserl maintains that they are. Phenomenology is a universal eidetic science of experience. However, in some texts at least, he seems to recognize that things are more complex. As long as we stick to elementary examples—sounds, colors, and so on—the eidetic method *may* be possible. But the more description goes on, the more complex it becomes, the less plausible it seems to maintain that phenomenological description proceeds as a mere report of laws of essence. "The *a priori* knowledge that we possess in advance for a given determined object, according to which an essence . . . belongs to it, is only a task, only an indication of goals for a practical effort . . . We will easily grasp pure concepts of essence such as 'color' or 'tone,' 'brightness,' 'timbre' as a moment of a sound, etc. But if we speak of a thing in general, in pure generality, of a body in general, of an animal being, of a man in general, it may well be that pure generality is only realized in the verbal intention, in an empty, non-intuitive way."[53] In short, the more we rise from simple essences to complex ones, the less eidetic variation can serve as our only methodological device for description. There are probably *limits to the eidetic method* that Husserl hardly recognized, but that needs to be recognized if we wish to question the very possibility of phenomenology (see chapter 11).

A third and final problem concerns the relationship between the eidetic method and language. Can we accomplish an analysis of essences without conducting a parallel analysis of the meanings of the terms we use? When I look for the essence of color, am I not at the same time looking for the meaning of the word "color" in my own language? This question is crucial, and it will receive more attention later (see chapters 6 through 8). An analysis of essence seems to be an undertaking far too complex and subtle not to involve our linguistic abilities. As Reinach emphasizes, "When we aspire to essence-analysis, we will naturally set out from words and their significations. . . . Moreover, I no longer need to especially stress the fact that the essence-analysis which is required is in no wise exhausted by investigations of significations."[54] As Husserl says, considerations of essence are not "grammatical hypostatizations";[55] but to what extent are they really independent of language and the conventional rules underlying it—independent of what Wittgenstein was to call its "grammar"?

At this stage, what matters is obviously not to accept all aspects of Husserl's doctrine of the *a priori.* It is rather to understand exactly wherein its originality lies. Without the idea of *necessary structures of experience* pertaining neither to the domain of the empirical discoveries of natural science nor to that of the analytic axioms of logic, the very idea of a "phenomenology" would no longer make sense. It may be that the identification of these structures is far more subtle an operation—much more dependent on language, history, and interpretation—than Husserl acknowledged. It may be that eidetics is only the first word and not the last word of phenomenology. The fact remains that if phenomenology has a meaning, there must be to some extent an autonomy of the pure morphology of our experience, of its style of organization and immanent structuration, with respect to language and the higher forms of thought and judgment. By attacking Kantianism, and through it the neo-Kantianism that triumphed in his time in the Marburg school, Husserl was at the same time attacking a very intellectualist version of what gives sensible experience, our first and corporeal openness to the world, its distinctive features. He denounced "transcendental constructions from on high"[56] that would make all the patterns of experience depend on intellectual functions, and opposed them by championing instead "the old idea of an *a priori* ontology" that Kantianism and empiricism had derided.[57] While neo-Kantianism, in denying the very idea of an independent faculty of intuition, held Kant's transcendental aesthetics to be a mistake, and conceived of knowledge as a constitution of the object by the subject's forms of judgment alone; while it considered, to use Paul Natorp's expression, that "the entire work of knowledge resides in thought,"[58] Husserl maintained on the contrary that "experience with its demands precedes conceptual thinking and its demands,"[59] that there is a regulated order of the preconceptual as such, irreducible to the logic of the understanding, and in which the latter has its origin. He strove to renew, by properly phenomenological means, the idea of a "transcendental aesthetics" de jure prior to "transcendental logic," and dedicated himself to "the eidetic description of the universal *a priori* without which, in simple experience and before categorical acts . . . objects could not appear."[60] Thus, he brought to light what he called, in a remarkable and oft-repeated expression, the "logos of the aesthetic world [*Logos der ästhetischen Welt*]."[61]

Phenomenology is therefore "a logic of the world" (*Welt-Logik*);[62] but this "logic" is not derived from logic in the usual sense. Its discovery was the result of a radical overhaul of the relationships between the *a priori* and the empirical that I have tried to echo in these pages. Phenomenology is no longer content to perpetuate the opposition between the domain of experience with its *a posteriori* contents, and the domain of the forms of thought; it seeks within sensibility itself, within experience as it declares itself to us, with its immanent logos prior to all intellectual and discursive order, a sensible reason, a "broad reason" behind the "narrow reason" of the intellect. Through the highlighting of "the invariant universal form, the pure *ratio* of the world,"[63] what is at stake is nothing less than a rethinking of the status of *ratio* in general. Phenomenology, which Husserl one day qualified as a "super-rationalism" (*Überrationalismus*),[64] can thus provide a fruitful alternative to approaches—notably exemplified in the present course of analytic philosophy—that remain dominated by a mixture of empiricism and neo-Kantianism, conceive of all order and all unity in experience as conferred by language, and consider the opposition between a raw sensory given and a linguistic-oriented reason to constitute the ultimate divide.

2

Husserlian Intentionality

Phenomenology is the analytic description of intentionality in its *a priori.*
—Martin Heidegger

In the previous chapter, I left out a difficulty which, when examined closely, might well constitute a major aporia. On the one hand, I stated that Husserl's *a priori* was objective, that it was valid for all possible subjectivities, not just for our factual psychological and anthropological subjectivity; in other words, the *a priori* is a characteristic *of objects* (in the field of sound and color, for example) and not of the subjectivity that experiences them. On the other hand, I argued that the characteristic specific to the material *a priori* is that it depends intrinsically on the content of our experience, so that material *a priori* necessities are at the same time structural regularities *immanent to that experience.* But isn't that contradictory? We seem to be faced with an alternative: either the *a priori* is a feature of objects, or it is a feature of our experience. And if it is a feature of our experience, the *a priori* is subjective and not objective. We have only seemingly freed ourselves from Kantianism.

Are we, then, confronted with an inconsistency on the part of Husserl? Surely not. To understand this, we must clarify what he means by "experience." If experience, in the phenomenological sense, were nothing but the way a psychological subjectivity appears to itself, the secret fold of an interiority, the objection I have just raised would be fatal to the above analyses. But Husserl conceived of consciousness not as an intimate sphere closed in upon itself, but as an openness onto an exteriority. Experience, in the sense in which Husserl takes this term, is always the experience *of this and that*; it is oriented toward things and the world; it is the mode of givenness of objects. Husserl gave a name to this feature: "intentionality." The situation—somewhat paradoxically—then becomes the following: to understand in what sense the *a priori* is objective, we need to understand what it means for consciousness to be intentional.

The intentionality of consciousness is what guarantees the objectivity of the *a priori* and protects it from all relativity associated with the de facto constitution of our psyche. But intentionality, in turn, is an *a priori* structure of consciousness and is identical with what Husserl calls "the *a priori* of correlation," the *a priori* by virtue of which all consciousness is correlated with objects, that is to say, is consciousness *of* something. Intentionality is therefore an instance of *a priori,* but the *a priori* in its objectivity rests on intentionality. Only that necessary structure of our consciousness allows us to see how the *a priori,* while being a determination of our experience of objects, is also—*and by this very fact*—a determination of the objects of our experience.

Intentionality thus bears within itself the seeds of an overcoming of *all* psychology, even though it is not clear that Husserl advanced that far—even though this overcoming was, in his work, no more than a progressive conquest, constantly threatened by moments of relapse. Although Husserl made the problem of intentionality "the work of [his] whole . . . life,"[1] the problem was not new. It is almost as old as philosophy itself. The whole mystery of intentionality is condensed in book 3 of Aristotle's *De anima* in the cryptic formula according to which *hē psukhē ta onta pōs esti panta,* "the soul is in a way all that is."[2] What does it mean, for the soul, that it *is* what it is not—namely all the rest, the totality of entities? The answer is contained in the little word "*pōs,*" "in a way." For if the soul is "*in a way*" all things, all things are not the soul. Aristotle's assertion does not entail a panpsychism; the "is" cannot be understood here in the sense of the "is" of identity. The soul can only be said *to be* all things in the sense that its presence is at the same time the very presence of things, in the sense that the soul and things *share the same being-at-work* and show up together, in such a way that perceiving, for example, is a "common being-at-work" or actuality—that of the sense and of the perceived. In other words, the presence of the soul does not modify the presence of things in the least, for example the presence of the celestial bodies, which would continue to shine even if there were no one to see them.[3] The presence of the soul adds nothing to that of things, nor does it subtract anything from the presence of things; it lets their presence unfold and blossom forth as presence. Or rather, the being of the soul is nothing but "the very presence of things," in the words of Rémi Brague.[4] Here, there is no interiority opposite an exteriority, but only the one, same actualization of a power to perceive that is in the soul and a power to be perceived that is in the thing, a *common* being-at-work that brings it about that the soul *is* the thing—"in a way." On this point, however, Aristotle seems to hesitate. He dismisses a first solution, which would be to say that the faculty of perception when it is actualized is "the thing itself,"[5] and agrees with the idea that what the soul receives "into" itself, what it is impressed by, is only the form of the thing, its *eidos*. To perceive is for the soul to receive the form of the thing without its matter, like a signet ring that impresses a piece of wax. For if the soul *became* the perceived, if no difference were maintained between them, the very idea of *perception* would become unintelligible.

The medieval commentators on Aristotle will notice this gap and try to fill it. The history of intentionality is the story of this gap and its successive iterations. Scholastics, from Henry of Ghent and Duns Scotus on, since they read Aristotle in light of the Augustinian doctrine of the *verbum mentis*, will separate what Aristotle maintained was inseparably united: the form or the face presented to us by the thing and under which the thing lends itself to vision, and the form that is imprinted in the soul as "the place of forms," *topos eidōn*. Aristotle's *eidos* becomes the *species*, and this "species" soon qualified as "intentional" is no longer the very face of the thing, but its presence by proxy in the soul, its *ens diminutum*, its "diminished being," that is to say, actually, its represented being. The Scholastics thus introduce a completely new problem, that of the *similitudo*, the resemblance between the thing as it exists *ad extra*, outside the soul, that is, the thing in its "real being" (*esse reale*), and the thing as known, in its "objective being" (*esse objective*), or, equivalently, in its "intentional being" (*esse intentionale*). To know the thing is no longer to grasp it as it presents itself, outside of the soul, in the world, but only to relate to an inner *species* which is its duplicate, as it were, and the shadow cast by it; the problem of intentionality becomes that of the *repraesentatio per speciem*. On the occasion of this metamorphosis of the problem, the genesis of which I cannot retrace here, the thing becomes object, *objectum*, and this term literally means what lies before me, what is placed in between and plays the role of a screen for knowledge, that against which knowledge stumbles and which is not the thing itself, but its "raison d'être" (*ratio rei*) in the soul, that is to say, what the medieval thinkers will call its *intentio*.[6] The "object" understood in this sense is thus always the "internal object,"[7] the *intentio* or immanent *species* which is a third item, distinct from both the knowing principle and the thing known. With this doctrine, culminating in the Scotist opposition between *esse reale* and *esse objective*, only a relation of resemblance remains between the thing that exists outside the soul, possessing real being (*esse secundum rem*), and the thing present inside the soul, the thing as known, which possesses objective being, that is to say, "represented being."[8] "The act of knowledge is related to the object as the resemblance is related to the [item] it resembles."[9] In short, the doctrine of intentionality becomes a doctrine of mental representation, in which the "object" means literally the opposite of what it means for us since Kant: not the external thing, but its mental duplicate, its internal stand-in.

It is of this entire legacy that Brentano claims to be a follower when, in his *Psychology from an Empirical Standpoint*, he rehabilitates the Scholastic concept of intentionality, or more precisely, since the term "intentionality" does not appear in the text, when he advances as a criterion for the differentiation of psychic and physical phenomena their relationship to an (immanent) object, their being directed to an object: "Every mental phenomenon is characterized by what the Scholastics of the Middle Ages called the intentional (or mental) inexistence [*Inexistenz*] of an object, and what we might call, though not wholly unambiguously, reference to a content, direction toward an object (which is not to be understood here as meaning a thing), or immanent objectivity. Every mental phenomenon includes something as object within itself, although they do not all do so in the same way."[10] Thus, to follow the three classes of psychic phenomena distinguished by Brentano, in any representation something is represented, in any judgment something is judged, in any feeling, for instance in love and hate, something is loved or hated. But what does it mean that an object is contained "in" each of these acts? What is the meaning of this enigmatic *intentionale Inexistenz* that Brentano mentions but does not explain? "In-existence" is to be understood at the same time and indivisibly in two senses that are nonetheless distinct: in the sense of an immanent existence, an inherence *in* the psyche (*existentia in*), and in the sense of a possible nonexistence (*non existentia*) of the object onto which mental acts are directed. The first sense is emphasized by Brentano when he emphasizes that the object as he defines it is not the reality (*Realität*) itself, the *esse reale* of the Scholastics, but an immanent objectivity, the *esse objective*. In other words, in this definition we must not understand "object" in its modern sense, but rather in its medieval sense of an immanent terminus of the act of knowing.[11] As for the second sense of "inexistence," it derives from the fact that the relation to an object characterizing psychic phenomena as such does not depend on the real existence of this object. Thus, all imagination relates to an object, but most of the time that object does not exist; love is necessarily directed to the beloved, but the latter can be a pure fantasy, and so on. The object is not reality, for there are intentional objects that have no counterpart in reality, and even necessarily so. I may desire something that does not exist or even that cannot exist; I can try to calculate the square root of minus one ($\sqrt{-1}$), even though the number is "imaginary," in mathematical parlance.

But Brentano is not content to revive the Scholastic doctrine; he adds a new exegetical layer, so to speak, to the medieval commentary on

Aristotle. Since psychic phenomena, according to Brentano, are characterized by their indubitability in principle, while the evidence of physical phenomena is subject to doubt, intentionality is reinterpreted and transposed into a Cartesian context. However, what is the meaning of this enigmatic inherence of the object in acts intending it? Can we go beyond mere metaphors here? Brentano does not so much provide a coherent doctrine of intentionality as bequeath a problem to his successors. Indeed, how can we affirm both that every psychic act is characterized by its intrinsic relationship to an object—which implies that this object exists—and that the object in question may not exist? If intentionality is indeed a *relation*, its two *relata* must exist: A is greater than B only if there is something that is B and that is smaller than A. But this does not hold for intentionality: "In other relations both terms—both the fundament and the terminus—are real, but here only the first term—the fundament—is real."[12] How can a relationship involving only one *relatum* be thought? Brentano does not solve this problem. He only emphasizes that, unlike in other relations, in intentionality we are dealing "with something somewhat similar to something relational in a certain respect, which might, therefore, better be called 'quasi-relational' [*Relativliches*]."[13] In short, Brentano does not say how it is possible to reconcile the idea that every psychic act is necessarily directed towards an object with the view that this direction or orientation could continue to characterize that act even in the absence of the object in question. Nor does he specify how to interpret the *immanence* of the intentional object. Brentano only emphasizes that he rejects a solution that would consist in distinguishing *being* from *existence*, and in maintaining that in the case of a *nonexistent* object such as a square circle, the object under consideration does have a being, since it is perfectly possible to assign properties to it, even contradictory ones (circularity and squareness), without its having the least existence, the least actuality. Brentano retorts that he cannot find any sense in that distinction.[14] After him, in 1904, Meinong, in his *Theory of Objects* advances a more radical solution. He accepts to speak of "pure objects," having no form of being whatsoever, neither existence nor ideal being, in such a way that their givenness (*Es gibt*) operates "outside being," and is that of an *Außersein*. Hence the so-being (*So-sein*) of logical *impossibilia*, that is, their *pure objectivity*, is not affected by the non-being of these objects. The field of objects exceeds not only that of existence, but that of being in general: "There are objects of which it is true that there are no such objects."[15] As for Brentano, he does not venture in that direction, but neither does he offer any solution to the problem he himself raised.

As for Husserl, he rejects in advance the solution that Meinong will accept: "the concepts of 'object' and of 'existing object' are equivalent."[16] But to understand how deep his transformation of Brentano's intentionality goes and to what extent it is even a complete turnaround of this notion, we must stop to consider the solution that another "Brentanian," Kazimierz Twardowski, recommends for this same problem. In 1894 Twardowski published a study, *On the Content and Object of Representations,* in which he took a position on the question of "representations without object." Instead of maintaining that there are objects such that they transcend all being altogether, as does Meinong, he distinguishes *two objects,* and correlatively *two senses of existence*: the object as it exists in representation, which he also calls the represented "content," and which has only an "intentional existence," and the external object which, in the case of contradictory representations, has no existence at all. Twardowski believes he can thus solve the paradox of nonexistent objects by splitting the correlate of the psychic act, henceforth distinguishing act, content, and object. The immanent content of consciousness, which has contradictory "marks" or properties (circular and square), is not the actual object which would normally correspond to the content but which, in this case, does not exist, since these two "marks" are mutually exclusive. Twardowski posits a general principle which governs its solution: "We must hold fast to this: for each representation, an object becomes represented, whether it exists or not; even representations whose objects *cannot* exist are no exception to this law."[17] The strength of Meinong's solution in 1904 was to preserve the *unity* of the meant or intended object, thus preserving what characterizes psychic phenomena: their being-directed toward something. Its weakness was to turn existence into a predicate, just like any other predicate.[18] Twardowski's solution presents nothing but weakness. By distinguishing between content and object, that is to say, between intentional and real existence, Twardowski, like Brentano before him, makes the intentional object into an immanent object, distinct from the transcendent object that can be or not be. But, in contrast with Brentano, Twardowski thinks of intentionality as a true relation necessarily comprising two fundaments, the act and the immanent content, but which in certain cases lacks all external reference. Twardowski does indeed free Brentano's thesis of its most paradoxical aspect, the idea of a *relation* to something nonexistent, but only to fall into the most classic aporias of a theory of mental representation with the relation it assumes to hold between a picture (*Bild*) or a picture-copy (*Abbild*) and the object.[19] The truth is that, far from solving Brentano's problem, he merely transposed it to the realm of consciousness, for how could there even be an *immanent content* "square circle," when these two properties are incompatible? It is not by internalizing the object that we can make it comprehensible how that object can possess two contradictory properties, nor how it can take on an *existence*, even only an "intentional" one. If in addition, the relation of this immanent content to the object is that of a picture-copy, as Twardowski claims, what can that picture-copy be a copy of?

It is this kind of objection that Husserl raises against both Twardowski and his predecessor. To be sure, the student ventured further than the master, but in the eyes of Husserl he only expresses the heart of the latter's conception: the view that the intentional object must be an inner object connected with the external realities only by a representational link. Now, we must deny both that it makes any sense to split the intentional correlate into an immanent and a transcendent object, and that the former object is connected to the latter by a relation of resemblance. "That all representation is linked by means of a mental 'picture-copy' to its object," writes Husserl, "we take to be a theoretical fiction."[20] It follows that there are not two, but one single object, which is the real object, transcending consciousness: "*the intentional object of a presentation is the same as its actual object, and on occasion as its external object, and . . . it is absurd to distinguish between them.* The transcendent object would not be the object of *this* presentation, if it were not *its* intentional object."[21] Therefore, the theory of intentionality cannot be a doctrine of mental representation. It must be exactly the opposite. It must demonstrate that consciousness in its phenomenological essence is a "relation to some 'transcendent' matter,"[22] and that "the immmanent, mental object is not therefore part of the descriptive or real makeup [*deskriptiven reellen Bestand*] of the experience, it is in truth not really immanent or mental."[23] The theory of intentionality must take us back to Aristotle, with the soul as openness to things, beyond the palimpsest of the accumulated misinterpretations of the text of *On the Soul* by Scholasticism and modern philosophy.

Husserl advances several arguments to show the absurdity of a theory like that of Twardowski. First, there is an argument that takes on a hypothetical form, and could be called the *argument of intersubjectivity*. If an intersubjective knowledge is possible, if the ideal of a truth resting on an intersubjective basis makes sense, then we must not be locked up within the circle of our representations, but rather have access by means of intentionality to the others' actual world, with its real, ideal, but also fictive and even absurd objects. For example, when I imagine Greenland's icy expanse, my fantasies are surely different from those Nansen may have produced, but they still relate to *the same object.*[24] *In order for us to have access to the* same *world* [*même monde*], *we must have access to the* world *itself* [*monde même*]. This argument, it must be stressed, is still hypothetical in form. It has not yet been established that an intersubjectively founded knowledge of the world and the different types of objects it comprises is possible. But *if* it is possible, then a theory of Brentanian inspiration cannot account for it.

A second, stronger argument, the *argument of infinite regress*, consists in showing that the thesis equating the intentional object with an internal representation is simply incoherent. This argument remains unchanged from the *Logical Investigations* through *Ideas I*.[25] It may be formulated as follows. If the intentional object is only a "picture-copy," it must meet the requirements of a picture. What requirements? A picture, a photograph for example, only represents something for us because we can—at least ideally—gain an access to what it represents that is unmediated by that picture. It is an eidetic necessity that where all self-givenness of the thing is lacking, all possibility of an image-givenness of that thing is also lacking. Indeed, in order for the image function to appear, Husserl says, it is not enough that there be as great a resemblance as you like between the picture-copy and the object of which it is a copy; it is also necessary that I intend or mean the latter through the former—therefore that there be an intentional relation between the supporting picture (a photograph, for example) and what it represents (the thing perceived or the thing imagined). "Resemblance between two objects, however precise, does not make the one be a picture of the other. Only a presenting ego's power to use a similar as an image-representative of a similar—the first similar had intuitively, while the second similar is nonetheless *meant* in its place—makes the image *be* an image."[26] Under these conditions, talk of an "internal" picture that would *replace* the thing entirely, since that thing would remain forever inaccessible, is just nonsense. To the theoretician of internal representations who tells us that we have *nothing but* immanent picture-copies, one should always ask: "internal representations of what?" Whence two possibilities: either the representation is a representation of something, in which case it should be possible to grasp the thing directly (without representation), or else there is nothing of which the representation is a representation, in which case the concept of representation becomes inconsistent.

Husserl's argument shows us why it is impossible to retain Brentano's intentionality. But it does not yet say how we are to conceive of intentionality positively. Indeed, how to understand that intentionality is both at the same time a necessary feature of consciousness, "an inward peculiarity of certain experiences,"[27] on the one hand, and a relation to the transcendent thing as it exists outside consciousness, on the other? Does it really make sense to say that there is only one object, the transcendent one, and at the same time that this object may *not* be? What solution can be given to the paradox of nonexistent objects on the basis of this completely renewed concept of intentionality that has broken away from its sources in Scholasticism and from any mentalist theory of representation? Husserl retains two lessons from Twardowski. First, intentionality is indeed a relation, and even an *a priori* relation, "the *a priori* of correlation," in the words of Husserl, which is distinct from any contingent relation between lived experiences, understood as mental episodes, and real events of nature. Intentionality, which is an internal relation, cannot in principle be confused with a causal, and therefore external, relation. "Closer consideration shows it to be absurd in principle, here or in like cases, to treat an intentional as a causal relation, to give it the sense of an empirical, substantial-causal case of necessary connection."[28] In a rather unfair way, Husserl accuses Brentano of having supported such a doctrine, and, being blinded by his naturalism, to have conceived of intentionality as a kind of "interlocking" between a mental and a real event.[29] Second, Husserl takes over Twardowski's triad act/content/object, while reinterpreting it through and through. Twardowski, having inherited this triad from Bolzano, subordinated it to a false theory of the content (*Inhalt*) that conceives of it, in a psychologistic vein, as a mental picture of the object, distinct from that object itself. Now, it was from a radically anti-psychologistic perspective, which Husserl embraces here, that Bolzano had introduced the distinction between (a) acts, (b) their objective content—that is, "representations in themselves" and "propositions in themselves" that persist even if nobody thinks them, and that mediate the relationship to objects, and (c) these objects themselves. In §49 of his *Theory of Science*, Bolzano distinguishes between the "representation in itself" (*Vorstellung an sich*) which refers to one, several, or no objects, and the objects to which this representation refers, which may or may not be.[30] Thus Bolzano makes the content of representations into Platonic identical-ideal entities (or Stoic *lekta*) that transcend the contingent psychic acts through which they are grasped. These ideal contents are analogous to the "meaning" (*Sinn*) of linguistic statements. This analogy with the linguistic sense allows Husserl to explain how the intentional relation, as relation to a content that mediates the relation to the object, is not immanent to consciousness, since such content has no "psychological status," but only an "ideal status," identical for every consciousness.[31]

Husserl's solution is therefore to reinterpret the notion of content (*Inhalt*) ruling out any idea of representation by resemblance, and to adopt, in order to conceptualize it, a *semantic* model. The content is not a picture of the object; it is the sense according to which an object is meant or intended; it is the object according to the mode of its being meant, and hence something about which it is absolutely nonsensical to speak of "resemblance" in any sense whatsoever.[32] Every consciousness relates to its transcendent intentional object through a mode of intending that is its "meaning" or its "intentional matter," and this meaning is already something ideal, which is not part of the stuff of the psyche, which is "nothing individual, nothing real, never in any way a *psychic* datum."[33] We must rethink the intentional content, or, as Husserl also calls it, the "intentional matter" of the act, which is defined as what confers on the act in relation to an object *in a mode that is in each case specific*,[34] by applying the model of meaning to it. "Meaning is the *essentia*, the essence of representation as such . . . A relation to objects belongs to each representation; but what is involved is a property of meaning."[35] This semantic, and no longer iconic character of the intentional matter must not, however, suggest that what Husserl calls here "meaning," "apprehensional sense" (*Auffasungssinn*), "intentional matter," and what he will later, from 1908 on, call "noema" and "noematic sense," is *intrinsically linguistic*. It is true that between linguistic meaning (for which Husserl tends to reserve the term *Bedeutung*) and apprehensional sense (or the matter of acts in general), a strict analogy is drawn—an analogy whose meaning and consequences we must analyze later (see chapter 4); but "analogy" in no case means identity. Thus, just as a single object, Napoleon, can be meant through changing nominal expressions—"the victor of Jena" or "the vanquished of Waterloo"—similarly, the city of Berlin can be taken as object by several intentional acts—acts of perception, imagination, or recollection—while remaining a single object, despite the changing intentional matter according to which it is meant and apprehended. The object is in all cases the same, but the modalities of its being intended and given differ. These "modes of givenness," these "apprehensional senses" are not necessarily linguistic. They extend to the entire sphere of acts: perception, recollection, imagination, image-consciousness, ideation, and so on.

This conception of intentionality opens the path to a solution to the paradox of nonexistent objects. Intentionality is a *relation*, and this implies that all intentional acts refer to an intentional content, a "sense" or "matter," regardless of whether the object intended through this matter exists or not. In order to understand this formulation, which prima facie seems paradoxical, one must grasp an essential phenomenological difference that pervades the entire domain of acts: the difference between an "empty" intentional act and its fulfillment. Husserl replaces the metaphor of resemblance used by iconic (that is, mentalistic) theories of intentionality with this metaphor of emptiness and fullness, according to which it becomes possible to escape all duplication of the object. An object can be intended emptily, that is to say, *without any corresponding intuition*. For example, the name "Ubud" is pronounced in my hearing. I recognize this name, having heard it before, and I know it refers to a town on the island of Bali. But suppose that I not only have never been to Bali—so I have no recollection of places on it—but I never had the opportunity of seeing any pictures of Ubud nor of hearing any stories that would enable me to imagine the architecture of the city, the style of its temples, the customs of its inhabitants. In that case, although I can intend the city of Ubud "emptily," as Husserl puts it, that is, in a purely "signitive" way; although I can intentionally relate to the same object as anyone who understands this proper name and is able to use it appropriately, it is nonetheless impossible for me to bring about the least intuition to its object, that is to say, the least givenness *in person* of it, in the form of perceptions, memories, or imaginings. I have the same intentional content as anyone who understands the name "Ubud" and, through it, I relate to the same object, but unlike someone returning from a trip to Indonesia, my intention remains empty or symbolic, and thus no object is given to me. Therefore, in all intending of an object, there is indeed an object that is *intended* in a specific way—that *object in its mode of being intended* is what Husserl calls "intentional matter" and which is identically the same for any consciousness relating in this mode to the object in question; but, in every intending of an object, there is not necessarily an object that is *given* in an intuitive manner.

How does this distinction apply to the problem of so-called "representations without object"? When I relate intentionally to contradictory objects, such as a square circle, or to impossible objects such as the square root of minus one, ($\sqrt{-1}$), it is indeed to these objects themselves, as transcendent objects identically thinkable by any consciousness, that I relate through a determined intentional matter—for example, by trying to imagine that figure or to calculate that number. And yet the content of my intentional acts is such, in this circumstance, that the "sense" through which I intend these objects is a contradictory one, is nonsense, and consequently a content such that it cannot receive, by virtue of an *a priori* necessity, any intuitive fulfillment. It is this *a priori* impossibility of an intuition, that is, of a givenness of that object *in person* or in the *original* that compels me to recognize that the object in question does not exist. In other words, even in the boundary case of the alleged "representations without object," I do intend the object itself in its transcendence with respect to consciousness, but I intend it in the modality of an "object" that is contradictory or in any case *a priori* impossible, and therefore necessarily nonexistent, that is to say *deprived of intuitive content.* This leads Husserl to support both the view that everyone who thinks of a square circle necessarily thinks of the same thing, and the idea that this "thing," contrary to what Twardowski thought, possesses no form of *existence* whatsoever, since it excludes *a priori* any possibility of intuition. Husserl holds this view without conferring upon the object in question the status of an *Außersein*, as Meinong does. We think the same thing, which means here that we *intend* the same object *emptily*, but since this object is deprived of any intuitive content, since it is an *a priori* impossible object, we are actually not thinking anything, in the sense of *not intuiting anything*: there is no "object" of our thought. We are thinking the same thing, but there is no such thing as what we are thinking. "'The object is merely intentional' does not, of course, mean that it exists, but only in an intention, of which it is a real [*reelles*] part, or that some shadow of it exists. It means rather that the intention, the reference to an object so qualified, exists, but not that the object does. If the intentional object exists, the intention, the reference, does not exist alone, but the thing referred to exists also."[36]

This distinction between thinking in the sense of intending (in an empty or symbolic way) and thinking in the sense of intuiting helps us to give meaning to a statement such as this: "We are thinking of the squared circle, but there is no square circle." Here, "we are thinking of" simply means "we grasp the meaning of the expression 'square circle,' we have an understanding of that *symbol*"—and certainly not "we are referring with these words to an object having such and such a property, and existing either in that form, or otherwise." What exists in this case is only the intending, as Husserl says, and not the object; the latter is "merely entertained in thought, and is nothing in reality."[37] More generally, this distinction can significantly refine the analysis of intentionality and its forms. In his *Psychology from an Empirical Standpoint*, Brentano wrote that "every psychological phenomenon contains something as object within itself, although they do not all do so in the same *way*,"[38] but he did not really succeed in giving a meaningful content to this assertion. What are these various modes of intentionality, and how are they to be described? Intentionality refers not only to a relationship between consciousness and objects. To each type of act there corresponds *a specific mode of givenness* of its object: to perception, a specific mode of givenness of the perceived object; to imagination, of the imagined object; and so on. Hence a description of intentionality must be a description of the modes of consciousness and of the correlative modes of givenness of its objects. A theory of intentionality is a theory of *forms or modes of intentional correlation*, that is, of the connection between types of object, modes of intending, and corresponding modes of givenness. This doctrine Brentano and his heirs have not been able to develop. In short, as Husserl writes, "reference to objects is possible *a priori* only as being a definite manner of reference."[39] Here again we see a kind of Aristotelianism surfacing: phenomenology is a *doctrine of forms*—forms of the intentional relation in its specific modes, and forms of the givenness of the correlative objects. It is a pure *a priori* morphology of experience in its intentional modes. The essential task of phenomenology is to describe and classify these modes.

To clarify this point, we must leave the mainly historical perspective that has hitherto been ours and adopt a more systematic one. What Husserl qualifies as "intentional" are sometime acts, sometimes objects, sometimes certain lived experiences (*Erlebnisse*), and sometimes consciousness itself. This terminological ambiguity is due to the fact that intentionality is a structural feature of consciousness as such, determining each of its moments or aspects. These aspects are descriptive characteristics and not real elements of lived experience. They are five in number. For every intentional lived experience we may distinguish (1) the act by which an object is intended (the noesis, in the vocabulary of *Ideas I*); (2) the doxic or positing qualities attaching to that act; (3) the intentional matter of that act, its content (later called "noema"); (4) the intuitive fullfilment of the intention, which admits of various degrees; and (5) the intentional object. Without going into a detailed analysis of these various moments of intentionality, let us examine a few examples that will enable us, as it were, to grasp them in vivo.

The last time I went to New York, I stayed in an apartment located along the East River, close to the Brooklyn Bridge. I would wake up, and there was the bridge I had seen so often in photographs, framed in the opening of a window, and I enjoyed going down to the riverbank to see its powerful architecture in the fresh air and morning sunshine. Some days, when it was cloudy, its silhouette, barely visible, would emerge from a thin fog. What difference was there between my perception of the bridge and the reproductions I had so often seen? In perception, Husserl says, "it is the thing itself that we perceive,"[40] which means that we don't have any consciousness of a picture or representation of any kind: it is near the bridge that we are ourselves standing, and its pilings with their neo-Gothic arches can only stand out in the fullness of their indisputable presence, their style at once massive and aerial, and their unswerving strength of reality, because they are here, as we are, right in front of us. The bridge itself is given *originaliter,* in person, unlike when I see one of its reproductions. But in the case of perception, this givenness in person is also a givenness "in the flesh [*leibhaft*]," in which the thing itself is present before me as I run my gaze over it. Here, the act is characterized by "the intuitive persuasion that a thing or event is itself present before us [*gegenwärtigen*] for our grasping";[41] thus it is paired with a matching doxic thetic quality. The positing in existence of the object is part of the act of perceiving. I cannot perceive something without perceiving it as existing—even if that assumption should prove inadequate after the fact. Perception is thus characterized by the highest possible degree of intuitiveness: it is a presentation (*Gegenwärtigung*) of the thing itself before my eyes in its bodily selfhood (*leibhaft*). Moreover, when I move further along the riverbank, the perceived object remains the same, but its mode of givenness (the intentional matter with which it presents itself) is continuously changing. This "object in its mode of givenness" actually depends on what Husserl calls "the real content of consciousness," that is, the data of sensation (or *hyletic data*) that are "lived" by me but not perceived as objects or pertaining to objects. Hyletic data, in the sense attributed to them by Husserl (for example, red as a sensed quality, distinct from the red as an objective quality of the flag flying in the distance), differ from the empiricists' sensations since, unlike the latter, they are not the ultimate elements constituting the very stuff of the psyche, inferred as an explanatory hypothesis, but only *descriptive* characteristics of lived experiences. These hyletic data are not intentional, unlike the object that presents itself through them according to changing modes of givenness. Only the object appears, only the object is perceived, never the sensory givens. "I do not see colour-sensations but coloured things, I do not hear tone-sensations but the singer's song."[42]

Now what happens if I try to remember the Brooklyn Bridge a year later? First of all, I remember the same bridge as the one I perceived at the time, and now, as then, it appears to me in recollection from changing perspectives. I can intend the bridge in this or that mode—as it appeared to me in the morning, suspended and motionless, within the window frame, or as it majestically soared above me when I walked the banks of the East River. The intentional matter is not the object itself, which remains one single object in all its perspectives. But neither is the intentional matter a second object. It is the object according to a specific mode of intending (and a specific mode of givenness). The recollection is of the Brooklyn Bridge itself, just as perception was. To this extent, it is an intuitive act, in which the object is given to me *in person*, or in the original. To be persuaded of this, I just have to try to remember a reproduction of the Brooklyn Bridge, for example a photograph I took at the time: in this case, the intentional object of recollection is not the bridge itself, but its reproduction, that is, a copy representing it. Consequently *recollection itself is not an image-consciousness*, because an image-consciousness presupposes a duality between the image that represents and the object represented by it. In recollection, by contrast, I have no consciousness at all of such a duality, although the object that I remember, and intend directly, without intermediaries, is not of course present *in the flesh* before my eyes. The recollection is an intuitive relation to the object itself, but one in which the object is not given in its bodily presence—but only "given again" or restored, in a modified consciousness, *as if it were present* again before my eyes. This modified givenness, in the mode of "as if," is what Husserl calls "re-presentation" (*Vergegenwärtigung*). Representation is a specific mode of consciousness, irreducible to either perception or image-consciousness. In perception, the thing is given in person *and* in the flesh: in re-presentation, the thing is given in person, but not in its corporeal presence (*leibhaft*); in image-consciousness, the thing is not given itself in the original, but only through something else, a more or less similar copy: what is given in person is only an image, and not what this image represents. Lastly, as we have seen, there are intuitionless modes of consciousness, in which the thing is only intended in "symbolic or blind" thought, as Leibniz would have it. In this case, the thing is not given at all; only the symbol referring to it is given.

What is the difference between an act of recollection and an act of imagination—and between their respective intentional correlates? At first sight, memory is very similar to imagination, so that their borders can sometimes blur. As Nabokov has observed, the writer, especially the novelist, whose art draws on memory, but who continually transforms it to fit his plot, ends up not knowing what he lived through and what he imagined. "I have often noticed that after I had bestowed on the characters of my novels some treasured item of my past, it would pine away in the artificial world where I had so abruptly placed it. Although it lingered on in my mind, its personal warmth, its retrospective appeal had gone and, presently, it became more closely identified with my novel than with my former self, where it had seemed to be so safe from the intrusion of the artist."[43] Between imagination and recollection, however, there remains a fundamental difference, an insurmountable eidetic disparity: recollection *posits* its object as having existed in the past, while imagination suspends or "neutralizes" all positing of existence. Therefore, while recollection and imagination are both re-presentations, they differ in their doxic quality: "*imagination* in general is the *neutrality modification* applied to '*positing*' *re-presentation,* and therefore to recollection in the broadest conceivable sense."[44] Recollection is a second givenness (*Wiedergegebenheit*) of the thing as it was lived; imagination is a givenness of the thing *as if* it were being lived, in the world of pure fiction. It follows that imagination (*Phantasie*) is not image-consciousness (*Bildbewußtsein*), contrary to what is advanced by most psychological theories, which make imaginary representation into a sort of internal "icon." Imagination is indeed concerned with the *original object,* and not a copy of it. If I imagine an episode taking place at the Brooklyn Bridge, the bridge itself becomes a kind of protagonist of my story. To imagine something about the Brooklyn Bridge is neither to perceive a picture (even an "internal" one) of the bridge, nor to present to oneself such a picture in the imagination. (This second possibility exists, but differs from the first one.) In image-consciousness, on the other hand, we have two distinct things: the image-object (*Bildobjekt*), that is to say, the picture that I see, and that generally has a material substratum, such as a canvas to which pigment has been applied, and the image-subject (*Bildsubjekt*), that is to say the thing portrayed in the picture, the subject represented by the painting. The first image is perceived, the second is intended *in the imagination* through the perceived image, which has been previously "un-realized," that is, neutralized in its objective properties, to become the mere support of an imaginary projection. Image-consciousness is a complex consciousness: an intertwining of a perception—hence an intuitive presentation, that of the image-substratum—and a re-presentation—that is, an imagining or imaging consciousness that is directed to a "world in the image" through the former. Imagination, *Phantasie,* intervenes as an auxiliary to a perception in image-consciousness, but is nowise identical with it. Imagination is *not* image-consciousness, because when I imagine the landscape presented to me in a painting, I do not imagine a second painting in turn depicting a landscape for me, and so on. Of course, I can always (but this is different) *imagine an image-consciousness,* as when I imagine myself walking through the Grande Galerie of the Louvre and stopping before this or that painting.

These analyses of examples, which could be continued, show the complexity of the concrete descriptions of intentionality in its several modalities, its positing or non-positing qualities (to which should be added the intermediate qualities such as doubt and questioning), the respective sorts of objects (simple and complex, sensible and ideal) and their modes of presence (presentation, re-presentation).

Some of these differences may be represented synoptically in the following table:

Type of Lived Experience	Intentional Character	Degree of Intuitiveness	Doxic Quality
sensations (hyletic data)	no		
perception	yes	presentation (*Gegenwärtigung*): given in person and in the flesh	positional (belief in the existence of the object or state of affairs)
imagination	yes	re-presentation (*Vergegenwärtigung*): given in person but not in the flesh	neutral
recollection	yes	re-presentation	positional
image-consciousness	yes	re-presentation on the basis of a presentation	neutral
ideation	yes	presentation	neutral

We can now give a more precise content to the idea that in every perception something is perceived, in every judgment something is judged, in every imagination something is imagined, and so on. To these various types of acts there correspond several types of objects in their mode of givenness, that is, several intentional contents—but also several doxic qualities (thetic, negative, or neutral, corresponding respectively to a positing of existence, a positing of nonexistence, and a neutrality with respect to existence or nonexistence), and several degrees of intuitive fullness, ranging from the mere empty ("signitive" or symbolic) intending to the highest degree of intuitiveness, presentation (*Gegenwärtigung*) in person and in the flesh, through all intermediate degrees: the several sorts of re-presentation (*Vergegenwärtigung*), and the complex modalities of consciousness that articulate a presentation *and* a re-presentation as in the case of image-consciousness. In Husserl's view, givenness in the flesh is not the exclusive privilege of sensible objects, but can apply equally to ideal objects. Essences are also given to intuition in acts of ideation; thus they are general objects of a certain type (simple, such as material essences, complex, such as states of affairs). These ideal objects are atemporal, or rather omni-temporal. They are identical to themselves and ideally reproducible for all thought that thinks them. Above all, they have the same non-psychological objectivity as do real-world objects. Intentionality has not only made it possible to understand how consciousness can "get out of itself" to intend and reach reality, how it "is" intrinsically nothing but its openness to things and the world, how it is "*in a way* all that is." It has made it possible to guarantee the objectivity of objects, sensible but also ideal, in contrast to the contingent lived experiences of a consciousness. Intentionality, which is an *a priori* structure of certain lived experiences (not of all, as we have seen, since hyletic data are an exception), guarantees the objectivity of all *a priori*, and consequently forearms the doctrine of the *a priori* against any possible relapse into psychologism. The existence of *a priori* structures of phenomenality makes possible the description of intentionality as one of these structures, and inversely, intentionality guarantees the independence of the *a priori* vis-à-vis our contingent psychic constitution.

Before we provisionally take leave of Husserl's intentionality, two points should be made. The first concerns intentionality, the second, Husserl's method.

There is a potential danger threatening the conception I have presented above. If intentionality is indeed a *relation*—not of course a contingent relation between two terms independent of each other, but an internal relation between an act and its content; if to every intentional act there necessarily corresponds—not an object, since the latter may very well not exist, but an object according to its mode of being intended, that is, a content that is not to be thought of as a copy but as a *meaning*; if consequently the presence of a content *is essential to intentionality*, while the presence of an object is *accidental* to it—the following question arises. Could not this semantic content continue to be present for a consciousness even in the absence of *any* object, and—why not—of any world? Going yet a step further, what would prevent us from maintaining that the world is nothing more than an intentional content, a "noematic correlate," according to the vocabulary of Husserl's *Ideas I?* In other words, a tendency toward idealism already begins to manifest itself in this conception of intentionality as a relation to a content—even to a semantic, not to a representational one. By this, I do not mean that this idealism is already present in *Logical Investigations* in the form it will take later on—which would be manifestly false—but its place seems already hollowed out, so to speak, by the thesis that intentionality is a *relation* to a content that is nevertheless *distinct from the object*—a content which has no need for the existence of this object in order to be intended and grasped as such. I will have more to say on this problem later (see chapter 14).

In the final analysis, the outcome of our attempt to reconstruct the "logic" that led Husserl to adopt his fundamental positions regarding the problem of intentionality is that the eidetic method, as described in the preceding chapter, is far from being the only actual method of phenomenology. This is probably obvious, but nonetheless deserves to be emphasized: we do not yet know whether Husserl's conception of eidetics is tenable, nor whether even one single *purely* eidetic analysis (or one single eidetic analysis without qualification) has ever been carried out in phenomenology; but what we cannot ignore, from this point on, is that the description of phenomena cannot be based on the eidetic method alone, in the absence of a closely argued discussion with the philosophical tradition, and consequently with earlier theories and descriptions. This intertwining of description and argumentation is not only a characteristic of Husserl's style: it belongs to the style of every phenomenology.

3

The Linguistic Criteria of Intentionality

"If you think of your brother in America," Wittgenstein wonders, "how do you know that what you think is, that the thought inside you is, of your brother being in America? Is this an experiential business?"[1] The problem raised by Wittgenstein is that of intentionality. But the suspicion he immediately formulates is directed against conceptions which, like that of Brentano and Husserl, see intentionality as a *phenomenon* of a particular nature that could be experienced and described as such. Without saying more about it, Wittgenstein's remark beckons in a very different direction. What if the intentional relation was primarily a property of language, or rather of our use of language, rather than being a property of consciousness? And what if that which allowed us to think of our brother in America was not a mysterious feature of consciousness—that of directing itself toward its object and being transported, so to speak, to his proximity, even though that would require crossing the Atlantic—but only a characteristic of the expression "my brother in America" when used appropriately? Without coming to a clear conclusion, Wittgenstein raises a problem that will be in the background of all the linguistic critiques of the phenomenological approach of intentionality.

It is not only a matter of intentionality. This, as we have seen, is a specimen of material *a priori*, of necessary structure of phenomenality. If it could be established that intentionality is a mere linguistic mirage, this consequence could be extended to include all the structures of appearance that phenomenology undertakes to describe. The "phenomenological problem" could then become a pseudo-problem. To address this difficulty, we can take as our starting point its formulation by Ernst Tugendhat. Tugendhat will prove to be an outstanding guide in this case for several reasons. First, unlike other analytic philosophers, he takes phenomenology seriously and has a firsthand knowledge of it. Let us not forget that he was a student of Heidegger, to whom he dedicated his *Traditional and Analytical Philosophy*, the work in which he formulates this critique. In Tugendhat's view, phenomenology is not just "nonsense" as Schlick and Carnap would have it. It is a project that is hampered from the outset by the unquestioned semantic presuppositions that it shares with the philosophical tradition as a whole; it constitutes the ultimate achievement of the possibilities opened up by that tradition. Furthermore, in the course of this whole discussion, Tugendhat has circumscribed the main issues of the debate between the analytic / linguistic and the phenomenological approach in philosophy. His critique, whether we accept or reject it, is exemplary.

The concept of intentionality Tugendhat examines is Husserl's. Not, of course, that it would be necessary to adhere unconditionally to Husserl's conception of intentionality to do phenomenology. As we know, Husserl's intentionality has been the subject of considerable controversy even within the phenomenological movement. Let us consider Husserl's description as a mere sample of his philosophical method, without concerning ourselves about what internal criticisms we could address to it from within the field of common problems and preoccupations. Let us rather ask ourselves whether the characteristic of being directed toward objects can be rightly regarded as a characteristic *of consciousness*—and not of what we can *say* about it.

According to its simplest definition, intentionality is an essential characteristic of consciousness. It means that "all consciousness is consciousness of something." How is that formulation to be understood? Does it even make sense? Such is the suspicion expressed by Tugendhat. If you want to give a meaning to that phrase, he says basically, you must perform the linguistic turn. Intentionality is not a structural feature of consciousness; it is a structural feature of our way of speaking about it. If we want to say what intentionality is, we find nothing in the description of our experience or our lived experiences (*Erlebnisse*) that would justify the application of this concept. Its application depends on criteria that are "exclusively linguistic."[2]

Let us consider the list of examples given by Husserl. "A perceiving is a perceiving of something, perhaps a physical thing [*Ding*]; a judging is a judging of a predicatively formed affair-complex [*Sachverhalt*]; valuing of a predicatively formed value-complex [*Wertverhalt*]; a wishing of a predicatively formed wish-complex, and so forth."[3] This list can be extended, but how far? Indeed, Husserl immediately adds: "Acting bears upon action [*Handeln geht auf Handlung*]. Doing bears upon the deed [*Tun auf Tat*]. Loving bears upon the loved one." But acting does not seem intentional in the same sense as loving. Consider for example the case of writing. To write, I must blacken paper; therefore there must be paper that is blackened, or rather covered with signs. But to love, it is not necessary for an object of love to exist. I may very well love an idle fancy. We find here again what might be called "the Brentano criterion," according to which the intentionality of a lived experience of consciousness is not affected by the nonexistence of its object. This criterion is what prompted Brentano to say that the intentional relation is merely a "quasi-relation," because a true relation presupposes the existence of each of its *relata.* But then the property of being directed to an object, the being-oriented (*Gerichtetsein*) toward an object is an *equivocal* property, not exclusively possessed by intentional states. In fact, as Tugendhat emphasizes, it is a property of all transitive verbs that require an "object" in the grammatical sense of the word. It is true that in all love something is loved, in every desire, something is desired, in every perception, something is perceived; but it is no less true that in every action of eating, something is eaten, and in every action of cutting, something is cut. Now eating and cutting are actions, but they are nowise "intentional lived experiences." Did not Husserl content himself with "discovering" under the name "intentionality" a grammatical feature common to a number of verbs: transitivity? As long as it does not tell us—to formulate the problem in the terms imposed by the linguistic turn—what differentiates an *intentional* transitive verb from an ordinary transitive verb, Husserl's (Brentano's) criterion of intentionality remains empty. He says nothing at all. Now, it is not possible to give a response to this problem on the basis of a description of phenomena; that response, Tugendhat claims, can only come from an analysis of language.

To begin with, it seems that the verbs delimiting the domain of intentionality, in the sense that Husserl bestows on this term, possess a common characteristic—that of pertaining to the domain of the "mental," in a sense requiring further clarification. Tugendhat, on this point, follows Wittgenstein's suggestion that there is a strictly linguistic criterion according to which we can make a distinction between psychological and non-psychological verbs, and consequently propose a "grammatical" equivalent of Husserl's concept of lived experience (*Erlebnis*) without, however, adhering to the Cartesian presuppositions underlying this concept, particularly the questionable idea of lived experience being accessible to an indubitable *knowledge.* In the case of psychological verbs, Wittgenstein writes, "psychological verbs [are] characterized by the fact that the third person of the present is to be verified by observation, the first person not."[4] For example, it is the observation of the other person's behavior that allows me to say that he is anxious, or that he intends to behave in a certain way, but it is not on the basis of a similar (external) observation, nor on that of an internal observation, that I attribute intentions or emotions to myself. Let us leave aside the difficulties raised by this criterion.[5] Intentional verbs are psychological verbs, but not all psychological verbs are intentional verbs. Indeed, verbs of sensation, such as suffering (feeling pain) or seeing the color red, pass Wittgenstein's test, but they do not put us in relation to any object or state of affairs in the world. They do not exemplify what Husserl means by "intentionality." As for verbs that express intentionality (desiring, believing, wondering, knowing, remembering, judging, wishing, imagining, perceiving, etc.), and therefore require a grammatical "object," their object can be of two types: either a nominal expression referring to a concrete object, individuated spatiotemporally, or a nominalized sentence of the form "that *p*," that is to say, an expression that refers to an abstract object, to what Husserl calls a "state of affairs" (*Sachlage, Sachverhalt*). When he writes, for example, that in all judging, something is judged, that "something" is not a concrete object. It can only be expressed in a propositional clause. Judging means judging that a state of affairs obtains; it is judging *that* p. But other intentional verbs admit of both of the aforementioned constructions. I can want an ice cream cone, or I can want to eat an ice cream cone. Similarly, I can see the tree beside the road or I can see that a tree is standing beside the road.

If all intentional transitive verbs had, always and necessarily, abstract objects as their object, that is to say, nominalized sentences of the form "that *p*," we would then have a strictly linguistic criterion to distinguish between intentional and non-intentional transitive verbs. For cutting, sawing, breaking, building, gathering, eating, and so on, can only admit of a concrete object. What do I eat? I do not eat a state of affairs. I eat *this* piece of bread. Unfortunately, however, this is not the way things are: most intentional verbs admit of the double construction, nominal and propositional. Tugendhat's strategy is to show that this is not in fact how things are. Indeed, while the nominal construction can always be expressed in propositional form, the converse is not true. Intentionality would thus be a property of what Anglo-Saxon philosophy calls, since Russell, "propositional attitudes." Or, to put it in the words of Tugendhat, the thesis to be defended is "that the non-propositional modes of consciousness [*nichtpropositionalen Bewußtseinsweisen*] are only apparently non-propositional, that in reality they imply propositional consciousness."[6]

We can desire something, but this is only an elliptical way of saying we desire that something be the case. Victory may be desired, but to desire victory is to desire *to win* the battle, that is to say, to desire a state of affairs: *that the battle be won.* The same is true of the other intentional verbs. This helps to understand the special status of objects that "exist only in the mind." By this metaphor, we mean that the objects in question are merely objects of belief. Sganarelle may fear the Surly Monk, even though the Surly Monk does not exist, but in this case it is because *he believes that the Surly Monk exists.* In other words, fear can be intentional only because it is subtended by a belief, and belief is clearly a propositional attitude. To fear the Surly Monk means to believe him to exist *and* to fear that he will harm us in this or that way. Tugendhat acknowledges that this claim raises serious difficulties for one mode of intentionality at least, imagination; for to imagine is precisely to consider what one imagines as nonexistent, fictive. To overcome this difficulty, he defends an analysis of the imagination according to which to imagine means to relate intentionally to something in the modality of "it is not so, but I imagine that it *were* so."[7]

Let us leave the additional difficulty posed by imagination aside, and restrict our attention to the question of whether or not the linguistic criterion of intentionality advanced by Tugendhat is defensible. Let us take an apparently less problematic example, that of perception. To perceive is to perceive something, for example, a tree in the garden. But what does this mean? To see the tree in the garden, Tugendhat replies, must be analyzed as a "propositional consciousness," that is to say, as the knowledge of the truth of a state of affairs. To see something is to hold an existential proposition to be true. "When we say *of X* that he *sees N* this means: he knows [*er weiß*] on the basis of his optical perception (1) that there is something which = *N*, (2) that here (in his optical surroundings) there is something, and (3) that this = *N*."[8] Tugendhat interprets perception as a form of *knowledge.* This knowledge is about the truth of an existential proposition and, in fact, of a complex existential proposition. To be convinced of this, it will suffice to ask ourselves how we can deny the statement "He sees a tree." The answer is that we can do so not just in one, but in many ways. These various negations thereby reveal the complexity of the assertion masked beneath its surface simplicity: we may say either that there is no tree, or that there is nothing there, or that what is there is not a tree. Seeing, therefore, is not a mere relationship between a subject and an object referred to by a name; it is an "implicitly propositional consciousness [*implizit propositional Bewußtsein*]";[9] it consists in the endorsement of an existential statement, namely the statement that the class to which a predicate ("_ is a tree") applies is not empty, that something in our environment falls under this predicate, and that we know this on the basis of a perception. It follows that only linguistic analysis puts us in a position to decide what does or does not satisfy the criterion of intentionality. Not only is this criterion the only criterion, but it tells us something about the nature of consciousness, namely that "a consciousness of something that is not founded in a holding to be true [*Fürwahrhalten*] of an existential sentence does not exist. The peculiar 'quality' of consciousness which Husserl called 'intentionality' and which in supposedly intuitive description he characterized as a being directed toward an object turns out to be *sentence-understanding* [*Satzverständnis*]."[10]

In reality, if we accept Tugendhat's demonstration, not only must we say that linguistic analysis alone gives us the tools to understand what is specific to intentionality, but we must add that any other approach to it leads to a dead end, since intentionality simply *isn't* a phenomenon, but only a way of speaking. Not only is it the case that to analyze intentionality "I have no intuition at my disposal—only linguistic usage,"[11] but the very idea of a prelinguistic relation to the world is an illusion. "If all that is given to us of something is our speaking about it then we can only elucidate it by examining how we can speak about it."[12] Under these conditions, Tugendhat has not only established, as he claims, the superiority of linguistic-analytic philosophy over phenomenology, but in addition the futility and even the absurdity of the latter.

To the phenomenologist, this linguistic reformulation of the problem of intentionality is characterized by a double hypostatization: that of language, and that of knowledge. Perception, says Tugendhat, is an endorsed belief, that is to say, the "holding to be true" of an existential proposition. Now, phenomenology has developed entirely against the identification of perception with a belief, and *a fortiori* with a *true* belief or judgment, that is to say, a propositional *knowledge*. Experience is *not* knowledge: the former, which is defined by Husserl as "the self-giving of individual objects,"[13] precedes the latter de jure. Thus, "the being of the world as a whole is that which is taken for granted, is never put in doubt, and is not the result of any prior activity of judgment, but rather already forms the presupposition of all judgment";[14] or, as Husserl says even more clearly: "*The world as the existent world is the universal passive pre-givenness of all judicative activity*, of all engagement of theoretical interest."[15] In the eyes of the phenomenologist, perceptual experience not only is prior to all judgment, and thereby to any theoretical interest; it is also prior de jure to all linguistic expression; it belongs to the sphere of the "prepredicative." For Tugendhat, on the other hand, only the one who possesses a *Satzverständnis* can also have a perception. An animal or a child before language acquisition cannot be said to *perceive*. This consequence, however radical, follows strictly from Tugendhat's premises. The question raised by Tugendhat's endeavor is therefore whether, through this "translation" of the whole problem into linguistic terms, something vital to both our pretheoretical and prelinguistic relationship to the world is not lost; whether, in other words, what is at stake is not an illegitimate intellectualization of perception and, more generally, of experience. To show that this is indeed the case, we must dwell on several important points of his argumentation.

First, we must ask ourselves whether Tugendhat's criterion can actually perform the function assigned to it, that of delimiting the class of intentional verbs. To do this, it would have to admit of no exceptions. But is this the case? The answer is clearly no. There are verbs that, according to Brentano's criterion, manifest intentionality (their object may not exist) and that are nevertheless not "implicitly propositional." This is the case with loving, admiring, esteeming, hating, or worshiping. Indeed, as Tugendhat himself acknowledges, but without drawing all the inherent consequences of this fact, "loving, pitying, and admiring can undeniably have as transitive object [*als transitives Objekt*] only a singular term which stands for a concrete object."[16] It is true that I can love visiting museums or hiking in the mountains. Therefore there is a use of "loving" that is clearly propositional. But in its main usage, that of "loving someone," "to love" simply does not mean to love some given predicate to be true of that person—for example, to love *his being alive,* to love *his having such and such a quality,* nor even to love *her loving me.* In an article on Tugendhat, Vincent Descombes, in an attempt to save the former's criterion, maintains the opposite. "In saying 'I love that woman' we have not yet said what the object of that love is. For it suffices to ask ourselves in what case that love will be felicitous and in what case infelicitous to observe that there is an implied predicate. One person, using the word love, means that he loves *seeing* that woman, another that he loves *chatting* with her, while a third is not satisfied with that."[17] But how could loving a person, just loving her, mean loving *to chat* with her, or *preferring to do something else*? For when does "to love" ever mean *not to be satisfied with chatting with someone*? We have only to ask the question to see how arbitrary such a paraphrase is. It may be that love comes down to the hope of physical possession, perhaps forever impossible, as in certain post-Schopenhauer theories, but in any case it is not *grammar* that will decide the issue. Love is *not* a propositional attitude. The point is even clearer in the case of hatred. The French have two verbs here requiring different constructions. One hates [*hait*] someone, one can upon occasion hate [*haïr*] something—hypocrisy, or travels (we have only to recall the opening line of *Tristes tropiques,* "I hate travels and explorers [*Je hais les voyages et les explorateurs*]"—but one hates [*déteste*] taking a trip [*partir en voyage*], listening to operas, hunting. In no case would it be possible to say that one *hates* [*hait*] taking a trip. The French verb "*haïr*" *excludes* the propositional construction. This is an objection to be taken seriously for a philosophy that keeps assailing us with the doctrine that the only rigorous criteria are linguistic. By "criterion" in this context, Tugendhat apparently means a necessary and sufficient condition for the intentionality of specific verbs. His intention is to establish that *all* intentional verbs are propositional, and that *only* intentional verbs are propositional. But if some of these verbs violate this condition, his criterion collapses.

Moreover, the group of "intentional verbs" is much more heterogeneous than Tugendhat seems prepared to admit, thus making any formulation of a linguistic criterion of intentionality a perilous undertaking, to say the least. Since Chisholm and Quine, it is generally held that the distinctive trait of intentionality is inten*s*ionality (with an "s"), that is, non-extensionality. A statement is extensional on the following conditions: first, if it is truth-functional, that is to say, if its truth is a function of the truth of the statements that compose it, and secondly, if the substitution of expressions having the same reference retains its truth-value. Consider the case of belief. The linguistic contexts governed by "believe that" are inten*s*ional, which amounts to saying: (A) that a statement such as: (1) "Peter believes that Émile Ajar is the author of *Gros-câlin*" fails the test of the substitution *salva veritate* of co-referential terms, because (1) may be true despite the falsity of (2) "Peter believes that Romain Gary is the author of *Gros-câlin*" (because Peter does not know that Romain Gary = Émile Ajar); (B) that such statements are not truth-functional because the truth of the statement "A believes that *p*" does not depend on the truth of the embedded proposition *p*. The truth or falsity of this embedded proposition has no direct incidence on the truth or falsity of the statement of belief. In addition, the law of existential generalization is valid in extensional contexts, but not in intensional ones: from the proposition "Romain Gary is the author of *Gros-câlin*" we are justified to infer "There is at least one *x* such that he is the author of *Gros-câlin*." But this rule does not apply in inten*s*ional contexts, including those governed by "believe that," "wish that," and so on. From "Paul believes that Moby Dick is a white whale," nothing can be inferred concerning the existence of a white whale. Starting from these characteristics of inten*s*ional statements—and, although inten*s*ionality is not exclusively a property of "propositional attitudes," but is also found in modal contexts—it seems possible to propose, as Roderick Chisholm did in *Perceiving*, three logico-linguistic criteria for intentionality (with a "t"):

(1) The first case is when the main verb is followed by a nominal expression. In this case, the statement is intentional if neither the statement nor its negation implies that the nominal expression has a referent.

(2) The second case is when the main verb is followed by a propositional clause "that *p*." Here, the statement is intentional provided that neither the statement nor its negation implies either that the propositional clause is true or that it is false.

(3) The third criterion stipulates that in an intentional statement containing a referential expression, the substitution of a co-referential expression does not retain the truth-value of the statement.[18]

The trouble with these logico-linguistic criteria is that they do not apply equally to all verbs that are intentional in the sense of Brentano and Husserl. For example, there are many contexts in which perception involves no referential opacity, and therefore does not meet the third criterion. If Peter has been introduced to Romain Gary, and if the statement "Peter saw Romain Gary" is true, then the substitution of a co-referential expression, "Émile Ajar," retains the truth-value of that statement: if Peter saw Romain Gary, then, by this very fact, regardless of whether or not he is conscious of it, Peter saw Émile Ajar. We can also discover some notable exceptions to the first two criteria. "See that," "perceive that," and "know that" *imply* the existence of the referent: if I see that the snow is white, there is, therefore, snow such that it is white, and such that I see it. The same is true for "to know" and "to perceive": the truth of the statement implies the truth of the propositional clause, thereby violating Chisholm's second criterion. If "I know that snow is white" is true, then necessarily "Snow is white" is true. "To know that *p*" implies "*p*," just as "to perceive that *p*" implies "*p*," while "to believe that *p*" implies neither "*p*" nor "not *p*." But, contrary to what is suggested by Tugendhat, statements of perception and of knowledge do not have the same logical status; they differ as to their referential opacity, and this makes any formalization of perception as a knowledge that is about a complex existential proposition problematic. "To know" does not allow the substitution *salva veritate* of co-referential terms, because "I know that the Tower of Pisa is in Pisa" does not entail "I know that la Torre di Pisa is in Pisa." Perception, on the other hand, is referentially transparent in many contexts. This is the case of statements of perception that can be qualified as "non-epistemic,"[19] following Fred Dretske's terminology, and in which the truth of the statement that something is perceived does not entail that the perceiver is aware that a particular predicate applies to it. I may have perceived a silhouette, which happens to be a fox, and therefore I perceived a fox, though without *knowing* that what I perceived was a fox. Non-epistemic statements of perception, therefore, are extensional; they do not satisfy any of the three criteria of Chisholm. Consequently, to propose to formalize perception as the "holding to be true" of a complex existential statement poses logical problems even before posing philosophical problems. This would lead us to think of all perception as a perception in which *I know* what I perceive, that is, in which I am able to apply a correct description to it. All perception would thus be transformed into an epistemological perception which is expressed in referentially opaque statements.

It is clearly very difficult, using a logico-linguistic criteriology, to determine the specificity of intentionality in the sense attributed to it by Brentano and Husserl. Unless we deny that perceiving and knowing belong in the sphere of intentionality—but then the price to be paid is exorbitant, since it amounts to ratifying the total dismantlement of the typology developed by Brentano. If, additionally, verbs such as "admire" or "love" do not admit, in some of their uses, a propositional construction, we realize that the analysis of language is far from providing us with anything resembling an exact criterion, and even less a necessary and sufficient condition. As Davidson is forced to admit, in the case of intentionality the criterion provided by the philosophy of language "is not precise,"[20] and thus linguistic philosophy is far from succeeding where phenomenological description is supposed to have failed. Perhaps it is because Tugendhat is conscious of these limitations that he does not enter into the thorny problem of inten*s*ionality in the logical sense. He sticks to a more modest criterion, that of the possibility of reducing the non-propositional forms of intentionality to its propositional forms. But despite this cautious strategy, the difficulties he faces are no less serious.

Indeed, Tugendhat is not content with maintaining that abstract objects must be allowed a place alongside concrete ones in order to think intentionality—which Husserl could easily concede to him, since he himself clearly emphasized that perception, for example, is directed not only on spatiotemporally individuated objects, but on states of affairs: "We say likewise that the whole statement gives utterance to our percept: we do not merely say '*I see this paper, an inkwell, several books,*' and so on, but also: '*I see that this paper has been written on, that there is a bronze inkpot standing here, that several books are lying open,*' and so on."[21] That perceiving can be "propositional," according to Tugendhat's terminology, is not an objection to Husserl, quite to the contrary. But Tugendhat does not only mean that perception, *when expressed in statements*, has a propositional form; he means that perception *is* something propositional; that is to say, that perception necessarily includes an assertion on a state of affairs, and therefore that its truth conditions are those of the corresponding proposition. It is not the linguistic account of perception, but rather perception itself, according to Tugendhat, that includes the understanding of a proposition. "Any alleged intentional consciousness is implicitly or explicitly a propositional consciousness."[22] This conclusion is questionable, to say the least. It is a curious principle, indeed, to attribute a property to something on the sole ground that a *description* of that thing has specific logical characteristics. The logical characteristics of the *statements* of perception still tell us nothing about the nature of perception. The fact that the statements of perception are propositional does not entail that perceptual consciousness itself is (no more than the fact that the concept of dog applies to Fido entails that Fido is conceptual in nature). However, this conclusion is anything but a slip on Tugendhat's part. Rather, his entire argumentation is based on this inference. Indeed, what is the point that is being established here? That the only thing given us of "things themselves" is our way of talking about them; and that therefore no direct description of experience is possible that does not borrow its resources from an analysis of language. If all consciousness is propositional, if it implies the holding to be true of an existential statement, if it is intrinsically connected with linguistic abilities, it is impossible not to admit that whatever is given to us to experience is given through language, through the way we talk about it, and the linguistic turn seems legitimated. But there is a real circle here: in order to be able to legitimate the linguistic turn, understood as the thesis that "the question of consciousness is reduced to the question of propositional understanding [*Satzverstehen*],"[23] Tugendhat must be able to show that all consciousness is implicitly propositional (and therefore to perform the questionable logical inference from the logical properties of the description to the properties of the thing); but in order to show that all consciousness is propositional, he must already have reduced consciousness to the linguistic criteria of its description—that is, he must already have taken the linguistic turn. In order to be legitimatized, the linguistic turn must appeal to an additional premise (according to which if a description possesses determinate properties, these same properties apply to the described thing as well), which can be legitimated—if it can be legitimated—only by the linguistic turn.

To see this, it suffices to compare Tugendhat's position to that of Chisholm. For the latter, the logico-linguistic criteria of intentionality do not allow any "ontological" conclusion. Chisholm's "ontological" thesis is not that all consciousness, including perceptual consciousness, is a linguistic matter, but *on the contrary* that primordial (intrinsic) intentionality is that of consciousness (or, as he says, of thought) and that linguistic intentionality has only a derivative status. "Thoughts would be intentional even if there were no linguistic entities."[24] To be sure, this statement could be challenged. But the essential point for the problem at hand is that Chisholm, unlike Tugendhat, does not believe it is possible to draw any conclusions of an ontological nature from a linguistic criteriology. And it is hard not to agree with him. Is it not just as absurd to say that I perceive a propositional content as that I eat a state of affairs? Husserl, in any case, would not have said that we perceive a propositional content, but only that we perceive a state of affairs, that is to say, a complex abstract *object*—which is accessible only to a being endowed with language, of course, but is not intrinsically linguistic in kind. We shall return later to this doctrine of states of affairs and the objections that may be addressed to it (chapters 4 and 5). Nonetheless, in Husserl's view, no perception can consist in an attitude toward a proposition; it is, at most, an attitude towards what makes a proposition true, and which can give it intuitive fullness. Thus, the mere *possibility* of expressing a perception in such and such a form does not tell us anything on the nature of perception. But then it is not granted at all that the refusal to reduce all experience and all reality to the modalities of our discourse is as naive and superficial as Tugendhat believes: we should be able to explain, he writes, "how something like 'reality' can be given to us, if not in linguistic usage [*Sprachgebrauch*]."[25]

Tugendhat's argumentation, which is, incidentally, that of many analytic authors,[26] can be reconstructed as follows. Nothing is given to us outside of language. Why? Because if we were given something outside of language, we would still need language to be able to say that this is given to us outside of language, that is to say, to be able to think its mode of givenness explicitly. But if we need language to be able to think its mode of givenness, this amounts to say that the thing is not given to us outside of language. So there must be something contradictory in the (linguistically formulated) claim that something could be given to us before or independently of language. The moment I express this claim, it refutes itself, since I have to *say* how what is supposedly given to me independently of language is given to me, and hence I demonstrate, against my own claim, that it is not given to me independently of (or prior to) language.

Must we endorse this *reductio ad absurdum*? To be sure, in order to *say* that something is given to us prelinguistically, that is, prior (de jure) to its expression—in order to *think* its givenness explicitly, we need language. But we do not need language for the thing to be so *given* to us. It is one thing to maintain that what is given to us prior to language cannot be *thought* as given in that way unless we possess language, cannot be *said to be* "given prior to language" otherwise than by means of language (which is tautological), and quite another to argue that all that is given to us is given through language and language alone. It is this kind of consideration that allowed Husserl to extend the concept of meaning beyond language. From the mere fact that only language can enable us to say what has meaning for us it does not follow that everything that has meaning for us pertains to language alone. Incidentally, if nothing made sense for us before our mastery of a language, it is hard to see what could induce us to want to acquire one.

For all perception to be propositional in nature, that is to say, for it to presuppose the possession of language, language would have to be independent from perception. But it is clear that language (whether in graphic or phonetic form) must be *perceived* in order to be understood. This perception must be educated, and is part and parcel of language proficiency. Thus "everything is given to us by the intermediary of language" is an assertion that borders on absurdity. Does "everything" include language as a reality among others? But then language is given to us through language, and we fall into an infinite regress. Does "everything" exclude language? But then there is at least one thing, language, which is not given to us through language. And if language is given to us directly, perceptually, why not everything else? In wanting to repatriate the whole reality within language, the linguistic turn loses the very specificity of the notion of language, a notion that makes sense solely by contrast to "world," "perceived reality," "experience," and so on. If all experience is nothing but a linguistic affair—that is to say, if there are no facts or data that are not already linguistic, then we no longer understand the adjective "linguistic," because we no longer understand its opposite, "non-linguistic." And since we are asked to consider our experience as being linguistic through and through, we have no choice but to rename "experience" our old language.

It is precisely this kind of difficulty that underlies phenomenology's opposition to any form of linguistic turn. Such a turn has also occurred in other philosophical trends. Gadamer's thesis of a "linguisticality" (*Sprachlichkeit*) of our experience of the world, and Ricoeur's claim that "it is *language* that is the primary condition of all human experience"[27] end up, as we shall see, in similar aporias (chapter 22).

But Tugendhat's endeavor brings out something like a permanent temptation on the part of analytic philosophy: the intellectualization of our being-in-the-world in the form of this twofold hypostatization of language and knowledge. It is no accident. The search for strict linguistic criteria leads in the end to the idea that there are no strict criteria other than linguistic ones. The analysis of perception statements ends up in a theory of perception as the implicit assertion of statements. This temptation transcends the divisions and debates within the philosophies of the linguistic turn and establishes itself as one of their most permanent features. From Wilfrid Sellars, for whom "all consciousness," whether of abstract entities or individuals, "is a linguistic affair,"[28] to Davidson, for whom our being-in-the-world boils down to sensations exerting a blind causal impact on our senses and to "propositional perceptions" which alone pertain to "the logical space of reasons"[29] and are also "perceptual beliefs," to Dennett, who maintains that every conscious experience is a judgment or a belief that something is the case, thus denying "the possibility in principle of consciousness of a stimulus in the absence of the subject's belief in that consciousness"[30]—in all these cases, it is as if our originary relationship to the world could be analyzed in terms of sensations shaped by language skills. It is as if language, playing a structural role similar to the one Kant assigned to the understanding in his "transcendental logic," were the only thing capable of imparting form to a "sensible manifold." This proximity of many analytical approaches to a (neo-)Kantianism, which, in a number of cases, is unconscious, will occupy us more fully later (chapter 19).

Even philosophers who, like John Searle, diverge from the mainstream of analytic philosophy by refusing to think of perception as a belief, do not hesitate to argue that perceptual contents are "propositional." Indeed, on the one hand Searle argues that the relation of dependency is not that of intentionality on language, but the other way round. On the other, he argues nonetheless that "the content of the visual experience, like the content of the belief, is always equivalent of a whole proposition."[31] On this view, to see, for example, is always and necessarily to see that things are such and such. But what justifies, despite the rejection of the idea that intentionality is an "essentially and necessarily linguistic" characteristic,[32] the amalgamation, so to speak, into the content of perceptual experience of the forms of its expression? The question seems to arise especially as Searle recognizes quite rightly that there is "a mistake which is apparently endemic to the methods of linguistic philosophy—confusion of features of reports with features of the things reported."[33] Is what is true of the statement about a belief true of that belief? The answer is no. A belief report in the third person in the form "Peter believes that Venus is a planet" is inten*s*ional, but the belief itself is extensional. It is expressed as: "Venus is a planet." Searle is right to denounce this endemic error, but does he himself succeed in avoiding it? His strategy is to extend the notion of "conditions of satisfaction" from language to intentional acts in general. As a consequence, to say that perception is "propositional" no longer amounts to saying that its content is itself linguistic, but only that its "conditions of satisfaction" are those *specified* by a proposition. These conditions of satisfaction differ in the case of a perception and a belief. While belief has as its conditions of satisfaction the fact or the state of affairs that make it true, what satisfies perception, the perceived state of affairs, must also be the *cause* of the perceptual experience. When I perceive that the apple tree is blossoming, not only does my perceptual experience present me with a blossoming apple tree, but it also represents to me the fact that the apple tree is the cause of my visual experience. Therefore the content of a perception, unlike that of a belief, is self-referential.[34] Perception represents to me that what it represents is the cause of my representation. This causality relation holding between the representation and the perceived state of affairs belongs to the "propositional content" of perception, but is missing in that of belief. But, yet again, this theoretical construct leads to an extreme intellectualization of perception. If we follow Searle, in order to have a visual experience, we would have to possess the *concept* of a self-referential intentional content, *hence the concept of visual experience itself.*[35] I would have to *know* that what my perception represents to me is the causal impact of what it represents to me on my representation. Furthermore, has Searle done anything other than redefine perception as a *belief of a particular kind,* whose content is the effect of the state of affairs it represents? It is hard to see how this thesis can be reconciled with that of the non-linguistic nature of perceptual intentionality. The danger of such a theory is not only that it over-intellectualizes perception, but also that it lapses into a mentalism that the phenomenological conception of intentionality was precisely attempting to overcome.[36] According to such a theory, perceptual intentionality becomes a property of "mental states" whose characteristic is to "represent" reality. It belongs, like judgment and belief, to a theoretical relationship with the world.

To perceive is not to judge or think that we perceive. There are countless ways in which the same perception can be linguistically formulated or *thought.* If perception were a "propositional consciousness," to a single perception there would correspond a single proposition. But, as Husserl points out, this is not the case. I can express my perception as "A blackbird is flying away," but I might just as well have said "This is black, it is a black bird," "This winged creature is flying," and so forth.[37] Moreover, what does "a single" perception mean? Perception is a *continuum,* while a proposition is a closed semantic unit. "But if we see what we judge," noted Merleau-Ponty, "how can we distinguish true perception from false perception? And after such a conclusion, how will we continue to say that the person suffering from hallucinations or the madman 'believe they see what they do not see'? Where will the difference be between 'seeing' and 'believing that one sees'?"[38] If vision were a kind of belief, seeing would always be more or less believing that one sees, but ordinary language rightfully distinguishes them. If I know that a proposition is false, it is impossible for me to believe it, as is emphasized by Moore's paradox; but if I know that a perception is false, it persists regardless of my beliefs and *even though it contradicts them.* In the Zöllner illusion, I am forced to *see* the lines as slanted toward one another, although my belief is that they are parallel. The difference between true perception and false perception (illusion or hallucination) cannot be of the same type as that obtaining between true judgment and false judgment. Moreover, it is not entirely accurate to describe the Zöllner illusion as if the lines were simply "parallel" and that we wrongly judged them to be convergent. It would be more accurate to say that the lines are *at once* parallel and inclined, depending on our way of looking at them, thus manifesting a characteristic ambivalence. "It is impossible to *see* them as oblique when we focus on them," Merleau-Ponty writes. "It is when we glance away that they silently tend toward this new relation."[39] Actually, Zöllner's lines are parallel *and* oblique according to the attitude we adopt toward them—according to whether we examine their position using a ruler or run our eyes freely over them; it is *the same lines* that possess both of these changing properties, that reorganize themselves spontaneously before our eyes, independently of what we judge true or false about them. This indetermination and this floating movement [*bougé*] are remarkable properties of our perceptual experience to which there is nothing corresponding in judgment. "There is here, preceding objective relationships, a perceptual syntax constructed according to its own rules: the breaking of old relationships and the establishment of new ones—judgment—only express the outcome of this deep operation and are its final report. Whether we consider true or false perception, it must first be constituted in this way in order for predication to be possible."[40] Judgment consists in the taking up of a theoretical position, subject to the alternative of true or false, and objectively valid. Perception is not thinkable in those terms. Perceiving is "the giving of oneself over to the appearance without seeking to possess it or to know its truth."[41] It is, then, "to grasp, prior to all judgment, a meaning immanent to the sensible."[42] To rely on the appearance, to see the line sometimes leaning toward, sometimes parallel to the line next to it, has nothing to do with any belief, justified or not, nor with any judgment on what we see.

One last argument can be advanced against an analysis like that of Tugendhat. One of the key aspects of our perceptual experience is that it is not entirely thematic, that is to say, it is structured by what might be called, following Husserl, "horizons." My look lingers on a face that strikes me by its beauty or its ugliness, standing out from the crowd; I see the crowd surrounding it and slipping imperceptibly into the background without noticing every gesture, face, or expression; I *see* the passersby without fully seeing them, just as, perhaps, certain features of the face will be seen without arresting my gaze, without them being *noticed*—the eye-color, for example. It belongs to all perception to be structured according to this polarity of what is thematic and non-thematic, of what stands out and retains our attention and what plays the role of a horizon, of an implicit halo, in the absence of which nothing could stand out or be noticed. What remains in the background is neither fully seen nor completely ignored, but it can, in principle, always be thematized. In an example from Scheler, I enter a familiar room and am suddenly struck by a change, I don't know what; it affects me as a vague uneasiness, enveloping all the objects without singling out any particular one, until it ends up locating itself on the absence of a painting which was formerly there. The horizon is experienced without being noticed, present by a ubiquitous presence without imposing itself to our attention. But if seeing is not necessarily noticing what we see, neither is it *thinking* or *judging* that such and such is the case, because to think or judge is to be conscious of what one thinks or judges. Descartes and Tugendhat notwithstanding, to see is not to think that one sees.

These remarks, which could be extended to other intentional modalities such as recollection or imagination, still do not tell us how to conceive of intentionality positively. They merely indicate that the attempt to construct a linguistic criteriology raises at least as many problems as it solves: internal problems, since none of the criteria suggested is adequate for all the specimens of intentional "relation" identified by Brentano and Husserl; and external problems, since this attempt leads to a problematic intellectualization of our prelinguistic openness to the world. It is far, at least, from being a neutral undertaking, free from presuppositions. We shall have to verify it again on several occasions.

4

The Prepredicative

> And some certain significance lurks in all things, else all things are little worth, and the round world itself but an empty cipher, except to sell by the cartload, as they do hills about Boston, to fill up some morass in the Milky Way.
>
> —Herman Melville, *Moby-Dick*

For a long time (and particularly in the tradition of empiricism), reality was conceived by philosophy as similar to those hills of Boston of which Melville speaks. All was clear: on one side, there was language and its meanings; on the other, brute, meaningless facts, announcing themselves to consciousness by the intermediary of sense data or "ideas." A good part of contemporary philosophy considers this division as settled; it rises in protest against a use of "meaning" and "signification" that would extend these notions beyond the linguistic sphere. Do you want to scout out a phenomenologist? Take a philosopher, examine the way he uses the word "meaning" and you will soon know the truth; if he only speaks of giving a meaning to a sign and of explaining the meaning of a sentence, you have an analytic philosopher; if "meaning" is used in a wider sense, you are dealing with a disciple of Husserl. Denunciation of the "phenomenologist's extraordinary use of words,"[1] starting with the use of the word "meaning," has become, since Gilbert Ryle,[2] a commonplace in linguistic philosophy—that is, in that branch of philosophy that considers philosophical problems as problems it is possible to solve (or better yet, to dissolve), either by submitting our language to the canon of a perfect logical notation, according to the hope of the Vienna Circle, or by bringing words back from their metaphysical to their ordinary use, as Wittgenstein and his heirs would have it. To allude, as Melville does, to a significance that might be possessed by things, or to evoke, after the example of the phenomenologist, a meaning inherent in experience, would be to succumb to typically philosophical confusions—after all, does not Melville don the cloak of the philosopher in this passage?

To speak of perceptions that would possess meaning in themselves, for example, would be absurd in Austin's view. "Sensa are dumb, and only previous experience enables us to identify them. If we choose to say that they 'identify themselves' . . . , then it must be admitted that they share the birthright of all speakers, that of speaking unclearly and untruly."[3]

What are we to think of this diagnosis? It is still too soon to answer that question. In any case, there is no doubt that if it is a symptom we are talking about, the phenomenologist has it, because it is the "still dumb" experience that he has assigned himself the task of allowing to speak. According to Husserl's famous motto, which epitomizes his entire project, "The beginning is the pure—and, so to speak, still dumb—experience, which now must be made to utter its own sense with no adulteration."[4] But what does it mean to speak of experience as *dumb*, if it makes no sense to attribute speech to it, and therefore to qualify it as speechless either? To reply that this is just a metaphor scarcely helps; we would still have to explain of what this metaphor is the metaphor. In order to shed some light on this, we must begin by asking ourselves how linguistic meaning has been conceived in the phenomenological tradition. Again, if Husserl's phenomenology can serve as our guideline, it is not because its solution to this problem does not lend itself to criticism—we will have to assess its limitations—nor because Husserl's semantics somehow foreshadows the whole panoply of solutions that follow in its wake, but because it opens up a field of problems and research into which subsequent phenomenology has delved. To return to Husserl is to think with him, which frequently means to think against him, and beyond him as well.

The logico-linguistic analyses with which the second volume of *Logical Investigations* begins have a twofold objective. First, their goal is to furnish the conceptual groundwork of a "pure logic," that is, "a science of meanings as such"[5] that is subdivided into a pure theory of validity (logic in the usual sense of the term, focusing on the laws of formal truth in general) and a pure morphology of meanings (or a pure logical grammar);[6] secondly, to enable phenomenology itself to develop as an autonomous "science," to be precisely a phenomeno-*logy*—in other words, to show how language is an organon for the description of phenomena and for the theory of knowledge as a whole. This second aspect of the inquiry is no less important that the first: all the "logical analyses" developed in connection with the problem of meaning are inscribed within the larger framework of a "*pure phenomenology of the lived experiences of thinking and knowing*"[7] or a "theory of knowledge"[8] of phenomenological inspiration. This epistemic perspective that ceaselessly shadows the logical one should not be overlooked, on pain of missing the overall significance of all these developments—more specifically the meaning of the two fundamental concepts that govern its economy: *meaning* and *intuitive fulfillment.* Indeed, because a fundamental epistemological orientation underlies all of Husserl's logical analyses (logic itself being conceived not as an *ars combinatoria,* a technique for the combination of signs, but as a science devoted to a specific domain of objects, namely ideal objects, that grant its objective validity: meanings and formal essences), and because that epistemology is of Cartesian inspiration, all knowledge being conceived as *an intuitive grasp of objects* according to the criterion of *evidence*—the problem of evidence is constantly intertwined with that of meaning. In a word, given that language is first and foremost, in Husserl's view, the medium of knowledge, the latter being defined not as a set of justified beliefs, but as a grasp of its object that is intuitive and in some cases evident, the aim of language is to relate meanings to objects susceptible to conferring intuitive fulfillment upon them. Language is a *revealer,* an *organon* for knowledge; it must bring "into view" objects that are sensible or ideal, simple or complex, temporal or atemporal, as well as the objective relations—contingent or necessary, formal or material—that constitute the infrastructure of the world. Therefore it must possess a sufficient transparency to "fit what we intuit like a garment."[9] Language is, to this very extent, *intrinsically phenomeno-logical.* Heidegger's insistence on the *apophainesthai* of the *logos apophantikos,* on its "bringing into view" character, is just a further extension of Husserl's fundamental orientation.

We would do well to keep in mind this dimension of Husserl's research, not only in order to grasp its coherence, but to assess its limitations. Indeed, in order for the meaning of expressions to fit or coincide with the objects susceptible of being given to consciousness, in order for "the object of intuition [to be] *the same* as the object of thought,"[10] to use the phrase that constitutes the leitmotif of all these analyses, intuition must have its own order of meaning. Experience in its various dimensions, sensible as well as ideal, must shelter within itself an immanent *meaning* which can coincide with that of its expression, without, however, being identical with it. Thus secretly, at the heart of the nascent phenomenology, a tension, a discrepancy emerge, pervading and fashioning it through and through. In a sense, it might be said that Husserl, throughout his work, accomplishes the great tradition of classical rationalism which culminates in Leibniz's *characteristica universalis* and goes up to Russell and Wittgenstein's *Tractatus*; a tradition whereby, in keeping with the polysemy of the Greek concept of logos, which signifies not only "discourse," "proposition," and "language," but also "meaning" and "order of things," the order immanent in language is destined to reproduce and reflect an order of the world, and the logic of language to echo a logic of things. But it must immediately be added that Husserl decenters this entire problematic by the proclamation—of empiricist inspiration—according to which, if language is a revealer of the world, the order of the world possesses both a *priority* and an *autonomy* with respect to any linguistic or logical order, for it is rather the latter that is, in part at least, derived from the former. "Logical concepts . . . must have their origin in intuition":[11] here we have, in a nutshell, the entire problematic of a genealogy of logic starting from prepredicative experience that was to be developed in Husserl's late work, particularly in *Experience and Judgment.* Thus phenomenology springs from this tension between the claim that language is entirely at the service of an intuitive knowledge of the world, and the idea that things, taken at the level of prepredicative experience, display a "logic" older than the one that structures our discursive intelligence—a "logic" that, although it is not refractory to language, is not derived from it, either.

These remarks, however vague and preliminary, will facilitate our understanding of Husserl's guiding thread when he approaches the problematic of language, not in its empirical diversity, but in its ideal universality: the question of the relations between thought and intuition. These relations are complex, and can be circumscribed by means of three theses:

(1) "The realm of meaning is . . . much wider than that of intuition."[12] Every thought has essentially the possibility of being expressed in language, and thus articulated in meanings, but to every meaningful expression there corresponds not necessarily the possibility to receive a fulfilling intuition.

(2) Nevertheless, every thought tends toward intuition—"intuition" meaning here a requirement of full and entire rationality, since intuition is the telos of knowledge. To every thought that is not an absurdity or a contradiction there corresponds an at least ideally possible intuitive fulfillment.

(3) The intuitive world, that is, the world of (sensible and ideal) experience, contains its own *a priori* laws, which do not essentially depend on language but are rather prior to it.

These three theses also reflect the three types of approach that Husserl coordinates in these passages: (1) a logico-linguistic point of view; (2) an epistemic thesis; and (3) an ontological approach. They are, in his view, inseparable.

Since these theses concern the ties between thought and intuition, in other words, meaning and its fulfillment, we must begin by asking ourselves what meaning is. Husserl's response stands in diametric opposition to a mentalist claim that would equate meaning with mental images or contingent lived experiences. Meaning cannot consist in the mental images that spring up on the occasion of the hearing of a word or the reading of a sentence, because such lived experiences are volatile, fleeting, and differ from one individual to the next, while meaning must be identical and invariable for anybody understanding these expressions. Meaning is an ideal intentional content, which is identical in all circumstances for any consciousness capable of grasping it, whereas images are contingent psychological accompaniments of understanding: they "lie outside the essence of an expression."[13] Not only do we have no consciousness of such images in most cases in which we understand an expression, but if, in order to understand a sentence, it were necessary to recover the lived experiences associated with it and which differ from one individual to another, in what would the *identity* of that sentence consist? Clearly it could not consist in the material component of the signs used, for signs change continually (a change from one graphic style to another, from one pronunciation to another, and so on); it must therefore reside in the identity of their meaning across different contexts. To understand a sentence is to understand *the same sentence* as anyone who understands the sentence in question. And to understand the same sentence is to grasp a self-identical ideal meaning that is objectively (intersubjectively) the same for any member of a community of understanding, and which is therefore not of a psychological or mental nature. Only this ideality of meanings that remain identical through time makes it possible for logic to escape all psychologism, and therefore all relativism, by precluding any reduction of the ideal and universally valid laws of logic to empirical laws of thought, that is, to the contingent generalizations of a science of facts.

Thus the theory of meaning is integrated into a general theory of intentionality, of which it is a particular case. Meaning finds its place within the general act/content/object schema, the progressive conquest of which I have described: it is a *content* that is not immanent in consciousness, but constitutes *the mode according to which* consciousness relates to objects. Thus, the passage from an iconic to a semantic conception of intentionality, that is to say, the overcoming of a conception of intentional contents as mental stand-ins for the object, in favor of an understanding of the content/object difference which conceives of the content as a mode of givenness of the object, sheds light on the new status that meaning receives and allows us to distinguish sharply this meaning from all mental image. Conversely, the analysis of semantic intentionality corroborates and confirms the general analysis of intentionality by extending but also completing it: for semantic intentionality is a sui generis mode of the intentionality of consciousness.

In what does its specificity consist? The answer is fairly simple. What makes signifying an original mode of the intentional relation to objects is the fact that in this case intention is *intertwined with signs* in a characteristic manner. Signification, as Husserl writes in 1908, is the consciousness "of meaning this and that with a [sign]."[14] In the signifying act, the meaning-intention and the sign present themselves in an indivisible unity. To describe this unity, Husserl has recourse to Stumpf's vocabulary of *Verschmelzung*, "fusion." "The appearance of the expression, on the one hand, and the meaning-intention . . . on the other, do not constitute a mere aggregate of simultaneously given items in consciousness. They rather form an intimately fused [*innig verschmolzene*] unity of peculiar character."[15] This "intimate [*fusionnelle*]" unity, so to speak, confers on signitive intentionality its sui generis character as consciousness of intending an object through a meaning that is itself inseparably united to a sign.

This is the reason why, contrary to what might have been expected, Husserl does not begin his analysis of meaning in the first *Logical Investigation* with a description of intentional acts and their objective correlates; he begins it with a description of the different sorts of signs. The *linguistic expression* for which he reserves the word "*Ausdruck*" (to the exclusion of everything that could be called "expression" in current usage) is a sign of a particular, remarkable nature. Indeed, expressions differ fundamentally from indications (*Anzeichen*) whose function is to manifest (*kundgeben*) something: tracks in the snow manifest an animal's passing, smoke the presence of fire, archeological remains the existence of a pre-Columbian city. How does this function of manifestation (*Kundgabe*) differ from that of expression? Without going into all the details of Husserl's analysis, the essential point is the following. The relation between the indication and the object it indicates or points out is an external one, because it is an empirical (causal) one. On the basis of footprints in the snow I must *infer* that an animal has passed by with a more than zero probability of error. In Husserl's terminology, the existence of the indication "furnishes one with an *empirical* motive or ground,"[16] for the conviction of the existence of what it indicates. Things are quite otherwise with the relation holding between expression and meaning (and therefore relation to the object) which is an internal relation. When I hear a sentence in a language that I have mastered, I do not infer its meaning, with risks of error. The sentence gives me its meaning, or rather, the sentence is only a sentence, a linguistic expression, if it has a meaning. "The essence of an expression lies solely in its meaning."[17] An expression is only the expression it is on the condition of being meaningful for the one who understands it. Accordingly, "that white with" is not an expression at all.

But does it not sometimes happen that I understand a sentence without understanding it entirely? Of course, but Husserl's whole strategy, which consists in unraveling what is essential and what accidental in the expression, leads him to maintain that this sort of incomprehension is parasitic on language; it results from the circumstance that in ordinary communication the linguistic signs possess at the same time a signifying function and a manifesting one. They are at once expressions and indications. In the properly linguistic manifestation, the relationship between indications and what they manifest is also an empirical one; it no longer rests on natural regularities (smoke/fire), but on psychological, cultural, and anthropological ones. For example, in the middle of a discussion, I may wonder what my interlocutor means. So I make conjectures or hypotheses on the thoughts he associates with his words. Is he serious? Is he making fun of me? But in order to wonder about his motivations, his intentions or his unspoken reservations in this way—that is, about what his words *manifest,* I must begin by understanding the sentences he is uttering. This difference constitutes one of the resources of Kafka's art. His novels are full of bizarre dialogues that never surprise any of the characters, but make the reader increasingly uneasy. What is said is perfectly clear, the meaning of the expressions presents no difficulty, and yet the further we progress the less we understand what the characters mean—that is, what they think, what they are getting at. This is a way of introducing the reader into the heavy, oppressive climate, into that meaning-saturated absurd that is the distinctive trait of Kafka's fantasy world. In Husserl's terminology, one might say that we understand the expressions perfectly; we grasp their meaning, but remain strangers to what they are supposed to *manifest* about the thoughts of the characters. We understand neither the allusions nor the innuendos that become increasingly plentiful, drawing us into a spiral of uncanny angst. The function of manifesting the thoughts of other persons possessed by language as indication remains a dead letter for us. Other people remain impenetrable. But this opacity of foreign subjectivities could never strike us if we had not first dealt with meaningful expressions. The function of manifestation and that of expression remain thus distinct in language.

What reveals this best is the example of monologue. When I soliloquize, I speak to myself, but it would be absurd to say that I communicate thoughts to myself, that I manifest to myself intentions or emotions: these thoughts, these emotions, I already know them, since they are my own! Here, consequently, the manifesting function of discourse disappears; all that remains is its expressive function. This is why it is not even necessary for the inner discourse to be embodied in actual signs. Mere imagined words suffice to express my thought when it is addressed to me alone. The soliloquy thus makes possible an *analysis* almost in the chemical sense of a separation of the expressive component of language from the indicative one. Indeed, in the case of indications in which I infer the existence of something else on the basis of the indicative function of the material sign, the latter *must necessarily exist* in order for the inference to be valid: there can be no indications in the imagination.

If the linguistic expression possesses a meaning by essence and only accidentally an indicative function, the precise status of this meaning remains to be understood. How can expression and meaning be united and merge into one? Husserl's solution is to say that meaning is something that *is conferred* on signs (phonic or graphic complexes), or rather that *constitutes these signs into signs,* by means of a meaning-intention (*Bedeutungsintention*). In other words, "It is in this sense-bestowing act-character [*sinngebenden Aktcharakter*] . . . that meaning consists."[18] Or yet again, meaning only pertains "to an expression by virtue of the mental acts which give it sense."[19] This point could be further elucidated by saying that perceived words/things are "animated" by sense-bestowing acts that constitute them into *signs* and allow them, by virtue of the meaning that is thus conferred on them, to relate to objects. But does not making meaning depend on psychic acts amount to a relapse into psychologism? Does Husserl not "psychologize" meaning once more, although the vocation of intentional analysis was to de-psychologize it?

This genuine difficulty has indeed led some interpreters to conclude that Husserl's doctrine was incoherent. In *Origins of Analytical Philosophy,* Michael Dummett contends that "it is difficult to acquit Husserl of maintaining a view of the matter like Humpty Dumpty's: the view, namely that an utterance assumes the meaning that it bears in virtue of an interior act of investing it with that meaning."[20] Humpty Dumpty is that character in *Alice's Adventures in Wonderland* who says in Lewis Carroll's tale: "When *I* use a word, it means just what I choose it to mean—neither more nor less." This is the expression of an "essentially private" conception of language, as Wittgenstein would have it, according to which one could say anything with any sign, in the absence of all convention and common use. If we are to believe Dummett, Husserl's theory would lead us into these waters, at least tangentially; it should be contrasted with that of Frege, according to whom, on the contrary, "the word *has* a meaning"—*period.*[21]

Such an interpretation rests on an almost complete misunderstanding. There is no doubt that certain formulations of Husserl, taken in isolation, could lead a reader to a conception of this sort. It is as if consciousness were the depository of meaning and conferred sense on spoken phonic complexes which, in themselves, would have none. "In certain mental acts," Husserl writes, "[the speaker] confers [on the articulate sound-complex] a sense he desires to share with his auditors."[22] Does this mean that I signify whatever I want to signify regardless of the signs I use and of the rules that govern the use of these signs? Not only did Husserl never support such a view, but he defended one that is exactly the opposite. If words have the meaning that I give them, no one can understand anyone—there is no more language. Now, Husserl's thesis is that *meanings are objective by nature*; they transcend the particular psychic acts through which they are grasped. Not only do I not give words whatever meaning I please, but there is a "pure logical grammar" that spells out the *a priori* laws governing the combinations of meanings[23] according to the various categories of words (nominal forms, adjectival forms, and so on), thereby prescribing the limits of sense and nonsense. To state that a meaning is conferred by an intentional act is nowise equivalent to maintaining that the meaning is created by that act independently of any objective rule or human institution. What matters, on the contrary, in what Husserl calls "the meaning-intention" or "the sense-bestowing act" is less the intention or the act (contingent, psychological, individual) than the ideal, universal, atemporal meaning that is intended through it. "The essence of meaning is seen by us, not in the meaning-conferring experience, but in its 'content', the single, self-identical intentional unity set over against the dispersed multiplicity of actual and possible experiences of speakers and thinkers."[24] Bolzano, with his notion of *Sätze an sich*, is the inspiration behind Husserl's Platonism. "Meanings 'in themselves' are . . . specific unities, however much the act of meaning may vary."[25] It would be difficult to be clearer: the fact of being thought or not is indifferent to the essence of expression, and therefore to its meaning.[26] A specific sentence has a specific meaning within a given language even if no one has ever uttered, written, or thought it. The ideality of meaning goes hand in hand with its transcendence vis-à-vis all consciousness, therefore also with its atemporality or omnitemporality of principle, which forbids its assimilation to the temporally individuated psychic acts of which it is the content.[27] Thus, what "is meaningful" (*bedeutet*) primarily and primordially is not the subjective act, but the expression itself. "*Are we to seek the meaning*," Husserl asks, "*as something that is given in the sense-bestowing acts? Cleary not* . . . Meaning . . . is not an act, nor a real moment in the act. The expression 'means' ['*besagt*'] this or that, and this is what makes its meaning; and to the extent that it is in general expression, it has its meaning, for that is what makes up its essence."[28]

There is no reason to view Husserl and Frege as being at odds on this point. Both share the same semantic Platonism, even if their way of formulating it differs substantially. But while Frege does not specify what it means for an objective "thought" to be grasped, or give no positive characterization of the nature of that grasp—beyond vague comparisons (to grasp a thought would be akin to seizing a hammer),[29] thus suggesting that the link between the objective sense (*Sinn*) of a proposition (which he calls *Gedanke*, "thought") and its understanding is a contingent matter, Husserl—here lies undoubtedly the superiority of his theory—refuses to dissociate the psychological from the objective side of meaning: all meaning is determined essentially by the possibility—at least in principle—of being understood by a listener and of playing the role of intentional content of the meaning-intention of a speaker. All meaning is meaning *for* a competent user of signs susceptible of meaning something through them and *for* the person capable of understanding him.

However, there is one point on which Husserl's conception, at least in the formulation of it found in *Logical Investigations*, remains problematic. Husserl, in order to forearm logic as a pure science of meanings against all psychologism, conceives of meaning as a *species* (*Spezies*) and the individual act conferring that meaning as a singularization or an exemplification of this species.[30] On this view, meaning would be the *type* of which the individual act would be the *token*. This view is unsustainable. The species under which the meaning-intention is subsumed is obviously the species *meaning-intention*, and by no means the species *meaning*. To maintain the opposite, as Heidegger remarks, "to say that the *content* of the judgment is the γένος, the universal, the Platonic idea for the *acts* of (actual or possible) judgment, is as absurd as saying that the genus or concept 'table in general' is the genus for a bunch of teacups."[31] Furthermore, to make meaning a species is to confer on it the status of material essence; now, meaning cannot itself be an essence for the simple and good reason that it is that which finds its *fulfillment* not only in individual sensible objects, but also in formal and material essences. Meaning is not an object; therefore it cannot be an ideal object, an essence, either; it is rather what makes it possible to relate through intentionality to any object, to intend it *in such and such a mode* through a sign. The particularization of a species has nothing to do with the temporally conditioned grasp of an ideal meaning in an act that is itself temporally individuated. These difficulties would lead Husserl in 1908 to to no longer assimilate meanings to eidetic generalities and to draw a radical distinction between two senses of ideality: ideality as opposed to the reality of the act and ideality as the generality of the *eidos*. Meaning pertains to the former and not the latter. The ideality of meaning, Husserl points out, "is not ideality in my originary sense (with which I confused it), that of the *eidos*, of essence qua 'generality.' General objects in the sense of meanings and general objects in the sense of species must be strictly distinguished."[32]

There is nevertheless one point on which Dummett's critique is justified. To characterize meaning, Husserl sets out from an isolated consciousness, which leads him to overlook—at least to a point—the social dimension of language. The methodological function of solipsism aggravates this situation. To bring out this social dimension, the analysis of meaning should have been based on the concept of rule, in the sense of *public* rule, linked to institutions and forms of life, as Wittgenstein will do. Indeed, what is specific to rules is that they are from the outset a social institution that anyone can follow or not follow, but that, by definition, can never be of an *essentially* private nature. I may follow a rule all by myself, as Wittgenstein stresses, but I cannot be the only one *to be able* to follow a rule—otherwise that rule is not a rule.[33] It belongs to the essence of rules that there are *necessarily public* criteria making it possible to establish whether or not one has followed them. Wittgenstein's argument, inasmuch as the notion of rule is pivotal to it, ends up de-psychologizing meaning far more radically than did Frege and Husserl. For Wittgenstein as well as for his predecessors, meaning cannot consist essentially in a psychological lived experience or in an inner image—both of these being, as Husserl had already insisted, merely accompaniments (*Begleitungen*)[34] of meaning. But rather than conceive of meaning as a Platonic entity, distinct from both words and lived experience, Wittgenstein brings it back to the rules of use of expressions in language. As for Husserl, he is not completely oblivious of the notion of rule and the normative dimension of what he calls a "pure logical grammar" and a "pure morphology of meanings." Nor does he entirely overlook the pragmatic dimension of the *use* of signs. He even mentions "the much favored comparison of mathematical operations to rule-governed games, e.g., chess. Chessmen . . . become . . . counters in the chess-game, through the game's rules which give them their fixed games-meaning."[35] From here it is but a short step to comparing language itself to a game; but Husserl refuses to take it, for he esteems that neither logic nor universal grammar can be pure normative disciplines, resting on a conventional basis. There must be a domain of ideal objects corresponding to them, making it possible for the validity of their norms to be founded in an apodictic manner. "One can only say 'must' ['*muß*'] because something *is* . . . [*nur darum ist es ein Muß, weil jenes Etwas eben . . . ist*]."[36] Therefore, without denying that many rules are related "to contingent linguistic habits, to matters of mere fact concerning language, which develop in one way in one speech-community and another way in another,"[37] Husserl does not take the pragmatist turn that would have led him to lead meaning back to the rules of use of expressions in language. He wants at all costs to retain the possibility of an intuitive relation to objects, to mathematical objects, for example, but also to the formal idealities of logic that can be given themselves "in person" through these meanings. One might wonder whether this element of intuitivity does not condemn his theory to a solipsistic understanding of meaning. For example, when Husserl writes of the term "red" that "in so far as it names a phenomenal object as red, it belongs to this object in virtue of the moment of red that appears in this object,"[38] does he not fall into the trap of an analysis of meaning in terms of "private ostensive definitions"? Wittgenstein would address him the following objections: (1) the adjective "red" does not apply *in the first place* to the *phenomenal* object, because the use of "*x* seems red" is more complex, and hence logically derived from, the use of "*x* is red";[39] (2) the word "red" is not learned according to private criteria, and therefore not on the basis of the intuition of something like the *eidos red.*

From a Husserlian point of view, several responses would be possible. First, the notion of phenomenon does not refer to a private appearance, but to the perceived object itself, which is transcendent to consciousness, and therefore "public." Even the intuition is not a *purely* private affair. The intuition of red *in specie,* as intuition of a certain type of object, can ideally be reproduced identically by any consciousness possessing language, that is, understanding the meaning of the word "red." Above all, Husserl's theory would most certainly fall into the myth of private ostensive definitions if it held that the meaning of "red" *consisted* in the intuition of the abstract moment *red* or of the *eidos red.* But that is not what it states. For this theory, the meaning of "red" is as "public" as it can be, since it is what any individual who understands the term in question grasps identically. The meaning is *not* the intuition that fulfills it. That said, it is not at all certain that the strategy of semantic Platonism is the best one, nor the most effective in order to vindicate the *intrinsically* social character of language (see chapter 21).

With this question of the fulfillment of meaning, we reach the last step in Husserl's analysis. It remains for us to understand the last moment that completes the triptych act/content/object: the relation of meaning to the object. As we have seen, Husserl conceives of meaning in general as what mediates the relation of consciousness to objects. "Each expression," he writes, "not merely says something, but says it *of* something; it not only has a meaning, but refers to certain *objects.*"[40]

This claim immediately raises difficulties. Is it really valid for "*all* expression"? A noun refers to one or several objects: the noun "cyclamen" to cyclamens and the noun "peony" to peonies. But to what object do the expressions "if," "then," "maybe," "and," and "or" refer? If we distinguish, as does Husserl, after the example of the medieval Scholastics, between categorematic expressions, which can stand in the position either of subject or predicate in propositions of the form "S is P," and syncategorematic expressions, that is, auxiliary words only possessing a meaning dependent on that of categorematic expressions, and signifying only in relation to them and to the proposition taken as a whole, what then is the *object* to which the latter refer? Is it by chance that names and definite or indefinite descriptions (Husserl proposes to treat both these descriptions as names), such as *the equilateral triangle* and *the isogonal triangle* for example, constitute "the plainest examples"[41] of the meaning/object distinction, since they both refer to the same object(s) while having different meanings? Do they not rather furnish *the only* clear examples? And what about sentences taken as a whole? Husserl attributes an object called "state of affairs" (*Sachverhalt*) to declarative sentences. But is it possible to do the same thing for speech acts such as orders, requests, and promises? Is the object of a request—that which must be the case in order for it to be satisfied—an *object* in the same sense of the word "object" as the objects referred to by a name or a declarative sentence? Is the universalization of the meaning/object distinction legitimate? Does it not rather betray the exorbitant primacy Husserl's analyses confer on statements at the expense of other linguistic acts?[42] Husserl would probably concede this point, while emphasizing that this primacy is partially due to the general framework of the inquiry, that of logical analyses in the context of a phenomenological theory of knowledge, as opposed to investigations on ordinary communication and particularly on what Austin calls "speech acts." But shouldn't the taking into consideration of speech acts lead to abandoning the meaning/object distinction, or in any case to limiting its scope? Shouldn't it bring about a recasting of the whole Husserlian conception, which is not far from considering language as being only destined to the formulation and communication of knowledge, according to what Austin has rightly qualified as a "descriptive fallacy"?

I will leave most of these questions aside, since they go beyond the framework of Husserl's semantics, and return to them later. If we concede the restrictions inherent in that semantics, the decisive point in Husserl's view is the following. *Meaning in no way can be conceived of as an object*, and consequently cannot be designated by the term *Gegenstand*; it is an "ideal unity,"[43] ideally graspable, no doubt, and remaining self-identical through time, but not the terminus of an intending act—rather the medium in which this act is performed. "In the act of meaning we are not conscious of meaning as an object."[44] Not only do meaning and object differ, but Husserl's analysis as a whole is intended to show the inadequacy of a theory that, like those of Sigwart and Erdmann, define the *objects* meant by an expression as "meanings."[45] According to this doctrine, an expression referring to an impossible object would be a meaningless expression. Now Husserl makes a clear distinction between the absence of an object (*Gegenstandslosigkeit*) and meaninglessness (*Bedeutungslosigkeit*). An expression such as "square circle" is a well-formed expression, according to the *a priori* laws of pure logical grammar; as such, it has a specific meaning, and it is through this meaning that it refers to an object; but the presumptive intending of an object is no more, in this case, than an empty intending, which can receive no intuitive fulfillment (and this is true *a priori*), so that the presumed object is actually *nothing*. This expression is a contradiction (*Widersinn*), which must be distinguished from a sheer nonsense (*Unsinn*), that is, from a pseudo-expression that violates the pure logical grammar.[46]

This distinction between meaning and object according to which two descriptions, analyzed as names, "the evening star" and "the morning star," have one and the same object but different meanings, irresistibly brings Frege to mind, with his differentiation between *Sinn* and *Bedeutung*, sense and reference. Just as for Frege, sense (*Sinn*) is the "mode of presentation" (*Art des Gegebenseins*) of the reference (*Bedeutung*),[47] so for Husserl, who does not, however, adopt Frege's terminology,[48] signifying is "the determinate manner in which we refer to an object."[49] Whatever the truth may be about an eventual influence—which is controversial[50]—of the German logician on the phenomenologist, their proximity has given rise to "Fregean readings" of Husserl (and probably Husserlian readings of Frege). It may be well to insist here on how much the overall perspectives of these two authors differ. Husserl's doctrine is not a strictly semantic one, since within it the semantic and epistemological elements are constantly superimposed. What shows this best is the case of reference. Husserl's theory is a *referentialistic* theory of meaning, but it is not truly a theory of reference. The paradigmatic problem a semantic theory of reference should solve is whether a (material) contradiction in terms such as "square circle" does or does not have a referent. Now it is difficult to find a univocal response to this problem in Husserl's texts. Husserl argues, on the one hand, that *all* expression that is not purely nonsensical (*Unsinn*) refers to an object through its meaning, but he adds that this reference may be "realized" (*realisiert*)[51] or not; in the case of a "square circle," for example, "the reference of expression to object is now unrealized [*unrealisiert*] as being confined to a mere meaning-intention."[52] It seems then that the reference (or the mere relationship: *Beziehung*) to the object does not have to be realized in order to be. An expression whose reference cannot be realized—that is, whose object cannot be intuited, whether in perception, imagination, or ideation—still refers to something. Conversely, the fact that the reference of an expression is unrealized does not entail that this expression has no reference at all. There is a fundamental ambiguity here. *In a sense,* "square circle" does have a reference; but since that reference cannot be realized, that is, occasion an intuitive fulfillment, *in another sense* that expression does not have a referent. Does it or doesn't it have a referent? Husserl does not settle the issue. What interests him is not so much the problem of reference per se as that of evidence in its phenomenological sense, that is, of the adequate fulfillment of a meaning-intention; it is therefore the problem of how language can become the medium of an apodictic knowledge—for example, how to a judgment of perception there may correspond a self-evident state of affairs that shows us by this very fact that it is true.

As for this last problem, his position comes down to two complementary assertions:

(1) Meaning is essential to expression, whereas intuitive fulfillment is not.[53] I understand perfectly the meaning of a judgment of perception ("That bird is flying away") without having to perceive the state of affairs to which it refers, or to represent it intuitively by imagination. As a consequence, the realm of meaning is wider than that of intuition.[54]

(2) Intuition, nevertheless, is the goal to which all thought aspires: "The perfection of thought lies doubtless in intuitive, i.e., in 'authentic' thinking, in that knowledge in which our thought-intention is 'satisfied' (as it were) by passing over into intuition."[55]

This assertion is nothing but the revival of the Cartesian ideal of a knowledge entirely justified by evidence. It implicitly conditions the broadening of the field of "objects" beyond individual, sensible ones to ideal ones: eidetic generalities, formal or categorical idealities, and finally states of affairs (*Sachverhalte*).

One might wonder what the true motivation is for this considerable extension of the domain of objects, or, as Husserl prefers to put it, of "objectivity" (*Gegenständlichkeit*).[56] Is it the primacy given to the name, which by Husserl's own admission plays the role of prototype[57] in his theory of meaning? Is it the Cartesian epistemology by virtue of which to each expression that is not nonsense or a contradiction there corresponds an at least possible intuitive fulfillment? As we shall see in the following chapter, Ernst Tugendhat subscribed to the first of these two exegetical options. But Husserl suggests that it is rather the second that is the right one. Indeed, he argues that *in order to maintain the strict parallelism between meaning and its possible fulfillment,* it is necessary to acknowledge new objects, or rather a new type of objects: categorial objectivities, eidetic generalities, and states of affairs. It is the concept of *truth* itself understood as adequation between the intended meaning and its fulfilling intuition that leads to that reform. "If these truths hold, everything presupposed as an object by their holding must have being."[58]

The doctrine that best illustrates the necessity of this broadening of the field of the object is that of the categorial intuition developed in the sixth *Investigation.* How should we interpret, in conformity with the motto that meaning is the mode of givenness of the object, a statement of perception of the form "this curtain is red"? "Curtain" is an expression that can receive an intuitive illustration on the level of perception or imagination. The meaning of this noun is different from the object I imagine, but the imagined object *illustrates* the meaning of the noun, conferring on it its intuitivity. However, there already is in the expression "curtain" something that has no equivalent in sensible intuition, namely the *nominal form.* What about the other words? What about the adjective "red," for example? The red of that curtain, *this* particular shade of red is an "abstract moment" of the perception of the curtain, as opposed to its concrete parts, the weave of the texture of the cloth or the folds it forms as it hangs. Yet it is not "*this* red" that plays the role of predicate here, but *red* in general. Now, red *in specie* is not a moment, even an abstract one, of sensible perception; it is an ideal object, an essence. The meaning of "red" thus finds its fulfillment in eidetic intuition. To the broadening of the concept of *object* there necessarily corresponds a broadening of the concept of *intuition.*[59] There is an intuition of the non-sensible, of the ideal, in which the ideal is given "in person." Can the analysis be carried further in this way? Yes, Husserl replies. The demonstrative "this" and the copula "is" are syncategorematic expressions that have no meaning independently of the syntactic function they assume in a sentence. But an intuition corresponds nonetheless to them: an intuition of the formal as such, a categorial intuition. Thus, "*forms, too, can be genuinely fulfilled*"[60] in an originary giving intuition. Even the form of being as copula is *given*—not, it is true, as something perceptible, for nothing in what we can *perceive* corresponds to being[61] (an assertion from which Heidegger will draw the whole problematic of the "ontological difference"), but as an object of a different sort than perceived objects, an object intended through acts that *are founded* or built upon those of perception. The same analysis must be valid in principle—Husserl scarcely tells us how to conduct it—for the deictic "this" that relates to a formal object within the state of affairs. Generally speaking, categorial forms are formal idealities that furnish an intuitive fulfillment to intentional acts of a new kind, not simple acts but "founded" ones.

Consequently, each of the words of which the statement is composed has a dependent or independent meaning, which puts it in relation with an object, be it sensible or ideal, and, among the ideal objects, material or formal. Alongside simple objects there exist complex objectivities, states of affairs, which derive from a combination of these simple objects and confer an intuitive fullness to the meanings of *statements.* What makes the proposition "this curtain is red" true, and makes it possible to grasp intuitively the evidence of the truth of this proposition, is the state of affairs *that the curtain is red.* "In the judgment, *a state of affairs* 'appears' before us, or, put more plainly, becomes intentionally objective to us."[62] Here we reach the most original element in Husserl's semantics, but also the most problematic. According to Husserl, when we say "this curtain is red," we are speaking about the curtain that is there in front of us with its moment of color, we are not only concerned with a proposition or the meaning of a proposition (a "thought" in Frege's sense). The state of affairs is indeed a complex ideal *object* made up of simple sensible objects (like the curtain that I am looking at, or the one I can imagine), of simple ideal objects (like red *in specie*), and of categorial forms (like being in the copulative sense). When he qualifies the state of affairs as an "object," Husserl means that it is a sui generis entity, possessing sensible and ideal parts; something that in some way is there in front of us—a *Gegen-stand.* In short, the state of affairs is not an element of discourse but of reality, in the same way as the curtain or its moment of color; it does not belong to the "real constituents of judgments."[63] How are we to understand this paradoxical claim? How can the state of affairs be an object and present itself intuitively to us as such *independently of its identification by language?*[64] Indeed, *what is it* that appears to me in this way, if not *that the curtain is red*? That is to say, precisely what I assert when I assert the corresponding statement? But it should be emphasized that Husserl never maintained, contrary to Reinach for example,[65] that a state of affairs could exist independently of any judgment, or at least of the *possibility* of formulating a judgment. A state of affairs is assuredly a type of object with which only a being endowed with linguistic proficiency can be involved.

However, if a complete statement refers to a complex ideal object having sensible and ideal parts, does it not follow that the kind of analysis of meaning that was valid for names is hereby extended to entire statements, each component of which is understood, in a sense, as a name—in short, does it not follow that the complete statement must henceforth be analyzed as *naming* a state of affairs? Some passages might lead us to believe this. For example, in §34 of the fifth *Logical Investigation,* Husserl states that "the analogy between nominal and propositional acts must necessarily be complete."[66] But actually the situation is more complex. What plays a role analogous to that of a name in Husserl's view is not the proposition "the Reichstag is open," but the nominalized form of this proposition, the propositional clause "that the Reichstag is open," for it alone can play the role of subject in another proposition: "That the Reichstag is open is a good thing."[67] *The proposition is therefore not a name*; it possesses properties that no nominal form can have—for example that of being true or false. It refers to a state of affairs, but one cannot conclude from this that it *names a state of affairs,* for "naming" (*Nennen*) is not identical in its meaning to "stating" (*Aussagen*).[68] We understand that the "parallelism" between meaning-intentions and simple or founded intuitions that fulfill them by no means signifies that the proposition is a sort of name, even less an image (*Bild*) of reality. Husserl forcefully rejects, on several occasions, the idea that will be that of the *Tractatus,* according to which there is a one-to-one correspondence between the elements of a statement and those of reality,[69] for there is no thinkable similarity or dissimilarity between a statement and its object. The metaphors of "fulfillment," "covering," "fusion," "unity of coincidence," "synthesis of fulfillment," "synthesis of concordance" (*Übereinstimmung*), or "synthesis of identification" are intended precisely to dismiss any iconic conception of the proposition. The theory of fulfillment is a theory of evidence, and it differs from psychological theories of the "feeling of evidence" insofar as it defines evidence, in the relevant phenomenological sense of the term, as "*the act of th[e] most perfect synthesis of fulfilment,*"[70] that is, as self-givenness and, on occasion, *adequate* givenness of an object. In this givenness, the "fulfilling sense" (*erfüllende Sinn*) that comes to coincide with the meaning-intention *is not itself of a linguistic nature.* Thus, the correlate of this entirely de-psychologized evidence is nothing other than truth itself,[71] that is, the intuitive givenness of something. The whole problem raised by this conception is whether the definition of truth on the basis of evidence doesn't come down to furnishing a *private* criterion of truth, and thus actually no criterion at all.

With these remarks, we better see the limitations of the Husserlian conception, specifically the three following limitations. (1) Husserl's analysis is only valid for declarative statements; it disregards all the uses of language in which we don't express or communicate knowledge. (2) The principle of the ideality of meaning, that is, of its identity through time, makes the status of deictics such as "this," "I," "now," and so on (i.e., "essentially occasional expressions," as Husserl, among the first to attempt their analysis, called them) hard to grasp. Indeed, what is specific to the meaning of a deictic is that it varies according to the context. Now, Husserl defends the view that if an expression does not have *one* meaning, it does not have a *meaning* at all. "Logically considered, all shifts in meaning are to be adjudged abnormal."[72] This is why he claims on the one hand that logic can purge ordinary language of this category of words—a project he shares with Russell, and that is, as we know, bound to fail—and, on the other hand, that deictics do in fact possess a self-identical meaning although the object to which they refer varies continuously. As a consequence, in his view, deictics are "much like *proper names*."[73] Again, this reduction is a failure. As Wittgenstein argues, if the deictics were names, it would be possible to learn them in the same way as names, that is, by ostensive definitions. But this is impossible. "This" is not a name, because "this is this" makes no sense.[74] (3) But the most serious limitation of all these developments is the one concerning the conception of logic itself. Husserl remains captive to the limits of Aristotelian syllogistics. He continues to analyze all propositions according to the fundamental form "*S* is *P*." He conceives of predication as the *synthesis* of a subject and a predicate by means of the copula "is." He overlooks the asymmetry of subject and predicate that has paved the way to mathematical logic. By extending the notions of function and argument beyond the sphere of arithmetic and by distinguishing unsaturated expressions (functions that refer to concepts) and arguments that saturate them (objects), Frege eliminates the notion of copula, because he analyzes it as a part of a predicate.[75] Whence two fundamental differences with respect to Husserl. First, his functional or predicative definition of concepts rules out the possibility to make them into objects.[76] The *Begriffsschrift* makes it possible to represent a quantificational hierarchy of functions of an order greater than 1, and thus to speak of concepts of concepts without ever equating concepts with objects. It is true that Frege claims a Platonism and that he conceives of concepts and thoughts as entities independent of the language in which they may or may not be expressed.[77] But he rejects the view that predicates stand for objects analogous to sensible objects, thus paving the way for a reappropriation of his theory in the framework of a new nominalism claiming that a predicate is only *a word* insofar as it applies to objects, the meaning of which is its rule of use. Secondly, by refusing the old doctrine of "states of affairs" that goes back to Gregory of Rimini, Frege conceives of the reference of a proposition as being either the true or the false. He makes possible a semantic analysis of statements in terms of truth conditions. Husserl did not recognize these major logical innovations. If it may be said that the ambition of his pure morphology of meanings is analogous to that of Frege's formalism, the "adjectival" and "nominal" forms, for example, being meant to be valid beyond the contingent grammar of any given language and thus constituting the equivalent of the *Begriffschrift*'s saturated and unsaturated expressions, his conception, with respect to its logical power, remains nonetheless far behind that of Frege.

We may now return to our starting point. Our initial problem was to determine whether it was possible—and on what conditions—to speak of a prelinguistic sense and to differentiate it from linguistic meaning. Is the extension of the concept of sense beyond the linguistic sphere possible? Is it legitimate?

According to Dummett, it is precisely "the generalization of the concept of sense"[78] that dealt a fatal blow to phenomenology, in preventing its taking the analytic turn. With this thesis, Dummett adopts the central point of the Fregean readings of Husserl: the view that the noema, which is qualified as "sense" in *Ideas I*, and the "noematic sense" as the innermost moment of the noema[79] deserve to be characterized as "sense" only because they share some characteristics with Frege's *Sinn*; and therefore the idea that there is on Husserl's part, as was already asserted by Dagfinn Føllesdal, "a generalization of the notion of meaning"[80] beyond *linguistic meaning*, on which phenomenological conceptuality depends in its entirety. If Husserl's procedure did in fact consist in extending the notion of meaning beyond language, its homeland, there would be good reasons to denounce, following Ryle, what is vague and adventurous about such an extension or generalization. But the whole problem is whether Husserl's operation is to be thought in these terms.

It is true that Husserl exposed himself to these criticisms, since, in at least one text, he presents his own innovation as if it were limited to applying the linguistic concept of meaning to the whole sphere of intentional lived experiences. Indeed, we read in *Ideas III*: "The noema in general is, however, nothing further than the universalization of the idea of signification to the total province of the acts."[81] In other passages, this "generalization" is determined more specifically. "Originally, these words ['signifying' and 'signification,' '*Bedeuten*' *und* '*Bedeutung*'] concerned only the linguistic sphere, that of 'expressing.' But one can scarcely avoid—and this is at the same time an important cognitive step—*extending the signification of these words and suitably modifying them* so that they can find application of a certain kind to the whole noetic-noematic sphere: thus application to all acts, be they now combined with expressive acts or not."[82] The insistence on the *modification* that the concept of "meaning" must undergo in order to be extended to the perceptual sphere mitigates to some extent the impression of a pure and simple *extension* of this concept from a domain in which it is legitimate to another in which it isn't. Even this last formulation, however, is somewhat deceptive. It might imply that it is one single concept (almost unmodified) that would be valid both here and there. This is not at all the case. To speak of a meaning of experience as such is not to equate this meaning with linguistic meaning; it is even to make the strictly opposite move. It is to mark the autonomy of the prelinguistic sphere, which is that of intuition, from the domain of meaning and thought in general; it is to emphasize the fact that experience bears within itself "its own sense," as the formula from *Cartesian Meditations* insists; in sum, it is to maintain that the logos of the world is not *projected* onto the world by the articulated logos, nor is identical with it. Merleau-Ponty was perfectly right to answer Ryle: "As if Husserl had first conceived of meaning as strictly tied to language, and had afterwards wanted to put everything into the framework of *Wortbedeutung*! But in truth, from the start, beginning with *Logische Untersuchungen*, Husserl is concerned precisely with differentiating between *Wortbedeutung* and *Bedeutung*."[83] For example, nothing on the side of the noema as sense (or on the side of "matter," in the terminology of *Logical Investigations*) corresponds to the intension/extension distinction that is valid in the sphere of linguistic meaning and more generally in the domain of the conceptual. The perceptual "sense" remains the determined mode of *presentation* of an object, and not something that is *thought* about it.

Husserl did not wait until *Ideas I*, in which he openly proposes a terminological distinction between linguistic *Bedeutung* and prelinguistic *Sinn*, to make a clear distinction between these concepts. Already in *Logical Investigations*, the notion of "fulfilling sense" is only intelligible if the sense that fulfills the meaning-intention differs from meaning itself. The intuitive fulfillment belongs to our prelinguistic consciousness of the world. It resides in a "sense" that precedes de jure its expression, and toward which our entire corporeal existence is polarized. To be sure, one could object to my interpretation of the very formula that I have qualified as the "leitmotif" of Husserl's analyses of meaning: "The object of intuition is *the same* as the object of thought." If we have here an identity between the thought object and the intuited one, isn't it because the linguistic and the fulfilling sense are one and the same? But this objection misunderstands the entire conceptual economy of these analyses. First, its conclusion would involve an infinite regress: if the fulfilling sense were linguistic, how could it confer upon meanings their fullness and upon language its relation to the intuited world? Secondly, we must counterbalance the claim that the object of thought and that of intuition are "the same" by the fundamental axiom of Husserlian phenomenology according to which "to intuit is plainly not to think."[84] The object may well be "the same," but the sense with which it is apprehended perceptually *in a preconceptual manner*[85] is only the *analogon* of the meaning that can be expressed and understood linguistically.

Whatever Husserl's hesitations on this point are, what matters in his analyses for the subsequent history of the phenomenological movement is the idea of an autonomy of prepredicative experience—and of sense such as it is present in the native state in things—with respect to the linguistic articulation of this sense, the idea of a meaningful order of our experience that does not coincide with that of our "grammar." If there is one claim that seems to be shared by almost all phenomenologists—perhaps the only one—it is that according to which phenomena are presented to us with an autochthonous meaning that is not projected onto them by our language patterns. Whether it be the face, which, in Levinas, speaks to us before any word, the flesh and expressive gestures, which are, according to Merleau-Ponty, at the root of language itself, affectivity, the event, and even Heidegger's *Sinn des Seins*—in all these cases, it is indeed with a prelinguistic meaning that we are dealing. This makes it all the more surprising to read in a Husserl exegete as well informed as Rudolf Bernet that the determination of the perceived as "sense" was "a terminological false step."[86] It is, rather, phenomenology's first step, the one that gives it its first thrust, its impulsion and fundamental orientation. What must be shown before anything else, as Husserl notes, is that "what presents itself as an operation of thought [*Denkleistung*] and can be expressed linguistically, rests on deeper operations of consciousness."[87]

Did Husserl, then, extend the concept of meaning beyond its original sphere? There is good reason to doubt it. His operation is a different one. What has prevented many interpreters from noticing it, from the ranks of analytic philosophy, is precisely the analogy with Frege—and in fact, with Frege reread in the light of a new nominalism. Let us start with the account that the logician gives of perception, and that is based on the distinction between private impressions, the objective outside world, and the ideal "third realm" of thoughts. Our visual impressions vary, writes Frege, "and yet we move about in the same outside world. Having visual impressions is certainly necessary for seeing things, but it is not sufficient. What is still to be added is not anything sensible"[88]—it is a thought (*Gedanke*). But how is this "addition" to be understood? Dummett comments on this passage as follows. "Plainly, the non-sensible component of perception, which converts it from a mere sense-impression, belonging to the inner world, into the perception of a material object, and so opens up the external world to us, belongs to the 'third realm.' But it is left unstated whether it must be a complete thought, for instance to the effect that there is a tree in a certain place, or whether it may be a mere thought-constituent, for instance the sense of the concept-word 'tree,' involving our seeing the object as a tree." In light of the contextual principle formulated at the beginning of *The Foundations of Arithmetic,* Dummett concludes, "almost certainly, Frege meant that a whole thought is involved"; therefore "in normal cases, the perceiver will judge this thought to be true."[89] If one leaves aside the fact that, for Frege, thought is not *essentially linguistic* in kind, and if one reinterprets what he says in the framework of a post-Wittgensteinian nominalism by maintaining that thought = the proposition, one inevitably ends up with the dominant analytic position according to which perceptual content is "propositional" (Sellars, Davidson, Dummett, Searle, Tugendhat). But Husserl's solution—and that of phenomenology as a whole—is quite the opposite. It consists in denying all identity between "experiential" sense and its linguistic homologue. It thus opens a field of research on the relationships between our discursive intelligence and our sensible, embodied intelligence.

It is not astonishing that many interpreters, approaching Husserl from the context of a linguistic philosophy foreign to both his interests and his preoccupations, have gone astray. The consequence is the sophism according to which, since all sense in Husserl is expressible in meanings (his "expressibility thesis"), sense *is* meaning.[90] This is a bit like saying that, since the world is expressible in language, the world is itself language.

5

A *Reductio Ad Absurdum* of Phenomenology

Husserl never fully realized (nor did Heidegger, for that matter) the advance of the new logic of Frege and Russell beyond Aristotelian syllogistics. The founder of phenomenology, despite his familiarity with Frege's *Begriffsschrift*, continued to conceive of the propositional statement as the union, the *sunthesis*, of a subject and a predicate by means of the copula, that is, to understand its basic form as being "*S* is *P*." He did not take seriously the difficulties and limitations of this formalization for the logical treatment of existence or relations. Furthermore, he had a tendency to think the proposition as a combination of terms possessing independent meanings (the subject and the predicate) and standing for sensible or ideal objects, and therefore to conceive of their meanings on the model of the meaning of names. "The prototype for the interpretation of the relation between signifying and intuiting"[1] is furnished by the relation of a proper noun, such as "Cologne," to the city itself, as it is given in a perception. This would be a good example of what Wittgenstein labeled at the beginning of his *Philosophical Investigations* the "Augustinian picture of language."

Are these limitations of the phenomenological inquiry in the area of logic and logos in general incidental? Prima facie it would seem so. After all, what would prevent a contemporary phenomenologist with sufficient patience and daring from rewriting *Logical Investigations* from the point of view of mathematical logic as it was developed by Frege, Russell, and Wittgenstein? The thesis of Tugendhat in his *Traditional and Analytical Philosophy* is that things aren't that simple. If Husserl and Heidegger were never able to give contemporary logic its due, let alone take the "analytic turn," it is because their conceptions of the object of philosophy—for the former, his transcendental legacy, and for the latter, his ontological legacy—are far from being neutral, as one might assume, with respect to *semantic* presuppositions. The whole point of Tugendhat's work is to show that, on the contrary, it is precisely semantic presuppositions that are responsible for the particular form taken by the fundamental philosophical question since the Greeks: *ti to on hēi on*, and its modern, transcendental counterpart: how are objects given to a consciousness? The whole framework of phenomenological thought is nothing but the contemporary prolongation of this "object-oriented [*gegendstandtheoretische*] semantics." Its dead ends derive from too narrow an understanding of language. Thus, from Tugendhat's point of view, breaking away from that semantic tradition, carrying out a "step-by-step 'destruction' [*Destruktion*] of the conceptuality available from the tradition,"[2] is tantamount to taking leave of phenomenology altogether.

The error affecting the whole philosophical tradition, according to Tugendhat, consists in understanding *all* expression on the model of a name, that is, on the model of an expression that *stands for* something. On this view, not only do "singular terms," namely deictics, proper nouns, and definite descriptions, refer to objects, but also predicates and even logical connectors. While a proper noun stands for a singular object, a predicate stands for a general object (or a general property), and this general object can be in turn understood as a Platonic entity subsisting in itself, while predication is understood as an *attribution*, that is to say, as a synthesis between two items. Thus, in the view of what Tugendhat calls "the traditional, object-oriented approach [*traditioneller, gegenstandstheoretischer Ansatz*]"[3] to meaning, the meaning of an expression is analyzed in the following way: "The expression *stands for* the meaning which the person who understands the expression *represents* to himself, and what one represents to oneself is an *object*."[4] Tugendhat gives few historical examples of this conception, but it is easy to see that it corresponds for him to a general tendency stretching from Aristotle's *De interpretatione* up to and including Husserl and Heidegger. Once all expression is understood as standing for an object, language itself appears as a medium between the world and us, while the view emerges that in order for language to be able to signify, we must already have access to objects *independently of language*. Hence the starting point of ontology in being as being or of transcendental philosophy in the object in general as *given* to a consciousness in an extra-linguistic manner—and hence the predominance of an "optical model"[5] that Heidegger had already made one of the distinctive features of Western metaphysics, but that Tugendhat henceforth extends to include Heidegger himself, *via* the implicit semantics underlying fundamental ontology and, actually, Heidegger's *Seinsfrage* as a whole.

In opposition to this dominant view, Tugendhat proposes a doctrine which forms, according to his own characterization, an original synthesis between the view of the later Wittgenstein according to which the meaning of a word is its use in language,[6] and the view of Frege, the early Wittgenstein, Carnap, and Tarski, according to which the meaning of an assertoric statement is its truth conditions.[7] In Tugendhat's view, meaning must be understood in terms of employment-rules and truth conditions, and not in terms of objects or their proxies. More precisely, if Tugendhat does not deny that singular terms stand for objects, he refuses to extend that affirmation to predicates, and *a fortiori* to the entire proposition. Since the reference to objects "is essentially an element in the truth-relation, just as the function of singular terms is only to be understood in terms of their role in a sentence,"[8] it follows that the employment-rules of singular terms are not the same as those of predicates, that their contribution to the truth of the statement differ, so that there is no *general* answer to the question of what the meaning of a word is—in an unqualified way: this is a pseudo-question.[9] As Tugendhat points out, "in the main part of my book, I try to show that one must conceive of both the comprehension of the logical subject and that of the logical predicate as comprehension of linguistic rules: the rule of the identification of the corresponding object, in the case of the subject-term, the rule of verification for the predicate. Contrary to the traditional conception, it follows that the predicate in no way stands for an object. The subject-term, on the contrary, does indeed stand for an object, but the latter is not accessible in any extra-linguistic way."[10]

Does Husserl fall beneath the blow of the arguments that could be developed against an "object-oriented" semantic theory, as Tugendhat calls it? The issue of lessons 9 and 10 of *Traditional and Analytical Philosophy* is to answer this question in the affirmative and thus conclude that Husserl's undertaking is a "failure." At first sight, however, it seems difficult to place the doctrine of meaning of *Logical Investigations* beneath the banner of semantic objectivism in the sense just specified, that is to say, as the doctrine maintaining that "the expression *stands for* the meaning which the person who understands the expression *represents* to himself, and [that] what one represents to oneself is an *object*," for at least two reasons. The first is the decisive break of intentional analysis from any doctrine of mental representation; the second is the fact that if there is indeed an author who has formally refused any identification of meaning with an object, that author is Husserl. Let us recall the important passage of the first *Logical Investigation*: "Each expression . . . not only has a meaning, but refers to certain objects . . . But the object never coincides with the meaning."[11] We shall have to return to the importance of this passage. For the moment, one thing is certain. This kind of response to Tugendhat's objections misses the point made by *Traditional and Analytical Philosophy*. Tugendhat does not blame Husserl for falling prey to a Cartesian conception of representation or the interiority of consciousness, but rather for remaining captive to an "Augustinian picture of language," that is to say, to a *properly semantic* conception that leads him, by considering all expression as referring to objects, to overlook the asymmetry between singular terms and predicates, and to conceptualize all expression on the model of a name. Furthermore, Tugendhat is quite aware of the fact that Husserl refused *strictly speaking* to conceive of meaning as an object. Nevertheless, meaning remains, for the phenomenologist, an ideality, which is by definition identifiable and indefinitely reproducible in all meaning-intentions and all understanding of the same statement—hence an ideal self-identical entity. To stick to the letter of this sole passage from *Logical Investigations* would be to underestimate the difficulty, and be satisfied with a verbal solution.

It is probably in order to avoid this type of objection that Tugendhat, to characterize the position he criticizes, chooses the rather indeterminate expression *gegenstandstheoretischer Ansatz,* "theoretical objectual approach." What he groups under this designation is a set of doctrines—among which Husserl's stands out by its coherence to the point of being able to be considered "exemplary [*exemplarisch*]"[12]—that supports the claim that all linguistic expression relates to objects; singular terms relate to sensible objects, predicates to general objects, and statements that attribute a general predicate to a logical subject by means of the copula "is" stand for a complex object, the state of affairs (*Sachlage, Sachverhalt*). In Tugendhat's view, no one has provided a better analysis of meaning within this philosophical framework, and no one in doing so has better shown the limitations of this same framework, than Husserl. The confrontation with his doctrine represents a truly decisive step—probably the most decisive—in Tugendhat's entire argumentation in his book.

It is Husserl who has gone farthest along the road to a semantic objectivism, to the point of revealing its fragility and its impasses. He "made an effort, unique in the pre-analytical tradition, to solve by means of the traditional conceptuality the problem of how the meaning of a complex expression (in particular that of a sentence) arises out of the meaning of its components."[13] Indeed, as Tugendhat will show, Husserl's doctrine of states of affairs is superior to that of Wittgenstein in the *Tractatus,* because, as opposed to the latter, it does not conceive of the state of affairs as "a connection between objects,"[14] therefore as a complex *concrete* object,[15] itself made up of simple ones, but as an *ideal* object. It avoids therefore the difficulty into which the author of the *Tractatus* inevitably falls: that of what concrete objects a fact, defined as the being-the-case (*Bestehen*) of a state of affairs,[16] is made of.[17] But Husserl's theory is also superior at least in one way to Frege's. As we have seen, instead of excluding the subjective side of language to give priority to its objective side, Husserl attempts to articulate these two dimensions. Now, "a satisfactory theory of meaning cannot confine itself to talking abstractly about meanings; it must also take into account the psychological or anthropological factor of the sign-user."[18] Of course, in Tugendhat's view, the sign-user is actually a man in the world possessing physical and practical abilities, capable of *using* signs in agreement with public rules; he is not the still Cartesian consciousness of which Husserl speaks.

Husserl conceived of meaning as a modality of the consciousness of objects or as that through which objects are given to consciousness. Since this frame applies to *all* meaning, it must be valid not only for proper nouns, through which singular objects are intended, but also for common nouns or adjectives playing the role of predicates, through which ideal objects, *eide* or essences, are intended, for deictics ("essentially occasional expressions"), for logical connectors (such as "and," "or," "if . . . then,"), and finally for propositions themselves: their object is a complex object, a state of affairs. If we leave aside the problem of deictics and that of definite descriptions, which Husserl does not distinguish from mere names, following Frege and in opposition to Russell,[19] the trickiest problem is the one raised by the syncategorematic expressions, which have meaning only in connection to categorematic ones, that is, to singular terms or predicates. Since it must be possible for each component of an expression to receive a fulfillment that gives it intuitive evidence, it follows that syncategorematic expressions—and among these, logical connectors—must also refer to objects, even if only to objects pertaining to a formal ontology. Thus, even being as a copula, as the doctrine of categorial intuition makes clear, is given to consciousness, and given by virtue of a necessary parallelism between the meaning-intention and its objective fulfillment. Is this theory tenable? Would we not do better to prefer Wittgenstein's claim according to which the logical constants, because of their interchangeable character, have no representative function?[20] Probably. "If . . . then," "and," and "or" clearly do not refer to any object: we understand these expressions if we understand the truth conditions of the statements in which they occur, that is, if we understand *a rule* that can be symbolized by a truth table—namely the rule according to which, for the conjunction "and" for example, the statement "p and q" is true if and only if "p" is true and "q" is true, and false in the three other cases. Furthermore, "$p \supset q$" is equivalent to "$\neg (p \wedge \neg q)$." Here, conjunction and implication have the same truth conditions, and therefore the same meaning: they do not, by themselves, represent anything.

This point is surely an important one, because it manifests the essential limitation of the object-oriented theory of meaning. This limitation actually goes hand in hand with Husserl's mistrust of mathematical logic such as it is elaborated by Frege.[21] But even if the solution that consists in understanding the meaning of a statement in terms of rules and truth conditions is superior to Husserl's, that doesn't necessarily make it totally incompatible with a phenomenological approach. The obvious embarrassment Husserl would feel in explaining what object the expression "or" stands for does not, for all that, constitute a *reductio ad absurdum* of his entire semantic doctrine. It is true that the doctrine that makes ideal formal objects correspond to syncategorematic expressions, providing a fulfillment for them in situations of evidence, has something baroque about it—producing, as it does, a profusion of ideal objects. It is also true that such a doctrine provides no more than a pseudo-clarification, for to say, as Husserl does, that the meaning of the expression "or" finds a fulfilling intuition in a "disjunctive form," which is certainly not an object in the ordinary sense, but can be intended and given as "an objective form in logic,"[22] does not improve in the least our understanding of the meaning of this logical connector. Nevertheless, this theory, as baroque and insufficient as it is, is not incoherent. Now, Tugendhat's aim is to show, first, that this theory is absurd, and secondly, that it is indissociable from the phenomenological approach, so that to reveal its "failure" is ipso facto to show the failure of phenomenology itself.

In order to see this incoherence, we must take an additional step and consider the object supplying an intuitive fulfillment for an assertoric proposition: the state of affairs. Actually, there is an ambiguity, a "fundamental uncertainty"[23] in Husserl's position, since he sometimes makes the claim that the object that the proposition "this chair is heavy" stands for is the one to which the subject-expression ("this chair") refers; and sometimes, on the contrary, that this object is the entire state of affairs corresponding to the proposition taken as a whole: namely, for a proposition "*p*," the state of affairs *that* p, which corresponds to the "nominalization" of this proposition.[24] However, as Tugendhat points out, these two responses are only apparently contradictory. In the first case, the object of the proposition is defined as "any subject of a possible predication";[25] but precisely the state of affairs to which the nominalized form of a proposition refers has the function of an "object" in this acceptation, that is to say, of a logical subject; for example, "That this chair is heavy is annoying" is a meaningful sentence.

The problem faced by Husserl's doctrine is far more serious, and it is on this point that the argument which is decisive from Tugendhat's standpoint comes into play—an argument that purports to be valid against phenomenology as the prototype of any semantics attempting to construct meaning objectively. Indeed, if the state of affairs is the object that "fulfills" the meaning-intention of a proposition, in the same way as a sensible object fulfills the meaning-intention of a singular term, what criterion do we have for identifying such an "object"? Clearly not the ordinary identity criteria for a perceived object, which are spatiotemporal. The state of affairs does not exist in time in the way concrete objects do. The state of affairs *that the assassination of Caesar took place in 44 B.C.* did not itself take place in 44 B.C. It is a supertemporal, ideal object that is valid *at every instant of time*—supertemporal in the sense of omnitemporal. How can we identify, then, the objective correlate of a proposition? How do we know, for example, that the states of affairs *that* a *is greater than* b and *that* b *is smaller than* a are one and the same? Tugendhat points out that Husserl, as opposed to Frege, has no formal criterion to establish such an identity, while his predecessor, by proposing the theory intuitively less plausible according to which the reference of the statement is truth and falsehood, can dispose of this difficulty: the statements "*a* is greater than *b*" and "*b* is smaller than *a*" have different senses, but one sole reference: truth. By stipulating that the object of a proposition is truth or falsehood, Frege breaks with the traditional concept of "object" as it is used in object-oriented semantics; he takes the first decisive step towards an analytic approach.[26] Husserl, who maintains that the object of the proposition is the state of affairs it stands for, and that the latter is given extra-linguistically, has no other option, however, in order to identify this state of affairs, than to repeat the proposition expressing it. How can one identify the fact to which the statement "snow is white" refers otherwise than by saying that it is the one that makes the proposition "snow is white" true? Indeed, unlike an object that can be pointed at, and that one can learn to name by "ostensive definition," a fact cannot be shown by pointing at it. Indeed, we cannot know *what* is being pointed at unless we already understand the statement that expresses the fact in question. As Wittgenstein insists, "facts cannot be *named*"[27] in the sense that "there is no ostensive explanation of *propositions*."[28]

One could, however, respond to this first objection that it tends to simplify what Husserl says. The phenomenologist does not say that states of affairs are given *extra-linguistically*, independently of all signifying articulation that already brings in categorial forms; he maintains, on the contrary, on many occasions, that the state of affairs is not extra-linguistic, but rather *prelinguistic*, and that the categorial shaping of this state of affairs which occurs in judgment—for example of a perception in a judgment of perception—is nothing other than an explication or a making explicit (*Explikation*) of perception,[29] and more precisely of a "sense" that perception already shelters within itself, without this sense being entirely independent of the (at least ideal) possibility of its expression. In other words, even if the categorial shaping in judgment does not "create" the state of affairs, nor is identical with it, nevertheless, the state of affairs, albeit prelinguistic, is always conceptually or logically dependent on its linguistic explication, on its categorial articulation, since it is precisely that which fulfills the categorial synthesis expressed in the judgment.

But this response remains superficial. Tugendhat's argument, strictly formulated, is the following. If the (complex) object that a proposition "*p*" stands for is a state of affairs, the state of affairs *that* p, this object should be able to be identified independently of the proposition that refers to it. But is this possible? Clearly not. It is impossible to understand what the state of affairs *that* p is, without already understanding *p*. Thus it is not the state of affairs that explains the meaning of the proposition, but quite the contrary. Husserl commits a *hysteron-proteron* here that causes the collapse of his entire semantic theory. In fact, this theory is not even coherent. Indeed, *that* p cannot provide an explanation of the meaning of *p*, since these two expressions *do not mean the same thing*. The former expression lacks the "assertive moment [*Behauptungsmoment*]" that belongs to the latter, or yet again, the former is an *incomplete* expression, which must be completed by a predicate in order to be a statement, whereas only the latter is a complete expression.[30] This central argument is formulated several times in Tugendhat's study. Let us quote the most explicit passage. For Husserl,

> the object *that* p is the meaning of the sentence "*p*." This idea could appear plausible, for it is natural to say that two states of affairs *that* p and *that* q, are identical if the two sentences "*p*" and "*q*" have the same meaning (it is of course assumed that the sentences "*p*" and "*q*" contain no deictic expressions). But even if we disregard deictic expressions the identification of the state of affairs *that* p with the meaning of "*p*" is not tenable. We can already see this from the linguistic usage: we cannot translate statements on the states of affairs with statements about meanings. For example, one cannot say instead of: "the state of affairs that it was snowing yesterday is pleasing," "the meaning of the sentence 'it was snowing yesterday' is pleasing."[31]

This is followed by the decisive argument:

> We can now return to Husserl's thesis that the state of affairs *that* p is the ("objectified") meaning of "*p*." It is now clear why this thesis is false. The meaning of "*p*" always contains more than that for which the expression "that *p*" stands. However justified and however natural it is to say that an expression "that *p*" stands for something—whether one calls

> it a state of affairs, a proposition or a thought—it is false to say this of the unmodified expression "*p*." Someone who says "*p*" is not simply designating a state of affairs, but at the same time asserting that it is true or "obtains" [*besteht*]; and this additional factor which is included in the meaning of "*p*" can no longer be construed objectually.[32]

It was worthwhile quoting this passage in its entirety before raising the question of its relevance. Does Tugendhat's argument truly establish that Husserl's doctrine is incoherent? The response is an unequivocal no. Tugendhat's argument is unacceptable, because it rests on a change in what Husserl says. After having emphasized that in *Logical Investigations* "the object never coincides with the meaning,"[33] because the meaning does not have the status of an intentional object, and that conversely the object is not the meaning but that which confers on it an intuitive fullness and, when the intuition is adequate, a full and complete evidence—that distinction being valid, in the *Logical Investigations,* for *all* meanings, however complex and stratified they may be—Tugendhat seems now to "forget" this essential point. In his argument, he *identifies* the state of affairs *that* p with the meaning of the proposition "*p*," instead of defining the former as the fulfilling object: "the object *that* p is the meaning of the proposition '*p*',"[34] he writes; or yet again, "the identification [*Identifizierung*] of the state of affairs *that* p with the signification of '*p*' is not tenable."[35] That identification probably isn't tenable—but as a matter of fact Husserl never performed it! Husserl could not be clearer on this point. There is a rigorous and strict parallelism between the meaning-intentions of expressions and the apprehension of objects—sensible or categorial, simple or complex—which subsequently provide the former with an intuitive fullness.[36] By virtue of this parallelism, to each meaning, when it is correct from the point of view of a pure logical grammar, there *may* correspond an object that fills it. Therefore there is no doubt that the state of affairs is a fulfilling object and nowise the meaning of the proposition as such. The texts speak for themselves: "In the judgment *a state of affairs* 'appears' before us, or, put more plainly, becomes intentionally objective to us."[37] "*As the sensible object stands to sense perception, so the state of affairs stands to the 'becoming aware' in which it is* (more or less adequately) *given.*"[38] The state of affairs is therefore a complex object which is apprehended on the occasion of a complex judgment, a judgment of perception, for example, and which confers on that judgment its evidence. The state of affairs *that the bird is on the roof* is what fulfills the signifying intention of the judgment of perception "the bird is on the roof"; in sum, "in the *fulfilments of judgments themselves* lies the true source of the concepts State of Affairs and Being (in the copulative sense)."[39]

One could not say more clearly that the state of affairs is not the meaning of the judgment, but the object that confers on this judgment an evidence through an act of intuition no longer sensible but categorial. The state of affairs pertains to "objects of higher order,"[40] that is, ideal objects.

But then it is not possible to make this transition from the assertion that every proposition "*p*" endowed with meaning refers to an object, that is, to a *possible* state of affairs, which, if it obtains, confers its intuitive fullness on it, to the assertion that the meaning of a proposition *is* its state of affairs. Now, this is indeed what Tugendhat does, and it is on this point that his entire reasoning hinges. The argument is the following:

> Let us suppose that *that* p is the meaning of *p*
> But *p* is an assertion (complete expression) and *that* p is an expression devoid of assertive force (incomplete)
> Therefore *p* and *that* p have distinct meanings
> Therefore *that* p cannot be the meaning of *p* (nor can it explain it)

All the force of this *reductio ad absurdum* rests on the initial identification of the state of affairs with the meaning of the proposition. But Husserl never made such a claim. He even said exactly the contrary. Tugendhat is forced to recognize this, since, shortly after having asserted that Husserl *identified* the state of affairs with the meaning of the proposition, he specifies, adopting this time Husserl's conceptuality, that "states of affairs as composite objects . . . are nonetheless objects of another order than the objects of which they are composed."[41] It follows from this that states of affairs are *objective* correlates of meaning, and nowise meaning itself. This is why they cannot "explain" the latter. Tugendhat speaks as if the goal of resorting to states of affairs were to *explain* the meaning of the corresponding proposition or the comprehension we have of that meaning. But this is not the case. If the doctrine of states of affairs, as a descriptive doctrine, may be said to "explain" anything, it could only be the way the existence of a corresponding complex object can make the proposition *evident*—can confer an intuitive tenor on its meaning.

Furthermore, if Husserl identified states of affairs with the meaning of the corresponding proposition, he could not maintain that a proposition may very well be meaningful, be *sinnvoll* from the point of view of the pure morphology of meanings, without being able to be made intuitive by any state of affairs—and therefore, be meaningful and at the same time necessarily false, as in the case of a material contradiction ("this circle is square") or a formal one ("A and not A").[42] For a proposition, to be meaningful and to have a relation to possible objects of intuition are two different things. Thus, Husserl specifies, one must not confuse "the true absence of meaning . . . with something completely different, which is the *a priori impossibility of a fulfilling sense*";[43] in other words, "meaninglessness [*Bedeutungslosigkeit*]" with "objectlessness [*Gegenstandslosigkeit*]."[44] The meaning of a proposition is not the state of affairs to which it refers, but that which eventually finds its fulfillment in the corresponding state of affairs. But, this being the case, it would be best not to give too much importance to what Husserl presents as an *analogy*, the analogy between the name and its object, on the one hand, and the proposition and its object, on the other. The state of affairs taken as a whole, writes Husserl, "is the *analogon* of the object named by the name, and what distinguishes that object from the meaning of the enunciative proposition."[45] It is mainly on this text that Tugendhat grounds his argument. But he is wrong to infer from this analogy that the proposition is only a name for a state of affairs. Indeed, if the expression of a state of affairs is in fact a name, in Husserl's view,[46] it does not follow that the proposition in which that expression can play the role of subject is itself thinkable on the model of a name. "Naming [*Nennen*] is not identical in its meaning with stating [*Aussagen*]."[47] What demonstrates this is the fact that the proposition (*p*) possesses properties that the expression of a state of affairs (*that* p) does not. Among other properties, it can be true or false, and, when it is true, intuitively evident, while a name considered in itself cannot be true or evident. One and the same state of affairs can be asserted with changing "positional qualities" ("I think that *p*," "I desire that *p*," and so on), but a proposition possesses an assertive positional quality and then cannot be asserted with changing positional qualities. As a result, even if Husserl has a tendency to attribute—probably wrongly—a positional quality to acts that are not assertions, and especially to the act of naming,[48] he nevertheless does not confuse assertion with designation.

Not only does he not confuse them; the criteria he advances to distinguish between them are the very ones that Tugendhat emphasizes. The difference between names and statements, Husserl argues, must be held to be "fundamental,"[49] because "an assertion can never function as a name, nor a name as an assertion, without changing its essential nature, i.e., its semantic essence, and therewith its very meaning."[50] In what does this modification consist? In the judgment "we perform a thesis [*Thesis*]"[51] that is, we take a position vis-à-vis the intended state of affairs. In the nominalized statement, the state of affairs "becomes for us an object in a totally different manner,"[52] because "the judgment is no longer carried out."[53] The expression is therefore devoid of all assertive force. In sum, the difference between the expressions "that *p*" and "*p*" consists, not assuredly in the fact that the first is complete and the second incomplete (since Husserl does not adhere to Frege's contextual principle), but in the fact that the first lacks the *Behauptungsmoment,* the "assertive moment," as Tugendhat will say, that the second does possess.

It could probably be objected that Tugendhat only allows himself to equate meaning and object in Husserl because he has shown in the first part of lesson 9 that Husserl did not succeed in distinguishing them from each other *by a strictly semantic analysis.* To the extent that "the concept of meaning remains dependent on the concept of an object . . . from the outset we must expect that it is simply not possible for the object-oriented approach to develop a concept of meaning which would be independent of the concept of an object."[54] This point is certainly accurate. But why should all identification of an object or a state of affairs meet *exclusively* semantic criteria? Here we come to what constitutes a begging of the question in Tugendhat's argumentation. At first sight, the demonstration of the "failure" of Husserl's semantic theory is supposed to lead us to adopt the linguistic-analytic perspective. But the recognition of this alleged failure itself presupposes the adoption of this same perspective, that is, the claim that, if we do not possess strictly semantic criteria of distinction and identity, we possess no criteria *at all.* It is only because he adheres to this view that Tugendhat can conclude, from the impossibility of distinguishing *semantically* the meaning from the object, that it is necessary to identify them, and so to reduce the state of affairs itself to the "objectified meaning" of a proposition. In sum, "formal semantics" as first philosophy presupposes itself. If we are to believe Tugendhat, the nominalization that leads from the proposition to the state of affairs corresponds to "the semantic modification of the objectification of meaning,"[55] and as a result "Husserl construes the meaning of the sentence *as an object.*"[56] But Husserl would respond that nominalization is a *semantic* modification of expression; in no case does it transform the expression of the state of affairs (or the meaning of that expression) into the *object* it stands for—the state of affairs.

It may be that Tugendhat's reading has yet another explanation. As early as in lesson 5, as we may recall (see chapter 3, above), Tugendhat proposed an interpretation of intentionality in terms of propositional attitudes. To him, the content of an act of perception is already "propositional"; it is a content that depends on language by its very nature. The state of affairs, then, consists merely in the ("objectified") sense of the proposition expressing it, that is, in what Frege calls "a thought." Now Husserl conceives of the state of affairs, when it is realized, as a characteristic of the world, an ideal object founded on perceived objects, and not at all as an (objectified) "meaning"—neither as the content of a proposition, nor as a Fregean "thought." He even formally opposes this kind of interpretation in §34 of the first *Logical Investigation*: "If we perform the [meaning]-act and live in it, as it were, we naturally refer to its object [the corresponding state of affairs] and not to its meaning. If, e.g., we make a statement, we judge about the thing it concerns, and not about the statement's meaning, about the judgment in the logical sense."[57]

This is what separates Husserl radically from all interpretation of intentionality in terms of propositional attitudes: what the intentional act intends is not a proposition, nor the meaning of a proposition, and even less that meaning objectified, but "the thing it is about," that is, the state of affairs as ideal object which, if it obtains, is given intuitively as an object founded on real objects in the world. This does not in the least prevent our saying that the grasping of a state of affairs is partly dependent on the language in which this state of affairs is formulated, although this grasp can in no case be reduced to the comprehension of the meaning of the proposition expressing it. The identification of the complex object of a proposition with an objectified meaning is not acceptable, no more so than is the "translation" of the problem of intentionality in Husserl's sense into the conceptuality of propositional attitudes. Obviously, if that translation is not tenable, the rest of Tugendhat's argument isn't either: for if the state of affairs is not the meaning of the nominalized proposition "that *p*," then it is not possible to infer that it is only by understanding the proposition "*p*" that we can understand the state of affairs, rather than the other way round.

The author of *Logical Investigations* has not adopted the Fregean distinction between function and argument. He continues to understand the statement as a *sunthesis* of a subject and a predicate. The predicate *names* an ideal entity and, consequently, the proposition is the union of two names by means of the copula. But that union, as Husserl points out, cannot be a real relation of the same type as those uniting the parts of a concrete whole, that is, what Husserl calls in the third *Investigation* its "pieces"; it constitutes an ideal (or, as he also calls it, a categorial) synthesis. Since Tugendhat's task is to show the incoherence of an object-oriented semantics when applied no longer to singular terms standing for objects but to the complete statement, the problem becomes to show that this doctrine of the categorial synthesis is incoherent.

Before getting down to this last moment of his critique, Tugendhat reminds us once more that the semantic doctrine he is attacking remains, within its own presuppositions, one of the most insightful. The doctrine of the categorial synthesis "represents the most far-reaching attempt so far made to explain states of affairs and the meaning of sentences from an object-oriented position."[58] It is less naive, as we have seen, than the approach of Wittgenstein's *Tractatus*—although the *Tractatus* has the superiority of advancing a claim that already breaks decisively with this semantics: the claim of the non-representative nature of logical constants. However, the doctrine of the categorial synthesis fails for precisely the same reasons as does the doctrine of the states of affairs (both doctrines being closely connected): it holds, in conformity with the entire post-Aristotelian logical tradition, that predication must be conceived as a *relation.* That relation is more precisely the one holding between the whole and the part, the predicate, which designates an ideal object, a generality of essence, being a "part" of the subject, in a non-real sense, that is, an *abstract* part of the subject. In §2 of the third *Logical Investigation,* Husserl writes: "We take the word 'part' in the widest sense: we may call anything a 'part' that can be distinguished 'in' an object, or, objectively phrased, that is 'present' in it . . . Every non-relative 'real' [*real*] predicate therefore points to a part of the object which is the predicate's subject: 'red' and 'round,' e.g., do so, but not 'existent' or '*something.*' "[59] Consequently, a predication such as "this ball is red, round, etc." must be analyzed in the form "*A* is *b, c,* etc." in the sense of "*A* possesses *b, c,* etc." as dependent, abstract parts.[60] The relation that comes in here between the concrete object, the ball, and its dependent part, red, round, etc., being a form of connection not sensible and real, but categorial and ideal.[61] "Sensible combinations are moments of the real object . . . As against this, forms of categorial combination go with the manner in which acts are synthesized; they are constituted as objects in the synthetic acts built upon our sensibility,"[62] acts by virtue of which "we bring new objects into being, objects belonging to the class of 'states of affairs.' "[63]

To this theory of predication as an ideal relation (between the whole and its parts), Tugendhat makes the same kind of objection as to the doctrine of the states of affairs analyzed in lesson 9. Let us assume that the subject and the predicate are indeed names standing for certain objects (real, e.g., this ball, or ideal, e.g., red). Let us assume that predication is a relation between whole and part (in the abstract sense of "part"). If such an ideal (predicative) relation obtains, within the state of affairs intended, between the object that the subject-term stands for and the object that the predicate-term stands for—let us say between this perceived ball and red *in specie*—how could such a relation be identified? For example, how could we distinguish this relation from the relation, not ideal this time but real, that exists between the concrete parts of the ball—let's assume for our purposes that the ball is a soccer ball, and that it is made of pieces of leather sewn together—that give it its spherical shape? What criteria do we have to identify this relation and to distinguish it from other (real) relations such as that of spatial contiguity? The answer, again, is that we have none. If we want to determine what kind of relation obtains here between the object the subject-term stands for and the one the predicate-term stands for within the intended state of affairs, we have no other solution than to repeat the sentence or proposition that expresses it. This relation is precisely the one that holds when the ball is red; that is, when the predicate under consideration is applied to the subject under consideration in a predicative statement. Here again, if we are to believe Tugendhat, Husserl commits a *hysteron-proteron*; because what is first is the proposition, and what is derived is the "relation" that holds within the state of affairs, the latter never being anything but the nominalization of the former.

> We are thus at the turning point [*Wendepunkt*] of the whole discussion. If it is true that we can only define the relation between attribute and object by means of the original predicative sentence then we cannot seek to explain the understanding of the predicative statement itself by means of that relation. But then this means that we require a completely new explanation of the understanding of a predicate, an explanation which does not have recourse to the nominalized form of the predicate and which does not take the form of saying that the predicate stands for something . . . We must therefore completely abandon the object-oriented explanatory model of a composition or sunthesis.[64]

Is Tugendhat's argument here any better than the one he advanced earlier? The answer, once again, is no. The *hysteron-proteron* argument would only have the force Tugendhat attributes to it if Husserl's intent had in fact been to "explain" the type of relation (between the whole and its parts) that links subject and predicate in the proposition by means of the type of relation obtaining between sensible and non-sensible objects within the state of affairs—thus, if his concern were to account for the *meaning* of the predicative statement by recourse to its objective correlate, the state of affairs. But this is not Husserl's ambition, neither in this passage nor in any other. Husserl does not propose a new analysis of predication; he proposes a new analysis of the way the predicative proposition finds a fulfillment in the givenness of a state of affairs. If he claims to explain anything, it is not the meaning of the proposition (or the way we understand it), but solely the possibility of its evidence. Tugendhat's persistent but erroneous assertion notwithstanding, one cannot say that, in Husserl, the predicate "stands for that object [redness], and [that] this object is its meaning,"[65] nor can one say it about the proposition as a whole. But if one cannot say that, then it is not the *meaning* of the proposition that has thereby been explained. Incidentally, it may be that the meaning has not been explained at all. But if such an explanation is not given in Husserl's text, the *hysteron-proteron* simply disappears.

This is not to say that Tugendhat's remarks are without relevance. On the contrary, Tugendhat is perfectly right to argue that Husserl, in interpreting the proposition as "composition," that is, in taking his orientation from the Aristotelian concept of *sunthesis*, misses the importance of Frege's formalism and is no longer able to account for the logical status of relations. For a predicative proposition is *not* a relational proposition. As Russell has demonstrated once and for all, "this ball is red" does not have the same logical form as "Peter is taller than Paul," or "Paul is giving Peter a ball." The first statement must be rendered by a monadic, the second by a dyadic, and the third by a triadic predicate. The *properly logical* critique that must therefore be addressed to Husserl closely resembles the one Tugendhat formulates: if the alleged "relation" between subject and predicate cannot be explained by the corresponding state of affairs, it is because in reality *we are not dealing with a relation at all!* But that critique only *resembles* Tugendhat's critique. It amounts to saying that Husserl's formalism is flawed, not that the philosophical doctrine that underlies this flawed formalism is itself flawed: this doctrine is only hampered by its logical presuppositions. The question remains: what prevents us from adapting the sort of approach recommended by *Logical Investigations,* the phenomenological approach, to the formalism of mathematical logic?

Tugendhat is right to impugn the assimilation of the predicative structure to a relational one—but the target of his criticism is then far more Aristotle than Husserl. Heidegger, who was familiar enough with the logical investigations of Frege and Russell to devote one of his very first texts to them,[66] stresses in *Being and Time* that "in the long run the phenomenon to which we allude by the term 'copula' has nothing to do with bond or binding."[67] Unfortunately, it is not at all certain that, in this passage, Heidegger had in mind the kind of problem raised by Tugendhat. Heidegger very quickly adopted the indefensible claim that "logic has not taken a single step farther in what is essential and inceptive."[68] Why didn't Husserl and Heidegger, despite having read Frege, Russell, and Carnap, understand the importance of what was happening before their eyes? This problem remains a major mystery, still unsolved, in the history of phenomenology.

There is another point on which it is not at all sure that Tugendhat's critique is acceptable. The fact that relations holding within states of affairs are not real, but ideal, leads him to question the very possibility for Husserl to give an account of real relations. Has that author not idealized relations to the point of denying that there are any real relations?

"There is no reason not to conceive of all relations between two real objects as a real relation."[69] But did Husserl ever maintain the doctrine ascribed to him by Tugendhat? As early as in *Philosophy of Arithmetic,* he emphasized on the contrary that certain relations are directly perceived, which in Husserlian terms constitutes the criterion of their *reality.*[70] We *see* for example a *flight* of birds, a *row* of trees, a *gaggle* of geese;[71] we *perceive* here "figural moments," just as we perceive the spatial relations of contiguity or succession that are given on a strictly sensible plane. When we perceive a basket of fruit, the "whole" that we have before our eyes does not have the same sense it does in mathematical set theory. Similarly, the unity formed by the fruit and its moment of color is not an ideal relation, like the one between *this* red, the red of this apple, and its type, red *in specie.* The former is perceived, while the latter relies on an eidetic grasp, a non-sensible intuition. Far from denying the distinction between real and ideal relations, Husserl makes it the cornerstone of his entire doctrine of categorial intuition. I see (sensately) this lamp and this yellow, but I do not see the state of affairs *that the lamp is yellow,* for the simple reason that the corresponding judgment involves an ideal, non-sensible relation, between this lamp and the *eidos* yellow. What this judgment expresses is no longer the concrete relation between this lamp and its color, but an abstract one, that by virtue of which this lamp falls under the extension of the concept "yellow." Thus, the state of affairs expresses an ideal relation *founded* on real, perceptually given relations between real objects.

Moreover, it must be emphasized that the relations holding between the subject and the predicate, or rather between their meanings, are not at all homogeneous with the relations taking place within the state of affairs itself. Husserl draws our attention to this difficulty in his theory. One cannot transpose what is valid for meanings to objects, and vice versa. For example, it is false that "categorematic expressions refer to independent objects, syncategorematic expressions to dependent ones."[72] While at the level of *meanings* categorematic terms are independent, and syncategorematic ones dependent, at the level of the *objects,* on the contrary, the essences corresponding to general categorematic expressions are (because abstract) dependent objects, and only sensible objects corresponding to *some* categorematic nominal expressions are independent, that is, given perceptually in simple acts, and not in founded acts. Indeed, dependence at the level of meanings is interpreted—probably mistakenly—by Husserl as dependence of the part on the whole, while it has a different sense in the state of affairs: it is the dependence of the ideal on the real, and not that of the whole on the part.

Perhaps Tugendhat draws his conclusion from a sentence that is in fact ambiguous in Husserl: "This exposition," we read in *Investigation* 6, "obviously applies to all specific forms of the relation between a *whole* and its *parts*. All such relationships are of a categorial, ideal nature."[73] But what does Husserl mean here? Only that the *making explicit* of the whole/part relation in statements brings categorial, and therefore ideal, formations into play, and not that these categorial formations do not ultimately rest on a "perceptual grasp of this whole" and of the part,[74] and therefore on real relations. In other words, *ideal relations do not exclude real relations,* but confer a new articulation on them: "Sensible combinations are aspects of the real [*realen*] object . . . As against this, forms of categorial combination . . . are constituted as objects in the synthetic acts built upon our sensibility."[75] But the latter do not cancel out the former: "In the sensible whole, the parts A and B are made one by the sensuously [therefore real] combinatory form of contact. But the emphasizing of these parts and moments, the formation of intuitions of A, B and contact, will not yet yield the presentation A in contact with B. This demands a novel act which, taking charge of such presentations, shapes and combines them suitably."[76] Once again, the articulation of the linguistic with the prelinguistic is more subtle and complex than a superficial reading of these texts might lead us to believe.

As long as Tugendhat critiques Husserl on the basis of purely logical considerations, blaming him for having reduced predication to a relation, for example, he is right. But as for the properly philosophical aspect of his critique, it is not at all obvious that the inferiority of the phenomenological doctrine with respect to the analytical one (assuming that there is such a thing) could be established by so direct an argument. The aim of the doctrine of states of affairs is to acknowledge a level of prelinguistic, intuitive experience, governed by *a priori* structures and laws, which corresponds to the linguistic level of expression and meaning. This prelinguistic plane harbors relations either real (sensible) or ideal (categorial) that precede their being made linguistically explicit, even though doubtless they are not entirely independent of language. They are *logically* dependent on language, for only language, in expressing them, can allow them to be grasped explicitly, but they are not *really* dependent on language, in the sense that they are not created by it. A doctrine of states of affairs is not intrinsically committed to an adhesion to the old logic, as is shown by the example of Wittgenstein in the *Tractatus.* It is, on the other hand, inseparably linked to a conception of language that sees in language the highlighting of a preestablished order. In other words, the world possesses structures—in Husserl's view, phenomenal structures—that are not reducible to the structures of language. This is the central idea around which all Husserl's analyses gravitate in *Logical Investigations* and in his later work. It is also the idea that Tugendhat challenges in the affirmative part of his work. To him, any conception of the object as a prelinguistic (or extra-linguistic) given is false, because the concrete object is what a singular term stands for, and the explanation of any relation to that object requires the explanation of the employment-rules of the expressions referring to it—and therefore the explanation of their contribution to the truth conditions of a statement. In short, only what is *identifiable by language* is an object.

It is this more general claim that would need to be further discussed; it bears the weight of the entire *disputatio,* of which we have analyzed only the most visible portion. It is not certain that phenomenology stands disarmed before such a claim; it might address several questions to Tugendhat. Is it possible to carry out his nominalistic-minded linguistic reduction of all the "ontological" structures of the world to the structures of language, that is, to the employment-rules of the expressions which enable us to express and identify those world structures? Has not Tugendhat, in so doing, merely changed the problem into the one of the conditions of verification of statements—since these conditions necessarily involve perceptions and behavior ultimately based on perception? Is it possible, for example, to reduce the problem of what it is to identify an object perceptually—to recognize a face, for example—to the following: According to what semantic rules do we apply to such an object a singular term, a name or a description? That both are genuine philosophical problems is certain, but are they one and the same? Or perhaps we should assume that our relation to the world is *exclusively* linguistic in nature, and that all that is given to us of the world is our way of speaking about it. Would Tugendhat finally suggest that *the whole idea* of a relation to the world, and of an understanding of the world prior to linguistic understanding, is but a consequence of the object-oriented semantic tradition?

6

The Synthetic *A Priori* Dispute

> There are some things in philosophy of which we want to say that we know they are so—or even that we can discover or come to know that they are so—as contrasted with merely deciding arbitrarily that they are to be so; and yet, we do not seem to know that these things are so by any observation of empirical fact.
>
> —Richard Mervyn Hare

In order for a description of experience to be possible, that description must be of *experience*, and not of some other thing. It is worth remembering this obvious fact before we approach one of the most crucial moments of the brief dialogue that took place at the threshold of the 1930s between phenomenology and logical positivism. Indeed, what gives us an assurance that in describing experience—or in claiming to do so—we are not in reality doing *something else*, namely describing the rules underlying the language in which we describe that experience? This objection, which has been formulated in various forms by what may be collectively referred to by the general term "linguistic philosophy," will occupy us for several chapters; we will have to examine its variants and attempt to respond to each of them. In other words: what gives us any confidence that we are really able to describe the laws pervading and structuring experience, and that beneath what we take for a description we are not simply inventorying the linguistic conventions that govern our linguistic usages, and thanks to which all description is carried out?

As we saw in chapter 1, Husserl calls these structural laws of experience as such "material *a priori*." These material *a priori*, essences and relations of essence, which phenomenology seeks to discover, belong to the domain of synthetic truths. This amounts to saying that all material truths are synthetic *a priori* and that all synthetic *a priori* truths are material. Therefore the objection I mentioned took, in the Vienna Circle, a first form, which consisted in denying altogether the possibility of synthetic *a priori* propositions. Moritz Schlick addressed this issue in 1932, in his well-known paper "Gibt es ein materiales Apriori?" ("Is There a Material *A Priori*?"), which is the counterpart, so to speak, of Carnap's article, "The Elimination of Metaphysics through Logical Analysis of Language," the intention of the latter being to show the fundamental absurdity of Heidegger's assertions relative to nothingness in "What Is Metaphysics?" Schlick's text appeared one year after Carnap's, and its purpose was basically the same: to establish the incoherence of the phenomenological doctrine of the material *a priori*, and thus furnish a full-fledged refutation of the phenomenological project as a whole.

It is not rare to find, still recently, historians of philosophy who consider this issue as definitively settled: according to them, the Vienna Circle achieved its goal. To restrict our purview to the French scene, Maurice Clavelin does not hesitate to write, for example, that "Hahn clearly showed the indefensible nature of such a claim [of the existence of synthetic *a priori*]."[1] Pierre Jacob, in his *Logical Empiricism* (*L'Empirisme logique*), states that the positivists' "reasons" for rejecting Husserl's claim are quite "simple" and their argumentation quite "reasonable";[2] he doesn't raise even the slightest question on the outcome of the debate. But are things that simple and the discourse of logical empiricism that transparent? I will show that this is far from the truth. If I had to characterize Schlick's argumentation—probably the most precise and developed on this point—in one word, I would have to say that on the contrary it is mostly rhetorical, and perfectly innocuous toward the thesis it attacks. Thereby, I will not have positively established the soundness of Husserl's thesis, nor the existence of material *a priori*. At most, I will have contributed to a better understanding of the sort of problem the elaboration of this concept aims to solve.

It has become common practice in analytic philosophy, particularly since the works of Saul Kripke, to distinguish three pairs of concepts: (1) the epistemological distinction between *a priori* and *a posteriori*; (2) the semantic distinction between analytic and synthetic; (3) the modal distinction between necessary and contingent. Thus, there could be necessary ("essential") propositions that would be nonetheless *a posteriori*, for example.[3] This typology, let it be said from the outset, does not allow us to enter into Husserl's conceptuality. Here we have no choice but to let ourselves be guided by his own terminological distinctions. First, Husserl qualifies both *concepts* (or essences) and *judgments* as "*a priori*" (and, within the realm of the *a priori*, as either "material" or "formal"), although the criteria of their apriority, as we shall see, differ. Second, he refuses to separate the epistemological from the ontological dimension of the problem. The *prius* of the *a priori* applies not only to our knowledge of objects but equally to the objects of our knowledge; one might even say that it is ontological *before* being epistemological. Indeed, the problem of the *a priori* must be entirely dissociated from that of the innate, with which empiricism, and even to some extent Kantianism,[4] have tended to confuse it. In Husserl, "*a priori*" does not mean "known prior to all experience" but "preceding *from the point of view of their validity* all facts."[5] The point of view of validity (which, as far as the *a priori* is concerned, is "unrestricted," that is, not restricted to the actual world, but extending to all possible worlds) is contrasted, here, with that of genesis. If we take up the point of view of genesis, *a priori* truths—be they formal or material—must be *discovered*, and so they should rather be qualified as "*a posteriori*." A blind man cannot formulate the necessary relations holding between colors if he has never seen red, green, or yellow. But, significantly, it is not the point of view of genesis that most interests Husserl; it is that of validity. "*A priori*" means, for a judgment, "true independently of any fact," no matter by what psychological pathways one may have been led to the formulation of this judgment. In other words, necessity is the distinctive feature of the *a priori* and is indissociable from it, whether we place ourselves at the semantic level of judgments or at the ontological level of essences. Finally, "*a priori*" as used by Husserl is so little opposed to "known through experience" that there is a possible experience of the *a priori*: the *Wesensschau*, the intuition of essences.

Before attempting to specify the nature of the analytic/synthetic distinction, which will be our main concern in this chapter, two general observations should be made.

First, the material *a priori* doctrine supports the entire edifice of phenomenology, not just in Husserl, but—whether they say it or not—in most of his successors: Scheler, Heidegger, Fink, Merleau-Ponty, Sartre, Patočka, and many others. To take but one example, nothing of what gives *Being and Time* its originality, even in relation to Husserl himself, would be possible without the Husserlian doctrine of essences, despite all the shifts and reorientations performed by Heidegger with respect to it. As the latter acknowledges in a significant note, "Edmund Husserl has not only enabled us to understand once more the meaning of any genuine philosophical empiricism; he has also given us the necessary tools. '*A priorism*' is the method of every scientific philosophy which understands itself."[6]

Second, there is nevertheless a controversial point within the phenomenological ranks: that of the *intuitive* character of the access to the *a priori*. It is assuredly an intrinsic part of the idea of a phenomenology that there are necessary and *a priori* structures of phenomenality, irreducible to logico-linguistic *a priori*, but it is far from being unanimous among the representatives of this method that access to these *a priori* must occur through intuition—an intuition that would bring us "eternal truths," free of all historical and even linguistic conditioning. It is on this whole issue that the discussion between an eidetic and a hermeneutic phenomenology hinges. For the moment, we need not enter into this debate, but we can draw one consequence from it. It would be methodologically recommendable, if we want to look into the significance of Schlick's criticisms for *the possibility of a phenomenology in general*, to dissociate the two aspects of the problem; the first being of a broader significance, the second concerning phenomenology solely in its Husserlian version: (1) the problem of the very possibility of synthetic *a priori*; (2) the more circumscribed question of the possibility of an intuitive access to these *a priori* by means of an eidetic grasp. Incidentally, Moritz Schlick devoted an article to each of these questions: "Is There a Material *A Priori*?"[7] and "Is There an Intuitive Knowledge?"[8] In the reflections to follow, I will concentrate exclusively on the first problem.

I have stressed that the *a priori/a posteriori* distinction, as well as the one derived from it, between formal and material *a priori*, was used both in the domain of concepts and in that of judgments. Generally, Husserl prefers the term "material" to qualify essences and "synthetic" for judgments, but that terminological distinction is not applied systematically in his works. Nevertheless, the *reasons* why concepts and judgments can be qualified as "material" (or "synthetic") are not identical.

As for concepts, a decisive point of clarification is presented in §11 of the third *Logical Investigation*. What characterizes a material concept is that it strictly depends on the "contingent singularities" that it subsumes (for example, for the concept of color, on the colors that I am able to encounter and experience), which is not the case with formal concepts, which concern only properties that are absolutely indifferent to all "concrete matter," to all content.

> Concepts like Something, One, Object, Quality, Relation, Association, Plurality, Number, Order, Ordinal Number, Whole, Part, Magnitude, etc., have a basically different character from concepts like House, Tree, Colour, Tone, Space, Sensation, Feeling, etc., which for their part express genuine content. Whereas the former group themselves round the empty notion of Something or Object as such, and are associated with this through formal ontological axioms, the latter are disposed about various highest material Genera or Categories, in which *material ontologies* have their root.[9]

The concepts in the first group apply to all possible worlds without exception. They are not bound to any contingent particularity of this world; this is why they are purely formal, and their *a priori* connections belong to purely formal, and therefore analytic, necessities. Those in the second group also have universal application; they apply to all possible worlds. But it must immediately be added that they apply *to all the possible worlds with characteristics sufficiently close to our own.* The concept of *color* is not dependent on any particular perception of color, but it would have no application in a world in which there was no color at all (a black and white world). Whence a certain tension within Husserl's theory that we have already noted: material essences and their necessary relations cannot possess an *absolutely* unrestricted generality, contrary to what Husserl sometimes says, and in contrast to formal essences. They are necessarily linked to at least some "contingent singularities" of our world as it exists in fact—and as we exist in it. As for a concept like *tree,* we are dealing rather with an empirical generality, as Husserl puts it elsewhere, for a world in which there were no trees, as opposed to a world without any spatiotemporal form, for example, which is perfectly thinkable.[10] What gives the *eidos* its originality is therefore that it applies to a domain of pure possibilities—whence the primordial role of fiction in the eidetic variation—independent (or at least *relatively* independent) of the existence of any particular fact in the world. This "relatively independent" refers to what Husserl will increasingly have to recognize as an "archfacticity" that *binds* material essences to our world, constituting in the end an essential feature of these essences. Every material *a priori,* even if it governs pure possibilities, is ultimately bound to the *factum* of the world.

Husserl does not characterize further the formal/material distinction at the level of concepts; but the originality of §11 and §12 of the third *Logical Investigation* resides in its proposing a more rigorous criterion with respect to judgments. This criterion is logical, and is borrowed, in its principle, from Bolzano:[11] it consists in the possibility of a complete formalization of these judgments. Husserl writes in §12:

> We may *define analytically necessary propositions* as propositions whose truth is completely independent of the peculiar content of their objects (whether thought of with definite or indefinite universality) and of any possible existential assertions. They are propositions which permit of a *complete "formalization"* and can be regarded as special cases or empirical application of the formal, analytic laws whose validity appears in such formalization. In an analytic proposition, it must be possible, without altering the proposition's logical form, to replace all material which has content, with an empty formal *Something* . . .[12]

In other words, *an analytic proposition is a proposition that can be completely formalized,* in which the concrete terms can be replaced *salva veritate* by the empty form of the "something" (*Etwas*) in general, and consequently whose truth conditions remain unchanged when all the material terms are replaced by variables. A synthetic *a priori* proposition, then, is a proposition whose truth-value depends on its material concepts; in other words, whose formalization (the substitution of variables to its concrete terms) does not preserve its truth. "Each pure law, which includes material concepts, so as not to permit of a formalization of these concepts *salva veritate*—each such law, i.e., that is not analytically necessary—is a *synthetic a priori law*."[13] Thus, a judgment such as the one frequently cited by the logical empiricists: "An object cannot be at the same time uniformly red and green" is synthetic *a priori*. Indeed, the substitution of concrete terms, such as "spherical" for "red" and "big" for "green," would make this proposition false. It cannot be completely formalized *salva veritate*.

The key concept in the domain of judgments is *analytic*, since synthetic *a priori* judgments are defined as those not satisfying the criterion of analyticity. Let us consider, to begin with, two examples of analytic judgments.

(1) "A whole cannot exist without parts."

(2) "There cannot be a king (master, father), if there are no subjects (servants, children)."

The first of these judgments possesses an analytic necessity that Husserl qualifies as "pure" in the reedited (1913) edition of the work, the second an analytic necessity that is not further specified. The reason for this disparity is probably the following. The terms present in the first judgment ("whole," "part") relate to formal concepts, while those appearing in the second judgment ("king," "master," etc.) refer to material concepts, although in both cases, the sort of necessity expressed by the judgment is of a purely formal or analytic nature. How so?

In the first example, "whole" and "part," as "empty" concepts, pertaining to a formal ontology, are *correlative* terms: there cannot be a part without a whole of which the part is a part, no more than there can be a whole without parts of which it is the whole. As Husserl writes: "A part *as such* cannot exist at all without a whole whose part it is."[14] In other words, the negation of that proposition is not materially false; it is a logical contradiction, a "'formal,' 'analytical' absurdity [*Widersinn*]."[15] It is contradictory to speak of a part without a whole, and vice versa. The second judgment also presents an example of analytic necessity, although the concepts it contains are material concepts. In the proposition "there cannot be a king without a subject," the terms "king" and "subject" are relative to one another, since it belongs to the concept "king" that all kings exercise their kingship on subjects, and to the concept "subject" that all subjects are only subjects to the extent that they are subordinate to a king. Using a formulation that is not that of Husserl, it is a formal-analytic truth that, if there exist an x and a y such that x is the king of y, then there exist an x and a y such that y is the subject of x. The judgment "there can be no king without a subject," that is, "if someone is the king of someone, then someone is the subject of someone," can be reduced to a theorem of the logic of relations: if x has the relation R with y, then y has with x a relation that is the converse of R. Even if it contains material concepts, the truth of the judgment under consideration *does not depend, therefore, in any way on the material content of these concepts.* In short, this judgment is entirely formalizable, as all of its material terms can be replaced by variables (x, y), that is, by "the pure form of *something.*"

The situation is different in the case of a proposition of the type: "there is no color without extension." "The difference leaps into view," Husserl writes.[16] Indeed, the concept of "color" is not relative to that of "extension," nor vice versa. It is only in relation to the possible experience of color in general that the *a priori* necessity of that proposition arises. This necessity is therefore material. "'Color' is not a relative expression, whose meaning includes the idea of a relation to something else. Though color is 'unthinkable' without something colored, the existence of the latter, and more definitely that of a space, is not 'analytically' founded on the notion of color."[17]

But why not conclude from these premises that this proposition is an empirical, contingent one? Let us recall the answer I have already given in chapter 1: because it is not even *conceivable* (*imaginable*) that we might one day have the experience of a color existing without any corresponding extension (which is not to say without a *surface,* for there are "atmospheric," non-localizable colors, like the blue of the sky). This proposition, therefore, is *a priori.* It differs radically from empirical propositions, obtained by inductive generalization, for which there always remains open the possibility that we may one day observe a counterexample. But its necessity is not analytic; it is based on "the essential specificity of the contents";[18] it depends on the fact that all the colors *that we see,* and that we learn to name, are offered to vision as occupying a certain extension, a certain portion of space. We can understand *a priori,* without having ever experienced a king, the necessity, in order for there to be a king, of there being subjects over whom he reigns; but we cannot understand *a priori,* without having had the experience of any color, that all color is extended. A blind man can *accept* that proposition as belonging to the "definition" of colors, but not *grasp its eidetic necessity.* That proposition is dependent on experience, but it is not derived from experience; it is valid *a priori* in all possible worlds, for all possible experience.

Husserl seems thus to have reached his goal, which was to furnish a criterion for the analytic/synthetic distinction, free from all psychologism, unlike Kant's criterion. Indeed, as Kant puts it, "either the predicate B belongs to the subject A as something contained (though covertly) in the concept A; or B lies outside the sphere of the concept A, though somehow connected with it. In the former case I call the judgment analytical, in the latter synthetical."[19] The Kantian definition rests on the difference between acts of thought which add something to a concept, and others, which only unfold its immanent content. But Kant never specifies how these two psychological operations are carried out. Husserl, by contrast—following Bolzano—advances a *formal*, non-psychological criterion for this difference. To the (semantic) difference between analytic and synthetic *a priori* in judgments there correspond, from the ontological point of view, two types of necessity. *Neither of them is dependent on experience in the sense that it could be invalidated by experience.* But one of these necessities, while being *a priori, is not of a logical nature*: it is a "factual" necessity, which depends on the particularities of our experience and of the material concepts that enable us to describe it. It is a material impossibility for us to encounter a color without extension, but this is not a logical contradiction, because it is not analytically contained in the concept of *color* that it cannot exist otherwise than extended. This is what reveals the impossibility of a substitution *salva veritate* of variables for each of the material terms in the judgment "all color is extended."

With this distinction between two types of necessity, we have reached the core of Husserl's conceptual work in these pages. It matters little how the second necessity is designated. Stumpf, as we may recall, proposed to call it "analytic," but distinguished between two senses of "analytic," formal and material analytic, one might say—which, by the way, would not be such a bad way of expressing it, since Husserl uses the term "material contradiction [*Widersinn*]" to designate a proposition such as "this color is non-extended," "this tone is devoid of pitch (of timbre, of intensity)," "this circle is square," and so on. The important thing is just to realize that such a contradiction *is not a logical contradiction*, as it cannot be reduced by formalization to a proposition of the form *A and not A*. Thus, it is best not to become obsessed with Husserl's terminology to the point of losing sight of the "thing itself," as if the definition of "synthetic" and "analytic" were written somewhere in the stars, independently of the way Husserl characterizes these terms and uses them. One might even argue that material necessities can be said to be in one sense *a priori* and in another *a posteriori*: *a priori*, because their validity is not derived from an empirical generalization and because no counter-example is conceivable here; *a posteriori*, because they depend after all on a general fact, that of the existence of a world possessing such and such characteristics (for example, in it we encounter such a thing as colors). Analytic truths, by contrast, are *a priori* in both these respects.

Do these definitions really allow us to progress toward a justification of the analytic / synthetic distinction that is no longer psychological? Yes and no. Yes, certainly, because the attempt to provide a criterion of analyticity by the possibility of a complete formalization no longer has anything psychological about it. No, in that—as Peter Simons[20] stresses—neither Husserl nor, for that matter, Bolzano, Leibniz, or Kant before him, solved the problem of what Quine calls "hidden analyticity." Are there not cases in which the substitution of the form of "something" for concrete terms does not retain the truth-value of the proposition, even though we have the intuition that the proposition is indeed analytic (as in "no bachelor is married," to borrow Quine's classic example)?[21] Here, isn't "not married" strictly equivalent to "bachelor"? Can that statement be given the same status as "all color is extended," in view of the fact that extension and color are clearly not the same thing? Indeed, it seems not. The proposition on bachelors seems intuitively much closer to Husserl's proposition, "there is no king without subjects," that is, to an analytic proposition. And yet Husserl's criterion does not allow us to establish it: such are its limitations.

With the material *a priori* and the intuition of essences giving us access to it, we have, according to Husserl, a conceptual knowledge that is neither empirical (obtained by generalization), nor purely linguistic (relative to the employment-rules of certain terms or to their definitions); a knowledge that, on the one hand, can be neither confirmed nor invalidated by experience, since it bears upon the invariable structures of experience, and that, on the other hand, is not merely bound to linguistic conventions. Philosophy, in its phenomenological version, has as its "realm" this domain of material truths, located between the domain of the empirical sciences and the purely formal one of logic. Such a domain does not exist, Schlick counters. This is what he sets out to demonstrate in his article.

In taking on this problem, Schlick implicitly makes phenomenology—which he qualifies as "the most influential school of philosophy in contemporary Germany"[22]—the main adversary of the Vienna Circle. He claims that the *a priori* of the phenomenologists is the supreme challenge to the theses of logical empiricism—"a more serious threat to its position than those [positions] with which the *Critique of Pure Reason* is concerned."[23] Thus he is prepared to make the entire outcome of the debate hinge on the answer to the question: are there, or are there not, synthetic *a priori*? As he writes, logical empiricism "is ready to revise its standpoint, if the result of the test should not be in its favor."[24] This dramatization of the stakes, which belongs to the rhetoric of the *disputatio*, must not hide the fact that Schlick doesn't have the slightest doubt about the outcome of the dispute. He doesn't want to establish that there are no synthetic *a priori* because they haven't been discovered yet, or because those ostensibly discovered really aren't what they were thought to be, but because, for logical reasons, there can be no such things. Thus he believes he can demonstrate not only the falsity but the absurdity of the phenomenological doctrine.

His starting point is a defense of the Kantian identification of the *a priori* with the formal, despite the fact that in this context the formal should be understood differently than in Kant. In Husserl's view, Kant was wrong in leading the *a priori* back to the formal (whether we are speaking of the *a priori* forms of sensibility, time, and space, or the pure forms of the understanding, the categories); he failed to recognize the existence of *a priori* contents of experience and objectivities. Contrary to what Kant maintained, the *a priori* must not be *inferred* by means of a transcendental argumentation; it is *given* to an eidetic intuition. Taking Kant's side against the phenomenologists, Schlick opposes Scheler, who denounced this identification of the *a priori* with the formal as "a fundamental error of Kant's doctrine."[25] As for Schlick, he blames the author of the *Critique of Pure Reason* for having accepted the existence of synthetic *a priori* propositions in mathematics, but he praises him for having managed to perceive that no content of experience could be *a priori*. "Kant's insight was quite correct, and his opinion that logic as a whole is to be understood in terms of the principle of contradiction can accordingly be interpreted as recognition of its purely tautological character."[26] Kant's only mistake was to fail to equate the formal with the logico-formal, and to have accepted, alongside the formality of formalisms, that of *a priori* forms of sensibility and *a priori* concepts of the understanding, thus postulating an ambiguous compound of the formal and the empirical, "a strange mixture of form and content."[27] But on the condition of avoiding this pitfall, logical empiricism can claim to be following Kant in its absolutely strict delimitation of the respective domains of the analytic and the synthetic, that is, of the formal and the empirical, a delimitation by virtue of which there can remain no room for a third possibility. "There is no *a priori* except in tautology, and there is nothing synthetic, no real knowledge, except on the side of the *a posteriori*."[28]

In order to understand Schlick's thesis (and logical empiricism's in general) according to which "all propositions are either synthetic *a posteriori* or tautologic" (from which it follows that synthetic *a priori* propositions are "a logical impossibility"),[29] we must understand his doctrine of meaning in its overall characteristics. What do "analytic" and "synthetic" mean for the Vienna Circle? These terms are used to characterize propositions and nothing but propositions. As Schlick puts it:

> An analytic proposition is one which is true by virtue of its form alone. Whoever has grasped the meaning of a tautology, has in doing so seen it to be true. It is because of this that it is *a priori*. In the case of a synthetic proposition, on the other hand, one must first understand its meaning, and afterwards determine whether it is true or false. It is because of this that it is *a posteriori*.[30]

In other words, analytic propositions are restricted to revealing the rules that govern the use of their constitutive terms—rules of a logical nature which are necessarily imposed on all language users. As a result, these statements say nothing of the world or of any state of affairs. "It is raining or it is not raining" tells us nothing about the present weather conditions; it merely expresses the rules governing the use of the disjunctive ("or"): when that disjunctive is inclusive, the statement is true if and only if at least one of its constituents is true. The truth of that proposition is therefore independent of the weather. It does not depend on any state of the world. It expresses nothing about the world. It is limited to expressing (Wittgenstein would have said: *to showing*) a purely formal rule inherent in the use of language, or a method for applying the propositions "it is raining" and "it is not raining" to reality; a method for speaking about things. Accordingly, that statement, which contains no factual content, is true by virtue of its form alone. It is a tautology. To understand such a statement means nothing but to grasp a rule. To understand its meaning and to understand its truth are consequently one and the same thing.

With synthetic statements, things are otherwise. To grasp their meaning is one thing; to be able to say whether they are true or false is another. For example, "All copper bodies conduct electricity" is a proposition whose validity must be tested by adequate experiments. The problem of determining whether this statement is meaningful differs, then, from that of determining its truth or falsity. This statement has meaning if it expresses a conceivable state of affairs, and it is true if that state of affairs obtains and false otherwise. Furthermore, it expresses a possible state of affairs if it can be deduced from more primitive statements, from observational statements or "protocol statements." The terms it contains ("copper," "electricity") are themselves meaningful if a proposition such as "*x* is made of copper" can be deduced from more elementary propositions bearing upon facts directly accessible to observation. Since the validity of a synthetic statement cannot be established by a purely formal criterion, it therefore necessitates the intervention of a nonlinguistic factor, experience. Consequently, such a statement is necessarily *a posteriori.* According to the watchword of logical empiricism, "the Meaning of a Proposition is the Method of its Verification."[31]

Relying on this distinction between analytic judgments (or tautologies) and synthetic (empirical) judgments, Schlick endeavors to show "the logical impossibility" of any synthetic *a priori.* According to the phenomenologists, there are *a priori* statements or laws that are not formal or empty—that are therefore not tautologies, but rather possess an *intrinsic* relation to experience and its content. In "Form and Content," Schlick gives the following examples: "Every musical tone must have a pitch and an intensity," "the surface of a physical body (or a patch in the visual field) cannot be both red and green at the same place and at the same time," "orange as a color quality ranges between red and yellow."[32] These examples are not exactly the same as those chosen by Husserl in §§11–12 of the third *Logical Investigation,* but they constitute without possible hesitation examples of the synthetic *a priori* for the phenomenologist.

Consider the proposition: "The same surface cannot be at the same time green and red." What is its status? It is certainly not an empirical proposition, Schlick answers, even though we do, clearly, learn to recognize the difference between red and green by experience.

> Nobody denies that it is only through experience that we can come to know that a (uniformly colored) dress worn by a given person at a given time was green or red or of some other color. But it is equally impossible to deny that once we know it to be green we need no further experience in order to know that it isn't red. The two cases stand on completely different levels. Every attempt to explain the difference between them as one of degree, by claiming, perhaps, that while in the first we have to do with a direct report of experience, the second, in the last analysis, can be traced back to experiences (on the ground that only through such could we know that red and green cannot be associated with the same spot), is fruitless.[33]

Let us note that Husserl never claimed that this difference was one of degree. He said that there is a necessity that, although universal, is not of a logical nature but depends on experience. Now, we must understand that the experience in question is not that of empiricism. Husserl certainly does not mean that we would need new experiences, given that a dress is uniformly red, to *learn* that it is not green. He claims, just like Schlick, that we know it necessarily *a priori.* But he adds that the sense of this *a priori* is irreducible to its strictly logical sense. For him, this *a priori* is an *a priori* of experience as such, a structural law immanent to experience. For the "experience" of phenomenology is not in itself without structure. It is not the bare reception of sense data of the empiricist tradition, nor even a succession of contingent lived experiences, certain of which might possess "gestalt qualities" as Schlick concedes to the proponents of Gestalt psychology.

Schlick points out in passing that the concept of "experience" in Husserl and the phenomenologists is irreducible to that of empiricism—"they also give a new meaning to the term 'experience'"[34]—but he does not delve into the matter. He says neither how the two concepts differ, nor what makes the one he uses superior. He is as little inclined to explore how the concepts "empirical" and "*a priori*" differ in phenomenology and logical positivism as was Carnap, a year earlier, in elucidating in what sense Heidegger used the word "*Nichts,*" and whether it was possible, consequently, to paraphrase his statements by means of negative existential propositions.[35]

For Schlick, it is as if to state that the proposition about colors is linked to our experience could mean but one thing: that this proposition can be either confirmed or invalidated by experience. Now, for Husserl, the material *a priori* can be neither confirmed nor invalidated for the simple reason that we cannot even conceive (imagine) what would be the case if it did. The necessity of the material *a priori* is not *inferior* to logical necessity (nor is it superior to empirical probabilities); it is of a different nature. Material impossibility is not only the impossibility of thinking or imagining things otherwise; it is the impossibility of things *being* otherwise. Schlick overlooks this when he maintains that the impossibility for one and the same spot to be at the same time (uniformly) red and (uniformly) green can be of only two orders, empirical or logical. "Red and green are incompatible, not because I happen never to have observed such a joint appearance, but because the sentence 'This spot is both red and green' is a meaningless combination of words."[36] Here Schlick "forgets" his own remark on the heterogeneity of the two concepts of experience: his own, and the one he challenges. He proceeds as if Husserl had maintained that the incompatibility between the colors came from empirical generalization. He *does not even take into account* the specificity of the phenomenological response, even for the purpose of refuting it.

The fact is, Schlick's argument is based on premises that he does not bother to make explicit, but which are the following. First, all necessity is logical in kind, in conformity with the thesis defended by Wittgenstein in the *Tractatus*: "There is no compulsion making one thing happen because another has happened. The only necessity that exists is *logical* necessity." "Just as the only necessity that exists is *logical* necessity, so too the only impossibility that exists is *logical* impossibility."[37] The example chosen by Wittgenstein to illustrate these assertions is, as it happens, borrowed from the domain of color. "For example, the simultaneous presence of two colors at the same place in the visual field is impossible, in fact logically impossible, since it is ruled out by the logical structure of color." ("The statement that a point in the visual field has two different colors at the same time is a contradiction.")[38] Unfortunately, Wittgenstein does not specify here in what that "logical structure" consists, let alone what reasons he has to maintain that this necessity is of a *purely logical* nature. The consequence it seems legitimate to draw from these assertions, in Schlick's view, is in strict keeping with empiricist doctrine. If there is no other necessity than logical necessity, all that pertains to the domain of experience must be contingent. Hence, *all structure is only the result of a projection onto experience of a logico-linguistic framework.* Therefore the detour through the *Tractatus* allows Schlick to rejoin the founding theses of classical empiricism and especially the latter's association of a sensualist atomism with a nominalism such as one might find, for example, in Hume. It is Hume's distinction between *matters of fact* and *relations of ideas*—at least if we consent to reading it, as is the dominant tendency within the Vienna Circle, as a prefiguration of the claims of logical empiricism—that is here the leading clue. The propositions of the sciences that rest on relations of ideas (geometry, algebra, and arithmetic) may be discovered, wrote Hume, "by the mere operation of thought, without dependence on what is anywhere existent in the universe."[39] They correspond to Schlick's "propositions of a purely conceptual nature." Propositions which refer to matters of fact, on the other hand, and whose negation is not contradictory, are of an empirical nature and have no necessity. Such is the relation of cause to effect. Consequently, for Schlick as for Hume, any "intermediary" discourse between the demonstrative and the empirical sciences is meaningless. One must say of phenomenology what Hume said of metaphysics: "If we take in our hand any volume; of divinity or school of metaphysics, for instance; let us ask, *Does it contain any abstract reasoning concerning quantity or number?* No. *Does it contain any experimental reasoning concerning matter of fact and existence?* No. Commit it to the flames: For it can contain nothing but sophistry and illusion."[40]

We cannot understand a single word of Schlick's undertaking, of his critique of the synthetic *a priori,* but also, more generally, of his denunciation of phenomenology as a perfect sample of "metaphysics," if we know nothing about the historical background against which his thought develops. The antithesis of the analytic-formal and of the synthetic-empirical is but the reformulation of Hume's antithesis in light of modern mathematical logic. Setting out from the double premise that (1) there is no necessity other than logical necessity, and (2) experience is entirely contingent, Schlick makes the following argument. Since the assertion that a uniformly red dress cannot at the same time be uniformly green can be neither confirmed nor invalidated by experience, *it has no relation to experience and is therefore analytic.* It expresses an impossibility that, being an inconceivability in principle, can only be a *logical* impossibility. From this we must conclude that it does not express any fact—that it is a tautology. "Our 'materially' *a priori* propositions are in truth of a purely conceptual nature, their validity is a logical validity, they have a tautological, formal character."[41] From this it follows, first, that these statements which are considered by phenomenology as profound truths, evident principles on which are grounded regional ontologies, are actually "trivialities," that have nothing but a "rhetorical" usage; and second, that the negation of these tautologies does not lead to false empirical propositions, but to logical contradictions, that is, to completely meaningless propositions. A proposition such as "the same surface is at the same time uniformly green and uniformly red" is not empirically false; it violates the laws of logical syntax; it expresses a logical impossibility, so that we cannot give any meaning at all to this combination of words. "The logical rules which underlie our employment of color-words," Schlick writes, "forbid such a usage, just as they would forbid us to say 'light red is redder than dark red.'"[42] For Husserl, there would be a difference between that last proposition, which is analytically false, that is, which is a formal contradiction (*Widersinn, Widerspruch*), and which he would not have called nonsense (*Unsinn*), and the first proposition, which is *a priori* false but not contradictory, since its falsity does not depend on strictly logical criteria. In Schlick's view, there is no difference of this kind: both propositions are nonsense.[43] For him, there is no distinction to be made between what Husserl would call a "formal contradiction" (for example, "a whole can exist without parts") and what he would call a "material contradiction." But as a consequence, Schlick has to account for the *logical* impossibility of the proposition that attributes two different colors to a selfsame surface by postulating that logic extends much farther than formal logic in its classic acceptation (which is still that of Husserl), farther than the domain of propositional connectors, variables, quantifiers, and truth-values; he must assume, in agreement with Wittgenstein, that there is something like a "logical grammar of color words,"[44] while being no more able than was his predecessor to specify exactly what it is that makes that grammar a *logical* one.

This is why, after having read Schlick's exposition, the reader can hardly resist the impression that its whole argumentation unfolds parallel to that of Husserl, but does not really come to grips with the latter. Schlick has defined experience, logic, analyticity, the meaning of statements differently. But has he accomplished anything beyond that? Has he proved that Husserl's synthetic *a priori* statements were actually analytic, or has he not been content with renaming the material *a priori* of the phenomenologists "analytic"? Has he provided a decisive argument against their thesis, or has he simply developed his own argumentation starting with different premises? In the latter case, his argumentation would remain purely verbal. It would not have demonstrated anything. It would in no sense constitute a *refutation* of the phenomenological position, let alone a demonstration of its meaninglessness, its "metaphysical" status, in the sense the positivists give this term. This is what we must now examine.

As we have seen, Schlick's claim is not only that nobody has yet discovered any synthetic *a priori* propositions, but that it is impossible to discover any—that the notion of the synthetic *a priori* proposition is as absurd as that of a square circle. "All propositions are either synthetic *a posteriori* or tautologous; synthetic *a priori* propositions seem to it [the Vienna Circle] to be a logical impossibility."[45] But is Schlick in a position to establish positively this point? And what would it take to establish it?

The answer to these questions is not in doubt. In order to succeed, Schlick would have to be in a position to give a definition of what he calls an "analytic proposition" distinct from the one he gives of "*a priori* proposition," and a definition of "synthetic proposition" distinct from the one he gives of "*a posteriori* proposition," because failing that, his claim that a synthetic *a priori* proposition is logically impossible would be no more than begging the question. Let us examine, for example, the following passage by Schlick:

> A synthetic sentence, that is to say, one that actually gives expression to a cognition, is always used in science and life to communicate a state of affairs, and, indeed, that state of affairs the cognition of which is formulated by the sentence. On the other hand, an analytic sentence, or, to put it more clearly, a tautology, has a quite different function . . . A tautology is naturally an *a priori* truth, but gives expression to no state of affairs, and the validity of a tautology rests in no way upon experience.[46]

It is clear that Schlick is defining here the analytic by apriority and the synthetic by aposteriority; but then his assertion that only analytic propositions are *a priori* is strictly nothing more than a tautology that follows from its initial definitions. This being the case, his thesis that "all propositions are either synthetic *a posteriori* or tautologous" cannot in any way be considered a *refutation* of Husserl's thesis. Once Schlick initially posits that the only *a priori* is of a logical nature and that all that is not *a priori in this sense* is empirical, it is a simple matter to draw the conclusion that the very idea of a synthetic—*i.e., an empirical—a priori,* is contradictory. But of course that "demonstration" has demonstrated nothing at all. As long as things are left at this point, if there ever was a "truism," to use the expression Schlick applies to the synthetic *a priori* of the phenomenologists, it is indeed the thesis of Schlick himself!

Can we get beyond this? It seems that the only way to do so—that is, the only way to positively establish the validity of Schlick's thesis—would be to set out from definitions of the analytic and the synthetic that do not make that thesis trivial. But is that possible? Yes, probably, or at least that is the approach Schlick himself seems to take at the beginning of his reasoning, by rehabilitating the Kantian definition of the analytic by the principle of non-contradiction. In the *Critique of Pure Reason,* Kant proposes the following definition. "In an *analytical judgment,* whether negative or affirmative, its truth can always be sufficiently tested by the principle of contradiction."[47] In formal terms, this means that a proposition *p* is analytic if and only if one can derive from its negation *not p* a logical contradiction, that is, a proposition of the form *p and not p.* Schlick begins by allying himself approvingly with this Kantian criterion of analyticity. "Kant's insight," he says, "is quite correct," that is, "his opinion that logic as a whole is to be understood in terms of the principle of contradiction." In thus siding with Kant, Schlick, whether he realizes it or not, is once more in opposition to the *Logical Investigations.* In that work Husserl refuses to define logic on the basis of the principle of contradiction alone, not only because there are properly logical objectivities that must be able to be given intuitively themselves,[48] but especially because Kant "never [saw] how little the laws of logic are all analytic propositions in the sense laid down by his own definition."[49] Indeed, what proposition of formal logic can actually be derived from the principle of non-contradiction *alone*? Practically none. At the very least, the Kantian formulation would have to be completed by stipulating that analytic propositions are those that it is possible to derive from the principle of contradiction *and from the whole class of logical truths* (identity principle, law of double negation, etc.). Thus, the Kantian definition should be modified as follows: *p* is analytic if and only if it is possible to derive from *not p* a contradiction of the form *p and not p by means of logical truths alone.* The domain of the synthetic would then be that of propositions which do not lend themselves to such a derivation. Schlick, in contrast to Husserl, does not raise this difficulty; nor is he preoccupied with the need to complete Kant's definition. But even supposing such a reform were carried out, in order to supply a definition of the analytic that didn't already involve the *a priori* and a definition of the synthetic that didn't already involve the *a posteriori,* would that be sufficient to legitimate Schlick's claim—and thus refute Husserl's?

Can it be said of a proposition such as: "One single object cannot be uniformly green and red at the same time" that it is analytic in the sense we have just specified? In that case, it would have to be possible to establish that by means of an adequate formal derivation. As long as that demonstration has not been made (and we have no guarantee that it could be), the claim that Husserl's synthetic *a priori* statements are actually analytic has not received the least justification. Indeed, the problem immediately arises of the presence in that proposition of apparently *unanalyzable* terms that would preclude its being reduced to a contradiction by means of logical truths alone. The presence of such terms would then reinforce the position Schlick opposes.

Schlick, in fact, does not express an opinion on this problem. But another member of the Vienna Circle, Hans Hahn, took it seriously. In his view, the negation of the proposition of the phenomenologist—if we may call it that—namely "one selfsame surface can be at the same time red and green" amounts to the logical contradiction: "One selfsame surface can be at the same time red and not red." Hahn writes:

> We learn, by training as I am tempted to say, to apply the designation "red" to some of these objects, and we stipulate that the designation "not red" be applied to all other objects. On the basis of this stipulation we now can assert with absolute certainty the proposition that there is no object to which both the designation "red" and the designation "not red" is applied. It is customary to formulate this briefly by saying that nothing is both red and not red."[50]

If we follow this suggestion, its consequence is that Husserl's apparently synthetic *a priori* is actually an analytic proposition in the (modified) Kantian sense, since it is nothing but the expression of the principle of non-contradiction: "$\neg (Rx \wedge \neg Rx)$." But should we follow this suggestion? The answer is no, and for at least two reasons.

First, the domain of synthetic *a priori* truths as conceived by Husserl includes a large number of propositions whose negation cannot be reduced prima facie to a logical contradiction. How should we handle "all color is extended"? "All tones have pitch and intensity"? Or "orange as a color quality ranges between red and yellow"? Neither Schlick nor Hahn tells us this. To be sure, such a reduction would be possible if we chose to define color, for example, as a visual quality of extension, in such a way that it would follow analytically from that definition that a non-extended color would be contradictory; but in so doing we would again be begging the question. For there is no such thing, *logically speaking*, as *the* definition of color, nor, for that matter, of any material term.

Second, even if we were to stick with the one example Hahn chooses to examine, it is not at all certain that things are that simple. What prevents us from saying that a single object can be at the same time uniformly blue and uniformly green, if we mean by that that it is turquoise, that is, if we designate its color, turquoise, by a combination of primary colors? On the other hand, it is true that we cannot say *in that sense* that a single object is at the same time red and green. Red and green are incompatible colors; so there is nothing that is red-green. But this is precisely the point. How are we to account for *this* difference? Is it not precisely this type of difference that Husserl has in mind when he speaks of material *a priori*, for example of necessary and *a priori* relations between colors that cannot be derived from the principles of logic alone? Thus, from the point of view that interests us here, that of the possibility of the material *a priori*, it would be rather the irreducibility of the given example to a logical contradiction that gives food for thought. May this irreducibility not indicate that the truth of the proposition under consideration, without being empirical, is nonetheless unanalyzable? That is, that there is indeed a synthetic *a priori*? But in that case, not only does Hahn's attempt fail to reach its goal, but it would lead to exactly the opposite conclusion from the one he comes to. For it seems that colors have precisely relations of compatibility and incompatibility that do not arise from the laws of logic alone, but depend rather on our experience of colors, even though they do not come from an inductive generalization based on that experience. Judgments such as "blue is closer to green than to red," "orange ranges between yellow and red," and "we can speak of an orange-red, but not of a red-green" express just such relations.

The outcome of these considerations is that it is very difficult—not to say impossible—to apply the narrow ("Kantian") definition of the analytic to Husserl's synthetic *a priori* propositions. It is very difficult to derive a logical contradiction from the negation of the propositions that Husserl qualifies as synthetic *a priori*, in order to prove that they are analytic.[51] Schlick, incidentally, as opposed to Hahn, does not even try to do this, either because he sees from the outset that it is impossible, or because, to further his cause, he carefully sidesteps the problem. His strategy consists in passing immediately from that first definition of the analytic to a second one, which, equating the analytic with the *a priori* in general, enables him to derive analytically the impossibility of the synthetic *a priori* from the very definition of the analytic. By this legerdemain, Schlick gives the impression of having solved the problem; but should these two definitions of the analytic turn out not to be equivalent, his whole argument, in the final analysis, would be based on an amphiboly.

The passage on which I have already commented, but which is of central importance in this respect, reads: "Kant's insight was quite correct, and his opinion that logic as a whole is to be understood in terms of the principle of contradiction can accordingly be interpreted as recognition of its purely tautological character."[52] In it, Schlick passes without saying it from his first (narrower, "Kantian") characterization of the analytic—according to which all analytic propositions are indeed *a priori*, because formally derivable from logical truths alone, but all *a priori* propositions are not necessarily analytic—to his second, much broader characterization of it: every proposition for which whoever understands its meaning immediately grasps, by this very fact, that it is true, is analytic ("analytic," in this sense, thus becomes synonymous with "true by virtue of its form alone," i.e., "tautological"; and "synthetic" now means: whose truth cannot be established by the mere comprehension of its meaning but requires recourse to experience). By this change of definition alone, Schlick has now *equated* the domain of the analytic with that of the *a priori* and the domain of the synthetic with that of the *a posteriori*, whence it logically follows that the idea of synthetic *a priori* is a contradiction in terms. If we restrict ourselves to the first definition of the analytic, the task remains pending, for it remains to be *demonstrated* by appropriate formal procedures that all *a priori* propositions are *by this very fact* analytic. Now if we move on to the second definition, this formal demonstration has become superfluous, since the domain of the *a priori* has been *defined* by analyticity. By making this transition from one definition to the other, Schlick has sidestepped the problem of the demonstration of his thesis by merely changing its definitions.

But of course Schlick has provided no justification for these new definitions. Now, as long as he has not established *what justifies* our considering Husserl's synthetic *a priori* propositions as true *by virtue of their form alone*, independently of all consideration of facts, he has established nothing at all. Indeed, it might very well be that here the *descriptive terms possess an unanalyzable conceptual content*, and that it is by the *a priori* knowledge of this content that we know these propositions to be true without the need of any empirical knowledge. This is even precisely what Husserl would maintain. For him, there is no difficulty in saying that whoever understands the meaning of the propositions in question also knows, by this very fact, that they are true. On the other hand, however, he would refuse to conclude from this that they are true by virtue of their *form* alone, and that they are therefore tautologies, for the simple reason that he would reject the identification of the domain of the *a priori in general* with that of the analytic. But Schlick obfuscates the difficulty by slipping from the narrow sense of "analytic" to its broad sense, that is, by extending the use of "analytic" far beyond its Kantian (and Husserlian) usage, in such a way that propositions that would never have been considered analytic by Kant, such as "all color is extended," "the same surface cannot be at the same time green and red," and so on, can now be thus characterized. Hence his whole argumentation rests purely and simply on an equivocal use of the term "analytic," on a broadening of its meaning such that it ultimately coincides with that of "*a priori.*" As long as the "demonstration" goes no further than this, we must make the following assessment. First, the type of objection Schlick addresses to Husserl, namely that he has reduced the question of principle (*quid juris?*) to a question of fact (*quid facti?*)—in other words, that he has not questioned the conditions of possibility of the synthetic *a priori*, but been content with asserting its existence, applies just as well, if not better, to Schlick's assertions. Second, Schlick's criterion for the analytic, namely that "whoever has grasped the meaning of a tautology, has in doing so seen it to be true" is insufficient: as it stands, it remains no more than a psychological criterion.

In sum, the alternative is as follows. Either (1) the assertion that analytic propositions are true by virtue of their form alone, in such a way that whoever understands them knows thereby that they are true without recourse to experience, is a *definition* of these propositions; in which case Schlick has merely *renamed* "analytic" Husserl's synthetic *a priori* propositions without having established *for what reason they are analytic*; or (2) their analyticity is a *property* possessed by these propositions, in which case it must be possible to demonstrate by what logical procedure the terms "color" and "extension," for instance, can be eliminated from the proposition "all color is extended" and replaced by predicate variables making the proposition true for all their possible substitutes; a task which Schlick has not fulfilled, however. It must be possible to demonstrate, on the basis of this substitution of variables, that the negation of that proposition is contradictory by virtue of its form alone; and thus, that this proposition is deducible from the principles of logic alone. But where has this been shown?

Of course if this has not been shown (and probably cannot), we are back to our original starting point, that is, to the problem of unanalyzable terms. *Now, that was precisely Husserl's starting point.* If there are indeed terms whose descriptive content is unanalyzable (and Schlick has nowise established that there are none), then the distinction between analytic *a priori* propositions (which remain true for all possible substitution of variables) and synthetic *a priori* propositions, which are not the result of a generalization (and therefore cannot be invalidated by experience), but which are not open to such a substitution *salva veritate*—this distinction retains all its force. These propositions are indeed *a priori*, but it is very doubtful that they are analytic. Far from the impossibility of a synthetic *a priori* having been demonstrated, Husserl's thesis seems to emerge rather reinforced by the holes in Schlick's argumentation.

Furthermore, in order for the propositions of the phenomenologist to be reducible to tautologies and their negations to logical contradictions, we should be able to reduce all material concepts in Husserl's sense to a very small number of primitive concepts, and perhaps even to one. Let us examine a relation that is as simple and fundamental as non-identity. "A C is not a color" may probably be reduced by analysis to "a tone is not a color," but we then run up against the impossibility of reducing these two concepts to a *common* primitive concept that would allow us to reduce the original proposition to a tautology of the form "A or not A," and its negation to a contradiction of the form "A and not A." In sum, even propositions expressing non-identity are not, as things stand, instances of logical truths; they are therefore not "analytic" in the sense relevant here.[53]

Of course we must acknowledge that Husserl's criterion of distinction also remains, as strictly formal criterion, insufficient. It runs up against the problem of *hidden analyticity* brought out by Quine. In "Two Dogmas of Empiricism," Quine has shown that all definitions of analyticity are hopelessly circular: the notion of analyticity rests on that of meaning; the notion of meaning rests on that of synonymy; the notion of synonymy rests on that of analyticity. Nothing Husserl says makes the overcoming of this difficulty possible; but perhaps we would be wrong in concluding from this that we should refuse any meaning whatsoever to the concept of "analyticity" itself. As Putnam emphasizes, we can accept Quine's idea that there is no infallible test for determining in the case of any given proposition whether it falls on one side or the other of the analytic/synthetic distinction, without rejecting the more modest idea that there is a sense in which certain propositions can be said to be true by virtue of the meaning of their terms alone.[54] Therefore also that there may be "many types of 'non-analytic'[55] propositions" that do not all have the property of being "descriptions of fact," contrary to what logical positivism claimed.

Basically, what Husserl tells us comes down to the following. (1) Since material truths cannot be reduced to tautologies and (2) since they are clearly not the result of empirical generalization, given that their negation expresses an unthinkable state of affairs, it follows that they must possess a status that is neither that of logical truths nor that of empirical truths. There is not much to be said by way of criticism about this argumentation, except that we lack a *formal* criterion to give positive support to its conclusion. As Peter Simons remarks,

> The Bolzano-Husserl concept, despite the admitted difficulties about implicit analyticity, seems to be no worse than the usual concept of the logical positivists, and has the advantage that logic does not have to [be] expanded to include concepts with specific empirical content. The philosophical investigations of Wittgenstein and the Vienna Circle are usually portrayed as representing a great leap forward in exact philosophy. However, it has to be admitted that in some points preceding traditions, such as early (pre-transcendental) phenomenology, were considerably more exact.[56]

But we should not give in too quickly to the temptation of opposing the early Husserl, rigorous and enamored of logic, to a later one, supposedly vague and metaphysical, in keeping with a certain Anglo-Saxon exegesis. On the contrary, the significant fact is that Husserl does not abandon Bolzano's criterion even after the transcendental turn. We read, for example, in *Ideas I* that, for synthetic truths, "the substitution of indeterminate terms for the related determinate ones does not yield a law of formal ontology, as it does, in characteristic fashion, in the case of any 'analytic' necessity."[57] Although Bolzano is not cited, this is precisely the definition of the third *Logical Investigation.* The lesson to be drawn from all this is clear. Even if it is difficult to establish positively the existence of material *a priori,* that is, of necessary structures of phenomenality as such, and even if Husserl tended—wrongly—to think of *all* phenomenological descriptions as being based on such *a priori,* thus missing all that depends, in phenomenology, on historical presuppositions, the fact remains that it is not only Husserl's first (pre-transcendental) phenomenology that survives Schlick's critique intact; it is phenomenology as such *in its possibility.*

7

Phenomenology or Grammar?

> We certainly know—though it is difficult to say how we know—that two different colors cannot coexist at the same place in one visual field. . . . This incompatibility is not logical. Red and blue are not more *logically* incompatible than red and round. Nor is the incompatibility a generalization from experience. I do not think that I can *prove* that it is not a generalization from experience, but I think this is so obvious that no one, nowadays, would deny it. Some people say that the incompatibility is grammatical. I do not deny this, but I am not sure what it means.
>
> —Bertrand Russell

"Is there a Wittgensteinian phenomenology? This question has often been asked in the course of the last decade, and has received different answers. It is now a well-known, documented fact that Wittgenstein was tempted by a project that he himself qualifies as "phenomenological" in the course of the year 1929, shortly after his return to philosophy. But it may be that, all in all, Wittgenstein's true phenomenology is situated less in this transitional stage than in the last, properly "grammatical" period of his thought. However, it is not in this way that I wish to address this problem. Rather than seeking in the work of the philosopher who wanted to cure himself of philosophy what might, almost in spite of himself, evince some affinities with a tradition that he never really studied in its own right, and in which he did not show an overwhelming interest, to say the least, it may prove a more fruitful approach to focus on what constitutes the most anti-phenomenological aspect of Wittgenstein's thought: the autonomy (or the arbitrariness) of grammar.

The natural place for this inquiry is the problem of colors, for reasons both internal and external. From an internal point of view, we know that it is a difficulty with the logical status of the incompatibility of colors that led Wittgenstein to an in-depth overhaul of the fundamental theses in the *Tractatus* and to the project of the elaboration of a "phenomenological language," to such a point that it has been said that "Wittgenstein's first philosophy collapsed over its inability to solve one problem—colour exclusion."[1] It is also dissatisfaction over his own solution that led Wittgenstein, a little later, to the abandonment of his "phenomenology" and to his grammatical conception of philosophical activity. From an external point of view, the domain of colors forms a field of material or synthetic *a priori* for the phenomenology stemming from Husserl: colors sustain relations of essence; for example, relations of opposition or exclusion (green/red, blue/yellow.) Among the most penetrating analyses of color we find in the phenomenological tradition, let us mention those of Wilhelm Schapp,[2] and especially those of David Katz in his 1911 essay, *The World of Color.*[3] Finally, as we saw in the last chapter, it is on this problem of color incompatibility that the great *disputatio* putting the Vienna Circle and phenomenology at odds was centered. Color is the basic, elementary instance (but not simply an instance among others) making possible the questioning and evaluation of the respective positions of the three major philosophical trends of the last century. As we shall see, Wittgenstein's solution to the problem of color exclusion is quite different from that of Schlick, though the latter drew his inspiration from the *Tractatus.* It consists in taking seriously the irreducibility of incompatibility propositions to pure tautologies. Consequently, Wittgensteinian grammar represents a much stronger alternative to the phenomenological doctrine of material *a priori* than the so-called analytic propositions of the Vienna Circle.

But what exactly is meant by "grammar"? Should Wittgenstein's "grammar" be accepted without further examination, and does it really, as it claims, harbor no philosophical presupposition? And what are we to make of the critiques of "grammatical" inspiration that have been advanced against phenomenology?

"The grammatical approach," Descombes writes, "is not the conclusion of a meta-philosophical argument intended to establish the truth about human speculation and the cognitive powers of reason as such. We don't have to decide *a priori* that all speculation is futile, that all intellectual difficulty is brought about by grammar's having bewitched us. The diagnosis must be carried out on a case by case basis, and has no other justification than the effectiveness of the prescribed treatment."[4] On this widely accepted view, in order to accept the idea of "grammar" and the grammatical method in philosophy coming from it, it is not necessary to do meta-philosophy but only to gauge the relevance and fruitfulness of this idea by the ability or inability of the one applying it to dissolve philosophical perplexities. However, this view is false, both in fact and in principle: in fact, because the idea of grammar does indeed derive, in the development of Wittgenstein's thought, from meta-philosophical arguments, even if these arguments are not the ones evoked by Descombes, and even if they are only partially developed and remain most often implicit in Wittgenstein; in principle, because it is not possible to evaluate the relevance of a method in philosophy by its results only—let alone to furnish a "justification" of that method on the basis of its alleged "effectiveness." How are we to know whether a philosophical perplexity has been truly "dissolved" without having previously taken a position on the soundness of the method of dissolution, and therefore on the acceptability of its underlying meta-philosophical premises? This circle concerns not only the grammatical method; it applies, as we have seen, to *all* method in philosophy. How can we accept a phenomenological description if we do not adhere to the premises of this method? How can we accept a logical analysis in the style of the Vienna Circle without having subscribed to a certain conception of analysis?

Without trying to reconstitute the genesis of the idea of grammar in detail, a perilous and complex project if there ever was one, it is nevertheless possible to give a few major landmarks, even if that enterprise cannot fail to provide matter for controversy, as is always the case when one tries to reconstruct the thought of an author whose philosophical legacy has occasioned so many different interpretations. As a precaution, let me point out that this reconstruction involves less Wittgenstein than the way he has been understood within the orthodox Wittgensteinian school; that of Elizabeth Anscombe, Anthony Kenny, Peter Geach, and Georg Henrik von Wright, and in the monumental commentary of Peter Hacker and Gordon Baker. What interests me is less Wittgenstein himself than the trend to which he gave birth—less historical problems than conceptual ones, although the formulation of the latter is indissociable from historical considerations.

If there is one indisputable point of continuity between the *Tractatus* and the later philosophy of Wittgenstein, it is the conviction that "the only necessity that exists is *logical* necessity" (*Tractatus,* 6.37), although the adjective "logical" takes on different meanings before and after the grammatical turn. This assertion is the axis around which all Wittgenstein's thought gravitates, and which has allowed that thought to undergo deep change without belying itself. Indeed, the edifice of the *Tractatus* rests entirely on the distinction between a "Humean" world, made up of facts logically independent of one another and lacking any *a priori* order, and an "empty" logic made up of tautologies that say nothing about this world and are not even, strictly speaking, true—a distinction between the radical contingency of the world and the necessity of logic, which is absolutely independent of the world. "It is an hypothesis that the sun will rise tomorrow: and this means that we do not *know* whether it is true" (6.36311); "There is no compulsion making one thing happen because another has happened" (6.37); "Outside logic everything is accidental" (6.3). However, the main point of the *Tractatus* is to show that logic penetrates the world, is "all-embracing" (5.511), without depriving the world of its absolute contingency. The logical form of the states of affairs in which the world consists is not expressed, but shown by the propositions that express these states of affairs. To satisfy the requirement of a radical contingency of facts, Wittgenstein advances the idea of a logical independence of elementary propositions. At first blush, this idea is difficult to accept. If I assert a contingent truth such as "Socrates is at the Agora," it follows logically that Socrates is not in Piraeus, at the Lyceum, or anywhere else. To overcome this difficulty, Wittgenstein advances the rather obscure doctrine of simple objects, whose connections are facts or states of affairs (2.032). If the proposition "Socrates is at the Agora" is not logically independent from other propositions, this is because it is not elementary. Elementary propositions, whatever they may be (Wittgenstein gives us no examples of them, nor of simple objects), are concatenations of names (4.22) referring to simple objects (3.203); complex propositions are truth-functional combinations of elementary propositions. Every proposition is the description of a state of affairs, and therefore a picture of reality (2.1; 2.12). All propositions are therefore empirical, or synthetic. As for the tautologies that constitute logic (5.43), they describe nothing, nor are they pictures of any reality: to say "It is raining or it is not raining" does not provide us information about any fact of the world, even meteorological. Insofar as having a sense (being *sinnvoll*) for a proposition is depicting a possible state of affairs, a tautology is senseless (*sinnlos*) (4.461), but it is not for all that nonsensical (*unsinnig*) (4.4611). Outside of *a posteriori*, that is, synthetic propositions, and *a priori*, that is, tautological or analytic propositions,[5] there is nothing. Thus there are no propositions such that they would be *a priori*, therefore absolutely necessary, and at the same time have sense—be a picture of reality. Consequently there are no synthetic *a priori* propositions: "There are no pictures that are true *a priori*" (2.225).

The *Tractatus*, by its whole architecture, presents itself, then, as an anti-phenomenological work. Of course, this claim is inaccurate from a historical point of view. Wittgenstein does not discuss the synthetic or material *a priori* of the phenomenologists. But this claim is not an unreasonable one, since the entire edifice of the *Tractatus* aims at undermining (and showing the absurdity of) the view that philosophy could be a science concerning a domain of *a priori* truths, a view of which the phenomenological doctrine of essences is but a reformulation. According to Wittgenstein, only the natural sciences furnish "the totality of true propositions" (4.11) and philosophy has no domain of its own, distinct from both empirical truths and logical necessities; it is reduced to the activity of "logical clarification of thoughts" (4.112). But the *Tractatus* runs up against the problem of internal relations and internal properties, among other difficulties. Is it not an *a priori* truth that every tone has pitch and intensity, or that, for two different given reds, one is darker than the other? Wittgenstein's answer is that these propositions are mere pseudo-propositions, tautologies. They assert nothing about facts and their negation is a contradiction. "A property is internal if it is unthinkable that its object should not possess it. (This shade of blue and that one stand, eo ipso, in internal relation of lighter to darker. It is unthinkable that *these* two objects should not stand in this relation.)" (4.123); or yet again: "For example, the simultaneous presence of two colors at the same place in the visual field is impossible, in fact logically impossible, since it is ruled out by the logical structure of color. . . . The statement that a point in the visual field has two different colors at the same time is a contradiction." Thus, in the perfect logical notation proposed by the *Tractatus*, internal relations and properties are not *expressed* in propositions (which Wittgenstein has just done), but they *show themselves* in the logical form of the expressions that depict states of affairs and refer to objects (4.122). Of course, the recognition of the fact that the *Tractatus* says many things that it itself declares to be inexpressible opens the chasm of an enterprise in which philosophy stages its own disappearance in favor of an ideal logical notation. That matter is too well known—or rather too little known and too controversial—for us to dwell on it.

What Wittgenstein claimed in these texts about internal relations—internal relations between colors, for example—would no longer satisfy him when he returned to philosophy. And it is quite easy to see why. First, the independence of elementary propositions is more asserted than explained in the *Tractatus.* It rests in fact on the obscurity which envelops the notion of "simple object" (and thus that of "elementary proposition"); for none of the empirical propositions that we can formulate possesses this logical self-sufficiency. Secondly, it is hard to see how an affirmation such as "every color has lightness, hue, and saturation" could be a tautology and its negation a logical contradiction.[6] This is even the main argument given by Husserl in support of the existence of materially necessary truths, that is, truths that, although *a priori, cannot be entirely formalized,* and consequently cannot be derived from the theorems of formal logic. Wittgenstein's change of perspective in 1929 is due to the fact that he now takes this difficulty seriously. Contrary to what the members of the Vienna Circle, with rare exceptions, will continue to hold for the following two decades, up until the publication of Quine's article, "Two Dogmas of Empiricism" (1951), a proposition like "one selfsame surface can be uniformly red and uniformly green" *is not a logical contradiction.* But instead of saying, along with Husserl, that it must be the negation of a synthetic *a priori* proposition, a "material contradiction," Wittgenstein says that such a proposition puts our canonical logical notation in crisis. It remains within the precinct of logic, but of a logic that must be substantially amended in order to be able to accommodate it.

This is the program put forward by "Some Remarks on Logical Form," in spring 1929. The truth tables of the *Tractatus* which give the meaning of the logical connectors are insufficient to analyze a conjunction as simple prima facie as "(a color *R* is at a certain patch *P* of our visual field at a time *T*) and (a color *B* is at a certain patch *P* of our visual field at a time *T*)," namely, "*RPT* and *BPT*." Why? If that proposition is a logical contradiction, its truth table will be the following.

RPT	BPT	
T	T	F
T	F	F
F	T	F
F	F	F

However, this notation proves to be "deficient," because the top line, "TTF," "gives the proposition a greater multiplicity than that of the actual possibilities."[7] Indeed, the combination "TT" "represents an impossible combination,"[8] since, as a matter of fact, it is excluded that two spots of different color could be located at the same time in the same place. It is an *impossible* combination, and consequently we cannot apply the sign "false" to it: "That is to say, there is no logical product of *RPT* and *BPT* in the first sense, and herein lies the exclusion as opposed to a contradiction."[9] The only option we have, in a logically well-constructed language, is to remove the first line of the truth table, in order to account for the difference between that "exclusion" and a logical contradiction:

RPT	BPT	
T	F	F
F	T	F
F	F	F

But how do we know that the first line is an impossible combination of signs—a combination corresponding to nothing in phenomena? Wittgenstein's answer is: by an investigation of the phenomena themselves. Consequently, without abandoning the project of the *Tractatus*, the quest for a logically clarified notation that does not disguise thought, Wittgenstein advances an idea that, if taken seriously, is rather disconcerting. The discovery of the logical language we need to express the logical multiplicity of phenomena—a language that would possess the same logical multiplicity as these phenomena, a "phenomenological language," as Wittgenstein calls it—is based on an extra-linguistic, and hence *a posteriori*, element. "Now we can only substitute a clear symbolism for the imprecise one by inspecting the phenomena which we want to describe, thus trying to understand their logical multiplicity. That is to say, we can only arrive at a correct analysis by what might be called the logical investigation of the phenomena themselves, i.e., in a certain sense *a posteriori*, and not by conjecturing about *a priori* possibilities."[10] Wittgenstein is here very close to the idea that there is a "logical" necessity that nevertheless depends on the properties of the phenomenal world and is, to this extent, *a posteriori*. He is close to the material *a priori* of the phenomenologists, which is both necessary and "chained" to the *factum* of the world. Still, he never takes the step of abandoning the logical character of all necessity, nor the *Tractatus* program of a perfect logical notation. "Phenomenology," in Wittgenstein's sense, remains the investigation of phenomena "in a certain sense *a posteriori*" necessary for the elaboration of the logical syntax of an entirely clarified notation. It remains therefore the search for an ideal *language*, and not an activity that could be carried out in everyday language rendered more accurate by philosophical concepts. Wittgenstein's phenomenology has little to do with the phenomenology of the phenomenologists, even though the former arose from a problem that both have in common, that of not (entirely) formalizable *a priori* necessities.

The solution offered by "Some Remarks on Logical Form" is hardly satisfactory. As Hacker remarked, Wittgenstein adopted, under the constraint of a real problem, a solution that contradicts "the very spirit" of the *Tractatus*,[11] which explains why he was very critical toward his text, to the point of refusing its publication. Indeed, how could logic "take care of itself" if logical syntax now depends on an *a posteriori* investigation of phenomena? Furthermore, this "phenomenological" solution is paradoxical. By making "A is uniformly red and A is uniformly green at the same time" not a logical contradiction, that is, a proposition which, like tautologies, is senseless (*sinnlos*), but a nonsense (*Unsinn*), Wittgenstein gives it the same status as the one he attributes to metaphysical propositions in the *Tractatus*. Now, this proposition contains no "formal concept" (*Tractatus* 4.1272), and therefore nothing that cannot be said and must only be shown. Furthermore, if this proposition has the same logical status as its negation, "A is not red and green at the same time" should be *nonsense* too. But is this the case? It seems that this proposition makes perfect sense and is even true. Moreover, if Wittgenstein is right, as Hacker points out, the colors do not all belong to the same "grammatical" category, since, while the statement "if A is scarlet, A is red" is true, when we replace "red" with "green," it becomes nonsense.[12] Finally, Wittgenstein did not solve the problem he began with; he rather made it insoluble. This problem was to account for the fact that "A is red" logically excludes "A is green"—and therefore that the assertion of the first proposition entails the negation of the second. But this inference is only possible if the conjunction of these propositions is a logical contradiction. If, on the other hand, their conjunction is nonsense, then we can no longer conclude from "A is red" that "A is not green."[13]

All these paradoxes help us understand why the phenomenological moment is nothing but an interlude. Wittgenstein preferred to make the claim that the notation of truth tables that supply the meaning of logical connectors required an *a posteriori* investigation of the phenomena rather than abandoning his "logical atomism"—to borrow Russell's expression. But another possibility was open: to abandon the axiom according to which all necessity is logical and accept a necessity that does not come from an inductive generalization, thus being authentically *a priori*, and that nevertheless depends in its essence on a fact: the fact of the existence of the world. "If Wittgenstein had been inclined to accept an expressible form of non-logical necessity," Hacker remarks, "whether it was attributable to the world or to the constitution of the mind, it would have been possible to keep the essential part of the structure of the *Tractatus* . . . [But] that all necessary truths are logical truths is one of the rare doctrines to which Wittgenstein remained faithful to the end, although keeping it after 1930 was only possible after an in-depth modification of his conception of logic and of its domain proper."[14] Why did Wittgenstein never abandon what even Hacker qualifies as a "doctrine"? The answer is probably the following. If he had given way on this point, the entire critical impact of his early work would have been dissipated. Were one to grant philosophy even one single non-logical *a priori* truth, the whole Tractarian tracking down of nonsense would have lost its systematic character. Metaphysics could no longer be *defined* by the fact of advancing nonsensical claims. In it, nonsense would only be *local*, and the notation of the *Tractatus*, although it might remain useful in dispelling this or that perplexity, could no longer lead philosophy to its own annulment in favor of an ideal logical notation. The only method that would remain would be the classical one: refutation. The *Tractatus* would have missed its point.

All this allows me to draw attention to a point that is both essential and neglected by commentators: the *extreme generality* of the thesis underlying not only the entire edifice of the *Tractatus*, but the whole subsequent philosophy of Wittgenstein, his grammatical period included. I say "extreme generality" and might add: a generality that is no less extreme than the most extreme generalities of which, according to Wittgenstein, philosophers (metaphysicians) are guilty. This generalization is perfectly *metaphysical* in the various senses of the word: (1) rooted in metaphysics, a particular metaphysics, namely Humean empiricism: neither the world nor the inner features of our experience contain the slightest necessary structure: "No part of our experience is at the same time *a priori* . . . . There is no *a priori* order of things (*Tractatus*, 5.34); (2) based on what can hardly be considered otherwise than as a kind of (philosophical?) *knowledge*; for, after all, how does Wittgenstein *know* that everything, in the world and/or our experience is contingent? Is this not something that cannot be qualified otherwise than as a *thesis*, and in the strong sense of the term? This claim is located precisely on the same plane as the claim of the phenomenologists: there are material *a priori* necessities. Later, we will examine the question of whether Wittgenstein's claim can or cannot be justified. In any case, it subtends everything he will say about grammar.

But before addressing this issue, a word about the conversations with the Vienna Circle, and especially about a passage titled "Anti-Husserl" is in order.

At the request of Schlick, in 1929 Wittgenstein answered the question of whether it makes sense to speak of a synthetic *a priori*.

> Wittgenstein: Now let us take the statement, "An object is not red and green at the same time." Is all I want to say by this that I have not yet seen such an object? Obviously not. What I mean is, "I *cannot* see such an object. Red and green *cannot* be in the same place." Here I would ask, what does the word "*can*" mean here? The word "can" is obviously a grammatical (logical) concept, not a material one.
>
> Now suppose the statement "An object cannot be both red and green" were a synthetic judgment and the words "cannot" meant logical impossibility. Since a proposition is the negation of its negation, there must also exist the proposition "An object can be red and green." This proposition would also be synthetic. As a synthetic proposition it has sense, and this means that the state of affairs represented by it *can*

> *obtain.* If "cannot" means *logical* impossibility, we therefore reach the consequence that the impossible *is* possible.
>
> Here there remained only one way out for Husserl—to declare that there was a third possibility. To that I would reply that it is indeed possible to make up words, but I cannot associate a thought with them.[15]

In this text, Wittgenstein is trying to defend the principles of his logical atomism and the logical character of all necessity, while at the same time implicitly recognizing that the statement "An object is not red and green at the same time" is probably not a tautology, contrary to what he said in the *Tractatus* (6.3751). As Peter Simons has shown in his reconstruction of Wittgenstein's argumentation,[16] the premises of the argument are five in number:

1. The only kind of possibility or impossibility is *logical.*
2. If a proposition has sense, it can be true.
3. The negation of a synthetic proposition is itself synthetic.
4. The negation of a proposition with sense itself has sense.
5. A proposition is synthetic if and only if it has sense.

Wittgenstein's argument is therefore the following.

A. Assume the proposition p is both synthetic and necessary.
B. Then p is logically necessary (by virtue of 1 and A)
C. p has a sense (A and 5)
D. not p has a sense (C and 4)
E. not p could be true (D and 2)
F. p could be false (E)
G. Now, p cannot be false (A)
H. Therefore (*reductio ad absurdum*) there are no synthetic necessary propositions.

The trouble is that this whole argument rests on two premises that Husserl would have formally rejected: the one according to which all necessity and all impossibility are logical, and the other professing that a false synthetic *a priori* proposition would nevertheless have to represent a possible state of the world. As Simons writes, "Clearly everything of importance in this argument is already there in the principles employed or presupposed, and the argument serves only to tease out their import."[17] But the "Anti-Husserl," while it reiterates the main claims of the *Tractatus,* seems to mark a modification in Wittgenstein's position, as indicated by the interpolated reflection about the word "can" having to be understood in a "grammatical (logical)" sense. Of course the *Tractatus* already mentioned a "logical grammar" (3.325), but in 1929 Wittgenstein seems to be reluctant to understand *logical* necessity in a sense of "logical" referring to mathematical logic, because he realizes, since "A Few Remarks on Logical Form," that it is difficult, if not impossible, to reduce the proposition on color incompatibility to a contradiction *stricto sensu*. Hence the emerging motif of the idea of "grammar," which will take on such a great importance in his subsequent work.

Consequently, since Wittgenstein wants to keep the axiom on the logical nature of *all* necessity, while recognizing that the proposition that asserts the presence at the same place and time of two mutually exclusive colors is not a logical contradiction, contrary to what Schlick will maintain in "Is There a Material *A Priori*?"; since, on the other hand, his "phenomenological" project initiated at the beginning of the year 1929 goes against the spirit of the *Tractatus*, only one avenue remains open: to abandon the logical independence of elementary propositions, their truth-functional status, and consequently the principles of logical atomism themselves. Wittgenstein draws this conclusion in a famous text in which he holds that one cannot compare a proposition to reality, but only a system of propositions.

> Once I wrote, "A proposition is laid against reality like a ruler. Only the end-points of the graduating lines actually touch the object that is to be measured." . . . I now prefer to say that *a system of propositions* is laid out against reality like a ruler. . . . If I say, for example, that this or that point in the visual field is blue, then I know not merely that, but also that this point is not green, nor red, nor yellow, etc. I have laid *the entire color-scale* against it at one go. This is also the reason why a point cannot have different colors at the same time. For when I lay a system of propositions against reality, this means that in each case there is *only one* state of affairs that can exist, not several—just as in the spatial case.[18]

During the same period in which he wrote these lines, Wittgenstein realized that mathematical logic has only a limited range for solving philosophical problems. "For certain purposes, e.g., for representing inferential relations, an artificial symbolism is very useful. . . . Frege, Peano, and Russell paid attention solely to its [logic's] application to mathematics and did not think of the representation of real states of affairs. . . . But as soon as you start to examine real states of affairs, you realize that this symbolism is at a great disadvantage compared with our real language."[19] By an irony of history, the same year that Heidegger denounced "the rule of 'logic' in philosophy,"[20] Wittgenstein abandoned any idea of a translation of natural languages into an artificial formalism, reaffirming that language "is completely in order, as long as we are clear about what it symbolizes."[21] The problem of color exclusion is no longer a matter of logic, but of grammar, in the sense that Wittgenstein henceforth confers on this term: "The proposition 'In one location and at one moment only one color has its place' is naturally a disguised proposition of grammar [*ein verkappter Satz der Grammatik*]. Its negation is not a contradiction, but it *contradicts* a rule of our accepted grammar."[22]

In thus descending from the Platonic heaven of the *Tractatus* with its simple, eternal objects and its ideal symbolism (its "sublimated" logic) to the "rough ground" of *Philosophical Investigations* made up of conventions and usage, Wittgenstein not only breaks with his phenomenological project; he also reconnects with his beginnings. Indeed, contrary to what he maintained during his short phenomenological interlude, the grammar as well as the logic of the *Tractatus* is completely independent of the properties of the world, so that grammatical analysis, taking up where logical analysis left off, will be able to constitute itself into an antiphenomenology.[23] Of course Wittgenstein breaks here with an essential point of his prior philosophy: the isomorphism between language and reality. Grammar does not represent any state of affairs; rather it is concerned with the norms that govern all possible representation. Thanks to the transition from logic to grammar, that is to say, thanks to a broadening of the meaning of "logic," Wittgenstein can preserve the two pillars of the *Tractatus*:

(1) All necessity is logical (which means, henceforth, grammatical).
(2) The negation of a grammatical proposition is not necessarily false; it is nonsense.

One must henceforth say that "A cannot be uniformly green and red at the same time" is not a proposition which can be true or false (empirical), nor is it a true *a priori* proposition (synthetic *a priori*), since there are no such propositions; it is not really a proposition, because it is a rule for the use of color terms, a norm of representation for the description of phenomena. And its negation is not a proposition either, but, since it contradicts this grammatical rule, a sheer nonsense (in a sense that has been modified with respect to the *Tractatus*: something that cannot be said, not by virtue of the say/show distinction, which has been abandoned in the meantime, but quite simply because it violates a grammatical convention).

We have thus arrived at the position that will be Wittgenstein's to the end: "A cannot be red and green at the same time," "Something can be greenish yellow, but not bluish yellow," "The four primary colors are red, yellow, green, and blue," "There are transparent green objects, but not transparent white objects"—all these propositions state employment-rules for our color terms and do not describe any state of affairs. Their necessity is that of a convention stipulating that a combination of symbols such as "the four primary colors are violet, orange, turquoise, and rose" has no usage, and hence no meaning. Their necessity is purely linguistic, and does not refer to any fact in the world. As the *Philosophical Investigations* will put it: "What looks as if it *had* to exist, is part of the language" (I, §50). And also: "Consider: The only correlate in language to an objective necessity is an arbitrary rule" (I, §372).

The first thing to do, before such assertions, is to avoid minimizing their paradoxical and even provocative character. Moore's astonishment expressed in his summary of Wittgenstein's 1930–1933 courses speaks for itself. "According to what he said elsewhere, he could only have been talking sense, if he was talking, not about the colors, but about certain words used to express them; and accordingly he did actually go on to say that 'red is primary' was only a proposition about the use of the English word 'red,' which, as I said, he cannot seriously have held."[24] And yet this is indeed what Wittgenstein maintained clearly and repeatedly. The grammar of colors, like grammar in general, pays no tribute to reality. It has only a conventional character. The propositions on colors do not describe properties of the world or of the experience of the world, nor do they rest on such properties. They fix the employment-rules, and therefore the meaning of our color terms. Thus, not only does grammar not depend on phenomenology, but it is itself the only genuine phenomenology, provided we understand the latter, not as a description of phenomena, nor as a description of the essences that govern phenomena, but as a description of the (grammatical) conditions of possibility for all description of phenomena.[25]

Wittgenstein's grammar might be characterized by the following three features. (a) The rules of grammar *constitute* the meaning; they are constitutive and not normative rules. Like the rules of a game, they say how the game is to be played, so that if one does not follow these rules, one is not playing *badly*, but it is not the same game that one is playing. By contrast, cooking rules, for example, tell us how to cook *well*, and not how to cook without qualification.[26] (b) What contradicts grammar is nonsense; and since grammar delimits the boundaries of sense and nonsense in language, there is but one kind of nonsense: that which violates grammar. There is, therefore, no nonsense that would be "deeper" or more "superficial" than others: "green is or" is not a different sort of nonsense than "this circle is square," Husserl notwithstanding.[27] (c) There is only one grammar. Philosophical grammar is not a different grammar than the grammar of the grammarians,[28] but it is a grammar guided by different *interests*: the dissolution of philosophical pseudo-problems. (d) Grammar is "arbitrary." This assertion is essential; it constitutes the anti-phenomenological affirmation par excellence. Grammar represents nothing, reflects nothing—no necessity of the world or of our experience of it, no synthetic *a priori*.

The fourth characteristic comes back to the first: the rules of cooking are answerable to reality; they depend on it, even though they also have a conventional aspect. Grammatical rules, on the other hand, are entirely autonomous with respect to all facts and all reality, and consequently *purely* conventional. "Grammar," Wittgenstein writes, "is not accountable to any reality. It is grammatical rules that determine meaning (constitute it) and so they themselves are not answerable to any meaning and to that extent are arbitrary."[29] Here we touch on the decisive point in the confrontation of grammatical analysis with the phenomenological analysis of colors. We should not say that there is no greenish red or yellowish blue because nothing in our experience of color corresponds to that combination of hues. It is not because we cannot experience anything of the sort that there are no such colors; it is because these expressions, by virtue of "grammatical conventions," are meaningless that we do not know what to associate them with in our experience. It is not because we cannot imagine these colors, as would transpire from an eidetic variation, that they are impossible: it is because they are *grammatically* impossible that we cannot imagine them. "When dealing with logic, 'One cannot imagine that' means: one doesn't know what one should imagine here."[30] A phenomenologist would completely agree with this last assertion, but without accepting that this necessity—in which the impossibility of imagining is the sign not of a contingent failure of our faculty of imagination, but of an objective impossibility, and in which, as a consequence, the "incapacity-to-represent-things-otherwise" is the indication, for the state of affairs, of an "inability-to-be-otherwise"[31]—is of a purely *logical* nature, in the relevant sense of "logical," and therefore purely conventional. He would respond that "the 'must' ['*Muß*'] plainly rests on the fact that [something] *is*."[32] It is the *a priori* constitution of our experience—to the extent that this *a priori* is not a formal "empty" *a priori*, but a material *a priori*, chained to the facticity of this world—that accounts for this impossibility. Grammatical conventions may perhaps explain our propensity to associate or not certain color terms (for example, to form compound names of hues), but not to combine *certain names of hues and not others*. Here, it is experience and it alone that decides. Not in the sense of *one or several specific experiences* being the deciding factors, but in the sense that what is decisive is the invariant style of our experience, the structural lawfulness that governs our perception of color *a priori*. Indeed, it is our experience of colors that shows us that nothing, in that experience, corresponds to a combination of green and red, to a greenish red or to a reddish green. And to say that these rules of association of color terms are conventional is to say nothing at all, since it would remain to be explained how it may have come about that these conventions were adopted, if not by virtue of invariable universal structures of experience.

To sum up, Husserl would agree with Wittgenstein in saying: (1) that the opposition between red and green, for example, is *necessary*; (2) that it is *a priori*; (3) that it therefore does not derive from an inductive generalization, and does not require the framing of empirical hypotheses. Husserl and Wittgenstein disagree, on the other hand, on what status should be given to this a-hypothetical necessity. For Wittgenstein, this necessity is the expression of a convention of our language; it is "logical" in a broadened sense of the term that equates it with "grammatical"; for Husserl, it is a "material" necessity that is in no way a mere linguistic convention (although obviously it *is expressed* though such conventions), and bears upon *a priori* structures of experience.

This response on the part of the phenomenologist reveals, first of all, the heterogeneity of the concepts of experience that are mobilized on both sides. Wittgenstein only recognizes contingent experiences taking place successively in time and deprived of all links other than hypothetical ones. He would probably retort, in substance: how can we know, for example, that green is a primary color and not a compound of blue and yellow? If we answer that "this is something we can only recognize immediately, by looking at the colors," this response is not acceptable. "But how do I know that I mean the same by the words 'primary colours' as some other person who is also inclined to call green a primary colour? No—here language games decide."[33] Let us spell out the meaning of this objection. It contains two distinct elements. It is one thing to say that the criteria for the use of color words are necessarily external, public, and consequently that there is no private language, neither in general, nor in this particular case: I do not learn the color system by "private ostensive definitions." We have seen that Husserl never held such a doctrine, for he never equated meaning (by definition public) and intuition (eventually "private"), even if it may be that he did not give the social dimension of language its full importance. It is quite another to say that it is language games, and *they alone*, that are decisive here. In this case, we end up with an extreme conventionalism,[34] which is precisely the target of the phenomenologist's critique. Is there any way of deciding the issue? Does Wittgenstein offer justifications for the kind of grammatical conventionalism he defends?

The answer is unequivocally in the affirmative. We do indeed find, in his writings, a general argument—which incidentally attests to the fact that he does not refuse to venture onto the "meta-philosophical" terrain.[35] There are several identical versions of this argument in *Philosophical Remarks*, in *The Big Typescript*,[36] but also in *Zettel* (§331). Let us consider the version from *Philosophical Remarks.*

> If I could describe the point of grammatical conventions by saying that they are made necessarily by certain properties of the colours (say), then that would make the conventions superfluous, since in that case I would be able to say precisely that which the conventions exclude my saying. Conversely, if the conventions were necessary, i.e., if certain combinations of words had to be excluded as nonsensical, then for that very reason I cannot cite a property of colours that make the conventions necessary, since it would then be conceivable that the colours should not have this property, and I could only express that by violating the conventions.[37]

In *The Big Typescript*, this text is immediately followed by another that sheds light on it. "Let's assume that someone wanted to justify a grammatical convention by saying, for example, that colours have such and such qualities and that therefore certain rules had to be valid for the use of colour words. Then, in accordance with this grammar it would also be conceivable, i.e., sayable, that colours do not have those qualities, and, in accordance with this grammar, everything that would be the case would have to be sayable."[38]

In order to establish that grammar is arbitrary, that is, that its necessity is a free creation of language, impossible to justify and produced by our conventions alone, Wittgenstein proceeds along two lines. First line: let us suppose that grammatical conventions are justified by properties of the world. For example, one could not combine the words "green" and "red" in the expression "a reddish green" because no object in the world (or no phenomenon) could be green-red. What follows from this? A manifest absurdity. At the very moment when we furnish the justification, when we state the *apparently empirical* proposition "No object in the world can be green-red," *we have already spoken of a green-red object*, that is, of what the conventions forbid, or more precisely, of what they make nonsensical. If the conventions were grounded on properties of the world, it should be possible to say (in meaningful expressions) what the conventions exclude. And if it were possible to say what the conventions exclude, these conventions would be pointless. What Wittgenstein thus critiques is the idea of a phenomenological language such as the one he himself tried to elaborate. Second line: let us admit, on the contrary, that our conventions are necessary, which is clearly Wittgenstein's claim. If these conventions are necessary, if they have a *constitutive* function for the meanings of the expressions "green" and "red," such that "green" excludes "red" and vice versa, it follows that their incompatibility is not an empirical property possessed by these colors. If "green and red exclude each other" were an empirical proposition, its negation should have meaning. Now, its negation has no meaning (by virtue of grammatical conventions). Therefore that proposition is not an empirical proposition, and as a result, it is not of such a nature as to justify the rules of our grammar.

Wittgenstein shows in that way that all attempts to justify our grammatical conventions violate these conventions by claiming to justify them. I cannot ground a grammatical rule such as "nothing can be red-green" on a description of the properties of the world: for if I wanted to ground this rule by saying that "nothing is red-green," this proposition would be either a rule—it would simply *restate* the rule, and therefore would in no way *justify* it—or an empirical proposition: the description of a state of affairs. But if it were the description of a state of affairs, its negation would make sense. Now, this negation does not make sense; it is excluded by our grammatical conventions. Thus grammar cannot be justified.

Is this reasoning compelling? Yes and no. Yes, if we accept Wittgenstein's premises; no, if we reject them. The argument, stated differently, is the following. *If* the propositions on color incompatibility express grammatical rules, and *if* the negation of such rules is nonsense (since it is excluded by the rules), *then* the propositions on color incompatibility cannot be justified. But these "ifs" must give us pause. Wittgenstein seems to take them for granted, because he takes for granted two ideas that go back to his first philosophy.

(1) All necessity is logical (only rules can be necessary).
(2) All empirical propositions (all descriptions of states of affairs) cannot be true unless they can be false, and vice versa.

The first, as we have seen, is that of the *Tractatus* 6.375, the second is formulated as early as in the *Notebooks* of 1914–16. "In order for a proposition to be capable of being true, it must also be capable of being false."[39] All propositions that are not logical rules are binary, because contingent. It is not then difficult to conclude that there are no empirical propositions that are at the same time necessary, no descriptions of states of affairs such that they are at the same time *a priori.* But all that is important in this argument lies, once more, in its premises. Now it is these premises that are in question in the debate with phenomenology.

These premises are not "trivial," to say the least. They are heavily metaphysical, at least in the sense that they constitute *substantial theses* that cannot themselves be drawn from an analysis of language alone. They clearly contradict Wittgenstein's assertion according to which "if there were theses in philosophy, they would have to be such that they do not give rise to disputes. For they would have to be put in such a way that everyone would say 'Oh yes, that is of course obvious.'"[40] Not only are these premises not obvious; but in Wittgenstein's entire work there is not a justification of them to be found that is not circular. The argument concluding that a grammatical justification would have to violate the grammatical conventions in order to justify them *follows* from these premises (there is no necessity other than grammatical, all empirical propositions are contingent) and does not justify them. It is, at the very least, paradoxical that the philosopher who relentlessly denounced the metaphysician's craving for generality should be caught in the act of defending on his own behalf one of the most outstanding generalizations of which metaphysics has been capable—the one consisting in assigning *one sole possible status to all necessity,* that of a grammatical rule, and consequently one sole possible status to all impossibility, that of a violation of that rule. To cure us of the "metaphysician's" generalizations, Wittgenstein asks us to accept a generalization that is no less *metaphysical* than the others. If we accept his view, a phenomenological description such as that of Katz—claiming that there are three kinds of colored phenomena, namely film colors (*Flächenfarben*), surface colors (*Oberflächenfarben*), and volume colors (*Raumfarben*)—must have exactly the same status as an empirical generalization of the type: "irises are violet and poppies are red." Conversely, "this object is greenish red" is nonsense of the same sort as "green is or." Wittgenstein, an admirable provider of distinctions when it is a matter of analyzing our forms of expression, proves to be astonishingly poor in distinctions here. But nothing, in what he asserts, compels our agreement, and nothing can persuade us that his whole philosophy does not rest on premises as general and problematic as those of authors whom he would readily consign to grammatical therapy. Might not grammatical philosophy itself be in need of therapy?

There is a paralogism too frequently (implicitly or explicitly) committed by Wittgensteinians to be left aside here. Since grammar cannot be justified by facts, it follows that there is no need to seek a justification for the idea of grammar. On this view, grammar is what it is, without further ado; we only have to aknowledge it in our ordinary forms of expression. In a word, recourse to the concept of "grammar" harbors no substantial claim. But this is absurd. We must not confuse arguments that are valid *within the framework of Wittgenstein's thought* and that allow him to say that grammar, in the sense in which he understands it, cannot be justified, and the problem of how Wittgenstein can justify—assuming he can do so—his recourse to the idea of grammar and what he says positively about it. It is not because grammar does not need to be justified by a description of phenomena that it is not necessary to justify the recourse to this idea philosophically. For if nothing legitimates that idea—and the consequences that Wittgenstein draws from it—why should we adopt it? That grammar cannot be justified does not entail that the idea of "grammar" does not *have to* be justified. Otherwise, we would cease doing philosophy; that is to say, we would cease submitting our discourse to the norms of all rational discussion and legitimation.

It will certainly not do to reply that the assertion that grammar is "arbitrary" is itself a "grammatical remark." That response is at best another begging of the question, and at worst a lot of empty words. It is only after having admitted that the proposition "there are four primary colors" is a grammatical rule, and that its negation is therefore nonsense, that we can infer from this that this proposition cannot be justified in the sense of verified by any fact whatsoever. To hold that the assertion that this proposition is grammatical is itself grammatical would be to inject an entire substantial metaphysics into the conventions that govern language, and therefore, by a true sleight-of-hand, pass off philosophical theses for rules of English usage.

The difficulty we run up against was clearly seen by Putnam. It is typical of conceptions of rationality that he has dubbed "criterial" that they violate their own criteria in being stated.[41] Just as the proposition of the Vienna Circle according to which every meaningful proposition is either analytic *a priori* or synthetic *a posteriori* is neither analytic nor synthetic, thus violating the criterion it advances, similarly, the assertion that the only necessary propositions are disguised grammatical rules and all the other propositions are empirical, and therefore contingent, is itself neither contingent nor necessary—that is, grammatical. But then what is its status? Wittgenstein is no more able to answer this question than is the Vienna Circle, and thus the self-destroying character of the *Tractatus* finds an analogue in his last philosophy. To these "criterial" conceptions of rationality it must be countered that all rationality is finite, that every *logon dinonai* comes to an end (as Wittgenstein, incidentally, has made us aware) and that consequently there is, in philosophy, no method capable of dispelling all our perplexity, no procedure that could offer us anything like "complete clarity,"[42] in the sense that, thanks to it, philosophical problems should totally disappear.

Furthermore, the dogma according to which all necessity is grammatical suffers from the same sort of weakness as all general theses: *it takes but one counter-example to refute it.* If it turned out that one sole necessary proposition on colors was not *only* a grammatical convention, that proposition would not thereby become empirical (contingent): doubt would be cast on the very disjunction between the empirical and the grammatical.

Before attempting to take a step in this direction, we must pause to consider a possible objection. So far, we have limited ourselves to relying on Wittgenstein's declarations, including their most paradoxical aspects. Our interpretation has followed, in its general lines, that of Hacker, who insists, in *Insight and Illusion,* on the influence of Brouwer's intuitionism on the elaboration of Wittgenstein's second philosophy and in particular on what he calls its "extreme voluntarism."[43] The thesis of the arbitrariness of grammar, he specifies, "is firmly located in the voluntarist tradition of European metaphysics" according to which "the mind forms nature."[44] Thus, he adds, "essences are a product of will, not a discovery of reason. All talk of essence is talk of conventions, and what seems to us to be the 'depth' of essences is in fact the depth of our need for the conventions."[45] But should one not be more cautious about the interpretation to be given of the notion of "arbitrary"? If to maintain that grammar is arbitrary certainly means, for Wittgenstein, that it is impossible to justify, this claim does not necessarily entail that our conventions are pure decrees. Wittgenstein says, for example: "But grammar is not a question of arbitrary choice. A proposition must have the same multiplicity as the fact which it expresses: it must have the same degree of freedom."[46] Perhaps there is a place, here, for a certain recognition of the idea, not that grammar is justified by facts, but that it depends on facts; not in the sense that these facts would make grammar *correct* or *incorrect,* but in the sense that these facts would make grammar easy or hard to follow, applicable or inapplicable, well suited or not to our goals. Moreover, the notion of "convention" is not univocal in Wittgenstein, either. The rules of grammar are not conventional the way the rules of a game are, because they must be applied to reality. "'Are you then talking in this case of 'pure convention,' of pure convention in the sense that the rules of chess or any other game are 'pure convention'? Grammar is decidedly not the conventions of a language in this sense, the game of language. What distinguishes language from a game in this sense is its application to reality."[47] One may, therefore, wonder whether the radical conventionalism of Hacker's reading should give way to a more moderate conventionalism.

Jacques Bouveresse, in a recent work, suggests a reading of this sort. As he stresses, "it is probably not sufficiently noted that Wittgenstein . . . excludes solely *one* specific possibility, for a proposition of grammar to be justified, namely the one that would consist in showing, as one does in the case of an ordinary descriptive proposition, the fact that verifies it. And it is a misconstruction of the true meaning of the autonomy of grammar to deduce from the fact that grammar cannot have this type of justification, that it can unilaterally impose its decrees on reality, allow itself to ignore the facts, or deal with them at will."[48] According to Bouveresse, we must distinguish between the *justification* of grammar by the facts (which is absurd) and the *dependency* of grammar with respect to facts, which Wittgenstein only ostensibly rejects. "[Wittgenstein] of course never denied that the truth of a proposition such as 'There is no reddish green' essentially depends on the way things present themselves in empirical reality."[49] But how, then, are we to characterize that dependency, or, as Bouveresse also puts it, that "constraint" exerted by the facts? Certainly not as a dependency of grammar on real necessities to which it should conform, and that would make it correct or incorrect; for such a dependency leaves no room for the arbitrariness Wittgenstein speaks of. "What Wittgenstein opposes," Bouveresse answers, "is, once more, a deceptive way of conceiving of the constraint that reality is capable of bringing to bear on the structure of language, not the existence of such a constraint."[50]

We may wonder whether this response doesn't make the problem more acute, rather than solving it. First, the idea of a constraint exerted by facts on grammar seems to contradict Wittgenstein's most explicit statements. "These rules are not answerable to a reality in the sense of their being controlled by it [*diese Regeln nicht einer Wirklichkeit verantwortlich sind, so daß sie von ihr kontrolliert würden*]," he writes for example in *The Big Typescript*;[51] or yet again "grammar doesn't owe reality any accounting [*Die Grammatik ist der Wirklichkeit nicht Rechenschaft schuldig*]," "grammar is answerable to no reality [*Die Grammatik ist keiner Wirklichkeit verantwortlich*]."[52] We must emphasize, "*no* reality." But let us leave these declarations aside and assume that facts do orient our grammatical "choices," or rather the grammatical choices of our linguistic community. The decisive question is, then, the following. Are these facts empirical, contingent facts, relative to the constitution of our visual apparatus, for example, or to the physics of light, as Bouveresse suggests? In that case, the facts that orient grammar without determining it possess no intrinsic necessity (other than hypothetical), and therefore all necessity in the strong sense still comes from grammar. Not only has the initial conventionalism not been abandoned, but it is difficult to say *in what* the constraint of the facts in question *consists*. Bouveresse says, for example, that the proposition "there is no reddish green" "surely depends in a certain sense on the empirical fact that there is actually no color sensation that we are disposed to recognize as constituted by a mixture of green and red."[53] But is it grammar that is dependent on the fact that we are inclined to recognize this or that? Is it not rather the other way round? Is it not the fact that depends on the grammar? There is no doubt that, for Wittgenstein, it is the latter assertion that is the correct one. Grammar describes nothing and no description of *contingent* facts can constrain it, since that description itself *presupposes grammar*. Thus there remains but one solution: the constraint comes from a necessity belonging to the domain of colors as such—a necessity that does not itself derive from a hypothesis and cannot be invalidated by a new experience, and that nevertheless is "factual," or, as Husserl says, "chained" to a certain facticity, that of colors such as we experience them. Thus we return to the synthetic *a priori*, that is, the very thing grammar was supposed to have ruled out.

Bouveresse's solution leaves us in midstream, so to speak. It is unclear, for example, whether one can construe as he does the admittedly enigmatic passage from *Zettel* in which Wittgenstein seems to nuance the notion of arbitrariness. We read at §§357–58: "We have a colour system as we have a number system. Do the systems reside in *our* nature or in the nature of things? How are we to put it?—*Not* in the nature of numbers or colours. Then is there something arbitrary about this system? Yes and no. It is akin both to what is arbitrary and what is non-arbitrary."[54] Bouveresse interprets this text as affirming that the system of colors "is related (and perhaps even closely related) to the non-arbitrary, because it is confronted with reality in a different way, through a multitude of facts that, if they do not have the power to make it correct or incorrect, nonetheless exert a very real constraint on it."[55] But the constraint of multiple facts seems either too weak or too strong. Too weak for those who, following the phenomenologist, would point out that, whatever the linguistic conventions adopted, the primary colors are always the same four, insofar as the only ones that can be called "primary" in the relevant sense[56] are colors that do not tend toward any of their adjacent colors within the spectrum, and the only ones to satisfy this requirement are red, yellow, green, and blue—there is a blue that tends neither towards green, nor red, a green that tends neither toward yellow nor blue, and so on (while there is no orange that tends neither towards red nor yellow); and this depends *on our perception of colors*, and not on conventions we adopt about them. Too strong, for those who would defend the point of view of Wittgenstein, for whom grammar, once more, "is answerable to no reality," that is to say, is *purely* conventional. Moreover, there is a passage in Moore's notes that sheds light on the nuance introduced in *Zettel*, and the elucidation we find there does not seem to square with that of Bouveresse: Wittgenstein "often asserted without qualification that all 'rules of grammar' are arbitrary. But he expressly mentioned two senses of 'arbitrary' in which he held that some grammatical rules are *not* arbitrary . . . : (1) a sense in which . . . single words are significant only if 'we commit ourselves' by using them, and (2) a sense in which to say that a rule is an established rule in the language we are using is to say that it is not arbitrary."[57] None of these senses is that of Bouveresse. The second sense, the most important, consists in saying that a rule is no longer arbitrary the moment we actually follow it, the moment it becomes an integral part—if not of the nature of things, at least of *our own* nature. Here there is but one kind of fact: *anthropological*. Therefore there is no fact that can temper in the slightest way Wittgenstein's extreme conventionalism—nor make grammar dependent on any reality that concerns the domain of colors, considered from a physical, physiological, psychological, or phenomenological point of view.[58] If the facts Bouveresse speaks of, and that "constrain" grammar, are not those anthropological facts, what are they? Not natural facts, in any case, since all description of those facts rests on grammar. And although the end of *Philosophical Investigations* (II-*xii*) contains an allusion to the "correspondence" between our concepts and "very general facts of nature," Wittgenstein nonetheless refuses there to explain the formation of our concepts, our concepts of color, for example, by these facts—"I am not saying: if such-and-such facts of nature were different people would have different concepts"—and, more generally, he dismisses any inquiry into the origin of our concepts as irrelevant from the grammatical viewpoint.[59]

However, the contribution of Bouveresse moves in the direction of a question that seems difficult to avoid: is there really an argument allowing us to adjudicate between Wittgenstein's extreme conventionalism and the essentialism of phenomenology, to determine whether the non-hypothetical necessity governing color relations, for example, is only *de dicto* or *always also de re*? "Always also," because there clearly can be no question of denying that we are dealing *in part* with linguistic conventions.

Let us examine a basic example. "In the sense in which orange is a mixture of red and yellow, there isn't a mixture of orange and violet at all."[60] This remark draws attention to the difference between binary colors (that is, colors that are a combination of their contiguous colors within the spectrum) and simple or unitary colors, for which there is a pure hue that is not the combination of the two adjacent hues. There is a blue that tends neither toward red nor toward green, whereas there is no violet that does not tend either toward blue or toward red. But why is this? Is it just a linguistic fact? The phenomenologist would be inclined to reply in the negative: the way we use color words depends on what we see, and not the other way round. It depends not on our contingent experience of a specific red or yellow, but on the distinctive content of red in general, as phenomenologically identifiable content—what Husserl would call "the essence" of red. As for Wittgenstein, he would say that it is "the language games that decide": it isn't because we don't *see* red as a combination of orange and violet that we don't call it an orange-violet, but because our grammar excludes this last combination of words that we are disinclined to characterize it that way. Can we go further? Probably so. There is indeed a *reason* why we don't call red violet-orange: red is not violet-orange because orange and violet are hues that both contain red, and one cannot define red as a combination of two different reds without circularity. Consequently, if we wanted to define red as a binary color, we would have to find within the spectrum its two contiguous colors that *do not contain red,* that is, yellow and blue; and we would then have to say that red is blue-yellow. But of course that definition is absurd, because yellow and blue are mutually *exclusive*: there is no such thing as a "blue-yellow." *Ergo* red is a simple, unitary color.

Have we made any progress with regard to our initial question? No, for the question whether the distinction between unitary and binary hues is purely conventional now becomes that whether chromatic exclusion is purely conventional. Each interlocutor has a prepared answer: the phenomenologist will say that color opposition is a necessary structure of our *perception*; the follower of the grammatical approach, that it is a necessary rule of our *language.* The former ascribes this characteristic to essences and their necessary relations, essences being what accounts for the distinctive feature of color *phenomena*; the latter to a system of concepts, that is, to the employment-rules of color terms by virtue of which, once it has been posited that there are four primary colors, it follows that there are unitary and binary hues, but also that red is not orange-violet (nor a yellowish blue). It is not obvious that there is a decisive argument in this matter. But then the problem becomes the following. Basically, aren't Wittgenstein and the phenomenologist speaking about the same thing? Must we truly decide whether that necessity is only *de dicto* or whether it is also *de re*? Must we not emphasize what brings grammar and phenomenology together, rather than what sets them in opposition? For the reasonable phenomenologist will not deny that his *a priori* relations between perceived colors, although prelinguistic, do involve the mediation of grammatical conventions *in their formulation*; and it also seems to me that the sensible "grammarian" cannot deny that the *experience* of colors is not anarchic; that it presents constants, invariants that cannot be ascribed to language alone.

Hence we must, in conclusion, wonder whether the phenomenological approach and the grammatical one are not closer than is generally admitted, on the condition that the interlocutors abandon one of their premises: the phenomenologist of Husserlian inspiration, the idea that there could be an intuition of essences *prior de jure to language* (by means of an eidetic variation free from all linguistic constraint); the "grammarian," the idea that there is no isomorphism of any kind between grammar and reality. Of course a variety of grammars are possible, and to this extent all grammar possesses a conventional element, but the grammars must nevertheless be constrained by structural invariants that come—in a case as little conventional as that of color—from necessary structures of experience itself. Thus revised, grammar and phenomenology would both describe "the '*possibilities*' of phenomena,"[61] to borrow Wittgenstein's expression, and not empirical phenomena. But these possibilities of phenomena, while containing a conventional element, would not amount to *pure* conventions. In suggesting this possibility, it is not my intention to make all difference between these two approaches disappear into that "night in which all cows are black" of which Hegel speaks. I merely wish to draw attention to the fact that Wittgenstein's grammatical solution is actually much closer to Husserl's phenomenological solution than it is, say, to that of the Vienna Circle, because Wittgenstein recognized by 1929 that grammatical necessities, which he continues to qualify as "logical," *are not reducible to mathematical logic*, to "formal" logic in general—which is precisely Husserl's starting point in his elaboration of the concept of the synthetic *a priori*.

Actually, if one had to fix a point at which the phenomenological undertaking diverges substantially from the grammatical one, it would probably be in what Elizabeth Anscombe has dubbed Wittgenstein's "linguistic idealism." The idea underlying linguistic idealism is that all the identities, differences, and necessities that we *think* we are finding in reality or in phenomena are in fact no more than by-products of language. Anscombe distinguishes three levels at which this problem arises: (1) that of concepts; (2) that of rules, rights, and promises as social institutions; (3) that of "metaphysical necessities." She says that with respect to concepts, Wittgenstein is only a partial idealist: the existence of colors and their phenomenological differences are not a product of our concepts of color;[62] on the subject of social institutions, Wittgenstein is idealist—and *rightfully so*: there could not be such things as rights, contracts, or promises if there were no linguistic conventions. In short, the Nietzschean definition of man as "the animal that may promise" is but a consequence of the classical definition of him as *zoon logon echon*. But the more difficult and interesting point for us is that of "metaphysical necessities." Are they a free creation of language? This is indeed what Wittgenstein seems to assert: "Reflect on this: 'the only correlate in language to an intrinsic necessity is an arbitrary rule.'"[63] Anscombe draws our attention to the fact that the form of this remark is the one to which Wittgenstein resorts whenever he advances points about which he is not sure. Similar hesitations may be found in his writings on the subject of color. "Does everything depend on my range of possible language games with the form '. . . ish'"?; "Here it could now be asked what I really want, to what extent I want to deal with grammar"; or yet again: "But I have kept on saying that it's conceivable for our concepts to be different than they are. Was that all nonsense?"[64] Nevertheless, Anscombe concludes that, on this point, "Wittgenstein was a linguistic idealist. He insists that these things [grammatical rules and necessities] are the creation of human linguistic practice."[65] But must we share his linguistic idealism?

This idealism is linked to the therapeutic function Wittgenstein assigns to philosophy. It is necessary for grammar not to be conditioned by anything in order for it to be a sufficiently powerful weapon to replace, in philosophy, any search for necessary truths. The abandonment of this linguistic idealism would lead to maintaining that "grammatical" necessities are conventional in one respect and factual in another. It is a convention that the so-called "primary" colors are simple or unitary, but it is a factual necessity (synthetic *a priori*) that, among the colors that I perceive, only four hues satisfy this criterion, and that these four hues are red, yellow, blue, and green (if we exclude, by convention, from the colors' domain white and black). In other words, from the fact that there is something conventional in the color system one cannot conclude that everything in it is conventional: some conventions express necessities of the world or of our experience. We are, then, rather far from the idea, proper to Wittgenstein's linguistic idealism, which may be formulated as follows. *The only necessities that can be expressed by means of conventions are those of these conventions themselves.* On the contrary, nothing forbids the recognition of non-conventional, and at the same time non-hypothetical necessities, that can only be *expressed* by means of conventions, but are not reducible to the conventions through which they are expressed.

The abandonment of linguistic idealism would allow us, then, to understand why Wittgenstein's grammatical necessities are also phenomenological necessities, but also why many phenomenological necessities are *not* grammatical ones. The domain of phenomenology is larger than that of grammar. As David Katz remarks, the origin of the distinction between the three types of colors—film, surface, and volume—for example, "cannot be found in everyday language."[66] But if we were to follow this path, we would also have to abandon the idea that philosophy has no more than a critical function, a therapeutic utility—which has sometimes been referred to as Wittgenstein's "quietism." An odd quietism, indeed, that brings him to say: "If my name lives on, it will be only as a *terminus ad quem* of the great Western philosophy. Like the name of the one who burned the library of Alexandria."[67]

Perhaps, we should make a different use—phenomenological, not therapeutic—of the grammatical distinctions he proposes. The critical significance of his work would be, if not diminished, as least different from the one often attributed to him. Not that Wittgenstein did not set fire to the library of Alexandria, that is, to traditional metaphysics. The flames are visible there; they rise, already reaching the shelves. But fire has another power than that of consuming: the power to shed light.

8

Transparent White

> The notion that our words and life are constrained by a reality not of our own invention plays a deep role in our lives and is to be respected.
>
> —Hilary Putnam

In days of old, the philosophers' pride consisted in passing for men of great knowledge, and in placing their discipline on a par with science; today, it consists in passing for medical doctors. The pharmacopoeia of this medicine is what Wittgenstein called "grammar." I would like to go back over that concept in light of concrete examples. Since there probably is no direct argument to establish the superiority of the phenomenological idea of *a priori* structures of appearing, all we have left is an apagogic method in order to show the limits of the grammatical approach.

As I have attempted to establish, there is a greater proximity between Husserl and Wittgenstein than between these two philosophers and Schlick. Even before the *Tractatus,* Husserl defined analyticity in terms of purely syntactic validity, in a manner that foreshadows the conception of the early Wittgenstein. As he emphasizes in appendix 3 of *Formal and Transcendental Logic,* his definition of analyticity by syntactic validity and the possibility of an integral formalization anticipates "the concept-forming that comes to the fore in modern logistics, and the logistical doctrine of '*tautology*' as including every closed analytic complex."[1] But Husserl stresses as early as in 1901 that certain necessary propositions, such as that on the incompatibility of colors, are *not* analytic, which Wittgenstein denied in the *Tractatus* and will be forced to recognize several years later, possibly persuaded by Ramsey's critique. While Schlick will go on believing (and the majority of logical positivists along with him) in the analytic, that is, tautological character of these necessities, extending the sphere of the "logical" though unable to specify *why* the "phenomenological" propositions belong to it, and therefore what legitimates such an extension, Wittgenstein, in full agreement with Husserl on this point, admits that these truths are not analytic; but he refuses to consider them synthetic *a priori.* Attached to the idea that all necessity is of a logical order, but giving up the idea of grounding logic on an examination of phenomena that is "in a sense *a posteriori,*" contrary to what he himself had suggested during his brief phenomenological interlude, he is forced to abandon logical atomism at the same time as the *tautological* character of all necessity. He, too, extends the domain of "logic," not—and in this he differs from Schlick—in order to include in the sphere of the analytic the synthetic *a priori* of the phenomenologists, but rather, thanks to a modification of the concept of "logic" itself which gives up defining its domain by analyticity, by making the "logical" coincide with the "grammatical." Grammar is a domain of rules that are neither true nor false, but which delimit the domain of sense and nonsense.

The superiority of this solution compared to that of logical positivism is obvious. Schlick held that the statement "A cannot be uniformly green and uniformly red at the same time" was true by virtue of its form alone. When pressed to explain, he answered: by virtue of the very *meanings* of the words "red" and "green" (or of their *definitions*). But what does that mean? Does the incompatibility of red and green belong to the *meaning* of these words of color? But then what does not belong to that? Why not argue that everything sensible that can be said about red and green also belongs to the meaning of the corresponding expressions? We then end up with a "metaphysics of meaning," to borrow Hacker's expression. Wittgenstein's solution is incomparably stronger. It consists in the claim that this sentence is not a proposition, even an analytically necessary one, but a grammatical rule; its necessity is that of a *convention* governing the use of the terms "red" and "green." Henceforth we should not say that the necessity of the incompatibility proposition *derives* from the meaning of "green" and "red"—*what* meaning?—but that it belongs to the rules that *constitute* that meaning, that is, that govern the employment or use of these terms. And it is no longer necessary to rush into the desperate attempt to show that this proposition is analytically true, that is, tautological, to be able to maintain that it is necessary. Its necessity is simply that of conventions that describe nothing, are neither true nor false, but constitute norms for all possible description. Its necessity is therefore *grammatical.*

Is this solution not also superior to that of phenomenology? Does not grammar give a better account of *phenomenological* necessities than the synthetic *a priori* of the phenomenologists? It gives an account, in any case, of the conventional character of the use of color terms; and it frees us from an almost insoluble problem, that of how to "compare" language with reality. Actually, the proposition on the incompatibility of colors is not a *proposition* at all, in the sense of a statement that could be true or false (nor is it therefore a statement that could be *necessarily* true because it would express a *necessary a priori* state of affairs); it is a *rule* of which it makes no sense to say that it "reflects" reality or does not reflect it. Thus we end up with a new nominalism whose watchword is "the *essence* is expressed by grammar."[2] There is no need to describe or analyze phenomena, but only language usage.[3] In short, "Phenomenological analysis (as e.g., Goethe would have it) is the analysis of concepts"[4] and nothing else; that is, an analysis of our use of signs. In the strict sense (let us say the sense used by Goethe, Husserl, and Wittgenstein in his middle period), there is no such thing as phenomenology, but only phenomenological problems[5] that can be solved *without remainder* by grammatical analysis. At the same time, if we perceive the proximity that remains between this nominalist retranslation of the problem and its formulation by Husserl, we can also understand the attractive, not to say tempting, aspect of phenomenology, on which Wittgenstein insists on several occasions. There is nothing comparable to this temptation (*Versuchung*) in the framework of logical positivism. "Here the temptation to believe in a phenomenology," writes Wittgenstein, "something midway between science and logic, is very great [*sehr groß*]."[6] The task of grammatical analysis is to *deliver* us from that temptation.

This proximity concerns another point—that of method. Both phenomenology and grammar are descriptive disciplines. They are neither doctrines nor systems, but rather, with all that this has of the oxymoronic, descriptive doctrines, or "systematic" analyses of examples. Consequently, it is not only possible, but necessary to set out from examples in order to bring phenomenology and grammar into mutual dialogue and inquire into the eventual superiority of one over the other.

In the preceding chapter we examined the difficulty in principle attaching to the declaration that statements such as "there are four primary colors," that is, four colors "that tend neither to one side nor the other"[7]—for example, a green that tends neither toward yellow nor blue, a blue that tends neither toward green nor red—would be merely *grammatical conventions.*[8] Indeed, they are entirely different from an empirical proposition of the type: "the three primary colors of the additive colour mixing [that is of the mixing of light] are blue, green and red." By "primary colors," what is meant in this last case are those colors whose mixture with other primary ones make it possible to obtain the totality of the colors. In order to know that the primary colors of light (additive color mixing) are not the same as those of the mixture of pigments (subtractive color mixing), namely yellow, cyan, and magenta, we must rely on experience. Perhaps we are inclined to believe *a priori* that yellow is one of the primaries of the additive mixing, but that is false. Using only blue, green, and red, it is possible to get all the colors of the spectrum, and even non-spectral colors, such as purple and rose: this is an empirical fact. Husserl would agree that a proposition such as "There are four primary colors" (in the first sense of "primary") is both necessary and *a priori*; it plays the role of a *norm* for all possible description—that is of a "law of appearance"[9]—but he would refuse to conclude from it that this norm is *purely* conventional, and therefore *arbitrary* in Wittgenstein's sense. It possesses, he would conclude, a *fundamentum in re.* Is it possible to pursue the analysis further? Are there arguments to support that Wittgenstein is wrong? That the view according to which, in the domain of phenomena, *all* necessity is of the grammatical order is at the very least fragile, if not untenable? Perhaps not a general argument, but particular ones. Let us examine a few examples.

In order not to make the list unnecessarily long, I will limit myself to two of them, hoping that their examination will allow us to draw a lesson from them that will also apply to others: that of brown and transparent white.

Borrowing his inspiration from an observation of Philipp Otto Runge, Wittgenstein remarks: "Why is it that a dark yellow doesn't have to be perceived as 'blackish,' even if we call it dark? The logic of the concept of colour is just much more complicated than it might seem."[10] The logic of colors is indeed complex, if it is derived from grammatical conventions alone. These conventions are not always, or even for the most part *explicit* conventions, but rather rules that we follow by virtue of a social "training" without being necessarily able to formulate them explicitly. To follow a rule it is not necessary to be able to express it in language—otherwise it would be impossible to learn language, because that learning process would presuppose itself. Our grammatical conventions are *tacit.* As Wittgenstein rightfully insists, language is not a theoretical possession. But if all necessity in the domain of colors is an *arbitrary* implicit rule to which no necessary state of affairs corresponds, it becomes indispensable to master an incredible number of rules—about which we might wonder how they could have been instituted in the first place—to be able to apply the concepts of color. For example, we must master the rather bizarre use of "blackish," since it authorizes an association such as "blackish brown" (for dark brown), but not this other one: "blackish yellow." And, according to this view, this convention has nothing to do with the fact (that is, finds no *justification* in the fact) that yellow will never *look* "blackish" to us.

Is this the way things are? In the case of the paradox Wittgenstein is thinking about, the solution seems much simpler, easily within reach, so to speak, and it has nothing to do with convoluted conventions. Yellow is a light color, even at its highest degree of saturation: this is a *phenomenal* property of that hue. A desaturated and dark yellow is nothing but a brown. Thus we can speak of blackish brown, if what we mean by that is a dark brown that tends to this extent to black, but not of a blackish yellow, because the darkest yellow remains relatively light compared to other dark colors. And this is not grammar; it is phenomenology. Indeed this "explanation" does not rest on empirical hypotheses. It arises from the laws of appearance, not from the physical explanations of these laws. A dark yellow is *unimaginable* due to the fact that we would call such a yellow "brown," and perhaps this is still grammar. But there is nothing arbitrary about this grammar: it is a phenomenal fact that there is, in the field of color, a manner of qualitative leap between saturated and light yellow, and this same yellow, desaturated and dark that *no longer appears to us to be yellow,* but brown. The reason why this "yellow" has a different name, "brown," is precisely because it is difficult to see it as a variety of yellow in its most characteristic sample. Let us compare a lemon and dark chocolate: does the latter appear yellow to us?

Wittgenstein writes: "What does 'brown contains black' mean? There are more and less blackish browns. Is there one which isn't blackish at all? There certainly isn't one that isn't yellowish at all."[11] But is this accurate? First, there are browns that are reddish and not yellowish. Second, brown is *dark,* which means that its lightness and saturation are low (if they were high, it would be yellow or orange), but to say that it is dark does not amount to say that it is black. There are obviously browns that are "light" (for browns), beiges for example.

On the other hand, it is true that brown is never a color of light: "'Brown light.' Suppose someone were to suggest that a traffic light be brown."[12] But, again, the reason for this particularity has nothing to do with grammar. It lies in the fact that brown is a contrast color. Let us observe, through a tube lined with black velvet, a surface that is initially brown. After a while the brown fades away and is replaced by a greenish yellow, a plain yellow or an orange, according to whether the original brown tended more to olive or, on the contrary, to ochre. This is because our perception of brown depends on its environment. If, by some artifice, that environment is made significantly darker, the brown becomes lighter until it becomes yellow. Once we stop looking through the cylinder, it returns to its initial color.[13] The fact that brown is a contrast color (and this again is phenomenology, since it is not necessary to resort to empirical conjectures on the nature of light or of our visual apparatus to establish it) suffices to solve Wittgenstein's paradox. A light source always looks lighter than its optical surroundings if it is a *light* source. But a brown brighter than the surrounding colors looks necessarily yellow. Thus there is no brown light. As Jonathan Westphal notes, "Brown is a kind of shadowing. . . . So brown can never stand out from its surroundings; it can never appear blazing or brilliant, although it can be glossy. A brown traffic light would be lower than the surroundings in brightness. It would not shine. In dark surroundings, at night, the traffic light would be brighter than its surroundings, and *it would turn yellow.* Brown light is yellow."[14] Grammar, here, is only a weak metaphor to speak of necessities that belong to the very way in which things appear to us. Taking refuge in the obscurity of conventional rules that we would master without even having to know them, Wittgenstein proceeds *ad obscurum per obscurius* because he overlooks the necessary laws governing *a parte objecti* the *phenomena* of color.

However, it is not certain that Westphal is right on an essential point. In his view, the adequate explanation for Wittgenstein's (apparent) "paradox" is borrowed from a physics of color inspired by that of Goethe. Westphal sets out from a *real* or *physical* definition of color in general as a phenomenon of absorption of certain wavelengths of the electromagnetic spectrum, and consequently, as a phenomenon of shadowing of light, and then gives us a definition of colors that manifests determinate necessary relations among them—a definition showing that a fair number of Wittgenstein's paradoxes can be reduced to formal contradictions. His explanation thus derives from a *physical* theory of color (which is in no way a physicalist one), and therefore from empirical hypotheses. Although the physics to which Westphal refers is a "phenomenological physics"[15] for, similarly to the ecological optics of James Gibson, it rests on elementary physical concepts in close connection with the way we *perceive* things, it remains nevertheless a *physics.* Now it is not at all certain that we have to frame the slightest hypothesis in order to solve Wittgenstein's paradoxes. As we have seen, the essential characteristic of brown's being a contrast color must indeed be *discovered,* but this does not entail that its discovery is based on empirical considerations on the nature of light, the physical phenomena of the absorption of certain wavelengths, let alone the atomic or molecular properties of reflective surfaces or the neuro-physiological processes involved; no more so than the fact that a mathematical theorem must be discovered entails that it is not *a priori.* In the phenomenologist's view, it is indeed an *a priori* property of brown to be a contrast color; and therefore it is a material *a priori* necessity that there can be no such thing as brown light.

Who, between Westphal and the phenomenologist, is right? Westphal's position seems to contain the following difficulty. For him, the impossibility of a brown light has exactly the same status as an empirical impossibility: the same as that of water, say, that would hypothetically not be made up of hydrogen and oxygen atoms, or of a whale that would not be a mammal. In Kripke's terms, the necessities he is trying to bring out are "metaphysical," and nonetheless *a posteriori*, necessities. Hence what he intends to show is that "grammar flows from the essence, and [that] essence is revealed by science"[16]—and by "science" he means empirical science. But if it were possible to *justify* grammar by means of truths possessing this status, we would have to conclude that a justification (even partial) of grammar would make it (partially) *a posteriori*. Is this conceivable? As Marie McGinn emphasizes, after all we can't make the rules we follow in our use of color words depend on what science has discovered—or will discover someday! Either grammar is *a priori* or it is nothing: its necessity is that of internal relations governing the *concepts* of color. In short, to ground the impossibility indicated by Wittgenstein's paradoxes "in a scientific theory of colour leaves completely inexplicable our ability to grasp the impossibility in complete ignorance of the theory that allegedly grounds it."[17] If, according to Westphal's claim, the grammar of color terms as we use them derives from essence, in the sense in which he understands it, how are we to understand that origin? This difficulty disappears if the relevant concept of "essence" is Husserl's and not Kripke's; that is, if the necessities that justify grammar have their origin in structural laws that are immanent to the phenomenal field and independent of any hypothesis.

Thus, on the one hand, Husserl would agree with Westphal in rejecting Wittgenstein's assertion that "our ability to explain the meanings [of color words] goes no further"[18] than a definition of the type: " 'brown' is used for *that* color" (followed by a pointing gesture). There is indeed a *real definition* of brown that might go this way: "a group of colors between red and yellow in hue, of medium to low lightness, and of moderate to low saturation."[19] On the other hand, Husserl would differ from Westphal in his claim that, if this definition must be discovered, it is in the sense in which the properties of the triangle are discovered in geometry and not in the sense in which the membership of whales in the class of mammals is discovered in biology. That this characterization of the essence of brown must be discovered does not contradict its *a priori* character, because the *a priori* is not the innate. Let us leave aside, for the moment, the difficult problem as to whether an eidetic variation is able to reveal an essential truth of this sort (see chapter 11). Furthermore, it may well be that experimental protocols might *help* us to discover that truth, but it is hardly plausible that this discovery would be empirical in the sense that a *counterexample would be conceivable here,* thus in the sense that a hypothesis would have to be formulated. This essential truth is non-hypothetical, because it is independent in its validity from all facts (excepting, of course, the fact of the existence of that essential truth itself, and of the whole class of kindred essential truths), and this is indeed what "*a priori*" means in Husserl. Thus we can understand that this essential truth can subtend the use of "brown" in language. Of course, Wittgenstein is right to remind us that we do not need to know the essential definition of brown to be able to use the corresponding word. We do not learn how to use the word "brown" by learning the definition of that color. But having mastered the word does not mean that we have learned all there is to know about brown, as the new nominalism would have it. We can go on to inquire into the real definition of that color, and do so *a priori.* The essential properties that appear in that definition are the properties of brown as *color,* not disguised employment-rules of certain *words.* However, they are not falsifiable empirical hypotheses. If brown were one day to cease appearing to us as such, with the properties included in its definition, if it were no longer this "group of colors between red and yellow in hue, of medium to low lightness, and of moderate to low saturation" it would no longer be *brown.* Phenomenology does seem to be an intermediary discipline between grammar and empirical science.

There are more contentious cases for which the question arises as to whether grammar suffices to dispel the paradoxes. What of transparent white, which keeps cropping up almost like an obsession in Wittgenstein? The greater complexity of that example will, perhaps, allow us to better sift through the intricate interconnections between grammar, phenomenology, and physics.

"Why is it," Wittgenstein asks, "that something can be transparent green but not transparent white?"[20] This problem is borrowed from Runge, who writes in a letter to Goethe: "Both white and black are opaque or solid . . . We should not be misled by the expression 'white' glass, by which expression it is clear glass that is meant. White water, which is pure, is as inconceivable as clear milk."[21] Runge ascribes this peculiarity to the *color* white. But he is wrong from Wittgenstein's point of view. The necessity involved here is grammatical; it is not a property of white but of the *concept* of white[22]—by which we are to understand the rules governing the use of this *word.* "But we should not express this ['It cannot seem white and transparent'] by saying: white is not a transparent color."[23] "Opaqueness is not a *property* of the white color. Any more than transparency is a property of the green."[24]

Before deciding whether Wittgenstein is right in presenting things in this way, let us consider whether the impossibility of transparent white doesn't admit of exceptions. At first sight, there are some. Certain kinds of cloth, made of very light material, certain nettings, for instance, let the light filter through, making it possible to see by transparency; and of course these materials can be white. So aren't they white *and* transparent? Not in the sense Wittgenstein and Runge have in mind. "A body that is actually transparent can, of course, seem white to us; but it cannot seem white and transparent,"[25] that is to say, it cannot seem *transparent-white* the way a bottle seems transparent-green. The things we perceive through a bottle look *tinted green*; whereas through white netting things do not look tinted white. So it is in a certain sense of "white" and of "transparent" that it is out of the question to say that something is transparent white. Something that is white and transparent is not therefore *transparent white* in the sense in which Wittgenstein understands the expression in this context.

We cannot find elementary exceptions in everyday life to the "law of appearance" formulated by Wittgenstein. It remains to be seen, however, whether this is for the reason he alleges. Wittgenstein's problem is formulated as follows. "If 'white' is a concept which only refers to a visual surface, why isn't there a colour concept related to 'white' that refers to transparent things?"[26] Three broad types of answer could be given to this problem. (1) The grammatical answer: green and white do not have the same logical grammar; they are structured differently *as concepts,* and solely by virtue of linguistic convention. (2) What is involved here is a physical impossibility, which calls for a physical explanation, and which is consequently only known *a posteriori.* (3) Here we are dealing with a phenomenological necessity that does not depend on any empirical discovery, or any explanatory hypothesis that might turn out to be false. This descriptive necessity precedes de jure all empirical hypotheses, and, to this extent, it affords their ground.

From the point of view defended by Wittgenstein, there is no need to furnish a justification for grammar. All we have to say is that we use the words "white" and "transparent" in this way: it is language games that decide. Here we are coming very close to linguistic idealism, the position according to which nothing can be said to be *necessary* in phenomena that is not the shadow cast on them by language, no *essential* property can be found in them that is not actually a mere convention. "The only correlate in language to an intrinsic necessity is an arbitrary rule";[27] for the essential is "the mark of a concept, not the property of an object";[28] and therefore, "if you speak of the *essence*—you are just noting a convention."[29]

But one might, after the example of Westphal, propose an empirical solution to Wittgenstein's puzzle.[30] What is white from a physical point of view? Answer: "We can define a white object as *one which does not* darken the light—by absorbing it,"[31] that is, as an object that, by virtue of its atomic and molecular structure, does not selectively absorb some wavelengths of the electromagnetic spectrum and not others, which it reflects, but rather reflects almost all of the light falling upon it, its level of refrangibility being as high as 80 percent or more. Now what is transparency from a physical point of view? Solids or liquids are said to be transparent if they transmit light, producing neither reflection nor diffusion nor selective absorption. Once again, it is atomic properties that explain this phenomenon. Glass, for example, is an "amorphous solid" in which the atomic order is less developed than in most opaque bodies, as a result of which light behaves in it almost as it does in a vacuum, moving in a straight line without obstruction and almost without obscuration. According to Westphal, Wittgenstein's puzzle may then be reduced to a double contradiction. "A transparent white object would transmit almost all the incident light and reflect almost none of the incident light (it is transparent) and reflect almost all the incident light and transmit almost none."[32] Let us take note of the fact that Westphal, in holding that we are dealing with a contradiction, is not trying to win us over to the side of the Vienna Circle's (tautological) analytic propositions. To be sure, we are dealing with a contradiction, but a contradiction involving a physical, and therefore empirical, definition of whiteness and transparency, and not with a proposition contradictory "solely by virtue of the meaning of the terms used" (whatever this may mean, and assuming it means something).

Is this solution acceptable? It raises several difficulties.

First of all, non-selective reflection (and refraction) of light cannot by itself explain the whiteness of many solids and liquids in the absence of another property: diffusion. Ice is transparent, but the moment I begin scratching it, it loses its shiny surface and becomes opaque, as a result of the diffusion of light. It becomes white. Snow and milk are white by diffusion. Now, the transparency of a body is defined by the fact of its maintaining the distinctness, colors, and contrast of the objects seen through it. It is a non-selective transmission of light *without diffusion effect.* Conversely, where diffusion does occur, the affected body is no longer transparent, but *translucent,* that is, semi-opaque. To take an example from Katz, pour milk into a glass of water and the liquid will no longer appear white, but only *cloudy,* that is, translucent.[33] Among colors, white is therefore the only one that is insufficiently characterized by selective or non-selective reflection, without an additional property: diffusion. And it is that property that explains why white is opaque; that is to say, why a transparent white is physically impossible. Non-selective reflection of light with a diffusion effect produces white as a surface color; non-selective transmission accompanied by diffusion produces translucence, which downgrades visibility by transparency in blurring the detail of objects seen, at the same time as it diminishes achromatic contrast. Whiteness, consequently, is in inverse proportion to transparency.[34]

We have then a first solution to Wittgenstein's problem; whether it is the only one remains to be seen. Ice, glass, and crystal are transparent because they transmit light without diffusion and because they absorb (almost) no wavelength of the spectrum, as a result of which the objects that we see through these media keep all their colors intact. But the presence of a pigment can absorb certain wavelengths and produce *tinted* transparent bodies. Schopenhauer gives the following example. In the glass that is called "white," the white is "produced from an actual combination of two chemical colors, although in a transparent state . . . In the glassworks, almost all glass, as everybody knows, originally turns out green—the cause of which is its iron content. This green that tends toward yellow is left only for glass of inferior quality. In order to eliminate this and to produce white glass, as an empirically found remedial, an addition of manganese is needed. But manganese oxide, as such, colors glass violet-red, as can be seen in the red streams of glass and also when, by the production of white glass, too much manganese has been added to the green mass and the glass tinges reddish like in many beer glasses and especially English windowpanes."[35]

There are, consequently, transparent media which do not reflect light selectively and through which objects retain all their colors, and transparent media which do, nonetheless, absorb certain wavelengths of the electromagnetic spectrum due to chemical substances contained in them. The latter are tinted green or red; as a consequence, the colors of objects perceived through them look altered or faded (for example, through a green glass, red surfaces will appear almost achromatic, gray or a dirty brown). This is what physics teaches us.

Is this the last word? First, we should think about the fact that it is difficult to replace "white" as a *phenomenal* property, as a "morphological essence of the life-world" as Husserl would have it, with a physical property—the diffusive and non-selective reflection of light—for the simple reason that there is no such thing as a single physical explanation for white, nor for any other color. A bar of steel at white heat is not white for the same reason that a star is, or for the same reason that snow is: these three whites have different physical origins. Furthermore, the physical properties of diffusion and non-selective reflection do not account for essential properties of *perceived* white, such as the phenomena of opposition (white appears as the opposite of black in the continuum of achromatic colors), contrast (the perception of a white square on a black background makes the white look brighter and the black more intense), and constancy (a sheet of white paper placed in shadow reflects a quantity of light considerably smaller than does that same sheet placed in full midday sunlight, and yet it does not look gray, but white, although its whiteness probably undergoes a slight qualitative alteration). A number of structural properties of perceived color, such as the phenomena of exclusion (green/red, yellow/blue), contrast, complementarity, and constancy have no equivalent in physics.

It is difficult to solve the enigma of transparent white from a physical point of view alone, without considering white as a characteristic of our world experience. This clearly does not entail that white is merely "subjective," after the fashion of a secondary quality. It may be that it is neither an objective physical property, nor a subjective property, but a relational property whose description only has relevance at the level of the interactions of a living organism with its environment—at the ecological level in Gibson's sense of the term[36]—or in reference to what Merleau-Ponty calls "sensing" [*le sentir*] (as opposed to sensation), "this living communication with the world that makes it present to us as the familiar place of our life."[37] Moreover, the foregoing remarks can be classified as pertaining to "physics" only in a very specific sense of the word; for the concepts to which I had recourse are inseparable from the world of our daily experience. As Larry Hardin is right to insist, the explanation furnished "rests on no theoretical assumptions about the micro-mechanics of transparent and opaque substances, or about the physical constitution of light, or about the physiological workings of human visual systems. It is theoretical only in that it conceptually regiments a set of optical phenomena that lie open to ordinary experience . . . It would be incorrect to think of the account as a physicalistic reduction, and in talking about human experiential capabilities as they are revealed in everyday life, it certainly introduces a phenomenological element of sorts."[38] In other words, it is not at all obvious that this "physical" explanation that avails itself of elementary optical concepts intrinsically linked to our everyday experience falls within the category of *empirical* explanation strictly speaking. Here we cannot replace "white" (our *explanandum*) with "that produces a diffusion effect" (our *explanans*) for the simple reason that, as we have seen, the diffusion effect appears sometimes as whiteness, and at other times as translucence. The "physical" explanation is therefore only intelligible if we already know what we are to understand by "white," to what perceived phenomenon that adjective is applied; in short, if we take into account the distinctive character of certain *phenomena*—which falls de jure within the precinct of a phenomenology.

Our question was the following: do we have to make the grammar of "white" and "transparent" depend on empirical discoveries? Not necessarily. It could be that there is a simpler and more economical explanation of the fact that white never looks transparent and transparent media never look white, if by "white" we mean the color whose paradigmatic examples are milk or snow—an explanation that doesn't resort to *any physical concept,* even borrowed from a simplified, "phenomenological" physics. Let us sum up the problem. What interests Wittgenstein is not whether there are transparent things that are white, but whether there is something that is transparent white, as there are transparent green and transparent blue objects, and so on. A transparent glass that is green and a green surface have probably something in common from a physical point of view (the same spectral absorption), but they also have a common phenomenological property: they *look* green. Moreover, in the case of a transparent green medium, the objects that are seen through it possess a common visual property: they appear tinted green. A white surface and white glass (since that is how transparent glass is designated) also have a common physical property: non-selectivity. But, as opposed to the preceding case, *they have no common phenomenological property.* Transparent glass does not look white in the paradigmatic sense of "white" exemplified by milk or snow.

But what exactly would be necessary for "white glass" to appear white? The objects perceived through a transparent medium would have to look *tinted white,* as they were, just a moment ago, tinted green, blue, or red.—*Tinted* white? What does that mean? White cannot be a hue that would be added to other hues (the hues that objects possess originally) quite simply because it isn't a *hue.* White, like black or gray, is an *achromatic* color. This means that, while the other colors have by essence three characteristics, hue, saturation, and lightness, according to which they vary and are ordered in relation to one another, the achromatic colors have neither hue nor saturation. Hue refers to the quantity of red, green, or blue, and so on, in a given color; saturation refers to the proportion of hue in a given color in relation to a neutral achromatic point (saturated colors have a greater proportion of hue, while desaturated colors tend toward gray); finally, lightness refers to the proportion of white or black contained in a particular hue. Thus white, possessing no hue, cannot *tint* the colors of objects perceived through transparent media *with white.* White, then, cannot, by essence, be added to preexistent hues to alter or modify them. At most, it can "lighten" them. It is exclusively an empirical question as to whether certain optical instruments, for example glasses producing a magnifying effect, are capable, by intensifying the luminosity, of provoking a slight lightening effect on colors.[39] But whatever the case may be with respect to this empirical problem, even slightly *lightened* colors would not appear *tinted white*. It is not that we wouldn't be inclined to *call them* thus; we would simply see nothing in those colors that *looks* white to us. The assertion that a transparent white object is an object that tints the objects seen through it with white, in the way that a transparent red object tints them with red, is phenomenologically incoherent. It is a material contradiction in Husserl's sense, because it overlooks the phenomenological difference of essence between chromatic and achromatic colors. Not only can we not even imagine what a transparent white glass that would tint the objects seen through it with white would be (What would we see? A snowy landscape?), but we *don't know what to imagine*, which here indicates an essential necessity. White cannot add its hue to that of other colors for the very good reason that it has no hue to add in any possible sense. And that is not because of our use of the expressions "white" and "transparent," but because of a material *a priori* that structures the domain of colors as such, and therefore because of the essential properties of color.

But that being the case, we do not have to introduce the notions of transmission, reflection, diffusion, and selective and non-selective spectral absorption from physics to solve Wittgenstein's problem. It suffices to turn to a pure description of our experience of colors and their *a priori* structure, to what Meinong already dubbed a "geometry." As a matter of fact, Wittgenstein's problem is not even strictly speaking a problem from the point of view of a phenomenology of colors, quite simply because it rests on a "possibility" that is *a priori* inconceivable (unimaginable). And the *a priori* character of the solution to this problem makes it possible to maintain that grammar is partially justified without falling into the absurdity of an *empirical* justification of grammar.

Actually, we probably must go so far as to say that the impossibility emphasized by Wittgenstein is *strictly* phenomenological, and *not at all* grammatical; because grammar, here, is more complex and less monotonous than Wittgenstein seems ready to acknowledge. In ordinary language, "white" is used in at least *two ways* that are incompatible with each other. "White" is applied to what presents an appearance of a particular color, the paradigm of which is snow, milk, lily, and so on. But white is also used for what presents an appearance that is *neutral with respect to all hue*, for what is both light and achromatic; and in this sense, there is no difficulty in speaking of "white glass," "white wine," and "an egg-white." Why shouldn't white glass be both white *and* transparent? Indeed, it is, but "white" is not used here in the same way as in the expression "white marble." If one of the two uses is probably paradigmatic, it is not clear that we must maintain that the other is merely derivative, analogical, or metaphorical. Neither of these two uses is entirely arbitrary, since each emphasizes one characteristic of white. To put it in phenomenological terms, one insists on the characteristic appearance of the lightest color in the absolute, while the other puts the emphasis on the dimension of neutrality in relation to all hue that transparent substances can have; or, to put it in terms of physics, the first usage insists on a property connected with the diffusion of light, and the second seems to be motivated by the property of non-selectivity possessed, for example, by the transmission of light by crystal. Between these two usages, grammar does not decide. Or rather, it decides case by case, reflecting a very fluctuating usage that has nothing systematic or especially coherent about it. Why is glass white and not crystal? Why can wine be white, but not water, even though almost colorless wine exists? It is as if the language were hesitating between two possibilities: milk is white, but not water; glass is white, and yet it looks more like water than milk. Light has no hue, since it makes all of them appear; it is consequently "transparent," so to speak; yet it is white: *to leukon,* in Greek, means both white and brightness.

But then what, we are prompted to ask Wittgenstein, has happened to "grammar"? If grammar is supposed to be akin to a geometry or a logic, it must be admitted that what is most striking, in usage, is rather its *incoherence,* almost to the point of concurring with Descartes: *fere decipior ab ipso usu loquendi—"I am almost deceived by everyday language."*[40] It is true that Wittgenstein continually reminds us of the vagueness of the rules of ordinary language, but does he not tend nonetheless to homogenize grammar when he makes it into the instrument of philosophical clarification par excellence? Does Wittgenstein *discover,* regarding the words "white" and "transparent," the grammar of ordinary language, that is, a set of employment-rules that are coherent and constitute a genuine "geometry of colors" by virtue of which "transparent white" is nonsense, a grammatical impossibility, or does he not rather "*invent*" that grammar, idealizing ordinary language, which is far less consistent than he says it is? Do his analyses reveal the logical infrastructure of our natural languages or do they not rather elevate them to the rank of an ideal language?

This suspicion is of limited importance as long as we remain within the domain of color. But it takes on a very different significance the moment certain grammatical distinctions are invested with crucial importance for philosophical therapy. To take but one example, is it certain that, when doubt is not logically possible, one cannot speak of "knowledge"? Is it really the grammar of our ordinary language that is so constituted that "I *know* I have a headache" is nonsense, or is it an already philosophical analysis, itself motivated by an anti-Cartesian strategy, that inclines *the philosopher* to maintain that it is nonsense, with the paradoxical consequence that "I am in pain" is not an assertion nor the expression of a knowledge of any kind?[41] Is Wittgenstein revealing the logic of our language or is he idealizing our everyday usage to make it artificially consistent for allegedly therapeutic purposes?

Whatever the answer to these questions may be, one thing seems almost certain: "There is a logic of color," as Cézanne[42] said, but it is far from being arbitrary. There are *reasons* why yellow is not blackish, why brown is not a color of light, and why the whiteness of snow and the transparency of ice do not occur at the same place. These reasons are varied, and it would be hasty to pretend to unite them under one heading. They are situated at the crossroads of the *a priori* and the empirical, at the border between strictly phenomenological necessities and explanations pertaining to a naive physics, that is, a physics still imbued with the "morphological essences" of the life-world from which it is indissociable; for we must already know what transparency or whiteness are from the phenomenological viewpoint in order to begin explaining them as a physicist. Here there is a greater compatibility between the phenomenological explanation of the impossibility of transparent white by the *a priori* properties of the system of colors and the empirical explanation by the phenomenon of diffusion than between these two approaches and that of Wittgenstein. For the former, the arbitrariness of grammar is a myth, and, like all myths that lack self-awareness, it has something philosophically pernicious about it. As Putnam makes clear, "*everything* we say is conventional in the sense that we might have said something else, perhaps something verbally incompatible; and *everything* we say is factual in the sense that we could not have said just anything else."[43]

For these reasons, it is insufficient to claim, as can frequently be read in the work of Wittgenstein's disciples, that an assertion is either empirical or grammatical. This disjunction itself proves problematic. It is not true that there are either instituted rules that *we* follow, and that depend on nothing outside ourselves, or facts independent of us that cannot exert any *necessary* constraint on language. There are necessities that are of the world without being empirical, that can be grasped only through language and its conventions, but are not of a linguistic and conventional nature. For if *all* necessary structure in the world and in our experience were of a grammatical nature, and therefore concerned with sense and nonsense, if, as Wittgenstein writes, "the genuine criterion for the structure [for *all* structure?] is precisely which propositions make sense for it—not, which are true,"[44] it should not be possible to speak, for example, of necessary structures of language (as the spatiotemporal structuring of the symbols themselves) without contradiction. Every structure of experience cannot be of a linguistic nature, without one of these mutually exclusive alternatives being true: either language has no experienceable structures, or the perception of language (of linguistic structures) presupposes itself.

9

The Concept of *Concept*

> We demand a somewhat keener analysis of what lies behind such "ways of using a name."
> —Edmund Husserl

In the preceding chapters I have tried to show that there is nothing absurd or incoherent about the idea of *a priori* structures of experience that phenomenology endeavors to describe. These *a priori* structures are also qualified by Husserl and his followers as "structures of essence." It remains for us to inquire into the status of these essences. This inquiry seems all the more necessary given that the idea that philosophy could proceed *a priori* to an analysis of the concepts that articulate our prescientific understanding of the world is not restricted to phenomenology. The philosophy of the analytic tradition has often taken the view that philosophy's task was to carry out "conceptual analyses," and by that it meant, at least in one of its major branches, an analysis of our use of expressions in language. Hence a confrontation of phenomenology with linguistic philosophy inevitably entails an investigation of the status of concepts, of the concept of *concept* itself. Is the possession of concepts equivalent to the capacity to apply the corresponding words? To address this question let us limit ourselves to "material" concepts (in Husserlian terminology): those on which the possibility of phenomenology depends in principle. These concepts are expressed by general predicates of the form "—is red," "—is a man," and so on, that allow us to identify and classify objects. Husserl's thesis is that the concepts understood in this sense, the predicates corresponding to the general terms of ordinary language such as "red" or "man," are not mere linguistic creations; they express *objective properties* pertaining to the corresponding *eidos*. If "we understand by concepts the *meanings* [*Bedeutungen*] *of names*,"[1] *eide* or essences cannot be reduced to concepts. Rather, the *eidos* is "*prior to all 'concepts,'* in the sense of verbal meanings; indeed, as pure concepts, these must be made to fit the *eidos*."[2] At first blush, Husserl only has the right to speak of essences distinct from concepts because he adopts a realist position with respect to universals: a concept can refer to a multiplicity of individuals only because these individuals share a *common general property* that exists independently from language. If our concepts are conventional creations, the eidetic properties and the *eide* to which they correspond are not.

We will examine a bit later the concept of essence for its own sake (see chapters 10 through 12). Husserl's position raises the following questions:

1. Must we postulate the existence of essences (or *eide*) in order to be able to account for the nature of our concepts?
2. Is access to these essences achieved by the intermediary of an intuition or "vision," a *Wesensschau*?
3. What, exactly, is the status of these essences—assuming they exist? Must we conceive of them as *ideal objects* of a certain sort?
4. Are essences *a priori*?

Let us reserve the three last questions for the following chapters, and inquire, for the moment, into the reasons that led phenomenology to a realism of universals, as opposed to a nominalist tendency dominating the tradition of linguistic analysis. Husserl's eidetics in its entirety derives from a critique of classical nominalism, which nonetheless concedes certain essential points to it. This critique has more than just a historical interest; it will serve as our guiding thread when we compare the essentialist position of Husserlian and post-Husserlian phenomenology with the new nominalism stemming from Wittgenstein.

To the view that there are common universal properties that are exemplified by various individuals, traditional nominalism counters by arguing that there are no general ideas, but only particular ones—expressed by names—that stand for several individuals, and that come to be associated with them by a process of habituation. Classical nominalism thus rests on three main theses: (1) an ontology of individuals: all that exists is of an individual nature;[3] (2) between these individuals there is only a set of resemblances, but no identity in the strict sense; or rather, identity, when it exists, is nothing but a borderline case of identity; (3) general ideas are actually only *names* used in a general way, and therefore "creatures of the understanding," or "creatures of our own making" (Locke)[4] to which nothing corresponds in reality.

Of course there are many versions of nominalism. To Locke, who nonetheless defends the notion of abstract ideas, that is, of ideas obtained by the abstraction of what constitutes the particularity of individuals (for example, the abstract idea of a triangle in general is that of a particular triangle that would be neither equilateral, nor isosceles, nor scalene), Berkeley and Hume will object that the very notion of "abstract idea" is indefensible. An abstract idea, in Locke's view, must be a *particular* idea, for example the idea of a lemon placed before me on the table, having such and such a color, size, stage of ripeness, giving off a captivating smell or being almost odorless; and at the same time it must be that particular idea *stripped of all its particular attributes*, the idea of *that* lemon, but without any of its characteristics, for they would have been removed by the abstracting process. It is easy for Berkeley and Hume to object that a particular lemon which would have none of the particular properties of a lemon is not even imaginable: it is a contradiction in terms. Besides, this contradiction is indeed present in Locke's text. On the one hand, Locke says that particular things do not share common properties (the universals of the tradition) and have only relations of resemblance; on the other hand, he maintains that in order to obtain an abstract idea one must make abstraction of all the differences between individuals, and only retain the *common* element.[5] This is why, retorts Berkeley, we must reject Locke's abstract ideas and replace them with singular ideas that, once associated to a name, become capable of evoking a multiplicity of objects between which no other relation has been claimed to obtain than that of resemblance. The alleged general ideas are thus reduced, via particular ideas, to the use of the corresponding words: "A word becomes general by being made the sign, not of an abstract general idea, but of several particular ideas, any one of which it indifferently suggests to the mind."[6] Hume will go even further than Berkeley, by eliminating the mediation performed by singular ideas insofar as they stand for several ideas (for example, the particular representation of a triangle that would be either right-angled or isosceles and that would stand for all the other triangles), to identify without remainder the general ideas with the names themselves. "A particular idea," he writes, "becomes general by being annex'd to a general term; that is, to a term, which from a customary conjunction has a relation to many other particular ideas, and readily recalls them in the imagination."[7]

Husserl is far from overlooking the importance of the critiques of Berkeley and Hume. The radical nominalism of the latter, he points out, "contain[s] valuable trains of thought."[8] At the same time, these doctrines rest on a false premise, according to which a general idea would be an "idea" in the sense that empiricism confers on that term, that is, a *particular* representation or image. Once we assume that the triangle in general must possess the characteristics of an individual triangle, we fall into a gross contradiction. But that contradiction is only a contradiction as long as we assume that we are right to give the general idea of the triangle the properties of a particular triangle, and even something like triangularity. Indeed, "a triangle is something which has triangularity, but . . . triangularity is not itself something that has triangularity."[9] The general idea of a triangle is therefore not the idea of *a* (particular) triangle *in general*, which is a *contradictio in adjecto*. There is no reason to attribute to the species *triangle* the properties of objects that fall under it. In the end, "it is absurd to treat a concept's content as the same concept's object, or to include a concept's content in its own conceptual extension."[10]

The unacceptable presupposition of classical empiricism consists, then, in maintaining that a general idea should possess the same properties as the exemplars it subsumes. This presupposition, which underlies Locke's entire conception, is not challenged by Hume's and Berkeley's critiques; it is rather confirmed in its rights by them, making these critiques themselves problematic. The theory of abstraction advanced by Locke and rejected by his heirs, Husserl argues, confuses the selective attention that highlights certain aspects of an individual object and leaves others in the background with generalization in the strict and authentic sense. Indeed, it is always possible to fix one's attention on the yellow of the lemon, the grainy quality of it skin, its odor; it is always possible, by contrast, not to pay attention to them; but even when I "make abstraction" of the particular determinations of the object I am examining, I obtain at best a vague perception of *this* lemon, and in no case a consciousness of the lemon *in general*. Attention by itself cannot be the source of consciousness of generality. To grasp an essential generality has nothing to do with apprehending an individual in an indeterminate and vague way. The content of the *eidos* lemon is the set of essential properties that apply to every lemon as such. These properties are themselves *general*; they are in no way comparable to the properties I perceive. To summarize, Husserl follows the lead of the critiques of Berkeley and Hume, but in doing so he arrives at a conclusion diametrically opposed to theirs. The impossibility of abstracting in imagination the particular properties of an object without destroying that object itself becomes the main argument, not against general ideas, but in favor of those same ideas; and this occurs because the unacceptable nominalist presupposition that general ideas—assuming they exist—are at the same time particular representations is rejected. Whether it is a matter of a pure *eidos*, such as that of the triangle, or of an empirical generality like the lemon *in specie*, the possibility of varying certain properties of the object in the imagination and the limits imposed on this variation, limits by virtue of which certain essential invariants are revealed, provides a basis for the procedure of eidetic variation. Whatever triangles I imagine, the variety of their characteristics will remain within certain limits that are prescribed *a priori* by the nature of the triangle in general: for example, they will be plane figures, the figures will have three angles, the sum of these angles will equal two right angles, and so on. As for the properties of essence of the lemon as a vague, inexact generality (or, as Husserl will later say, a "morphological essence of the life-world"), they reside, for example, in the gamut of color shades that range from green to yellow, in a characteristic form, a more or less acidic taste, a transparent flesh, a grainy skin that the lemon shares with other citric fruits. The properties that cannot be separated even in imagination from the totality of imaginable exemplars of the triangle or of the lemon are their *essential properties* and belong to the content of their respective concepts.

But Husserl's critique does not stop there. Indeed, what can be said in response to the radical nominalist who claims to dispense not only with all abstract ideas, but even with all general ideas, who is content with *names* standing for several particular ideas (or several individuals), associated with the latter by means of custom and on the basis of their *similarity* alone? In order to be able to speak of "similarity," Husserl retorts, one has to be able to specify *in what respect* two things are similar. Two horses can be alike with respect to color, size, or their ability to jump over obstacles. In other words, one same individual belongs to several "circles of similarity [*Ähnlichkeitskreisen*],"[11] which means that it shows resemblances of several *sorts* to other individuals. It is not the same thing to be similar in form and in color. Now, in order for there to be differences of several sorts, there have to be sorts or species: the form-species, the color-species—and this is precisely what the nominalist denies. Two horses are similar from the point of view of color, but their colors are not similar from the point of view of color; they are *identical* from this point of view. Their colors *are* both colors. They fall under a common species: color in general. And it is only because they fall under the species *color* that they can be subsequently classified according to their greater or lesser degree of similarity. From this it follows that "wherever things are "alike," an identity in the strict and true sense is also present. We cannot predicate exact likenesses of two things, without stating the respect in which they are thus alike. Each exact likeness relates to a Species (*Spezies*), under which the objects compared are subsumed: this Species is not, and cannot be, merely "alike" in the two cases, if the worst of infinite regresses is not to become inevitable."[12]

It is not because two things are similar that they are of the same nature; it is because they are of the same nature that they are similar. The argument stated by Husserl as early as in *Logical Investigations* finds an echo in Russell's *The Problems of Philosophy* (1912) in a slightly different form. There, too, the issue is to show that nominalism, which, at first blush, accepts only as a primary relation similarity, is actually forced to reintroduce identity at the level of similarities themselves. Two things that are similar must have something in common, *be it only their similarity.* "Since there are many white things, the resemblance must hold between many pairs of particular white things; and this is the characteristic of a universal. It will be useless to say that there is a different resemblance for each pair, for then we shall have to say that these resemblances resemble each other, and thus at last we shall be forced to admit resemblance as a universal."[13] And if we begin by conceding a first universal, that of similarity, what reason do we have for rejecting all the others?

But the nominalist might reply to the argument as stated in its Husserlian form that it rests on a begging of the question; for the nominalist denies that there are any specific identities in addition to the array of likenesses. He denies that "'alikeness' is the relation of objects falling under one and the same Species."[14] He refuses to speak of resemblances *in some respect,* and argues that there is nothing but resemblances that are designated by different *words,* without there being any identity of nature or of essence hidden behind the use of these words. As for the form that Russell gives the objection, it must be admitted that is hardly compelling. What is common to all similarities, the nominalist would reply, is nothing but the use of the word "similarity," and not a common universal property, similarity. The begging of the question appears clearly in the transition made by Russell from "resemblances that resemble each other" to "resemblances that are identical with respect to resemblance"; hence to resemblance as species or common universal. It is precisely to this transition that the nominalist objects.

But his defense is fragile, and the infinite regress spoken of by Husserl and Russell does in fact occur. Indeed, the nominalist implicitly assumes that what applies to non-relational properties, such as whiteness or triangularity, must also hold for relational properties such as likeness. Hence the consistent nominalist must maintain not only that two objects that resemble each other by their color have nothing in common, but that two pairs of objects that resemble each other (by their color) have nothing in common, not even resemblance, and only *resemble each other* from the point of view of resemblance. Resemblances, on this view, are therefore resemblant relational properties—so that one would have to speak in each case, to borrow Husserl's phrase, "of a similarity of this similarity with other similarities."[15] But if what brings together two pairs of green objects is only a (second-order) similarity between their similarities, the similarity between this second-order similarity and the similarities to which it is similar will force us to postulate a third-order similarity, and hence to postulate similarities of similarities ad infinitum.

The whole problem here is whether this regress is logically vicious. It would certainly be vicious if it were a regress *in the explanation*, that is, if we had to postulate, in order to explain the least similarity, an infinite number of similarities of similarities. But the nominalist has no intention of *explaining* each particular similarity by means of a similarity of a higher order. For him, all the cases of similarity are nothing but instances of the application of the *word* "similarity," period. In other words, infinite regress *in the explanation* is immediately blocked, for it ends with the word "similarity." For the rest, the consistent nominalist would, without hesitation, accept that the world is intertwined with an infinite number of similarities, and of similarities of similarities, but he would add that there is nothing logically vicious about this regress: it tells us nothing about the impossibility of such similarities, no more than the infinitely repeated mutual reflection of two mirrors facing one another constitutes an objection to the existence of mirrors.[16]

Still, his answer is less convincing than it seems, and it is at this point that a stronger argument comes in. Nominalism tells us that the similarity between colors can be reduced to the use of the word "color," and that the similarity between similarities can be reduced to the use of the word "similarity." The trouble is that what he tells us is not intelligible. The use of *the* word "similarity"? But to speak of *the* word similarity, in the singular, can be understood in two ways. A first possibility would be to understand this expression as meaning the word as a particular phonic complex (or sign) uttered or written *hic et nunc* by a particular person. In that case, if, in conformity with the nominalist ontology, only individual words exist and the word "similarity" uttered by me at this moment and the word "similarity" uttered by someone else at a different moment *are two different words*, it becomes impossible to agree about the least word, and the very possibility of a *language*, of a communication of thoughts by means of signs, is destroyed in principle. In order for that possibility not to be destroyed, that is, in order for what the nominalist says to remain intelligible, he must speak about the word "similarity" (or any other) as *one and the same* word that I utter and that someone else utters, that is, he must speak about this word considered in its specific identity—about the word as species and not about its exemplifications (about the word as *type* and not as *token*, in Peirce's terminology). But then, the nominalist is forced to reintroduce a specific identity *at least at the linguistic level.* Perhaps similarities are nothing but what is signified by the word "similarity," but to speak about *the* word "similarity" presupposes that one is speaking of a certain *species* of word, and therefore about the word in question as universal.

Hence the nominalist finds himself caught in a dilemma: if he carries his reasoning through to its logical conclusion, he must say that all words are only individuals connected by similarity relations, and therefore that it is impossible to speak of "the *same* word"; yet at the very moment in which he seems to adopt this thesis and asserts, following Locke, that things "are all of them particular in their existence, *even . . . words*,"[17] the universal, driven out through the doorway of language, climbs back through the window, because he must concede right away that the same words are used by all speakers of a given language, and that these identical words are associated with identical ideas: "unless a man's words excite *the same ideas* in the hearer which he makes them stand for in speaking, he does not speak intelligibly."[18] Excluded from the real world, the universals must thus be reintroduced at least into the linguistic domain, since "when we have found a resemblance among several objects, that often occur to us, we apply *the same name* to all of them, whatever differences we may observe in the degrees of their quantity and quality, and whatever other differences may appear among them."[19]

The strategy of classical nominalism is therefore untenable. This strategy consists in considering specific and generic identities as boundary cases of similarity. Thus, Mill writes in his *Logic*: "Resemblance, when it exists in the highest degree of all, amounting to undistinguishableness, is often called identity, and the two similar things are said to be the same."[20] But a specific identity cannot be the same thing as a resemblance, however great, because the concepts of *identity* and of *resemblance* possess distinct logical properties. The relation of membership within the same species is transitive: if A is specifically identical to B and B is specifically identical to C, then A is specifically identical to C. But this transitivity does not apply to the relation of resemblance: if a white cube is similar to a white sphere and a white sphere is similar to a black sphere, it does not follow that a white cube is similar to a black sphere.[21] Therefore it is not by chance that the classic nominalist always ends up contradicting himself, and recognizing that words must be the *same,* or have the *same* meaning, in order to fulfill their function in language. As Husserl says in one sentence: "we merely push the problem back a stage when we reduce the unity of the Species to the unity of a verbal meaning."[22] And if there are indeed identities "in the strict and true sense," as Husserl writes, in the linguistic domain, if two occurrences of the word "resemblance" are two occurrences of the same word endowed with one identical meaning, why should we deny to things what we began by granting to words? Two triangles not only resemble each other; they are identical as triangles. They are also identical as plane figures, in the sense that they share a common property and belong to the same species. Two different numbers, 5 and 3, are identically numbers in the sense of a specific identity. This specific identity is not merely a case of resemblance—no more, incidentally, than is numerical identity. It is the same Prelude by Scriabin, whether interpreted by Horowitz or Sofronitsky. It is *The Red and the Black*—the same novel—that goes through successive editions and is read by various readers. In all these examples, the nominalist reduction of identity fails. It is impossible to speak of "resemblance" in the cases in which there is no identity in the strict sense. All resemblance is a case of partial or complete identity.

The only solution that remains for the nominalist is to introduce into his theory the concept of exact resemblance. The exact resemblance between particular properties (sometimes called "tropes" in contemporary philosophy, and which Husserl called "moments"), for example the resemblance between two shades of yellow, the shade of lemon *A* and that of lemon *B*, then becomes *an Ersatz of specific identity*. Exact resemblance, like identity, instantiates the logical property of transitivity: if the yellow of lemon *A* exactly resembles the yellow of lemon *B*, and if the latter exactly resembles the yellow of lemon *C*, then the yellow of *A* is ipso facto exactly similar to that of *C*. This relation is also symmetrical. With this solution, however, the very substance of the nominalist thesis is lost, for it is no longer a "name" that stands for a missing identity. Furthermore, the coincidence between the logical properties of exact resemblance and those of identity becomes a mystery. Is this coincidence not rather due to the fact that the nominalist has gone no further than renaming identity "exact resemblance"?

This critique of classical nominalism allows us to shed light on Husserl's positive doctrine and specifically on his conception of the intuition of essences. There exists, according to the phenomenologist, an apprehension of the general as such that is given "in person" in founded intuition of a new kind. "The idea seen is here said to be seen," he writes, "because it is not meant or spoken of vaguely, indirectly, by means of empty symbols or words, but is precisely grasped directly and itself."[23] How is such an apprehension possible?

To answer this question, it will be helpful to remove a few ambiguities that might be an obstacle for an understanding of the *Wesensschau*. First of all, to speak of the *eidos* as "a beheld and beholdable universal"[24] presupposes that we clarify our ideas about the concept of *intuition*. In the phenomenologist's view, intuition is neither a psychological faculty nor the characteristic of an inner, lived experience. Nor is it a feeling that might occasionally be associated with a lived experience. Understood in its strict, non-psychological sense, intuition designates rather *a mode of givenness of the object itself*, the mode by virtue of which it presents itself in person, is self-given (*selbstgegeben*) and, eventually, is given in the flesh (*leibhaft*).[25] The universalization of the concept of intuition and its application to the domain of *generality*, that is, the assertion that "intuition of an essence is consciousness of something, an 'object' . . . which is 'itself given' in the intuition,"[26] is consequently accompanied by a universalization of the notion of *object* itself: "The essence (*Eidos*) is a new sort of object. Just as the datum of individual or experiencing intuition is an individual object, so the datum of eidetic intuition is a pure essence."[27] To say that the *eidos* is an object of a new kind is obviously not to maintain that it is an "object" in the same sense of the term as a concrete individual, spatiotemporally individuated. In this regard, nothing is more removed from Husserl's essence than this *contradictio in adjecto* of the empiricist theory of abstraction: a *general individual*. The relevant concept of "object" is rather a minimal concept that may be specified by means of two characteristics: (1) object is anything that can be given in an intuition; (2) object is any subject of a possible predication.[28]

Although both sensible and ideal objects are available to a potential intuition, that intuition varies as to its nature in the two cases. A first major distinction resides in the different role played by language with respect to these two kinds of intuition. If there can be a prelinguistic—"still dumb"—experience in the order of perception, there is no dumb experience in the domain of essences. Indeed, as we have seen, the intuitive apprehension of categorial objects (formal idealities) and of eidetic generalities (material idealities) presupposes a meaning-intention that it fills. The *eidos* of red is inseparable from the meaning-intention that means this general object via an expression: "red" (or its equivalent in other languages). Thus the relation between an apprehension of essence and its *at least possible* expression is an internal, necessary relation. "Even in our case, nonetheless, and in the generic field as such," Husserl specifies, "intuition has an essential relation to expression and to its meaning."[29] This situation is different from the one occurring in the sphere of sensible intuition: I see the blue sky, but I do not need to have the concepts of *blue* and *sky* to see it thus. If the possession of language can occasionally inform my perception, that is, allow me to perceive otherwise, all perception is not of a linguistic order, since the perceptual sense as such contains "nothing pertaining to expression and conceptual signification."[30] This is why Husserl will distinguish with increasing clarity between the mere empty intention that is operative in the perceptual order, when we intend the unperceived sides of an object at the same time as those perceived, for example, and the properly *signitive* intention that finds its place in the linguistic realm. As he emphasizes in a course in 1908, "the fact of being tied to sensible intuitions of signs, to symbols, is not essential to the empty intention. Consequently, the term *symbolic representation* is not entirely appropriate as a designation for the entire class of empty representations."[31] Thus, if eidetic intuition is always an intuition that is linguistically (conceptually) articulated, the same cannot be said of perception. But of course the fact that all eidetic intuition presents itself as intrinsically tied to meaning-intentions[32] does not cancel out the difference that is established elsewhere between the *eidos* as intuitionable object and the concept as verbal meaning, tied to its expression by a predicate. It is the concept that conforms to the *eidos*, and not the other way round

This first distinction brings with it a second, in its wake. The sensible intuition is "simple," while the eidetic intuition is "founded." The latter possesses this particularity "that [it] has as its basis a principal part of intuition of something individual . . . ; certainly, in consequence of that, no intuition of essence is possible without the free possibility of turning one's regard to a 'corresponding' individual and forming a consciousness of an example."[33] In order to seize an eidetic generality a perceptual or imaginary perusal of variables is *necessary*, in which each specimen is intended as an exemplification of the essence in question.[34] There is no intuitable essence that does not announce itself as the essence *of* a multiplicity of exemplars that fall under it. Thus the tie between an *eidos* and its exemplification is still an *internal* relation.

A third characteristic follows. Far from being a simple and immediate contact with its object, the eidetic intuition is an articulated intuition, and in many respects it is *mediate*, since the access to the *eidos* is indissociable from the imaginary perusal of its exemplifications. As Eugen Fink emphasizes, "the often misunderstood 'essential insight' is in no way defined as some sort of mystical act, as a receptive intuition or a pure 'seeing,' as it were, of the nonsensible. Rather, the *eidos* is the correlate of an operation of thought, or of a spontaneous intellectual act."[35] The misunderstanding to which Fink alludes underlies, for example, the entire critique by Schlick, who conceives of the Husserlian intuition not only as simple and "immediate," but as "ineffable."[36] The eidetic reduction is rather an operation comprising several steps, and it is the strict correlate of the eidetic variation without which no essence could be given in any possible sense. This applies not only to simple essences, such as the essence *red* or the essence *spatial object* in general, but also to essences that include in their contents themselves an operative diversity. The essence of the number 2^3 can only be given in an intuition by means of a series of arithmetic transformations: $2^3 = 2 \times 2 \times 2$ and $2 = 1 + 1$. It might be objected that these operations are themselves symbolic, but Husserl would reply that these operations, though they are in fact symbolic, nonetheless possess their own intuitive content.

In the fourth place, every essence prescribes to thought its possibilities and impossibilities. Essence possesses a *normative* content, in the sense that the impossibility of thinking things otherwise is inseparable from a not-being-able-to-be-otherwise of the objects it subsumes. Husserl rejects both a "Platonic hypostatization,"[37] that would conceive of ideal objects as entities absolutely independent from the thought processes through which they are revealed, and a "grammatical hypostatization"[38] which would make these idealities into mere products of language—that is, both a naive Platonism and a naive nominalism. There is a constitution of idealities that makes them inseparable from our thought processes, but these processes, partly symbolic, far from producing these idealities, merely bring them to light.

Lastly, contrary to another misinterpretation on Schlick's part, the intuition of which Husserl speaks is not a *knowledge* but only a *legitimizing source* for all knowledge. As it is unambiguously expressed in the "principle of all principles" of phenomenology, formulated in §24 of *Ideas I*: "*every originary presentive intuition is a legitimizing source of cognition.*"[39] As for knowledge, it is propositional in nature, for it must be communicable by essence. According to the maxim of *Logical Investigations*, "to intuit is not to think"; now, to know is to think something and to be able to express it in linguistic form.[40] Thus, as Rudolf Bernet emphasizes, the act of knowledge is a signitive act endowed with intuitive fullness: "The intuitively fulfilled speech-act, that is, the assertion which has been justified by the intentional givenness of its object, proves to be the authentic paradigm for the act of cognition in the strict sense."[41] Therefore, as Reinach remarks, "essence analysis is no ultimate goal, but rather is a means"[42] of phenomenology. It is nonetheless true that for Husserl—and this point already raises problems—intuition, as "legitimizing source," constitutes by itself a first *justification* for knowledge. Thus it is possible to speak of "justifying intuition [*belegende Anschauung*]"[43] or "legitimizing fulfillment [*auswisenden Erfüllung*]."[44] These assertions raise the question of whether a private justification of knowledge is not an absurdity in principle, and whether all justification does not presuppose language as the public, intersubjective element of thought.

The complexity of the Husserlian doctrine of the intuition of essences resides, in sum, in the following aspects. Eidetic intuition is (1) dependent on language by essence; (2) indissociable from exemplification;

(3) articulated or mediate; (4) escaping the mere alternative of a naive Platonism or a naive nominalism; and (5) a legitimizing source for knowledge and not knowledge properly speaking. To these characteristics, it should be added that "essences" are of several kinds, and that all are not "exact" after the manner of mathematical essences. This theme, which will take on its full proportions in the *Crisis*, is already present in the third *Logical Investigation.*[45] Husserl sometimes calls the vague and inexact essences "types"[46] or "morphological essences"; and he insists on the fact that, from the point of view of their role in knowledge, the vagueness of concepts and of their correlates, their "fluid spheres of application," do not constitute an imperfection and "are not a defect that [should be] imputed to them."[47] To return to our example, the fact that after successive grafts it is possible to obtain a variety of citrus fruits about which it is difficult to decide whether or not they fall under the concept *lemon*, the fact that these exemplars only differ as to the *more* and the *less* with respect to a paradigmatic case—that of the "*trombe d'oro della solarità*" of which Eugenio Montale speaks[48]—cannot constitute an objection to the claim of the reality of essences.

The doctrine of the intuition of essences is complex. It is superior to the doctrine of traditional nominalism. Whether it is defensible remains to be examined. Here, Husserlian phenomenology must face a second wave of critiques, emanating this time from a new nominalism that is expressed by the Wittgensteinian school.

Traditional nominalism replaced the universals of the tradition by names employed in a general way, standing for various objects with which they are associated by custom. In doing so, it conceived of each word on the model of a name (*nomen*, in Latin, meaning both "name" and "word" in general). The ideas to which the word refers are characterized sometimes as general abstract ideas (Locke), and sometimes as particular ideas (Berkeley). This conception, which should perhaps be called the "Lockean picture" of language rather than the "Augustinian picture," now constitutes the target of the new nominalism. It is quite simply inadequate to maintain that all words only signify by virtue of their association with the ideas they stand for. In comparing language to a toolbox and emphasizing the great variety of uses that several types of words possess, Wittgenstein rejects the traditional primacy of nominal expressions for the analysis of meaning. The unity of an expression resides in its meaning, but its meaning is in no way an "idea" that would coexist with the word, a representation that would be associated with it, be it particular or general: "For a *large* class of cases—though not for all—in which we employ the word 'meaning' it can be defined thus: the meaning of a word is its use in the language."[49] Wittgenstein's reservation ("for a *large* class of cases") immediately restricts the scope of his characterization. What applies to the meaning of words does not necessarily apply in the same way to the meaning of sentences: at least not, as Peter Geach insists, "if 'use' is here taken to mean 'established usage.' For in general there is no established usage for a sentence as a whole."[50] But words do indeed have employment-rules, which determine their contribution to the meaning of the sentences in which they appear—so that these rules constitute their meaning. What we explain when we explain the meaning of a word is its employment-rules in our language.

These semantic considerations cast a new light on the nature and status of concepts. The approach to meaning in terms of use makes it possible to dissolve the problem raised by traditional nominalism: for what kind of ideas do words stand in order to be able to signify as they do? This whole problem rested on the implicit assumption that a word only has meaning as long as it stands for something—an idea or a representation. Let us consider even the most favorable case from the point of view of traditional nominalism, that of general terms ("book") or of predicates ("__ is a book"). According to traditional nominalism, I only understand the word "book" because I know the "thing" it represents, that is, because I am able to place before my mind's eye a book stripped of its particular attributes and reduced to its "abstract idea" (Locke), or, on the contrary, a particular idea of book standing for all others thanks to its customary association with this word (Berkeley). However, counters the new nominalist, it is not correct to maintain *in general* that to understand a word is to grasp the "thing" for which it stands. To understand a word is to know how to use it, to master the rules of its usage, and this is equally true in the case of predicates. The function of the predicate is not to stand for a "general idea," but to be applied to a plurality of objects in order to classify and identify them. Consequently, having the concept of book is nothing but knowing how to apply a predicate, to master a rule of use, so that if I wanted to teach someone this concept I would not need to appeal to an "idea" present before the inner eye of his mind; it would suffice for me to resort to examples and exercises. "If a person has not yet got the concepts, I shall teach him to use the words by means of examples and by practice.—And when I do this I do not communicate less to him than I know myself."[51]

The error flagged by Wittgenstein in this passage is the one consisting in conceiving of the concept as an "idea" in the empiricist's sense, namely, as a mental representation present before an "inner eye," in such a way that the awareness of this idea would make possible the use of the word, and hence its explanation as well. If this were the nature of the concept, the explanation by examples (examples of correct use, or the showing of specimens in the case of a general term) would amount to no more than an *indirect* explanation procedure, which would palliate the impossibility of communicating to others the direct vision of the idea as I possess it within myself—for example, the vision of what all books have in common (Locke's abstract idea): "One gives examples and intends them to be taken in a particular way.—I do not, however, mean by this that he is supposed to see in those examples that common thing which I—for some reason—was unable to express; but that he is now to *employ* those examples in a particular way. Here giving examples is not an *indirect* means of explaining—in default of a better. For any general definition can be misunderstood too."[52] Because the explanation of the meaning of a predicate is nothing but the explanation of the way it is used to characterize objects, that is, to classify and identify them, we need nothing but the rule and examples to understand this meaning; for, what we teach through these examples is precisely the mastering of this rule. If we wish to teach the meaning of "book" to someone, we can, for example, present him with objects that are books and others that aren't, and ask him to continue by himself. *The rule and the examples suffice*, and there is no need for any special faculty of abstraction or of representation for such learning.

As we see, the target of Wittgenstein's critique goes far beyond traditional nominalism, and includes the critique of this same nominalism by Husserl. Indeed, if Husserl is right to oppose the classical theories of abstraction by saying that we do not acquire a concept (the concept of red for example) by focusing our attention on one aspect of our experience and by making abstraction of all the others, he is wrong to conclude from this, in agreement with the traditional semantic prejudice, that the word "red," in order to signify, must *stand for* a *general* object, an idea or an *eidos* given to a non-sensible intuition, and that, contrary to what empiricism maintained, possesses none of the characteristics of the objects it subsumes. It is basically of little consequence that the Platonism of Husserl leads him to conceive of the *eidos* in general not as a representation or a lived experience, but as a self-identical object, an ideal intentional object transcending all individual consciousness; what is decisive is that, in conformity with the tradition it critiques, he maintains that this universal, this *eidos*, is *given* to consciousness as a content of experience. This idea of a "given concept"[53] is precisely what Husserl shares with empiricism. Now, nothing of what can be given as a content of experience can be a *concept*, the new nominalism would retort. As Elizabeth Anscombe writes, "no concept is simply given; every one involves a complicated technique of application of the word for it, which could not just be presented by an experience-content."[54] A concept is, consequently, what is possessed by someone who has mastered a practical competency, the ability of using a word in an intelligible manner. Whoever can use the terms "chair," "negation," or "this" possesses these concepts. To possess a concept is nothing other than to know how to apply *a word*—whence the qualification "new nominalism."

From this it follows that the criteria for the possession of a concept are necessarily *public*. No private faculty, no private access to a content of experience constitutes the criterion for the possession of a concept. Let us recall that for Wittgenstein the criteria for "I have the concept *x*" are the circumstances in which I would be justified in uttering that sentence.[55] Thus, my ability to give examples of trees is not just an *indication* that I possess the concept "tree," but the *criterion* for my possessing it, that is, the reason that justifies me in thinking that I have the linguistic mastery of this word (or that I understand it). To put it differently, the relation existing between the concept and its application is not external, but internal. Indeed, if this connection were external, it would still be necessary to *explain* how one having "access" to a concept in a private manner is also capable of applying it. But the ability for application, the capacity to provide examples or to use meaningful sentences in which the word appears is *constitutive* of the possession of the concept. This capacity to apply the word in following a rule cannot be identical with any representation, any private episode.

In making the case in this way, the new nominalism has not yet demonstrated positively that there are no common properties or universals that correspond to our (linguistic) concepts, that is, to words' meanings. Nor has it demonstrated that any idea of an intuition of these eidetic generalities is incoherent. What it has done is rather to shift the *onus probandi* onto the adversary. For even if we assume that an intuition of essences is possible, that intuition remains extrinsic to the possession of a concept. The nominalist could therefore ask the realist of universals the following questions: (a) Are there aspects of concepts, the existence of which he postulates in the form of universals or *eide*, that cannot be accounted for by an analysis in terms of the use of linguistic expressions? (b) Of what *criterion* other than the use of linguistic expressions could the realist avail himself or herself in order to answer the first question in the affirmative?

Let us take the example of eidetic variation as thematized by Husserl. By submitting examples of book to an imaginary variation and by grasping the characteristics that remain invariable throughout this variation, it must be possible to bring out the content of the *eidos* book. But, the Wittgensteinian would object, how do you know that the specimens of book that you are imagining, whose invariable or essential qualities are to be extracted, are indeed instances *of book*? Isn't the only criterion you have to make this claim that you have mastered the meaning, and therefore the use, of the word "book" in English? And that therefore you already possess the *concept* of book—in the relevant sense from the point of view of the new nominalism? Accordingly, far from eidetic variation making it possible to reveal the essential characteristics of a book, to which all language must conform, it is rather the mastery of the employment-rules of the word "book" in English that makes possible something like eidetic variation. It is the rule governing the use of the word that explains the regulated character of eidetic variation, and not the other way round. Thus, even if it were conceded that an eidetic intuition is indeed possible, even if it were conceded that intuition enables us to determine what is or is not a book, the problem would remain as to whether the normativity of intuition is not only the shadow cast by the normativity of language. As Rorty suggests, "In my Wittgensteinian view, an intuition is never anything more or less than familiarity with a language-game."[56]

Thus the new nominalism is not even forced to deny the existence of an eidetic intuition. It suffices that it shows that such an intuition, assuming it exists, remains extrinsic to the possession of a concept; and therefore that it offers no real alternative to the concept of *concept* advanced by the nominalist. Indeed, no private intuition can teach me how to use a word correctly: the only way I can learn this is by mastering the rule and the examples, and in conformity with public criteria. The idea of an intuition that would at the same time provide a private justification for the possession of a concept does not make sense. Furthermore, eidetic intuition, far from protecting us from any erroneous use of the word, is itself subject to error. Far from intuition being of such a nature as to dispel all doubt, there is always a possibility of doubting one's intuitions: "And how do I know that it [intuition] doesn't mislead me? For if it can guide me right, it can also guide me wrong." This is what leads Wittgenstein to conclude: "Intuition is an unnecessary shuffle."[57]

Intuition does not take us one step forward because, unless we resort to the mythology of an infallible intuition that would shield us from all risk of error, the rule that we follow in using a word can be followed correctly or incorrectly—like any rule. And therefore intuition adds nothing to our ability to follow a rule according to public criteria—an ability that *constitutes* the possession of the concept. Moreover, the main problem raised by the procedure of eidetic variation is the following. While recognizing an internal relation between concept and application, *the idea of eidetic variation leads to conceiving application too narrowly, that is, solely as imaginary exemplification,* whereas the criteria that justify my assertion that I possess a concept are much more varied, and include different ways of using it—which all presuppose my possession of language.

The superiority of the nominalist-behaviorist analysis of concepts in comparison with their analysis in terms of eidetic intuition lies, therefore, in the following assumption: while it is impossible to justify the possession of a concept understood as eidetic intuition without resorting to public criteria, be they linguistic or behavioral (saying this or that, pointing to such and such a specimen, etc.), it is perfectly possible to justify the possession of a concept on the basis of public criteria without ever resorting to objects called "essences" or to eidetic intuitions. Here there is a "logical" priority of the external over the internal, or, to put it differently, "an 'inner process' stands in need of outward criteria."[58] The nominalist-behaviorist analysis of concepts proves to be more powerful than their analysis in terms of eidetic intuition, because it explains what eidetics explains, while eidetics alone is insufficient to account for what analysis explains in terms of employment-rules and grammar.

To respond to this line of argument, the phenomenologist might bring several points to bear. First, he might remind his interlocutor that the Husserlian doctrine of the intuition of essences is more subtle and complex than the version given by the nominalist. Indeed:

(1) In contrast to the empiricist theory of abstraction, Husserl, as I have said, does not claim that the relation that exists between the *eidos* and its exemplifications is an external relation, and therefore that we could grasp an *eidos* without knowing to what it applies.[59] The theory of eidetic intuition is characterized, on the contrary, by the internal relation that it postulates between the *eidos* and what falls under it, between the essence and what is able to illustrate it on the occasion of an eidetic variation. Since eidetic intuition is an intuition founded and articulated—founded on a free perusal of examples, indissociable from the syntax that is revealed through it, that is, from the possibilities and impossibilities that it brings to light—the *eidos* possesses a normative content; it is also necessarily a *rule* that prescribes to the free variation of examples its limits de jure, which are thereby the limits of the corresponding concept.[60] That the *eidos* possesses a normative function, that it bears within itself a rule of application to examples—this is what is implied by the "and so on" that belongs essentially to any eidetic variation. As Wittgenstein notes, "Essential to the expression of the rule is the occurrence of the words 'and so on' or of the dots used in the same sense."[61] For example, for the series of natural integers, three examples are as good as a thousand, but

the essential thing here is precisely that they are *examples* of the same general rule: "the generality lies precisely in the rule's specifying some examples of series of numbers with dots and its then saying: and so on."[62] Husserl says exactly the same thing, except that the "and so on" of eidetic variation derives from an objective necessity that belongs to the essential content of the thing and not solely to the meaning of words, that is, to the concepts that we use to describe it. The question that remains open, at this stage, is whether all possibility and all necessity are rooted in the meaning of the terms of our language, and are consequently purely conventional, or whether we shouldn't recognize in the domain of the conceptual the existence of possibilities and necessities other than those of our conventions themselves.

(2) As we have seen, eidetic intuition is not at all a mute intuition that could do without a linguistic mastery of "concepts" in the sense of "verbal meanings." Eidetic reduction is too subtle and complex an operation to be able to be carried out without the help of language. On this point, the Wittgensteinian is right, but as it turns out Husserl never said anything different. Despite some residual ambiguities, his thesis is not that the "real concepts" he speaks of, the *eide*, are offered to an intuition *independently from all language*, but rather that he or she who possesses a concept in the sense of a "verbal meaning" can always in principle turn toward the corresponding intuition, and thus obtain, for the meaning-intention intertwined with the verbal expression, an intuitive fulfillment. In other words, Husserl would hardly be embarrassed by the "grammatical" remark that intuition, if it exists, is extrinsic to the possession of a concept, in the sense that it does not constitute the criterion that justifies me in saying that I possess it. His thesis is not, as we saw in chapter 4, that every time I understand or use the word "book" I apprehend a general object, the book *in specie*, but only that to every concept understood as "verbal meaning" there *may* correspond an intuition of this object. Nothing in what Husserl says calls into question the autonomy of what Leibniz called symbolic or blind thought, that is, the purely operative use of signs.

Actually, the outcome of the whole debate depends on the way one interprets Husserl's already quoted sentence: the *eidos* is "*prior to all 'concepts,'* in the sense of verbal significations; indeed, as pure concepts, these must be made to fit the *eidos*." The nominalist objections reach no further than a naive conception of what this "fit" of concepts to the *eide* might be. Of course, if this assertion means that a concept must be acquired by means of a dumb eidetic intuition of private objects called "essences," the Wittgensteinian critique is on target. But since this reading is indefensible, the debate remains at least partially open.

It is on this basis that it becomes possible to formulate more precisely the phenomenologist's response. It is true that the nominalist has shown that the criteria for the possession of a concept are public. But a criterion is not a necessary and sufficient condition.[63] It is perfectly possible to concede that the criteria for the possession of a concept are public, without conceding that the concepts *are* by their very nature anything but the capacities that provide their criteria, and therefore that there is nothing more in a concept than the ability to use the word. At no time has the nominalist positively established that there are no objective common properties (the universals of the tradition) on which the acquisition and mastery of concepts, in the sense of verbal meanings, rests at least in part. At no time has he produced a decisive argument that would exclude the possibility that objective properties and objective material necessities may condition the rules, at least up to a point.

On this subject, let us consult §§66–67 of *Philosophical Investigations.* There Wittgenstein considers the well-known example of games—chess, card games, ball games, games of battle, and so on—and formulates the question as to whether it is possible to discover in this diversity a property shared by all these games. The belief in the existence of such a common property, so hints the text, is no more than a grammatical prejudice: "Don't say: 'There must be something common, or they would not be called *games*'—but look and see whether there is anything common to all.—For if you look at them you will not see something that is common to all, but similarities, relationships, and a whole series of them at that." The only thing that this examination reveals to us, Wittgenstein concludes, is "a complicated network of similarities overlapping and criss-crossing"—which he calls "family resemblances."[64]

It is difficult to separate the question of family resemblances from the critique of the Augustinian picture of language as developed by Wittgenstein. The strategy of this text, however, is somewhat reminiscent of that of the classic nominalist, which consisted in holding the relation of resemblance to be ultimate and unanalyzable. Perhaps after all there is nothing between the various uses of "game" but similarities or family resemblances. But the whole question—beyond the strictly Wittgensteinian framework—is how this notion of "resemblance" must be interpreted. What if the resemblances mentioned by Wittgenstein are to be understood as resemblances *in certain respects?* What if they belong to "spheres of resemblance" that in turn rest on an *identical* element? Nothing, in what Wittgenstein says, allows us to rule out that possibility. There is an interpretation of Wittgenstein's example that is perfectly compatible with a realism of universals: we can draw up the topography of the properties common to *some* games (chess and checkers are *identically* games with pieces, although the pawns in these two games are not the same), properties that sometimes overlap (for example, tennis is both a ball game, a game of endurance, a game of skill), while at the same time ruling out the idea that there is a common property running through the entire domain of games, that would make them *identically games.* There are common properties that intersect and overlap among the various games, without there being any one common property that corresponds to what it is to be a game in all these cases. But then, as David Armstrong remarks, from the point of view of the realism of universals, the only positive conclusion that is to be drawn from Wittgenstein's example is that "there is no automatic passage from predicates (linguistic entities) to universals."[65] To every predicate there does not *necessarily* correspond a common property. But even if a universal does not correspond to each predicate, it does not follow that universals do not correspond to at least *some* predicates; and this is all that is required to satisfy the realist.

Thus, the strategy of the new nominalist can only reach its goal if it has already been established that similarities (or family resemblances) rest on no identity in the strict and authentic sense. But it is not at all certain that this lesson can be drawn from Wittgenstein's example. Now, it suffices to admit *one sole universal,* one sole identical property common to all numbers or all triangles, for example, to refute nominalism. Wittgenstein seems, moreover, to hesitate between two positions that are not equivalent. Sometimes he asserts that the conception according to which concepts are common properties (or based on common properties) is "too primitive"[66]—which leaves open the possibility that *some* common properties exist on which the use of *some* concepts rests. At other times he seems to reject this last possibility: "To say that we use the word 'blue' to mean 'what all these shades of colour have in common' by itself says nothing more than that we use the word 'blue' in all these cases."[67] And even: "every species of tree is a 'tree' in a different sense of the word."[68] But the notion of resemblance thus extended to the entirety of the words of language is well-nigh absurd. How can it be said that the word "tree" has *a determinate use*—therefore a determinate sense—if all we have here is the infinite scintillation of language games and their family resemblances?

Part of the verisimilitude of Wittgenstein's position comes from the nature of the example he chooses. The fact that the word "game" designates a conventional activity is not indifferent to the plausibility of the thesis that there is no essence of game independent from what we understand by "game" on a case-by-case basis, according to our linguistic practice. But it is not at all certain that what is valid for concepts related to activities as conventional as games applies with the same right to concepts relating to entities as "natural" as trees or colors. To take other examples, is it certain that what we understand by "spatial object," "right angle," or "number" depend solely on a bundle of resemblances à la Locke between the uses of these expressions? This is the problem that the phenomenologist Karl Bühler already brought up in connection with the doctrine of Johannes von Kries, which anticipated, in some respects, Wittgenstein's "family resemblances." This doctrine, he said, may be valid for words like "house" or "burglary," but not for "red" or "blue."[69]

Basically, all that the phenomenologist needs for his descriptive undertaking to retain its meaning is to be granted the existence of some common properties that, moreover, are structured by necessary relations, by material *a priori* laws. In short, the phenomenologist does not have to yield to what is indeed probably a "grammatical prejudice," the belief that there is always something in common, an ideal object, "behind" each concept. There probably is no identical property that is common to a beautiful flower, a beautiful face, and a beautiful car, allowing all three to be qualified as "beautiful"; and it is precisely because the invariant features that phenomenology seeks to describe are generally not as obvious that phenomenology is a difficult undertaking. But to say that there is no property common to all these cases does not amount to saying that there is absolutely nothing common to them. It is here—if anywhere—that the work of the phenomenologist begins.

In any case, the position of the new nominalist harbors indeed a substantial claim and is nowise reducible to Wittgenstein's "Oh yes . . . , that is of course obvious."[70] Nothing is further from a mere "grammatical remark" than the idea, which actually goes as far back as Locke and is inseparable from the whole nominalist tradition, according to which "the mind *makes* concepts."[71] This conclusion derives from a whole arsenal of premises that ultimately lead back to the "arbitrariness of grammar," to the idea that the only necessities (hence also the only possibilities and impossibilities) that our conventions manifest are those of these conventions themselves. On the one hand, conventions and usages (habits, human institutions); on the other, an amorphous universe with no other binding element than hypothetical and therefore conjectural ties: this Humean framework is the product of a particular metaphysics. But we should refuse to jump to conclusions: because the relation of language to the world is conventional, it would be *purely* conventional; because there are grammatical necessities, *all* necessity would be grammatical. Nothing the nominalist says is of such a nature as to dismiss as absurd the search for universal properties, for structural invariants of our world experience, nor the search for necessary relations that may hold between these properties and that are not in the least derived from our conventions.[72]

Thus, it is perfectly possible to maintain at the same time that (1) we learn to use the word "triangle" without necessarily knowing any of the properties common to triangles—without knowing, for example, that the sum of their angles equals two right angles (similarly, we learn the word "color" and arrive at an understanding of its meaning without necessarily knowing that the chromatic colors are structured according to three axes: hue, lightness, and saturation)—and that (2) we can nevertheless *discover* in certain cases such properties, which the phenomenologist would call "essential properties." What we discover in this way is not a property of the meaning of the word "color," a property of the *concept* of color understood as "verbal meaning"; it is a property of color as such. The fact that to possess a concept means, among other things, to have mastered the employment-rules of a word, does not entail that all there is to know about a concept comes down to employment-rules, or that it is impossible to make (non-empirical) discoveries in the conceptual domain, or rather in the domain of essences, since the latter are not identical to our concepts. And of course if it is possible to make discoveries in the domain of essences, this means that there are non-empirical necessities that are not merely conventions forged and instituted by us: the material *a priori* of phenomenology.

It seems, moreover, that there is a true incoherence on the part of the new nominalist when he attempts to reduce all necessity to the conceptual sphere and all essence to grammar. The error he commits is to confuse the necessities that apply to our concepts with those that apply to the things of which these concepts are the concepts. Now, this difference is of the utmost importance. It is one thing to assert a truth in the conceptual domain, a truth about the concept "bachelor" for example ("all bachelors are unmarried" is a truth of this kind); it is quite *another* to assert an essential truth that rests on the specific identity of the objects pertaining to a certain domain (according to a recurrent example in Husserl, "all material things have spatial extension" is an essential truth belonging to the domain *material thing*). The difference of modal status between these two necessary truths—the one being relative to our concepts, the other relative to the things that fall under these concepts—can be clarified as follows. When we assert that the former truth (the one relative to our concepts) is a necessary one, we do not mean that bachelors cannot marry, but just that they cannot marry and *continue to be called "bachelors."* The impossibility in question concerns only the correct application of a word. With the latter truth, things are different. In saying of this truth that it is necessary, we do not mean that material things cannot cease occupying spatial extension *and continue to be called "material things."* We mean (for it is indeed of the thing, and no longer of the concept that we are speaking), that a material thing cannot exist without spatial extension—*period.* This necessary truth is no longer about language and our use of words; it is a truth about things and their natures. As Husserl insists, "the sentences 'based purely on the concepts (essences),' and 'springing from a mere analysis of word-meanings,' are only by equivocation equivalent."[73] It is, consequently, illegitimate to pass from the assertion that a bachelor as bachelor is necessarily unmarried to the assertion that it is necessary for a bachelor not to be married: the first assertion is about the concept of bachelor and it is true; the second is about bachelors themselves and it is false.[74]

Not only is the position that claims to reduce all necessity concerning the properties of things to a necessity concerning our concepts incapable of making this decisive distinction, but it ends in fact in an absurdity. Given that language itself is a "thing" of a specific sort, there must be necessary truths about that "thing" and its essence that are not truths about the concepts that we apply to it and about our language, because otherwise, if all the truths about language were only truths about the concepts we apply to it (hence truths about the language in which we conceive of language), it would follow that all truth about language would be a truth about a second language, and so on ad infinitum. As Jonathan Lowe remarks, the nominalist (whom he calls "conceptualist") "is at least committed to affirming that *concepts*—or, in another version, words—exist . . . *These, at least, are things* that the conceptualist must acknowledge to have identities, independently of how we conceive of them, on pain of incoherence in his position. The conceptualist must at least purport to understand what a concept or a word is . . . and thus grasp the essences of at least some things. And if of these things, why not of other kinds of things? Once knowledge of essences is conceded, the game is up for the conceptualist."[75] It is difficult, for example, to understand what the assertion underlying the new nominalism as a whole, "for a broad class of cases in which it is used, the meaning of a word is its use in language," could mean, if that assertion tells us nothing about *what a meaning is,* and consequently *what a word is.* Otherwise, what is its purpose? Is it limited to taking note of a convention, the one underlying our use of the *words* "meaning," "word," or "language"?

At this stage, the proponent of universals may shift the *onus probandi* onto his adversary. Indeed, when the new nominalist advances that for a broad class of cases meaning is use, or when he claims that a concept is the capacity to use a word intelligently, is he truly noting a convention or is he not rather, without admitting it, seeking a common property, a universal, an essence? That the word "dog" is a convention of English to refer to dogs, that is a fact; but that the word "dog" is a convention, is that in turn a convention of English? Is it conventional that language is conventional? Is it conventional that the word "dog" is conventional? Is it conventional that the meaning of a word is, in most cases, its use in language? It is easy to see the absurdity that characterizes the thesis (it matters little whether or not it is Wittgenstein's) that would do without any possibility of speaking of common properties necessary for the identity of anything, and would purport to replace them *always and everywhere* with the necessity of our norms of description.

Thus we are led to a variant of the argument already used by Husserl against traditional nominalism. Resemblances, he argued, cannot be unified solely by resemblances; otherwise language would become impossible, for there is at least something that cannot be unified solely by resemblances—the word "resemblance," and in fact the totality of words. Now it must be agued: even if our language games are often unified by family resemblances, it is absurd to say that the fact that our language games are unified by family resemblances is in turn something like a convention belonging to a language game—the one that we play with the expressions "family resemblance" and "language."

10

Essentialism without Essences?

The journey we have taken through the quarrel between realism and nominalism has brought us the first elements of a response. First of all, even the most radical nominalism, inaugurated by Wittgenstein, cannot claim any status other than that of a substantial philosophical thesis. Secondly, there is no decisive argument to dismiss the idea of common properties that would correspond to at least *some* concepts. Lastly, the most radical conventionalism, which reduces all search for common properties and essences to grammatical remarks, fails precisely where traditional nominalism did: with language and concepts. For the fact that meaning is use, to take but one example, cannot be merely a convention about the meaning of the word "meaning." Sooner or later, even the linguistic philosopher must ask himself questions about real essences, be it only about the real essences that configure the field of language.

For all that, the debate between realism and nominalism is far from being settled. But perhaps it does not have to be, in order for the possibility of descriptions of essence of the kind advanced by phenomenology to receive a methodological elucidation. Indeed, could there not be descriptions of essence without there necessarily being *objects* or *entities* endowed with a particular status that would have to be called "essences"? On this hypothesis, one could maintain that phenomenology discovers essential necessities in the phenomenal field, without thereby supporting any realism of universals. A defense of the notion of "description of essence" would no longer have to subscribe to the legacy of Platonism. There would be an *essentialism without essences.* The task of this chapter is to give consistency and credit to that formula.

At the beginning of *Ideas I,* Husserl defines phenomenology by three characteristics that he takes to be equivalent: "phenomenology will become established here as a science of essence—as an '*a priori*' or, as we also say, an eidetic science."[1] Let us leave aside the title "science" and examine that equivalency itself. In Husserl's view, to interrogate oneself about essences amounts to interrogate oneself about *eide,* that is, general objects, Platonic entities. These essences are, moreover, *a priori.* Let us reserve the problem of the *a priori* for the next chapter. What does the first equivalence suggest to us? It is part of a tradition that goes back to Plato himself. It was Plato who first called essences "ideas"—that is, who used *eidos, idea,* and *ousia* almost interchangeably. The presupposition underlying his conception may be formulated as follows: as soon as we apply a predicate to objects—the predicate "blue," for example, to several shades of blue, it is necessary that there exist a property common to these shades that makes them shades *of blue,* and that general property is nothing other than the idea under which they fall, the *hen epi pollōn,* the *eidos* that bears within itself the specific identity for all the shades in question. In other words, *to every concept as verbal meaning there* must *correspond one and only one essence.*

It is this prejudice that the detour through the nominalist objections began to undermine. After all, there may not be any property common to all the games, making them all identically *games* and constituting their essence. But then Platonism in its strict form, which equates concept (idea) with essence, becomes problematic. It may be that in the case of games we can enumerate everything to which the word "game" applies, imagine all kinds of games, without grasping anything constituting the one, identical essence of game. On this hypothesis, the only thing an "eidetic variation" could do is to remind us of the arbitrary rules that we follow in the application of the word "game" to a set of human activities. It is true that all games are human (or eventually animal) activities, but there is no common property essential to all games in which their *specific* difference consists within the genus of activities in general. To every predicate there corresponds not *necessarily* a common property, nor, *a fortiori,* a common essence.

But this assertion does not suffice to make any search for essential truths futile; it only leads to calling into question the received equivalency between essence and *eidos.* Indeed, Husserl defends both the view that individuals and general properties (species and genera) *have* essences, and that these genera and these species *are* essences, so that whenever we speak meaningfully of "game," for example, we can grasp one or more properties essential to all games constituting the content of this concept. But it is perfectly possible to defend the first claim without adhering to the second. It suffices to maintain, with the nominalist, that the use of a number of predicates of our language does not require the existence of any (essential) property common to all the individuals to which this predicate applies—and so requires no *eidos* that would necessarily duplicate the concept, understood as verbal meaning; and that, nevertheless, essential common properties do exist in a number of cases, properties that *can* become the subject matter of an essential description. In the latter eventuality, the essences wouldn't have to be conceived of as *eide,* universals, or general objects of any kind. We could also abandon the simplistic image of meaning condemned by Wittgenstein, according to which whenever a predicate is applied to objects, universals distinct from the linguistic concepts—that is, from the meaning of predicates—must be postulated. *Essence is no longer a general object.* As a result the possibility of a coherent essentialism no longer depends on a commitment to the realism of universals. Instead of Platonism, that is, of a doctrine that makes an essence, conceived of as an ideal object, correspond to each concept, or instead of an *essentialism of essences*, what must be elaborated is an *essentialism of essential properties* claiming that essential properties are properties of a specific kind, but that not all applications of a predicate rest on an essential property.

To attempt to give form to this possibility, it is indispensable to sort out what must be kept and what abandoned in Husserl's doctrine of essences. In the process of doing so, we will see that this doctrine contains elements that are not specifically attached to Platonism. The consequences of this reform may in turn influence the phenomenological method itself, leading to a conception rather different from Husserl's of what a description of essence is (and isn't).

Of what is there essence? What is an essence? What is the status of an essential necessity? In the following analyses, I will try to address these questions without taking a stand for or against the existence of universals. Indeed, it is one thing to determine whether we should accept properties (being a color, for example) conceived of as universals, as distinct from particular properties, sometimes called "tropes"; it is quite another to determine whether we should accept essential properties as distinct from accidental ones. The first question involves considerations about ontological economy: an ontology that accepts universal properties alongside particular ones may be simpler than a nominalist ontology that must account for these universal properties in terms of resemblances without identity. The second problem leads to an inquiry into the existence of essential necessities as distinct from necessities that govern the use of our predicates, that is, from Wittgenstein's "grammatical" necessities. In any case, *even if it were conceded to the new nominalist that properties in general have no other "existence" than a linguistic one (through the predicate that expresses them), it would not follow that essential necessities are no more than linguistic necessities, that is, necessities relative to the use of our predicates.*

In what follows, I will express myself most often in a way that conforms to realism, and yet, as we shall see, the characterization I propose of essence is compatible with a refusal of general objects. Even if essences are not eternal, changeless objects, propositions of essence and descriptions of essence remain possible.

Two kinds of essentialism are to be found in Husserl: an essentialism regarding individuals, and an essentialism regarding properties, and therefore two kinds of essences: individual and general. "Individual existence of every sort is," he explains, "quite universally speaking, '*contingent.*' . . . [Now] *it belongs to the sense of anything contingent to have an essence.*"[2] For example, Socrates has an individual essence that makes him the individual he is, differing from other individuals who share with him the common property of being human beings. But the property of being a human being also has an essence, which makes of that property the property that it is, in contrast with other properties.[3]

How can essence as such be characterized more precisely? For an individual object, Husserl writes, it consists in "its stock of *essential* predicates which must belong to it (as 'an existent such as it is in itself.')"[4] This characterization of essence—probably the most precise to be found in Husserl's entire corpus—is prima facie circular. To define essence by a stock of *essential* predicates is to define essence by essence. But to stop at this apparent circularity would be tantamount to missing what is most interesting about this definition, namely the specification contained in the parenthesis: essence is the manifold of predicates essential to a thing (or a property), *that is,* the manifold of predicates necessary to the thing's being "such as it is in itself [*als "Seiendem, wie er in sich selbst ist"*]." It suffices to replace "essential predicates" with "predicates necessary to a thing's being what it is" or "predicates necessary for the identity of that thing" for the appearance of circularity to disappear. To speak here of *what a thing is,* of its *ti esti,* or of *what it is to be that thing,* that is, of its identity, does not amount to speaking of identity in the logico-formal sense of the *relation of identity* which that thing maintains with itself and with no other thing. Essence, in Aristotelian terms, is what answers the question *ti esti?*—namely the set of predicates that define the *to ti ēn einai,* the "what" that the thing "is" or better, the "what it is to be [that thing]" or yet again the "what it is [for that thing] to be the thing it is [it was]"[5]—what Latin expresses as *quidditas.* The identity in question is therefore the one that appears in a definition (*horismos*).[6] But, as Aristotle himself specifies, if the definition is the logos of the essence, it does not follow that the essence pertains to logos alone: there is essence in the case of *real* definitions, which tell us what the thing (*res*) is, while some predicates (goatstag, square circle) can only have a nominal definition, because they have no corresponding essence.[7] The essence is about the thing and not only about the predicates. Consequently *a property is essential if it is necessary for the thing's being what it is*, and if not, it is accidental. Since individual objects can have an essence as well as general properties, the individual essence, that is, the set of predicates necessary for an individual to be the *individual* it is, distinct from all other individuals falling under the same genus, must be distinguished from the generic essence, the set of predicates necessary for an individual's being the *kind* of individual that it is, or for a property's being the *kind* of property it is.

But what does the clause "necessary in order for *x* to be what it is" mean? Husserl makes an important clarification on this point: essence is defined in terms of necessity, but necessity does not suffice to define essence. "Now, it is important," he writes, "to respect distinctions of meaning and above all not to designate generality of essence [*Wesensallgemeinheit*] itself as necessity [*Notwendigkeit*] (as is customarily done)."[8] This clarification is crucial, as it sets up a strict demarcation between essential necessity and necessity without qualification. It rules out *a strictly modal definition of essence.* Indeed, to say that a predicate is essential is to say that it is necessary, but the converse is not true: it is not enough for a predicate to be necessary for it to be essential. Or, to put it differently, a proposition of essence is a proposition true in all possible worlds, and therefore necessary, but all necessary propositions, that is, true in all possible worlds, are not propositions of essence. Why? Husserl does not answer this question in §6 of *Ideas I*, but one of his disciples, Jean Hering, endeavors to do so in a 1921 text that constitutes a long commentary on the first chapter of *Ideas I.* There are properties, he stresses, that derive necessarily from essence, while not being a part of its content. "From the essence of a sphere with a diameter of one meter, it follows with absolute necessity that it is smaller than a cube with an edge of one meter; now, this does not *belong* to its essence; for its essence is what it is, regardless of the existence of other solids or the lack thereof."[9] Thus, the pair necessary/contingent does not coincide with the pair essential/accidental, because the mention of essence introduces an extra-logical element, an element of *relevance* of the property under consideration, which is contained in the clause "for the thing's being what it is"—that element having no equivalent from the point of view of modal logic. The truth of the proposition that attributes an essential property (or that attributes a property essentially) is not necessary *in an unqualified way*; it is necessary *by virtue of the identity of the object.* We might even possibly agree about all the necessary properties, and still not agree about those that are essential. To take another example, it is a truth of set theory that, necessarily, each element belongs to at least one set. Therefore it is *necessary* that a given cat (Felix) belongs to a set (for example, to the singleton containing Felix as its only member). But it is not *essential* to Felix, or to cats in general, to belong to any sets whatsoever. Even if it is essential to the singleton containing Felix as its sole element that it contains Felix as its sole element, it is not essential to Felix that Felix belongs to this singleton. Here we find an *asymmetry* that is a distinctive feature of assertions of essence. In modal logic, there is nothing that corresponds to this asymmetry, since the proposition that "it is necessary that the singleton 'Felix' contains Felix" is indifferent to the fact that the one or the other—the cat or the set—plays the role of the logical subject of the proposition.

The outcome of these considerations is that Husserl would reject a modal characterization of essence like the one favored by many contemporary authors, according to which an object's property can be called essential if and only if it is necessary (that is, true in all possible worlds) that this object possesses this property.[10] Husserl would accept to say that if a property is essential to an object it is necessary for that object to possess that property (or to possess that property *if it exists*), but he would reject the converse. We are therefore witnessing a true reversal of perspective in respect to any modal characterization of essence, since we must henceforth say that *unconditional necessities have their source in essences, and not the other way round.* In Husserl's terms, material necessities are rooted in "material essences," and formal necessities in "formal essences," each of these two kinds of essence constituting the object proper, respectively, to material and formal ontologies. Let us bear in mind that what Husserl means by "ontology" is an *a priori* doctrine of the object[11] (in which "object" must be taken in the most formal sense of "subject of true predicative judgments").[12] Formal ontology is *formal* in the sense that it bears upon objects conceived of as pure, undetermined variables, that is to say, reduced to the pure form of *something.* "The *province* of a formal ontology," Husserl writes, "is said to be the 'formal region' of the object as conceived universally."[13] Indeed, formal idealities (object, state of affairs, unity, plurality, number, property, relation, whole, part, essence, genus, etc.) apply to any domain of objects whatsoever, regardless of the material content of these objects, that is to say, of the region of reality to which they belong. Since formal essences (obtained by the substitution of variables for all the material terms, or by "formalization") only apply to the pure form of *something in general,* formal ontology—like formal logic[14]—is governed by analytic necessities. Material ontologies, on the other hand, introduce considerations on the "nature" of their objects; they take into account the dependency of these objects with respect to general properties that delimit the various regions of reality (material thing, lived experience, consciousness, tones, color, and so on); therefore these ontologies are governed by synthetic *a priori* laws.

The reversal of perspective by virtue of which essence is not defined in terms of modality but rather that modalities are founded in essence gives the Husserlian conception all its originality. It is stated in §6 of *Ideas I*. We find in this passage the following two claims. (a) Although eidetic generality and eidetic necessity are strict correlates, since eidetic generality is an *unrestricted* generality (valid for all possible worlds) and the necessity of a proposition of essence signifies its truth in all possible worlds, eidetic generality and necessity *in general* cannot be considered identical. (b) This particular sort of necessity, essential necessity (*Wesensnotwendigkeit*), is a "particularization" (*Besonderung*) "of a state of affairs endowed with eidetic generality,"[15] that is, a particularization of "essential laws [*Wesensgesetzen*]."[16] *Essence is therefore at the foundation of all necessity in the strong sense of the term, of all unconditional necessity.* Thus, for example, the necessary propositions that "every ashtray is a material body" or that "every ashtray has spatial extension" draw their necessity from "regional axioms" that govern the highest generic essence of the corresponding material domain, namely the essence *material thing*. Since it results from the essence of the material thing in general that every material thing has spatial extension,[17] and since every ashtray is a material thing, it follows that every ashtray is also a spatially extended object, so that the necessity of this last proposition *follows* from the necessity of "regional axioms," that is, from the most universal truths of essence of the region under consideration. The same is true of the essential formal (analytic) necessities that have their source in formal essences: "2 + 2 = 4," "There is no whole without parts," and so on. In sum, as Jitendra Nath Mohanty remarks, the singularity of Husserl's position is not only to hold that the essential modalities are irreducible to logical modalities, but to add that logical modalities are particular instances of essential modalities: "For Husserl, essential possibility is the key concept, 'logical possibility' is subordinated to it. A notion of 'essential possibility' that is irreducible to the merely logical, is his original contribution."[18]

This reversal by virtue of which the unconditional necessity of the propositions that are valid in all possible worlds is rooted in essence, instead of essence being defined in modal terms, was already present in *Logical Investigations*, since in that work Husserl understood objective necessity in terms of pure lawfulness (*Gesetzlichkeit*) and defined pure lawfulness in terms of essence: "The essence of all objective necessity resides and finds its definition in a lawfulness [*Gesetzlichkeit*] determined in each case,"[19] he wrote. Now, the laws are subdivided into empirical (*a posteriori*) laws, and "pure laws"[20] (either analytic-formal, or material, that is, synthetic *a priori*). These pure laws have their source in essences, in material essences, for example: "The 'necessity' relevant to our discussion of non-independent 'moments' stands for an ideal or *a priori* necessity rooted in material essences."[21]

This analysis of the concept of essence is not in the least a mere doxographic curiosity. Some of its main aspects—its general characterization of essence, the irreducibility of necessities of essence to logical necessities, the reversal by which, if essence cannot be defined in terms of necessity, necessity *can* be defined in terms of essence—have been "rediscovered" in the course of the last two decades and serve as a starting point for an undertaking that stands apart from the dominant presuppositions of analytic philosophy in the way it approaches the complex relations between essence and modality.

In a paper that has contributed much to a resurgence of a form of essentialism in contemporary philosophy, and especially in what is generally known as "analytic metaphysics," Kit Fine has produced a logical analysis of essence astonishingly close to Husserl's, even in the choice of examples. Fine, although he never refers to the characterization of §2 of *Ideas I* (the permanent stock of necessary predicates for a thing to be "such as it is in itself"), coincides with it almost word for word, since he characterizes essential properties as those which an object "must have 'if it is to be the object that it is.'"[22] "A property of an object is essential," he writes, "if it must have the property to be what it is; otherwise the property is accidental."[23] Even more significantly, Fine rejects a modal characterization of essence—"the contemporary assimilation of essence to modality is fundamentally misguided"[24]—on the basis of examples analogous with Hering's: "Consider two objects whose natures are unconnected, say Socrates and the Eiffel Tower. Then it is necessary that Socrates and the Tower be distinct. But it is not essential to Socrates that he be distinct from the Tower; for there is nothing in his nature which connects him in any special way to it."[25] The class of necessary truths is therefore broader than that of essential truths. Since the essential predicates of an object cannot be equated with its necessary predicates, Fine even concurs with the *apparent* circularity of Husserl's definition: "The essence of an object can be identified with the class of its essential properties"[26]—to be understood, of course: with the class of properties necessary for it to be what it is. But above all, Fine agrees at the conclusion of his analysis of essence with Husserl's central intuition: all essential attribution of a property gives rise to a necessary truth, nowise to a truth that is necessary *in an unqualified way*, but to a truth that is necessary by virtue of the identity of the object in question, so that "the necessity has its source in those objects which are the subject of the underlying essentialist claim";[27] and therefore, Fine concludes, "it seems to me that far from viewing essence as a special case of metaphysical necessity, we should view metaphysical necessity as a special case of essence. For each class of objects, be they concepts or individuals or entities of some other kind, will give rise to its own domain of necessary truths, the truths which flow from the nature of the objects in question."[28] On this point, Fine refers explicitly to *Logical Investigations*—this is in fact the only mention of Husserl to be found here—and especially to §7 of the third *Investigation* in which Husserl speaks about an "*a priori* necessity rooted in material essences."[29]

It is true that on this point the conceptions of Fine and Husserl diverge. Fine does not adopt the distinction between formal and material essences. To him, all cases of essential necessity are cases of "metaphysical" necessity, and metaphysical necessity is neutral with respect to the Husserlian distinction between the analytic-formal and the synthetic-material. It is a "logical necessity in the broad sense"[30] that is, a necessity that is valid for all objects whatsoever,[31] which is to be understood as including both things and concepts. Thus, there are metaphysically necessary truths that concern mere concepts, that is, verbal meanings, or—as Fine also says, using an expression that irresistibly brings Husserl to mind—"the meaning's essence" of the terms. "All bachelors are unmarried" is a necessary truth of this kind.[32] As for logical truths, they are metaphysically necessary by virtue of the nature of all logical concepts.[33] But in addition to these necessary truths in the conceptual order, there are truths that are necessary by virtue of the (real) objects to which they refer. The former give rise to "a sentence which is true in virtue of the meaning of the term while [the latter] result in a proposition which is true in virtue of the identity of the object."[34] In sum, the necessities Fine continues to call "analytic" are particular instances of metaphysical necessities: they are metaphysical necessities that exist "in virtue of the meaning of all the terms"[35] (there are also *local forms* of analyticity in the case of propositions that are true by virtue of the meaning of *some* terms: "All bachelors are unmarried"); while the metaphysical necessities that Fine does not further specify, but that follow, not from the essence of the meanings, but from the essence of the objects, are those which Husserl would have called "material." The essential necessity in this last case is a local form of metaphysical necessity that rests on the identity of *some* objects.

Although the conceptualities of Fine and Husserl are not homogeneous, the fact remains, to revert to an expression of the former, that "the underlying idea is the same."[36] What Fine rejects in Husserl is, first, the commitment to Platonism that makes essences universals, and, second, the apriority of these essences. But Fine shares the main idea with Husserl, namely that necessities in the conceptual (logical-semantic) order and necessities in the real order (those necessities involving the introduction of real definitions) are two *distinct* cases of "metaphysical" necessity, or, as Husserl would have it, *unconditioned* necessity, as distinct from the conditioned—because hypothetical—necessity of the empirical sciences.[37] The idea that analytic metaphysical necessities are those which rest on the meaning of our concepts, and Fine's unqualified metaphysical necessities are those resting on the identity of objects, presents a striking analogy to the Husserlian idea of necessities of equal rank, sometimes rooted in formal essences, that is to say, relative to the pure form of *something* in general, and sometimes rooted in material essences.

Fine's main break from Husserl is his refusal to make the commitment to the idea of essence depend on the hypothesis of the existence of entities that would themselves *be* essences. To be sure, Husserl points out that essences are not "*objects upon which* [*Gegenständen-worüber*]" the description of essence bear,[38] but he maintains nonetheless that essences *are* objects. Why is it preferable not to hypostatize essences, but rather to define them in terms of essential properties (that is, of properties necessary to the identity of something)?

A first reason is that the Platonist hypostatization inevitably leads to an infinite regress. If essences are ideas or species, that is, ideal objects, these objects must possess essences. But if these essences of essences are in turn objects, they must possess an essence, and so on. We could not know the least essence without knowing by this very fact an infinite number of essences. This argument, on the face of it, does not seem to apply to Husserl's conception. Indeed, by virtue of his distinction between material essences, which are arranged by genera and species according to different degrees of generality (for example, animal in general and man in general) and formal essences (for example, the essences of *genus*, *species*, or *essence*) which are all situated on the same plane, Husserl can perfectly well maintain that material essences have a (formal) essence, which is *to be* essences, but that the regression stops at formal idealities which are ultimate in their own order and only belong to formal ontologies. In other words, from Husserl's point of view, a material essence does not *have* an essence in the same sense in which it *is* itself an essence (for several individuals falling under it), that is to say, in the sense in which it *is* an identical property common to several individuals; it does not have an essence that would in turn be a genus under which it would fall; it has no *material* essence, and thus an infinite regress cannot even begin. But the problem does seem to arise, at least at the level of the formal essences themselves; for these are ideal objects, that is, essences. But if the formal essences fall beneath the *formal* category of essence, and if that formal category is in turn an essence, then an infinite regress is inevitable.

A second, stronger reason is that the fact of attributing an essential property to an object does not amount to asserting that this object bears a relationship of ontological dependency with respect to a common property (a universal) that *would be* this essence.

This can be shown by setting out from the two main forms that a judgment of essence may take: (1) a judgment of essence can be formulated by means of a predicative modifier: "*a* is essentially *G*" ("Socrates is essentially a man"); or (2) this judgment can be expressed by a propositional modifier: "It is true by virtue of what *a* is that *p*" ("It is true by virtue of what Socrates is that Socrates is a man").

In conformity with these two formulations of essence, essence can be defined in two ways: (1) the essence of an object is the class of its essential properties; (2) the essence of an object is the class of the propositions that are true by virtue of what it is.

The problem now is whether the judgments of essence imply any commitment whatsoever to the idea that Socrates exemplifies a universal, the common property of being a man. Let us limit ourselves to the first of these two formulations. Is the assertion that (A) "Socrates is essentially a man" logically equivalent to the assertion that (B) "Socrates has essentially the property of being a man"? The answer is an unambiguous no. Indeed, the second formulation adds something to the first: it not only says that Socrates is essentially a man, but it goes further by saying that Socrates entertains essentially a certain relation, namely a relation of exemplification, with respect to a property, the property of being a man, and therefore that Socrates is ontologically dependent on that property: what it is to be Socrates depends essentially on what it is to be a man. But it is perfectly possible to hold that what it is to be Socrates does not depend essentially on any property. The difference results from the fact that in proposition (A) Socrates appears in subject (or argument) position, while the property occupies the position of the predicate, whereas in (B) the property of being a man appears in subject (or argument) position: this proposition tells us that there is a property of which it is true, and essentially true, that Socrates possesses it. As Fine remarks, "We are not merely appealing to the property in order to say how Socrates is; we are also explicitly saying how Socrates is related to the property."[39] We are no longer only saying that Socrates is essentially a man, we are asserting in addition that there is a property to which Socrates is related in a specific way, in that he exemplifies it. Now, it is perfectly possible to think that Socrates is essentially a rational animal without thinking that he is essentially related to any universal property whatsoever by any relation, be it that of exemplification.

Naturally this logical argument does not allow us to *exclude* an interpretation of the assertions of essence in terms of the exemplification of certain properties—thus ruling out a *philosophical* claim, that of the realism of universals. But it allows us to establish that a commitment to essentialism is not intrinsically dependent on a commitment to that philosophical claim, and consequently that it is possible to retain the guiding principle of Husserl and of phenomenology in general according to which descriptions of essence are possible, while avoiding recourse to ideal, immutable, and eternal objects in which essences *would consist.* And therefore to escape the essence-*eidos* equivalency, which seals the fate of Platonism from its origin up to and including Husserl.

This point brings us back to the suspicion with which this chapter began. If all essence is an *eidos,* the temptation is strong to think that for every predicate there must necessarily be a corresponding essence, *that is to say,* a general property; thus we are brought back to one of the most important aspects of "the Augustinian picture of language" strongly criticized by Wittgenstein. Now, there are clearly predicates to which no universal property can correspond, be it only the predicate "__ is a property that does not self-exemplify." There can be no property such that it is the property of not self-exemplifying, since, if such a property exists, it self-exemplifies if and only if it doesn't self-exemplify; and yet even if no property can correspond to this predicate, it does not follow that a property that does not self-exemplify has no essential properties; it is by essence at least two things: a property, and a property that does not self-exemplify. Therefore an essential attribution does not always necessarily entail the existence of a universal property.[40] In short, an essentialism of properties is nowise forced to subscribe to a realism of essential properties.

There is thus no longer any difficulty in defending an *adverbial* conception of essence: there are no essences as ideal objects, but things are *essentially* such and such.[41] This conception has non-negligible consequences for a characterization of the phenomenological method. Indeed, the last, and probably the most important of the reasons conducive to the greatest suspicion with respect to a Platonism of essences within the framework of phenomenology is the following. Once the existence of atemporal or supertemporal ideal entities has been granted—and furthermore of ideal entities which are graspable by means of an intuition of essence (*Wesensschau*)—it is no longer possible to consider phenomenological description otherwise than as an ahistorical activity. One sinks into a form of extreme dogmatism from which Husserlian phenomenology has not been entirely able to escape. To do phenomenology would be to seize atemporal essences that exist independently from us, and to express them in pure descriptions. But if essences *aren't* anything, no entity of any sort but solely *that which is brought to light in a description of essence,* a new avenue is opened up for a completely reconsidered essentialism—a possibility we shall try to explore in chapters 11 and 12—beyond the dogmatism of principle of *Husserlian* phenomenology. Essences will no longer appear as those atoms of eternity whose disclosure might be conceived of as being independent from any interest, any presupposition, any historical perspective. Descriptions of essence become an infinitely more complex activity than that foreshadowed by Husserl's eidetics.

We must conclude by pointing out a number of limitations that seem inherent in Fine's analysis of essence.

First, Fine's approach only concerns itself with the essential properties of objects, and not the essential properties of properties. Now, it is especially the latter that interest the phenomenologist. Phenomenology is not particularly interested in the question of what it is to be Socrates or what it is to be the number 3; but rather in what it is to be an object of perception, imagination, or recollection. The kind of essential relation from which a phenomenological description sets out is exemplarily that between the fact of being a spatial thing and the fact of being perceived by silhouettes or adumbrations (*Abschattungen*), or the fact of being a tone and that of having a pitch, a timbre, and an intensity. Therefore it is necessary to broaden Fine's analysis of essence to include the case of *essential properties of properties*—hence to examine, in addition to individual essences, generic ones.

The two forms taken by generic judgments of essence—that is, judgments about essences that are relative to properties—are analogous to those we have just noted for essences relative to individuals. Judgments about individual essence can be expressed, let us recall, either by means of a predicative modifier, or by means of a propositional modifier. The same is true of judgments about generic essence: (1) (a) "An ashtray is essentially a spatial thing," (b) "A spatial object is essentially an object given by adumbrations"; (2) (a) "It is true by virtue of what it is to be an ashtray that ashtrays are spatial things," (b) "It is true by virtue of what it is to be a spatial object that spatial objects are given by adumbrations." The two examples mentioned in (1) and (2) are not equivalent. For the first two cases (1a and 2a), we have a relation of subsumption between essences: every ashtray is a spatial thing, but every spatial thing is not an ashtray. In the two last cases (1b and 2b), on the contrary, what is at stake is, as Husserl would have said, a relation of "reciprocal dependency" between essences: every spatial object is perceived by adumbrations and every object perceived by adumbrations is spatial.

It is important to emphasize that the argument applied above to individual essences, by virtue of which it was established that being a man, for Socrates, was not logically equivalent to exemplifying the property of being a man, now applies to properties. *To say that there are properties essential to properties is not necessarily to assert that it is essential to properties to exemplify properties; therefore it is not necessarily to subscribe to a realism of universals.* To say that red is essentially a color and to say that it is essential to red to exemplify the property of being a color do not amount to the same thing, since the latter of these two assertions makes the property of being red essentially dependent on the existence of a second property, being a color, which the first property exemplifies. But it is perfectly possible to defend the idea that the property of being red is not ontologically dependent on any other property whatsoever.[42] Of course it can be argued that a realism of universals is the philosophical position that has the most "affinities" with this analysis of essence, but the important thing is to grasp why it is not *necessary* to its formulation. Even if the most "natural" idiom for the expression of an essentialism of essential properties is that of properties understood as universals, it is not excluded that this essentialism could be formulated in another idiom, that of particular properties (Husserl's "moments," or the "tropes" of contemporary metaphysics), and therefore in an idiom that would itself be compatible with a form of nominalism.

A second questionable point in Fine's analysis is that it does not settle the issue, to which we will return in the next chapter, of whether all essences and all descriptions of essence are or are not *a priori*. Fine sides against the assignation of an *a priori* status to every essence, but says nothing further about it. For Husserl, and probably for every consistent phenomenology, a description of essence—in the sense relevant here—must precede de jure the empirical developments of science; it is prior to any empirical hypothesis in the sense that it makes it possible.

Thirdly, Fine speaks as if essence *were* either a class of essential properties, or, more problematically, a class of propositions that are true by virtue of what *x* is.[43] But it is difficult to see how essence could *be* a class of propositions—it is rather *that which is expressed by that class.* This remark is not just incidental. The refusal to make essence, that is, what something (object, event, property) *is*—or what it is to be that thing, or yet again what it is for that thing to be the thing it is—into an entity or a being of any kind, must not lead, on the other hand, to relegating this essence to language alone, or to those paradoxical "objects" called propositions. Essence is neither an entity, of which we would have to wonder in turn how it is, nor a characteristic of the statements that express it. It is quite precisely this "neither . . . nor . . ." that constitutes one of the most important aspects (not the only one, to be sure) of what Heidegger has called "ontological difference." What a thing is, its *ousia,* in the terminology of Plato and Aristotle, or its Being in that of Heidegger, is precisely not something, an entity or a manifold of ontic properties, but neither is it an ontic characteristic that would be possessed by statements or by the meaning of those statements: Being *is nothing that is.* Regardless of whether or not the Heideggerian approach to the problem is satisfactory, it is not unrelated to the considerations that have occupied us throughout the present chapter.

In light of these analyses, we can characterize phenomenology as the discipline whose goal is the uncovering of essences, essential relations and essential necessities that are operative in the field of phenomena, that is, in the field of our experience as such. This characterization requires further clarification on several points. It could prove to be partial and even insufficient. Nevertheless, already at this point I can stress that the overall perspective of phenomenology, even reinterpreted in light of a characterization of essence like the one Fine has elaborated in the wake of Husserl, does not coincide with the overall perspective of a *metaphysics of essence* that implicitly stands in the background of Fine's analyses. Indeed, although "metaphysical necessity" as understood by Fine does in fact enable us to distinguish truths that are necessary by virtue of logical concepts alone, truths necessary by virtue of the meaning of *some* concepts ("All bachelors are unmarried"), which are not identical to logical truths *stricto sensu,* and lastly truths necessary by virtue of the identity of *objects,* marking off the domain proper to an "analytic metaphysics"—a domain that corresponds pretty well to the one that Husserl claimed for his material necessities—it should not be hastily concluded that phenomenology is merely a province within metaphysics conceived as a science of essences in general. From its very origin, phenomenology has always refused to understand itself as *ancilla metaphysicae.* It pursues the Kantian critique of metaphysics by claiming that what it is possible to furnish a description of essence of is not reality in itself, envisaged from a quasi-divine point of view—the point of view which still dominates in the contemporary versions of "analytic metaphysics"—but only reality *for us.* It is from the viewpoint of our experience and from this viewpoint alone that analyses of essence are possible. Hence phenomenology firmly criticizes the hubris of any method that would claim to tell us what things are, regardless of the way they *appear to us* in relation to our finite experience.

11

Essence, Necessity, *A Priori*

For Husserl and most of his successors, there is no doubt that descriptions of essence in general and essential descriptions of phenomena in particular are *a priori*. But is that claim of the *a priori* character of descriptions of essence tenable? The question seems all the more legitimate, since contemporary analytic philosophy was the theater of the upsurge of a new essentialism that epitomizes Kripke's assertion that "one might very well discover essence empirically."[1] According to Kripke, an assertion such as "water is H_2O" is certainly an empirical discovery; which does not prevent its being necessary in the strongest sense of the word. It is valid in all possible worlds in which water exists. And since essence is characterized by Kripke in modal terms, this necessary proposition about the molecular constitution of water is also, by this very fact, a proposition of essence.

Are essences *a priori*? On what concept of essence is such a view based? Does this claim of the *a priori* character of essences conflict with the scientific essentialism that is presently the object of a renewed interest in the mainstream of analytic philosophy? Furthermore, is the presumed *a priori* character of essences in contradiction with the idea that descriptions of essence may eventually depend, at least partially, on considerations foreign to essence: interests that underlie description, historical presuppositions, the formulation of philosophical problems to which descriptions of essence are intended to respond? Moreover, can we speak of *the* essence of something, in an unqualified way?

Jean Hering, in the passage in which he attempted to explain why essential necessity is irreducible to necessity without qualification, furnished not one, but two examples of a necessity that *derives* from essence but is not itself an essential necessity. We have already examined the first of these examples: "From the essence of a sphere with a diameter of one meter, it follows with absolute necessity that it is smaller than a cube with an edge of one meter; now, this does not *belong* to its essence; for its essence is what it is, regardless of the existence of other solids or the lack thereof." The text continues as follows: "*Necessary to essence relatively* to certain circumstances is for example the fall of a stone (this reveals itself to be necessary to essence the moment certain conditions are met). Similarly, *founded* on essence, though not taking place necessarily, is for example the fall of a stone *purely and simply*, regardless of any particular condition. On the basis of the essence of stone, it is manifest that this event *can* take place. Assuredly, essence prefigures what destiny its bearer *can* undergo, in what relations it *can* be found."[2] The necessity under consideration in the first example is a pure necessity, that is, an *a priori* necessity. In the second example, on the other hand, we have a case of empirical necessity. Neither the one nor the other, Hering tells us, belongs to the content of essence properly speaking, although they both have—differently—their source in it. However, Hering does not specify further how empirical necessities can be grounded in essential necessities.

To address this problem, we must return briefly to the results of chapters 1 and 10. We have seen in the last chapter in what sense, in Husserl's view, all necessity in the strong sense, that is to say, all unconditional necessity (what is necessary, in this sense, is what is true in all possible worlds) follows from essence: a proposition is necessary because it is essential, and not the other way round. Essences are subdivided into formal and material. Necessary formal truths are analytic: they are true of *something* in general, that is, they authorize the substitution of variables for all material terms. "There is no whole without parts," "If *a is* greater than *b* and *b* is greater than *c*, then *a* is greater than *c*" are truths of this kind. The other necessary truths, which Husserl calls "material," are synthetic *a priori*. They rest on "material axioms" that delimit the possible and the impossible within a given kind of object, within a particular ontic region, for example: "All material things have spatial extension." Thus, a statement such as "all statues are extended" is an (absolutely) necessary truth, because it follows from that material axiom of the region *material thing in general*. That proposition is true in all possible worlds and its negation is a material contradiction (*Widersinn*) since the state of affairs it expresses, that of a statue lacking all spatial extension, is inconceivable. By this assertion, we do not mean that we cannot use the words "statue" and "spatial thing" in that way, by virtue of our linguistic conventions, but that—whatever our conventions—the state of affairs itself is *a priori* impossible.

Unconditional necessities derive from pure essences and pure essences (which must be distinguished from mere eidetic generalities) are all *a priori*, whether they are formal or material.[3] Consequently, essential necessities are themselves *a priori*: "An *a priori* necessity [is] a necessity grounded in pure essence."[4] Why is this so? The answer is that it is not even possible to conceive a state of affairs opposed to the necessary state of affairs according to which all material things are spatially extended. The knowledge of this state of affairs rests on no empirical generalization, no hypothesis that could be invalidated by a new experience, because a counter-experience (a counter-example) is not even *thinkable* here. This remark helps us to understand further the particular meaning that Husserl and his successors give to "a priori." This "multisignificant expression,"[5] as Husserl calls it, must be explained in the following way: a truth is *a priori* and, therefore, unconditionally necessary (true in all possible worlds) if and only if it cannot be invalidated by any conceivable experience (hence if it does not rest on any empirical generalization). It would not be an objection, for example, to point out in opposition to Husserl, that in order to know a formal-analytic truth of the type "*A and B* is true if *A* is true and *B* is true, and false in the three other cases," I can consult a handbook on logic, or even rely on hearsay and public opinion, and consequently know that truth *a posteriori*. "*A priori*," as that expression is used by Husserl, does not characterize the way in which I happen *in fact* to acquire an item of knowledge, but the way I *can* acquire it de jure. A truth (an item of knowledge) is *a priori* if I *can* acquire it without having recourse to an inductive generalization, that is to say, if it is not *necessary*, in order to acquire it, to resort to experience. This does not in the least imply that I cannot *also* have recourse to experience (in the case just mentioned, glance at a handbook on logic) to learn this truth. And this applies, of course, to analytic-formal truths as well as to material ones.

If laws of essence are necessary *a priori* laws, the laws of nature that belong to the precinct of the empirical sciences are not necessary in the same sense. They are merely contingent regularities. "These laws of Nature," writes Husserl, "express only *de facto* rules [*faktische Regelungen*]."[6] And therefore, "'Natural laws', laws in the sense of the empirical sciences, are not laws of essence (ideal, *a priori* laws): empirical necessity is no necessity of essence."[7] Or, since necessity can be formulated in terms of generality (necessary is that which is true in all possible worlds, contingent what is true in at least one possible world), "the *unrestricted generality of natural laws* must not be mistaken for *essential generality*."[8] The contingent regularities of the laws of nature are valid in this world, but other worlds governed by different laws are *thinkable*. For example, it is perfectly thinkable for the molecular constitution of water as revealed to us empirically to be H_3O. Or there is no intrinsic absurdity in imagining an experimental situation in which water would not dissolve sodium chloride, in a world in which the physical constants would have values slightly different from their actual ones and in which water molecules would not be able to overcome the electrostatic forces that ensure the cohesion of salt crystals. The regularities of nature are perhaps "necessary," but in a different sense: *on the condition* that the world is what it is. Their necessity is therefore conditional.

However, this conditional or *de facto* necessity is rooted in turn in truths of essence. Indeed, in order for *de facto* regularities to be the *actual* regularities of this world, they must first be possible regularities. In order for an empirical truth such as "the molecular composition of water is H_2O" to describe a real state of affairs, it must first describe a possible one. To be possible, these facts and these regularities must be neither formal (analytic) nor material contradictions. In other words, by virtue of the axiom according to which "*the cognition of 'possibilities' must precede the cognition of actualities* [der Wirklichkeiten],"[9] we must maintain that empirical truths and empirical necessities depend on pure truths and pure necessities, that is to say, on truths of essence and necessities of essence. As Husserl insists in the most important passage for his characterization of essence that I have already commented on, an individual object, a contingent This here (*ein Dies da*), "as qualitied '*in itself*' thus and so . . . has its *own specific character* [*Eigenart*], its stock of *essential* predicables which must belong to it (as an 'existent such as it is in itself') *so that other, secondary, relative determinations can belong to it.*"[10] It is on this point that Hering, too, insisted. Every contingent fact and every contingent regularity can only be what it is on the condition that it first satisfies the requirements of truths of essence: "*It belongs to the sense of anything contingent to have an essence.*"[11] More precisely, "The sense of this contingency . . . is limited in that it is correlative to a *necessity* . . . When we said that any matter of fact 'in respect to its own essence,' could be otherwise, we were already saying that *it belongs to the sense of anything contingent to have an essence, and therefore an* Eidos *which can be apprehended purely*; and this Eidos comes under *eidetic truths belonging to different levels of universality.*"[12]

The knowledge of essences precedes and grounds all empirical knowledge. As Husserl explains, "Although every eidetic science is necessarily independent of every science of matters of fact, the reverse holds, on the other hand, for the latter sciences. There is *no science of matters of fact* which, *were it fully developed as a science*, could be pure of eidetic cognitions and therefore *could be independent of the formal or the material eidetic sciences.*"[13] Thus, all facts must conform to the requirements of formal ontologies, of course, but also to the requirements of material ontologies. "Any matter of fact includes a *material* essential composition [*Wesensbestand*]; and any eidetic truth belonging to the pure essences comprised in that composition must yield a law by which the given factual singularity, like any other possible singularity, is bound."[14]

We can present, in synoptic form, Husserl's doctrine through the following theses:

(1) Pure necessities, pure possibilities and impossibilities derive from essence and laws of essence.
(2) Pure essences (formal and material) are *a priori*.
(3) Necessities of essence, possibilities and impossibilities of essence are *a priori*.
(4) They are subdivided into formal (analytic) and material (synthetic *a priori*): formal impossibilities are contradictions, material impossibilities "material contradictions [*Widersinn*]."
(5) Essences delimit the domains of the possible and the impossible.
(6) Empirical facts and empirical laws are contingent.
(7) Empirical necessities are not laws of essence; they are conditional (hypothetical) necessities and not unconditioned necessities.
(8) The knowledge of possibilities precedes the knowledge of realities.
(9) Everything that is contingent implies the possession of an essence.
(10) The knowledge of possibilities and impossibilities of essence must precede the knowledge of *de facto* (empirical) possibilities and impossibilities. Empirical necessities are founded in essential truths.
(11) The empirical truths of the empirical sciences are grounded in truths of essence.

The question arises as to whether this set of theses is coherent and whether some objections might not be fatal to it. Indeed, this entire edifice rests on the idea that the laws of nature are *contingent* laws, that is, laws such that it would be conceivable that they might not obtain in some possible worlds. Or, more profoundly, this entire edifice rests on the equivalency between *a priori* and necessary (in the unconditional sense) and *a posteriori* and contingent (necessary only as long as it is not invalidated by a new experience). For Husserl, what is epistemologically contingent (*a posteriori*), that is, what is such that it could have been found to be other than it is, is also ontologically contingent. Similarly, what is epistemologically necessary (*a priori*), that is, what is such that it is inconceivable for it to have been otherwise, is also, and by this very fact, ontologically necessary. According to his formulation, the "incapacity-to-*represent*-things-otherwise" signifies the objective necessity of an "inability-to-*be*-otherwise."[15] But is this double equivalency of the *a priori* and the necessary, of the *a posteriori* and the contingent, tenable? Are the empirical truths of the natural sciences, despite their empirical origin, truths such that they might conceivably not be the case? Are they not on the contrary necessary truths in the strong, "metaphysical" sense of the term, as Kripke contends?

This question is difficult, because, as we shall see, Kripke's conceptuality is so far from Husserl's that it is rather difficult to compare their positions. I shall limit myself in the following passages to some remarks that claim neither to be exhaustive nor systematic.

The key point in Kripke's demonstration consists in dissociating the *a priori* from the *a posteriori* on the one hand and the necessary from the contingent on the other, by pointing out that the former notions are epistemological, while the latter are modal. His argument consists therefore in challenging the double equivalence that we have found in Husserl. Indeed, on the one hand Kripke maintains that the truth of a proposition of identity such as "water = H_2O" is *a posteriori,* and therefore epistemologically contingent: a different empirical discovery on the molecular constitution of the liquid that flows in our rivers is conceivable; by this Kripke does not mean that the molecular constitution of water might have been different, but that the liquid that flows in our rivers could have revealed itself as being other than water. On the other hand, he argues that the *a posteriori* character of the truth "water = H_2O" does not entail its being *metaphysically* contingent: it is an essential character of water that it has as its chemical composition H_2O, because the identity "water = H_2O" is true in all possible worlds. The fact that we could have made a different discovery concerning the molecular constitution of the liquid that flows in our rivers does not entail, once it has been posited that water is H_2O, that this proposition of identity is contingent, that is to say, that it is conceivable that water could have in other possible worlds (or, in conformity with the minimalist interpretation of "possible world" advanced by Kripke, in other counterfactual situations), a different molecular constitution; for as Kripke counters, if it had a different molecular constitution, *it would not be water.* And therefore it is absolutely necessary—necessary in the strongest sense of the term—that water be H_2O. This is true for many other empirical truths (heat is the average kinetic energy of molecules, light is a flow of photons, and so on), but also for the laws of nature deriving from them.

At first sight, Kripke's view seems to contradict our most common intuitions, since it confers on an empirical truth the same character of necessity possessed by "2 + 2 = 4" or "*A and B* is true if *A* is true and *B* is true." What arguments does Kripke bring to bear to support such a paradoxical claim?

Without going into all the logico-semantic sophistication of the series of lectures that made Kripke famous and the transcription of which was published under the title *Naming and Necessity*, we can say that this claim results from two great principles:

(1) A certain conception of the reference of names conceived of as "rigid designators."

(2) The logical theorem of the necessity of identity. Setting out from two premises: (a) every *x* is necessarily identical to itself; (b) all that is true of something is true of everything identical to that thing, it follows that if *a* is identical to *b*, then *a* is necessarily identical to *b*.[16]

If we consider, on the one hand, that "water" and "H_2O" are expressions that function as rigid designators, that is to say, as terms that, if they refer to anything, refer to the same object in all possible worlds,[17] and if, on the other hand, we assert the judgment of identity "water = H_2O," it follows that this identity, by virtue of the demonstration of the necessity of the identity, is itself valid in all possible worlds, and therefore is metaphysically necessary.

In Kripke's view, it would be of no avail to object that this necessity is discovered empirically. For Kripke would refuse, as we have seen, the transition from epistemic modalities to "metaphysical" modalities. From the fact that I have discovered something empirically, *a posteriori*, that is, from the fact that I could (in the epistemic meaning of "can") have discovered a different one, it does not follow that what I discovered is not necessary in the strong sense of the word, that is, true in all possible worlds. Therefore it is futile to object that, since my discovery is empirical, I could conceive of a world in which water would not have a molecular constitution of two hydrogen atoms and one oxygen atom. For we must clarify first what "I could conceive" means here. There is no doubt that, since the truth in question is *a posteriori*, it is epistemologically contingent: a different discovery would have been possible. But *given that water has that constitution*, it has that constitution necessarily, because anything that does not have that molecular constitution in other possible worlds, whatever *resemblance* it may have to water, just *isn't* water. Of course, physics may have been wrong until now about the chemical composition of water and even about all the fundamental physical constants: it might even discover someday that what the name "water" refers to actually possesses a radically different atomic composition—let's call it *xyz*; but once we know that the atomic composition of water is *xyz*, if Kripke is right, we can no longer *conceive of* a world in which that constitution is not *xyz*, because any substance that we could conceive of and that would have a different atomic composition would be something other than water.

We may wonder whether this conclusion is not trivial. Indeed, if we set out from the idea that a rigid designator is an expression that, if it designates an object, designates the same object in all possible worlds, it becomes trivial to conclude therefrom that, if *a* and *b* are identical, then they are necessarily identical, since it has already been postulated at the start that "*a*" and "*b*" referred to the same objects in all possible worlds, and therefore that, if they were identical, they were necessarily identical. Actually, the whole problem lies in the additional clause: "once we know that water is H_2O." It is this clause that introduces a new element, thereby rendering the preceding demonstration non-trivial. Indeed, through this interpolated clause, Kripke seems to consider as already established the assumption that the only way we can identify something in all possible worlds, that is to say, the only way we have of knowing its nature, is by what science teaches us about it (and in this case, what a particular empirical science, physics, reveals). It is science that discovers essence, *and science alone*. If we do not concur with Kripke on this point, if we maintain that there are other ways of knowing what water *is* than via the empirical discoveries of science, it is no longer so easy to conclude that what is not H_2O in a different possible world "resembles," but "is" not water. In other words, as Filipe Drapeau Viera Contim and Pascal Ludwig remark, "the essentialism [of Kripke] comes from scientific presuppositions, and not from a philosophical reasoning. Indeed, on what conditions can we assert that it is necessary that water possess the property of being H_2O? When we can reasonably think (i) that we are making a rigid reference by means of the word 'water' to the liquid substance present in streams, seas and lakes of our planet, and (ii) that science has established that each molecule belonging to a sample of that substance was composed of two hydrogen atoms and one atom of oxygen. Point (ii) implies that science has discovered the *nature* of the substance in question, that is, a characteristic which that substance possesses in all possible worlds in which it exists."[18]

There are several ways to reject Kripke's conclusions: either by rejecting his theory of reference, or by denying the logical theorem of the necessity of identity, or merely by denying that science *and science alone* is entitled to teach us *the* nature of something. Perhaps there simply isn't any such thing as *the* nature of something, independently from any theoretical interest and any presupposition.

Indeed, if science alone could tell us what water is, we would have to infer that men never knew what water was before the discovery of its molecular composition. But if that were the case, it would be difficult to see what contemporary science could have *discovered*, because one must already know what water is to be able to discover something about it. This would undoubtedly have been part of Husserl's response: if I didn't already know what water is in a prescientific way (a transparent, colorless, odorless, tasteless liquid, which can sometimes exist in the solid form of ice, which evaporates when heated, and so on), I could never discover anything about it empirically, because I could not even say *about what sort of thing* I discover whatever I discover. (Empirical) science cannot possess the monopoly of essence. There must, in other words, be material essences, even inexact ones, even merely reduced to "types" as in the case of water—essences that, in order to be grasped, require no particular physical theory—in order for there also to be "essences" in Kripke's sense, that is, ultimate constituents of reality discovered empirically. But all the prescientific essences that structure our ordinary experience of the world are not, for all that, vague and inexact. For the essence "water" belongs to the genus "material thing" or "physical thing" and is thus subordinate to regional ontological axioms. In order to know what water is in a prescientific way, we must know *a priori* other things, for example, what a material body is, that every material body is spatially extended, and so on.

In sum, in response to Kripke, it is possible to adopt two strategies. The first consists in entering into all the sophistication of his logical-semantic construction and in critiquing specific aspects of it. For example, one may deny that the judgments of identity he takes as examples ("Water is H_2O," "The atomic number of gold is 79," "Light is a flow of photons") do in fact contain two rigid designators. One may object that they actually contain at least one description: "water is H_2O" is just an elliptic way of saying "water is *the physical substance* composed of the molecules H_2O"; the proof of the necessity of identity cannot apply to this case, because it applies only to identities between two rigid designators. One can then inquire into whether everything in this proposition ("Water is *the physical substance* composed of the molecules H_2O") is known empirically. Of course, it is empirically that we discover that water is made up of molecules composed of two atoms of hydrogen and one of oxygen. But we certainly do not empirically discover that water is a physical substance or that it is a material thing of a certain sort; for if we also discovered *that* empirically, it would be impossible for us to say what such a discovery is about. And if one concedes that at least some essences are not discovered empirically, but that they delimit what a thing is before any empirical discovery about it, it is no longer possible to assert that once it has been posited that water is H_2O, what is possibly not

H_2O isn't water either; for there is no longer one and only one way of apprehending *what water is*, independently of any particular theoretical interest (that of physics being only one interest among others).

But this complex strategy is perhaps unnecessary. A second, more direct way is to argue that, even if we grant Kripke his sophisticated logical-semantic apparatus, the conclusion does not follow, unless we are committed to the idea of positivist inspiration, that only science can discover *what water is*. In order to clarify this response, it is probably useful to try to elucidate further the points of disagreement between Kripke and Husserl. There are at least four of them: (1) the *a priori/a posteriori* difference; (2) the necessary/contingent difference; (3) the characterization of essence; (4) the question of whether or not phenomenological and scientific concepts should be distinguished.

(1) For Husserl, truths of essence are *prior* to truths of experience; possibilities of essence precede realities. This does not mean that the *a priori* cannot be discovered (in the sense of a *non-empirical* discovery: it is in this sense that the Pythagorean theorem was "discovered"), for it should be stressed once more that what is *a priori* in Husserl's view is not what *in fact* is not known through experience but what does not need empirical research (nor empirical hypotheses) to be known. Therefore, *a priori* is what *can* be known without recourse to empirical research or hypotheses. Now, Kripke expressly rejects this use of *a priori*—which was already that of Kant—according to which *a priori* truths are those "which *can* be known independently from all experience,"[19] and, in defining the expression "*a priori*," he limits himself "to the question of whether a particular person or knower knows something *a priori* or believes it true on the basis of *a priori* evidence,"[20] that is, to the way he *actually* knows this truth. Why does Kripke reject this traditional sense of "*a priori*"? This refusal is clearly essential to his whole project: indeed, if one chooses the traditional interpretation, what *can* be known without recourse to experience is also that which cannot be contradicted by any other experience, and therefore is true in all possible worlds; "*a priori*" becomes a *synonym*[21] of "necessary"; now Kripke wants to show that all that is *a priori* is not necessary and that all that is necessary is not *a priori*.

(2) To Husserl, the *epistemological* distinction necessary/contingent is closely connected with the *ontological* necessary/contingent distinction, on the grounds that the *a priori* is somehow "analytically" necessary and the necessary somehow "analytically" *a priori*. To Kripke, things are otherwise, precisely because he rejects the "synonymy" in question.

(3) Kripke defines essence in modal terms. A property true in all logically possible worlds is essential. "Some properties of an object may be essential to it, in that it could not have failed to have them."[22] "Essen-

tial" is, therefore, synonymous with "necessary" for him. Thus, on the one hand, Kripke breaks the equivalence between *a priori* and necessary, between *a posteriori* and contingent, and on the other hand he institutes a new equivalence—this time between "necessary" and "essential." If science succeeds in discovering necessary properties, it therefore also succeeds in discovering essential properties, and vice versa.

To Husserl, this consequence does not follow, as we have seen, because he explicitly refuses all modal characterization of essence. "Necessary property" and "essential property" are simply not synonymous. Consequently, even if "water is H_2O" expresses a necessary property of water (Husserl would not concede that the truth of that proposition is *necessary* in the same sense as *a priori* material truths are), this still does not, in Husserl's view, make it a property of essence; it is rather a property that is *grounded in* essence—and therefore that *presupposes* this essence in order to be able to be discovered empirically. Husserl would probably argue that, if we follow Kripke, the *discovery* of empirical truths becomes a rather mysterious fact, since if it is not metaphysically possible for water to be anything but H_2O, it is hard to see what remains *empirical* in the discoveries of the so-called empirical sciences. Those discoveries must have the same status as those of logical or mathematical truths (Kripke, of course, would not accept this formulation of the problem).

But the conceptions of essence of the two authors differ on still another point. If we examine the examples with which Kripke illustrates his remarks (the atomic number of gold, light as a flow of protons, the tiger as a mammal, heat as the average kinetic energy of molecules), we see that all these examples are rooted in a very specific conception of essence: the one that emerged within the Lockean tradition, according to which "essence" actually means "the real constitution of things."[23] Kripke's essence is only a variant of Locke's: essences are the deep properties that a thing must necessarily have, and that explain its surface properties. As Locke writes, "the real internal, but generally in substances, unknown constitution of things, whereon their discoverable qualities depend, may be called their *essence.* This is the proper original signification of the word"[24]—a signification distinct for that of the School. Thus, implicitly, the Kripkean essentialism has its origin in the Lockean tradition and not in the Platonic-Aristotelian tradition to which Husserl belongs. Husserl would, of course, admit that science allows us to discover the real constitution of things empirically, but he would refuse to call that, without further precautions, their *essence.* He would say once more: in order to be able to discover empirically that water is H_2O, one must already have an understanding of its essence, for example one must know *a priori* that water is a physical substance, and a physical substance that has such and such phenomenal characteristics, for otherwise it would be impossible to discover through experience *what* is actually H_2O, that is to say, to identify the liquid in question.

(4) Finally, Kripke rejects one point that truly constitutes the heart of Husserl's conception, namely the view that it would make sense to distinguish phenomenological concepts from scientific ones. He writes, for example: some philosophers advance the view that "there are really two concepts of metal operating here, a phenomenological one and a scientific one which then replaces it. This I reject."[25] If indeed essences are the hidden constituents of things, they are accessible only to science and everything that enables us to say *what* something *is* from the point of view of our primordial and ordinary experience of the world does not deserve the name "essence." This is what I have called the "positivist" element in his conception.

I do not pretend, in what follows, to discuss each of these points. Some aspects of Kripke's conception rest on extremely insightful questions that he raises in opposition to the philosophical tradition, such as the possibility of a distinction between necessary and *a priori*. Others, on the other hand, seem more like unquestioned presuppositions of his own doctrine. For example, his Lockean definition of essence, or the idea according to which it is science and science alone that teaches us the true nature of things. This idea follows neither from the analysis of rigid designators nor from the theorem of the necessity of identity brought to light by Ruth Barcan Marcus. Now, it is because Kripke contends that science enables us to know *the* nature of things (in the singular, and without qualification) that he can infer from this that, if that is indeed the essence of water, heat, and so on, in this world, it is also their essence in all possible worlds.

For, after all, is there really such a thing as *the* nature of water? Must we not distinguish between the nature of that element as it is presented to us in our everyday experience and the nature of water as analyzed by the physicist or chemist? Must there not first be prescientific essences (and, among them, pure *a priori* essences) in order that there may be subsequently essences in the empirical sense—essences in Locke's sense? To take another example that Kripke comments on at length, is the truth of the proposition of identity "Hesperus = Phosphorus" (in which "Hesperus" and "Phosphorus" are the Greek names for the evening star and the morning star, that is, two names of Venus) known—or knowable—entirely *a posteriori*? As Jonathan Lowe remarks, that "identity was established because astronomers discovered that Hesperus and Phosphorus *coincide in their orbits*: wherever Hesperus is located at any given time, there too is Phosphorus located. However, spatiotemporal coincidence only implies identity for things of appropriate kinds. It is only because Hesperus and Phosphorus are taken to be *planets* and thereby *material objects of the same kind* that their spatiotemporal coincidence can be taken to imply their identity. But the principle that distinct material objects of the same kind cannot coincide spatiotemporally is not an empirical one: it is an *a priori* one implied by *what it is* to be a material object of any kind—in other words, it is a truth grounded in *essence*."[26] These are precisely the material axioms of Husserl, which are prior to all the hypotheses of science, governing all our prescientific experience, and making possible only subsequently all the empirical discoveries that we can make about them.

To be sure, one might object that the scientific/prescientific distinction is a vague one: does science not begin with perception? Furthermore, Husserl called the *phenomenological* doctrine of essences a "science." We must return to the questions raised by this point. But the important thing to be pointed out is that nothing, in what Kripke advances, has furnished the slightest argument for ruling out the idea of *a priori* essences. Perhaps all essences do not have this status. Perhaps there are essences that are discovered empirically (I shall return to this in a moment), but, in any case, it does not seem that the nonexistence of *a priori* essences, particularly of material *a priori* essences, follows from the arguments he advances. In fact, at no time does Kripke envisage that possibility.

Actually, in some rare texts, Husserl does seem to recognize that some essences can be discovered empirically, but those are not the ones that hold the most interest for the phenomenologist. For example, we read in *Experience and Judgment*: "The membership of the animals called 'whales' in the class of mammals is masked by the outward analogy which whales have with fishes with regard to their mode of life, something already indicated in the verbal designation [*Walfisch* in German]. In such cases we speak of *nonessential types* . . . . Necessarily underlying it [i.e., science] is *the prescientific and multifariously nonessential typification carried out by natural experiential apperception*."[27] Here, the naive typification that ascribes the status of fish to the whale is only *a nonessential* typification: it belongs neither to essences properly so-called (since it is empirically false) nor *a fortiori* to pure essences. When the marine biologist discovers that whales are mammals, he replaces this naive typification with a scientific concept. He discovers an essential trait of the species "whale" empirically. This empirical discovery is, then, a discovery about essence. Therefore not all essences are *a priori*. These essences that are not *a priori* are designated in Husserl's terminology as "empirical generalities."[28]

Consequently, only *pure* essences are authentically *a priori* in Husserl's view. And if there are "empirical essences," or at least essences discovered by the empirical sciences, they presuppose *pure* essences and do not have the same kind of necessity as them. What exactly is the status of the necessity of the truths discovered empirically, or at least of some among them? Are there physical truths, for example, that are unconditionally necessary? On this point, the debate remains open, and the purpose of these pages was not to conclude it.

Surely it is to Kripke's great credit to have disrupted the allegedly self-evident equivalence *a priori-necessary,* and *a posteriori-contingent,* and in this regard his major philosophical contribution consists first and foremost in compelling us to refine our concepts, rather than pretend to return to a pre-Kripkean, "Adamic" state, in which there would not even be room for such questions. There is another point of great importance that is evinced by the questions raised in *Naming and Necessity.* Regardless of whether one endorses or not his overall conception, Kripke has shown, convincingly in my view, that the fact of something's being conceivable does not necessarily entail its being possible; or, to express it in his own terms, the fact that something is epistemologically conceivable does not necessarily entail its being metaphysically possible. Thus he has restored to the relationship between conceivability and possibility its full complexity.[29]

No doubt, it is a limitation of Husserl's conception of essence that it simply equates conceivability—and actually *imaginability*—and possibility. On this view, all that is conceivable is possible and all that is possible is conceivable. The entire procedure of eidetic variation rests on this equivalence. Now, two objections must be raised against Husserl. First, all that is imaginable prima facie is not thereby possible, nor all that is unimaginable impossible. Isn't it possible to imagine impossible things? H. G. Wells's time travel machine, for instance? Isn't it possible to imagine someone going back in time and changing the course of history? But does its being imaginable entail its being possible? Husserl would probably reply that such a state of affairs is empirically impossible, but not eidetically impossible. But that answer is not tenable if the only criterion we have for discovering the *eidetically* possible is precisely what it is possible and impossible to *imagine* (without further specification). Secondly, it seems very difficult to say what is conceivable and inconceivable, imaginable and unimaginable, without introducing further considerations. For the Kripkean, by virtue of his initial presuppositions, a water that would not be H_2O is not conceivable in the strong sense of the term, that is, metaphysically possible; for a Husserlian, on the contrary, by virtue of his or her characterization of essence, it is. How can the issue be settled?

The only way to settle it brings a philosophical argumentation into play. But if there is no other way to settle this issue than by argumentation, the consequence to be drawn is that eidetic variation cannot be *the* method, let alone *a* method, for discovering essences and necessities of essence. Eidetic variation would be a good method for phenomenology only if it could be established by an *a priori* argument that the conceivable (the imaginable) and the eidetically or essentially possible are coextensive. But this demonstration, even if it could be successfully carried out, would already bring a philosophical argumentation into play, and hence partly unquestioned implicit premises. In philosophy—this is perhaps the problem, but a problem that must be recognized and addressed—there is neither beginning nor end to the *logon didonai.* This is why any dogmatic method that would claim to rest on a presuppositionless procedure and would pretend to provide us with truths beyond any possible doubt is nothing other than a philosopher's dream and a fanciful method.

The discovery of essences necessarily presupposes an argumentative dimension. There is only one way in philosophy to discover essential truths: by means of more powerful and more convincing arguments. The essential properties are not inscribed once and for all in the eternal spirit of some tutelary god. They call for the only possible method in philosophy: that of an argumentation-based discussion, hence of a critique of competing conceptions.

12

Essence and History

> It is easier to think opposites than degrees.
> —Friedrich Nietzsche

What is a phenomenological description? The preceding chapters have suggested the beginning of an answer. The moment has come to recapitulate their conclusions and to try to go a step further.

Chapter 10 has shown it to be perfectly possible to defend the possibility of judgments and descriptions of essence without subscribing to the Platonism of phenomenology's founder, that is, without assuming that essences are ideal, atemporal, or supertemporal *objects*; and consequently, that it is possible to sunder the equivalence essence-*eidos*, whose roots reach down into all of Western metaphysics, since its Platonic origins.

Chapter 11 established that eidetic variation cannot be the method of phenomenology, but it also contributed to highlighting the fact that the idea of *a priori* essence, that is, of essences independent of any empirical research, and therefore of any hypothesis that could be falsified, has nothing intrinsically incoherent about it. These essences are phenomenological essences, that is, they are tied to the world as it appears to us, to what Husserl called the "*Lebenswelt*." To recognize that the things that present themselves to us are *essentially* this or that way amounts to maintaining that the empirical sciences do not have a monopoly on discourse concerning essence. The method that allows us to draw a boundary between what deserves to be called an "essence" in this sense and what doesn't is the most obvious method in philosophy, that of argumentation. Finally, chapter 11 has shown that there is not one sole answer to the question of *what* a thing or a property *is essentially*. Now it is time to clarify this last point.

Even in the case of an empirical essence (of an "empirical generality" in Husserl's terminology), there is not one and only one possible answer to the question *ti esti*?—"what is it?" The molecular composition

"H_2O" is essential to water, but relative to a particular interest, that is, to a specific kind of inquiry—the one that asks about the *fundamental physical properties* of this liquid. But other properties of water from a macrophysical point of view, or, more precisely, from the point of view of the way we apprehend this liquid in our daily experience, may be valid with the same right as properties of essence, even if these properties (transparency, tastelessness, drinkability, and so on) are considerably less "exact" than those analyzed by physics. For our ordinary purposes, pre- or extra-scientific, these phenomenological properties fulfill very well their function, which is to allow us to identify this liquid, to say precisely *what it is.* All essence is relative to a kind of description, which is carried out according to specific interests, and the interests of fundamental physics are no less *interests* than others. Things have essences (although their essences are not to be thought of as things), but this assertion must not lead us to say that descriptions of essence could be freed from all relativity with respect to particular interests and reflect things as they are "in themselves," from the point of view of a divine understanding, or, as Merleau-Ponty says, from the point of view of a *cosmotheoros.*

This, however, does not make judgments of essence relative, in the sense of a relativism. Indeed, we should not conclude from the fact that different descriptions of what is essential to something, each depending on different interests and conceptual schemes, are possible, that these judgments of essence have no objectivity. Such a consequence would be unavoidable only if the conceptual schemes by means of which we describe essential properties turned out to be necessarily incompatible or incommensurable. But such is not the case: some properties of water that are of interest to the biologist (for example that it is potable, or that it is a necessary factor for life) can be reduced to "fundamental" physicochemical properties. And the same should hold, ideally at least, for phenomenological properties.

But how, it may be asked, does all this concern phenomenology? Phenomenology is concerned not with empirical essences, but with *a priori* ones. These essences are "naive" in the sense that they are prescientific. They are about the world as we experience it before any idealization and theory. If a description of essence is always relative to an interest, the interest of our daily practice is no less compelling than that evinced by physics. But does not the mention of an interest, that is, of a way of questioning that underlies all description of essence, jeopardize the very notion of essence: that which a thing *is*—without further qualification?

It is probably this concern that led Husserl to a dogmatic conception of phenomenological description. If such a description is true, he argues, it must satisfy the requirements of truth in general and therefore be valid absolutely for anyone. "Talk of what is true *for* this one or that one is absurd. . . . What is true is true absolutely, is true 'in itself.'"[1] This is why only an *intuition* of essences free from all relativity can put us in the presence of essential truths; it alone can constitute the organon of a phenomenology that, as a science that is "grounded on an absolute foundation, and absolutely justified,"[2] is also, by this very fact, a science free from all presupposition, having achieved "genuine freedom from prejudice [*die echte Vorurteilslosigkeit*]" which requires "as the foundation of all proofs, immediately valid judgments which derive their validity from *originally presentive intuitions*."[3] Thus, not only does eidetic intuition constitute "the principle of principles" of the phenomenological method, but that intuition is capable of furnishing us with descriptions that, as Husserl says (building on an entire rhetoric of the "immediate" and the "directly" apprehended), draw their descriptive legitimacy from intuition and it alone. The vision of essence, assuming it is possible, *determines the description through and through*, so that there is only one way of describing whatever there is to describe. But this idea of an *absolut getreuen Beschreibung*,[4] of a description that would possess something like an "absolute faithfulness" to the phenomena to be described, that would in no way transcend the given but be a pure tracing of it, is nothing but a myth. As Heidegger insisted already in 1919 in opposition to his master, "one identifies intuitive behavior with description itself, as if the method of description were ultimately a kind of intuition: but I can only describe if I have already seen."[5] Description is always an account that, because it is formulated in a particular idiom, because it introduces a conceptuality that is at least partially inherited, because it implicitly asks questions about the state of affairs to be described, irremediably transcends every possible "given." There is no description that would be a tracing of essence. On the contrary, a description is only possible and faithful on the condition of forsaking all "absolute faithfulness," and the absence of prejudices that goes with it—two ideas that are no more than additional prejudices. "We must free ourselves," writes Heidegger, "of the prejudice according to which, because phenomenology requires that we grasp the things themselves, these things should be grasped point blank, without adding anything: it is rather the case that progress in the direction of the things themselves is slow and progressive, and must before all else eliminate the prejudices that obstruct access to what is in question."[6]

The idea of a description that would legitimate itself in intuition and be perfectly adequate to the phenomenon, that would leave no room for an alternative description, is an absurdity. A description always involves (1) interests, that is, implicit questions; (2) given that it is formulated in a specific language, conceptual schemes, which may also be called a (linguistically articulable) pre-comprehension of the phenomena; (3) in the majority of cases (especially in instances of a complex description with underlying philosophical stakes), beliefs or presuppositions, sometimes even an entire tacit theory. It is precisely this complexity that forces us to conclude that there is a necessary pluralism in descriptions. It belongs essentially to every description that there are always, for a given description, competing descriptions. A description that would be the one and only description would no longer be a *description* at all. Naturally this pluralism does not mean that there are no criteria to decide between descriptions, or that some of them are not more adequate than others.

This applies, to begin with, to nonessential descriptions. It is related that the young Maupassant went to see Flaubert at Croisset; he was going to get advice from the master. The latter is reported to have said—probably to get rid of him: "Stand in front of a tree and describe it." It is easy to imagine the young artist obeying, holding a leaf in one hand like a canvas, dueling with the Herculean task. Sartre doesn't believe the anecdote. "The advice, if it was given, is absurd."[7] Is it really? That injunction would indeed be nonsensical, if describing were similar to performing a topographical survey: there would be nothing to be learned from it. But in doing no more than detailing the particularities of a tree—its branches, its curves, its bark, its size and shape, its look and its proportions—a writer finds himself, that is to say, he finds his style. In selecting certain aspects, in featuring some more than others, he brings the mark of his personality, his tastes, aspirations, and artistic sensibility. We do not know whether Giono was familiar with the anecdote, but he practices the principle in *A King without Diversion.* The novel begins with a description of a beech tree in the roadside: it is by the very way of depicting it, by the intentions that come out in the description, and by the whole atmosphere this creates, that the novel gets its impetus. Giono claims that when he began the description he had no idea of what the novel would be, and the plot was born, so to speak, from the intertwining of the branches.[8] To describe is always an inventive operation: it is to invent what is before our eyes.

This applies equally well to descriptions of essence. Let us consider one of the plainest phenomenological examples. There is a vase on the table; I perceive it. The vase shows itself to me by changing adumbrations (Husserl's *Abschattungen*) as I walk about in the room, moving closer or farther away, changing my perspective. The vase I perceive is the same, but its *Abschattungen,* its outlines, are always different. This is an essential feature of this perception, of *all* perception of this kind. Indeed, a vase is by essence a material thing, and as such, a spatially extended thing (synthetic *a priori* truth). I cannot perceive all its aspects at the same time, but only successively. Still, once this truth of essence has been stated, I am assailed by a host of questions. How will I describe these adumbrations themselves? How will I describe their relation to the thing, one and identical, that is adumbrated through them? Will I say that they are characteristics of my perception of the vase? And, assuming that I choose this last option—how is their status to be conceived? Are they subjective characteristics of my lived experiences (*Erlebnisse*) considered in themselves, or relational characteristics of my perception-of-this-vase? In other words, are *Abschattungen* objective, subjective, or neither—*relational*, that is, belonging to the relation that, in perception, is established between this vase and me? This is where a philosophical decision takes place. Husserl tells us that the adumbrations are lived experiences. He specifies that these lived experiences are immanent to consciousness. The argument he invokes to support this claim is borrowed from the arsenal of skepticism: it is that of an illusion, eventually generalized. I may be wrong about this vase, about its determinations and even about its existence, but I cannot be wrong about the adumbrations themselves. I may believe that this vase is porcelain, while in fact it is earthenware or glass; there may not even be a vase before me; but I cannot be wrong about the fact that I perceive at this moment this opalescent, bluish form, continually changing its aspect, its look, its perspective, as I move toward it or away from it. As for these adumbrations themselves, there is no room for doubt, for their being is nothing beyond their appearance: for them, *esse est percipi*. Here we are no longer in the domain of mere description, but already in that of explanation and even theory: their borders thus appear porous. Husserl's description presupposes the validity of the skeptic argument (a problem to which we shall return in chapter 15) and, actually, a whole Cartesian background postulating the validity of a generalized doubt and drawing conclusions from it for the distinction between interiority and exteriority, immanence and transcendence. As a result, the adumbrations are subjective, while the vase being adumbrated in them is objective. The former belong to consciousness, the latter to reality. The adumbrations are given "adequately," in an infallible evidence; reality is given inadequately, so that it is always possible to raise a doubt about it: a doubt about the existence of the vase, the objects surrounding it, and even the world as such.

For now, we don't have to ask ourselves whether Husserl's description is tenable. Whatever difficulties it raises, it constitutes an excellent specimen of description; it allows us to inquire into the status of description in general, and of phenomenological description in particular. According to Husserl, what we have here is a description of essence *through and through*, having the same apodictic validity as the *a priori* synthetic judgment—"every material thing is endowed with spatial extension"—from which it sets out. But clearly things are more complex. We do have, *at the beginning*, necessities of essence that establish a connection between a material object and spatiality, between spatiality and perception by adumbrations; these essential truths are part of a "science of naiveties" that achieves a return to a *second* naïveté, that is, a naïveté that is vindicated and consciously assumed; but, having reached this point, description goes a step further. Not only does it bring in a certain kind of interest (we describe *in order to bring essences and relations of essence to light*), not only does it put into play a partially invented terminology (that of *Abschattungen*, adumbrations, or outlines) partly inherited from the philosophical tradition (that of reality as opposed to lived experience, of the objective as opposed to the subjective, of transcendence as opposed to immanence)—a terminology that is anything but naive—but it ends up incorporating entire philosophical theories. In describing, we are not only enabling phenomena—however "dumb"—"to speak" and giving them voice such as they present themselves of themselves, but we apply concepts to them, question them, and are drawn willy-nilly into theory.

Does this mean that we are no longer dealing with a "mere" or "pure" description? But the idea of a *pure* description is absurd, if by that we mean a description perfectly adequate to its object, that would ultimately limit itself to putting that object on stage, and erase itself as description. Therefore let us try to say, in precise form, what we have done. We started with a description at the same time minimal and naive, in the sense that it rests on no particular theory—either scientific or philosophical; it expresses a bundle of essential truths: a spatial thing *must* present successive adumbrations to the perceiver. This description is "obvious," not only because it is "self-evident" (*selbstverständlich*), but also because it is necessarily true by virtue of *what it is* to perceive a spatial thing. At that stage, we were content to make explicit something that remained tacit in our daily perceptual experience—something we were perhaps even totally unaware of before expressing it, for, in general, we don't pay attention to it when we are immersed in perceptual activity. Given that the language we use every day is not intended to convey this sort of discovery, we introduced a new, philosophical concept, that of *Abschattung*. But this recourse to an invented terminology (the word is not current in German) does not yet mean that we have introduced philosophical beliefs or presuppositions into the descriptive content itself. Furthermore, the minimal description that is thereby sketched out neither follows analytically from the meaning of the words "spatial thing" and "perception," nor is it derived from grammatical conventions, and even less is it an empirical discovery.

The trouble is that essential truths of this kind are rare in the practice of phenomenology. The moment that the description proceeds, we leave these reassuring shores to be cast adrift in mid-ocean. New questions come up, regarding the conditions of possibility of the state of affairs described. On what conditions can we perceive one *same* vase through *changing* adumbrations? It is here that Husserl ventures a response: on the condition that we distinguish between a transcendent object that does not change and belongs to reality and its adumbrations that keep changing, that belong to consciousness and are "immanent" to it. "Immanent in what sense?" is the next question to be asked. And so, one question leads to another.

Each of these formulations commits us to a whole implicit description of the "subject" of perception. Shall we say that this subject is a self-enclosed sphere of being, a psychological consciousness? Shall we say that it is an intentional consciousness, or a corporeal, practical subject, like the one favored by Merleau-Ponty? How will we decide? By argumentation. Naturally, considerations concerning the subject of perception immediately impinge on the way we will describe the object perceived and its adumbrations. The more distant these considerations are from the point at which the description is anchored in essential truths, the more urgent the question of whether we have correctly described things becomes.

Thus an essential aspect of the phenomenological method is revealed. Phenomenology proceeds by means of transcendental questions and transcendental arguments. We may, following Kant, qualify as "transcendental" a question that inquires into the "conditions of possibility" of our experience, that is, on *conditions necessary for our experience to possess the (necessary) characteristics that it possesses.* Consequently, a transcendental argument is, as Charles Taylor remarks, "a regression from an unquestionable feature of experience to a stronger thesis as the condition of its possibility."[9] Here several points must be emphasized. (1) First, the unquestionable feature is, in the case we are considering, one of those that are circumscribed by essential truths. We have seen that assertions of essence are necessary; they draw the boundaries between the possible and the impossible. A transcendental question in turn inquires on these possibilities and impossibilities that are prescribed by essence or have their origin in it. It asks what the necessary conditions are for these possibilities and impossibilities to be what they are.[10] (2) Therefore, a regression toward a "stronger thesis" does not mean a regression toward a *less controversial* thesis (we will see that it is exactly the opposite), but only an ascent toward a *less trivial* thesis. Indeed, as previously stated, transcendental questions can only be settled by transcendental arguments, and transcendental arguments are not better than others; their relevance and significance must be evaluated on a case-by-case basis. Wherever there is a transcendental argument, there is always room for a counter-argument and a better one. A transcendental argument *should* ideally possess the same degree of apodicticity as the *a priori* features of our experience in which it is anchored; but for that, it must be valid. And it is not always obvious whether a transcendental argument is valid, nor if it offers an interesting conclusion. A transcendental argumentation does not enjoy in this regard any superiority over any other argumentation in philosophy. (3) Lastly, in Kantian terms, a transcendental argument says nothing about the "in itself" of things, but only about our experience of them. Inasmuch as its premise is borrowed from experience, the conclusion it reaches cannot take us outside the limits of experience; all that argument can do is highlight conditions necessary to the characteristic feature of experience identified in its premise, and thus tell us not how things are, but how they should be described. But in telling us how we should describe experience, it has also an indirect impingement on the way certain empirical problems (for example, the problem of how our perceptual apparatus is constituted) must be posed.

The conditions of possibility brought to light by transcendental arguments are generally "subjective": they concern necessary characteristics of the *subject* of experience. Many examples could be given of this kind of argument in phenomenological literature. That the object of experience differs, by its identity to itself and its exteriority, from the lived experiences through which it is announced, entails that consciousness is intentional (Husserl). That all manifestation of beings occurs in conformity with the way of being that belongs to them has as its condition of possibility the existence of a remarkable being, *Dasein*, which possesses an understanding of Being (Heidegger). That perception has an essential connection to movement, or that it is characterized by a "sensorimotor intrication" requires that the subject of perception be a corporeal subject capable of movement and endowed with practical abilities (Merleau-Ponty). In certain cases, the "stronger" thesis, which gives an account of the feature of experience that has served as the starting point of the argument, is itself a transcendental *thesis*. After Husserl's "transcendental turn," for example, the subject that is held to be necessary to account for the characteristic features of experience is a *constituting* subject, that is, an ego who plays the role of *condition of possibility* for the very appearing of the world. Some elements of transcendentalism remain present in *Being and Time*, and in the work of Merleau-Ponty, Patočka, Henry, Marion, and many others. But it is important to stress that a transcendental *argument*, to be valid, does not require any commitment to a transcendental *the-*

sis. Nothing rules out the possibility that transcendental arguments may reach radically anti-transcendental conclusions, as we hope to be able to show in the second part of the present work.

Since phenomenological description sets out from necessities of essence that are themselves *a priori*, a transcendental argument is an argument that inquires into the conditions necessary for a state of affairs that is essential in this sense, hence *a priori* necessary, to be what it is. There is no strict demarcation, however, between assertions of essence and the transcendental assertions that account for them. For example, the property of the perceived spatial field to possess a left-right lateralization and a distinction between "high" and "low" is an essential property of the perceived space as such. But is the claim that only a bodily "subject" endowed with a sense of left and right, high and low, is able to perceive such a space still an assertion of essence? Yes, *on the condition* that there is no decisive argument to support an opposite claim. Once again, only argumentation, and not a doubtful eidetic intuition, can constitute the organon of a characterization of the essence. And if there is no strict demarcation between initial judgments of essence and transcendental descriptions that make explicit their conditions of possibility and that, in complexifying the description, introduce additional concepts and conceptions, we can now understand why it was important not to make essences immutable objects that it would suffice to seize or recognize (see chapter 10).

But if a transcendental argument is an argument such that some of its premises can always, in principle, be questioned, it is much less infallible than the descriptions of essence from which it sets out. Though *a priori*, it is only valid on the condition that each of its premises is accepted, and it is only relevant to the extent that the conclusion it reaches is not trivial. This is why, as Taylor insists, "the conclusions of transcendental arguments are apodictic and yet open to endless debate."[11] This leads us to what is probably the most interesting characteristic of phenomenological descriptions: they are *a priori*, like the assertions of essence in which they originate, and yet they are a matter of controversy to the precise extent that they rest on transcendental arguments. They are *a priori*, and yet they are open to a revision that is always possible in principle, because one cannot *a priori* rule out the possibility of a more convincing argumentation.

Have we correctly described what a phenomenological description is? In sum, it is a description that sets out from at least implicit assertions of essence—from material regional axioms, as Husserl would have said. From these, it formulates transcendental questions and arguments, and, to that extent, it is both *a priori and* subject to revision. For example, all of *Being and Time*—the "essential result" of which is recapitulated by Heidegger through the sentence "the constitution of the *Dasein*'s Being is grounded in temporality"[12]—rests implicitly on the assertion that *temporality is an essential characteristic of the being that we ourselves are.* This assertion can be made more explicit by saying that the way in which time belongs to *Dasein* is distinct from the way in which it belongs—to a chair, let's say. For *Dasein,* to be temporal means to have an experience that unfolds temporally, *to exist time* as a fundamental modality of its Being and the horizon of the meaning of Being in general. Fundamental ontology, to account for a necessity of essence that it does not state explicitly, thus forges a new conceptuality, that of the *modalities of being* of the entity that we ourselves are, *Dasein,* and of the entity whose revelation occurs only as long as *Dasein* exists. But *Being and Time* further states a transcendental *thesis,* or rather a thesis of transcendental inspiration: "Only as long as Dasein *is,* that is, as long as an understanding of Being is ontically possible, 'is there' Being."[13] The understanding of Being as ontological characteristic of *Dasein* is the condition of possibility for there being Being in general, and, therefore, for the entity *as entity* to be able to manifest itself to *Dasein.* And since the "sense of Being" is temporality, the finite temporality of *Dasein* becomes the *origin* of the time of things, the condition of possibility for beings that do not have the way of being of *Dasein* to be able to be qualified as "temporal" in a derivative sense. Nothing of all that would be possible if the phenomenological description did not get its impetus from apodictic truths of essence that it is absurd to call into question, because their negations form material contradictions in Husserl's sense. The transcendental argument underlying the description is formulated *a priori,* and yet reaches a truth that is subject to revision in its very principle. Nothing guarantees that the new concepts introduced in the description—and to begin with, that of *Dasein*—are adequate to the phenomena to be described. Nor is there any guarantee that the description, or what Heidegger sometimes called the "phenomenological construction,"[14] has not surreptitiously introduced substantial philosophical theses (in reality, this is inevitably the case) that shackle it to historically conditioned presuppositions, which can themselves become the subject matter of a deeper discussion. But such presuppositions are quite simply inevitable in philosophy if we do not want to remain at the level of the triviality of characterizations of essence. To take up the formulation in *Phaedo,* it is the "beautiful risk" that philosophy must run. In a phenomenological description, essence is surely the first word of the description, but it cannot be the last word, on pain of insignificance.

This manner of characterizing the phenomenological method is not without affinities to the one Heidegger developed in his critical dialogue with Husserl. It is possible, however, that Heidegger's fundamental methodological considerations generate at least as many aporias as they do solutions. It is to this question that we must now turn our attention.

It is no accident that Heidegger spoke on occasion of phenomenological "construction" rather than "description." In his view, phenomenology cannot, any more than can any philosophy for that matter, be exempt from presuppositions. The idea of a "science of absolute beginnings" that would free itself from all prejudice and supply truths emancipated from all historical anchorage, valid once and for all and impossible to put in doubt, is nothing but a fiction that in turn has its historical roots—thus inheriting its own presuppositions—in the Cartesian theory of science. To speak of "phenomenological construction" is a way of taking one's distance from the Husserlian idea of a *pure* description, that is, a description that, because it purports to originate directly in intuition, would be "absolutely faithful" to phenomena. But under the pretext of rejecting one specific concept (or one specific ideal) of description, must one reject the idea of description altogether? If phenomenology does not describe, what does it do? There are several ways to describe, and this includes ways to describe what a description is, but there is no other way to describe what phenomenology in fact does than to qualify its method as "descriptive."

In reality, Heidegger tells us, what characterizes a description in general is that there is no airtight separation between describing and explaining. "Description is unthinkable without an underlying explanation [*zugrundliegende Erklärung*]."[15] Heidegger also calls this *Erklärung*, this "explanation," which, in this case, has nothing of an empirical explanation about it, an "*Auslegung*": a laying out or interpretation. The defect of this concept of interpretation could be at first sight to blur any demarcation between the various moments that I have distinguished in the operation of description: first, the questions and the interests, second, the conceptuality by means of which the preliminary understanding of what is to be described is articulated, and third, the presuppositions of theoretical origin subjacent to the description itself. A conceptuality is more or less *adequate* to the phenomena, whereas presuppositions are *true* or *false*. But if to describe is always to interpret, must one not conclude that presuppositions, beliefs of which we are partially unaware, are already amalgamated in the least description? Surely not. However, presuppositions do belong to all descriptions that are *at all complex*, and especially to philosophical descriptions.

In the actual practice of interpretation, when it is a question of interpreting a text, for example (and more specifically a text that sets up a claim to truth), it is impossible to separate entirely the question of meaning from that of truth; it is therefore impossible to separate the two operations that are the strictly linguistic understanding of a *meaning* and the understanding of the *thing* on which the text focuses. I understand the meaning of a text by interpreting it according to what seems to me to be the truest reading, and I understand the truth of the text according to what seems to me to be its most plausible meaning. In other words, linguistic understanding never goes without an agreement about the "thing," and conversely the agreement on the thing depends on the understanding of the text.[16] There is nothing vicious about this circle, since we are not, here, in the domain of inferences and definitions in which the notion of logical circularity is relevant. Such a circle does not constitute a limit or obstacle to understanding, but rather one of its conditions. The same is true when we are dealing with the interpretation of *phenomena*: the bringing to light of their mode of givenness or of their meaning is never carried out, not only outside any questioning and independently of any particular conceptuality, but also in the absence of any presupposition and any commitment to philosophical theses.

What is specific to interpretation (*Auslegung*) as analyzed by Heidegger is that it proceeds from a preliminary understanding of the phenomena to be understood, from a pre-understanding (*Vorverstehen*). This pre-understanding is rooted in historically conditioned presuppositions (*Voraussetzungen*). The task of a phenomenological description is not, as Husserl believed, to get rid of all prejudice, and thus guard against "all interpretations transcending the given"[17] but rather, to renounce all *Voraussetzungslosigkeit* (presuppositionlessness) and accept the necessity of the prejudices that orient understanding and description, to elucidate the nature and origin of these prejudices as far as possible. "Philosophy" writes Heidegger, "will never seek to deny its 'presuppositions,' but neither may it simply admit them. It conceives them, and it unfolds with more and more penetration both the presuppositions themselves and that for which they are presuppositions."[18] But then, if "the λόγος of . . . phenomenology . . . has the character of a ἑρμηνεύειν,"[19] that is, if phenomenology is in its essence hermeneutic, the task of describing and that of "destroying" the inadequate presuppositions that block the access to phenomena are one and the same. As *Being and Time* illustrates it in an exemplary way, the phenomenological procedure is, in one and the same gesture, critical "deconstruction" (*Abbau*) of the inherited presuppositions that conceal phenomena and prevent their adequate description, and "construction," that is, positive description of them. Phenomenology is always, at the same time as a description of the "things themselves," a historical meditation on what prevented them from being grasped.

Is it possible to maintain at the same time reference to the historical conditionality of *all* description-interpretation of phenomena and reference to the "thing itself," that the description-interpretation has as its goal to bring to light?[20] If all description-interpretation is historically conditioned, that is, valid solely on the condition of endorsing the presuppositions that orient it, can we still speak of an "adequate" description of "things" as they are revealed to us as phenomena? This is, in substance, the problem of relativism. Beginning in 1921, Heidegger emphasizes that the concept of relativism is inadequate in characterizing a philosophical position, because one can only charge it with relativism if one has already subscribed to the ideal of dogmatism—the ideal of a truth "per se," absolute and valid once and for all.[21] Relativism shares with dogmatism the same ideal of absolute knowledge, free from doubt and endowed with a universal validity; but the former proclaims the inaccessibility of this knowledge, while the latter claims to have achieved it. It remains to be seen whether this way of dismissing both relativism and dogmatism by playing them off of each other does not resemble a sleight of hand. It is hardly convincing as long as it has not been shown *positively* what status philosophical truths can be given.

How can Heidegger maintain at the same time that phenomenology, even in its hermeneutic version, has no other goal than to bring into view the phenomena, to bring them to light themselves, on their own behalf, and that all description is more or less a historically conditioned interpretation that hence cannot aspire to be a definitive, universal, unconditionally valid truth? That there is, to say the least, a strong tension between these two assertions appears in light of a supplementary consideration. *Being and Time* maintains at the same time a strict essentialism and the idea that philosophy is by essence a historical activity, resting on a hermeneutic procedure. It advances the two following theses, which may be incompatible:

(1) Phenomenology rests on interpretation.
(2) All phenomenological descriptions are essential descriptions.

The first thesis orients us in the direction of a conception of philosophical activity that is historical through and through. Because it rests on interpretation, phenomenology cannot rise above its own presuppositions; it is limited to elucidating them as far as possible. It only gives us historical truths that cannot be unconditionally valid.

The second, which goes hand in hand in *Being and Time* with the defense of the ideal of phenomenology as science, explicitly claims to follow Husserl's essentialism and apriorism. "Not just any accidental structures, but essential ones which, in every kind of Being that factical *Dasein* may possess, persist as determinative for the character of its Being."[22] This vindication of the essential character of phenomenological descriptions adopts the Husserlian equivalence of essence and of the *a priori*. The existential analytic has as its task the discovery of "the *a priori* character of Being and of all the structures of Being."[23] Thus it can explicitly claim to follow the "breakthrough" of Husserl's *Logical Investigations* in their characterization of the *a priori*. "Edmund Husserl has not only enabled us to understand once more the meaning of any genuine philosophical empiricism; he has also given us the necessary tool."[24] This "tool" is phenomenological essence, Husserl's material *a priori*. But an *eidetic* characterization of essence is no longer possible. Indeed, the Husserlian eidetic proves insufficient when it comes to apprehending an entity whose way of being is that of *Dasein*, an entity whose very essence is to exist in the sense that this verb possesses henceforth in existential analytics, that is, whose essence is to understand Being and *to be* in the mode of *In-der-Welt-sein*. To the extent that, according to the famous declaration of §9 of *Being and Time*, "*the 'essence' of Dasein lies in its existence*,"[25] the eidetic method, inasmuch as its purpose is to separate almost chemically the *quid* from the *quod*—the essence from the fact of which it is the essence—cannot account for the *essential* facticity (*Faktizität*) of that being—a facticity that cannot be separated from its *existing* itself. The eidetic method does not help us understand the *essential* intertwining that intervenes here between essence and existence—not the *existentia* of the Scholastics, but the ek-sistence as ontological characterization of *Dasein*: "This prohibits us from experiencing and interrogating this entity, Dasein, 'eidetically' . . . What is to be determined is not the '*eidos*' of this entity but from the outset and throughout solely *its way to be*, not the what of that of which it is composed but *the how of its Being and the characters of this how*."[26] Withdrawn from the horizon of an eidetic, essence and the *a priori* become specifications of Being as such. It is a question of understanding "the specification of the structure of the *a priori* as a feature of the Being of entities and not a feature of the entities themselves"[27]—in short, it is a question of apprehending the *a priori* itself, or better yet, the apriority of the *a priori* in light of what Heidegger will henceforth christen "ontological difference." Thus specified, essence need no longer be conceived of as ahistorical. Since Being is in its very "essence" finite, temporal, and historical, essences are only possible, as ontological features, insofar as they are endowed with the same characteristics. The rejection of eternal truths and of the "*fanciful idealization*" of the subject that accompanies them, in §44 (c) of *Being and Time*, marks the end of an eidetics conceived sub specie aeternitatis, and reintroduces essences into history without, however, as Heidegger stresses, taking away their "universal validity." Consequently, essential truths can no longer escape the fate of truth without qualification: "*because the kind of Being that is essential to truth is of the character of Dasein,* all *truth is relative to Dasein's Being*."[28] And since that Being is declined historically, the essences themselves are dovetailed to the historicality of *Dasein*; they cannot escape the historical conditioning of the being par excellence.

The problem is that Heidegger does not tell us—here or anywhere else—how to reconcile the "universal validity" of essences with their historical rootedness (no more, as a matter of fact, than he tells us how it is possible to maintain at the same time that Being is *a priori* and that *a priori* is a feature of Being). Not only does he not tell us this, but, taken literally, his doctrine ends up with insurmountable aporias. Can one "historicize" the essences (and along with them the essential truths) while at the same time retaining for the discourse on essence all its rights? In retaining, on the one hand, universal and necessary essences, and in stressing, on the other hand, the necessary historical conditioning of these same essences and of the essential truths that follow from them, Heidegger introduces into his conception all the ingredients indispensable to relativism. Indeed, relativism consists in the claim that truths are always relative to a given historical perspective. It is therefore caught in the following alternative: either this assertion itself is relative to a given historical perspective, which leads to a downright absurdity; or else this assertion is not relative to a historical perspective, and it is therefore false to say that *all* truths are. In trying to escape at the same time Husserl's dogmatism—by maintaining that *all* truth (and consequently also the truths of essence) is subject to historical conditioning—and outright relativism, which would claim that we cannot rise to the level of *any* super-historical truth, Heidegger winds up at an impasse. He tries to escape Husserlian dogmatism by "historicizing" essences and Diltheyan relativism (historicism) by considering historicality itself as an *essential* structure of *Dasein*. But the latter claim contradicts the former. If historicality is an *essential* structure of *Dasein*, there are only two possibilities left: either the "essence" in question is itself something historical, and the truth that follows from it is subject to historical conditioning and is not valid universally and necessarily (which is absurd); or the "essence" under consideration is an ahistorical essence, and in that case it is quite simply untrue that *all* truth is subjected to historical conditioning.

It is pointless to say that we must reject both dogmatism and relativism without explaining how you do so. It is pointless to hold that essences are historical if you don't say how this assertion is compatible with a discourse on essence. What is an essence? Or rather, what is a property of essence (and correlatively, a description of essence), since we have seen earlier that essences are not necessarily ideal *objects* of a specific kind—

and Heidegger has contributed positively to helping us think this, by leading back essence to Being and holding that Being is *nothing that is*? Answer: the properties of essence are properties necessary for a thing to be what it is; *they belong to it in all possible worlds, and therefore* a fortiori *at all possible times.* But if the properties of essence are properties that are *necessary* (in order for a thing to be what it is), how can they vary historically? Would Heidegger suggest, for example, that the judgment "all spatial things are perceived by adumbrations [*Abschattungen*]" is a truth that depends on particular historical presuppositions? There would no longer be any reason to speak here of a judgment of *essence.* Historicizing essences cannot be a solution, if essences specify the domains of the necessary and the universal *a priori.* To one who would argue that essences are historical, the following question should be asked: Is the assertion that essences are historical a truth of essence? If so, then that truth is in turn historical, and therefore it is not a truth *of essence* in the sense of a necessary and universal truth.

The only way out of this dilemma seems to be the one that I began to suggest at the beginning of this chapter. It consists in showing that the phenomenological description is a far more complex and refined operation than it seems, a "stratified" operation that *begins* with descriptions of essence but cannot be carried out from beginning to end as a description of essence. The essences in which description is anchored are necessary and universal, as Husserl rightly underscored, and in this regard they are indeed ahistorical or rather super-historical: their discovery is a historical fact but their validity does not depend on history. In formulating transcendental questions, in introducing a historically inherited conceptuality, and, most often, *theoretical* presuppositions that interfere with the description of essence while at the same time attempting to make its grounds explicit, phenomenology enters into its hermeneutic dimension, but without ever abandoning its original "home ground." Phenomenological descriptions are therefore not descriptions of essence *through and through,* and this is why they are not through and through apodictic descriptions, either. They are rooted in judgments of essence but do not derive their entire descriptive legitimacy from these judgments. The judgments of essence are ahistorical, but the descriptions that proceed from these judgments and attempt to elucidate their (transcendental) necessary conditions are not. The *a priori* on which phenomenological description is built, for example "human experience is temporal," or "man is mortal (finite)"—assertions without which nothing *Being and Time* says would make sense—are strictly necessary, and, if these *a priori* have been correctly identified, they are not subject to revision, as opposed to phenomenological descriptions that proceed from transcendental arguments; otherwise the very idea of essential truths from which the description *sets out* would be destroyed.

This seems to be the only way to understand how the *a priori*, essential element of the phenomenological description, and its historical element (the "hermeneutic" element), fit together. This last element comes into play at the very moment the transcendental argumentation begins. It is necessary at that point to introduce premises that are not all reducible to essential truths *stricto sensu*. That *Dasein* possesses an understanding of Being is a premise of this kind. After all, it is not certain that such a thing as "Being as such [*Sein überhaupt*]" makes any sense, because it is not certain that there is any sense in postulating a unity of the different acceptations of being ("being" in the sense of predication, "being" in the sense of identity, "being" in the sense of existence, "being" in the sense of being true). There are many premises of this kind in existing phenomenological descriptions, and that is precisely what makes them depend on an *interpretation* of phenomena. But if this interpretation is not arbitrary, if it has its starting point in genuine judgments of essence—if, in sum, it is not oblivious of its own presuppositions but strives to bring them to light as such, the specter of relativism is overcome. It is not true, then, that every interpretation is as good as any other; nor is it true that there are no phenomena, but only interpretations. We have criteria to decide between these interpretations, even if we do not have any kind of infallible method to succeed in this. The only method that remains is the one philosophy has always used: a critical and well argued discussion.

Perhaps at that point the reader will get the impression that phenomenology has betrayed its own principles. If all phenomenological descriptions are debatable, if every one of them rests in the final analysis on an implicit argument, on premises that can be challenged, is there still such a thing as a *description of the phenomena*—a phenomenology? But this objection has something rhetorical about it. There is no need to subscribe to the ideal of absolutely adequate and unconditionally true descriptions to commit oneself to the view that all descriptions are not of equal value and that some are truer than others. There is no need to believe that the "in itself" of things could be reached independently of the relativity of our descriptions in order to mantain that there are descriptions that put us on the right track toward the "things themselves." To those who deny that a description that does not give us the "in itself" could be qualified as "true" or "trustworthy," the reply should be that there is no sense in pretending to reach the "in itself" of things *independently of the descriptions that we can give of it*—relative though they may be to interests, queries, a specific conceptuality, and, often, implicit presuppositions. Perhaps the main achievement of the "hermeneutic turn" sketched out by Heidegger, all the possibilities of which should be filled in, is after all negative: there is no *unconditional* method in philosophy that would allow us to reach absolute truths, free from all relativity and beyond any possible doubt. As Gadamer wrote, "the idea of an absolute reason is not a possibility for historical humanity."[29]

This conclusion may lead us to reconsider a problem that has been left in suspense, closely tied to the one we are dealing with at present. In Husserl, the dogmatic conception of the phenomenological description is accompanied by the idea that there is a truth "in itself," a truth that is not only true for such and such a person—or even for such and such a *species*: "What is true is absolutely, intrinsically true: truth is one and the same, whether men or non-men, angels or gods apprehend and judge it."[30] This dogmatic conception of description and truth thus goes hand in hand with the rejection of "anthropologism," which constitutes, in Husserl's view, one of the forms of relativism. I stressed in chapter 1 that this rejection of anthropologism was ambiguous and problematic. It is difficult to consider the essences and essential structures that are interesting from the phenomenological point of view otherwise than as bound to phenomena such as they appear *to us*, that is to say, to the *human* experience. This problem, with which Husserl constantly struggled, is the problem of what he will call more and more insistently as his work advances "arch-facticity." Now, this problem is a variant of the one we were just examining.

Indeed, the rejection of the idea of a perfect conformity of our descriptions to the "things themselves," such as they would offer themselves *independently of all description*, and, what is more, independently of all interpretation, must sooner or later lead to the rejection of the idea of descriptions valid "for men and gods," the abandonment of all divine point of view—even as a mere methodological fiction—in philosophy. The experience that phenomenology can endeavor to describe is only the *factical* experience, or better yet, the "arch-factical" one, the experience possessed by those that we ourselves are as *human beings*. This apparently trivial assertion is so little self-evident that Heidegger, the first to reject forcefully the "acosmic" character of the Husserlian transcendental ego, also the first to confer upon facticity the rank of *essential* structure of existence, refusing thereby even the characteristic opposition of Husserl's eidetics between the fact and the *eidos*, continued to maintain that anthropologism was one of the main threats that jeopardized philosophy. *Dasein* is not man, as *Being and Time* emphasizes; *Dasein* is the essence, or, better yet, the Being of man. "In *Being and Time* the problem is set up outside the sphere of subjectivism . . . *the entire anthropological problematic is kept at a distance.*"[31] In what way is the problem raised by such assertions analogous to the one formulated above? Anthropologism is a variant of relativism, for Heidegger[32] as for Husserl; his rejection is therefore accompanied by a return to an essentialist position. It could be said that, just as Heidegger previously stressed the conditioned nature of all philosophical interpretation while at the same time maintaining a doctrine of essence inherited from that of Husserl, and without specifying how these two theses are to be reconciled, he now rises in protest against the abstraction of the Husserlian starting point in an idealized ego, restoring to facticity all its rights, not as a mere "limit" of *eidos* but as an *essential* constituent of human existence as such. There is no human being but factical—and by that we should understand: this or that human being existing *in fact.* And yet Heidegger refuses to consider that it is the *factical* man that must be the subject matter of a phenomenological description. That description concerns the essence of man, namely *Dasein.* Heidegger thus tends to reject anthropologism without rejecting altogether anthropology. He limits himself to derive the latter from an existential analytic of *Dasein,* which he considers to be more originary.

At this point, it is no longer possible to dodge the question of whether the distinction between the essence (or the Being) of man—*Dasein*—and *factical* man makes sense, whether it doesn't simply take us back to an essentialism akin to Husserl's, which radically separates the essence from the fact of which it is the essence, in contradiction with the very spirit of *Being and Time.* We find, for example, in Heidegger the following assertion: "If I say of Dasein that its basic constitution is Being-in-the-world, I am then first of all asserting something that belongs to its essence [*Wesen*], and I thereby disregard whether the being of such a nature factually [*faktisch*] exists or not."[33] Such an assertion puts *Dasein* and empirical man in diametric opposition, just as it does facticity (*Faktizität*) as an essential feature of the former, and factuality (*Tatsächlichkeit*) as a contingent characteristic of the latter. It *essentializes* facticity, which is no longer held to be identical to the pure fact of existence. It thus reaches the point where it essentializes existence itself (for which Heidegger will adopt a new spelling: ek-sistence), as ontological character of *Dasein,* which differs henceforth from the *factual* existence of man. This twofold operation makes something like birth literally unthinkable; for the "fact" that *Dasein* advenes in fact to existence (therefore also to ek-sistence) by the event of a birth cannot be of the order of a fact for that existence (ek-sistence). Consequently, *Dasein* is no longer thought of as the essence of factical man, but as its double, freed from the factuality (*Tatsächlichkeit*) that belongs to the latter. *Dasein* becomes an "essence" in a sense very akin to the one this word takes on in Husserl's eidetics, an *eidos* distinct from the fact of which it is the *eidos*. This strange doubling must be emphasized. Indeed, if the essence is distinct from the individual of which it is the essence, it can possess characteristics other than those of this individual—even opposite ones. And this is precisely what occurs in *Being and Time*. In that work, Heidegger ends up in a position that is ambiguous to say the least, since *Dasein* must be man and must not be man, have the essential characteristics of man and not have them: *Dasein* is "neutral," not only with respect to birth, but also to corporeity and sexual difference.[34] It is at once the essence of man and the bearer of characteristics (carnal and sexual neutrality, absence of birth) that *are diametrically opposed* to those of man, of whom it is nevertheless the essence.

An unstable, perhaps untenable position, as we see by the hesitations that abound in the existential analytic. Let us mention a few of them. What differentiates *Dasein* from the human being? Apparently, the answer is quite simple: *Dasein* is not man, but the Being of man: "*das Dasein, d. h. das Sein des Menschen*," we read in *Being and Time*.[35] But the lingering remnant of man that appears alongside *Dasein* is intriguing and troubling. Can one entirely divorce the question of the meaning of Being as it is formulated, taking *Dasein* as the guiding thread from the question of the Being of man, that is, of that entity that, as Heidegger says, "we ourselves are"? To whom does this "we" refer? Does not such a "we" strangely echo the "we" of the Kantian Transcendental Aesthetics, which prompts Husserl to say that Kant remains mired in the worst of contradictions (that of a transcendental anthropologism), and that consequently the authentic meaning of the *a priori* eluded him? Still more radically: *Dasein* is the Being of man, Heidegger tells us. But the question formulated by *Being and Time* is not, generally speaking, that of the Being of man, but indeed that of the Being of *Dasein*. Now, if *Dasein* is already the Being of man, then the Being of *Dasein* is the Being of the Being of man—a consummately absurd expression, and one that is excluded by the whole conceptuality of the ontological difference: Being is always the Being of an entity. Did Heidegger notice this difficulty? Probably so, because he asks, in a course immediately following the writing of *Being and Time*: "However, can we say then that Being itself has a mode of being?"[36] Only *Dasein* has a "mode of being" in the strict sense; but if *Dasein* is the Being of man, then Being has a mode of being—and the ontological difference, the axis around which all Heidegger's thought revolves, is destroyed. The least that can be said is that the articulation between the ontology of *Dasein* and (philosophical) anthropology does not stand out very clearly from these formulations. The same ambiguity returns in other passages. For example, *Dasein*, as opposed to man, is not a particular ontic region; it is defined as "the ontic-ontological condition for the possibility of any ontologies";[37] but at the moment of enumerating these ontic regions rooted in fundamental ontology, Heidegger once again mentions *Dasein*—and not man—as one of these particular regions.[38] How can *Dasein* constitute an ontic region among others, while being the ontico-ontological possibility for all regions, and for their respective "regional ontologies"? This cannot simply be a lapse—not *only* a lapse in any case. Man, the one who is born and dies, who has a body and sexual differentiation, does not cease haunting *Dasein* like a cumbersome doppelganger from which the latter is at pains to rid itself. Anthropology still haunts fundamental ontology, despite the repeated denials of its author. The supposedly faulty reading that sees in the analytic of *Dasein* a variant of philosophical anthropology cannot be just a "misreading."

These ambiguities probably originate in the fact that Heidegger remains more attached to the Husserlian conception of essence than he himself admits. He considers that if *Dasein* is the essence of man, that essence must be something—an entity?—that must possess different characteristics than that of which it is the essence. But if essence is not at all an entity, *it makes no sense to say of it that it has or does not have the characteristics of that of which it is the essence.* And this is what Heidegger himself taught us when he maintained that Being—that which makes understandable "essence" in the renewed sense conferred upon it by Heidegger—*is nothing that is.* The conclusion to be drawn from these difficulties is relatively simple and can be put as follows: a description of essence is not a description of *anything other* than what the essence is essence of; it is a description of that same thing *in a different respect.* The description of *Dasein* as essence of man—or whatever name we give it, including "the advenant"[39]—is not the description of any other thing than the empirical man, the *factical* man who is born and dies, who has a body, sexual differentiation, and so on; it is a description of this same man not in his contingent, empirical features, but *from the point of view of his essence.* To misconstrue this is to misconstrue the problem of which Husserl was aware, and that Heidegger did not solve—that of arch-facticity. It is an essential feature of all material essence that it is "chained to a fact," as Husserl used to say. But then the phenomenological description, insofar as it is understood as a description of essence at least at its starting point, is chained to *our* factical experience, to the factical experience of the human beings that we are; in no case can it rise above that experience. It is an *a priori* feature of the various phenomenological *a priori* that they can be evinced as such only *a posteriori,* that is to say, that they retain an ineluctable tie to our *factical* existence by virtue of our birth as men; for man only *is* man if he is *born* man.[40] The horizon of anthropology thereby turns out to be *impossible to overcome.* And we should be wary, at the very least, of the "ends" of man prophesied in the wake of Heidegger. Furthermore, Heidegger himself will revisit this point at the end of his itinerary; he will again speak of "men," of "mortals," and of their essence.

We have now reached the point at which we can recapitulate the main characteristics of a phenomenological description.

We have seen that phenomenology was a descriptive philosophy that proceeded *a priori* on the basis of initial descriptions of essence bearing upon the domain of experience as such, and that inquired into their conditions of possibility by means of transcendental arguments. We have seen what "description" meant here, what the status of these essences were, what reasons we had to hold them to be *a priori,* to what status the descriptions that start from them could pretend: that of *a priori* and revisable truths. We have called the procedure consisting in going beyond the initial descriptions of essence thanks to interpretations resting inevitably on historical presuppositions "hermeneutic phenomenology." We have seen, lastly, that the experience relevant for such descriptions was none other than *human* experience. It remains to be understood—and this is the most arduous task—how "experience" is best construed.

Part 2

Transformations

> The radicalism of phenomenology must act against itself and against everything that is expressed as phenomenological knowledge.
>
> —Martin Heidegger

Introduction

The Phenomenological Concept of Experience

The purpose of the first part of this book was to elaborate the idea of phenomenology as a descriptive discipline. The task of the part now opening will be to penetrate more deeply into that discipline focusing on its subject matter itself.[1] The thing or matter (*Sache*) of phenomenology is experience itself in its various modes. Therefore to begin with, we shall consider how "experience" must be understood.

This question goes beyond the confines of an introduction. It will concern us throughout the following pages. Seen in the perspective of the history of the phenomenological movement, the decisive fact seems to be Husserl's leading back of that polysemic expression, "experience," to one of its meanings taken as paradigmatic. *Erfahrung*, experience in its widest acceptation, is understood by Husserl as *Erlebnis*, lived experience. Now if every lived experience is obviously an experience, it is not at all certain that all experience is to be understood in terms of lived experience(s). One could, for example, consider a pain as being a lived experience: it wells up at a given moment, lasts for a certain time, and it is felt by the person undergoing it as being localized in a part of his or her body. According to the Cartesian criterion taken over by Husserl, a "lived experience" is everything that is offered to consciousness in such a way that it is impossible to doubt it; therefore in such a way that we have an *apodictic* knowledge of it. A pain, at first sight, meets this criterion: the one feeling it cannot be in doubt as to whether he or she feels it. But the word "experience" is normally used much more broadly. We can experience the emotions of other people, such as the anger or joy in their faces; we perceive the brilliance of a work of art and the beauty of a city; we may have experienced war, German occupation, illness, or happiness. There are experiences of disorientation, of love, and even experiences that "transport" us suddenly into the past—as when we see a loved one once again, or hear once more the song of a thrush; then, within the melancholy of the present song, another of long ago may be heard, echoing the depth of time that takes away illusions and hopes. Such is the song heard by Chateaubriand at Montboissier, bringing back to him the woods of Combourg and the "days lost in pursuit of that unachievable bliss. There is nothing more for me to learn; I have travelled faster than others, and made the tour of life."[2]

There is much to learn, for philosophy, in the examination of these broader, pre-philosophical uses of "experience." None of the uses we have just mentioned meet, at first blush, the Cartesian criterion of indubitability. Experience as used here is about *realities of the world*, and sometimes even realities of the past; and regarding these realities many doubts may arise.

We will have occasion to examine this broad concept of experience, and we will have to see why the narrow concept of lived experience, with its Cartesian ascendancy, cannot be an adequate guiding clue for the phenomenological project. Our experience of a stretch of blue sky above the rooftops has what we might call a phenomenal content. This experience is the very way in which we are conscious of something (in this case, of the sky and its color) and, reciprocally, what we are conscious of, what this experience is the experience of, is always revealed to us in such and such a way, that is, with the distinctive features belonging to it. To say that the experience is the very way we are conscious of something entails no commitment to the idea that the "subject" of the experience is *a* consciousness; the "consciousness" required here is an adverbial, not a substantive one. It is a *way of being conscious* and not an entity of any sort. "Experience has a phenomenal content" thus means prima facie that in every experience something is given to us to experience. What is given to us in an experience, what is *experienced* in it, is also, by this very fact, what appears—what to us is a *phenomenon*. Experience in its primary and original sense—the *Urerfahrung*, as Husserl would have said—is thus an experience in which something is presented to us "in person" in its irrecusable presence. This experience is classically called "perception," and for the time being we will leave aside the problem of whether it would be better for us to use other names: openness to the world, or being-in-the-world, for example. The defect in the concept of perception seems to be that it brings along with it a whole intertwined skein of distinctions—the one between "sensibility" and "understanding" to begin with—but also an underlying *epistemological* problematic. Now a painting or a symphony can be the object of an experience without our necessarily having to trace that experience back to the sole sphere of sensibility, of *aesthesis*. There is an experience of language; there is an experience of events that are meaningful to us; there is an experience of certain axiological properties (gracefulness, ugliness, femininity) without there being any reason to preemptively restrict the concept of experience to "perception" in the classic sense of the term, as reception of data of sensation—regardless of the precise meaning attached to this last expression.

All experience involves something that is presented to us with a distinctive feature, a determinate phenomenal content. The phenomenon, here, is nothing other than the "self-showing" of something. Of course, this does not rule out the possibility to speak also of experience (or quasi-experience) in the case of "things" that are fictive, or even illusions. This point will not concern us for now. In all experience something is self-given, present in person—as opposed to assumed or inferred. As a first approximation, we can characterize experience as having the following characteristics.

(1) All experience has a phenomenal content.
(2) A phenomenon is the way in which something appears.
(3) All experience is about something, which consequently shows itself to us.
(4) Originary experience is perception (being-in-the-world).
(5) What shows itself can be considered as given, as opposed to assumed or inferred.

With this brief characterization, we are far from having answered our initial question. Many points remain in darkness, many questions arise. What is the "subject" of experience? Is this subject psychological, transcendental, ontological . . . ? Is experience itself *experienced*? Do phenomena *appear*? Should we have recourse to the vocabulary of intuition and perception to qualify primordial experience? Should we speak of a (certain, evident) *knowledge* of experience or of phenomena (which seems to go hand in hand with the idea that phenomena appear); or should we rather say that to have an experience is *to be conscious* of its phenomenal content, and not to possess a *knowledge* about it in the strict sense of the term?

We will have occasion to return to these different issues. For the moment, let us dwell on the last one mentioned. It has divided philosophers and continues to do so. Wittgenstein has advanced famous arguments to reduce to the absurd the idea of a *knowledge* of our own lived experiences and sensations. These arguments allow him at the same time to oppose the Cartesian tradition and to retain something of the view that it makes no sense to doubt our experiences. Let us take note of the fact that Wittgenstein's arguments rest on a conception of experience that is at least as narrow as Husserl's, since it equates experiences to mental episodes possessing an "authentic duration," that is, a beginning and an end, a continuity or discontinuity, and, in relation to each other, simultaneity or succession. From a Wittgensteinian point of view, sensation—a pain, for instance—plays the role of paradigm for the characterization of experience in general.

The grammatical analysis of verbs of experience reveals that they form a subset of "psychological verbs" (verbs of intention, desire, emotion, belief, etc.), that is, verbs that are characterized by the asymmetry of their use in the first- and third-person singular. In the third person, the use of these verbs is based on observation: to tell whether someone else has a given intention or sensation, we must observe his or her behavior. But we do not attribute a sensation or an intention to ourselves on the basis of an observation of anything—neither of a private episode nor of public behavior. Wittgenstein's argument in order to establish this point is subdivided into two moments.

(1) In the case of that subclass of psychological verbs formed by verbs of experience (and, paradigmatically, in verbs of sensation), we are not dealing with assertions that could be true or false, allowing us to describe, when they are true, states of affairs, but with expressions (*Äußerungen*) that in the course of language learning come to replace other, more "natural" expressions. A child has hurt himself: he cries. Adults teach him to replace this cry progressively by an exclamation, and later on by a complete sentence. Therefore "I am in pain" is an *expression* of pain and not a *description* of anything.[3]

(2) For the class of psychological verbs in general (it being understood that while all verbs of experience are psychological verbs, the converse is not true), doubt is logically excluded, *and therefore knowledge as well.* Thus, it will be said of an intention or a sensation that I *have* it, but not that I *know* that I have it. More precisely, the expression "I *know* that I am in pain" (or "I *know* that I want to go out") have strictly the same meaning as the expressions "I am in pain" ("I want to go out"); they are either emphatic expressions or jokes, and—taken literally—grammatical nonsense.[4] It makes no sense to *doubt* one's sensations or intentions, and consequently, it makes no sense to *know* them, either.

The considerable influence of these arguments has turned some philosophers away from all idea of a possible knowledge or even of a possible description of our own experiences. But should they be given so much weight? Even assuming that these remarks are *purely grammatical*, that is, that they harbor no substantive claim about what "knowledge" is, for example, do they suffice to show the absurdity of a descriptive discipline that claims to enlighten us on our experience as such? This is quite unlikely, as Wittgenstein's gambit raises at least as many problems as it solves. To begin with, is it true that the verbal expression of our sensations is an *Äußerung* and not an assertion? Is it really *meaningless* to maintain that "I am in pain" is an assertion about my state or my sensations? If that were the case, it would bring about a cortege of consequences that would be bothersome, to put it mildly. If "I am in pain" is not an assertion, I cannot use that sentence in a meaningful way to *inform* someone of my pain. More seriously still, it is hard to see how the negation of that sentence, "I am not in pain," which by definition has the same grammatical status as the affirmative sentence, could have an expressive value: Would it *express* the absence of pain? But what is a "natural expression" of the absence of pain? Furthermore, if Wittgenstein is right, "I am in pain" can no longer appear in any valid inference. A reasoning of the type "all persons feeling a pain *x* are suffering from an injury *z*; I feel a pain *x*, therefore I am suffering from an injury *z*" becomes sheer nonsense. These consequences, counterintuitive to say the least, have led Wittgenstein's followers to try to mitigate his statements in various ways: (1) by admitting that "I am in pain," at least in some of its uses, does not have the same meaning as "ouch!" and therefore that *it is indeed an assertion*, even if it is an assertion without cognitive content (Tugendhat)[5]—and so we can rightly speak of "lie" here, and not just of "simulation" and (2) by postulating several meanings of the word "description," one epistemological and the other "intentional," having the nature of a *speech act*, by virtue of which "I am in pain" does indeed constitute a *kind of description* (Hacker).[6] Whatever reform it undergoes, Wittgenstein's gambit seems to have something dogmatic about it.

The situation is hardly better for the second part of the argument. First, it is not certain that for all psychological verbs doubt is logically excluded:[7] I can probably make a mistake in saying that this tea tastes like Lapsang Souchong or that I heard a C-sharp; I can also err in saying that at this moment I am feeling anger or jealousy—someone else can bring me to recognize that my anger was simulated and my jealousy a pose. Next, even if we were to concede for the sake of argument that *in all these cases* doubt is logically excluded, it would not follow that to speak of "knowledge" has no meaning in this context—or rather, that consequence would only follow on the condition that an additional premise were to be introduced, namely that all knowledge is empirical in kind (there is no *a priori* knowledge, nor, *a fortiori*, any knowledge of *essences*)—a premise that, as I have insisted, underlies Wittgenstein's whole philosophy. As attested to by §246 of *Philosophical Investigations*, what Wittgenstein rejects is the idea that I could come to *learn* something about my pain, to *acquire* a knowledge about it *by observation*—hence also be wrong in making the observation: "I cannot be said to learn of them [my sensations]. I *have* them." We may concede this point to Wittgenstein without conceding to him that to know, *in all cases*, is to come to *learn* something; therefore, that all knowledge of my experience (for example, all description that brings to light its essential *a priori* structures) is an absurdity. The phenomenology of pain gives us no new empirical knowledge, nor does it rest on such knowledge. It is *a priori* in the sense that its *justification* at no point introduces a hypothesis subject to eventual falsification, that is, in the sense that the phenomenological features of pain are not something that it would be possible to "learn" *in that sense*—although perhaps in another sense, a good phenomenological description might indeed allow me to "learn" something. In any case, we have discussed this problem enough in the first part of this work to leave it aside from now on.

Even if Wittgenstein's arguments are not conclusive, this does not necessarily entail that we must return to the Cartesian position. To describe the structures of essence of our experience—to do phenomenology—is not necessarily tantamount to postulating an *indubitable knowledge* of that experience. Perhaps there is no reason to apply the concept of *knowledge* in the strong sense to that of experience as we have defined it above, as consciousness of phenomenological contents. It is one thing to say that our experience of the world is already intrinsically a kind of knowledge (and, in addition, an indubitable knowledge); it is quite another to maintain that there is a *possible* phenomenological knowledge of that experience in the form of linguistic descriptions bearing upon structures of essence. These descriptions are carried out in the first person without necessarily resting on introspection, on "internal perception," or *a fortiori* on apodictic evidence. To reiterate, Wittgenstein's arguments do not seem of such a nature as to eliminate this possibility—the possibility of a *first-person description of experience as endowed with a phenomenal content.* It is not indispensable to postulate an infallible knowledge of our experiences as states of consciousness, or, better, as *modes of the awareness of something*, in order for the idea of a descriptive discipline shedding light on their essential structures to retain meaning.

We can conclude, at least provisionally, that Wittgenstein's remarks do not invalidate the idea of a description of experience in the sense I have conferred on that term. In order for there to be experience in general, something has to be given to be experienced: experience is *something we do*, rather than something we *have* (*Erlebnisse*, lived experiences); but what is experienced in an experience is something that is *given*, i.e., that is present for us through that experience. That which is thus given to us in an experience, that which is experienced in it, is also, consequently, that which appears, that which is a phenomenon. One can rightly wonder whether or not it is appropriate to say that the experience itself is "given," whether or not it is appropriate to say that phenomena "show themselves" or "appear," but in all experience something appears, is given according to a certain mode of givenness, and hence grasped without the least reasoning or inference. This simple and obvious sense is the one according to which it may be said that things are given to us, and even, up to a point, that phenomena are given to us—precisely, as *modes of givenness* of something. It is this concept of phenomenon that furnishes the leading clue to the phenomenological inquiry, and according to which the latter can present itself as a description of the things themselves in their phenomenality.

In the first part of this work, we purposely limited ourselves to very basic examples. Now we must leave that rarified atmosphere and reintroduce into our analyses all the complexity that gives phenomenology its worth. We must, to take up a geological metaphor dear to Husserl, undertake a series of probes into the thing itself. Whereas up until this point we have confronted phenomenology with its "others," interrogating it from the outside in light of queries not always its own, henceforth we can question it on its own terms, that is to say, setting out from its subject matter, from the "*thing itself*" of which it speaks, and consequently we can ask ourselves how it should be transformed from the inside.

13

Intentionality as a Problem

> "Intentionality" . . . is not a watchword but one that designates a central *problem.*
> —Martin Heidegger

Experience may be characterized as the very way in which we are conscious of things, events, processes, and so on, that, correlatively, appear to us "in" and "through" this experience; it has a phenomenal content. This relation to objects that, in all experience, are given to us to experience as phenomena has been given a name by Husserl: intentionality. To wonder in what sense experience is a consciousness of objects—is "about" these objects or "directed" toward them—constitutes the central enigma of Husserlian phenomenology. "The fundamental meaning of experience," as *Formal and Transcendental Logic* makes clear, is "*an original self-giving* [*einer originalen Selbstgebung*]."[1] Husserl calls this self-giving of objects in the flesh *perception.* But to speak of perception, as I mentioned previously, is not without its difficulties. When I listen to a tune, do I do no more than *perceive* it? To listen to it—is this not also to let it resonate affectively within me, to feel its gaiety and its sadness and—why not—to make analogies, to associate images and daydreams with it? Is this not, sometimes at least, to think something about it, to make comparisons, judgments? Where does experience end and thought begin? The answer to these questions has nothing evident about it.

Even less evident is the answer to the problem of what it means to describe our experience *as such.* If what an experience is about is what appears in it, to describe an experience does indeed seem to mean to describe what appears—what we are experiencing. The moment I try to describe my experience, it has already withdrawn before me like the sea, leaving no more on its palpitating shores than the washed-up waifs of the world. It is easy to describe the pen lying on my desk, but how to describe my experience of this pen? That experience is obviously not a "thing" that would be located somewhere between the pen and me, just as that pen is lying on the table between a notebook and a stack of books. Nor is it certain that it makes sense to say of my experience of the pen that it *appears to me,* or that it, too, is a "phenomenon." Is the experience an object of experience? Does the experience appear the way its phenomenal contents do? Probably not. Still, even if we refuse to subscribe to the idea of an experience whose phenomenal content would be that experience itself, the idea of a "reflexive" experience in which the experience would become its own object of experience, that does undermine the idea of a description—not of the things we experience, but of the experience of those things. I can describe the pen on the table, of course; but I can also be attentive to the way it appears to me, at this moment very close to me, within hand's reach, and perhaps in a little while farther away, from a different angle, in lighting that will have changed. To describe my constantly changing experience of this pen amounts to describing *modes* of appearance; not new things, nor things of a new kind, but that same thing from a different standpoint, according to a different way of considering it, when I am attentive not to what appears but to the *way* in which it appears. To describe experience is to describe the things themselves, but in reference to us, that is, to the one to which they appear, by incorporating the subject, so to speak, into the description. I can describe the pen by mentioning its "objective" properties: its form, its color, its tactile features. But I can also say that it looks close or far away, on a slant, to my right, shinier or duller than it was just now, and, when I move, taking on a reflected sheen that moves slowly along its edge, then dulls out. With these new predicates, we have already entered the realm of *phenomenological* description, a description of things as *we* see them, as they present themselves *to us.* The pen couldn't be "on my right" or "far away" if I myself were not situated here or there, in this room in any case, and if I did not have a body endowed with a sense of its own lateralization; it couldn't change its appearance if I didn't have a memory of its former ways of looking, and so on. In other words—and this is the essential point—in order to give meaning to the idea of a description of *experience,* at no time need we assume that to describe experience involves describing anything other than *the way* things look to us.

But historical phenomenology, that is, phenomenology as instituted by Husserl and espoused by most of his students, has hardly been sensitive to this nuance. It very quickly (too quickly?) inferred, from the fact that experience was the object of a description, that this experience was *of a different nature* than the things of which it was the experience—that it was a "thing" of a different kind than those with which the physicist, for example, was concerned. To describe experience, Husserl tells us, is to describe subjective lived experiences: *subjektive Erlebnisse.* That decision goes hand in hand with a terminological choice. The concept of *Erlebnis* favored by Husserl is not the "popular concept"; indeed, according to this latter concept, what experience—the fact of experiencing something (*erleben*)—is about is the event external to consciousness, or the thing experienced. "If someone says he 'experienced' the wars of 1866 and 1870, then what he has been said to have 'experienced' in this sense is a complex of outer events, and 'experiencing' [*Erleben*] consists here in perceptions, judgments and other acts."[2] According to this use of the term, our experience is of the world itself. But in the "phenomenological sense" in which Husserl understands it, the experiences we *have* (as opposed to the things we "live through") must be interpreted as the real components of consciousness belonging to its makeup.[3] "It is in *this* sense," he writes, "that what the ego or consciousness experiences is its experience. There is no difference between the lived or conscious content and the experience itself."[4] So not only is what we experience in an experience nothing but our lived experiences (experience experiences itself, which is paradoxical to say the least), but these lived experiences must be interpreted as "all that as real parts constitute any particular phenomenological flow of consciousness."[5] Thus, the objects or events of the world are not *experienced*, nor do they *appear*, in the strict, phenomenological sense of the term, since by "phenomenon" in *Logical Investigations* we must understand the real contents of consciousness, "the lived experience in which the appearance of the object resides."[6] Experience becomes henceforth strictly identical with the subjective lived experiences to which consciousness accedes reflectively and which differ *toto caelo* from the things and events of the world. Experience is characterized by two essential determinations: (1) its mode of access: "internal perception [*innere Wahrnehmung*]," to use an expression from Brentano;[7] and (2) its immanence (as opposed to the transcendence of the objects and events of the world), that is, its belonging to the "flow" of consciousness.

Yet Husserl is not content with tracing experience to lived experiences such as they take place in the immanence of consciousness. In an opposite movement, he opens that immanence up to transcendence, that is, to exteriority, since he attributes to some of these lived experiences the character of intentionality. To the Cartesian gesture that leads experience back to immanent *cogitationes* there corresponds an Aristotelian gesture that conceives of these lived experiences themselves as relating to things as they fill the world with their presence: lived experiences, then, are nothing else than the *very presentation of things.* "Intentionality" is the word referring to this enigma, the indication of a problem rather than its solution. It is not a *Losungswort,* a "watchword," that is, a solution (*Lösung*), Heidegger will say, punning on the proximity of the two terms in German; it is rather "the title of a central *problem*."[8] It remains to be seen whether this problem is not more difficult to solve than we thought at first (see chapter 2)—whether it does not constitute, strictly speaking, an aporia.

Are the two characteristics by which Husserl defines intentionality, namely (1) intentional lived experiences are *about something*, and (2) intentional lived experiences are such that their object *can* not *exist*, indeed compatible? The first determination breaks with the Cartesian tradition, since the aim of the description is to show that intentional lived experiences have an object that transcends the lived experience and belongs to exteriority. Against Brentano, and against the whole tradition coming from Descartes, Husserl understands intentionality as a "relation to the 'transcendent' thing."[9] But in order for intentionality to be a relation to the *extra mentem* thing, it has first to be a *relation*. Something is a relation only if its *relata* exist. In order for consciousness to be, in its very nature, a relation to the transcendent thing, it is therefore necessary for that thing to *exist* as one of the two end points between which the relation holds. Now this is precisely what the second characteristic denies. According to it, intentionality is precisely not a relation, but a quasi-relation. In intentional experiences, the *intentum*, the object meant by the *intention*, can always not exist: I can desire something without there being anything to which my desire corresponds or believe something without any state of affairs corresponding to my belief. Intentionality, according to this approach, is no longer a relation to something else, but a property of experiences considered in themselves. Can these two characteristics be reconciled? How can intentionality be both a relation to the transcendent thing (which implies that this thing exists) and a quasi-relation to an object that, at least in certain cases, does not exist? How can intentionality be at once a relational property and "an *inward* peculiarity of certain lived experiences"?[10] It suffices to raise the problem to see that it is insoluble in this form: either intentionality is an intrinsic characteristic of certain lived experiences (whether their object exists or not), or it is a "relation to the transcendent thing," which implies the existence of that thing. It is as if the object had at the same time to both exist necessarily and be able not to exist in order for such a thing as intentionality to be possible.

The difficulty is nowhere more manifest than in the case of perception. A desire can be a chimeric desire without ceasing to be a desire. A belief can be a false belief without ceasing to be a belief. But can it be said of a perception to which no object corresponds that it is still a *perception*? Should it not rather be called *illusion*, or even *hallucination*? Furthermore, if perception is defined by the self-givenness in the flesh of its object, how could it remain a perception in the absence of any object? Unless—and this is Husserl's paradoxical solution—we dissociate the givenness in the flesh, which is an *intrinsic* characteristic of the lived experience, from the existence of that object *ad extra*; but then, that means that a perception can give me the thing itself to experience, and in addition the thing itself in its bodily selfhood, without there being anything to be experienced—and consequently without it being in any way a *perception* in the usual sense of the term. There would be *perceptions* in which nothing would be perceived because there would be nothing to perceive. In short, there would be lived experiences that it would make sense to call "perceptions" (and not "hallucinations") and that would present the transcendent thing to me *in the flesh*—but in the complete absence of that thing!

Is there any way out of these difficulties? As I have shown in chapter 2, Husserl's "solution" consists in distinguishing in all intentional lived experiences three components (the act, the content, and the object) and in thinking the intentional content not as an internal duplicate of the object, a mental representation, but as the *mode of givenness* (which Husserl also calls "sense") of that object. It consists in replacing the iconic conception of intentionality in the Brentano tradition with a semantic paradigm. Thus, when I try to imagine a square circle, it is indeed *the object itself* that I intend, and that object is the same as the one intended by anyone who tries to do the same; but the intended object is in fact nothing, since it is contradictory; as a consequence, no intuition can correspond to my intentional act. It is indeed the object itself that is intended, but that object cannot be given; it remains the correlate of a signitive intention, as the expression through which I designate it reveals itself to be a *flatus vocis*. Yet it must be admitted that this solution is only an apparent one. Indeed, what does it mean that it is "the object itself" that is intended even when no intuition can fill that intention, that is, when that object is *nothing*? What object is being spoken of, since that object does not exist? A *nonexistent* object is not at all an *object*. The metaphors of intention and fulfilling do not modify the situation in the least. The content of the intending act is the object such as it *can* eventually be given in an intuition—when it exists. The content of the intending act is therefore the object in its mode of givenness (or its "sense"). But only an object that *is given* can have a "mode of givenness," and only an object that *exists* can be given. A nonexistent or impossible object can have no mode of givenness, and hence no "sense" that constitutes the content of an intending act. To be sure, I can always assert that I am intending the square circle in imagination—on the condition of adding that *I believe (mistakenly)* that I am intending it, since there is nothing here that is intended. To maintain that the square circle is intended with a certain "sense" that is its mode of givenness if it exists—amounts to saying something contradictory, since the square circle *does not exist* and therefore cannot be intended according to a "sense" (a content, an intentional matter) that is its mode of givenness *if it exists.* In short, the metaphors of fullness and emptiness, of intuition and intending, do not enable us to surmount Brentano's problem except verbally. It is not at all certain that it is possible to speak of the content as "sense" in the case of a nonexistent object (either necessarily or contingently). Hence, it is not certain that one can speak justifiably of an object's being intended according to a perceptual "sense," when there is no object to be perceived. The semantic paradigm has only ostensibly toppled the iconic paradigm of intentionality, since the content is quickly changed back into a mental duplicate that could "be," as correlate of an intending act, even despite the circumstance of the intended object's *not being.* Far from freeing intentionality from the idea of an internal substitute, the act/content/object triad reduces us to falling back into the same rut.

If this tension is constitutive of the Husserlian concept of intentionality, the question of how to surmount this difficulty—assuming that it is possible—becomes decisive for the fate of phenomenology as a whole. One of the ways to solve this conflict is to initiate the "transcendental turn" that takes place in Husserl's 1906–07 courses,[11] and still more clearly in his five lectures on *The Idea of Phenomenology.* Indeed, a part of the problem is that, for certain intentional acts, the first characteristic seems to apply perfectly: they are in their very nature "relation to the transcendent thing." That is the case with perception, recollection, and ideation. For others, on the other hand, it is the second characteristic that seems relevant: a desire, a wish, a belief, a judgment are such that their object—which in most cases is an abstract object, a state of affairs—can *not* exist. Finally, for still others, that object *must* not exist: and thus it goes—differently—with imagination, illusion, and hallucination. In other words, part of the problem lies in the fact that the field of intentional acts is actually much less homogeneous than Husserl seems ready to admit. To try to understand perceptual intentionality and the intentionality of beliefs on the same model can only lead to doing violence to both.

But Husserl's doctrine of intentionality was progressively elaborated in its entirety precisely by the combination of a perceptual and a semantic paradigm. In conformity with the former, intentionality puts us *necessarily in a relationship with objects* that are intersubjectively accessible and identifiable. It is the same object that I perceive and that he or she perceives; it is the same essence that I grasp and that he grasps; it is the same *fictum* that we both imagine, and so on. According to the semantic paradigm, by contrast, an expression can have a meaning without having an object. To understand that expression is to grasp its meaning and—*only when its referent exists*—to refer to something. Now Husserl was not content with juxtaposing these two paradigms; he undertook to unify them in a general theory of intentionality. Just as, in the theory of meaning, one can maintain that sense is the mode of givenness of the reference (Frege) or the mode of givenness of the object (Husserl), that is, that to one and the same object there may correspond several names or several definite descriptions ("the evening star" and "the morning star," for Venus), so one and the same perceived object is adumbrated or stands out through several modes of givenness that are the *analogon* of names and descriptions in the domain of expressive acts: the object remains self-identical, though the perceived content keeps changing. The semantic distinction between sense and relation to the object thus becomes the pivotal phenomenological distinction between the mode of givenness of the object (the intentional matter, the content, and the soon-to-be *noema*) and the object that is given.[12] But in thus wanting to unify in a sole model disparate modalities of intentionality with differing requisites, one runs the risk of doing justice to neither: neither to perception, which is a direct hold on the world, nor to language, which can signify and be meaningful even in the absence of any object.

The conjunction of the two models provokes difficulties both in the semantic and the perceptual domain. In the former, it constrains us to think meaning as a necessary relation to objects, and therefore to endorse, according to Tugendhat's expression, an "objectively oriented" semantics, which, if not straight out untenable (see chapter 5), becomes very problematic for syncategorematic expressions such as "and," "or," "if . . . then." To what kind of object do these expressions refer? And how does the mention of an alleged "object" enlighten us with respect to their meanings? Must we not prefer—by far—to this sort of analysis a conception that defines the meaning of these terms by their rules of use and their truth conditions? We will see further on that an analysis of this sort is not incompatible with the phenomenological approach, and that it has even been foreshadowed in it (see chapter 21).

In the perceptual domain, the analogy with the linguistic difference between meaning and relation to the object (reference) introduces a distortion that is no less problematic. It leads Husserl to maintain that I never perceive the thing in an unqualified way, but always the thing according to its mode of givenness, that is, according to the adumbrations (*Abschattungen*) through which it is presented, so that these adumbrations alone are given in evidence, and the object they present to us *can always not exist.* The existence of the perceived object is not necessary to perception—only the concordance of the flow of outlines is. For these reasons, perception does not truly open to the thing itself, since the experienced contents, on condition they are concordant, can be qualified as "perceptions" even in the absence of the thing they present—that perceived thing amounting in this case to nothing other than an ideal pole, an indeterminate "x," the telos of a process which, in principle, is endless. This idealization of the object, to which I shall have occasion to return in chapter 15, already contains the idealism of the late Husserl *in nuce.* "If idealism is already in intentionality, it is because the latter has been conceived from the outset as intending an ideal object."[13]

This idealization of the object does not come down to aligning its mode of being with that of ideal objects, that is, *general* objects, essences, or to denying that it is a *tode ti,* an individual. Nor does it amount to confusing the object of perception with that of judgment, which brings into play general predicates, concepts. The perceptual content is *preconceptual.* But this idealization of the object certainly ends up making the latter not that which at every moment is self-given in such a way that its presence entails its existence, but that whose presence is ever deferred by the indefinite mediation of concordant adumbrations or contents, the correlate of an indefinite—and indefinitely postponed—perceptual confirmation; in short, something the existence of which can never be secured, whose evidence remains forever presumptive. Between asserting that the object is merely a pole located at the outer limits of an infinite teleological process, and saying that the object is only the correlate of the operations of a transcendental ego, there is but one step: the transcendental turn is the transition from the first thesis to the second. All in all, according to this view on perception, perception does indeed contain something like a referential opacity, since it would have to do with modes of presentation of the object, or rather objects-according-to-a-mode-of-(preconceptual)-presentation and never objects without qualification. Whence the claim that a perception whose object does not exist remains a perception.

Husserl thus tries to reconcile the two at first sight irreconcilable requirements: intentionality must be a relation to the thing; intentionality is an intrinsic characteristic of lived experiences. Intentionality must be at once relational and non-relational: relational, since it puts us directly in contact with the world and takes us out of the closed and self-contained space of our representations; non-relational, for the object can in principle always not exist—and this holds true for all the modalities of intentionality without exception. But how can these two requirements be reconciled? Going beyond the letter of the texts, one might respond: by constructing intentionality as a double relation, or as a duplicated relation, at once internal (necessary) and external (contingent); an internal relation to a content, paralleled by an external relation of this content to an object that may or may not exist. The former is an *a priori* relation (the *a priori* of correlation, as Husserl calls it); to every *percipere* there belongs a *perceptum* and to every *cogitatio* in general, a *cogitatum*. The latter is a contingent relation: in spite of the *percipere*'s being such that a *perceptum* belongs to it by essence, this *perceptum* may or may not have a corresponding real object, existing in the world. As Husserl writes in *Ideas II*, "the real [*real*] relation collapses if the thing does not exist; the intentional relation, however, remains."[14] It is as if, through the concept of intentionality, Husserl wanted to maintain two theses at the same time: that these two relations—the "intentional" relation (in Brentano's sense) to the content and the real relation to the object—are inseparable from one another and that they can exist independently of one another.

The first relation, which "interiorizes" the object, since it reduces it to a content of consciousness, or rather to a potentially infinite number of indefinitely concordant contents of consciousness, leads to the *idealism of constitution*: the object is nothing but the system of lived experiences and subjective operations through which it presents itself to a consciousness, "is constituted" by and for it. The second maintains—timidly—a realist requirement: perception is about the thing itself as it exists outside and not about a mental or psychic duplicate. We have here the expression of the two poles that Husserl's entire effort is directed toward conjoining: transcendental idealism and empirical realism. According to the former, all real relation can only *appear* on the ground of an intentional relation (the thing itself must be "constituted" through multiple lived experiences that relate to it in different modes). According to the latter, the intentional relation is ultimately grounded on a real relation. But *how* is it rooted in that relation? Therein lies the whole problem. A genuine realism should maintain that a perceptual intentional relation can only *exist* on the basis of a real relation to a thing whose existence is, thereby, assumed. But Husserl, unable to break away completely from Brentano's criterion, will keep saying that even in perception the object is open to the possibility of nonexistence. The idealist requirement will constantly take precedence over the realist one. And Husserl will be increasingly inclined to say, no longer that in order to *appear* every real relation must be grounded on an intentional relation, but that this must be true of it in order for it to *be*.

It is still too soon to enter into all the subtleties of transcendental idealism, to inquire into its conditions and limitations. For now, it is enough to delineate in a formal way the problem to which this idealism is called upon to respond. The concept of intentionality is structurally ambiguous. And because it is ambiguous, because it harbors in its heart an unresolved tension between a Cartesianism and an anti-Cartesianism, between a theory of representation and its negation, between an idealist and a realist tendency, phenomenology has taken different pathways, which are so many ways of responding to the challenge of the unification of the various modes of intentionality.

In a schematic and preliminary fashion, we may distinguish three of these ways, only two of which belong to the domain of historical phenomenology—the third having been privileged by a trend in analytic philosophy.

The first is that of Husserl's transcendental idealism, with all its unresolved tensions. It consists in giving weight to the skeptical argument of a generalized doubt, and in so doing, in denying that perception is necessarily about something existent. It leads to establishing a parallel between perception, memory, and ideation, on one hand, and the modalities of intentionality for which the existence of the object, whether concrete or abstract, is not required, on the other. But this parallel has a limit, which is the insurmountable difference between experience and judgment, intuition and thought, expressed by the axiom of *Logical Investigations*, "intuiting is not thinking." Perception, for example, is indeed about the object-according-to-its-mode-of-givenness, distinct from the object without qualification, but it is not at all about a conceptual content, let alone a propositional one, that would necessarily entail the coming into play of language. There is an autonomy of the perceived world with respect to thought and judgment. On this point, Husserl stands diametrically opposed to Cartesianism, if Cartesianism is defined by the identification of thought with (conscious) experience. "By the word 'thought' I understand all those things which occur in us while we are conscious, insofar as the consciousness of them is in us. And so not only understanding, willing, and imagining, but also sensing, are here the same as thinking."[15] To Husserl, perceiving is certainly not thinking. If thought is of the order of a lived experience, every lived experience is not of the order of thought. While it is true that perceptual intentionality is constructed on a semantic model, it nonetheless remains preconceptual. It is not a confused or latent thought.

The second way, which is no longer phenomenological because it goes so far as to deny the existence of a phenomenal *given* that would be independent of thought and judgment, is dominant in contemporary analytic philosophy. In a word, it tends to *deny* the originality of perceptual intentionality (and of the intentionality of memory) with respect to the intentionality of belief and judgment. For it, as Davidson writes, "awareness . . . is just another belief,"[16] to the point where perception must be conceived of as "propositional" in its very nature (Sellars, Davidson, Rorty, Tugendhat, McDowell). This thesis, which we will revisit in chapter 19, derives at least in part from a different response to a difficulty analogous to Husserl's. Approaching the problem of intentionality from the point of view of a logic of "intentional" statements, it defines intentionality in the Scholastic-Brentanian sense by inten*s*ionality in the logical sense (see chapter 3). Most of the statements containing intentional verbs do not pass the logical test of substitution *salva veritate* of co-referential terms: they are referentially opaque. This is paradigmatically the case in contexts governed by "to believe that," "to judge that," "to desire that." This logical criterion is the *analogon* of Brentano's psychological criterion. But how will we handle "to perceive," and "to remember," which, in certain contexts at least, are referentially transparent? One often-used strategy is to align their status with that of verbs of belief, to conceive of perception as a kind of judgment and to characterize it in terms of "propositional attitudes." A belief doesn't need the state of affairs that makes it true to obtain in order to remain a belief. But at first sight, a perception cannot be false and remain a perception. But never mind that! If perception is an implicit judgment it can enter by brute force into the category of inten*s*ionality. Contrary to what Husserl maintained, our primordial experience of the world becomes a "linguistic affair" (Sellars) through and through.

There is a third way, probably the most interesting one. It consists in highlighting the gap between the various modes of intentionality instead of trying at all costs to trace them back into one common matrix. According to this way, to perceive is not an operation of thought, but of being; it is a corporeal hold on things, a way of being among them—of belonging to them—that does not require the mediation of language, but is instead one with behavior and conduct; it is a modality of transaction, of interaction with the world. This is why perception opens directly to the world; it is fundamentally being-in-the-world; its object *must* exist, precisely in order for it to be *perception.* Here there is no longer any room for a skeptic argument, for a suspension of belief or an *epochē*; for we have no need to *believe* in what we see or feel. Thanks to perception, we are immersed in immemorial being, held by and in hand-to-hand engagement with it prior to all belief and all knowledge. The same is true for the way we exist in time through memory: the latter may fail us, as can perception, but it is not a modality of belief. By widening the gap between the prelinguistic and linguistic modalities of intentionality, thus between perception and thought, in granting the perceived world an autonomy even greater than that already allotted to it by Husserl, in thinking our relation to the world as a relation permeated with meaning, but with a meaning that is practical rather than intellectual throughout, this third way leads us to frame the problem of the relations between intuition and thought afresh.

We see how, setting out from a central aporia, different pathways are born and stretch out in different directions. It remains for us to examine them, and, as far as possible, to travel them. And since what is at stake in Husserl's transcendental turn is a deepening of intentionality in its principle, it is with this turn that we must begin. Does that turn represent—still today—a possible way for phenomenology?

14

Can Phenomenology Be Transcendental?

One needs to start from something other than the *ego cogito.*
—Martin Heidegger

"Manifestly [one] . . . can start with nothing other than the *ego cogito,*"[1] we read in *Cartesian Meditations.* Many phenomenologists, and not the least among them, have considered this assertion as an unshakeable dogma. Sartre: "the sole sure starting point is the interiority of the cogito."[2] Levinas: "to be is to be isolated by existing. Inasmuch as I am, I am a monad"[3]—so that this absolute ontological separation (which is unthinkable in terms of relation) between an "I" that is "absolutely closed over upon itself"[4] and an Other, just as ab-solute, is attested to in the cogito.[5] Michel Henry: the Cartesian project coincides "with the project of philosophy itself" and its phenomenological reenactment requires a "repetition of the cogito."[6] But what justifies such an assurance? Why should phenomenology—of necessity—present itself, to use Husserl's terms, as a "neo-Cartesianism," "a twentieth-century Cartesianism"?[7] Because of what constraint brought to bear on it by the things themselves? Because of what unquestionable and indubitable force of evidence?

My claim will be in diametric opposition to the foregoing: nothing, absolutely nothing, binds the destiny of phenomenology to that of Cartesianism. In order to attempt to show this—or in any case to try, as a first step, to see why the Cartesian presuppositions that orient Husserl's phenomenology from the start and that are reinforced (and not in the least outstripped) by its transcendental turn, are not drawn from a description of the phenomena—we must inquire into that element of the phenomenological method that Husserl named "phenomenological reduction." In his view, it is from a correct understanding of the reduction that a proper grasp of intentionality in its principle depends.

Must phenomenology be a transcendental idealism? According to Husserl, there is no other possibility. "*The proof of this idealism,*" he writes, "*is . . . phenomenology itself.*"[8] Yet the phenomenological project at the beginning stage was oriented in a completely different direction. Not that the early Husserl was a realist, as some of his students, Ingarden first and foremost, believed. Rather, the phenomenology of the *Logical Investigations,* which remains an "intentional psychology," is not at all transcendental. It is not until around the years 1906–1907,[9] on the occasion of the discovery of the method of the phenomenological reduction and the profound upheaval it brought about, that Husserl began his idealist turn. The incomprehension of many of his students in the face of this evolution, and the resistance to it by the proponents of a realist phenomenology (Ingarden, but also Reinach, Daubert, Stein, Conrad-Martius) show that the ties between phenomenology and transcendental philosophy require at least further examination.

It is impossible to understand the particular form taken by transcendental idealism after 1907 without elucidating the motives leading Husserl to adopt it—therefore without beginning with the position held to be "metaphysically neutral" of *Logical Investigations.* In this text, phenomenology is concerned with the psyche, the soul and its lived experiences (*Erlebnisse*) as they are given in immanence or in interiority. The description of these lived experiences brings out what Husserl continues to call, after Brentano, "inner perception [*innere Wahrnehmung*]." But Husserl conceives of it otherwise than does Brentano. Instead of characterizing the distinction internal/external (or, as he prefers to say, immanent/transcendent) in terms of provenance, of empirical-causal genesis, Husserl prefers to limit himself to the purely phenomenological distinction, "which has its roots in the *pure* phenomenological essences of [lived] experiences," between adequate and inadequate perception.[10] A perception is adequate if the object "is apprehended totally as it is," inasmuch as "it is itself included in the act of perception,"[11] so that the appearance of the object and its being are one and the same. It is inadequate if the being of the object can differ from its being perceived. For example, while I remain seated at my desk, I hear at this moment the rain falling; what I perceive adequately is the neutral and muffled hammering of the rainfall against the rooftops and along the drainpipes. But now I approach the window: there is no trace of humidity in the street. I realize that what I mistakenly took for rain was the applause recorded on a record to which, after a while, I had stopped listening, and the last notes of which I scarcely heard, absorbed as I was in my work. Here two things must be distinguished. My adequate perception of a rapid, distant sound; my inadequate perception of an event in the world, the rain. When the rain comes, it is there, in the street, in the atmosphere, over the rooftops and not "in my consciousness." This is why my perception of it can always turn out to be inaccurate and even illusory when new perceptions come to contradict the former ones. But the sound heard is an adequate given; it does not leave room for error. If I heard that hammering sound, whether or not it is that of rain, and even regardless of whether acoustic vibrations were produced in the room or not, it remains no less true that I heard it. It is in the transition from "I hear a hammering sound" to "it is raining" that the possibility of error comes in—hence the possibility of a doubt. The adequate givens are such that it makes no sense to doubt them. Their being is nothing but their appearing, because that being is an immanent being. By contrast, inadequate givens are characteristic of transcendent being, which possesses merely "presumptive" certainty; it is valid only as long as the lived experiences through which it announces itself continue to mesh harmoniously with one another—as long as no conflict arises between them, which would relegate their object to the rank of illusion.

In reinterpreting Brentano's opposition between inner and outer perception phenomenologically, Husserl agrees with Descartes: transcendent objects are always open to doubt; only immanent lived experiences are indubitable. He takes up on his own behalf "the traditional estimate of the relative cognitive value for knowledge of the two forms of perception: *external perception is deceptive, internal perception evident.*"[12] In Husserl's typology, the indubitable givens are of two kinds: intentional acts (act of judgment, doubt, imagination, perception, etc.) and the contents of sensation. For example, it makes no sense to doubt that at this moment I am seeing the blue of a lamp placed on a stand not far from me, although I can always doubt that there exists before me at this instant a lamp possessing an objective property, that of *being* blue. It is on these concepts of immanence and transcendence that nascent phenomenology is built. A description will be "phenomenological" if it leaves aside all the questions qualified as "metaphysical" (concerning transcendent being), and limits itself to immanence, hence to consciousness.

But what does "leave aside" mean here? From 1901 on, Husserl uses the term "reduction" to designate this methodological operation. In *Logical Investigations*, we already find a pre-transcendental "reduction" that means an exclusion of all interest for considerations relative to transcendent being and a return to the phenomenological givens conceived of as immanent givens, therefore evident and indubitable. Thus, for example, "The question as to the existence and nature of 'the external world' is a metaphysical question"[13]—which means not phenomenological. Phenomenology, at the start, is neither idealist nor realist; it rejects this very opposition. In order to proceed in a purely descriptive way, to keep to the rule of evidence, it must suspend all empirical questions, all questions of fact, which are inseparable from the positing of realities in the world, beginning with the psyche itself as object of psychological inquiry. Husserl uses the expression "reduction *to* the phenomenological [*Reduktion auf das Phänomenologische*]"[14] rather than "phenomenological reduction" to refer to that "conversion from the psychological attitude . . . to the phenomenological attitude." "We exclude all empirical apperceptions and existential affirmations, we take what is inwardly experienced or otherwise inwardly intuited . . . according to it as pure reality of lived experiences and as the exemplary basis for acts of ideations."[15] The reduction to the phenomenological is reduction to the immanent, that is, to the adequately given, or yet again, to the evident in the sense of the indubitable: it is on this system of equivalences that the whole phenomenology rests in its early stages.

How, then, should we conceive of the work of phenomenology, and how should we understand the term "phenomenon"? As it is used in the natural languages, the term "phenomenon" is ambiguous, because it can mean *that which appears*, that is, the transcendent object or event, just as well as *that in which the appearing resides*, that is, the subjective lived experiences—intentional acts and contents of sensation—through which the object announces itself.[16] Husserl solves this ambiguity in favor of the latter acceptation: "As belonging to a flow of consciousness, we experience phenomena; as belonging to the phenomenal world, things appear before us. The phenomena themselves do not appear to us [*die Erscheinungen selbst erscheinen nicht*], they are lived [*sie werden erlebt*]."[17] "Phenomenon" in the phenomenological sense thus applies to *the lived experiences immanent to consciousness*, and not to their intentional correlates, transcendent objects. This decision is paradoxical. It entails that phenomena are not what appears, not what is "phenomenalized" [*se phénoménalise*] (*erscheint*), but what makes the appearing possible, and that, conversely, what appears or is phenomenalized, the objects in the world, are not "phenomena." Furthermore, since the phenomena do not appear but "are lived," and since the phenomena *are* themselves lived experiences that belong to the flow of consciousness, it must be concluded that the lived experiences are themselves lived, that experience is itself experienced—and not the objects of which that experience is the experience.

Consequently, the reduction of *Logical Investigations* is a limitation of the description to what Husserl calls "the real contents" of consciousness—meaning its really immanent contents, which are contrasted with intentional contents, that is, with transcendent objects.[18] Reduction is an *exclusion* of all that does not belong to consciousness, an *abstention* from any positing with respect to transcendent being as a whole, a parenthesizing or putting out of play of all metaphysical problems. This is the meaning of the famous "metaphysical neutrality" of *Logical Investigations*, which has led to so many misinterpretations. Such a neutrality means that the nascent phenomenology abstains from taking up any position toward classical problems, such as the realism-idealism opposition; but it obviously does *not* mean that this phenomenology would be neutral with respect to the presuppositions that have their origin in the *history of metaphysics*, since most of what Husserl says comes directly from a line of argument borrowed even word for word from Descartes. To maintain that phenomenology at its inception was "metaphysically neutral" *in that sense* would be more or less like saying that Cartesian metaphysics is metaphysically neutral.

The position of *Logical Investigations*, with its crystal-clear simplicity (which might be summarized in the form of the equivalence: phenomenological given = evident given = adequate given = immanent given = real [*reell*], that is, non-intentional content of consciousness), is actually *too* simple and will soon become unsatisfactory to Husserl, in light of difficulties it brings about. As he will admit in 1906, in a letter to Hans Cornelius, "I myself was grossly mistaken when I identified phenomenology and descriptive (immanent) psychology."[19] From this will come a radical recasting of Husserl's whole conceptuality, inseparable from the adoption of a transcendental idealism and its decisive methodological innovation: the *transcendental* phenomenological *epochē*. The two essential difficulties on which the system of *Logical Investigations* founders are an epistemological difficulty and a strictly phenomenological one.

As it is revealed by the 1906–1907 courses, in which the theme of the *epochē* appears for the first time in plain view, the epistemological problem to which all Husserl's efforts are devoted is how to eliminate all possible skepticism which might arise from the ever-provisional results of the empirical sciences—how to supply for these sciences an unshakable foundation in absolutely evident, apodictic, and definitive truths. This problem of foundations also concerns—in a different way—the pure sciences, the first principles of which do not suffice in themselves and require philosophical elucidation. The solution suggested by the *Logical Investigations* has, in the meanwhile, revealed itself to be an impasse: "Is psychology, therefore," Husserl wonders, "in the final analysis the *fundamental philosophical science*?"[20] The answer is an unambiguous no. Psychology is ultimately a science of nature, directed toward an entity in the contingent world, the soul, which is bound to a contingent spatiotemporal body and enclosed by its intermediary within a network of causal relations. Dependent in principle on other sciences, psychology cannot pretend to accede to a domain of truths de jure prior to those of the sciences to which it is tributary, let alone endowed with greater certainty. To want to draw from psychology, "that pre-established natural science,"[21] something like an *apodictic grounding* for the other sciences of nature (and even more so, we must add, for logic and mathematics) would be to claim to ground these sciences in truths that are themselves *relative*, which is a patent absurdity. Must we then abandon the very idea of a foundation for the sciences? Surely not. Husserl formulates the alternative as follows: "*Theory of knowledge with psychology and on the basis of psychology does not work . . . . Theory of knowledge without psychology does not work either.*"[22] But then what can the solution be? Husserl answers: To ground the sciences in "a psychology of a new kind,"[23] a psychology without psyche and, consequently, a psychology freed from all psychologism—a psychology without psychology, so to speak. The ego of the ego cogito that furnishes the sciences with their foundation will no longer be an empirical and worldly ego, that is, an ego conceived of as a specific ontic region, a fragment of nature, that depends on the existence of the world to be and succumbs as a consequence to a generalized doubt; it will be an ego that is neither in the world nor of the world, located beyond the reach of any doubt, even hyperbolic. The transcendental phenomenological *epochē* will be the "open sesame" giving access to this psychology of a new kind, and to the object most specific to it, an ego henceforth qualified as "transcendental."

But then the *epochē*, the phenomenological method par excellence in Husserl's view, only comes to light at the end of an implicit *argumentation* of an epistemological nature. "In that way," as Ingarden noted, "the purely methodological ideal of philosophy as rigorous science . . . prepared the ground for a transition to an essentially metaphysical solution, to transcendental idealism."[24] This implicit argument is the following. Since science, to escape skepticism, needs an unshakable foundation; since psychology, as science of a "natural" entity, can only provide relative truths, it follows that this absolute foundation, sheltered from all possible doubt, can be sought only in a non-psychological, and therefore a transcendental subjectivity. But of course that argument is only conclusive as long as one adheres to the Cartesian epistemology that underlies it. Today, empiricism has triumphed in the philosophy of science, and no one, or almost no one, considers the problem of the validity of the experimental sciences from that perspective. Husserl's thought has aged terribly by its epistemology, as it is the very idea of seeking a foundation for empirical truths that has become obsolete. As Davidson writes, "empirical knowledge has no epistemological foundation, and needs none."[25] Science is a process of permanent self-correction, in which "the ship must be rebuilt on the open sea," to borrow Otto Neurath's image; it is a set of propositions, each of which can be put in doubt separately, but not all at the same time. We may conclude at least provisionally that nothing forces us to take Husserl's transcendental turn. We must now consider a second series of reasons in its favor, of a strictly descriptive nature.

If only lived experiences immanent to consciousness, and not their intentional objects, possess apodictic evidence (in other words, if all evidence in the strict, phenomenological sense of the term, is *adequate* evidence), two serious difficulties arise that compromise the very possibility of phenomenology. First, the domain of evidence is restricted to the contents given in the present: the object of memory being a transcendent object, because past, it follows that all the "flow" of time-consciousness, with the sole exception of the present, falls outside the domain of evidence. Husserl thus reverts to a problem that had vexed Descartes: if science develops in time, how is a phenomenological science possible? In the second place, phenomenology is an eidetic discipline; but essences, as ideal objects, are also transcendent objects that remain self-identical for every consciousness intending them. As transcendent, these objects cannot be given apodictically. Eidetics as a whole succumbs to too narrow a conception of evidence.

In the face of these aporias, there is no other choice than to take up anew the characterization of the concepts of immanence and transcendence, and more generally, the question of evidence in the phenomenological sense. This re-elaboration of Husserl's fundamental conceptuality marks, at least at prima facie, a distancing from Cartesianism and a recasting of the very concept of subjectivity.

Husserl borrows the term *epochē* from the skeptic tradition, but the *epochē* as he understands it is not a suspension of judgment; it is a "universal inhibition from all taking of a position toward the objective world"[26] in which "I no longer hold the natural belief in being to be valid."[27] Indeed, in "natural," pre-theoretical life, the world presents itself to me as endowed with an existence that it would not even occur to me to call into question, that precedes and makes possible all judgment and all belief; the world is what exists for me prior to all the doubts that I might raise about it; it is characterized by its *Selbstverständlichkeit*, by the fact of its being entirely self-evident. The *epochē* breaks with this "evidence" or this pseudo-evidence (an expression that might serve to translate "*Selbstverständlichkeit*"). Henceforth, all taking of a position, negative or positive, toward the existence of the world is put out of action, held in suspense. Not only is the world no longer posited as that massive being that precedes me, but I place myself with respect to myself as existent in the world in that same attitude of "pure disinterested onlooker" who no longer takes part in any belief-position, for whom the world *and* himself as a human being, as a being in the world, and even as a soul, no longer appear as anything more than "mere phenomena." The *epochē*, the suspension of the "general positing of the world," thus appears as the first side of a methodological procedure that has a second side, the phenomenological reduction in the strict sense (although the two terms are often used as synonyms). The suspension of all belief in the world and in myself as part of the world means at the same time the reduction (*Reduktion*), that is, literally the leading back (*Zurückleitung*)[28] to a transcendental field purified of all existence-positing, that is, to the "realm of phenomena in the phenomenological sense" and to the transcendental ego to whom they appear. Considered in its sense of *re-ducere, re-ductio*, the phenomenological reduction is a leading back or a reorientation of the look from the world of the natural attitude to the world as pure correlate of a transcendental consciousness.

Of course, this characterization remains merely formal as long as it has not been made clear what "transcendental consciousness" means here, and in the absence of a description of how this transcendental consciousness, hidden by the natural attitude, is unveiled for the first time through the methodological operation of the *epochē*. But first let us pause to consider the differences—numerous and important—that separate Husserl's characterization from Descartes's doubt.

1. The phenomenological *epochē* is not the first step in a skeptic procedure that must be dropped at a second stage, when, doubt having been turned into certainty, a first truth has been reached from which it is possible to derive all the others. The *epochē* is not in the least an *argument*. It gives us access to the world in its pure appearing, and has no other goal than to implement its description.

2. The *epochē* is definitely not a suspension *of judgment*,[29] that is, the act of not holding a number of propositions bearing upon states of affairs to be true, nor even the act of *doubting* these propositions; it is concerned only with a spontaneous and pre-theoretical belief in the being of the world that is older that any taking of a position, any judgment, any explicitly formulated belief.

3. This is why to speak of a putting out of action of all belief is ambiguous, since, generally, the refusal to believe is equivalent to a doubt. But the *epochē* is not a kind of doubt. It consists in suspending *belief as well as doubt*, and in adopting a perfect neutrality toward any "positing," affirmative or negative—more specifically: it is neither a belief in the existence of the world, nor a doubt as to its existence, nor a belief in its

nonexistence, nor a doubt as to its nonexistence. By this methodological operation, we do not leave the natural attitude, but limit ourselves to "parenthesizing" it: "The annulment in question is not a transmutation of positing into counter positing, of position into negation; it is not a transmutation into uncertain presumption, deeming possible, undecidedness, into a doubt (in any sense whatever of the word). . . . *Rather it is something wholly peculiar. We do not give up the positing we effected, we do not in any respect alter our conviction* which remains in itself as it is as long as we do not introduce new judgment-motives . . . Nevertheless the positing undergoes a modification: while it in itself remains what it is, *we, so to speak, 'put it out of action,' we 'exclude it' we 'parenthesize it.'*"[30] Thus it is *all the doxic modalities* of our pre-theoretical relation to the world (doubt, belief, disbelief, questioning, etc.), and not just some of them, that are suspended all at once.

4. While Descartes's doubt was a provisional procedure, ending up in a proof of the existence of the world that rendered this doubt superfluous, the *epochē* is definitive. All phenomenological description rests on it after the transcendental turn, so that this operation must be constantly reiterated as long as the description goes on. Like the Cartesian doubt, the *epochē* makes a science of the world possible; but contrary to Descartes, this science does not establish itself *against* the *epochē*, but *in* the *epochē*.[31]

5. The *epochē*, precisely because it is not a doubt, nor the first step in an argumentation, leaves everything as is. Thanks to it, we do not lose the world, but limit ourselves to seeing it in a new light. The problem to which the *epochē* is a response is not that of uncertainty about the world, but that of its phenomenological *mode of givenness*. In doubting the existence of the world I am still taking a position toward that presumed existence—if only to disbelieve it; I am still making myself an accomplice of the natural attitude that is to be suspended. I act as if the phenomenological "meaning" of the world, its mode of givenness for my consciousness, were taken for granted. On the other hand, the phenomenological reduction is the indispensable methodological prerequisite for being able to raise the problem of the world and of its mode of givenness: the "problem of transcendence." Thus, as Fink noted, it is quite close to astonishment, because it brings us face to face with the "world-enigma [*Welträtsel*]."[32] An *enigma* to be assessed, that of transcendence, and not at all a *problem*—that of the existence of the world—to be solved.

6. Finally, as we have seen, the *epochē* is fully "universal." It leaves nothing outside itself, not even the ego that accomplishes it. Contrary to Descartes's doubt, which ended up in the position of an ego sheltered from doubt and conceived of as a *res cogitans*, that is, as a "little tag-end of the world [*Endchen der Welt*],"[33] the *epochē* bears at the same time upon

the world and myself as a piece of the world, a worldly ego. Hence it ends paradoxically in a doubling of the ego. To the psychological ego ("the soul") and to the ego as a psychophysical composite ("the ego-man"), which are both mundane realities, is henceforth contrasted a transcendental ego that is neither in the world nor of the world, but is its constituting origin. And since all being has been put out of action, this ego possesses only a "pre-being" (*Vorsein*), and occupies no specific ontic region, being the *Urregion* in which they are all constituted. This doubling leads to the paradox that the transcendental ego and the empirical ego are at once identical and different: identical, since they are both "me"; different, since the latter is an object-ego [*ego-objet*] *constituted* by the former. In the operation of reduction we actually even count three egos: the constituting ego, the constituted ego, and the reflecting ego who has placed himself in the attitude of a pure, disinterested onlooker to apprehend their relations.

The *epochē*, despite the fact that it has a goal, content, and a status that are entirely different from those of the doubt, is nonetheless elaborated in an ambivalent proximity to the Cartesian problematic, which, as we have seen, is that of the quest for an apodictic evidence capable of providing the various sciences with a *fundamentum inconcussum.* From Descartes to Husserl the vocabulary changes, but the goal remains the same, that "of attempting to find in transcendental subjectivity the deepest grounding of all sciences."[34] "The historical error of Descartes," as the *Crisis* calls it, was probably to conceive of the pure ego as a *res,* hence as an (inner) worldly reality; that error prevented the precursor of phenomenology from setting foot in the promised land of an authentically transcendental philosophy. However, to the extent that the phenomenological reduction remains subordinated to the epistemological motive of evidence, which has its source in the Cartesian procedure of doubt and the search for an apodictic grounding for the sciences, it becomes difficult to extricate the reduction as conceived by Husserl from the Cartesian doubt, contrary to what a still formal presentation of these methods could have suggested. The Husserlian critique of doubt remains ambivalent. As Heidegger remarks, "it is necessary to heed the fact that although the reduction, in view of its methodic sense, is fundamentally different from the path of doubt, it presupposes for itself precisely the result of the path of doubt in the sense of something self-evident. The proposition *'cogito sum,'* that emerges from the end-situation of the path of doubt, is now taken simply as a triviality and thus laid claim to at the outset of the reduction. . . . The *cogito sum* is not only *not discussed,* but is *taken over as self-evident* in Husserl's case."[35] Actually, the phenomenological reduction is less won against doubt than by and through it,[36] less as an alternative path to that of Descartes than as its deepening. This is why, as we shall see, far from the Cartesian motivations of the early Husserl being overcome by the transcendental turn, they come out rather confirmed and reinforced by it.

To understand this, it is necessary to pass from a still formal understanding of the reduction to a concrete description of the transcendental field that we reach through it. As long as we remain in the natural attitude, things are fairly simple: the immanence of consciousness stands *opposed* to the transcendence of things. "The immanent is in me, the beginner will say at this point, and the transcendent is outside of me."[37] But the carrying out of the reduction challenges that pseudo-evidence, making us conceive of the dichotomy between transcendent and immanent being differently. The whole purpose of the five lessons on *The Idea of Phenomenology* is to describe the transition from a naive and pre-transcendental understanding of these concepts to an authentically transcendental one. In order to attain this goal, Husserl takes the path of the Cartesian doubt, the shortcomings of which he emphasizes, without criticizing it in its principle. "Here the *Cartesian meditation on doubt*," he writes, "provides us with a beginning: the being of the *cogitatio*, of lived experience as it occurs and is simply being reflected upon, cannot be doubted."[38] The "ground" on which transcendental phenomenology is built is indeed that of the natural attitude; now, that attitude maintains an opposition between the interiority of consciousness and the exteriority of the world, because it equates evidence with adequate, that is, immanent, givenness. The natural attitude is, we might say, "naturally" Cartesian—this is Husserl's never-questioned presupposition. Given this starting point, two concepts of immanence, and correlatively two concepts of transcendence can be distinguished, valid respectively before and after the reduction: "At first [i.e., before the reduction] one is inclined to interpret, as if it were entirely obvious, immanence as real [*reelle*] immanence, indeed as real [*reale*] immanence in the psychological sense: the object of knowledge also exists in the experience of knowing, or in the consciousness of the ego, to which the experience belongs, as a real actuality."[39] Here a terminological clarification is in order. Husserl uses *reell* in opposition to "intentional," and he uses *real* in a narrower sense to define the mode of existence of natural things.[40] Real (*reell*) immanence includes all real (*reell*) contents in the sense of *Logical Investigations*, that is, all the contents that *are not intentional.* And consciousness thus conceived, is, in a certain sense, an object of nature, therefore real (*real*). In Husserl's view, the concept of immanence that is held to be evident by the "neophyte" is not *false*, but *one-sided*. As long as we remain in the natural attitude, we have access to a first sense of the reduction that means the *exclusion* (*Ausschluß*) of all that pertains to transcendence: "That which is transcendent (not really [*reell*] immanent) I may not use. For that reason I must perform the *phenomenological reduction; I must exclude all that is posited as transcendent.*"[41] At this stage, the reduction continues to be understood as a *limitation* of the inquiry to the sphere of real (*reell*) immanence, by virtue of which "everything transcendent (everything not given immanently to me) is to be assigned the index of zero."[42]

But we cannot stop at this first stage, which is that of a psychological reduction like that of *Logical Investigations*. Understood in the fullness of its meaning, "the phenomenological reduction does not signify the limitation [*Einschränkung*] of the investigation to the sphere of real [*reellen*] immanence, to the sphere of what is really [*reell*] contained in the absolute 'this' of the *cogitatio*."[43] In abandoning descriptive psychology and deepening "the enigma of transcendence," we understand that the naive concept of immanence cannot satisfy the objective of a theory of knowledge, which is to understand how a consciousness can "get out of itself," so to speak, to know something outside of itself. The performance of the authentically phenomenological reduction, which is one and the same as the deepening of the meaning of intentionality itself, reveals that consciousness is not a "box," to borrow an image already present in *Logical Investigations*,[44] is not a domain closed in upon itself that would be contained in the world as in a larger sphere; and that the world, conversely, is not located outside of that box, nor encapsulated within it. If the reduction led back to a "residuum," that is, to a particular ontic region, there would be only two possibilities: either that region should contain the world, which would lead to an absolute idealism; or that region would not contain the world, and it would remain to be explained how consciousness gets outside itself to know something. Either consciousness would be coextensive with the world and there would be no exteriority, or I would be closed up inside my consciousness as in a box, with no way of getting out. These two hypotheses are equally absurd, and the lesson of the reduction is to reject both of them. As Husserl writes in a manuscript, "The transcendental ego is neither inside nor outside of the world, and the world, in turn, is neither inside nor outside of it [the ego]."[45] The discovery of the transcendental *I*[46] goes hand in hand with the discovery of the inclusion in it of all the transcendences, but as a nonreal, that is, intentional, inclusion. It is inseparable from the elucidation of intentionality in its essence. "Just as the reduced ego is not a piece of the world, so, conversely, neither the world nor any worldly Object is a piece of my ego, to be found in my conscious life as a really inherent part of it, as a complex of data of sensation or a complex of acts. . . . If this 'transcendence,' which consists in being non-really included, is part of the intrinsic sense of the world, then, by way of contrast, the ego himself, who bears within him the world as an accepted sense and who in turn, is necessarily presupposed by this sense, is legitimately called *transcendental,* in the phenomenological sense."[47] To perform the reduction is to carry over the transition from narrow immanence to enlarged immanence, to perceive how intentional consciousness "bears" within itself all real transcendences. Correctly understood, the phenomenological reduction is neither a retreat to immanence in the sense of interiority, nor an exclusion of transcendences outside of that interiority that would allow it to subsist in itself as a residuum. As Eugen Fink expresses it in a play on words that is difficult to translate, the *epochē* is not a delimiting (*Einschränkung*) of consciousness, but a removing of limits, "de-limiting" (*Entschränkung*)[48] of it, at the end of which the very concepts of inner and outer become problematic. The loss of the world, its being put out of play as ground for the natural attitude, is then nothing short of the discovery of the world: "to give up everything is to gain everything."[49] The reduction is *the world lost and regained*: "One must first lose the world through *epochē* so as to regain it in universal self-examination."[50] But the world regained is no longer quite the same as the one that has been lost. It is no longer merely the vis-à-vis of consciousness, no longer that which stands opposite the subject in the way that exteriority stands opposite interiority, but, on the contrary, it is that which is inseparable from consciousness in its intentional character, the transcendental correlate of its constituting operations. In other words, it is only once the world is reduced that the structural solidarity between the world and consciousness can appear in full light, that is, that the *a priori* of correlation can reveal itself as such. This is what will prompt Merleau-Ponty to say, not without paradox, that the transcendental reduction, thought through all the way, ends up with Heidegger's *In-der-Welt-sein* (Being-in-the-world).[51]

Here it is important not to be led astray by the recurrent formulations that Husserl will end up rejecting[52] such as a "switching off of the world" or the ego conceived of as a "phenomenological residuum." Contrary to what these expressions suggest, the reduction does not consist in separating the ego from the world, in gathering up consciousness as a chemical precipitate by isolating it from what is not it, but on the contrary, in reuniting them, in understanding their structural unity—in Husserlian terms, in showing the non-real inclusion of the world in consciousness, and, reciprocally, the openness of consciousness to the world, that is, its intentionality. We must first have understood that the really transcendent world is also immanent to consciousness in the enlarged, *in-*

tentional sense of the term "immanence," in order to be able to grasp the meaning of the whole problematic of the transcendental constitution, to which I shall return later. For the ego to be "transcendental" means that it is the grounding for all transcendences—that it is their origin. Transcendental phenomenology, then, means constitutive phenomenology. The reduction can therefore be defined as the leading back from a narrow (Cartesian) concept of immanence to a wide concept (that of intentional immanence) by virtue of which all real transcendence appears as the transcendental correlate of an operation of constitution.

Two consequences follow from this, that help us to better understand the statute that phenomenology receives after the transcendental turn. First, it is no longer possible to equate, as in *Logical Investigations*, apodictic evidence and adequate evidence. Evidence can be defined in general as "a grasping of something itself that is [*Seienden*], or is thus [*So-seienden*], a grasping in the mode 'it itself,'"[53] that is, as a synthesis of fulfillment in which a self-givenness of the thing occurs. But Husserl distinguishes presumptive evidence that remains constantly exposed to doubt, and apodictic evidence that is beyond doubt. Endowed with "the signal peculiarity of . . . excluding in advance every doubt as 'objectless,' empty,"[54] apodictic evidence can no longer be the exclusive lot of *really* immanent, that is, adequate, givens. Eidetic necessities, for example, fall under the category of real transcendence, and yet they are apodictic. In sum, apodicticity "can occur even in evidences that are inadequate,"[55] which, of course, formally contradicts the dispensation in the early works. The second consequence concerns the necessity of redefining the phenomenological concept of phenomenon. Henceforth the equivocation of the phenomenon, far from being decided in favor of one of the two meanings, is shouldered as an inevitability. "Phenomenon" means both that wherein appearing resides (the immanent lived experience) and that which appears (the intentional object). This ambivalence becomes a structural property of the *a priori* of correlation as such: "The meaning of the word 'phenomenon' is twofold because of the essential correlation between appearing and that which appears."[56]

Up to this point I have presented the reduction in the manner most faithful to Husserl's intentions, in distinguishing it from Cartesian doubt. But doubt constantly parallels the reduction, accompanying it like a shadow. There are several reasons for this.

First, as we have seen, Husserl's overall epistemological perspective remains "Cartesian"; it is characterized by the search for a piece of indubitable evidence that would supply a ground to the various sciences.

This evidence is not that of a chain of truths deduced from a first principle, the cogito, but of a purely descriptive discipline, transcendental phenomenology. Here Husserl adopts an epistemological prejudice that goes hand in hand with the traditional skeptical argumentation, and more specifically with its central claim: "Since it is always possible to doubt something, it is always possible to doubt everything"—*the possibility of a punctual doubt entails the possibility of a universal doubt.* In accepting the validity of this inference, Husserl confers a philosophical significance and legitimacy to Descartes's entire procedure. He authenticates "Descartes' methodological attempt at universal doubt as the first radical method of reduction to pure subjectivity."[57]

The second reason concerns the internal economy of the reduction itself. In order to have meaning, the *epochē* presupposes the ground of the natural attitude: it must grant a validity, even if only a limited one, to the naive, pre-transcendental distinction between immanence and transcendence. From the transcendental point of view, that distinction is not false—it is insufficient. Why, it may be asked, once the reduction has been performed, does Husserl not conclude, as will Heidegger subsequently, that consciousness has no interiority at all, and therefore no exteriority either? Quite simply because that conclusion would make the entire procedure pointless. It would *disqualify* the Cartesian starting point, and, with it, the reduction itself. Husserl's conclusion is entirely different. Even though he brings out immanence in the intentional sense, he maintains, within that same "enlarged" immanence, the *pre-transcendental* distinction between really immanent contents (intentional acts and hyletic givens) and really transcendent intentional objects. Thus, even though in his view consciousness is no longer a box, we must continue to acknowledge within it an interiority peopled with sensory data differing by their mode of givenness from the objective properties of things. We must distinguish, for example, between a felt, "immanent" red and a "transcendent" perceived red, whose modalities of evidence differ. Instead of recognizing that these sensory data are nothing but fictions, a remnant of sensualism and especially of psychologism, Husserl remains faithful to the Cartesian framework of his early thought, explaining all the while that the reduction must lead to its overcoming.

Hence what cannot be called otherwise than "the fundamental ambiguity" of Husserlian transcendental concepts, to borrow Rudolf Boehm's phrase—the concepts of "immanence" and "transcendence" first and foremost. We are dealing with an *ambiguity* here because the new conceptuality does not replace the preceding one, but is added on to it. As Boehm remarks, phenomenology attributes "a new meaning to these two terms," and, at the same time, "a parallel use of these same terms in the traditional sense (of 'real' immanence and transcendence) will prove indispensable and will be retained."[58] And since these concepts have their roots in the procedure of doubt, Cartesian doubt is both rejected (because it ends up at the worldly ego) and confirmed in its rights by transcendental phenomenology. Because of that ambivalence, Husserl remains captive to the Cartesian dispensation while trying to blaze the trail to a non-Cartesian conception of the pure ego.

Still, even more than this structural ambiguity, what is perplexing about the phenomenological reduction is the almost complete absence of supporting arguments to justify both its necessity as a method and the results it ends up with. Indeed, how are we meant to understand that a mere "turning of the look" can *take us back* to the transcendental ego, which, in Husserl's opinion, we ourselves are? Let us examine things more closely. I put myself in an attitude of perfect neutrality with respect to the being and not being of the world, with respect to myself as a man, as a psyche tied to my own body, and so on. How can an *attitude* in which I place myself instruct me on what I *am*? How can a consequence involving my being follow from an attitude that I may or may not adopt? Yet Husserl seems to suggest that a connection such as this exists. "If I place myself above that entire life and if I abstain from any commitment about reality, specifically one which accepts the world as existing, and if I view that life exclusively as consciousness *of* the world," he writes, "then I reveal myself as the pure ego with its pure flow of *cogitationes*."[59] Husserl even seems to suggest that there is a *logical consequence* here: "I certainly do not discover myself as one item among others in the world, *since* [da] I have altogether suspended judgment about the world."[60] But what is the meaning of this "since"? From the fact that I no longer ascribe existence to my worldly ego, can I conclude that I *am* not a worldly ego? And why would I not be a worldly ego or simply a man who, because he has suspended all belief in the world, *wrongly* no longer believes that he is what he has never ceased being: a worldly ego, a man? It must be admitted that the consequence drawn by Husserl remains totally unmotivated. There is, strictly speaking, no argument here. The only thing Husserl says, basically, is that I *see* that I am such an ego. And what could be answered to one who would object that he sees nothing of the sort?

The difficulty here bears a formal resemblance to that found in Descartes, in the controversial passage from the *ego sum, ego existo* to the *sum res cogitans*—but it is a mere *resemblance*. Descartes's reasoning, *at first sight,* contains a leap. I doubt that a world exists, that I have a body, and so on. And since I doubt, I am. Who am I then, I who doubt? Descartes answers, in substance: I doubted that there was a world, that I was a body, and so on, therefore I am a thinking thing. He passes implicitly from the premise "I doubt that I am a body" to "I know that I am not a body."

If I *knew* that, I could indeed certainly draw the conclusion from it—assuming no other solution presents itself—that I am a thinking thing. Illegitimate inference? No, if we remember the methodological precept underlying the whole deductive order of *Meditations*: to consider as being false what is only subject to doubt. It is this precept that plays the role of additional premise and makes it possible to conclude that, since I *doubt* that I am a body, I *am not* in fact a body. Of course, one can reject this precept, perhaps one even *should* reject it; but at least there is an argument in Descartes. In Husserl there is nothing of the sort. The *epochē* is not a hyperbolic doubt, nor is it the first step in an argument; and yet it *does indeed function as an argument*, since it is supposed to teach us what we are, setting out from a suspension of all ontological commitment. But how? I put myself in the attitude of a pure, disinterested onlooker with respect to myself as a man in the world. What follows from that? Obviously nothing. Perhaps I am indeed a transcendental ego; perhaps I am a man who takes himself for a transcendental ego. How can I know? How decide? Not, in any case, by responding that I *see* what I am!

The transcendental turn remains fundamentally unmotivated in Husserl. The reduction "leads back" to a transcendental ego only on the condition that one has already admitted the existence of that ego (or its parenthesized existence, its "pre-being"). The reduction does not justify the adoption of transcendental idealism; rather, it presupposes its validity as self-evident. It is not a mere "turning of the look," but the motto of a substantial metaphysics. Far from being "metaphysically neutral" (which it never was, even in the pre-transcendental form of *Logical Investigations*), it is rather, as Köhler puts it, the "weapon of an ontological prejudice."[61] To the question, must we carry out the transcendental turn, the only possible response is no. Nothing of what Husserl says is of such a nature as to compel us to do so. For even if we accepted (1) the epistemological prejudice in favor of foundationalism and (2) the skeptical argument of universal doubt, we still would not see how from a suspension of our ontological commitment we could draw the least consequence of an ontological nature.

One possibility, however, remains. Even if we assume that the decision in favor of the idealism remains unmotivated, does not transcendental phenomenology constitute at least *a possible interpretation* of phenomena? Since we clearly do not *have to* carry out the transcendental turn, *may* we at least do so?

Confronted with the difficulties raised by the reduction, Husserl—and, after him, his disciples and his commentators—have often maintained that these difficulties were less attributable to the reduction itself than to the vestiges of a pre-transcendental understanding of the transcendental method par excellence. The obstacles to the genuine understanding of the *epochē*, on this hypothesis, originate in the residual instances of naïveté into which the neophyte phenomenologist falls—a naïveté that will be overcome in the subsequent developments of phenomenology when fully matured. This applies first and foremost to the Cartesian elements that surface at nearly every moment. The logic of Cartesianism consists in separating a domain of absolute certainly (real immanence) from a domain subject to universal doubt (real transcendence); the logic of the concept of intentionality, on the contrary, is to unite the two domains. Husserl, on this view, oscillates between these two logics, but ends up choosing the second: such would be the final outcome of the phenomenological reduction, rightly understood.

The Cartesian temptation triumphs in §49 of *Ideas I*, in which the ontological disparity between consciousness and reality is revealed through the hypothesis of the annihilation of the world, of its "explosion" into a chaos of discordant adumbrations. Even if such a cataclysm were to occur, Husserl argues, the existence of consciousness would not be touched. On the side of consciousness, we have a self-contained sphere of being, endowed with an absolute existential self-sufficiency, to the point that one might say of it what Descartes said about substance: *nulla re indiget ad existendum.* On reality's side, we have a relative being that, once consciousness has been crossed out, sinks into nothingness. According to the traditional interpretation, the principle of which I have recalled, the fiction of §49, with its Cartesian background, would be an *obstacle* to an authentic understanding (authentically transcendental) of the reduction. A perfect illustration of that reading may be found in Rudolf Bernet:

> 'The annihilation of the world' draws on the ontological dualism (of the Cartesian variety) between the (evident) being of immanent consciousness and the (doubtable) being of the transcendent world—a dualism that basically is an obstacle to the understanding of the meaning of the *transcendental constitution* of the world by the subject. The constituted world is neither purely interior nor purely exterior to the constituting subject; . . . [In §49 of *Ideas I*], the existence of the world is treated as if it had the reality of a particular thing such as it gives itself, confirms itself or, on the contrary, 'explodes' in the course of a particular and limited experience. Moreover, the subject is manifested in the deficient and undetermined mode of an immanent 'residuum' of the annihilation of the transcendent world, that is, once more, as a

> 'little tag-end of the world' [*Endchen der Welt*]. The hypothesis of the 'annihilation of the world' thus does not correspond in any way to the program of the phenomenological reduction: it brings to light neither the phenomenon of the world, nor the transcendental being of the subject, nor the 'correlation' or co-belonging of subject and world.[62]

On this view, the hypothesis of the annihilation of the world and its conclusion, the aseity or existential self-sufficiency of consciousness, would merely belong to a provisional, imperfect, purely propaedeutic exposition of the reduction, to be left behind in the subsequent stages of description and analysis, when the transcendental motif has finally been extracted from its naturalistic dross. This interpretation is scarcely tenable, due to the structural ambiguity to which I have alluded. Transcendental phenomenology remains fundamentally suspended *between* Cartesianism and anti-Cartesianism without ever really resolving that constitutive tension. To be sure, Bernet's reservations about the hypothesis of the annihilation of the world are legitimate; but it is possible to raise some doubts as to whether his conclusions follow. In his view, the Cartesian dualism of evident and doubtful knowledge, of absolute being and relative being, prevent us from fully understanding transcendental correlation, and, more profoundly, transcendental constitution. In order to understand the transcendental motif in its purity, this dualism should be abandoned. But is it really this ontological dualism that precludes a correct understanding of the transcendental thematic of reduction and constitution, or is it not the other way round? Is not the dualism of the two realms, the two regions, necessarily *presupposed* by the very idea of transcendental constitution? Indeed, the idea of constitution presupposes several things. First of all, it presupposes the relation of the constituting to the constituted to be asymmetric: the transcendental ego is constituting; the world and itself as empirical ego, constituted. Moreover, it presupposes, precisely in order to be able to account for the asymmetry of that relation, that the constituting instance is *ontologically independent from the constituted instance*, that it enjoys an existential self-sufficiency expressed by the formula: "*nulla re indiget ad existendum.*" Lastly, that priority is not only ontological, but also epistemic: not only is the constituting ego the first existent de jure, but it is the first knowable, for its self-knowledge, as attested in the cogito, is evident, whereas the knowledge of the world remains always subject to doubt. In other words, without the thesis of Cartesian inspiration according to which pure consciousness is a self-contained sphere of being, possessing a mode of being different from that of the world, there is no priority of consciousness; without that priority, there is no constitution; and without constitution, there is no transcendental reduction, since "transcendental reduction" means a leading back to the *constituting* ego.

Far from the problematic of the reduction freeing us from Descartes's ontological dualism, it presupposes its validity. The *epochē*, the parenthesizing of the general positing of the natural attitude, could not lead us back to any *constituting* transcendental ego, and in fact it would not in any way be a *leading back* to anything at all, if the ego were not conceived of as an instance prior de jure to the world in the twofold sense of an ontological and an epistemic priority—hence if the ego did not possess an existential self-sufficiency that makes it independent of the existence of the world (irrelative to the world), while the world is relative to it. But then it is illusory to pretend to separate conceptually the problem of the existential self-sufficiency of the ego such as it is revealed by the hypothesis of the annihilation of the world and the problem of constitution in general that is peculiar to all *transcendental* phenomenology. The ontological and epistemic aspects of the twofold primacy of the ego, aspects that are, moreover, inseparable, are attested in a twofold lexicon, that of "being" (or of the "existential validity") and that of "sense." The world, as *Cartesian Meditations* confirms, "gets its sense and acceptance or validity [*Sinn und Geltung*] in and from me, myself [*in mir und aus mir selbst*]";[63] "The Objective world, the world that exists for me [*für mich*], that always has and always will exist for me, the only world that can exist for me—this world, with all its Objects, . . . derives its whole sense and its existential validity, . . . from me myself [*aus mir selbst*], from me as the transcendental ego, the ego who comes to the fore only with transcendental-phenomenological *epochē*."[64] Phenomenological idealism rests entirely on this reversal of the *für mich* to the *aus mir* to which I will return. In light of these texts, it is impossible to understand Husserl's transcendental position independently from his "ontological dualism," to borrow Bernet's expression.

And yet, on the other hand, this ontological dualism, with the "abyss of meaning [*Abgrund des Sinnes*]"[65] it brings about between reality and consciousness—and in this regard Bernet's remarks are accurate, showing us, not how to get out of the difficulty, but how deep it is, deeply anchored in Husserl's Cartesianism—is hardly compatible with the idea of a *constitution* of reality by consciousness. How can reality be separated from consciousness by an abyss of meaning, and at the same moment be *nothing other* than the transcendental correlate of a multitude of constituting appearances? If reality is the correlate of a concordant system of lived experiences, an "intentional production" of the ego, and if reality is separated from consciousness by an ontological abyss, then the ego is separated from itself by an abyss! In sum, as Ingarden will remark, the tension existing between Descartes's reality/consciousness dualism and the idea of constitution ends up in something that looks very much like an aporia: the world possesses, as in Descartes, a mode of being that is *heterogeneous* with that of consciousness, and at the same time, in contrast with Descartes's claim, this world is not known by the intermediary of an "idea" possessing only mental existence; it must be experienced directly in its incommensurability with consciousness; what is more, it must be constituted *in* and *by* consciousness. Though different from consciousness, the world must be made from the same stuff as it, since the world is intentionally *included* in it as the correlate of a constituting system of lived experiences. So we end up in what is very like a square circle: *a constitution of the world by consciousness as something absolutely heterogeneous with respect to consciousness and nevertheless enclosed or included in that consciousness.* This is what will make Ingarden conclude that there are only two viable solutions to the dilemma of Husserlian phenomenology: either return to ontological dualism, abandoning the whole idea of constitution, or "enclose the physical world, in its essence, in pure consciousness."[66] The constituted world is then no longer the actual, real world, as it was there before the reduction, and this reduction, far from leading back to the *In-der-Welt-sein,* turns us definitively away from it. The "world" to which it leads back is but an ever subjective one, "a being posited by consciousness in its experiences . . : *beyond that* it is nothing."[67] "The reduction becomes a *subjectivization* of being,"[68] as Levinas will observe.

The idealist turn does not supply a solution to this tension, but it rather increases it in a paradoxical way. On the one hand, the transcendental reduction rests on the Cartesian dualism of the realms of being, which is inseparable from the validity of a universal doubt; on the other hand, the authentic understanding of that reduction *excludes* that dualism that is the logical consequence of doubt, since the world can only be a transcendence included in intentional immanence, the correlate of a constituting system of appearances, if its being is not entirely heterogeneous with that of consciousness. It is as if Husserl were trying to broaden Cartesianism to the point of making it assimilate its own negation.

His transcendental idealism attempts to articulate three theses that are not easily compatible:

1. A thesis of realist inspiration, according to which what we perceive is the thing itself: knowledge does not modify the nature of the object, as Husserl says in *Logical Investigations.*[69]

2. A thesis of Cartesian inspiration: there is a duality, a heterogeneity of essence between pure consciousness and reality.

3. A thesis of Kantian inspiration: pure consciousness *constitutes*

reality as its transcendental correlate—a thesis stripped of its Kantian corollary, the existence of a thing in itself.

The two last theses, if combined, circumscribe the position of *Ideas I*, namely the idea that there is a heterogeneity of essence between pure consciousness and the world, but that heterogeneity does not mean opposition, since reality depends both ontologically and epistemologically on consciousness. In this way Husserl saved, as it seems, the *transcendental* distinction between immanence and transcendence—the idea that consciousness opens onto the world; he also saved *in a certain sense* the idea that the being of consciousness is different from the being of the world, since the former is absolute while the latter relative; but it is at the price of the realist thesis of *Logical Investigations*, according to which knowledge is not a modification of the object—since henceforth reality *in its very being* is a meaning formation of constituting subjectivity, the indefinitely postponed horizon of an ever-incomplete process of constitution. Far from consciousness not modifying the world, the world is now literally *nothing beyond* the ultimate horizon of all transcendental constitution, the horizon of all its horizons, "a being posited by consciousness in its experiences, which, of essential necessity, can be determined and intuited only as something identical belonging to motivated multiplicities of appearances: *beyond that* it is nothing."[70] Knowledge cannot leave the being of reality intact, since that being is absolutely "nothing" beyond the process of its being known.

As if by a magic trick, reduction has not only changed our point of view on the world; it has modified what we meant by "world" prior to its performance. Let us use the expression "pre-given world" to designate the world of the natural attitude, a world that precedes us, survives us, and that is neither affected nor altered by our knowledge. Let us call the world as it appears after the reduction "constituted world." The former is independent of our knowledge; the latter has no being outside the process of its constitution, and therefore outside its being known in and by the ego. These two worlds, Husserl tells us in substance, are but one: the pre-given world *is* the constituted world. But how is that possible, if the former is defined by its independence and the latter by its dependence with respect to consciousness? Husserl has not so much solved the problem of intentionality—he has not so much shown positively how consciousness can exit itself to reach reality—than he has made reality entirely dependent on consciousness to the point of becoming the latter's intentional product.

This is why the concept of "constitution"—like all transcendental concepts—also remains structurally ambiguous. Constitution means the absolute dependence of the world with respect to consciousness ("If we cross out consciousness, then we cross out the world," as Husserl liked to repeat during his Göttingen seminars),[71] and at the same time, Husserl constantly warns us against an interpretation of constitution that would make it into a *real* production or genesis: reality is not a *product* of the transcendental ego. Speaking of the pure ego as "origin of the world," Husserl gives among others the following specification: "Never have I understood origin genetically, and nowhere . . . did I wish to demonstrate a genesis."[72] Basically, the concept of constitution merely expresses the difficulty involved in reconciling the three theses that I have enumerated, since it signifies at once the manner in which consciousness lets the thing appear itself by itself, to give itself as it is, according to a *Selbstgegebenheit,* and inseparably, but also probably contradictorily, a "transcendental production"[73] in conformity with which "every type of being . . . is understood as a formation which is constituted in . . . [an] act of transcendental subjectivity."[74] About constitution, Husserl tells us rather what it isn't than what it is. Even the explanation in the famous letter of 1903 to Hocking remains programmatic, and above all *negative,* and it is uncertain whether it can be maintained as it is after the transcendental turn: "The expression that occurs so frequently, that 'objects' 'are constituted' in an act, always refers to the property of the act to make the object representable; it is not about 'constituting' properly so called."[75] If it has a meaning, constitution must mean something different and something more than the mere intentional correlation, that is, the relation of functional correspondence between a manifold of lived experiences and acts and the characteristics of the appearing object. How are we to think this "more"? As a mere sense-bestowal (*Sinngebung*)? That is not enough, because it is not only the sense but the being of what is constituted that originates in transcendental consciousness.[76] As a true production? Husserl rules this out. But how, then? It must be remarked that the ever-increasing insistence on Husserl's part—both in his working manuscripts and his published texts—on the passive and pre-egological nature of constitution changes absolutely nothing with respect to the problem I am raising, which is that of the dependence of reality, not on the activity of the ego, but on subjectivity itself, regardless of *whether the operations of subjectivity are active or passive.* The passive processes take place before, and independently of, all egological activity, that is, without the participation of the *I,* but they remain *formally egological,* that is, subjective; they are "processes that flow forth of themselves, yet that remain subjective," as Husserl specifically states.[77]

Consequently, it is not at all obvious that the *problem* of intentionality—how intentionality can be both a relation (presupposing the existence of its *relata*) and an intrinsic property of consciousness that is only *apparently* relational (a quasi-relation to a possibly nonexistent object)—finds a solution, or even the beginning of a clarification, thanks to the transcendental turn. On the one hand, the description of perceptual intentionality in terms of *Selbstgegebenheit,* of self-givenness of the thing itself and of itself, seems to presuppose that this thing exists independently of consciousness and its constituting work; on the other hand, if we are to believe *Ideas I* and many other texts, the thing has no "itself," no autonomy; it "lacks self-sufficiency [*Selbstständigkeit*],"[78] it is *nothing beyond* an intentional correlate.[79] Intentionality must be both a relation to the transcendent thing and the basis for the constitution of that thing as a pure ideal pole remaining identically the same as correlate of consciousness *regardless of whether the real thing exists or not.* Intentionality does not so much solve the problem from which Husserl had set out as it dissolves this problem, since the word "thing" has not at all the same meaning when we say that intentionality is a relation to the transcendent thing (meaning, to the thing existing in the world) and when we say that this thing is nothing but an ideal pole in the process of constitution (regardless of whether the "thing" in the first sense exists or not). Husserl succeeds in reconciling these two meanings of "thing" only at the cost of an equivocation, refusing to adjudicate between incompatible requirements. The Husserlian doctrine of intentionality is the focal point of these unresolved tensions.

If I am right, these tensions have a common source—the acceptance of the skeptical argument. "Since it is always possible to doubt something, it is always possible to doubt everything": this is the watchword of universal doubt. Applied to the problem of perception, this doubt leads to claiming that, since all perception can always turn out to be deceptive, perception as a whole is constantly threatened by the specter of illusion, and a generalized doubt with respect to perception is legitimate. But does such doubt really make sense? Do we not doubt a particular perception against the background of the continuity and permanence of the world as that which escapes all reasonable doubt? We will have occasion to return to this question in chapter 15. In conclusion, let me simply stress that the hypothesis of a generalized illusion, that is, of a world entirely chaotic because of a conflict between its appearances, seems to enter into contradiction with one of Husserl's main claims, that of the existence of material *a priori,* that is, of necessary structures of phenomenality that confer on the latter an immutable order and cohesion. If the world in its phenomenological meaning is neither a mere addition of phenomena, nor a mere sum of objects or facts, and therefore something contingent, but rather *the necessary spatiotemporal* a priori *structure of all appearing of something,* how could it ever dissolve into a chaos, according to the fiction of a generalized illusion? In any perception, an isolated error is always thinkable, but a global illusion is absurd, for it is contradictory with the material necessities that structure perception, conferring on it its unchanging phenomenal features. Either perception is governed by non-empirical laws that furnish its *contents* themselves with a necessary structuration, and the idea of complete chaos is absurd, or else such a chaos is thinkable, and the idea of *a priori* material structures must be ruled out.[80]

The transcendental turn is based in its entirety on the possibility of a universal doubt. If that possibility is "empty," if the very possibility of doubting something *excludes* the possibility of doubting everything, it may be that the cogito represents neither *a* starting point, nor, *a fortiori*, *the* starting point for an authentically descriptive philosophy. The fate of phenomenology may not be one and the same with that of Cartesianism.

15

The Intentionality of Perception

> A phenomenon isn't a symptom of something else: it is the reality.
>
> —Ludwig Wittgenstein

The olive tree shimmering in the heavy heat, the blinding distances harried by the sun appear precisely where they stand, in a mute and self-sufficient adequacy to themselves; they are neither in my head nor in a chimerical consciousness. Their presence requires nothing beyond itself, it seeks no justification, asks for no supplement of soul. And the same goes for myself: I do not appear to myself elsewhere than immersed in this space beaming outward from this place, making me equal to my surroundings; located *alongside* things, not on the other bank of I know not what Lethe, but rearing up suddenly in this same phenomenal field in which they, too, stand erect, and in which, seen from here, they do not appear to me *otherwise* than my own body; bodily bonded to them, so to speak, concretions of a common network of appearance conferring upon us a primordial, indefectible parity.

Yet phenomenology has had a tendency to fail to recognize this starting point of all description, interpreting it instead according to Cartesian premises. Thus, the tree would be only over there in the world because it would be inadequately given. By contrast, consciousness would be given to itself adequately and, to that extent, it would retain a fold of interiority. Despite the breakthrough of intentionality beyond a philosophy of representation, Husserl "remains trapped in immanence," as Heidegger writes.[1] In order to determine precisely when description began to deviate from its path and lose its way in the shifting sands of metaphysics, we must return to our starting point and proceed, as much as possible, in a phenomenological manner. This starting point is a characteristic of essence of perception as such. Every perception of a material thing, hence of an extended thing, as Husserl puts it, is carried out by silhouettes or adumbrations (*Abschattungen*). This assertion is neither a linguistic convention that would govern the use of the words "spatial thing" and "perception," nor a contingent empirical discovery. Nor is it a geometrical truth, and this is the case not only because the perceived thing, as opposed to a geometrical solid, presents a certain opacity, keeps hiding itself in the perception we have of it, but more deeply because the very idea that a thing appears *from a specific angle* presupposes that we are ourselves situated *some place,* and because the notions of perceptual situation and of perspective from which something appears to us have no equivalent in geometry. Even a transparent glass cube, the six sides of which I would see simultaneously, would not be a pure geometrical solid, because it would still appear to me through changing profiles, according to whether I get closer or farther away from it. And even if it is always possible to formalize that optic property thanks to a projective geometry, that formalization is only meaningful for someone who possesses an *experience* of vision, since the notions of point of view and of modalities of appearance make sense only in relation to that experience.

Husserl's triviality—for it is indeed a triviality[2]—is therefore an essential property of our visual experience of spatial objects, to the extent that this experience is characterized *a priori*: it is part of *what it is to be* a spatial object grasped at the level of our daily experience of the world, to be unable to be perceived otherwise than by adumbrations. But what does this last assertion mean? Phenomenological description, in order to be carried out, proceeds on the basis of transcendental questions (see chapter 12). Hence we must ask: What is the status of these adumbrations? What is their relationship to the thing that presents itself in them? Are these adumbrations objective, subjective, or neither?

We know henceforth Husserl's response. If experience in its primary sense means "the self-giving of individual objects,"[3] perception is experience par excellence, the *Urerfahrung,* the primary experience, since it is characterized both by the givenness in person and by the givenness in the flesh of its object. Not only is the thing itself given, *originaliter,* and not through anything else, a substitute or a mental intermediary, but it is given *in praesentia,* so to speak, according to the fullness of the intuitive presence of what is lying or standing there, within reach, and whose "bodily" presence calls for the simultaneous presence of my own body. I see this ashtray, and the fact of *seeing* it implies precisely that I can walk around it, come closer or back away from it, pick it up, feel its weight, turn it this way and that: I would not be *seeing* it if I couldn't perform these acts toward it, at least in principle. And yet—and here the paradox begins—that presence in the flesh, within my reach, can never guarantee for me that the ashtray actually *exists,* because its mode of givenness, necessarily inadequate, is of a nature such as to give me only a "presumptive certainty." If at this moment I perceive this glass ashtray as having a milky transparency, the aspect it presents me with, and that transparency itself are indubitable; but as I make a movement, as the flow of adumbrations suddenly jolts forward, it is always possible that the following adumbrations may not coincide with the preceding ones; coming closer, I discover for example that this so-called ashtray was only a crumpled piece of paper on which a ray of light fell, giving it a characteristic form and look. We can go a step further: given that perception possesses a teleological structure and is always by essence exposed to the risk of illusion, we must maintain that I can come as close as possible, hold the ashtray in my hand this way or that, put my cigarette ashes into it, and even throw it against the wall to see it break into a thousand and one pieces—I will never be able to eradicate entirely the possibility of a perceptual error, nor, therefore, the legitimacy of a doubt about its existence; the presence in the flesh of the ashtray remains continually threatened by the specter of illusion, as if it stood vacillating on the brink of non-being.

The trouble with that description is that it is not very phenomenological. How can we reconcile the view that perception involves the very presence of the thing, with the view that that thing is constantly on the verge of disappearing into nothingness like a phantasm or a mirage—and the world along with it? On the one hand, Husserl tells us that the thing, in order to be *perceived*, must be given not only *in persona*, but *in praesentia* or in the flesh; on the other hand, he maintains that this presence in the flesh can never make us sure that the thing actually exists, that is, that we are really perceiving it (and not hallucinating it), and this is true whatever the care with which we examine it and scrutinize it in each of its profiles. In short, Husserl tells us both that the distinctive feature of perception is the very presence of the thing, and that perception never guarantees the presence of the perceived thing. Are not these two assertions contradictory? In order for a thing to be given to us *in praesentia*, does it not first have to *be present*, and in order for it to be present, does it not first have *to be*? As paradoxical as it sounds, Husserl's response is negative. "The foregoing characterization [called *Leibhaftigkeit*] is not to be understood in the sense that there would pertain to the essence of every perception as such the existence of the perceived object, the existence of that which stands there in the mode of presence in the flesh. In that case, talk of a perception whose object did not exist would indeed be countersensical; illusory perceptions would be unthinkable."[4] In order to spell out in what sense illusory perceptions are thinkable, Husserl proposes to distinguish two characteristics that are confused in ordinary language: *Leibhaftigkeit*, which belongs to every perception, regardless of whether it is illusory or not, and *Glaubhaftigkeit*, the belief which should be given to it—and which must be withdrawn from it in the case of an illusion. The former is independent of the latter: a thing may perfectly well be given in the flesh without *existing*. In other words, Husserl acknowledges that the use of the word "perception" that he proposes to adopt for the purposes of his description has nothing to do with the common use of that term. In the current use of "perceive," I can only say that I *perceive* something if there is indeed something that gives itself to be perceived. "To perceive that *p*" entails "*p*," whereas "to believe that *p*" does not entail "*p*," and "to have the hallucination that *p*" entails on the contrary "not *p*." In the case in which I "perceive" something and that thing does not exist, it is improper to speak of *perception*; we must rather speak of *illusion* or *hallucination*: "to perceive" *excludes* "to hallucinate" or to "be deluded," and vice versa. As Husserl notes, "if we take the word perception in the usual sense, then we will find that in our fundamental examples the moment of belief [*das 'Glaubhaft'*] is fused with the one of presence in the flesh."[5] It is precisely this ordinary use of "perceive" that Husserl rejects. But why depart from ordinary usage? The answer is henceforth well known: because Husserl adopts as his own the Cartesian premise of the dubitability of the external world and the indubitability of our "ideas" or lived experiences, and because this metaphysical prejudice leads him to conclude that it is possible to distinguish a characteristic of perceptual lived experiences from a characteristic of the objects that may or may not correspond to them, that is, "presence in the flesh [*die Leiblichkeit*], which is fundamental and essential to perception as such, and the presence in credence [*das Glaubhaftigkeit*], which can either supervene or be lacking."[6] We may perceive a six-story building standing there in front of us in the flesh, and at the same time not be certain at any moment that this building exists.

No infraction to linguistic usage, by itself, is a philosophical error, let alone nonsense. But it does happen that a reform of this sort leads to serious difficulties. Is it so easy to disconnect the givenness of a thing *in praesentia*, which is the mark of its having been perceived, from the existence that belongs to that thing? Merleau-Ponty writes:

> I am not certain that there is an ashtray or a pipe over there, but I am certain that I think I see an ashtray or a pipe. Is it as easy to dissociate these two affirmations as is often thought? On the contrary, this is impossible. Perception is just that kind of act where there can be no question of separating the act itself and the term upon which it bears. Perception and the perceived necessarily have the same existential modality, since perception is inseparable from the consciousness that it has or rather that it is of reaching the thing itself. There can be no ques-

> tion of maintaining the certainty of perception by denying the certainty of the perceived thing. If I see an ashtray *in the full sense of the word 'see,'* then there must be an ashtray over there. . . . To see is to see something. To see red is to see an actually existing red."[7]

To grasp the necessity of these assertions, we must ask ourselves whether Husserl's position is coherent. If we are to believe the founder of phenomenology on this point, we should be able to speak of the "perception" of a thing, even when the perceiving subject is not certain that it exists, and cannot make *absolutely* sure of its existence by any examination, no matter how attentive and scrupulous. But how can we conceive of the difference between a *real* perception and an *illusory* one (since it becomes possible to speak in all strictness of "illusory perceptions")? Their difference, Husserl answers, rests on two characteristics. First, perception is a *positional* consciousness, whereas the consciousness of illusion derives from a suspension of belief in the object and from a replacement of the original positing by "counter-positing" (*Gegenthese*).[8] Secondly, perception and illusion differ as to the mode of concatenation of the adumbrations: perception is a flow of concordant adumbrations, constantly confirming and corroborating one another in the unity of an experience; illusion, a flow of discordant adumbrations, denouncing the inanity of their object through the outburst of a conflict between them. These two distinctive characteristics are closely connected: it is because perception is a flow of confirmed adumbrations that a doxic modality of belief is attached to it, or rather a proto-belief that is not yet linguistic or propositional. Conversely, where a conflict breaks out between competing appearances, a doxic neutralization takes place, so that consciousness only relates to the alleged object as to a *mere appearance.*

The postulate of this whole analysis is that there exists an *element common* to experience and to pseudo-experience, to appearance and to mere appearance, namely the *Abschattungen* as indubitable givens, which remain identically the same, regardless of whether the thing they present to us exists or not. According to such an analysis, a perception and an illusion could be indistinguishable in all points during the time they are lived; their difference should therefore reside in an additional characteristic, the concordant or discordant concatenation of adumbrations. One and the same phenomenon would be now perception, now illusion, according to the way it coordinates with other phenomena. Let us call this conception *conjunctive.* According to the conjunctive approach to perception, there is a neutral sense of "to appear" prior to the distinction between appearance and mere appearance—a neutral sense to which the adumbrations as "modes of givenness" of the object correspond.

The ashtray that I am able to touch "appears" to me in the same sense of that term as does the mirage in the desert, except that the ashtray appears to me (in that sense of "to appear") in a concordant way, that is, as constantly confirmed and corroborated by its subsequent appearances, whereas the mirage appears to me (in this same sense) in a discordant or conflictual way, for the very moment I begin to direct my steps toward it its vaporous and trembling silhouette dissolves above the sands, leaving behind nothing but more desert scenes, other dunes similar to the preceding ones.

The paradoxical thing about this description is that it becomes possible to speak of adumbrations as "modes of givenness" of the object even when no object is given, as in the case of the mirage in the desert. But in order for an object to appear to us in a given way, is it not indispensable for it to *be*? Otherwise it becomes possible to "separate" the adumbrations from the object that is adumbrated in them; these outlines amount to nothing other than mental intermediaries, interfaces between the mind and the world, since they are still present even in cases in which no object is present. Thus Husserl relapses into a psychologism from which intentionality freed him only apparently. The *Abschattungen* are really immanent hyletic data that float within consciousness and about which it is hard to see how they could possibly open to the thing itself. To be sure, Husserl makes the claim that it is the apprehension or interpretation (*Deutung*) of these impressional data that enable consciousness to relate to objects. But this claim remains enigmatic. How could the interpretation of immanent data initiate us to the thing, transform these hyletic data into objects, give rise to anything more than these same data interpreted?[9] Furthermore, Husserl will end up conceding that the postulation of immanent contents *common to both perception and illusion* is merely a remnant of sensualism and psychologism: "Is not my original grasp of the sphere of immanence, thanks to the immanent data which come to be understood only with the passive accomplishment of association, a remnant of the old psychology and its sensualist empiricism?"[10] The consequence of this residual psychologism is the necessity of a Platonism that counterbalances it, and, consequently, the inevitable idealization of the object. In order to forearm transcendent reality against all relativity with respect to my consciousness and my factual lived experiences, there is no other solution than to ascribe to the object the status of an unreal, therefore ideal, content, or, as Husserl sometimes says in order to distinguish this ideality from that of eidetic *generalities*, of something "ideell [ideal]."[11] The object is henceforth an ideal pole in the flow of subjective or intersubjective life, an Idea in the Kantian sense.[12] It bursts in two, so to speak: immanent adumbrations, which are truly mental things, and the real thing *ad extra*, which is now no more than a teleological pole in a process of confirmation, always in principle incomplete.

This solution is untenable. There is nothing in common between perception and illusion, no neutral sense of "to appear," in which one might be able to say of a thing and of a mere appearance that they both *appear*. The thing that stands before me addresses itself to the potentialities of my body, giving itself corporally in a fullness of presence that stands in complete opposition to the vanishing point of an ideal. The illusion, in its phenomenological mode of givenness, is definitely not a contradicted and crossed-out perception; nor is perception a confirmed illusion, nor the world a "coherent dream."[13] Once we make the difference between perception and illusion depend on the mode of concatenation of adumbrations, we have already given skepticism the last word. If a perception can only rightfully be called a "perception" (in the ordinary sense of the term) *as long as* it remains concordant, it cannot in fact *ever* be called a "perception"; all concordance being by nature provisional, the distinction between illusion and perception is also provisional, so that I can never tell, for a given phenomenon, whether it belongs to the first category or the second. By placing that distinction at the end of an infinite process, that is to say, at the end of what is by definition endless, we fully agree with the skeptic, whose "thesis" is that it is impossible, on the occasion of a present lived experience, to decide whether it belongs in the category of truth or appearance. Far from the "purely phenomenological" character of concordance furnishing a response to the skeptic, it merely endorses the claim that his doubt is well-founded, and confers a supplementary plausibility on it. It is no use adding that the probability of a perceived thing admits of degrees, that the more the concordance is prolonged, the more the rational motives for believing in the existence of the thing gradually gain "weight."[14] The tenth time I turn this ashtray in my hands, will its existence be more certain than the first time? It is certain from the start, or it never will be—and this is what Husserl does not succeed in accounting for.

Husserl set out from a description of essence that is not controversial. Every spatial thing is perceived through a multiplicity of profiles or adumbrations. But at the moment of saying what these adumbrations are, due to Cartesian prejudices, he ends up with an untenable conclusion. The *Abschattungen* are neutral with respect to the illusion/perception distinction, and the counterpart of this claim is that illusion can be defined as a contradicted perception, whereas perception can be defined as a confirmed illusion. But we must call into question the presuppositions governing his analysis. Is there really something that perception and illusion have in common, or are the perceptual experience and the illusory quasi-experience intrinsically distinct? Can one reduce the givenness of the thing *in praesentia* to a synthesis of concordant adumbrations accompanied by a positing of existence or an indefinitely maintained proto-belief? Do we not see, do we not perceive *before believing* what we see or perceive—therefore before being able to doubt or not believe it?

In order to show that Husserl's analysis of perception is metaphysical and anti-phenomenological, we cannot rely solely on "grammar"; for the "logic of our ordinary language" cannot, by itself, convince the skeptic. If we say, for example, that the necessary condition for us to be able to speak meaningfully of "perception" is that material objects and other minds *exist*, skepticism about the existence of the external world is not in the least refuted. The skeptic can always reply that the necessary condition for our language's making sense is not that material objects and other minds *exist*, but that we *believe* they exist.[15]

Other transcendental arguments than grammatical ones are thus needed. The problem is not, in this case, that to speak of "perception" without anything being perceived is a violation of the logic of our language, but that this hinders a good description of the *phenomena* of perception and illusion. We must not say that the illusory object is transcendent, as is the object perceived, but that it is *apparently* transcendent. We must not say that there are modes of givenness corresponding to this pseudo-existence, because there is no mode of givenness possible for what does not exist in any way.

Let us start with a few examples of illusion. Sometimes we use the term "illusions" to refer to false judgments on true perceptions. Entering a café, I hesitate for a split second before a person blocking my path who turns out to be my reflection in a mirror. There is unquestionably a perception here, but it is accompanied by a mistake about the identity of the object perceived. There are very different cases of illusion, close to hallucination, in which I mistakenly believe I perceive something: a mirage in the desert, tyrannical voices that assail schizophrenics, effects induced by the use of certain drugs. In still other cases, what is perceived is changed: in the Zöllner illusion, the lines appear to converge although they are parallel. Each of these examples would require a detailed analysis. The Zöllner illusion presents me with real lines, and it is those lines that appear to me now oblique, now parallel, depending on how I look at them. If, with the help of a ruler, I undertake to measure their distance from each other, leaving out oblique lines that "deform" my perception, the lines straighten out beneath my eyes, seem to run parallel again, if only for a fraction of a second. It is these same real lines that change how they look according to whether I look at the drawing as an indivisible whole or I proceed in an analytic way, leaving aside, as much as I can, some of its elements. In this specific case, one can speak of "illusion" only if it has been previously decreed that perception must be a synthesis of isolated elements that are identifiable independently of one another and capable of appearing to us in the exact same way in all circumstances—in short, if the "syncretic" or holistic nature of all perception has not been recognized. The two ways of perceiving this figure, the one normally prevalent and the one resulting from a particular, "analytic" attitude, reveal two *objective* aspects or properties of the perceived lines, in relation to the overall context of perception and the intent of the observer. It is the perception of the figure itself that is ambivalent, unstable by nature, and this indeterminateness, this inherent motility, only represents an *illusion* for those who have already settled the issue by proclaiming that all perception must be determined and stable in principle, or that it must reflect by essence the geometric properties of its constituents.

Other examples of illusion would require a different analysis. The hallucinated object *looks like* a perceived object, but manifests itself differently, as if on a different stage from that of the real world. The victim of hallucinations distinguishes very well between a voice resulting from hallucination and a voice heard—which does not prevent him from "believing" in the former, from attributing a presence to it that is almost as full and obsessive as that of the second, and, as it were, a beginning of reality. "The voices are heard, but these voices differ from normal voices," Erwin Strauss points out. "The voices which torment the schizophrenic differ so strikingly from all other acoustic impressions (including linguistic sounds) . . . that most of the time the patient does not immediately understand that he is being asked whether he hears voices."[16] These voices are not pathological phenomena within an unchanged perceptual framework but the result of an alteration of that framework itself. The same is true of visual illusions. A schizophrenic, as Zucker reports,[17] thinks he sees a man standing beneath his window in the garden; he describes his location, his look, his clothing. Someone is placed in the same spot, similarly dressed, and asked to imitate as closely as possible the posture and gait of the person according to the descriptions given by the patient. The latter is surprised; he immediately perceives the difference. He exclaims: "It's true, there is someone there, but it is someone else." The fact is, "the illusory thing and the real thing do not have the same structure."[18] The illusion is by essence fleeting, labile, fluctuating, indeterminate: it shoots up like foxfire and almost immediately goes out. There is in it nothing like the ordered succession of facets that follow upon one another in an orderly and continuous way, forming a system within a dynamic succession in the course of which the thing is enriched by ever new determinations. Conversely, perception is in no case a hallucination with something else added on: the possibility of a dynamic exploration and the regulated character of the process of appearance. In perception, what appears is *inseparable* from the orderly pathway of the appearing. The rose of the dahlia is slightly modified by a change of lighting, but in a progressive and regular manner; its velvety flesh has a matte look and a consistency that, far from being affected by the change of circumstances, are preserved as I move closer and the lighting is modified, as if they were changed in themselves under changing conditions. None of these characteristics are present in the case of illusion. The dahlia produced by hallucination has neither a determined hue, nor any specific consistency; and it is *because it does not possess these properties* that neither its texture nor its color varies in a regular way. The phenomenon of the hallucination is a sui generis phenomenon: it "is not part of the world," as Merleau-Ponty emphasizes, "that is, it is not *accessible*, there is no definite road that leads from this phenomenon to all the other experiences of the hallucinating subject."[19] This is why there is nothing here corresponding to *Abschattungen*. "The majority of hallucinations are not things with different facets, but rather ephemeral phenomena, injections, shots, explosions, draughts, hot or cold flashes, sparks, points of light, glimmers, or silhouettes. When the hallucination has to do with real things, such as a rat, they are only represented by their style or their physiognomy. These inarticulate phenomena do not allow for precise causal connections among themselves."[20] Perception is dynamic and orderly, it is the very manner in which I have a hold on the world through my body, it accompanies and espouses my slightest movements. Illusion is static, and, to this extent, ephemeral, volatile, unstable. "The visual illusion is thus much less the presentation of an illusory object than the unfolding and, so to speak, wild fluctuations of a visual power henceforth lacking a sensory counterpart."[21]

But, it may be asked, how is it then that illusion *passes itself off* as reality? How are we to explain that there is an imposture in illusion in which the *illusio*, as is suggested by its etymology,[22] fools us in its play and deludes us? To be sure, it belongs to illusion to fool us, and it is only once it has been recognized and unmasked that it reveals itself as such; but we should not conclude thereby that nothing distinguishes it from a perception. From the fact that we are sometimes led astray by a false appearance, it is just as impossible to infer that the latter was indistinguishable from a true appearance as it is absurd to conclude, from the fact that we sometimes make a mistake in adding numbers, that the two results, the true and the false, are equivalent. The illusion tends to supplant perceptual reality without its being homogeneous with it. Mere appearance can pass itself off as appearance, without itself being an appearance *in the same sense.* Only true perception truly is a perception, that is, a mode of givenness of something. As for the falsity of illusion, it belongs intrinsically to the illusion's mode of manifestation, which does not in the slightest keep the illusion from fooling us, but on the contrary explains that it does so. For "false," here, means: that deceives, that passes itself off for something other than what it is. Strictly speaking, there is no illusory *experience*; there are only illusions of experience.

Furthermore, the difference between illusion and perception depends, first of all, on the different relationship they have to their contexts. By essence, illusion is only revealed as being such against the background of the perceived world. Illusion can only give itself away, take on the status of deceptive appearance, against the background of a true grasp of the world; it only exists as a borderline case within perception, and this is why it can only be *an isolated phenomenon.* The mirage that trembles in the distance reveals itself as being a mirage when I keep walking toward it, that is, when the sands stretching out before me in a vast, virgin expanse end up "reconnecting with" the distant panorama, when what a moment ago seemed to stand out and float on the horizon melts away like a dreamy wisp. Without the continuity of the walk, that coalescence of my gestures with their environment, this continuous passing by of the landscape as I move forward in it, that cohesiveness of the distant dunes whose texture gets finer as if condensed beneath the weight of distance, and in which each detail is situated in relation to all others—the dunes keeping their mutual spatial relationships while spreading out like a Chinese fan, streaming away to my left and right as I pass them one after another—without all this, the mirage could not *conflict* with the firm ground of all my perceptions, and so disintegrate. To grasp the illusion, we must have identified it; and that identification presupposes the background of the real world, on the hither side of all possible illusion. "It is this opening to a world," writes Merleau-Ponty, "that makes perceptual truth possible, or the actual realization of a *Wahr-Nehmung,* and permits us 'to cross out' the preceding illusion, to hold it to be null and void."[23] If it is permissible to speak of perceptual truth, it is because that openness to the world prior to all possible belief and doubt is of the order of a global grasp that offers no purchase to suspicion, and only in the background of which, all circumscribed doubt and all hesitation become possible. The whole is given before the part; the world is given before the partial perceptions that are cut off of it, and some of which, upon occasion, turn out to be subject to doubt. This is why illusion is necessarily an anomaly. It is also why the idea of an entirely illusory world is an absurdity in principle. If all were illusion, no illusion could betray itself, nor, *a fortiori*, could an illusion about the Whole itself. Husserl's error was to believe that a hallucination could be revealed as such by a conflict *internal* to the flow of adumbrations. But if, in hallucination, there are, strictly speaking, no longer any adumbrations; if, moreover, the only conflict that breaks out here is the one between illusion and perception, such a conflict cannot come to light where neither perceptual continuity nor perceptual cohesiveness exist. Illusion is an infringement of the general cohesiveness of the world. In illusion, *the world remains presupposed as the inviolable background* of all my perceptions and behavior. If an annihilation of the world were possible, according to Husserl's hypothesis, that annihilation by conflict should reveal itself against the background of a more fundamental cohesiveness, so that what survived the annihilation of the world would not be an acosmic transcendental ego, but rather the world itself.

Perception plays the role of a *basso continuo* on which the melodic line of illusion is superimposed. It is because the skeptic believes he can break down the being of the world into "lived experiences," into fragments of knowledge that are independent of one another and capable of revealing themselves severally as illusory—because he misunderstands, from the very first step of his reasoning, the fundamentally holistic character of all experience—because he leaps over the phenomenon of the world as a structural totality, indivisible into elements and preceding all partial perception, that he ends up with postulating something like a generalized illusion. But this way of proceeding is hopeless. Once our original and undivided openness to the world has gone unrecognized, it cannot be reconstructed by summation. The world is a structural whole that is defined by its intrinsic cohesiveness. This cohesiveness of the world, which belongs to its phenomenological *a priori*, is not the coherence of beliefs about the world. Coherence is logical, cohesiveness is phenomenal. The former is a formal relation of non-contradiction; the second, a necessary phenomenological characteristic of all *perception* as such, and the indispensable condition for every illusion to be able to reveal itself as an illusion. More precisely, this cohesiveness means a system of structural invariants—spatiotemporal, for example—that underlie all variation of phenomena; hence a system of possibilities of essence preceding realities. The world is a structural phenomenon. It is not first and foremost a totality of things, facts, or states of affairs; it is the totality of essential possibilities governing factical possibilities and realities. If "coherent" is understood here as characterizing that cohesiveness and not the coherence in the logical sense, it is no accident that reality is coherent; cohesiveness is what defines reality by essence. Thus illusion is not an incoherent reality, nor is reality a coherent illusion; the cohesiveness of the real is what *excludes* illusion and only allows it to reveal itself as such. The world is not presumed true; its cohesiveness is prior to any presumption of truth or falsity; it is that without which nothing could reveal itself as being illusory.

An accurate phenomenological description of illusion suffices to rule out the fiction of a generalized illusion, the "perceptual" variant of the skeptic argument. It is true that any perception can be doubted, but it is not true that perception as a whole can be doubted. "There is absolute certainty of the world in general, but not of any particular thing,"[24] Merleau-Ponty writes. This is because the uncertainty about a particular thing is only possible against the background of a certainty about the whole world. There is nothing theoretical about that certainty; it is neither a constantly confirmed belief nor a proto-belief. Heidegger emphasized very early that the very idea of a primordial openness to the world based on a primordial belief, an *Urdoxa*, was the symptom, in Husserl, of a remnant of theoreticism. "We saw that in environmental experience there is *no theoretical positing* at all."[25] And he specifies: "It becomes clear that nothing exists in our relationship to the world which provides a basis for the phenomenon of belief in the world. I have not yet been able to find this phenomenon of belief. Rather, the peculiar thing is just that the world is 'there' *before* all belief. The world is never experienced as something which is believed any more than it is guaranteed by knowledge. Inherent in the being of the world is that its existence [*Vorhandensein*] *needs no guarantee in regard to a subject* . . . . That it [the world] is real stands in opposition to any move to prove it. And even any purported belief in it is a theoretically motivated misunderstanding."[26] The reply to Husserl's thesis that in our primordial relation to the world, "we believe 'before we know it,' "[27] must be that we perceive before believing, that the perceptual openness to the world is "older" than any belief, and, *a fortiori*, than any knowledge. It is true, in a sense, that Husserl paved the way for this conception by distinguishing between experiencing (*Erfahren, Kennenlernen*) and knowing (*Erkennen*) strictly speaking,[28] the full and complete knowledge essentially involving language. He stressed that our commerce with the world was not first and foremost gnoseological, but he nonetheless subordinated experience to the telos of an evident knowledge. Now, the world is not certain with a theoretical certainty. Our pragmatic relationship with the world, our engagement in activities that take it as a goal and are absorbed in it precedes any relationship of belief and knowledge. To perceive is not to believe; it is to have no need to believe; it is to be destined to the world and chained to it by an indissoluble bodily bond.

Thus, the presence of the thing in perception, or what Husserl calls its *Leibhaftigkeit*, cannot be analyzed as an indefinitely confirmed presumption of existence. It is a "certainty" in a more originary sense. To perceive a thing is to live symbiotically with it, to be able to act upon it, to possess it in a pragmatic way. Perception is a pre-theoretical "living with [*Mitleben*]," as Erwin Strauss writes; it is a primordial commerce with the thing; in this commerce, we experience ourselves in and though this contact with something else in a continuous encounter. "In sensory certainty, the world appears unmediated, direct, not hypothetical—*before* doubt."[29] The world is not certain in the sense in which its existence could be demonstrated, silencing all possible doubt; it stands not beyond doubt, but on the hither side of it; it is something that, because it is given to be experienced before any belief, is such that a doubt about it does not make any sense. Hence, in this vital communication with the world, there is no room for the negation of existence or for unreality. "Sensing," Straus continues, "is a direct, non-conceptual living-with [*Mit-leben*]. All belief begins with or after doubting; even apodictic judgments which exclude doubt are still oriented with respect to doubt. Sensory experience, on the other hand, knows no doubting. It is before doubt. And it thus cannot be touched by reasons."[30]

That the existence of the world should rely on a certainty that is not based on reasons, but precedes them, is a critical point. Since the openness to the world envelops a direct contact with things older than discursive intelligence and knowledge, it is impossible to understand perception as a set of beliefs, or even as being subtended by a fundamental belief. We adhere to the world even before asking ourselves the least question about its existence (a question that only appears with language); we come to grips with our surrounding world before believing in it, and this is why the question of the world's existence simply doesn't arise for us. The skeptic is wrong on two counts: indeed, it is not true that we can doubt everything at will; nor is it true that *all* certainty is based on reasons. To really doubt, we need incentives to doubt, just as to believe we need incentives to believe. In this sense, there is no such thing as *voluntary* doubt. Let us suppose that someone tells us that he doubts this or that, and that to our question "why," he answers: "Because that is what I have decided, for no particular reason." His doubt would sound hollow. It would have something absurd about it. It could not engage him, nor could it engage us. Because the act of doubting needs reasons just as much as the act of believing, it is necessary for doubt or belief to be rooted in "certainties" that are not in turn motivated beliefs, but stand on the hither side of all reasonable doubt, since *they are not themselves based on reasons.* Our perceptual certainties are of this kind. Their status is analogous to that of the "certainties" examined by Wittgenstein (for example, "cats don't grow on trees"), which, more basic than the opposition justified/unjustified,[31] ground the language games of doubt and belief. But, by contrast with Wittgenstein's certainties, perceptual certainties do not belong to the problematic of language games but to that of our embodied being-in-the-world. It is certain that the paper I am writing on at this moment and the movement of my hand are real, and, more generally, that the room in which I am, the apartment, and even Paris, exist around me. Of course, I can always be mistaken in this or that respect, for an *isolated* and *local* illusion is always possible. But if this illusion takes place, it can only declare itself by opening a breach in the perceptual continuity of the world—and the world with its continuity and its cohesiveness gives itself with a certainty that leaves no room for doubt, because it is not produced by reflection and judgment, it is prior to any possible justification and plays, with respect to all belief and all doubt, the role of ultimate justification. There must be certainties that are not justified by reasons in order for other certainties and other beliefs to be. If the perception of the world is insufficient for its existence to be "believed in," not only will nothing ever be able to persuade us of that existence, but nothing will ever be able to persuade us *of anything whatsoever.*

It must be pointed out that the hidden aspects of things—the sides of this table not presently visible, but also the rooms gone through a moment ago and presently fallen into a kind of latent life—are no less certain than their manifest aspects.[32] The office that I perceive fits into an apartment, a building opening onto a courtyard, then onto a street; if all this became uncertain the moment I lost sight of it, I could never perceive the walls surrounding me as an *office.* These perceptual certainties, though prior to doubt, nevertheless do not result in any infallibility. They can always be corrected in detail, but it is the idea of correcting all of them (like that of justifying all of them) that is meaningless. Thus, we must not conclude, from the fact that the existence of the perceived is never necessary, that the perceived is only possible or probable. "Possibility and probability presuppose the prior experience of error, and they correspond to the situation of doubt. The perceived is and remains, despite all critical training, beneath the level of doubt and demonstration . . . Each thing can, *après coup,* appear uncertain, but at least it is certain for us that there are things, that is, that there is a world. To wonder if the world is real is to fail to understand what one is saying, since the world is not a sum of things that one could always cast into doubt, but precisely the inexhaustible reservoir for which things are drawn."[33] Thus Merleau-Ponty concurs with Heidegger, who had already stressed that "he [the skeptic] does *not* even *need* to be refuted,"[34] and who added: "The question of whether there is a world at all . . . makes no sense."[35] The skeptic hyperbole manifests a primacy of the theoretical attitude, the forgetting of our pragmatic and corporeal engagement in the world. It rests on the false assumption that all perception contains an element of belief (a "thetic character") that it is always possible to suspend or neutralize. But while all perception can *motivate* beliefs, it does not shelter within itself a belief. This is why, if the idea of doubting all perception is "empty," that is no less true of the idea of suspending the natural attitude by the *epochē,* since that methodological operation cannot be dissociated from the skeptical approach. One must not say that the world only is as long as we believe in it, but that the world is what we have no need to believe in. Or, in Merleau-Ponty's terms, "we must not wonder if we truly perceive a world; rather we must say: the world is what we perceive."[36] There is no perception but *in* the world and *of* the world, because to perceive is already to explicate our primordial engagement in it, our commerce with it, our inherence in it as body.

In that case, it is hard to see why Merleau-Ponty maintains the truth of the cogito, and even its "definitive" and "unassailable" truth.[37] The cogito in the sense it has in Descartes, but also in Husserl, that of an indubitable first truth, is only "true" on the condition that the validity of universal doubt is presupposed. If we abandon universal doubt, we must also abandon the cogito: the world's existence is as indubitable as mine. If Merleau-Ponty and Heidegger did not themselves go so far as to draw that consequence, it is because they always mistrusted realism and considered it a latent form of naturalism. In their view, all realism is a *causal* realism.[38] One is, to be sure, right in stressing the difficulties in which a causal realism gets bogged down when it claims to explain experience itself on the basis of objects or events gleaned from that experience, when it assumes, between these entities and experience itself, the existence of a *causal* tie that has strictly speaking no meaning except within that experience. One cannot solve the epistemological dilemma of the validity of perception envisaged as a form of knowledge by having recourse to objects that are themselves given in the modality of that knowledge. But this dilemma only exists as long as realism is presented as an attempt at *explanation* and not as a description of phenomena. A *descriptive* realism asserts only one thing: perception cannot be described otherwise than as openness to the world itself, in the absence of any mental intermediary. The perception of the world presupposes the existence of the world and is indissociable from it. Such a realism provides no explanation in the causal sense; it supplies the indispensable basis for all explanation, for it limits itself to excluding incoherent descriptions. It is a "naive" realism, in that it says nothing more, or nothing other than, what Merleau-Ponty's reversal of terms already expressed: we must not ask ourselves whether we perceive the world; the world is what we perceive. Consequently, the world exists—as we do.

In this preconceptual mode of communication, prior to all belief and all knowledge (if by "knowledge" we mean what is expressed in propositions and can be justified by reasons), I experience myself through the experience of reality, I exist as one of the poles of this continuous interaction and transaction with my surroundings. In sensing (*Empfinden*; a term that Straus prefers to "perception," because perception, in his view, is already a form of knowledge and of objectification), the perceiving subject experiences himself and grasps himself as existing *in* the world, belonging by right to the world as body. "In sensing, both self and world unfold simultaneously for the sensing subject; the sensing being experiences himself and the world, himself in the world, himself with the world."[39] There is here no priority of the subject over the world, or the other way around. The world only exists on the condition that I exist—I only exist on the condition that the world exists. Subject and world are equiprimordial; their structural cohesiveness is the first and the last word and perception is nothing other than their continuous encounter. The "and" of Straus's phrase already signals that equiprimordiality; the "with" indicates that, in all perception, there are two indissociable poles, so that the experience of the world always unfolds in two directions at the same time: toward the subject and toward the object. To see, for example, is always to be part of the spectacle, to grasp one's own situation in relation to what appears, to discover oneself inscribed within the visible. To hear is to be inserted in the auditory space, to perceive sounds as located within that space in relation to the absolute frame of reference of one's body. To touch is to experience oneself in bodily contact with what arises before one's body and touches it. Finally, the "in" expresses this inherence in the world as body, which is inseparable from all perception. The thing is that undivided fullness to which my embodied presence opens me. It is only in that experience of the world that I become certain of my own presence, so that it is perhaps not entirely false to invert the cogito: "I am only insofar as the object is."[40]

If the world is perceived without intermediaries of any kind, must we not consent to abandoning the *Abschattungen*? We must first, certainly, abandon the concept of sensation which has its source in traditional empiricism. This concept is an ambiguous mixture, since it is either the result of an attempted explanation, being the correlate of the concept of *stimulus*, and it is devoid of any descriptive relevance (such atomic sensations are nowhere to be found), or it possesses a real descriptive relevance, as in the case of pains, sudden bedazzlements, afterimages, and burns, but does not enable us to explain anything at all. The idea of sensation is merely a theoretical postulate. But the idea of immanent contents of a strictly phenomenological nature is hardly any better. Let us be clear: it is not a question of denying that a multifaceted solid is perceived successively and never from all points of view at once: this is an essential truth. What is problematic is the temptation to separate, from a conceptual point of view, the object that appears from a particular angle from the angle from which it appears, and thus the adumbration it presents to us; in other words, to understand that adumbration as an immanent content *distinct* from the object and neutral with respect to its existence or nonexistence (and therefore also neutral with respect to the perception/illusion dichotomy). In rejecting this temptation, we move from a conjunctive to a disjunctive conception of perception.[41] According to the latter, every phenomenon is *either* perception *or* illusion (exclusive disjunction). Such a conception holds therefore that the distinction between perception and illusion is an *intrinsic* one, even though it remains often unnoticed as such. Husserl's hyletic data are a useless and even absurd reduplication of the object's properties as characteristics of the perceived scene. This is why the perceiving subject has neither interiority nor exteriority: the world is neither inside nor outside it, since it exists only as being-in-the-world. "The world is entirely on the inside, and I am entirely outside of myself," as Merleau-Ponty emphasizes.[42]

Still, it is far from being the case that the rejection of *Abschattungen* that are neutral with respect to the appearance/mere appearance distinction denies all relevance to the concept of sensation, as it has sometimes been hastily concluded. Husserl's mistake was not to believe that there were sensations (which is an indisputable fact), but to have extended the notion of sensation to perception as a whole; in short, to have defended the view that *all* perception rests on sensations. When it refers to particular phenomena (burn, pain, tickling, afterimage, etc.) whose specific property is to appear solely in a private way, and not on the world's stage, sensation is in its place, it possesses an unquestionable phenomenological legitimacy. An afterimage is not in the surrounding space, it affects my vision, it floats in that indefinable place in which my body projects itself onto things. A sensation of burning is in my hand, yet differently from the muscles or the blood circulating in it. Not only is there no reason to assume that there are sensations everywhere at work in perception, but there is no reason to confer on these sensations the status of absolute givens of which we would have an infallible knowledge. Even for sensations, it is not quite true to say that their *esse* is their *percipi*. Projected pains (pain in the left arm for an infarct, pain in the shoulder indicating an inflammation of the diaphragm), or pains in a phantom limb—are these not the *analogon* of perceptual illusions? Can we truly *feel* a pain in our hand if we no longer have a hand? Without going to these extreme cases, we can fail to correctly identify a pain and be mistaken about it. Anyone who has experienced neurological pain knows that there are an infinite number of degrees stretching from a mere discomfort to an itch, from a prickling sensation to a burning, and that it is often hard to say where a pain begins and ends. That burning, that itching—are they already a weak form of a familiar pain? Perhaps. Should we nevertheless call them "pains"? There is no clear-cut answer to these questions. Even sensations have an indetermination that makes them not be everything they appear to be. Whatever may be our final conclusions on that point, which would require a longer examination, it can be maintained that perception does not admit of immanent givens, without going so far as to assert that such givens do not exist for *sensation* (and probably for imagination, dreams, and hallucinations). From the assumption that interiority is contrary to the very idea of being-in-the-world as originary openness to things, we should not go so far as to conclude that *all* interiority is mythological.

As for this disjunctive conception of perception, Heidegger and Merleau-Ponty came very close to it, however, without being able to attain it. It implies, as it has been emphasized, that the phenomenon understood as *mere appearance* and the phenomenon understood as appearance *in person* cannot be led back to a common element. In §7 of *Being and Time,* Heidegger endeavors to distinguish three concepts of phenomenon, which he calls, respectively, *Phänomen, Schein,* and *Erscheinung.* According to the first, the phenomenon is the very manner in which a thing shows itself: a *Phänomen* is what shows itself as what it is [*ce qui se montre soi-même à même soi*]. In that "*montrance*" ("self-showing"), to borrow Claudel's lexical invention,[43] the thing shows itself *as it is,* so that it may be said of the *Phänomen* that it is "what the Greeks sometimes identified simply with *τὰ ὄντα* (entities)."[44] The phenomenon as a self-showing corresponds to Husserl's self-givenness, and contrasts with the two other concepts. First, the concept of *Schein,* of semblance or mere appearance, that is, of an appearance in which something shows itself *as it is not,* simply looks like . . . this or that. Semblance, Heidegger insists, refers necessarily to the phenomenon in which the entity shows itself as it is, since it is only to the extent that the entity can show itself as it is, that is to say, be a *Phänomen,* that it can also on occasion show itself as it is not, look like . . . , seem different from what it is. The *Schein* refers, then, to the *Phänomen* as to the "original signification" of the appearing from the point of view of a phenomenology. Finally, Heidegger reserves the name *Erscheinung* for a third concept, which is in substance the Kantian one. Here, what shows itself indicates "something which does *not* show itself"[45]—in the Kantian terminology, the thing in itself. The concept of *Erscheinung* possesses a phenomenological relevance when we describe traces, symptoms, vestiges, indications: smoke indicating the presence of fire, footsteps in the snow revealing the passing of a chamois. But the error into which Kant himself lapsed was to conceive of *all* phenomena in that way. The *Erscheinung,* on the contrary, is only comprehensible on the basis of the *Phänomen,* since an appearance cannot indicate something that, in itself, does not show itself, unless that same thing is capable of showing itself in itself in other circumstances: the chamois may step out at a bend in the path, the fire may set the valley ablaze, and the bacillus whose presence is attested by the symptom may be revealed by a microscope.

The strength of the Heideggerian analysis lies in the fact that it rejects the whole assumption of a neutral acceptation of "phenomenon" with respect to the basic distinction between appearance in person and mere appearance. The phenomenon in the primary phenomenological sense is the self-showing of something: "'*Phenomenon,*' the showing-itself-in-itself, signifies a distinctive way in which something can be encountered."[46] This sense of the word is distinct from that of mere appearance or semblance, for which we should, moreover, distinguish the case in which a thing shows itself otherwise than it is (I mistook this for that, this sparrow for a chickadee), and the case in which, actually, *nothing* shows itself—the hallucination pure and simple. Yet in the same §7 of *Being and Time,* Heidegger seems to back off from his own conclusions. Indeed, if the phenomenon in its primary phenomenological sense is the self-showing of something, it follows that the phenomenon is the very appearing of the thing, which cannot be dissociated from the thing that appears. But then only the *thing* can be said to "appear," *and not the phenomenon.* To describe a *Phänomen,* a self-showing [*montrance*] is to describe nothing else than the appearing thing (and sometimes what is not at all a *thing*: change, event, horizon, and so on), but it is to describe that thing itself in another respect, that is, in its relation to the one for whom it appears. To describe phenomena is not to describe hypothetical intermediaries—mental entities located in the sphere of immanence of a psyche, or even noemata floating somewhere between the world and consciousness—for which it would in turn be necessary to say that they, too, "appear." Phenomena, modes of appearing of things (events, changes, and so on) *do not appear* on pain of infinite regress, no more than experience itself is experienced. If the phenomena are mistakenly taken as hypothetical intermediaries, a phenomenology of our being-in-the-world rigorously excludes them. Such a phenomenology must be a *phenomenology without phenomena.*

Heidegger, as I was saying, backed away from this consequence. Indeed, at the very moment he states that "phenomenon" means first and foremost the showing-itself of something, he adds that the phenomenon shows itself as phenomenon, that it must be defined as *Sichzeigen*: it is "*that which shows itself in itself,* the manifest."[47] But these two assertions contradict each other. Either the phenomenon shows itself, and, in that case, it is not the mode of appearing of things, or it is indeed this mode of appearing—in which case the only thing that shows itself is the thing that appears, not the phenomenon. Actually, there is nothing fortuitous about this backing away. Indeed, the whole conceptuality of *Being and Time* presupposes that Being as such is a phenomenon, and a phenomenon in an eminent sense—a sense different from the *Sich-an-ihm-selbst-zeigende.* Being shows itself as that which, initially, does not show itself, remains withdrawn, repressed by an essential forgetfulness. Thus understood, Being plays the role of a transcendental condition of possibility for the appearance of all that is; it is "that which is 'transcendental' for every entity."[48] Whence the ambivalence of the whole conceptuality of *Being and Time.* At the very moment in which Heidegger claims that that to which *Dasein* is open, that to which it relates, is the entity itself, he adds that it is not actually the entity, but the entity in its mode of givenness, and he thinks this "mode of givenness" as an ontological characteristic different from the entity possessing this characteristic. This is what we can note in Heidegger's reinterpretations of intentionality as they unfold in the courses contemporary with the writing of *Being and Time.* What is given in perception, Heidegger writes, is "not the perceived as an entity, but the entity in the how of its being-perceived, the *intentum* in the how of its being-intended."[49] Thus a new discrepancy [*écart*] is introduced between the Being of the perceived and the perceived, between the how of the being-given and the given itself. And Heidegger restores a form of idealism, no longer a subjective idealism, but, let us say, an ontological transcendentalism: the Being of the perceived plays formally the role of the noema in Husserl, that of a condition for the givenness of all given. While he introduces an entirely novel problematic, that of perceivedness (*Wahrgenommenheit*) as an ontological characteristic of the perceived as such, Heidegger does not break entirely with Husserl's conceptuality, since he writes that "the perceived in the strict sense for phenomenology is not the perceived *entity* in itself but the *perceived* entity insofar as it is perceived, *as* it shows itself in concrete perception"[50]—precisely what he calls "the perceivedness of the perceived." Thus, in the perception of a chair, he specifies, "the perceived in the strict sense is the perceived as such or, more precisely expressed, the *perceivedness*,"[51] that is, not the chair *in an unqualified way*, but the chair "*in the how of its being-intended*."[52] How could perception bear upon the entity as perceived, on the perceived in its perceivedness, *and not on the perceived (or the entity) itself?* The being of the perceived again plays the role of a transcendental condition for the appearing and we lapse back into an idealism. This idealism asserts not that the entity in general depends, in order to be, on the entity that we ourselves are, *Dasein*, but that it depends, in order to appear *as entity*, on the understanding of Being that belongs to *Dasein*, on its ontological openness (*Erschloßenheit*) as what possibilizes all manifestedness, all uncoveredness (*Entdecktheit*) of entity in general. This "ontological" idealism can be considered superior to Husserl's, in that it includes a strong realist requirement: the fact that perception bears upon the perceived as such, that is on the perceived in its perceivedness, "already requires the *existence* of the perceivable or the perceived entity."[53] However, Heidegger hesitates at the moment of completely abandoning the (necessarily idealist) terrain of a transcendental philosophy. He keeps saying, following the example of Husserl, that "the intentional relation . . . lies in the perceiving itself, *whether illusionless or illusory*."[54] Now, illusion, and *a fortiori* hallucination cannot be intentional in the same sense that perception is: in this latter case, we have a relation to the thing; in the former, on the contrary, that relation is lacking, since the object of the hallucination, strictly speaking, is nothing.

Basically, this difficulty, which is perpetuated in Heidegger, derives from the ambiguity of the concept of intentionality that I presented in chapter 13. Husserl, wanting at the same time both to overcome Brentano's Cartesianism in order to make intentionality a relation to the transcendent thing, and to maintain Brentano's criterion, the possible nonexistence of the object, ended up in an aporia. He was forced to assert that intentionality has the same identical structure, whether it relates to real objects, illusions, or *ficta*.[55] In other words, intentionality is a relation to the transcendent object, *regardless of whether or not that object exists.* But this assertion is far from being clear, since an object that does not exist can't be transcendent, either. Heidegger ends up with the same disastrous consequence. "If, in the dark," he writes, "I mistake a tree for a man . . . in this perceptual illusion the man himself is given to me and not, say, a representation of the man."[56] How could the man be given to me as a transcendent object, since we are dealing here with an *illusion* and there is actually no man? Of course, the illusion has an "object," but surely not in the same sense of the word "object" as perception has one. In the first case, the object is a mere *fictum*: in the second, an existing thing in the world. It is on this ambiguity that intentionality breaks down altogether.

Thus we have returned to our starting point, the problem of perceptual intentionality. All the analysis that I have carried out ends in one simple conclusion: the intentionality of perception must be conceived as a relation that needs its two *relata* in order to obtain. The world depends on the subject in order to appear; the subject depends on the world in order to be (and therefore also to appear to itself and to others). To perceive is to possess the thing itself before one; perception is not of the order of a knowledge, but of a "having" (*Haben*).[57] Just as there is no possession without something that is possessed, similarly, perception is not occasionally turned toward real objects: there is no perception except of the real. But of course this assertion raises a problem, for it obliges us to maintain that perceptual intentionality as openness to the world itself *is not "intentional," according to Brentano's criterion.* It forces us to aknowledge that the unity of intentionality is problematic. While for wishing, desiring, and believing, Brentano's criterion is unavoidable, perception necessarily departs from it.

At this point, we cannot avoid the question of whether intentionality constitutes a good guideline for thinking our openness to the world as such. The model of intentionality presupposes that we can isolate an intentional content belonging to a given intentional act. This condition is satisfied for modalities of the intentional relation to objects in which language plays a preponderant role. For example, it is fairly simple to say *what* is believed in the belief that *p*: its intentional object is "that *p*." Of course this intentional object is only determined to the extent that the propositional clause that expresses it is determined. If I believe *that Emily is going to keep our appointment,* what I believe is completely expressed by that clause; I don't have to believe that Emily will come in through this or that door, wearing a dress or a raincoat, cheerful or sad, and so on. Furthermore, I can only have that belief on the basis of other beliefs, practically unlimited in number. If these restrictions are left aside, the intentional content of a belief is whatever a propositional clause expresses.

But the content of a perception is difficult to understand in these terms. What I perceive is not an intentional object that could be specified in a univocal manner, nor, as a matter of fact, a plurality of objects of this sort, nor even an object that "would imply" other objects (just as my belief implies other beliefs) in order to be itself perceived; it is a global perceptual scene that is inexhaustible on the descriptive level, that is, that can be expressed linguistically in an infinite number of ways. What I perceive is always the world itself from such and such a perspective. Here the whole necessarily precedes the part. And this whole is not the sum of its parts, but a structural whole that cannot be decomposed into elements. This holistic character of perception is at least as marked as that of beliefs and desires. Indeed, even if we accept Davidson's claim according to which most of our beliefs are true[58] (because we possess a *system* of beliefs), it remains no less possible to have a belief that contradicts another belief, a desire that is incompatible with another desire, or a desire that contradicts a belief. I can desire to marry a woman even though I believe the marriage will be a failure; I can believe things are hopeless while being determined to change them. Incoherence, if it is not the rule, is at least *conceivable* here. But as I have stressed, a world that presented no cohesiveness would no longer be *a world* at all. In order for perception to open to the world, and therefore for it to be perception, it is necessary for any breaks of cohesiveness, any hiatus to be "explained," and thus classified as illusions. A belief that does not fit into a system of beliefs can remain, at least temporarily, a belief—until we decide whether we need to modify that belief or that system; but a perception that does not fit into the totality of perception is not a perception at all. The concept of intentionality can scarcely give an account of this *radically holistic* nature of our being-in-the-world, because it tends to break up the unity of the perceived world into multiple intentional objects capable of being given and grasped in isolation.

Before a more extended examination of this point in the course of the following chapters, we must pause to consider a series of objections that all take the same form. To counter the idea that perception opens by essence to the world in such a way that its "intentionality" (if the concept is retained) must be interpreted as an authentic relation, it is possible to bring up a number of phenomena that seem to attest to the "subjective" nature of the content of perception: optical illusions, the upsurge of the phenomenon of aspect perception, or the indetermination of the perceived itself.

In the Müller-Lyer illusion, for example, straight lines of equal length seem to me to be unequal. Is this not the proof that what I perceive is never the world *in an unqualified way*, but the world *as it appears to me* according to my subjective constitution and, consequently, a "phenomenon" that it is impossible to understand otherwise than as an interface between the world and myself? In the drawing of the duck-rabbit, I see the same outlines alternatively as duck or rabbit, but never both at the same time. Is this not another proof that what I perceive is not the "thing itself," that is, the outlines in their objective properties, but only a subjective phenomenon, or what is sometimes referred to as a perceived "aspect"? To take a less artificial example, when I stand still within a grove, the branches look to me like an inextricable network; but as soon as I start walking, the boughs disengage before my eyes, sprightly reattaching themselves to the trunks, the scene suddenly reconfiguring itself into a multitude of trees with distinct branches. Not of course that the scene would change entirely; it is the same grove, the same trees, but segregated and organized differently. Is this not proof that it is not the forest per se that I perceive, but a forest-for-me that depends on my way of moving around in it, of circulating within it, of arousing through my movement dormant "aspects" in things? Finally, does not the vagueness, the indetermination characteristic of all perception attest once again to its content being subjective? For there is no indetermination or vagueness in nature. The melody I listen to has a precise number of notes, and the words I read, a determinate number of letters; but I notice neither of these. I read the words perfectly, I hear the melody perfectly, and yet I do not read a determinate number of letters, nor do I hear a determinate number of notes. Is this not the infallible indication that phenomena are not reality?

To these objections, and to others of the same sort, the following response may be made. If, in saying that phenomena are "subjective," we want to say that they imply by essence a relation to a subject, that is, that they are always phenomena *for someone,* that point is indisputable. But it does not threaten my thesis. Rather it corroborates it, since that thesis consists in maintaining that perception is intrinsically *relational*: it is neither a determination of the subject taken in isolation, nor a determination of the thing considered in itself, but a characteristic of the system formed by their encounter. If, on the other hand, what we mean by "subjective" is that the phenomena are *intrinsic* characteristics of the subject, properties immanent to his or her consciousness, it must be denied that phenomena are subjective in that sense. The way the lines in the Müller-Lyer illusion look varies depending on my attitude toward them, on whether I just look at the figure, or examine severally each of its constituent lines, or yet again measure them with a ruler. The appearance of the lines is unstable; it contains an ambiguity, a floating movement, and is molded by its whole context. But the various aspects that the lines take on belong in every instance to *these lines themselves*; they are "objective" properties of these lines, the latter being considered in their relation to an observer and to a context of observation. Here there is *but one sole pair of lines,* the real ones, possessing different relational properties.

The situation with the trees in the forest is not different from this. To say that the perceived aspect of the boughs varies depending on my behavior, on my movement or immobility—this comes down to saying that I perceive things from a specific point of view, according to a certain mode of presentation for me; but this does not amount to saying that what is perceived is things-from-a-certain-angle *as distinct* from things in an unqualified way; we don't have to understand the mode of appearance of things as a subjective duplicate, conceptually separable from the things that appear. The fact is, both the idea of a thing-for-me distinct from the thing itself and that of a thing "in itself" in the absence of any subject for whom it would appear are, from a phenomenological point of view, empty. The error comes here from the circumstance that we remain prisoners to the classic alternative: either we perceive mere representations, or we perceive the physical realities themselves. But it is neither the one nor the other. What we perceive is the phenomenal thing—that is, the thing considered in its relation to ourselves, and grasped at the level of what Husserl dubs the *Lebenswelt,* the "life-world."

The same reasoning applies to the case of indetermination. It is true that the phenomenal world is "elliptic," having a constitutional indetermination about which we will have more to say in chapter 17. It is true that this indetermination is *for someone*; it is not a property of the *physical* world. But it does not follow from this that such a property of the phenomenal world is not a property of the *things themselves.* What we perceive in an elliptic way is the world itself, but it is this world *in its relativity to us,* and not the world of the physicist. The physical world is neither the perceived world nor a perceivable world; it is a theoretic construction, an idealization that rests on a number of methodological operations of abstraction (see chapter 23). But the world in its relativity to us is *the world itself.* It is not a new interface. It is the only thing that deserves to be called a "world."

16

Being-in-the-World

> For twenty years past I have mistrusted "consciousness" as an entity . . . It seems to me that the hour is ripe for it to be openly and universally discarded.
>
> —William James

Perception can only deal with the world itself, in the absence of any intermediary. To perceive the world is to perceive it existing. To doubt that existence is not to know what one is saying. With these conclusions, we ended up with the idea that perception was an authentic relation resting on the existence of its two *relata.* But doesn't this assertion make us fall from Charybdis to Scylla? In abandoning, for perception, Brentano's criterion, have we not thereby abandoned all possibility of qualifying perception as "intentional"? Have we not made the concept of intentionality burst apart to the point of losing all unity? If perception is authentically relational, is it still authentically intentional?

Before attempting to answer these questions, let us pause for a moment and try to take stock of the journey up to this point. What did we do in the preceding chapter? We inquired into the relevance of a *concept,* intentionality, for the description of perceptual phenomena, that is, of phenomena in an eminent sense from the point of view of a phenomenology. We asked a transcendental question: under what conditions can perception be qualified as "intentional"? Is the concept of intentionality commensurate with perceptual phenomena, that is, with experience in its originary sense? At no time have we assumed that intentionality was itself a *phenomenon* that it sufficed to describe. The question that is presently before us is whether the concept of intentionality suffices to the task we have assigned to it, whether it gives us the best guideline to approach our primordial openness to the world, our *In-der-Welt-sein,* according to Heidegger's expression.

But first, if perception is an authentic relation, how is that relation to be thought? A judgment may have no fact that verifies it, a desire no object that satisfies it: this is why they do not express a true relation. With perception, things are otherwise. To perceive *implies* the existence of the perceived. Not of course that the existence of the object is necessary. The existence of the desk that I perceive at this moment is contingent, but it is necessary for this desk to exist *if this is a perception.* Conversely, it is necessary that the relation *be able* to obtain if this desk exists. Not only, like every relation, does this one have its foundation in each of the *relata,* but it seems additionally that this relation is internal, that is to say, that it is (at least partially) constitutive of the essence of the related terms: no act of perceiving without perception of something; no thing grasped at the level of the life-world, of the world we experience every day (as opposed to the objects of physics) without at least the *possibility* of being perceived. This intentional relation is asymmetrical: it makes no sense to say that what I perceive in turn perceives me. The case of other people is no exception, because it is not as perceived that others perceive me, but as perceivers. Finally, the relation of perception has its converse. "I perceive this vase" has as its converse "this vase appears (perceptually) to me." In order to be able to appear to me, this vase must exist, but its existence does not itself depend on its being perceived; it depends, at most, as existence of a vase as *phenomenal thing,* on the mere *possibility* of being perceived. The internal relation—if it is an internal relation—thus holds between the act of perceiving and the appearance of something that, in other respects, exists, but whose existence is not itself dependent on that act of perception. If this were not the case, to speak of "internal relation" would lead straight to a form of idealism.

The relation of perception is not necessary for the existence of the perceived thing; but the existence of the thing perceived is necessary for the relation of perception. This existence is an *external* factor necessary for the holding of the *internal* relation between the act of perception and the appearing object. Indeed, a relation may be said to be "internal" to one of its *relata* under one description, and not under another. Under the description "desk," the perceptual relation to the desk is not internal to that object, because to be taken as the object of an act of perception is not constitutive of what it is to be a desk; but under the description "appearing desk" or "phenomenal desk" that relation is internal to it. In short, what depends intrinsically on that relation is not the desk itself, nor its existence, but its appearance. And of course the perceptual relation is also internal to the act of perception, because this act is a consciousness of the desk itself; it is identified by its phenomenal content.

In maintaining that perception is an authentic relation, are we not making it into a real relation, that is, actually, a *causal* relation, thus falling prey to a danger constantly denounced by Husserl, that of a naturalism? Is it not specific to the intentional relation to be the opposite of a real relation? As is emphasized in §55 of *Ideas II*, for example, the relationship between the ego and its surrounding world "is not immediately *a real relation* but *an intentional relation* to something real."[1] If Husserl can contrast the two relations in this way, it is, on the one hand, because he conceives of any real relation as an external relation of a causal nature, and on the other hand because he continues to subscribe to Brentano's criterion, asserting that "the real relation collapses if the thing does not exist; the intentional relation, however, remains."[2] But it is not true that the only choice we would have here is between an "extraordinary" relation à la Brentano, in which one of the *relata* could fail to exist, without the relation ceasing to hold, and an ordinary relation, which Husserl calls "real" (*real*), because it takes place between two *realities.* The intentional relation is internal as relation to a (perceptually) appearing object, and external as relation to an existing object. At the same time, the existence of the object is the sine qua non condition for the internal relation mentioned, the intentional relation, to obtain. But that condition is not in turn of a causal nature, that is, stemming from an empirical conjecture. It is *a priori*, for it belongs to *a pure description of perception in its difference from illusion.* The intentional relation is *also* a real relation, because it is a relation whose two *relata* exist necessarily *if that relation obtains.* The real relation needs the intentional relation in order to *appear*, but the intentional relation needs the real relation in order to *be.*

By the claim that the existence of the perceived thing defines perception by essence, we thus remain on a strictly descriptive level, on the level of a naive realism that has nothing in common with a causal realism. The problem with any causal conception of perception is that it constitutes a hybrid theory resting on a permanent confusion between the plane of a phenomenological description and that of a genetic explanation of the content of experience. For such a conception, to perceive an object, that is, to experience it, *consists*, for that object, in playing a causal role in the genesis of that experience. But this assertion is, to say the least, obscure. A phenomenological description says nothing against the idea of a causal basis of phenomena, but it rises in opposition to the thesis that this causal basis belongs *to the very content* of experience, and thus could make us understand *what it is to be* a perception, as opposed, for example, to what it is to be a recollection. In this regard, we must yield to Husserl's anti-naturalism on one point: the causal interconnections between consciousness and reality may be as complex and mediate as you like, but the perceptual appearance is a consciousness of the thing itself in its self-givenness *without mediation of any kind.* Intentional discourse is irreducible to causal discourse; the relation of appearance is irreducible to an external relation. Moreover, in confusing these two regimes of discourse, in forging a hybrid, unintelligible idiom, naturalism brings us back inevitably to psychologism. Since the alleged "effect" differs from its cause, what we perceive can never be the reality itself without intermediaries, but only sense data, representations, interfaces between mind and world.

Nevertheless, this approach in terms of relation (and logical properties of relations) reaches its limits rather quickly. It remains abstract. It doesn't tell us what is specifically *intentional* about the perceptual relation. If what is specifically intentional about that relation is *not* that it exists even in the absence of its object, as my argument in favour of a disjunctive conception of perception has established, in what does it consist? Have I not surreptitiously reduced the perceptual intentional relation to an average internal relation—the one obtaining between the numbers 2 and 5, for instance, since it belongs to the nature of these numbers that the former is smaller than the latter? And if not, how can we guarantee the specificity of this intentional relation without making it into an *extraordinary* relation à la Brentano, and, to tell the truth, a "relation" in an eminently paradoxical sense?

To be justified to speak of "intentionality," it might be suggested, a minimal condition must be filled. A discrepancy must remain between what shows itself, the object, and the way in which it shows itself—in such and such a mode, with such and such a meaning. As Husserl already noted, what makes perception an *intentional* relation is not only the presence of a lived experience (*Erlebnis*), but the fact that the thing is "intentioned" or meant and eventually grasped by consciousness, *in such and such a way*, hence the *modality of the relationship* that is established here between the thing and consciousness, the way consciousness is directed toward the thing, in a word, what Husserl calls the sense or meaning (*Sinn*) with which the thing is manifested: "To have a meaning, or to have something 'in mind,' is the cardinal feature of all consciousness, that on account of which it is not only experience generally but meaningful, 'noetic.'"[3] The problem of intentionality is therefore inseparable from the difference between the object in its mode of givenness and the object that is given. In §124 of *Ideas I,* after having specified that, if its meaning is suitably modified, the word "meaning" could be applied outside the strictly linguistic sphere of signifying (*Bedeuten*) and signification (*Bedeutung*), Husserl claimed that it was possible to speak of "meaning" for all intentional lived experiences without exception, and he clarified: "Let us suppose, to take an example, that there is a perceived object out there, an object with a definite meaning."[4] The meaning is what articulates a way for an object to present itself to a consciousness, before any linguistic intending, any meaning-intention, any "signifying" in the verbal sense. Husserl calls these modes of appearance of something "meaning." An intentional relation can, consequently, be determined as a relation that refers to something *in a certain modality*, that is, *according to a certain meaning* that is prelinguistic, and therefore—if by "concept" we mean "verbal meanings"—preconceptual. *A relation is intentional if and only if it relates to something according to a certain meaning.*

The interest of this formulation is that it enables us to dissociate two aspects of the concept of intentionality that are inseparable in Husserl, but should be separated. The first is the above mentioned "discrepancy" between what appears and the *modes* that articulate this appearance—its *meaning*. The second is the idea of an intending (*intentio*, *Meinung*) that prescribes in advance its conditions of satisfaction and therefore its possible fulfillment. In Husserl's view, the "perceptual sense" is always to be understood on the basis of the noetic-noematic correlation, that is, of the act/content/object pattern. The "meaning" is what mediates the act's relation to its intentional object, that is, what prescribes to an intention its conditions of satisfaction. The *Wahrnehmungssinn* as *Gegebenheitsweise*, as mode of givenness of the object, depends therefore by essence on a *Meinung*, that is, an intending—and more precisely an intending in one mode or another, according to such and such a meaning—according to which hyletic materials are apprehended in such and such a way, as exponents of such and such an object; in short, it depends by essence on an *Auffassungssinn*, an apprehending meaning. But this description raises great difficulties. It is hard to see why, in the case of perception, everything that presents itself to us in one mode or another should be *anticipated* by an intending. I open my eyes, the world gives itself to me with the perceptual field crowded with infinite details without my having the least consciousness of having anticipated its meaning by an infinite number of corresponding intendings. How, moreover, could I *intend*, that is, seek to reach what I already possess, what I have over there *before my eyes*? The difficulty here stems from the epistemic duality underlying Husserl's whole conceptuality, a duality between a given and a meaning that consciousness bestows on it. How can my act of apprehension, that is, this "surplus [*Überschuß*]"[5] that interprets the hyletic data, determine what meaning to bestow on this given? Can it bestow just any meaning on just any given, or is it constrained by the given itself—and if so, in what way? This problem runs parallel to the one we have already encountered in the context of Husserlian semantics. Granted, Husserl does not have a Humpty Dumpty conception of *linguistic* meaning, because sense and nonsense are delimited by a pure universal grammar that prescribes the possible and impossible combinations between meanings (see chapter 4). But the problem is more difficult when it comes to perception. If the world "gets its sense and validity [*Sinn und Geltung*] in and from me, myself,"[6] how do I confer them on it? And if, on the other hand, experience considered in itself has something like an *immanent* meaning, since it is to this meaning of the "still dumb" experience that it is phenomenology's goal to give voice, how can this meaning at the same time be *conferred* on experience by consciousness? How does consciousness "know" what meaning to confer on the given if the given has not already displayed it *its own meaning* by its very way of appearing?

The only response to these questions Husserl can provide consists in a revamping of the empiricist idea of association, transposed into a new philosophical setting. This "universal principle of passive genesis," as he calls it, is no longer to be conceived of along the lines of empiricism as the *psychological* principle of the association of ideas. Association designates an essential structure of all *intentional* life, the totality of sedimented intentionalities that account for the emergence of a meaning itself sedimented—a structure on which rest all the preconstituted indications from one experience to another that unify the latter in the "continual, passive and completely universal genesis" of temporality.[7] But association, even elevated to the rank of transcendental egological principle of passive constitution, is incapable of explaining what it is supposed to explain. The meaning of my present perception cannot *derive from* the association of what I perceive with my past perceptions, which it resembles and with which it is linked by an "intentional history," for the simple and good reason that, if my perception did not already possess in itself its meaning, it would be impossible for me to associate any memory with it that resembles it. Associationism, even in the refined intentional form conferred on it by Husserl, rests on a circle, since it must presuppose that experience already possesses an immanent meaning in order to account for the way it can be associated passively with past experiences *of the same sort*, and thus explain how it can "receive" from that association itself the meaning it possesses for me in the present. *Association presupposes meaning in order to account for its genesis.* And therefore the universal law of passive synthesis is incapable of accounting for the way association actually works.[8] Besides, if all meaning were indeed only immanent to my present experience because of its association with past experiences, it is hard to see how a meaning could accrue to these past experiences themselves if not by a new association, which would lead to an infinite regress.

We have not made much progress in understanding that *Sinngebung* which Husserl made the key to intentionality. The originality of Husserlian phenomenology has been to define experience by meaning; more precisely, to oppose the empiricist concept of experience as pure receptivity of sense data, but also the Kantian approach according to which all meaning in experience would be the product of the subject's spontaneity, would be of a conceptual or categorial nature. All experience is the grasp of a preconceptual meaning immanent to experience itself. However, Husserl did not go so far as to abandon the epistemological duality of a pure "given" prior to all intentional apprehension (the immanent hyletic data) and of a meaning assumed to be additionally conferred to this given, and supposedly coming from constituting subjectivity—whether in the mode of a patent intentionality, or in the (passive) mode of a universal synthesis of association taking place in the arcane recesses of time-consciousness, hence prior to any coming into play of an egological activity. Now, it is this duality itself that raises a problem. Once we adopt the view that a meaning must accrue to experience thanks to the active or passive operations of a subject, we make the immanence of meaning in experience, which defines that experience as such, unintelligible.

If we wish to attempt to understand the specificity of the phenomenological concept of *meaning*, and thus to respond to the question left in suspense of what is specifically intentional in the perceptual relation, we must abandon the idea of a determination of meaning by consciousness and replace the model of *intentio* understood as "aim," or prior "intending," with that of an *intentio* understood as *meaning* inherent in the thing and given to a practical intelligence that may be called "understanding," on the condition that this term is kept as far as possible from the idea of an intellectual or discursive apprehension. This understanding articulates a certain modality of relationship[9] with the thing that always necessarily depends on the context in which the latter is situated. Perception, as I was saying, is not only about the thing itself; it is about the thing according to differentiated *modes of presentation*. It always already understands the thing this way or another way, relating to it in such and such a way. How can this situation be analyzed?

First of all, what specifically characterizes the perceptual modes of presentation? We have seen that they must not be considered as givens immanent to consciousness, as adumbrations in Husserl's sense. They are rather properties of the thing *in its relation to the perceiving subject.* (Let me underscore that my use of "subject" will henceforth include no specific allegiance to any particular metaphysics. As important as it is not to yield to the Cartesian presuppositions that I have enumerated, it is not useful, in combating them, to fall into a fetishism of *words.*) The desk that I see, with its books sitting on top of it, its notebooks, the stray sheets of a work in progress, appears to me close or far away, on my left or right, indistinctly or clearly, according to such and such a perspective. To say that it appears to me according to a particular perspective is already to relate it to me, to the angle of my view, to my corporeal location in space. To maintain that it appears to me close or far away is not to carry out an objective measurement, because nothing is "close" or "far away" absolutely speaking, independently of a living being's range of action or visual capacities. Or yet again, to assert that the desk appears indistinctly to me is both to refer to parameters of the situation—let's call them "objective" (the intensity of the lighting, for example)—and to characteristics of the observer, his or her ability to see more or less clearly in the half-light. The modes of presentation are neither objective nor subjective (if by that is meant: *intrinsically* subjective or *intrinsically* objective), but *relational*. They specify the properties-of-the-thing-for-an-observer. But for what kind of observer? One of the essential aspects of these modes of presentation is that they appeal to norms, or that they are evaluable in relation to ends. These ends are not those of a transcendental subject but *of an agent in the world*. To see, this can mean to see well or badly depending on specific goals: for example, to find one's way around in a new environment. Even when I am content with admiring a landscape, the contemplation, the aesthetic pleasure taken in this scene already constitutes an *end*; it is in relation to this end that the presence of a fog spread out through the countryside will bring me to say that I didn't get a "good look" at the landscape—whereas I did get a very good view of the valley enveloped in the mist. In other words, to perceive is not just a *state* in which I find myself, but it is also an *activity* I perform, and that as such can succeed or fail (with all the degrees in between). If to perceive is conceived of as a state, we do not learn to perceive; but if to perceive is understood as an accomplishment, there is an education of perception. We can see well or badly; we can succeed in recognizing a motif in a sketch, identify the style and manner of a painter, or fail to do so. We can acquire an eye for painting, a palate for wine-tasting, an ear for music. Perceiving is then an activity involving a certain *understanding* of what is perceived, the aptitude to identify, to recognize, but also to grasp the infinite nuances of what manifests itself to us, to orient ourselves in the ocean—one and multifarious—of perception, putting down sea markers and opening up our pathways in it. Hence perceiving is an activity subordinate to other ends and evaluable in relation to these same ends.

Thus two characteristics emerge that make perception similar to other modalities of relation to objects which are generally qualified as "intentional": (1) like desire, judgment, wish, or belief, perception presents us with something *in some respect, according to a particular mode*, or yet again from *a certain aspect*—in the case of a wish, a judgment, a desire, that "aspect" being most often a linguistic description; (2) perceptual modes of presentation are subordinate to norms.

Let us begin with a brief examination of the second point. Just as a judgment can be evaluated in terms of truth and falsity, a desire or wish in terms of satisfaction and non-satisfaction, so the perceptual modes of presentation can present us the thing clearly or vaguely, adequately or inadequately, precisely or in a schematic way. But by contrast with other modalities of intentionality, "seeing well," for example, does not mean having something (a representation) that can turn out to be in conformity or not with an object, in the same way that a judgment can turn out to be in conformity with a fact or a state of affairs. Perception is not a *representation* at all. Why, then, is it subordinate to norms? If, in the case of judgment, the answer to this question is difficult, because we may consider that the truth of a statement is irreducible to any pragmatic criterion, in the case of perception adequation, or lack thereof, refers to our corporeal "hold" on things (as Merleau-Ponty would say), and therefore to possible or actual actions. The world that I perceive is the same as the one in which I act; it is a world that is "out there," and not a "world" within consciousness. Here, intentionality in the Scholastic-Brentanian sense coincides with intentionality in the practical sense of the term. Perception presents the world to us not only from varying aspects, but from aspects that are *evaluable* in relation to our intentional actions, and from the perspective of the ends we pursue, so that perception is not only a science of the world but primarily a way of moving around in it, of getting our bearings and having our being within it.

The first point calls for deeper analyses. What does it mean to say that in perception we are dealing with things *according to a particular* meaning? At first sight, it means that all perceptual activity brings into play an *understanding*, be it minimal, of what is perceived; not of course that all is recognized or identified in the least perception—there is always an element of the implicit, the non-thematized in it—but perception, precisely because it is linked to action, is a way of existing in the world, of moving and being oriented within it, always engages an apprehension of the meaning of what appears.[10] To say this is not to claim that perception is already a *knowledge*, but on the contrary that before knowledge in the strong sense a preconceptual perceptual meaning comes to light. This meaning is the way a thing *presents itself to us* against a background, and correlatively, the way we apprehend it without yet applying a concept to it, hence prior to all formulated *knowledge*, which alone lends itself to a justification by reasons. This *mode of presentation* is a property weaker than knowledge and the application of concepts properly so called. Considered in itself, perception is a recognition that is not yet cognition.

How can we characterize more precisely this prelinguistic meaning that arises in things and needs no deciphering or exegesis? In all perception, something can only be perceived, that is, given to consciousness in a certain way, if that modality of relationship is rooted in a practical intelligence which is, as it were, a prolongation of our bodily powers. To the different modalities of appearance there correspond an equal number of modes of understanding at work in perception itself. (a) Already Husserl's mere "adumbration," the way I perceive something identifiable beneath changing outlines, calls for an *aptitude for recognition* on which perception constantly builds. To see is not only, or even primarily, to be preoccupied with forms, colors, or surfaces; it is to recognize entities endowed with spatiotemporal continuity that offer themselves to be grasped in their constantly changing identity and their constantly identical variety. There are outlines or adumbrations only for the one who has *identified* them: to perceive this vase in a particular outline is already to have identified this outline as a mode of appearance of the vase, therefore to have identified the vase as what is outlined in its outlines. (b) The upsurge of aspect perception, that sudden and unpremeditated reorganization of my perceptual field, is another way for a *perceived meaning* to come to light. When I take the escalator that comes up under the pyramid of the Louvre, I know very well that there is a pyramid there, but at first sight all I see is a glass brick wall, with no recognizable geometric form; as I go higher, that pile of stacked bricks reconfigures itself on its own into a pyramidal form. The thing perceived has not changed; only its mode of presentation differs. In the first case—that of the vase—I immediately recognize the vase through one of its outlines; in the case of the pyramid, by contrast, the perceptual salience thrusts itself upon me all at once by a reorganization of the visual field itself. In the first example, I wouldn't say that I saw an outline *as* a vase, because I never saw an outline *by itself*; in the second, I would be more inclined to say that I see that imbrication of transparent wall *as* a pyramid.

These meanings of "perceptual sense" draw on recognition. But recognition can, in turn, be understood in various ways. (c) As is probably the case for many animals, I can identify an *individual* thing by its spatiotemporal continuity, that is, prior to any quantification or application of a general predicate.[11] Similarly, a bird will recognize its nest and find its way back to it. (d) But I can also identify an object as being *of such and such a kind*; I can distinguish, for example, between an animate being and an inanimate one—and I can do this, again, without having to apply a predicate to it, or a concept in the linguistic sense. A young child and some animals will not proceed otherwise. Must we postulate here prelinguistic *concepts* at work in perception itself? To be able to recognize and identify the individual and the typical—is this already tantamount to possessing "natural" concepts (in the sense of non-conventional concepts) that are not linguistic creations? A different solution would be to reserve the word "concept" for concepts properly so called, Husserl's "verbal meanings," and to qualify as "types" those concrete universals that come to light at the level of perception and whose criterion is our capacity of recognition alone.[12] The animal, too, is capable of perceptual discrimination; it is sensitive to the salient features of its environment that possess distinctive value for it. Many species of winged creatures and rodents react differently in the presence of an inoffensive, large bird, as opposed to a bird of prey. Of course the question of how this perceptual discrimination operates without resorting to linguistic resources is a delicate problem that falls to empirical research. But it is hard to see how this thorny issue can be sidestepped, how we can ignore the submerged portion of the iceberg of our corporeal, prelinguistic intelligence, without thereby making its emerged portion unintelligible: that of language and conceptual thought. To understand language learning, we cannot do without postulating preverbal capacities of perceptual discrimination that form its starting point and permanent background. Once we admit the existence of such capacities, it seems consistent to also admit *in perception itself* the existence of corresponding differences, hence types, natural concepts, that is, general properties (being a bird of prey) that are directly perceived. If we always had to have a word in order to have a concept, it is difficult to see how it would be possible to learn the use of any word, and thus to acquire the concept, and *a fortiori*, to invent new concepts. Language did not emerge from reasoning, nor is it the result of blind action. To understand its basis, we must, as Wittgenstein writes, "consider man as an animal," and more precisely, think animality as an irreducible dimension of humanity itself. All that is animal in man is not in-human, however. (e) Moreover, there is a recognition that concerns less individuals or common properties than *practical meanings*. A piece of fruit appears appetizing to me. A path winding through the rocks looks slippery, but passable: it invites me to follow it. During a heat wave, the sea itself, a bit sunken in, is seen as a call to cool off, an invitation to go for a dip. In what I perceive, in the mode of appearance of things, are manifested to me, before any judgment and reasoning, vital meanings, appetitive vectors addressing themselves to the potentialities of my body and testifying to some extent of a continuity between action and perception. We do not have on one side pure, neutral perceptions, and on the other a consciousness that would bestow meanings on them, or even an agent who would project onto them the ends that he or she pursues. There is but one sole, indivisible "hold" on the world, integrating my potential actions and permeating sensibility from the outset. I cannot *see* those rocks that border the green precipices of the sea otherwise than as slippery, dangerous; I cannot *see* that water otherwise than as refreshing, welcoming, and radiant at high noon. All these adhesive or "viscous" meanings are as if amalgamated with things, embedded in them, and it would be a vain enterprise to pretend to disengage them. An animal would notice them as I do, probably differently, but no less certainly: they appeal to that corporeal intelligence that arranges the surrounding world, making it habitable for me, that is, accessible and subjected to my practices. Whether we call them "valences," "vital significations" (Merleau-Ponty), "appetitive vectors" (Erwin Straus), *Aufforderungscharacter* (Lewin), *requisitions* (Köhler), or *affordances* (Gibson), the questions raised by these "meanings" are numerous and difficult. To what extent, after the example of Husserl's *Wahrnehmungssinn*, do they arise from a regime of intelligibility that is prior to that of verbal meanings, hence of concepts as linguistically articulated? What is their relationship with my ends and my praxis, and how can this praxis permeate sensibility from the start?

To recognize, identify, classify according to sensible types (if not concepts in the strict sense), to let oneself be guided by valences or vital meanings: in all this, perception brings out what we must call *meaning*. How does meaning come to things? We still have not understood it. Let us limit ourselves to these *affordances*, to take up Gibson's vocabulary. A tempting solution to our problem would consist in saying that perception does not harbor these meanings within itself, but that they are conferred on it by our free projections. If the sea appears to me in the distance with its eternally virginal air, winking and blinking in the morning light, casting the spell of its cerulean waters and turquoise depths across the distance, it is first of all by virtue of an "objective" situation consisting in the heat, already oppressive and rising, the accessibility of the beach through the path over the rocks; but it is also because I have some free time, because of that vacation atmosphere floating around me and to which it seems to me I am yielding, whereas in fact it is only a projection of my desire or my laziness. If this is right, instead of granting transcendental consciousness the privilege of bestowing meaning on a given, we should henceforth grant that privilege to the agent and his or her projects, with certain objective constraints dictated by the situation. Sartre has proposed an analysis of this kind. His example is famous:

> The situation is the free coordination and the free qualification of a brute given which does not allow itself to be qualified in an arbitrary way. Here I am at the foot of this crag which appears to me as "not scalable." This means that the rock appears to me in the light of a projected scaling—a secondary project which finds its meaning in terms of an initial project which is my being-in-the-world. Thus the rock is carved

> out on the ground of the world by the effect of the initial choice of my freedom. But on the other hand, what my freedom can not determine is whether the rock "to be scaled" will or will not lend itself to scaling. This is part of the brute being of the rock. Nevertheless the rock can show its resistance to the scaling only if the rock is integrated by freedom in a "situation" of which the general theme is scaling. For the simple traveler who passes over this road and whose free project is a pure aesthetic ordering of the landscape, the crag is not revealed either as scalable or as not scalable; it is manifested only as beautiful or ugly.[13]

On the one hand, according to Sartre, there is a brute, meaningless given; on the other, a discretionary freedom which "disposes of the situation," so to speak, or rather which disposes of the *meaning* of the situation and has full authority to decide of this meaning in light of its projects. Do I plan on going for an excursion? In that case the boulder that blocks my way will reveal itself to me in that practical situation with the meaning "scalable"—on the condition, of course, that this "brute given" does indeed lend itself to climbing: the only constraint that weighs on my freedom is that of a pure *factum.* Do I plan to enjoy the landscape? In that case the boulder will appear to me as "beautiful or ugly," and I will go on my way. What makes this description hopelessly simplistic is that despite my having left the cords, ice axes, and karabiners back at the shelter, this rock may very well appear to me as difficult to climb, and that might even be what will give it its icy beauty, its abrupt solemnity, that specific aesthetic quality that belongs to inaccessible peaks and elevations. The beauty of this rock is not just any beauty, and it is not true that one must in some sense "choose" between finding it beautiful and finding it steep—hence difficult to climb. For one passing through this area, the rock is all of this at once, and other things as well—and it matters little what his or her projects are at the time! The truth is, if a meaning awakens in things as I pass by, it is not only because this meaning depends on my projects, my actual and active intentions (otherwise the world would be nothing other than the mirror of my projections), but it is first and foremost because it depends on a whole repertoire of *capacities* and *aptitudes.* These capacities need not be actualized for the rock to take on this or that meaning, calling for a *possible praxis.* Even less than I would have to be involved in a project of aesthetic appreciation, when I am walking down the street, to find a woman beautiful, or in a project of conquest to find her seductive. The error of these analyses is to be entirely oblivious to the notions of disposition and capacity; Sartre's whole philosophy is a new Megarianism that reduces the possible to the actual because it rests on the principle according to which "freedom only exists *in actu.*"[14]

But let's leave aside the peculiarities of Sartrean philosophy. It is against the background of my capacities—multiple, varied, multiform—that the meaning of a thing in situation stands out. This meaning is in no way conferred from the outside on a raw given; it depends in its very nature on a subject endowed with practical capacities and exists only in relation to it—which does not mean that this subject would be its *origin*. Just as properties such as distance or orientation have meaning only in reference to the one perceiving them and who is himself inserted in space by his body, similarly, the practical vectors emerging from a situation depend in their essence not only on the actual behaviors and the present intentions, but also on the *possible* behaviors, and therefore on the capacities of the one experiencing that situation. But what, then, gives an analysis such as Sartre's its apparent plausibility? The assumption that our perceptions have to possess the same characteristics as the physical realities of which they are the perceptions, that is to say, must consist at the start in a manifold of *meaningless raw givens,* and its corollary, the view according to which these raw givens must be "completed" in a second moment by a consciousness or a practical subject in order to *acquire* a meaning. This presupposition is already present in Husserl's analysis of hyletic data. Sartre's analysis is probably superior to Husserl's in that it takes into account the fact that the meaning purportedly "conferred" on the raw sensible givens does not come from a theoretical consciousness but from an agent in situation. But it rests on the same almost ineradicable tendency to see in human experience only the reflection of a physical reality. Now, it is rather the exact opposite that is true. As Husserl will suggest in his last philosophy—without nevertheless drawing all the consequences from it—the physical "world" is a *theoretical construct* obtained by the methodological abstraction of certain features of the perceived world, beginning with those vital meanings adhering to things and addressing our spontaneous and pre-discursive intelligence; the physical world is not, to be sure, a world other than the perceived one, but it is this very world in which we exist, considered from the viewpoint of certain interests—relative to the study of matter and its fundamental laws—and thereby stripped of its own specific phenomenality. The physical "world" is an *idealization* indissociable from the perceived world, to which there therefore belongs an irreducible primacy (see chapter 23).

The epistemological duality of the given and meaning stands in the way of a good description of perceptual experience. We do not begin by receiving pure, neutral sensible givens that must subsequently be completed and fashioned by concepts and judgments in order for us to accede to the "world itself," to a structured and meaningful world. In abandoning that duality, we must also abandon a concept of perception that goes hand in hand with a whole inadequate philosophical framework which is content with setting in opposition theory and practice, sensibility and understanding, receptivity and spontaneity. What we perceive is already shaped by our commerce with the world, by our way of being "at home" and existing bodily in it, by practices that carve out space, making it into a place for us; by a manifold of *possible* behaviors that instill within things ends, practical vectors, attractions, repulsions, lines of force, dumb or tacit meanings obscurely deciphered by our bodies. We need, in order to think this, a concept of perception that does not succumb to the division between sensibility and a contribution foreign to sensibility (let us call it, for brevity's sake, "understanding"), nor to the dichotomy between receptivity and activity; a perception that would not be a nascent science, but a way of orienting oneself practically in the world and of arranging one's sojourn in it; a perception that would be a way of being in a world already articulated and meaningful, but not yet structured by language and knowledge. Such a perception has nothing to do with an immediate contact with being or an in-itself of things, nor is it a representation that we would give ourselves of it, because it is about the things themselves, on the one hand, and is not separable from all goals, interests, and practices on the other; it is a *vital communication with the world.* And since the "living being" that thus enters into communication with its surroundings is also a speaking being, endowed with culture, embedded in an individual and collective history, his practices appear infused, so to speak, in the very manner in which he understands that world, and himself on the basis of that world. Let us call, after Heidegger, "being-in-the-world" that openness to things that is not thinkable in terms of the traditional dichotomies understanding/sensibility, theory/practice. This being-in-the-world is, in turn, made possible by our inherence in the world as body; it goes hand in hand with a *finitude* in our access to things in relation to which the world itself reveals to us as inexhaustible.

Let us attempt to reach a better understanding of the relationship uniting this being-in-the-world to behavior in general. Heidegger sometimes makes a parallel between intentionality and behavior (*Verhaltung*) by thinking the latter as a modality of relation (*Verhältnis*) to something.[15] But how do intentionality in the Scholastic-Brentanian sense and behavior go together? None of the classical solutions to this problem is satisfactory. The three main ones are the following.

(1) Intentionality of behavior, practical intentionality (that is, what makes us say of a behavior that it is *intentional*) depends on intentionality understood as a property of consciousness: its relation to objects. This is the solution of the whole Cartesian tradition to which Brentano and

Husserl belong. As a consequence: intentionality of consciousness remains representative; and behavior is *caused* (in a way that remains enigmatic) by lived experience or intentional states.

(2) Intentionality of consciousness is reduced without remainder to intentionality of behavior. According to this approach, intentionality of belief amounts to a disposition to adopt such and such a behavior (Ryle). We end up with an incoherent logical behaviorism, since it is impossible to say to *which* behavior a belief disposes us. My belief that it is going to rain cannot be reduced to my disposition to take my umbrella when I go out; for I can take my umbrella without believing it is going to rain (to get it fixed) or not take it even though I think it is going to rain (because I like walking in the rain).

(3) Lastly, intentionality of consciousness can be defined by the role it plays in the *explanation* of behavior. Desires and beliefs, on this view, are only intentional states to the extent that they allow us to account for behavior. Indeed, to explain a behavior is to understand how, due to an initial desire that sets up a goal and certain beliefs relative to means, we arrive at a conclusion that is itself an *action*. Here we have a reformulation of Aristotle's practical syllogism. Let us call this solution "pragmatist."[16]

The pragmatist solution seems the most interesting insofar as it articulates practical intentionality with intentionality of consciousness without claiming to *reduce* the one to the other. Furthermore, it makes it possible to account for the normative nature of "intentional states" on the basis of their explanatory role regarding action. But it has two major drawbacks. First, it continues to conceive of intentional states, and of perception among them, as *representational*: the intentional content of a belief differs from the fact that verifies it: the intentional object of a perception differs from the state of affairs that may or may not obtain. Next, given that an intentional state plays an explanatory role in a practical reasoning, this view tends to attribute an inevitably *linguistic* character to the state's content; it will speak, for example, of the "propositional content" of a perception. In sum, it postulates that our being-in-the-world is always mediated by intentional states that are both representational and linguistic in nature, the contents of which do or do not match the course of things.

But our being-in-the-world cannot consist in a multiplicity of intentional, representational states, as well matched with the world as you wish. It is precisely in order to think that original "intentionality," which, contrary to the other intentional modalities, *possesses no representational content*, that Heidegger framed the expression "*in-der-Welt-sein*." Being-in-the-world is an openness to things without mediation of any kind. This is why it has nothing to do with a system of beliefs that would play an inferential role in a practical syllogism, either. Moreover, most of our actions do not bring any articulated belief into play, no explicit desire or reasoning properly so called. Quite frequently I am moved by the things around me; they form poles of attraction or repulsion, tropisms perceived or felt, mere motives and not reasons *stricto sensu.* This is why my body knows more about the world than I do. "To move one's body," Merleau-Ponty writes, "is to aim at the things through it, or to allow one's body to respond to their solicitation, which is exerted upon the body without any representation."[17] It is to think these solicitations that are neither causes nor reasons properly so called that Merleau-Ponty forged the concept of "motive": a motive is a practical meaning that arises at the level of things themselves without the intermediary of any judgment or reasoning. These "motives," he specifies, "are tacitly known to my perception in veiled forms; they justify my perception by a logic without words";[18] the motive is "an antecedent that acts only through its meaning" and "a sort of operative reason."[19] Let us not confuse such motives with reflex causal chains. I am sitting on the terrace of a café in springtime; I am waiting for a young woman. My wait modifies the very experience that I have of the street, of the passersby: suddenly, the dresses of unknown women stand out with a particular intensity, their colors look livelier, they stand out with the insistence conferred on them by my nervous, indeterminate waiting. The dresses of the passersby present themselves to me otherwise than they normally do because I am no longer indifferent to them, and I expect one of them to be the one I was waiting for. When it appears, perhaps I will make a hurried, solicitous movement, but I will not react like a Pavlovian dog. These motives that present themselves at the spur of the perceptual moment itself do not *set off* my movements; they *guide* them among the beings and things more surely than any reasoning. Far from being the result of an unconscious practical syllogism, that is, a kind of calculation (*logos*), as Aristotle said, most of our movements spring forth all of a piece, already attuned to the things that solicit them, and "the elements of the supposed calculation are not given to me."[20] Let us also take care not to confuse the way I often act when my behavior has nothing deliberate about it, with the rational reconstruction of my action if required of me, the practical syllogism I can reconstitute. Even when the intentionality of beliefs, desires, or wishes does in fact intervene in a deliberation, its bringing into play rests on a prelinguistic understanding of those motives, immanent in things, which make my behaviors immediately adjusted without the detour of any representation, and which are already a way of being attuned to the world and anchored in it.

We are now in a position to answer the question of the status of this meaning that offers itself to us at the level of our being-in-the-world without the intermediary of any representation. This meaning depends at once on our practical capacities and on the overall context in which we are situated, on our *situation* itself insofar as it is taking a particular turn or cast [*tournure*], that is, insofar as it presents to us a meaning both intelligible and opaque, that we can, of course, make explicit, but only up to a point. This turn or cast of our situation is always also determined in part by our affective dispositions, by what Heidegger calls *Stimmungen.* Our feelings and emotions people the world with dumb meanings—but how? Does the crag look dangerous to me because I am afraid? Does my fear confer on the steep, abrupt crag its quality of dangerousness? If this were the case, I would have to feel fear at this moment, in order for its menacing character to appear to me. But that is obviously not the case. I am sheltered, far from the rocky wall that plummets headlong into the sea; at the moment I feel no threat. The threat will only come alive if I try to approach. The cliff repels me like a vague zone of danger; it keeps me aside, so to speak, and it is only if I begin to move forward that I feel my legs waver. This does not mean that I must *know* the danger *objectively before* feeling the fear and in order to be able to feel it as such. In that intellectualist conception, fear is nothing other than the opinion of the imminence of a future evil.[21] But it sometimes happens that fear rises up in us without our even knowing exactly where the threat is coming from, that this vague and indeterminate fear precedes any explicit knowledge of what is to be feared, and sometimes that it even puts us on the right track to discovering it. I may find a situation disturbing without yet knowing what is disturbing me. Here we are on the hither side of knowledge and judgment, in that symbiotic union with the world in which we communicate before any word.

Let us take a more complex, and in many respects a more interesting example: that of an aesthetic quality, something about which it is difficult to say, at first sight, whether it belongs in the category of feeling or judgment. I find the woman sitting in front of me attractive. Perhaps part of her charm comes from the apparent detachment with which she proffers harmless but witty comments; perhaps that charm resides in her smile, pronounced, though not insistent, in that way of not avoiding my look, though not inviting it either, in that melancholy that I hear in her voice but does not seem to be addressed to me, and keeps me at a distance. It is probably that distance that stirs my curiosity, giving her an expression, an air of fleeting vulnerability, of fragility, that seems to say, "You can do nothing for me." The description could go on. Perhaps I should describe her particular gait, the paleness of her face, the tasteful way she features it—all beneath a studied negligence. The question is where all these attractive qualities come from. The first response to impose itself is that these are my own feelings toward that woman that bestow on her that impalpable quality only apparently emanating from her. Is she not charming because I am charmed? Because I have succumbed to her charm—in other words, because I desire her? That response is doubly wrong. If I had to be attracted to find that woman attractive, it is hard to see how desire could ever *be born.* Tell a man who is in love that the charm of the woman he loves amounts to nothing more than his love for her: his indignant response will be that this woman *is* charming. The charm is as intrinsic to her as is the sound of her voice or the color of her eyes. The reason why it is so is the following. While desire may be born and disappear, the enchantment grow or diminish, the charm of a person possesses a durability that makes it a quasi-permanent mode of being. I distinguish very clearly and very easily between the charm this person gives off and my own attraction toward her, because there are occasions on which I find a woman full of charm, wit, vivacity, and sensuality, without feeling any desire for her. One can see a loved woman again, feel once again her charm intact and yet have ceased being attracted to her. The charm is part of these meanings that inhabit beings; but it does not have the ephemeral character of the attraction exerted on me by other emotive vectors and other meanings. Are we to conclude that charm is a quality of the woman sitting before me of the same kind as her complexion or the precise nuance of her hair? If what is meant thereby is that this property belongs to her, yes; if what is meant is that it could belong to her independently from my own dispositions, no. I must *be able* to be charmed by a woman in order for her to appear charming to me. This meaning that is embodied in her as a person and in her whole way of being exists only in relation to me. It also depends on the overall situation. I am not charmed, for example, independently of any social code: the gesture of lowering the gaze while blushing and hiding behind a fan may be charming in eighteenth-century Japan; it is not so sure that it is in the Paris of the twenty-first century. There is something in the charm that a person casts over us that depends on circumstances, time, atmosphere, mood, and a thousand and one little details, so that the spell can be broken at every moment. This quality appears so tied to circumstances that it is usually necessary to describe all of them in order to convey the nuances of the quality experienced—as a good novelist will do. To tell the truth, a person's charm only acts and has its full sparkle against the background of my whole experience. This means that each experience is systematically consistent with the totality of one's experience and cannot be isolated from the latter. The meaning of the least experience is a function of the context of my experience as a whole.

The example of charm shows us how much these meanings that adhere to things and to persons are tied to our dispositions (and not necessarily to our actual desires, states, and emotions), but also how much they depend on circumstances and the overall cast of a situation; it also reveals to us how much, in certain cases, the feeling/judgment distinction is problematic. Is judgment based on feeling here? Is the birth of the feeling (of the attraction) concomitant with the formation of the corresponding judgment? There is here no clear-cut distinction between the level of experience, which includes our sensibility to meanings, and that of the judgment by which these meanings can be made explicit.

It will probably be objected that we only find meanings in things and living beings *because* we can express them thanks to language. On this view, it is in language and language alone that meaning resides primordially and even exclusively. Our two examples, those of steep crags and of feminine charm, are different in this respect. To find that someone has charm, one must certainly possess language and a whole culture. But that is not the case for perceiving rocky crags as being steep or dangerous. Nevertheless, the objector could go further: does not the simple fact of saying that we perceive the crags *as* dangerous already show that we have applied them a predicate, that we have subsumed them under a concept? Does this not reveal with sufficient clarity that the meaning I have been speaking of for a while is nowise *prelinguistic*?

This objection can be understood in two ways. Either (1) "to perceive *x* as *y*" means *to believe* or *to judge* that *x* is *y*. Then we fall back into the difficulties, already mentioned in chapter 3, of an intellectualism attributing a *propositional* content to perception. Now, a perceived situation can be expressed in many different ways, in a multiplicity of judgments, but we do not have to formulate these judgments, either in part or in totality, in order to *perceive* this situation. Perception can motivate beliefs, and it does so in general, but it does not itself consist in a belief, nor does it "harbor" within itself a belief: otherwise what would motivate our beliefs would in turn be a kind of belief and we could never get out of our beliefs to confront them with reality. Or (2) "to perceive *x* as *y*" must be taken in a weaker sense: to perceive the crags as steep, it suffices to apply a concept to them, but without judging this or that to be the case—or even, it suffices to possess the aptitude to apply a concept to them, without necessarily actualizing that aptitude. But this solution is no better than the preceding one. The point is not to deny that human perception is in fact most often permeated by linguistic meanings. The question raised is a question of principle: it is whether all perception *must* be thus permeated. Now there is a leap, to say the least, between asserting that the water appears to me at the perceptual level to be favorable for bathing, the path along the sea to be passable, and so on, and asserting that the reason why they appear thus to me is that I apply to them a concept. There is indeed a great difference between what I can *say* about my perception and the intrinsic properties of that perception. When I *speak* about my perception, when I try to *describe* it, as I am at the present moment, I do apply a great number of predicates, and thus, of concepts, to it. But this does not entail that perception is conceptual in its very nature.

In a Japanese tea-house, a tray of delicacies is brought to me: their surface is smooth, transparent, catching the light in a marvelous way that makes you want to touch it, and that almost makes them into a work of art; their texture is indefinable and presents a greenish tinge that traverses the shining surface, conferring on them a luster of jewels. That is how I may try to *describe* this strange delicacy—obviously with the help of the not very adequate concepts at my disposal. Is this a sugary cake? A salty one? What is its consistency? What is it made of? But can it be concluded from my inexperience in matters of Japanese delicacies that the dish placed before me on the tray does not *appear* to me as a *yōkan,* because I do not have the concept of *yōkan,* and all the gastronomic concepts associated with it? Doesn't it have the look, the consistency, the luster of a *yōkan,* as it would have for a well-informed gastronomist? It is true that, if I do not possess the concept of *yōkan,* I cannot *think* or *judge* that it is one; but to conclude that this cake does not appear to me as a *yōkan* appears to whoever perceives one constitutes as non sequitur. That concepts and knowledge can enrich and shape perception is one thing; that they constitute the meaning-content of perception is quite another. If I do not have the concept of *yōkan,* I cannot realize that what I am looking at is the traditional Japanese cake; but I do not need to possess this concept to *see* what is before my eyes. The same reasoning applies to the other concepts in our *description:* the smooth, bright surface, the green texture, the luster of a jewel. A child can perceive a green texture without having mastered the concepts of color and texture (and *a fortiori* without being capable of making a comparison with a jewel), for otherwise it would be strictly impossible to ever acquire them—which does not imply that acquiring them would consist *solely* in associating them with these perceptions.

But is not the assumption that a content of experience is already meaningful before being structured by concepts, after all, *incoherent* (and along with it the idea of a meaning of experience preceding verbal meanings)? It is true that, if what we are trying to do here is to account for linguistic meaning on the basis of prelinguistic meaning, this explanation is incurably circular. Indeed, we cannot say *what* prelinguistic meaning verbal meanings are the articulation or explication of, without already making use of language. And therefore prelinguistic meaning already presupposes language in order to be the "meaning" it is. But that objection rests in turn on the false assumption that we are trying to *explain* something—the origin of language. It is correct that, if the notion of prepredicative meaning has an explanatory status, this notion, conceived as an *explanans,* is incoherent, because it implies, in order to be understood, its *explanandum,* and there is, therefore, only an appearance of explanation. But the notion of prelinguistic meaning is purely descriptive, and comes in at the end of a transcendental argument. Its only purpose is to establish that the understanding in play here is actualized through and through in *the very way in which we experience* things, and not in any discourse that we might hold on them. In a word, the notion of prelinguistic meaning comes down to insisting on the fact that a description of language and experience *makes sense only on the condition that* experience is prior to language de jure—if only to be able to be "shaped" by it.

How can the nature of this meaning that is immanent to experience be further characterized? I have shown in the preceding paragraphs that, in order to think what is properly "intentional" in the perceptual relation, we had no other choice but to abandon the *intentio* conceived as a prior intending prescribing its fulfillment and, actually, to give up the concept of intentionality itself, replacing it with that of being-in-the-world. Grasped at the level of our being-in-the-world, the meaning presented to us by things always depends on the overall cast taken on by a situation. Such a "meaning" is not to be conceived as an entity floating somewhere within consciousness, or alternatively as an entity outside consciousness, situated in a Fregean "third realm." Psychologism and Platonism are only the obverse and reverse of the same coin: Platonism is a reaction to psychologism, which, by placing meaning outside the individual psyche and thus freeing it from the contingency and relativity of that psyche, continues nonetheless to conceive of it as a quasi-object, and consequently continues to make the understanding of it dependent on a psychological act that would take place every time understanding takes place. But understanding is only rarely an *act* (a "eureka"). It is more frequently a *capacity*: the capacity to say what is at issue in a given situation, for example, or more simply the capacity of knowing how to handle that situation. As Heidegger stresses, understanding (*Verstehen*) is of the order of a practical competency, a "being competent to do something [*etwas können*]."[22] As a capacity, it depends essentially on the circumstances of its exercise. Understanding is an "*existentiale*," that is, a way of being of *Dasein* as "subject" engaged in practices and susceptible to being emotively affected by situations; it is a modality of *Dasein*'s "potentiality-for-Being [*Sein-können*]." Meaning, then, is nothing but what an understanding brings to light: "Meaning is that wherein the intelligibility of something maintains itself."[23] This tautology (meaning is that which articulates the intelligibility of something, in other words, meaning is what is understood when something is understood) takes on a function that is analogous, in Heidegger, to the one devolved to Wittgenstein's affirmation according to which meaning is "what an explanation of meaning explains."[24] In both cases, the purpose of the two philosophers is to get rid of meaning conceived of as an *entity*, be it of an *ideal* or a *mental* nature. To limit ourselves to the linguistic level, the common root of the error committed by both psychologism *and* Platonism is described by Wittgenstein in the following terms. "We are looking for the use of a sign, but we look for it as though it were an object *co-existing* with the sign."[25] This hypostatization of meaning leads to insurmountable aporias. First, meaning must subsist identically *in all circumstances* in which a sentence is uttered, and therefore regardless of the pragmatic context underlying its understanding. Next, the way the meaning is supposed to "accompany" the words remains obscure. Must I say that I grasp the meaning that "accompanies" the sentence only when the sentence is finished? But in that case, I was not understanding it while it was still being uttered. Or during the entire duration of its utterance? But then if the speaker interrupts himself, I will have only a half understanding of the sentence, as I have only a half sentence. We must conclude that the meaning *does not coexist with the sentence*, nor is it grasped at any particular moment. Understanding, Wittgenstein would say, resides in the mastery of the rules of usage of expressions; it is nothing other than a practical competency. As Heidegger makes clear, we are never dealing with "word-Things . . . [that would only subsequently] get supplied with significations."[26]

There is no reason to restrict this point to just linguistic meanings. Things "mean" for us before language. *What* do they mean? Only language can tell us this. But language does not create that meaning. And our preverbal behavior already attests to our understanding of this meaning. To understand something may, for example, consist in being able to use it in such and such circumstances. We have good reasons to say that we "understand" a penholder on the condition that we know how to use it, but, as Wittgenstein points out, that does not mean that this understanding "contain[s] the whole system of its application"[27]—no more than understanding a word, or being able to use it correctly in a particular context, presupposes the mastery of the totality of its uses in all possible contexts. There is, therefore, a prelinguistic understanding of that implement that is, so to speak, in the very action of sticking one's quill pen in it, and that has no need to be expressed linguistically to be effectively at work as a practical modality of our transaction with it. Understanding addresses the thing *as* this or that; it determines it in light of our practical possibilities. This understanding bears upon the thing itself, and not upon representations or immanent givens; it consists in *a way of dealing with* things. To deal aptly with a penholder is to understand its function and use, that is, to understand it as an implement of a certain sort, taking on its meaning against the background of social practices, in connection with a multiplicity of other implements (pen, paper) that form with it an instrumental complex. Such an understanding has nothing to do with a knowledge that would have to be elaborated in the form of judgments, and still less with the making of a "theory" based on hypotheses (Davidson). "Understanding," Heidegger writes, "is not a mode of cognition but the basic determination of existing."[28]

Not only is this understanding a practical capacity, but it depends on other capacities as well. As a capacity to handle such and such a being, to approach it in such and such a way in light of practical possibilities, understanding in turn is only possible if it rests on other capacities and other "know-how" furnishing the practical possibilities in light of which something can be approached and understood. Without these other capacities, to be able to walk on rough ground, for example, rocky cliffs above the sea, could not seem easy for us to climb, that is, reveal themselves to us with the meaning they harbor. These background capacities present several characteristics. First, they are at least partially acquired. In this respect, they resemble Aristotle's "*hexeis*." What is specific to a *hexis* is, among other things, that it is immediately in the power of the agent, that it is up to him alone to actualize it. Second, these practical capacities are not possessed *independently of the circumstances of their exercise,* that is, of a global situation, a world. My capacity to orient myself in a dark room cannot be actualized in the absence of all room in which to orient myself. My capacity to keep my balance on steep rocks cannot be actualized in the absence of rocks or any other substitute. As Charles Taylor says, the "grasp of things involved in my capacity to move around and manipulate objects can't be [separated from the latter]." This is why this capacity is located neither in my mind nor in my body *regardless of the circumstances.* My capacity to open up a pathway for myself among passersby in a crowded street, for example, "exists not just in my body, but in my body-walking-the-streets."[29] This point is important, for if these capacities cannot be described without mentioning the circumstances in which they are actualized, they are capacities such that it makes no sense to attribute them to a subject independently from a world in which it is situated: these capacities are those of a subject that is *essentially* in the world. In order for such a subject to have the capacities it has, a world must exist in which these capacities are actualized—*end of the skeptical argument.* Being-in-the-world is the necessary condition for the description and the attribution to the subject of capacities of a certain kind, and these capacities are required for understanding as a capacity to be actualized, therefore for things to manifest themselves to us with specific meanings.

Understanding consequently requires background capacities that already imply the world (they are *world-involving,* as Taylor would say), in such a way that in order to understand the world, one has to be already bodily and practically situated in it. No acosmic subject adopting towards the world a bird's-eye view would be able to find a *meaning* in things. This understanding not only relies on background capacities; nor does it deal only with *isolated* things or entities, but always envisions them in light of an *overall situation.* An implicit understanding of the whole is prior to any explicit understanding of its parts; or rather, an understanding of the whole cast of the situation is prior to any understanding of a particular aspect of that situation. All understanding already brings to bear the whole domain of intelligibility of whatever it is dealing with.[30] This applies already to the mere understanding of a sentence. "To understand a sentence," Wittgenstein writes, "means to understand a language. To understand a language means to be master of a technique"[31]—and to be master of a technique, one might add, is only possible within forms of life. But that is true of all understanding, including prelinguistic. The expression of my interlocutor, the meaning of which I grasp, stands out from a background of tacit understanding, more or less rich and extensive depending on my familiarity with him or her, our common history, and so on—a background I do not have to thematize, but which remains constantly presupposed. There is never any isolated experience; every experience draws its meaning from experience as a whole. By contrast with the "perception" of the classical philosophers, being-in-the-world is a necessarily total structure, a "structural whole"[32] that cannot be broken up into elements. This structure is "always *wholly* there as itself," Heidegger writes, so that any highlighting of its constitutive moments is "only an *actual apprehension of the whole structure in itself.*"[33] Phenomenology can no longer consist in a description of isolated or isolable lived experiences; it can only be carried out as such as *structural phenomenology.*

The horizon of meaning against which all understanding stands out is articulate without being explicit, meaningful without being entirely understood. It is not an inert component of understanding, but rather that which gives everything that is situated "within" it its meaning. Indeed, a horizon belongs to a situation and a situation is nothing but the way *the world* shows itself to us, according to the aspect it takes on at any particular moment depending on our own situation and the modalities of our finite understanding. The situation is the individual face the world presents for each of us at a moment of his or her history. Meaning, as it comes to light in a given situation, depends on the interests and goals of a subject engaged in the world, and on the entire non-thematic context in which what appears finds its place. Meaning always depends on the *system* formed by the subject and its world. If the concept of being-in-the-world is superior to that of intentionality to understand our primordial openness to things, this is because it accounts for *the both relational and contextual character of meaning* as it arises in every experience, while giving to this experience its unique qualitative character. It is not the subject that structures experience by conferring on it a meaning whose key it holds; it is experience itself that *structures itself* in a particular way—that is, that presents the subject with objects, changes, events, and processes endowed with such or such a meaning, and it does so on the basis of the subject's experience itself as a whole.

We can recapitulate the various moments of our analysis as follows.

(1) To perceive is to perceive something in a certain way, according to a certain meaning: the "intentionality" of perception lies precisely in this meaning according to which something is perceived.

(2) Meaning is always the correlate of understanding.

(3) Understanding is a practical capacity that consists in being able (knowing how) to deal with something in a given situation; it depends on goals, interests, and background capacities.

(4) Both the capacity to understand and the background capacities on which the former rests already bring the world into play, so that they are the capacities of a being who is essentially in the world, that is, a being such that, if it exists, the world must also exist.

(5) The meaning brought to light by understanding does not depend solely on the capacities of the "subject," but on the overall cast of a situation—therefore, on a tacit understanding of that situation itself, preceding all understanding of this or that specific aspect of it.

(6) Meaning depends on understanding as a practical capacity, other background capacities, and the circumstances of their exercise: it is both relative to these capacities and contextual. All making explicit of meaning brings into play these different dimensions structurally united in the overall structure that I have called "being-in-the-world."

It becomes possible to better understand why a theoretical approach centered on the intentionality of perception finds its fulfillment in one based on being-in-the-world. Meaning is not bestowed on things by consciousness in an a-contextual way (or even on the sole basis of associative links with past experiences): the meaning that things take on reveals itself to me according to the possibilities in light of which I relate to these same things and the overall situation in which I am situated. Meaning depends on practical capacities, and thus on a repertoire of behaviors and ends that are those of a living being—and, in the human context, on a "living being" of an eminent species, on an *existent* who is historical "in the depths of his Being," as Heidegger would have it. *Only a living being capable of behaving in such and such a way can have a consciousness of the world of such and such a kind: and therefore it alone can grasp the things that surround it according to such and such a meaning.* Let us note that meaning depends on capacities, but it is not "conferred" on things by these capacities, as if the latter had, all by themselves, the power to give a cast to the world, to give it a meaning it would not already have. *Meaning is what comes to light in the continuous event of an encounter between a subject endowed with specific capacities and a being of a certain kind within a situation having a specific cast.* Each of these moments is integrated into the structural whole that I have characterized as "being-in-the-world." What one may call, along with Husserl, "intentionality," that is, the modality of the relationship of a consciousness with its objects, depends therefore more deeply, in its essence, on being-in-the-world.

The world, as the locus of a shared intelligence and of potential behaviors, is offered to us already infused with our practical capacities—beginning with that eminent capacity called "understanding." It is a horizon of possibilities, including possibilities of understanding, and therefore a horizon of meaning. This meaning takes on, in each occasion, a specific cast, that of a particular situation. It is never entirely ununderstood, although it remains for the most part implicit. The meaning that I can make explicit, linguistically formulate, presupposes a background of tacit meaning that can also be made explicit, but only up to a point, for otherwise it would cease being a background and be converted into a theme. *All explication of a horizon presupposes a horizon of explication.* Our understanding, like our perception, is finite; it is inscribed in the cast of meaning of a situation from which it can never be abstracted. The "relationship" with the world is not *instituted* by the "intentional acts" of an ego: it must be understood as an openness *to* and *of* the world absolutely prior to all intending, all anticipation, all sense-bestowal—positively *nonconstitutable.* All our capacities by virtue of which things are given to us in a meaningful way *rest on* this prior openness and cannot make it possible. Here, *any* transcendental framework reveals itself clearly as being inadequate to the phenomena. Inherence in the world and the world's openness transcend all the prerogatives of a subject; they cannot depend on him by their very nature, in the sense of being made possible by him. The world cannot get its meaning from any sense-bestowal of any kind, nor be formed, as world, by any project, of whatever nature.

This assertion leads elsewhere than to Heidegger's *In-der-Welt-sein*, at least as it is characterized in *Being and Time* and related texts. Being-in-the-world is not to be conceived of as a transcendental structure, that is, as an ontological characteristic of an entity, *Dasein*, regardless of whether that entity exists or not in fact, and regardless of whether there are or are not entities for this *Dasein*. Being-in-the-world is a relational structure of *Dasein-in-the-world*—if one may speak in this way[34]—and not of *Dasein* taken in isolation. In other words, the world's openness is a structural characteristic of the *system* formed by a "subject" and a world. It is that which absolutely transcends the subject's (finite) powers, its projects and its "potentiality-for-Being," so that it makes no sense here to say that the world is "formed" by *Dasein*, or that *Dasein* is "world-forming" (*Weltbildend*).[35]

Being-in-the-world understood as a relational structure comprises two moments. The inherence in the world of the subject as embodied is structurally dependent on the world's openness as transcending its powers absolutely (including that of understanding) and therefore displaying an inexhaustible meaning, that will never be able to be integrally made explicit, or rather, that it makes no sense to pretend to explicate integrally. *I am open to the world to the extent that I belong to it, and I belong to it to the extent that I am open to the world.* Belonging makes openness possible; openness makes belonging possible. Neither of these two poles is prior to the other. Subject and world are equiprimordial, so that this relational structure of being-in-the-world can only be what it is according to the nature of each of its *relata*. I cannot be open to the world by essence if there is no world, hence if there are no things, events, or states of affairs, and so on, belonging to it; and the world cannot be that openness to the totality of what there is, the possible as well as the actual, if it is not opened as such for a subject that belongs to it bodily and constitutively. The critique I am formulating is, up to a point, Heidegger's own self-critique on the occasion of the famous *turn* (*Kehre*) of his thought, at the end of which he will no longer make the world depend on Being-in-the-world as ontological characteristic of *Dasein*, but *Dasein* on its openness to Being.[36] What I have qualified as "descriptive realism" turns out to be the only way to give meaning to the idea of openness to the world; for, in the still post-transcendental perspective of *Being and Time*, that to which

I am open, the world, remains a formation of my ontological project and presents nothing of the alterity to myself that is characteristic of a *world.*

In leading us beyond perceptual intentionality, our path also leads us, by that same movement, beyond the residual psychologism that belonged to intentionality as such. Since the capacities in light of which things take on a meaning for us are practical and affective capacities that always already bring a world into play, one cannot set out from acts of a consciousness, even intentional ones, in order to understand meaning in its immanence in experience. Meaning is the correlate of our finite understanding insofar as understanding depends on our behavior in the world and our way of being emotionally affected by our entire surroundings. Meaning has nothing psychological about it, and nothing ideal, either. But then the question can be raised whether we shouldn't get rid of consciousness "openly and universally." Husserl, despite his critique of the Cartesian reification of the ego as *res cogitans,* continued nevertheless to apply to that ego the scheme of substance (*nulla re indiget ad existendum*), and the transcendental consciousness he ends up with still bears a great resemblance to a thing or an entity. Moreover, in his view, although the ego is not a substance, the psyche remains one—and that is already too much.

To be aware [*avoir conscience*] is not to have *a* consciousness [*avoir une conscience*], let alone to *be* a consciousness.[37] Perception is indeed an awareness of the thing itself without intermediaries. But that does not entail that what is aware is in turn a consciousness. The fact that "consciousness" is a noun should not incline us to conceive of consciousness as a kind of thing. What exists is not *a* consciousness, but rather a bodily subject engaged in practices, possessing capacities and open to the world through a situation, to a world that takes on such and such a cast in light of background capacities that orient its comprehension.

The main revolutionary element introduced by Heidegger into phenomenology is to have conceived of *Dasein* in this way. *Dasein* is the name for what Aristotle once called "soul," ψυχή,[38] but a soul that is in this case entirely *de-psychologized.* The German expression must be understood in its mainly verbal sense: *Dasein* designates primarily our very way of existing in the world, of engaging ourselves in activities, of "being our possibilities qua possibilities." *Dasein is a bundle of capacities inherent in a bodily "subject," or rather it is this bodily subject itself as a subject of capacities—capacities to which being-aware-of-the-world belongs: "'Consciousness of Reality' is itself a way of Being-in-the-world."*[39] Still, despite this considerable advance, Heidegger's *Dasein* retains something of a transcendental structure, of an ontological condition of possibility for the occurrence of all ontic manifestation. If, instead of *Dasein,* we posit a bodily and practical subject equipped with world-involving capacities, that is, of capacities such that it makes no sense to speak of them in the absence of a world in relation to which they are *capacities,* then Being-in-the-world can no longer designate a transcendental condition of possibility, nor the world a mere "moment" of that total structure or structural whole: Being-in-the-world as "ontological character" of *Dasein.*[40] The world is no longer something that might be understood as "formed" by *Dasein* in any sense whatsoever. The "subject" that is in the world, the world, and Being-in-the-world *form a system* and cannot be conceived of independently of one another. Here, there is no longer anything of which it may be legitimately said—not even *Dasein*—that *nulla re indiget ad existendum.*

17

Horizon (The Holism of Experience, I)

Perception does not possess cohesiveness accidentally, as I said in chapter 15: cohesiveness is what defines perceptual experience as such and differentiates it from its opposite, illusion. It is not the world that is the correlate of an indefinite perceptual confirmation; it is perception that is the correlate of a world possessing structural cohesiveness. In other words, there is not, nor can there be, an isolated perception. An experience is only a *perception* if it is integrated into the whole of perception and forms a system with it; and therefore a thing can only be *perceived* if there is a whole possessing the character of being perceived to which that thing belongs. Perception possesses a holistic character. It remains for us to attempt to better understand the meaning of this assertion.

In the preceding chapter, I have tried to take up the problem of perceptual intentionality afresh. If what defines the phenomenological concept of experience is the immanence of a prelinguistic meaning in it; if, moreover, meaning is defined as the correlate of understanding, which is a practical capacity, that capacity must be able to be actualized, at first sight, not only in actions, but also, in a "passive" way, in experience itself, in the very manner in which we relate to things, apprehend them with this or that meaning—before any behavior and any linguistic spelling out of this meaning. My analysis of being-in-the-world not only showed the problematic character of the epistemological duality of a raw given and of a meaning allegedly "conferred" upon this given by a consciousness or an agent, but it advanced that a meaning could only come to light in things by virtue of the *system* made up of the world and a subject endowed with practical abilities. The immanence of a prelinguistic meaning in experience is a characteristic of being-in-the-world, that is, of an undivided structural whole that is not the mere aggregate of "objects" on the one hand, and of a "subject" on the other. Not only is an experience only meaningful if considered in the context of experience as a whole, but it is only meaningful *for* a subject endowed with practical capacities, and by virtue of the system that this subject forms with its world. Again, meaning appears as a holistic characteristic of a system.

On several occasions the problem of holism has been touched upon in the preceding analyses. Now we must approach it head-on. Let us distinguish, in a preliminary way, two holisms that I will qualify as "horizontal" and "vertical," respectively. The first is stated thus: an experience can only have the property of being a perception if it presents a structural cohesiveness with other experiences that are themselves perceptions, that is, if it is integrated into the entirety of perception, which possesses *primarily* the property of cohesiveness already mentioned. All experience gives itself to us as a perception only against the background of perceptual experience as a whole. Therefore all experience depends on the whole of experience. As for vertical holism, it is based on the impossibility of a description of experience which would be made up of two heterogeneous elements: a "theoretical" element, perception, and a second element coming from our "practices," the additional meaning supposedly conferred on this perception; nor is experience analyzable on the basis of the sensibility/understanding dichotomy, since an understanding is always already at work in experience, even if that understanding is not always conceptually elaborated. The first holism can be approached and discussed in light of the phenomenological concept of horizon. The second has its locus classicus in the Heideggerian analysis of equipmentality, although it has, as we shall see, a broader significance. I will reserve the examination of this point for chapter 18.

To tackle the problem of the holistic constitution of experience comes down to investigating in depth the reasons that lead to replacing the concept of perceptual intentionality with that of being-in-the-world, in order to conceptualize our primordial openness to the world, things, and other people. As we have seen, and as remains in part to be further specified, what constitutes the superiority of the concept of being-in-the-world as compared with that of a multiplicity of intentional acts or lived experiences lies in the following two characteristics:

(1) To think perceptual experience as being-in-the-world amounts to refusing from the start what Heidegger calls, already by 1919, an "atomizing analysis [*atomisierende Analyse*]"[1] of experience, in order to replace it with a "structural analysis [*Strukturanalyse*]."[2]

(2) To give priority to being-in-the-world is to reject the dichotomy between a theoretical relation to the world allegedly established through intuition, and practical dealings built on the basis of that perceptual relation. Even perception already attests to our practical relation to things. In other words, the two main motivations for the conceptual reform at hand correspond to the two dimensions of the problem of holism, which we must now examine successively.

There are many versions of "holism" in contemporary philosophy, and many debates surrounding it. Some, among the most widely known, revolve around the Duhem-Quine epistemological claim according to which science confronts the tribunal of experience not as a collection of assertions each put to the test separately, but as a whole, as a *system of assertions.*[3] This holism of verification is extended in a holism of meaning in Quine and Davidson. In order to interpret one sentence, we must be able to interpret many others containing the same constituents: a sentence is only interpretable, that is, only has meaning, by virtue of the relations it bears with other sentences and with their interpretations, hence by virtue of its location within the infinite network formed by the sentences of a given language. Or, to put it in the terminology of "beliefs," it is impossible to have a belief without ipso facto having many others, and even without possessing a whole system of beliefs, since each belief necessarily bears logical relations with other beliefs: it is incompatible with some, can be inferred from others, others can be inferred from it, and so on. These varieties of holism are quite compatible with an atomistic view of experience reduced to a sum of *inputs,* stimuli, "sensations" that are themselves caused by objects, whether one adheres to Quine's behaviorism, or whether one adopts Davidson's view according to which the world acts *causally* on our beliefs.[4] Solidly anchored in the empiricist tradition, these different versions of holism are not even aware of the *possibility* of a holism of experience. But it is probably impossible to understand how our beliefs harmonize with the world, hence how a "radical interpreter," to borrow Davidson's expression, can understand the least sentence of someone whose language he does not share, and hence attribute beliefs to him, if one is mistaken about the way in which we are in contact with the world, dealing with it and its fundamental cohesiveness in a way that precedes and founds all our beliefs. It is only if our experience of the world is structured and meaningful that our beliefs can possess the coherence they do. And therefore it is only on the condition that we abandon the atomism of sensations and "surface excitations" that the order and the rationality that reign in our beliefs will become understandable.

In what sense is it possible to speak of a holism of experience? What would be the consequences of such a holism for a phenomenological characterization of that experience itself? "Holism" comes from the Greek *to holon,* "the whole." Experience forms a holistic system if, to use a classic expression, in it "the whole is greater than the sum of its parts." Let us take the example of a constellation. Against the background of the night sky, the stars do not stand out for us like a mere unstructured collection—a multiplicity of beams of fossil light; they appear rather as already grouped into recognizable figures: a chariot for Ursa Major, a cross for Cygnus, and so on. Of course, the stars do remain identifiable separately, but what Husserl calls, after Gestalt psychology, "figural factors" are added to them: each star only gets its figural factor, that is, the property of being a constituent of a *figure* integrating several stars, from its insertion into a whole possessing that figure. To put it differently, it is impossible to account for the configuration that makes up a constellation on the basis of properties of stars considered in isolation. Of course, the spatial relations of each star with all the others and with the next constellations are at the basis of the emergence of a perceptual shape; but that shape, that *Gestalt,* is an indivisible totality, and its gestalt properties cannot be reduced to the sum of those of its constituents. Indeed, each star has a particular *meaning* within the whole configuration: one star takes on the meaning of an *extremity* of the cross of Cygnus, while another is located at the *center* of the figure. Each star thus appears invested with a characteristic gestalt that it only acquires by virtue of its being integrated into a whole. Let's call such a property "holistic." A holistic property is *a property such that it is possessed by a part only under the condition of this part's integration into a whole.* Gestalt qualities—visible forms that stand out against a background, musical forms born of silence—are holistic properties in this sense.

Husserl recognized the existence of these gestalt properties, but seemed reluctant to confer a phenomenological status on them. First, in his mereology (his doctrine of whole and parts) developed in the third *Logical Investigation,* he took into account, as concrete parts, only the "independent" parts of an object, that is, the parts that can be separated from the whole in which they are included without losing any of their qualities—except of course that of being parts of this whole. While the concept of *Gestalt* requires that each part possess only certain of its properties (for a note, for example, its musical significance) in conjunction with the other parts, hence within a whole (the melody) to which it belongs and to the shaping of which it contributes—so that the whole is more than the sum of its parts, and its parts are not *elements* that could remain identical within the various wholes to which they may belong—Husserl does not seem to envisage any other whole than the one resulting from the sum of its elements. As Aron Gurwitsch puts it, "As to independent parts, Husserl accepts the traditional conception of wholes and parts in terms of elements. On the basis of that conception he asserts that the *same elements may, and do, exist and are experienced in two different modes,* in grouping and in isolation."[5] One of the reasons for that decision is probably the following. Husserl's analysis is part of a *formal ontology,* that is, an ontology pertaining to the "something in general," stripped from all material determinations. Now, the problem of what kinds of objects are grouped in holistic systems is a problem that involves material considerations; it is by virtue of their material content, as Gurwitsch points out, that notes can occur both in isolation and as parts of a melody, and that their musical significance differs accordingly.

Consequently, we cannot take Husserl's mereology as a starting point to address the problem aforementioned. Our question, let us recall, was the following. Given that holistic properties are encountered in the perceived object as such (a melody, a constellation), can we not go so far as to maintain that *perception itself* taken as a whole forms a holistic system?

But what is a holistic system? A system *is not* holistic if it is merely an aggregate of parts possessing their properties independently of one another. For example, a sand-pile is an aggregate of grains of sand, each one of which has properties (a form, a size, a mass, etc.) independently of the other grains and regardless of whether or not it is part of the sand-pile.[6] Things are otherwise in a belief system. Indeed, it can be claimed that some properties (having a meaning and being verifiable) only pertain to beliefs in conjunction with other beliefs to which they are bound by logical relations. These properties are *relational*, since they depend on other beliefs (and their properties) with which these beliefs form a system: a belief is meaningful if and only if there are other meaningful beliefs to which it bears logical relations. One can also qualify these properties as *holistic*, since a part only has them within a whole. Sometimes holistic properties, as relational properties, are only possessed by the parts of a whole if other parts possess *the same* properties—that is the case to which I have just alluded; sometimes these properties are only possessed by the parts if other parts possess *other* properties. For example, an individual can only be a lawyer within a judicial system in which other individuals exercise the same functions, but also other functions: judge, prosecutor, examining magistrate, attorney, assessor, clerk, and so on. Of course the fact that a system is holistic does not entail that all the properties of its constituents are holistic; it suffices that some be so. Therefore we can characterize a holistic system as a system in which all the parts only have at least some of their properties if other parts of the system have the same (or other) properties, and consequently only have these properties within the whole of which they are a part, and by virtue of their relations to other parts of the system.

As Michael Esfeld remarks, "for something to be a holistic property, it is necessary that the description of the property cannot be reduced to a description of non-relational properties and the description of a suitable arrangement."[7] The perceived constellation is not a group of stars possessing their properties each independently of the others, with, in addition, a suitable spatial arrangement between them; it is a configuration, a *Gestalt,* in which each point of light is endowed with a "gestalt quality" which it acquires only in relation to the other points of light and to the organization as a whole. For a star to have the gestalt quality it has, there must be other stars possessing other gestalt qualities and presenting a perceptual organization with it. Now we see what it means that the whole is greater than the sum of its parts: the distinctive property of this whole, namely its property of perceptual organization, is not reducible to the properties of its parts taken in isolation, but is the result of properties that these parts only possess on the condition of their integration into the whole of which they are parts. More specifically, as Esfeld notes, there are two ways to conceive of a holistic system: (1) either the holistic property in question is first instantiated by the constituents of the system, so that if the whole also instantiates that property, it is only to the extent that its parts instantiate it; for example, a belief system may be said to be meaningful because *each* belief, as dependent on the entire system of beliefs, possesses a meaning *in the first place*; or (2) the holistic property is instantiated first by the system, so that, if its constituents also instantiate that property, it is only derivatively from the whole: it is solely the system of beliefs that possesses *stricto sensu* a meaning, and only on that condition, the beliefs within the system.[8] The conceptions that adopt one or the other of these models may be called, respectively, "weak holism" and "strong holism."

We are now prepared to formulate our problem more precisely. Given that there are, within perception, holistic properties, such as the properties of form brought to light by Gestalt psychology, can we not further assert that perception *as such* forms a holistic system? Indeed, if we choose to use the word "experience" in its broadest sense, which includes not only experiences in the strong and "originary" sense, those in which the thing is given to us *in praesentia* (perceptual experiences), but also affective, emotive, remembered, imaginary, or oneiric, which are only "experiences" in a modified sense (and sometimes in the "as if" mode), we can advance the following thesis. For an experience (in the broad sense), being a perception is necessarily a holistic property. *An experience is a* perceptual *experience if and only if it is integrated without any break or hiatus into the whole of perceptual experience, and therefore if it presents a structural cohesiveness with the system of perceptual experience as a whole.* What is true of perceptual experience also holds for what it is the experience of: the world. Hence we can formulate the same principle *a parte objecti*: the property of being perceived depends on cohesiveness that is first a property of the whole before being a property of the part; only a whole possessing structural cohesiveness (a world) can be perceived, and only what is integrated without any hiatus within a world can receive, by derivation, the characteristic of being an object of perception. Thus characterized, the property of being perceived appears as a strong holistic property that belongs to the whole *before* belonging to the part, and *in order* to be able to belong to it as such. A particular thing can only present the cohesiveness of its concordant adumbrations to me because it emerges from a world necessarily endowed with structural cohesiveness.

This cohesiveness is a set of intangible *a priori* laws. These *a priori* laws are material: they belong both to the objects of experience and to the experience of these objects, since the latter refers to nothing other than the mode of appearance of the former. Such laws are first and foremost spatiotemporal. The spatiotemporal characteristics of the objects of our experience are themselves holistic characteristics: an event, for example, cannot be temporally situated unless other events are temporally situated, and in fact, unless there is a whole system of temporal situations governed by before/after relations.[9] The same applies to spatial properties. But the sphere of material law extends beyond the spatiotemporal form of the world (the world, as Husserl specifies, being "nothing but concretely filled time and concretely filled space"),[10] for example, to the essential relations between colors, between the pitch, timbre, and intensity of a tone, and so forth. Of course, experience does not have "structures" in exactly the same sense as perceived things do. In a thing, these structures, the interconnectedness of whole and parts, are immediately perceived. But experience, as mode of givenness or mode of presentation of "objects" (facts, events, processes, states of affairs) cannot itself be perceived, given, or experienced. The structures of a thing are the concrete (perceived) relations of its parts to one another, and of its parts to the whole thing. But the structural properties of experience are not concrete (perceived or perceivable) structures; they are abstract ones. They depend by nature on the understanding we have of experience and on the descriptions we can give of it. They are not so much structures of a kind of "thing" that should be called "experience" (which exists nowhere) as principles of the *description* of what we designate by that term, namely the mode of givenness of certain objects. Phenomenology only describes by accident the concrete structures of objects; it investigates the conditions of descriptiveness of experience itself, its modalities of meaning or of intelligibility. Such "structures" are lineaments of meaning, descriptive necessities and not experienceable concrete relations.

My tentative conclusion is thus the following. Being a perception is a strongly holistic property. For an experience to be a perception (and correlatively for its object to be said to be "perceived'), not only is it necessary that there be other perceptions, but it is further necessary that there be a *system* of perceptions governed by structural cohesiveness, so that perception (being perceived) is a property of the system (of the world) itself, and, only to that extent, a property of the part.

This conclusion, to be accepted, requires us to subscribe to the disjunctive conception of perception developed above, and therefore to dismiss as inadequate the form taken by the skeptic problem. In turn, it makes it possible to deepen that disjunctive conception, since the illusion/perception distinction rests entirely on the phenomenon of perceptual cohesiveness, which it devolves on a holism of experience to elucidate. If perception is a holistic phenomenon, the fact that we can doubt a particular experience excludes this experience from the domain of perception, rather than casting doubt or discredit on perception as a whole. If perception is by nature endowed with structural cohesiveness, then all that is not endowed with structural cohesiveness is not a *doubtful* perception: it is *not a perception at all.* As he still believes the skeptic problem to be well posed, Husserl falls short of reaching a holistic conception of perception in its continuity with memory. Husserl's implicit reasoning is basically the same as that of Descartes, and of Locke before him: since universal doubt is legitimate, perception must be an *indubitable* knowledge in order to give us access to a world and to objects. Now in order to be an indubitable knowledge, perception must consist in (and be divisible into) "truths" (or "evidences") *susceptible of being evaluated in isolation*; for, if truth resides only in the whole, it is nowhere. On this view, the only acceptable starting point is a multiplicity of at least ideally identifiable "lived experiences," about which the question can then be raised: By what "universal form of synthesis" are they interconnected? The view according to which lived experiences can be evaluated in terms of intrinsic truth and falsehood goes hand in hand with the foundationalist epistemology originating in Descartes and extending up to empiricism: ideally, we should be able to trace our knowledge of the world back to simple elements, to Descartes's clear and distinct ideas, to empiricism's mental atoms, that is, to the ultimate, indubitable elements on which the entire edifice of knowledge ultimately rests. This prejudice underlies most approaches to perception. The idea of sense data, for example, is nothing but the idea of a given that would be intrinsically a knowledge beyond doubt and would afford the foundation for knowledge as a whole. The Cartesian framework thus extends its influence up to the Vienna Circle, with its protocol statements playing the role of ultimate ground. In Husserl, the epistemic duality of indubitable hyletic data, on the one hand, and intentional acts, on the other, form the legacy of this same theoretical framework and give rise to the same difficulties. These Cartesian prejudices prevent Husserl from doing justice to a "phenomenon" to which he does, nonetheless, devote the first philosophical analysis worthy of the name: the phenomenon of horizon.

The problem of horizon is, in a sense, the central problem of phenomenology, because it is that of the limits of phenomenality as such—and thus that of our finitude. As Levinas remarks, Heidegger's Being is only a new name for this problem that Husserl was the first to raise: "All Heidegger's work consists in opening and exploring this dimension [or horizon], unknown in the history of ideas, to which he nonetheless gives the most well-known name of *Sein*."[11] But what is a horizon? How is horizon thinkable in the framework of a holism of experience?

Let us observe a chair: it appears to us over there, situated in relation to oneself and to other pieces of furniture, keeping its individuality when moved by virtue of its continuity in time and space. It is seen now with one outline, now with another; we can go through these outlines in succession by changing our position in such a way that the new outlines are linked to the preceding ones by specific spatial and temporal relations, while at the same time maintaining invariant structural ties between themselves. At no point do we have here a series of elementary perceptions whose law of composition we would subsequently have to discover, about which we would have to ask ourselves thanks to what "synthesis" they hold together. What we perceive is that chair taken in its global perceptual context, with definite relations between its parts, between the outlines it presents to us, and between itself and its surroundings. The way the chair appears to me now depends essentially on the way it appeared to me a moment ago and will appear to me in a moment if I move, if I come closer or move further away. Each appearance, in order to be precisely the appearance it is, depends on the entire system of appearances. The chair is a *system* of appearances and the perception of it, as Merleau-Ponty says, is "a structural phenomenon."[12] Without the fact of my being situated here, there could not be a chair over there; without a partially indefinite background, its form would not stand out with that cleanness and definition. Without the possibility of my perusing its successive outlines, it would not harbor that element of mystery that is its depth. Actually, the chair is nothing but this network of structural invariants, a system of appearances prescribed in advance, a spatiotemporal *continuum* that has its place in the spatiotemporal continuity of the world. Hence it is necessarily dependent on the world: by contrast with Descartes's ideas, the empiricist's sensations, and even Kant's objects, it does not appear in an abstract theater, that of my ego, my soul, or my consciousness, as the pure counterpart of a cognitive act. The world is not a stage, as vast as you please. That is also why the world is not an object either, a *Gegen-stand*, the counterpart of a gaze that would grasp it without remainder. I must be plunged into the world, in a continuous and coherent world whose truth, or rather whose certainty, is prior to all judgment, and in which error or illusion can only be local, in order for the chair to appear to me as this flow of outlines forming a system that, despite changes of perspective (or rather thanks to them), retains a recognizable style and face. I must be situated and included in this world in order for a ring of invisibility to arise, delimiting my access to things, restricting my empire over them, infusing my perception with finitude. That is what Husserl is probably the first in all of Western philosophy to notice and conceptualize under the name "horizon." The phenomenological horizon, far more than James's "*fringes*," achieves the overcoming of the concept of object understood as a correlate of a frontal vision, of a pure *theorein*, of a "seeing" that does not conceal itself by the very act of focusing on things. But to think this concept, which is probably the most significant in all of phenomenology, through to the end, we must understand how I am inserted in the world and how, symmetrically, the entirety of the world is present in the least perception as an implicit dimension underlying all the rest, how *the object is but a limited view on the world, rather than the world being an appendix to the consciousness of an object.*

To understand the horizon, we must start with the world and its way of showing itself to one corporally situated in it and belonging to it by its very situation. The horizon is only the finite way in which the world presents itself to us through a body, and hence through a perceptual situation. It is the way a totality (both of potentialities and actualities) underlies, without itself being perceived, every perceptual hold on it, every partial grasp, every limited and circumscribed view, making them possible as such; for without an invisible depth, there would be no appearing relief, and without an implicit background, no explicit motif. It is because of its inherence in a non-thematic whole, but remaining always present at the threshold of all vision, that a thing can deliver itself to us, thickened with the sensible mystery of its latency, and that it can be endlessly modulated while remaining constantly the same. The horizon is first of all that vague backwash of the world onto the beaches of manifestation, that indeterminate background against which the thing and its immediate thematic borders stand out, and it is only subsequently the unperceived depth that belongs to that thing: the potential totality of its "adumbrations." Because each object is a view on the world, it cannot reveal itself otherwise than haloed with a horizon; but the world is not thinkable as an addition of objects or a sum of horizons, no matter how numerous and indeterminate.

In Husserl, however, intentionality is cut out to the measure of the object. This is why the horizon can only be approached as a boundary phenomenon, the unobjectifiable remainder of all objectification, the unconstitutable residue of all constitution. Granted, as opposed to the atomism that triumphs in the empiricist tradition, Husserl refuses to break up the life of consciousness into ultimate elements. There is a *life of consciousness* that forms an indivisible continuity. "The life of consciousness," he writes, "is neither a mere aggregate of data, nor a heap of psychic atoms, or a whole composed of elements united through gestalt qualities [*Gestaltqualitäten*]. This is also true of pure introspective psychology, as a parallel to transcendental phenomenology. *Intentional analysis is the disclosure of the actualities and potentialities in which objects constitute themselves as perceptual units.* Furthermore, all perceptual analysis takes place in the transition from real events to the intentional horizons suggested by them."[13] By contrast with an "analysis of sensations" after the style of Mach, Husserl maintains that "transcendental subjectivity is not a chaos of intentional experiences, but it is a unity through synthesis," "one universal synthetic unity" whose form is that of time.[14] It is not certain, however, that the concept of synthesis doesn't presuppose precisely the kind of atomism that it seeks to overcome, or at least that it doesn't, in many respects, remain hostage to it. Is it possible to truly understand the *in each case total* character of our openness to the world as a "structural whole" (Heidegger)—which it would be better, therefore, to call "being-in-the-world" rather than "perception"—as the universal passive synthesis taking place between a multiplicity of lived experiences formerly given (or postulated)? Associative ties can only be *isolated* ties between *isolated* lived experiences that must remain at least in principle *identifiable.* But the wholeness of experience cannot be the sum of such isolated ties, even infinitely multiplied. And the horizon through which that wholeness is given to a necessarily finite grasp, by virtue of the inherence in the world of the subject of perception, cannot be grasped as a sum of associative ties between formerly given objects—and formerly given *independently of all horizon*—for the simple reason that the horizon cannot be conceived of as an appendix to object-consciousness; it is prior to it and makes it possible; it is of a different nature. This understanding of horizon as a synthesis would have a plausibility only on the condition that we could indicate the ultimate elements on which that synthesis operates: but if a perceptual field is a continuum that is indivisible into elements and, furthermore, a holistic totality in which the whole is more than the sum of its parts, such ultimate elements are elusive, and to speak of a "synthesis" makes no sense.

Because phenomenology is still a partial holism, Husserl resorts to the notion of passive synthesis in order to think of perceptions as concrete totalities. For instance, he gives the following description. "While taking an evening stroll on the Loretto Heights, a string of lights in the Rhine valley suddenly flashes in our horizon; it immediately becomes prominent affectively and unitarily without, incidentally, the allure having therefore to lead to an attentive turning toward. That in one stroke the string of lights is affective as a whole is obviously due to the pre-affective lawful regularities of the formation of unity; because of them possibly other groups of lights in the visual field will also simultaneously be there affectively as prominent special unities, and this *ceteris paribus*."[15] Here Husserl addresses the aforementioned problem of sensible totalities that are immediately perceived; in his example, a string of lights. The unity of these lights which are not first given separately, and then unified by a synthesis, pertains to those "gestalt qualities" revealed by the analyses or Ehrenfels, Wertheimer, Köhler, and others. But how does Husserl analyze this phenomenon? In a way that remains symptomatically ambiguous, since it oscillates between a form of atomism and a Gestalt-like approach. "Sometimes," Husserl writes, "the givenness of the wholes, their affective prominence and therefore the possibility of grasping them, precedes the parts, sometimes the givenness of parts the whole."[16] The case in which the parts precede the whole is the one in which the lights come on *successively*. But this assertion, when carefully considered, is untenable: even when the lights come on one after the other, unless they only come on after very long intervals, it is still *a row of lights* that I see twinkling in the valley; and that is so because the lights, thanks to their gestalt qualities, stand out as a whole against their nocturnal background. The whole must be perceived *as a whole* in order for the part to be perceived *as a part*, with the meaning it takes on within the whole. It seems that Husserl felt the greatest reluctance to accept the existence of these holistic properties. In some passages, he even rejects all holism as an excessive reaction to atomism, or even as an outright "prejudice."[17] In his view, what remains primary in principle if not in fact is the consciousness of objects, that is, of individual realities: "Granted, in order to grasp the world as an object of experience, we must have previously grasped single realities of the world. Therefore, in a certain manner the experience of single things precedes the experience of the world that is a grasping, noticing experience."[18] In other words, and even more clearly, there is a "priority of the experience of single real things to the experience of the world."[19]

Phenomenology remains, as a consequence, a partial holism in the works of its founder, and it is hardly surprising, under these circumstances, that the concept of horizon, so important in the economy of description, remains itself in the background, little or poorly thematized, a limit concept of phenomenology, just as horizon is a limit phenomenon. How does Husserl characterize horizon? Starting out from the object, and taking it as his guiding thread, he distinguishes between an "internal" horizon and an "external" one. The former designates the totality of potential perceptions to which the actual perceptions of an object implicitly refer, for example the facets of a cube which are now invisible, but are implied by the visible ones—a totality that is co-intended, co-involved in the present perception, since without it we would not have to do with the perception of *a cube*. The latter, the external horizon, is the indeterminate halo of potential perceptions that envelop present perception and form the background against which an object stands out. In both cases, these potentialities of intentional life possess the paradoxical characteristic of being at once prescribed and indeterminate. "Horizons," writes Husserl, "are 'predelineated' potentialities";[20] the horizon is an "undetermined-determinable," epitomizes Straus.[21] But how can these characteristics be accounted for? How can horizons belong to all object-consciousness without themselves being objects for a consciousness? Here, as Merleau-Ponty comments, "the whole Husserlian analysis is blocked by the framework of *acts* which the philosophy of *consciousness* imposes upon it."[22] Indeed, to the problem of horizon Husserl applies the generic intention/fulfillment distinction that runs through the entire domain of acts. For example, he thinks of the internal horizon as the structural excess of the empty intentions of consciousness over the intuitive given which confers their fulfillment on them: every intention intends beyond itself and its present fulfillment, it harbors a supplement of intention, a "more-meaning" (*Mehrmeinung*) by virtue of which it anticipates the hidden sides of an object, performing an *Über-sich-hinaus-meinen* (intending-beyond-itself),[23] a "*dépassement de l'intention dans l'intention elle-même*" (surpassing of the intention in the intention itself), in the free translation of Levinas and Pfeiffer. The act of apprehension being itself already a surplus (*Überschuß*), the horizon is the surplus with respect to any intending of the surplus inherent in every intending: the surplus of a surplus. It is that which exceeds all my surpluses of intention but only appears according to them. Now, it is not certain that, even for the internal horizon, the one of the two horizons that is the most easily approachable and describable as a pure appendix to object-consciousness, the Husserlian conceptuality is adequate. According to it, consciousness would progress, so to speak, from an unfulfilled intention to a fulfillment of intention, which would in turn elicit a more-meaning, summoning a new fulfillment, and so on; it would advance continually into reality "as one jumps from rock to rock in a riverbed," to borrow an image of Patočka's.[24] But this metaphor—like those of "intentions" and "fulfillment"—is misleading: it reveals the atomistic element in the whole description, which strains to reach the horizon, as it were, by adding up unfulfilled intentions and partial perceptions, rather than seeing that the horizon can only be given in its undivided totality prior to them. Jumping from intention to intention and moving from one lived experience to another, *we will never reach the horizon,* not because the horizon is in principle unreachable, but because it precedes, as a structural globality, all the appearances of the object that stand out against it, because it is a structural totality in which the whole is more than the sum of its parts. As for its internal horizon, the object appears to me from the first moment as an indecomposable totality that gives itself to me according to a finite view on it, and at no time am I involved with a sum of unfulfilled intentions that would carry me beyond present adumbrations—that mythology raises insoluble questions, such as how many co-intentions are there directed toward invisible aspects (and toward *how many* invisible aspects) of the object at every moment—nor with a sum of corresponding fulfillments. The visible and the invisible emerge together from the outset, and are of a piece. As for the external horizon, it is even less amenable to being conceptualized along these lines. It points us in the direction of a structural unity between the thematic and the non-thematic, a unity that cannot be reconstructed by summation. This horizon possesses the paradoxical property of being neither entirely conscious, for otherwise it would be given without breaks like an object of a new kind, nor entirely unconscious, in which case it would make no contribution at all to the present perception. It is co-perceived without being expressly grasped, apprehended without becoming thematic, seen without being known. Yet its role is major. Its enveloping presence remains constantly in the background, diffuse and undetermined, yet determining all the rest; it is not an object-perception, but it precedes and accompanies it. To say that the horizon "appears" or that it "does not appear" is unsatisfactory in both cases. The horizon *in-appears,* if I may forge this verb: its in-appearing signifies its appearing in withdrawal and not its outright occultation.

To Husserl's *negative* concept of horizon as ever-retreating limit of objectification, not-yet-thematized residuum of all thematization, lack or paucity of intuition—whence the choice of the word "horizon," from *horizein,* to delimit, to circumscribe—it therefore becomes possible to oppose a *positive* concept, which Heidegger (after Rilke), and subsequently Merleau-Ponty have called "the Open." The Open should not be conceived of as equivalent to the world itself, but as *the world's mode of appearance,* its phenomenalizaton for a finite, situated "subject." If the world were nothing but the Open, then indeed its being would boil down to its appearing for us, and we would again be drawn into idealism. Conceived from the starting point of the Open as mode of manifestation of the world, the horizon is not initially lack and paucity, the limit of phenomenality: it is full and complete positivity. It is that which brings all things to visibility, holds up and underlies appearing, conferring upon it its very characteristics. It is that full and all-encompassing presence of the whole insofar as this whole is included in each view, in each partial perception taken on it. The invisibility, the indetermination of that which does not appear, its necessary "withdrawal," are the milieu of all form, all visibility, all determination. As Merleau-Ponty insists, we should understand "the *Eröffnung*, the horizon, not as far off, but as the 'milieu' of things."[25] Furthermore, the horizon is not only this halo that encompasses and limits my vision, but also that indeterminateness that is lodged in its heart and on the background of which all that stands out stands out: when I read a sentence, I generally take note neither of the style nor the size of the letters; when I see a face, I don't notice the eye color. These unperceived milestones that prepare the ground for my perception fulfill a dynamic role in it—in my vision of distance, for example. The tree I perceive in the distance only looks as having a real size by virtue of structural invariants of which I am not aware but that border my perception like the sea borders the shore, in particular the density of the texture of the ground that increases in proportion to the distance, and, consequently, to the optical angle—what Gibson calls *texture-perspective.*[26]

This free, vast, and vacant field that flows out beyond me in all directions and borders my perception without itself having any precise limits—this openness in which I am myself located is primary. To grasp it, the description must be stripped from the primacy of object and objectification as it reigns unchallenged in Husserlian phenomenology. It is not by setting from the object and its mode of presence that we will be able to conceptualize the horizon negatively [*en creux*], but it is quite the reverse: only the fullness of the horizon, the entirely positive phenomenon of its constitutive indeterminateness or rather of its duplicity, that is to say, of its appearance in withdrawal that is not an outright occultation, will enable us to grasp the internal and external horizons of an object as particular cases. We must no longer set out from objectivity to end up with the world conceived as a sum of all the horizons, the "horizon of horizons," to borrow Husserl's expression; we must rather discover in the precedence of the world, in the pure positivity of an Openness that no subject can anticipate or constitute, the omnipresent and uncircumscribed background within which every particular horizon is carved out. *The horizon is the latency proper to all display of the world in its structural cohesiveness.* It is because the world is the consistent and unshakable background of all appearance that there are partially tacit *perceptual situations,* and that these situations give rise to finite views for a subject always already included in them, and whose movement among things continually flushes out horizons the way a hunter flushes out partridges—horizons that he or she at the same time never stops filling up and determining. Every view stands out against a situation, and every situation stands out against the non-objectifiable background of the world, whose withdrawal is not a boundary but the *source* from which all manifestation becomes possible and each thing begins to be. The Openness of the world conditions the appearing of a situation and the appearing of a situation always infused with indetermination conditions the appearing of things. That which is never missing but always escapes us, that ring of invisibility that circumscribes the gaze and eludes it endlessly—that "horizon," that is to say, that measure of latency ceaselessly fulfilled while at the same time giving rise to new latencies, can only befall an individual object because of its insertion in a situation that authorizes but one view at a time, and that situation only surfaces with its own latency because it is integrated to a world even more indeterminate, offered to a more finite perspective. *Cohesiveness and indetermination are characteristics of the mode of appearing of the world before being characteristics of the mode of appearing of the object or the situation—and in order to become so.* Therefore, the only coherent approach to the horizon is in holistic terms. The world is at once that which is constantly perceived and that which structurally exceeds all perception; it is that superlative presence, that omni-presence always remaining in the background and conferring upon all the rest its presence and its patency, but also, and by this very fact, that which is never given otherwise than in a fleeting and oblique manner, through a finite perspective on it.

Still, it may be objected, if perception forms a holistic system, doesn't the whole into which each perception is integrated have to be given, and given in an explicit way—while perception, as is revealed by the horizon phenomenon, is characterized by the fact that, as it unfolds temporally, it never ceases slipping away and escaping us? This objection rests on the presupposition that the whole must be thematic if it is to play the role that it does in a holistic system. But such is not the case. The world does not have to be entirely present to a consciousness in order for perception to form a holistic system, no more than a belief system has to be explicit down to the smallest detail in order for each particular belief to depend on it: beliefs that are systematically bound together always remain partially indeterminate; they form a vague background, and the idea of making them all explicit makes no sense.

We set out from the idea that perception forms a holistic system. That idea allowed us to move from an atomistic view according to which we have a plurality of intentional perceptual acts, each of which is focused on its object and possesses its characteristics in isolation (and is associated only subsequently with other acts and other lived experiences by means of passive syntheses, and, ultimately, through the universal synthetic form of time), to a view in which perception is a structural whole, indecomposable into elements. I have thus tried to give plausibility to the thesis according to which perceptual intentionality is better grasped in terms of being-in-the-world. If I am right, the passage from an atomistic phenomenology to a structural one is not just an option among others; it is the one and only option.

In a second phase, I advanced the view that the right way to conceive of horizon, that key concept of phenomenology, is not as the ever-receding limit of a process of objectification in principle endless, but as the positive (though structurally withdrawn) mode of givenness of the world itself—that is, in the modality of what Heidegger and Merleau-Ponty have called the Open. This view precludes all reification of our presence in the world based on naturalistic concepts such as causality. Not, of course, that there cannot be *causal conditions* for a subject to bear that holistic relationship with the world that I have called "being-in-the-world." Phenomenology says nothing against such causalities. But that openness to the world certainly cannot *consist* in a network of causal relations, because causality is, by nature, a non-holistic relation. The subject that is open to the world is not the center of a network of physical influences, but rather at once *in* the world and *open to it*: he belongs to the world inasmuch as he is open to it; he is open to it inasmuch as he belongs to the world. All openness to the world, because it goes hand in hand with a belonging to the world as a body, is finite through and through—a finitude by contrast to which the world presents itself, significantly, as inexhaustible. The Open is a characteristic of the relationship between a corporeal subject and a world, and nowise an intrinsic property of the subject alone, a transcendental condition of possibility that would belong to him as an instance prior by right.

Now the question is how to reintroduce into these analyses a dimension that I have deliberately set aside, the practical aspect of our *In-der-Welt-sein*; for a horizon is first of all a variety of available possibilities to be explored corporally and practically. This problem requires revisiting what, at the beginning of this chapter, I termed "vertical holism."

18

The World (The Holism of Experience, II)

An experience is only a perception if it forms a system with the whole of perception: thus is heralded the structural holism I presented in the last chapter. But we do not just perceive things; to perceive is always to perceive in such or such a way, according to a particular meaning. The phenomenological concept of experience is characterized by the immanence of meaning in experience itself—a meaning that is not yet an articulated thought, that is to say, a conceptually elaborated one, a meaning that draws on our affectivity and practices. It has become clear that experience, as understood here, has nothing mental or psychological about it. It is a way of being-in-the-world, a direct hold on things and beings in the absence of any intermediary, a continuous corporeal transaction with our surroundings. And the understanding that is constantly at work in our very way of experiencing the world is not a mental episode, but a practical competency tributary both to background competencies and to an overall situation. The meaning that comes to light through that understanding is not an entity of a new kind that would exist alongside things, or accompany the experience we have of it; it is not a self-identical object that would possess a sui generis mode of existence. Meaning is unreal, which is not to say that it is ideal; it escapes this alternative. It depends on a finite understanding such as it is exercised on each occasion on the basis of a given situation, or rather, such as it is at work passively in the very *modalities* of the experience of that situation: it is at once relational and contextual. This conception of meaning inaugurated by Husserl can be qualified as "modal";[1] but instead of asserting that the meaning depends by essence on a preliminary intentional act that would be fulfilled by an object in accordance with the latter's mode of givenness, I say that it is the holistic characteristic of a system: the system formed by the object (the fact, the event, etc.) taken in its overall context and a subject endowed with practical capacities, among which understanding itself occupies a prominent position.

It remains for us to better understand what the status of this meaning is. If it is not conferred in a unilateral and sovereign way by consciousness, regardless of the circumstances, that is to say, of the subject's immersion in the world, how are we to understand its nature? And if a thing, a situation, or an event have meaning only when approached in light of practical and affective possibilities, how are praxis and *theoria* articulated with each other in our primordial commerce with the world? This problem is that of "vertical holism." But to begin with, what are the relationships between the two atomisms? Indeed, to the horizontal atomism according to which experience is made up of "lived experiences" united by synthetic ties and subordinated to the deepest form of synthesis, that of time, there is added, in Husserl, a vertical atomism according to which it is allegedly possible to distinguish, in that experience, a "stratum" of pure perception and strata built upon perception, for example a layer of axiological predicates that make some objects into cultural ones having a useful function. These two atomisms are not merely juxtaposed: they respond to a common concern. Husserlian phenomenology, because it subscribes to an epistemology oriented toward the search for truths founded and justified in an absolute way, has tended to conceive of perception as knowledge, be it still naive and prescientific, and, as a consequence, as an impervious stratum of phenomenality that was in need of being completed by practical, emotional, or aesthetic value predicates.

The clearest expression of this conception is to be found in *Ideas II:*

> To begin with, the world is, in its *core*, a world appearing to the senses and characterized as 'present-at-hand' [*vorhanden*], a world given in straightforward empirical intuitions and perhaps grasped actively. The ego then finds itself related to this empirical world in new acts, e.g., in acts of valuing, or in acts of pleasure and displeasure. In these acts, the object is brought to consciousness as valuable, pleasant, beautiful, etc., and this happens in various ways, e.g., in original givenness. In that case, there is built, upon the substratum of mere intuitive representing, an evaluating which, if we presuppose it, plays, in the immediacy of its lively motivation, the role of a value-'perception' . . . in which the value character itself is given in original intuition."[2]

On this view, there is a straightforward, intuitive grasp of the thing as object of nature upon which subsequently an "axiological intuition"[3] is built. To the real predicates of the perceived object there are superimposed, as a supplementary stratum of intentional constitution, "meaning-predicates,"[4] giving rise to a value-perception (*Wert-Wahrnehmung, Wert-nehmen*),[5] by virtue of which that object henceforth pertains to the spiritual or cultural world. This is the case, for instance, for the mode of givenness of tools or implements. Some objects, Husserl says, are not only grasped as natural things in a natural world, but, in the personalistic attitude, that is, in the practical attitude (*praktische Einstellung*), they are grasped as fit for the satisfaction of a need, and thus as objects of use (*Nutzobjekte*): "For instance, I see coal as heating material; I recognize it and recognize it as useful [*dienlich*] and as used [*dienend*] for heating, as appropriate for and as destined to produce warmth.[6]

This *Dienlichkeit*, this appropriateness or serviceableness that makes some items appropriate for fulfilling a function, that makes them objects destined to a use, consists in a value-predicate added on a mere natural thing. The idea of intentional stratification makes us assume that, at least in principle, an object appears *primarily* as an object of knowledge, and thus as a mere thing in the natural world, and *only subsequently* as an implement embedded in cultural and historical practices. The question of how an ego can bestow its implement-meaning on a pure piece of *res extensa* appeals to the universal form of passive synthesis, and it raises all the difficulties that have been already emphasized. This is where Heidegger's critique comes in. A tool does not have a function all by itself, when considered in isolation from what it is used for, the user, the circumstances, a community of practice, and finally the totality of implements with which it forms an instrumental complex. Its meaning depends by essence on its entire context. There is no need for us to postulate, according to a temptation that goes back at least to Brentano,[7] a theoretical attitude that would precede by right the practical, axiological, or aesthetic one.

In *Being and Time*, the analysis of "the Cartesian ontology of the world" is a thinly veiled critique of Husserl, since it is only in the works of Husserl that the idea of "layers" or "strata" can be found, and not in Descartes. According to this ontology, "this [material Nature] would be the fundamental stratum upon which all the other strata of actuality within-the-world are built up."[8] The *res extensa* ultimately forms the underlying support "for such specific qualities as 'beautiful,' 'ugly,' 'in keeping,' 'not in keeping,' 'useful,' 'useless.' If one is oriented primarily by Thinghood, these latter qualities must be taken as non-quantifiable value-predicates by which what is in the first instance just a material Thing, gets stamped as something good. But with this stratification, we come to those entities which we have characterized ontologically as equipment ready-to-hand [*zuhanden*]."[9] In other texts of the same period, the allusion to Husserl is transparent. "Here too, a thing is approached as an object of observation and perception, and perception [*Wahrnehmen*] is then, as it is typically put, complemented by an apprehension of values [*Wertnehmen*]."[10] The personalistic attitude, which is supposed to complete the naturalistic one—the latter providing to the whole analysis its starting point—far from overcoming this naturalism, remains hostage to it. The Husserlian description, Heidegger objects, misunderstands both the mode of being of the tool (*Zeug*), that of its user, *Dasein*, and that of the surrounding world that belongs to the Being of the latter. As a consequence, the force of Heidegger's well-known critique lies less in the ontological reorientation imparted to the concept of *Dienlichkeit*, which becomes *Zuhandenheit*, the readiness-to-hand of the item of equipment, than in his insistence on the holistic character of equipmentality, and consequently on the fact that an entity can only be an item of equipment of a certain kind if inserted in a complex of items of equipment of a certain kind. In enlarging the concept of *Zeug*, "tool," to the point of giving it an extension approaching that of *ta pragmata* in Greek, the things with which we deal in our daily coping with the world, "our things"[11] (as one might say to a child "put your things in order!"), Heidegger stresses that these "things" with which we deal when we are absorbed in our daily tasks always refer one to another and can only appear to us with their meaning within the context in which they are used. Hence "there 'is' no such thing as *an* equipment."[12] Thus the analysis of equipmentality supports the weight of a more general critique of Husserlian atomism and allows its replacement by a holistic approach in terms of Being-in-the-world. Although that critique, as we shall see, fails in the form given to it in *Being and Time*, its principle is justified, and the 1927 opus unfolds some of the conceptual resources that are indispensable for that transformation.

Without getting into all the complexity and subtlety of the analyses of *Being and Time* devoted to the surrounding world (*Umwelt*) of daily life, let us sketch out its main features. The way of being of the tool (*Zeug*), namely usability or readiness-to-hand (*Zuhandenheit*), is approached in light of the idea of *Verweisung*, "reference." A tool is always a tool *for* (*um zu*) this or that; it refers in its very Being to a possible use. For example, hammers are *for* nails, nails *for* the rafters, the rafters *for* the roof, the roof *for* the house, and so on. With this *for*-structure Heidegger has in mind not thoughts strictly speaking, but possibilities of use that come to light at the level of items of equipment themselves in relation to other items of equipment. When *Dasein* is busy, "wrapped up in what it is doing," the *for*-structure and the expectation it raises, he points out, have "by no means the character of getting something thematically into one's grasp."[13] In this immanent reference of each item of equipment to what it is for (*wozu*), a meaning that precedes all articulate—that is, all conceptually elaborated—thought becomes manifest.

But that idea of "reference" is not without ambivalence. Sometimes the reference belonging to a given item of equipment is characterized by Heidegger as a reference *to other items of equipment* that make up, with the first item, an equipmental manifold; at other times it is defined as a reference to its *use* by and for a *Dasein.* In the first case, there is said to be a "reference of something to something,"[14] the "something" being here an item of equipment. The writing case is *for* the pen, the pen *for* the ink, the ink *for* the paper, and so on. In the second case, it will be said rather that every item of equipment is *for* a possible use: "the manufactured clock is *for* telling the time."[15] These two assertions are not equivalent, but neither do they conflict. It is because an item of equipment is *for* this or that task that it is also, and for that very reason, *for* this or that other item of equipment. This ambivalence testifies rather to Heidegger's attempt to grasp in one single concept, that of "reference," two distinct characteristics: that which would be classically referred to as "finality," and to which Heidegger prefers to give the name "purpose" (*Bewandtnis*), on the one hand, that is, the subordination of the item of equipment to ends that are only reached by human actions; and the insertion of the item of equipment within a manifold of items of equipment, on the other—an insertion that belongs to its way of manifesting itself. The notion of "reference" thus has a twofold function in the economy of the phenomenological description: (1) to furnish the ontological equivalent of the *ontologically indeterminate* notion of "finality," making the latter an essential characteristic of the mode of appearance of the item of equipment; (2) to stress that the equipmentality (*Zeughaftigkeit*) is a necessarily holistic property—Heidegger, it is true, would refuse to call it a *property*[16]—that only belongs to an item of equipment if other items of equipment possess it too, that is, if that item is part of a totality of items of equipment.

The first aspect of the description leads Heidegger to contend that we do not relate first to an item of equipment as something present-at-hand (*vorhanden*), in a purely theoretical consideration, and only subsequently invest it with value-predicates, but that we are dealing from the outset with that item of equipment as something that is revealed *through* its reference to something else. In our attitude primordially absorbed in tasks and busy which Heidegger calls "concern" (*Besorgen*), the item of equipment never shows itself, as a matter of fact, to a purely theoretical "seeing"; far from being the object of a thematic grasp, it *lets itself be forgotten* in its use, to the point of "disappearing," as it were, behind what it refers to. "The tool thus becomes absorbed in the reference. . . . Concern in a certain sense looks away from the tool as thing; it is primarily not even there as such a thing, but rather as a tool, as '*equipment for* [*Zeug zu*]' which is *used.*"[17] Conversely, the tool only appears as tool—and at the same time its mode of being, readiness-to-hand declares itself—in cases in which it fails to perform its function: for example, when it is damaged or left lying around in the workshop. This characteristic, which Heidegger dubs *Unauffälligkeit*, inconspicuousness (in the sense that the tool does not impose itself on our attention, is not grasped thematically when we use it), is important because it emphasizes the absorption in everyday tasks of existence interpreted by the guiding thread of concern. Far from constituting the primary way of being of *Dasein* as Being-in-the-world, knowledge *presupposes* the concerned acquaintance which relates to beings in light of everyday tasks, and apprehends them originarily as ready-to-hand. In short, it is their *purpose* that we grasp first of all when we are dealing with things and concern ourselves with them. The tool only "comes to light" through its reference or references, and each reference only possesses its reference-character insofar as it is part of a totality of references.

Thus we come to the second aspect of Heidegger's description. The readiness-to-hand of the item of equipment—which is not to be conceived of as a property, but rather as a way *of being*—can only be approached and described in holistic terms. The tool disappears behind its references, but these references, in turn, can only reveal themselves within a totality of references, and consequently within a totality of items of equipment, a *Zeugganzheit*. There is never, strictly speaking, any *isolated* implement. "Equipment—in accordance with its equipmentality—always is *in terms of [aus]* its belonging to other equipment: ink-stand, pen, ink, paper, blotting pad, table, lamp, furniture, windows, doors, room. These 'Things' never start by showing themselves as they are for themselves, and then make up a sum of *realia* [*Summe vom Realem*] to fill up a room. . . . *Before* this or that item, a totality of equipment [*Zeugganzheit*] has already been discovered."[18] Here takes place the transition from an inadequate characterization of the surrounding world in terms of sum (*Summe*) to a characterization in terms of whole or totality (*Ganzheit*). The world is not an addition of objects, have they the way of being of items of equipment; it is a structural totality in which each "thing" is only what it is insofar as it has the characteristics (those of referring to . . . or of being-for . . .) that it only has, in fact, when inserted in a totality of "things" possessing these same characteristics. Heidegger uses the word *Ganzheit*, literally "entirety," rather than that of "totality" (*Totalität*), probably in order to emphasize that a complex of equipment is an open totality, impossible to encompass in one's look, to which new items can always be added in principle. Commenting on an expression used repeatedly by Heidegger during this period, particularly in his courses, to characterize the world, "being as a whole" (*das Seiende im Ganzen*), Gadamer justly remarks that the goal of the philosopher was clearly to "avoid any and all thinking of 'totality' [*Totalität*], or 'absoluteness,' any thinking of a universal, comprehensive concept of Being."[19] The same is true here of the equipmental entirety (*Zeugganzheit*). The best translation of *Ganzheit* remains, however, "totality," for the essential reason that what Heidegger wishes to bring out is the priority of the whole to the part, which is the characteristic inherent in any holistic system: "In a workshop, for example, the totality of purpose that is constitutive for the ready-to-hand in its readiness-to-hand, is 'earlier' than any single item of equipment."[20] This totality of purpose ultimately refers to an entity that does not have the way of being of readiness-to-hand but that of a user, *Dasein* as Being-in-the-world. We must distinguish between the what-for (*Wozu*) which concerns a reference *among* items of equipment, and the for-the-sake-of-which (*Worum-willen*), which, for any equipmental complex, is necessarily *Dasein,* since every item of equipment only announces itself as such for the sake of a user that can make use of it, and that user himself possesses no purpose, no function; he is an entity that can *give itself* goals, that exists for its own sake (*umwillen seiner*), or yet again, to take up the consecrated formula to which we shall return later, it is an entity for which "in its very Being, this Being is an *issue.*" The ambivalence of the concept of *Verweisung* dissolves once we understand that there are references between items of equipment only insofar as there is a first "reference" of the items of equipment to a user and to its ends, the two kinds of referentiality, the *Wozu* and the *Worumwillen,* being conceptually distinct, though inseparable.

The surrounding world is therefore a "structural correlation" of references. "It is now a matter of discerning this peculiar structural correlation in which . . . references are encountered in a totality of the references and individual things are encountered in the references," Heidegger writes.[21] This structure is qualified as "surrounding world" (*Umwelt*) in *Being and Time.* The surrounding world, that is, the totality of the references of the *for* . . . , is more than the *sum* of these references: it forms an implicit, non-thematic background. Indeed, like the item of equipment, the surrounding world tends to go unnoticed when we are absorbed in it in the mode of concern.[22] This totality of references constituting the surrounding world can also be described in terms of "meaning." Indeed, the structure of the *for* . . . is a prelinguistic modality of meaning that use-objects present to me when I approach them in light of an understanding that is itself engaged in practices and inseparable from concern. These pragmatic meanings by virtue of which a thing appears to me as endowed with such or such function are prior to verbal meanings, which, in the conceptuality of *Being and Time,* do not, incidentally, accompany the utterance of words and sentences, but "found the possible

Being of words and of language."[23] The surrounding world, as totality of references preceding any particular reference and making it by this very fact possible, can, therefore, be characterized ontologically as "significance [*Bedeutsamkeit*]."[24] The world, though not thematic, manifests itself, "shines forth" as the permanent background of concern, to which belongs its own modality of consideration, its own "view," its own "knowledge" called by Heidegger *Umsicht*, overview, circumspection. Thus, the use of implements, as a power or a practical capability (*können* and *wissen* have meanings that are very close to each other in German),[25] possesses its own knowledge. This knowledge (being able) is a practical one that takes an overview on the totality of beings ready-to-hand and their references in order to make use of them for a given end. Circumspection, this knowledge or this seeing that is immanent in use as such, replaces from the point of view of "fundamental ontology" the classical concept of perception. To describe Being-in-the-world as sensible perception is to adhere both to a theoreticism and to an atomism of principle: on the one hand perception is a pure modality of the *theorein*, an observational grasp of the entity; on the other, in Heidegger's view, nothing forbids us to speak of an isolated perception. To advance that *Dasein*'s primordial relation to the world is pragmatic and concerned before being a mere perceptual observation amounts to saying that the world does *not* give itself on the basis of fragments of experience isolable from one another, but as an indecomposable, meaningful totality. What is more, the approach to the phenomenon of the world in terms of perception, because it misses the structural correlation of references, that is, the significance underlying the manifestation of the least implement as implement, misses the phenomenon of the world itself and ends up, to this extent, in a genuine "de-worlding" of experience. "This phenomenon [of the world]," Heidegger writes, "is really passed over when . . . the world is approached just as it shows itself in an isolated, so-called sense perception of a thing, and this isolated free-floating perception of a thing is now interrogated on the specific kind of givenness belonging to its object."[26] It is indeed of this "forgetting" of the world that Husserl was guilty. As a consequence, Heidegger's critique is less about Husserl's theoreticism for its own sake—since Heidegger pointedly emphasizes that concern's committed and absorbed way of being has its own "knowledge," its own "view" called "circumspection"—than about the atomism of a constitution by strata that pretends to reconstruct the whole world by an addition of heterogeneous layers of meaning. Mere perceiving (*Vernehmen*) is never primary, but is rather *derived* from circumspective concern: "The kind of dealing which is closest to us is . . . not a bare perceptual cognition, but rather that kind of concern which manipulates things and puts them to use; and this has its own kind of 'knowledge.'"[27] Pure perception is nothing but a limit-modality of our pragmatic commerce with entities which provides the background of our everyday existence. It is only when manipulation and use are no longer available that "the *perception* of the present-at-hand is consummated."[28]

As I said in the beginning, the analysis of equipmentality is not at all secondary for the purpose of *Being and Time*: it supports the entire weight of a holistically oriented critique of Husserlian phenomenology. Leaving aside the properly Heideggerian vocabulary, and to make it short, that critique may be presented as follows. It is not possible to reconstruct the experience of a hammer as I deal with it when I do some job around the house, for example, by distinguishing, in the phenomenon, an aesthesic or perceptual layer (the hammer-object with its form, its color, etc.) and a meaning (or a plurality of axiological predicates) that I would ascribe to it in addition. On the contrary, I have immediately to do with a hammer that only has its tool-meaning when inserted in its equipmental complex, which also includes the rules for handling it[29] depending on institutionalized practices. There is not, on the one hand, a given, and on the other a sense-bestowal, but rather the meaning of the hammer only becomes understandable in light of the overall context of its use by *Dasein*, be it mine or other, within a community of understanding and praxis. All meaning is *contextual* insofar as understanding is always concerned with a *totality of meaning*, a significance (*Bedeutsamkeit*), that is, a surrounding world (*Umwelt*) in which each entity announces itself as such, invested with the meaning that belongs to it.

It remains for us to ask ourselves whether this analysis of equipmentality can truly fulfill its function, that of leading us from a *partial* holism like Husserl's, for which experience remains a concatenation and a stratification of ideally distinct "lived experiences," to a true holism. To try to do justice to this question, we must examine some difficulties brought about by Heidegger's description.

(1) First, the ontology of equipment developed in *Being and Time* seems to furnish too narrow a basis to account for the diversity of human practices, and, correlatively, for the diversity of the meanings with which things, events, and situations can present themselves to us. Even if Heidegger extends the concept of *Zeug* beyond its normal meaning, tool (*Werkzeug*), his characterization of that "thing"[30] in terms of reference can only be valid for a very specific kind of "thing," and leaves out many aspects of our daily transactions with the entities that surround us. To say that our relationship with the world is primarily practical and engaged is one thing (for our practices are of several kinds); to say that it is primarily *instrumental* is quite another. Furthermore, at the very beginning

of §15 takes place a significant semantic shift. Heidegger begins with an analysis of *Zeug* in terms of use (*Umgang*)—a term whose meaning is very broad and can also be translated by "dealings," "acquaintance," "intercourse"—and subsequently replaces that notion with that of *Gebrauch,* "utilization," or even that of *Zeughaftigkeit, equipmentality or utensility.* But there is a significant difference between the use of the word in an Augustinian sense, on the one hand, and utilization or utensility, on the other, and the transition from the one concept to the other is neither made explicit nor truly justified by Heidegger. Now, many things that we understand prelinguistically and that take on meaning for us in light of our practical possibilities cannot be grasped in terms of functional references to something else: we understand actions, rites, intentional and unintentional gestures, facial expressions, works of art, games, and so on. None of the meanings these "things" take on for us can be interpreted in light of a tool's immanent referentiality. To understand the expression of a face or an unintentional gesture is to grasp the affective state, the mood or the ulterior motive they betray; to understand a painting can mean, among other things, to understand the motivations of the artist or the place of that work in the history of art; to understand a chess move is to grasp its strategic role, and consequently the intentions of the player. A painter has a practical relation to his subject; he even relates to it through *his entire practice,* that of painting. But this relation has nothing instrumental about it: the basket of fruit is not *for* the still life in the same sense in which the hammer is *for* hammering in a nail, nor the nail *for* hanging the painting on the wall. To be sure, Heidegger mentions entities that, although approached in light of the correlation of references of the surrounding world, do not themselves fully belong to that correlation. For example, some natural objects, he insists, do not belong to *readiness-to-hand,* but, as available "materials" or "forces," they are no less accessible in light of circumspective concern and its world. "In equipment that is used, 'Nature' is discovered along with it by that use—the 'Nature' we find in natural products. . . . The forest is standing timber, the mountain a rock quarry; the river is hydropower, the wind is 'in the sails.'"[31] In a sense, these natural materials may be called "present-at-hand [*vorhanden*]," but *that sense* of "presence-at-hand" does not coincide with the one pertaining to items of equipment that have become merely "present" due to a deficiency of circumspective concern, and therefore to a de-worlding of the surrounding world.[32] Nevertheless, the notion of "reference," inseparable from that of readiness-to-hand, cannot include all the diversity of meanings things can take on for us in light of the irreducible variety of our practices.

(2) The derivation of *theoria* from concern, which goes hand in

hand with the derivation of perception, is not itself without serious difficulties. It is true that for Heidegger it is not so much a question of *reversing* the traditional priority of *theoria* over praxis, such as it persists in Husserl, as of showing that praxis possesses its own *theoria*, its own "seeing": circumspection. Hence Heidegger's insistence that care (*Sorge*), that is, *Dasein*'s Being, "by no means expresses a priority of the 'practical' attitude over the theoretical. . . . 'Theory' and 'practice' are possibilities of Being for an entity whose Being must be defined as 'care.'"[33] Therefore, it is less a matter of conferring primacy to one of the two attitudes than of thoroughly rethinking their relationships. In a sense, it could be argued that the practical attitude, the absorbed coping that Heidegger calls "concern," is prior to conceptual and propositional thought which goes along with knowledge, strictly speaking. In another sense, however, if we consider that circumspection does pertain to prelinguistic *theoria*, that is to say, is a substitute for "perception" as a characterization of our primordial openness to the world—our experience—as such, then we should rather claim that theory and practice, perception and care, are *equiprimordial*. In short, what Heidegger undertakes to derivate in the economy of *Being and Time* is less the idea of "theory" in general than a naive conception of theory as an immediate contact with the entity, as a *pure* theory prior to all concerned coping with the world. It is *this* concept of theory that is still probably dominant in the Husserlian idea of a stratum of pure intuitive givenness of phenomenality preceding any interest and any practical position-taking (or evaluation).

But even on this point the analyses of *Being and Time* are not without ambiguity. Indeed, many passages suggest that the theoretical attitude, and particularly the scientific attitude, merely result from a deficiency of praxis, from a suspension of daily concern and dealings. "If knowing is to be possible as a way of determining the nature of the present-at-hand by observing it, then there must first be a *deficiency* in our having-to-do with the world concernfully."[34] This assertion raises problems both in itself and within the framework of *Being and Time*: (a) within the framework of fundamental ontology, since, if knowing is just a *deficient* modality of concern, demoted by this very fact to the level of improper or inauthentic existence, and if, furthermore, fundamental ontology itself is presented as a "science," a disastrous consequence follows: fundamental ontology is to be attributed to inauthenticity, to deterioration (*Verfallen*) of *Dasein*; (b) in itself, because the very possibility of a purely theoretical relationship with entities seems to have its source in *Dasein's* positive and specific capacities. As Heidegger objects to himself in a marginal note to his copy, this suspension of care, this "looking at [*Hinsehen*] does not occur merely by looking away [*Ab-sehen-von*]. Looking at has its own origin and has looking away as its necessary consequence. Observing [*Betrachten*] has its own primordiality. The look [*Blick*] to the *eidos* requires something different."[35] What must be said, then, is not that the purely observational notation of the entity *derives* from care, but conversely that care is always already at work in all *theoria,* in all observational view on something, whether prescientific (perceptual) or scientific. Not only does praxis possess its own modality of "knowing," but science itself is always *also* a praxis motivated by questions and interests, so that practice and theory must be conceived of, once again, as equiprimordial. Heidegger's self-critique coincides here with Husserl's critique in an unpublished manuscript of May 1931, titled "Against Heidegger," in which the founder of phenomenology points out that "intellectual curiosity," as an underlying motivation for scientific practices, cannot be reduced to the mere suspension of the "vital necessities" of concern. "No 'deficient' *praxis,*" he concludes, "is present here."[36]

But then the only thing that is really "derived," with regard to the practical-theoretical attitude of concern, is *a naive concept of theoria,* and it is this naive concept—and it alone—such as it continues to be expressed in the Husserlian conception of an intentional stratification of experience, that should be abandoned. Thus reformulated, the Heideggerian critique does not lose all its validity, but that validity is severely limited to a specific conception of *theoria,* and hence to a specific conception of perception. Only a perception understood as a science in its infancy—and a science itself understood as *pure theoria* which would be cut off from any practical interest—can be dismissed as a misconception of our primordial openness on the world. As Jacques Taminiaux remarks, "it is as if, from the outset, Heidegger imposed on perception a concept uncritically inherited from the tradition. . . . [His] deconstruction or its de-struction of the traditional theses reinforces them at the very moment when it might seem that it was shaking their foundations."[37] For, if perception is already structured by practices, as Erwin Strauss and Merleau-Ponty have suggested (see chapters 15 and 16, above), the project of deriving perception from an allegedly "more primordial" attitude loses all justification.

The questions that should be addressed to Heidegger are in substance the following. Would it not have been better to criticize the theoreticism at work in the Husserlian understanding of perception rather to try to *derive* perception itself, attributing it to *Dasein*'s deterioration and thereby conferring on the perceived thing the status of mere *vorhanden*? Furthermore, is it possible to do without perception? Did Heidegger succeed in this project? In speaking of the "encounter" (*Begegnung*) of *Dasein* with entities, or of the entities' "uncoveredness" (*Entdecktheit*) for

Dasein, did Heidegger replace traditional perception with a more adequate conceptuality, did he reform Husserl's descriptions, or did he not rather limit himself to change vocabulary? Did he succeed in eradicating the primacy of perception, that is, the primacy of an intuitive relation to things in which the latter present themselves in person and in the flesh, or was he content with *transposing* that intuitive givenness into the conceptuality of fundamental ontology?

(3) Heidegger's analyses raise one more final difficulty, by far the most serious. Heidegger basically shares Husserl's prejudice according to which it is meaningful to speak of an isolated perception. It is because Heidegger subscribes to an atomism of perception deeply rooted in the Cartesian tradition and its foundationalism, because he thinks of perception as a kind of knowledge that can be broken down into lived experiences—all intrinsically evaluable in terms of truth and falsity—that he opts for a holism of Being-in-the-world approached by the leading thread of equipmentality. Two problems follow from this. (a) If we are right in chapter 18, it is not necessary to assign a "derived" status to perception in order to promote a holism of Being-in-the-world; for perception *is* an intrinsically holistic phenomenon. (b) Conversely, there is no reason to assume that the property of being an item of equipment is a *sufficiently holistic* property to sustain all the weight of a holism of Being-in-the-world. Indeed, is it really true that there is never an isolated item of equipment? Let us imagine a new Robinson Crusoe shipwrecked on a desert island, who happens to have been able to salvage just one item of equipment from his cargo—a hammer, let's say. Would this hammer, stripped from the network of implements with which it makes up an equipmental complex, no longer possess the least function? To be sure, the use of this hammer would be radically modified: henceforth it would serve to break open coconuts or be a throwing weapon for the hunting of small prey, along the lines of aboriginal boomerangs. But just because the other items of equipment with which it is ordinarily used would have been withdrawn from circulation, it would not lose *all* function. It would not have any longer its usual use, but it would still keep *a* use. The new Robinson Crusoe would probably end up fashioning new implements, just as Daniel Defoe's hero did before him. But the idea that every implement, if it is to have a function, must take place among other implements, themselves possessing a function, is most debatable. So is the idea that what has a function in the first place isn't the implement itself, but the complex in which it is included. Heidegger, to tell the truth, furnishes no decisive argument to support this claim, and the existence of such an argument may be reasonably doubted. But then the consequence that Heidegger intends to draw from his example does not

follow. Even if we admit that *Dasein*'s relation to the world is primordially a practical one, and *in part only* an instrumental one, the analysis of the mode of being of implement does not furnish a phenomenologically sufficient basis for achieving an authentically holistic conception of Being-in-the-world.[38]

Moreover, Heidegger's holism, after the example of that of Husserl, remains a partial one. Just as, for the latter, the object serves as a "transcendental guideline" for the analysis of constitution, similarly, for the former, the tool plays an eminent role for the elucidation of the phenomenon of the surrounding world. "Ontologically," writes Heidegger, "'world' is not a way of characterizing those entities which *Dasein* essentially is *not*; it is rather a characteristic of *Dasein* itself. *This does not rule out the possibility that when we investigate the phenomenon of the 'world' we must do so by the avenue of an entity within-the-world and the Being which it possesses.*"[39] The avenue for the elucidation of the surrounding world passes through the implement (surprisingly in the singular) taken as a guideline. But the project consisting in "reconstructing," so to speak, the surrounding world (*Umwelt*) on the basis of a multiplicity of references between items of equipment, and therefore on the basis of the purposive relations that make of every tool a tool *for* other tools, is just as doomed to failure as the project of (re)constituting the world on the basis of a multiplicity of associative ties linking, within the universal passive genesis, at least ideally identifiable lived experiences. The world *must be already given as a unitary universal structure* for a plurality of tools to be able to refer to one another, to be functionally dependent one upon another, and thus to weave through their functionality that meaningful totality Heidegger calls *Bedeutsamkeit.* World cannot be *identical* with that functional totality. It is probably with that difficulty in mind that Heidegger actually juxtaposes *two* concepts of world: the *Umwelt* as the totality of functional references between tools, and the *Welt* as "characteristic of *Dasein* itself." This *Welt* is revealed for the first time by the mood of anxiety in §40 of *Being and Time,* but in fact it is tacitly presupposed by all the preceding analyses.

Heidegger will be led to acknowledge this in a 1928 course: far from making possible the elucidation of the phenomenon of world, the analysis of equipmentality *presupposes* it. "By the word 'world,'" he writes, "we cannot understand the ontical context of useful items, the things of historical culture, in contradistinction to nature and the things of nature. Yet the analysis of useful items and their context nevertheless provides a starting point and the means for first making visible the phenomenon of world. World is therefore not entities qua tools, as that with which humans have to deal, as if being-in-the-world meant to move among cultural items. Nor is world a multiplicity of human beings. Rather, all these entities belong to what we call intra-worldly entities, yet they are not the world itself."[40] The context of tools only provides a "starting point" for the highlighting of the phenomenon of world: the surrounding world cannot, therefore, *be identical* with that context itself. Incidentally, if the phenomenon of the world could be fully elucidated on the basis of a description of equipmentality, given that all tools are cultural and historical products, we would be led to the dangerously relativistic conclusion that someone who didn't share our culture (and did not understand our items of equipment) would not, strictly speaking, live in the same world as we do. But shouldn't we concur with Husserl on this point? Is not perceptual experience—whatever name we may give it—the common and universal ground of all our practices, a ground thanks to which we exist in the same world, in *a single and shared* world? This world that we share with others is inseparable from a common background of practices, at least in part "natural," without which there would be no living tie between men. Accordingly, even though it turned out to be true that perception is not a ground free from all praxis—Heidegger is right on this point—there is nevertheless a hierarchy in our practices, from the most elementary to the most complex and most dependent upon a culture, thanks to which there is no need to share all the "forms of life" of a given culture in order to share one and the same world with its representatives. Our primordial experience of the world cannot be cultural and historical *through and through* on pain of making the sharing of the world with other people, coming from other cultures, incomprehensible; and, at least on this point, Husserl should have the last word.

Still, it may be that Heidegger gives us—almost in spite of himself—"a next best course" as Plato would have said, to determine this enigmatic phenomenon of the world positively. In the same 1928 course, he makes the following characterization: the world is nothing other than "*das Ganze der wesenhaften inneren Möglichkeiten des Daseins*,"[41] the totality of the essential intrinsic possibilities of *Dasein*. The world is not only the *omnitudo realitatis*, the totality of the real, but also the *omnitudo possibilitatis*, the totality of the possibilities that come to light from a situation for a *Dasein*. Thus, openness to the world is always concerned by possibilities as well as actualities or presences: it is openness to what *can* be manifest to us as phenomenon at the same time as openness to possibilities in general. How is this assertion to be understood? How can we determine more precisely what is meant by "possibility" here?

Dasein is an entity that not only has possibilities as extrinsic characteristics, in the same way as a table "possesses" possibilities: it can be moved, damaged, restored, and so on. *Dasein* in its very Being *is possibility*. Its Being is a potentiality-for-Being (*Sein-können*) or a capacity to be—in this or that modality. It is this feature that Heidegger has in mind when he defines this entity ontologically by care, as the entity that cares about its Being, or rather about its to-be. *Dasein* is such that, in its Being, this Being is an issue for it. Therefore, it is such that, in its Being, its potentiality-for-Being is an issue for it. Far from it being the case that the Being of this entity is given it "ready-made," it is incumbent on *Dasein* to determine itself to be in this or that guise; its Being is a stake for it, about which it must continually decide. *Dasein* is the entity that must decide about itself and about its Being *sub specie possibilitatis* in order to make that Being possible for itself in existing (it) in a specific way. Its Being is first a Being-possible, in which "Being" and "possibility of being" are but one. *Dasein is* the possibility of its Being, that is, the possibility of determining itself as being in this or that modality, and more precisely, the possibility not only of determining itself as being in this or that way, but as being this or that kind of *Dasein. Dasein* has to be what it is. Heidegger characterizes positively in the following way this "possibility" about which it is incumbent on *Dasein* to exist it in the first person:[42]

> *Dasein* is not something present-at-hand which possesses its competence for something by way of an extra; it is primarily Being-possible. *Dasein* is in every case what it can be, and the way of being its possibility. The essential Being-possible of *Dasein* pertains to the guises—as we have characterized them—of concern with the 'world,' of solicitude for Others, and always already implied in all that, the being-able-to-be for itself, towards itself, for the sake of itself. The Being-possible which *Dasein* is existentially in every case is to be sharply distinguished from both empty logical possibility and the contingency of something present-at-hand considered as something to which this or that can 'happen.' As a modal category of presence-at-hand, possibility signifies what is *not yet* real and what is *not always* necessary. Such a possibility characterizes the *merely* possible. Ontologically it is on a lower level than reality and necessity. On the other hand, possibility as an *existentiale* is *Dasein*'s most primordial and ultimate positive ontological determinateness."[43]

Let us attempt to clarify what Heidegger means as concretely as possible. *Dasein* does possess an essence, Heidegger affirms, but that essence resides in its existence, that is, in its to-be (the one who it already is). *Dasein* always already responds to Pindar's injunction: "Become what you are!"[44] It possesses its Being in such a way that it has always to be (this Being) in a determinate and specific way by determining itself to be (it) this way, or otherwise. Here, "determining oneself to be" simply means: deciding about its ownmost, most intimate possibilities. More simply stated, *Dasein,* by essence, exists in such a way that it has to form not only particular projects, but *projects of life or of existence.* A project of life is a project that engages me totally, that is, that engages "the idea I have of myself," or again, that concerns who I aspire to be.

Up to this point, the concept of "possibility" has remained to some extent indeterminate in Heidegger's usage. Let us try to clarify that usage. And to do this, let us attempt to comment more closely on Heidegger's characterization of potentiality-for-Being or capability-of-being—in order to better understand the aforementioned characterization of the world.

1. First, in the passage we are focusing on, Heidegger attempts to elucidate the meaning of possibility that corresponds to *Dasein*'s way of being, existence (*Existenz*), as opposed to two ways of being which can only befall *Dasein* by confusion with the rest of entities: presence-at-hand (*Vorhandenheit*) and readiness-to-hand (*Zuhandenheit*). However, contrary to what has sometimes been suggested,[45] Heidegger does not deny that *Dasein* is *also* an entity that can rightfully be characterized as "present-at-hand." On the contrary, he claims that "human *Dasein* 'is' in such a way that, although it is an entity, it is never solely present-at-hand."[46] The characterization of *Dasein* as something present-at-hand is not false; it is not primordial enough. To be sure, the *Dasein* that "is co-determined by corporeality [*Leiblichkeit*]"[47] is *also* an entity that exists in the world in the same way as does a table or a chair. When a doctor orders a scan for his patient, he considers him *also* as a mere thing in the world, but he does not consider him *only* that way. Here the whole emphasis is on the "also" and the "only," just as when Kant says that it is our duty always to treat the other *also* as an end and never as a means *only.*

2. *Seinkönnen* might be better expressed in English as "capability-of-being." *Dasein* not only *has* capabilities, it *is* that fundamental capability to determine itself to be in this or that way—and to be this or that kind of *Dasein.* The assertion that *Dasein* not only has capabilities but *is* its capability (to be) is not merely a stylistic or rhetorical phrase. Heidegger's purpose here is that of entirely de-substantializing the "spirit" or the "soul" by conceiving of them, not as substances or entities, but as *a bundle of capabilities and powers* already involving the world (see chapter 16);[48] in short, Heidegger pushes Husserl's anti-psychologism to its ultimate consequences. Like other animals, man not only possesses capabilities; he also possesses the second-order capability of acquiring capabilities. But unlike other species, he has the capability of acquiring these capabilities *by himself,* and not only due to external circumstances or to passive socialization within a group. Man (or *Dasein*)[49] can, therefore, make himself capable of this or that—by deciding to do so. *Dasein* is "capable" in the sense that it possesses, in addition to its "natural" capabilities, capabilities

for existence, that is to say, the capability to give itself autonomously this or that form of existence.

3. The key point of this whole passage is the distinction—which remains elliptic—between different sorts of possibility. Heidegger mentions, alongside the existential possibilities of which he is speaking, logical possibilities, and he asserts that the existential possibilities are not accountable on the basis of a *modal* conception of possibility—namely, a conception of possibility that is formalizable within the framework of modal logic. This assertion seems surprising, and we could easily believe that it amounts to a mere rejection of logic. As we will see, this is far from being the case.

It must be recognized that Heidegger does not clarify further this distinction between several senses of "being possible." Let us try to perform this task in his place, since it is of the greatest importance if we are to understand what he means. If I say that I *can* now—or that *it is possible for me* now—to take the path through the rocks to go swimming, I could mean several things: (a) that is not logically contradictory; (b) that is not incompatible with my essence: it is possible with respect to what it is to be the kind of being I am; (c) it is physically possible, in the sense of empirically possible: that does not transgress the laws of physics—the laws of gravity, for example (as opposed to what would be the case if I said: "I can propel myself to the stars by my own power alone"); (d) it is physically possible in another sense of the word "physically": I have the bodily *capacity* of doing it; I *can* move, swim; (e) nothing in my situation prevents me from doing it: I have time and leisure for it; or yet again I have the *opportunity* to do so; (f) that is in accordance with my inclinations, my character; (g) nothing forbids me to do it, no "No Swimming" sign is to be seen. (This list is not meant to be exhaustive.)

It is important for us to distinguish between these different senses of "can" and of "is possible," because Heidegger seems to mean *several things at once* by his concept of "potentiality-for-Being." The meaning he gives to this expression is both very specific—I shall return to this point—and, at times at least, relatively indeterminate. Potentiality-for-Being in the sense in which *Being and Time* speaks of it indicates first *Dasein*'s capabilities (whence my translation: capability-of-being). Such capabilities refer to this ultimate "I can," as Husserl called it, that is formed by a living body in possession of its resources. All my powers (in that sense) refer to this fundamental power over myself that is given to me with the fact of having a body or of being a body, that is, a source of potential actions.

If the sense of "can" favored by Heidegger in "potentiality-for-Being" is that of capability, we can understand what distinguishes this meaning from several others mentioned above. For example, "it is physically possible for me to go swimming" is ambiguous because sometimes "physically" refers to the physical sciences (the possibility in question is based on an empirical generalization), and sometimes to the "physical" body. In this last case, it is not at all an empirical truth that I can actualize or not actualize, according to my will and the circumstances, that capability that I possess, but it is an *a priori* truth about *what it is* to have a capability of this sort: if someone has the capability to do something and the opportunity to do it, and if, furthermore, he has the will to do it—then, all other things being equal, he will do it. Such capabilities are within the power of the agent (which does not mean that it is entirely up to the agent to possess them or not); they are actualized at will, in the sense that no conjunction of circumstances can *necessitate* an agent's to actualize them.

Not only are practical capabilities not understandable in terms of empirical generalizations, but, as Heidegger overtly states, they are not even conceivable in conformity with the formalism of modal logic: they are not "logical possibilities." Why not? Heidegger does not answer that question, but we can try to do so for him. One of the fundamental theorems of modal logic is: *ab esse ad posse valet consequentia.* What is real is also thereby possible. But significantly, this theorem does *not* apply to capabilities. I can pull off a "hole in one" once in my life without ever being able to repeat such an exploit. From the fact this feat is actual it does not follow that I am capable of it. A single success is not a sufficient condition to attribute a capability to someone.[50] What is more, in modal logic disjunction is distributive: "It is possible that *p* or *q*" is equivalent to "It is possible that *p* or it is possible that *q*." In some cases this applies to capabilities as well. For example, "It is possible that I go out or that I stay home" amounts to "It is possible that I go out or it is possible that I stay home." But this is not always the case. From a pack of cards, I can pick up at will either a red or a black card, but it does not follow that I can either pick up at will a red card or pick up at will a black one.[51] If disjunction is not always distributive in the case of capabilities, it follows that capabilities are difficult to formalize within the framework of modal logic. Therefore Heidegger is on solid ground when he maintains that what he calls "potentiality-for-Being" cannot be accounted for in terms of "logical possibilities."

However, *Dasein* does not exercise its capabilities without qualification: it exercises them according to circumstances, that is to say, according to the possibilities that its practical situation affords it. Thus, potentiality-for-Being, that permanent capaciy of anticipation that structures human existence, goes hand in hand with "thrownness" (*Geworfenheit*) in the world, that is, with the fact of being immersed in a situation.

This connection is an essential one. "In every case," Heidegger writes, "*Dasein* has already gotten itself into determinate possibilities. As the potentiality-for-Being that it *is*, it has already passed other possibilities by, it comes to grips with the possibilities of its Being; it seizes them, and seizes itself, correctly or mistakenly."[52] In other words, "*Dasein* is Being-possible which has been delivered over to itself—thrown possibility through and through [*durch und durch geworfene Möglichkeit*]."[53] *Dasein* only has or *is* a Being-possible on the condition that possibilities are given to it from the context of a situation, that is to say, that it understands the overall cast of the situation as affording this or that possibility. Thrownness means being delivered over to myself and assigned to a world I neither wanted nor chose, to a situation into which I am thrust and the contours of which I do not always perceive clearly, but from which I must draw possibilities—*opportunities.* On the occasion of this clarification, we can see that Heidegger would have been well-advised to distinguish more sharply between various concepts of possibility. Granted, the opportunities that a situation offers *Dasein* are relative to its capabilities. Opportunities can only be seized or missed by an entity possessing the corresponding capabilities. But the converse is just as true: the capabilities of *Dasein* can only be exercised in relevant circumstances, that is, according to opportunities. Capabilities and opportunities are structurally linked and the latter cannot be reduced to the former. We have here two *different* senses of possibility. This remark will be of importance for what follows.

With these two senses of "possibility"—capabilities and opportunities—we have acquired the tools necessary to analyze a basic example such as the one brought up in chapter 16. I am at the edge of the rocky ledges and see the water down below. The sea appears to me adorned with the sparkle of sunlight and my joyful sense of bodily well-being: it invites me to go for a swim. At this point, no reasoning is necessary, and the appetitive vectors presented to me by the sea stretching out before me are given to me directly at the perceptual level. But sometimes things become a bit more complex. I may begin to think: Can I go swimming? Is it allowed? Is it appropriate? Here "I can" means: I am authorized to do it; no norm, no rule forbids me to do it . . . "After all," I may add, to myself, "I'm on vacation, there's nothing else I'm supposed to be doing." Here we have a sense of "possibility" that is related to specifically human social institutions; no animal would have such concerns. This sense also relates to *customs* that have a normative dimension. On the French Riviera, swimming became fashionable due to wealthy Americans just after the First World War. No one used to go swimming before their arrival. The beach at Gausse's Hotel is almost empty at the beginning of *Tender Is the Night.*

But it is not this sense of "possible" that Heidegger is mainly interested in. The meaning he wishes to highlight is one that he himself calls "existential." What is it? From my high perch in the rocks I can begin a new soliloquy, and address a different kind of issue. Assuming that I am capable of going swimming, that the circumstances are favorable (the sea is calm, accessible, I know how to swim), and that I have a real yen to go in; assuming nothing forbids me to do so, should or should I not go ahead? Can I? Yes or no? These questions no longer have anything to do with "proprieties," morals, conventions, with what I do or do not have the right to do (from the point of view of morals, swimming is intrinsically neither good nor bad): they concern an entirely different realm of considerations. The problem is whether or not I can go swimming from the point of view of the kind of *Dasein* (or human being) I aspire to be. Is it worthy of me to lie around all day in the sun doing nothing? Is that how I want to live? Is *that* what I want to do with my life? Wouldn't it be better for me to go home and get to work? To finish the book I am working on, for example? Here we have a new kind of possibility, an "existential" possibility, in Heidegger's terminology. Something is "possible" in the existential sense if it is compatible with the sort of "being" (of entity, of *Dasein*) I aspire to be—if it is in keeping with the way I understand myself, with the way I see or envision my own existence. In other words, something is possible, in the existential sense, if it is in conformity with a life project, or a project of existence.

Dasein is an entity such that, in its Being, that Being is in each case an issue for it: now we understand the meaning of that expression. It is an entity for which it makes sense to raise the question of its Being, that is to say, the question of what kind of *Dasein* it wants to be, how it should spend its lifetime, what it wants to do with its existence. This last question is entirely foreign to the animal. It requires a high degree of culture and is part of an interrogation involving language in an essential way. To be or not to be? To be this way or some other way? To do this or something else with its Being? All this is concealed to the animal. These questions bring into play a singular—and signal—capability, which is one with man's mode of existence itself, a mode of existence that consists in caring about one's own existence, in taking a vital interest in that existence as such, and therefore in having to decide about it. In being *umwillen seiner*: for the sake of itself.

It is this capability that Heidegger has in mind with the expression "capability-of-being," *Seinkönnen*. A practical capability *in general* is a capability exercised *ad libitum*, which nothing prevents us from attributing to other higher animals. A dog probably can't *decide* to go and find the stick thrown to him, if deciding involves a preparatory deliberation, that is, a reasoning about possibilities, the imagining of counterfactual situations, and so on. But a dog can either go after the stick or not do so. Having that capability, it can exert it *ad libitum.* Capability-of-being, however, is of a different nature, it concerns what Heidegger calls "existentiality," "to-be" (*Zu-sein*). Through this capability-of-being, it is a matter of taking over one's existence as such—or, on the contrary, of shifting its burden onto others—in order to give it this or that orientation. This is why Heidegger emphasizes that this capability-of-being has nothing to do with a specific plan, a project for action among others. It is rather something like a fundamental project responding to a deep aspiration regarding our existence as such and as a whole, a global project of existence. To understand oneself in light of a fundamental project (which can include several subordinate projects) is still "to understand" in the sense of "to know how to handle a situation," but it is in fact to know how to handle *one's existence itself,* so to speak, and not one or another of its aspects that would only concern *Dasein* under a spectific viewpoint. The way I understand myself is the very way I am, the way I exist my *Dasein,* the way I make something of my existence. A *Dasein* is certainly able to understand other things than himself, but its basic understanding as *Dasein* is about its own Being as such; what for it gives itself to be understood in the first place is its existence itself.

What would not apply to other capabilities deriving from its bodily constitution, from circumstances, and so on, does therefore apply to that signal capability: the possibility in question, as Heidegger specifies, "is the possibility it is only if *Dasein* exists in it."[54] Indeed, to refuse to decide on its Being is still, for *Dasein,* a way of deciding on it—in the modality of a decision by default of decision. Existence is the burden of *Dasein* not occasionally, but always, by virtue of its very essence. Hence the distinction—a capital one, in Heidegger's view—between occasional plans, which *Dasein* can have *or not have,* and the fundamental project of existence which it can never entirely escape.

> The character of understanding as projection is constitutive for Being-in-the-world with regard to the disclosedness of its existentially constitutive state-of-Being by which the factical potentiality-for-Being gets its leeway [*Spielraum*]. And as thrown, *Dasein* is thrown into the kind of Being which we call 'projecting.' Projecting has nothing to do with comporting oneself towards a plan that has been thought out, and in accordance with which *Dasein* arranges its Being. On the contrary, any *Dasein* has, as *Dasein,* already projected itself; and as long as it is, it is projecting. As long as it is, *Dasein* has always understood itself and always will understand itself in terms of possibilities.[55]

Dasein, as long as it is, is projecting: this means that *Dasein* does not limit itself to projecting itself occasionally toward the future by sketching out plans that it would later have to carry out, but that it *is* its fundamental project, the project of its Being, because it cannot be in the mode of a *Dasein*, that is to say, in the mode of existence, without determining itself to be in conformity with a fundamental project, a project of life or of existence. Existence is such that one must project oneself into it and make it possible in this or that way in order for it to be the *existence* it is.

Such a project involving existence itself as a whole only takes shape against the background of the closure of *Dasein*'s possibilities, that is to say, of *Dasein's* essential finitude or mortality. Heidegger gives the name "resoluteness" to the anticipation of death in the light of which *Dasein* grasps itself as finite, and, consequently, decides on the meaning of its existence. Indeed it is only because *Dasein* is finite, because it cannot "live all lives," that it must decide about who it has to be. Resoluteness, anticipation of death, confronts it with the *necessity* of choosing, that is, of determining itself to this or that existence, to exist its existence in the modality of a coherent project. Such a choice is inescapable, and this is why existential possibilities are possibilities that no *Dasein* can entirely elude. But *Dasein* can *attempt* to escape them by refusing to choose, that is, by delegating this choice to others, by letting the sense of its own existence be determined by the vox populi, or rather by what Heidegger calls the "they" (*das Man*). Resolving to exist in the first person, to decide for oneself on one's existence is the possibility opposing the renunciation to all decision in which *Dasein* leaves it up to the "they," to decide in its place. The first possibility, that of an existence that is one's own, in which *Dasein* decides on its Being because it has taken over its own finitude, is called by Heidegger "authentic [*eigentliche*] existence"; the second, in which *Dasein* alienates its decision, delegating it to "the voice of the 'they,'" to what *they* consider to be the best, is characterized as "inauthentic [*uneigentliche*] existence." But this refusal to choose remains a way of choosing, since an entity that *exists* in the strong sense Heidegger gives this term is placed before the *necessity* of deciding on its Being, and not to decide is still a way of deciding on it.

To exist properly speaking is therefore to resolve to decide on one's existence in the face of the surrounding indecision in which *Dasein* stands "primarily and for the most part," *to decide oneself against indecision and in favor of decision itself.* Resoluteness is that decision to decide. In it is rooted the possibility of a second-order choice,[56] as Charles Taylor calls it, that is to say, in the possibility of a choice not of this or that possibility, but of the kind of *Dasein* I aspire to be. Only a *Dasein* possessing the signal capability of resoluteness—of deciding oneself in favor of decision itself—can make second-order choices allowing it to form a fundamental project for itself, that is, a project bearing upon its existence itself as a whole.[57] Since the decision to decide about one's Being—and therefore the assumption of the necessity to which it is subjected by virtue of its very existence to determine itself in favor of this or that way of being—is what makes possible, for *Dasein*, the second-order choice of the kind of *Dasein* it wants to be, Heidegger argues that it is resoluteness itself that makes possible all *Dasein*'s factical possibilities. "When," he writes, "by anticipation, one becomes free *for* one's own death in anticipation [that is, resoluteness], one is liberated from one's lostness in those possibilities which may accidentally thrust themselves upon one; and one is liberated in such a way that for the first time one can authentically understand and choose among the factical possibilities lying ahead of that possibility which is not to be outstripped [death]." And therefore "the possibility is disclosed because it is made possible in anticipation [that is, in resoluteness]."[58] It is in the extreme and ineluctable possibility of death that all the factical possibilities of *Dasein* have their origin, because it is the acute consciousness of its own finitude that constrains that entity to put order in its possibilities, that is, to acquire such a thing as a coherent project of existence.

We are beginning to catch sight of the meaning of the Heideggerian characterization of the world as the "totality of the intrinsic essential possibilities of *Dasein*." The possibilities in question are existential possibilities that only "exist" if *Dasein* projects itself into them—and into which *Dasein* does not project itself in a contingent way, since it belongs to what it is for *Dasein* to *exist* that it *must* necessarily project itself into them. These possibilities form a coherent whole because *Dasein*, being mortal, cannot avoid the choice of *one* specific existence. All the factical possibilities, all the occasional projects that *Dasein* may or may not have also depend on this second-order decision, on this existential project. There are never for *Dasein* isolated possibilities: its possibilities are ordered according to a hierarchy of means and ends such that some possibilities are subordinated to others, some projects to other projects, the fundamental project upon which all the others depend being a global project of existence. *Dasein* thus possesses a *system* of structured and hierarchized possibilities in which the occasional projects refer *in fine* to a general project of existence by virtue of which they only acquire their unity and coherence.

Therefore, the world is clearly not a mere addition of entities, of facts, or of states of affairs ("ontic" concept of the world); it is an organized and structured totality of possibilities relative to capabilities of several kinds, in light of which all that can present itself to *Dasein* takes on a meaning—possibilities that are subordinated to this signal capability of *Dasein* to choose itself and its Being.

If this free reconstruction—in which I have tried, as much as possible, to leave aside some of the subtleties of the Heideggerian lexicon—is in conformity with the spirit of *Being and Time*, we can now better see the strength of Heidegger's position. His conception raises several problems, however, and I would like to address these problems in conclusion.

As I have emphasized, Heidegger does not distinguish clearly between the different senses of "possibility" that I have enumerated. He proceeds as if *all* the possibilities contained in the world, or rather, all the possibilities in which the world *consists*, were possibilities in the existential sense of the term, that is to say, possibilities such as *Dasein* makes them possible, or "possibilizes" them by projecting itself into them. As he writes, "what is possible only essentially prevails in its possibility if we bind ourselves to it in its possibilization."[59] By virtue of this hypertrophic conception of the powers of *Dasein* it is as if the exemplary being possibilized all the possibilities—according to a single meaning of the verb "to possibilize"—and, as a consequence, possibilized *the world itself*. Indeed, if the world is the totality of the intrinsic possibilities of *Dasein* (and "intrinsic" means: into which *Dasein* has always already projected itself, and which it itself *is* by existing), and if *all* possibility is made possible by the finite project of a potentiality-for-Being—that is, by what Heidegger calls "resoluteness"—it follows that *Dasein* configures the world by existing. And this is indeed the conclusion reached by fundamental ontology: *Dasein* "projects a world for itself, and it does this not subsequently and occasionally but, rather, the projecting of the world belongs to the *Dasein*'s Being."[60] Consequently, "the world is something *Dasein*-ish. It is not present-at-hand like things but it is *da*, there-here, like the *Dasein*, the Being-da [*das Da-sein*] which we ourselves are: that is to say, it exists."[61] The world is only a structural moment in the unitary structure Heidegger calls "Being-in-the-world."

Of course Heidegger does not mean that *Dasein* creates heaven and earth, the direction of the wind and the shape of the clouds. He rather stresses that *Dasein* "has been brought into its 'there,' but *not* of its own accord."[62] It must be born into a world that precedes it and that it did not itself want or conceive. But nothing is said of this world or of that birth. On the contrary, it is as if the only relevant world from the standpoint of a phenomenology were the one *Dasein fashions* by its finite ontological project. That world remains a "subjective" world in the sense of the "well-understood concept of the 'subject,'"[63] *Dasein* as Being-in-the-world. Here Heidegger is very close to Husserl: he *transposes* onto the "practical" level an argument that in Husserl's view was valid on a theoretical level. From the fact that there are only possibilities (in the sense of possibilities contained within a situation—that is to say, opportunities) *for Dasein*, in conformity with its capabilities, it would be legitimate to conclude that *Dasein*, on the basis of its existence, that is to say, on the basis of a manifold of capabilities and behaviors, "forms" these possibilities, "possibilizes" them, and consequently possibilizes and forms the world itself. Just as the Husserlian ego was not only the one *for* (*für*) which there is a world, but also the one *in* (*in*) and *setting out from (aus) which* the world in its meaning and validity is constituted, similarly, *Dasein* is not only, on the basis of its practical capabilities, the entity *for* which there is possibility, but the entity *through which* there is possibility and *by virtue of which* the world reigns, the "world-forming" entity, as Heidegger calls it. Hence the world remains a transcendental structure,[64] "a characteristic of *Dasein* itself."[65]

By distinguishing between various senses of "possible," it would have been relatively easy to avoid this consequence. *Dasein* cannot possibilize the possible *as such* for the very good reason that possibility can be taken in many acceptations. The world is the totality of what manifests itself to us, but also of what *can* manifest itself to us as meaningful in light of our practical capabilities. But in what sense of "can"? In *several* senses! Some of the possibilities that announce themselves to us in a situation are empirical possibilities. We can expect it to rain tomorrow on the basis of weather forecasting, that is, by means of generalizations belonging to that science. This possibility only pertains to the situation in which we find ourselves because we are *capable* of generalizations of this type. But of course the fact that this possibility only exists in relation to a capability of *Dasein*, that of making accurate forecasts grounded on empirical knowledge, or, to put it otherwise, the fact that this possibility depends on *Dasein in order to be grasped and understood as possibility*, does not entail that it depends on *Dasein in an unqualified way*, nor that it is "made possible" by it. Many other possibilities, necessities, and impossibilities depend on *Dasein* without being "formed" by that entity. Consider, for example, logical possibilities and necessities; or, alternatively, possibilities and impossibilities concerning essence. These possibilities and necessities are referred to corresponding abilities: the ability to think logically, the ability to bring essential necessities to light. The world, the structured totality of possibilities and impossibilities *in these various senses of "possibility"* (empirical, logical, essential), is always also a horizon of anticipations and expectations that remain in large part implicit and call upon these same resources.

For example, when it is a matter of the *opportunities* that present themselves to *Dasein* in a given situation, it makes no sense to say that they are *made possible* by it, because they pertain to a different meaning of possibility than the *capabilities* of this entity. It is true that all opportunities can only be grasped by a *Dasein* possessing the corresponding capabilities; but it is no less true that every capability can only be exercised if a situation is presented to *Dasein* that lends itself to it. Opportunity and capability are *mutually* interdependent. Furthermore, the capabilities of *Dasein* do not all depend on it in the sense that it could decide to have them or not: acquired capabilities can only be acquired on the basis of innate capabilities. Incidentally, these capabilities are different in kind, and cannot be reduced to one. While it is true that Heidegger makes a decisive contribution to the phenomenology of the *human* world in showing that man has a signal capability that separates him radically from the rest of the living realm, that of giving himself such a thing as a project of existence—a capability that is the product of the highest refinement of a culture and involves language in an essential way (by virtue of this capability-of-being, the possibilities that the world grants *Dasein* are far more ample and complex than those of any other living being)—it is no less true that Heidegger is wrong in collapsing the varied array of capabilities into that one sole capability-of-being, and in thereby reducing the "natural" world to the "existential" one.

As long as we remain at the level of "natural" aptitudes, such as going for a swim or eating a piece of fruit, a first concept of the world emerges: the totality of all that can appear to us as invested with meanings in light of our practical possibilities. Let us call it "natural world" or "surrounding world." Animals also have a world in this sense, though it might involve other abilities than the ones we have. That world is a structured and hierarchized totality of possibilities ultimately relating to biological ends. But while the animal's capabilities are a given—so that if it has the capability to acquire new capabilities, it does not have the capability to acquire them *by itself*, because it does not possess the signal capability of forming such a thing as a project of existence—the capabilities on the basis of which the world and things take on a meaning for man are far more complex. Man has in particular the capability of calling into question his own Being, of deliberating and deciding about himself *sub specie possibilitatis*. The possibilities in light of which things take on meaning for him are considerably more varied, and consequently the meaning in question is considerably more difficult to make explicit. The sea appears to me to favor a swim, but only if I allow myself to do it, and only if the fact of going for a dive and then lazing in the sun matches the kind of existence that seems desirable for me at that moment—that is, if it matches my deep aspirations and the idea I have of myself and of my Being.

But there is more. In stressing the capability-of-being and the power of self-determination of *Dasein,* Heidegger has tended to obscure another dimension, its *vulnerability to the event.* Indeed, *Dasein*'s ability to decide who it is to be on the basis of its factical situation is always rooted in propensities, tendencies, predispositions that it has not itself made possible, but that come from its entire past history. *Dasein* is not an autarkic freedom to choose itself in the face of a situation that is of the nature of a pure facticity; it is always involved in all kinds of histories, caught up in the complex web of a destiny originating in inaugural events—its own birth, to begin with. Its situation always appears to it in light of these events and its past history. Its freedom does not lie in the autarky of a pure ontological project that would have full authority over facticity and would utterly master it; it is rather an ability to come to itself [*advenir à soi-même*] out of what happens to it [*lui advient*], and thus to make of what is beyond it, of what definitively transcends its powers, the lever of a constitutive transformation, an ability to *become other* through what happens to him, and in so doing *to become itself.* Exposed to the reign of the event, human existence can only appropriate its possibilities against the background of its immeasurable exposure to what, in respect to its expectations and projects, remains strictly im-possible: the event as such. An event is not only an unimaginable change from the point of view of my expectations: it is first and foremost what puts the fundamental projects in light of which I understand myself and my own existence in crisis—my possibilities in the existential sense—reconfiguring them through and through. And since the possibilities that structure the world form a system, since for a *Dasein* there are never any isolated possibilities, some transformations in its existence strike the possible as such at its root: they no longer allow it to understand itself existentially as "the same." They upend possibilities as a whole—the world in the existential sense—by casting a new light on it. I will not pursue this question of the event further, which is strangely absent from *Being and Time,* since I have developed it elsewhere; it will suffice to refer the reader to these analyses.[66]

These remarks furnish the initial elements of a solution to the problem I raised at the beginning of this chapter. The question was: what status should we attribute to meaning understood as immanent to experience itself? With Heidegger, I stressed the difficulties inherent in a conception of meaning (1) as conferred by a consciousness by means of an a-contextual sense-bestowal; (2) as being layered in heterogeneous strata: at the lowest level, perception, and, built upon it, so to speak, a pragmatic commerce with things, which invests them with value-predicates and elevates them to the level of a "spiritual" and cultural world. In opposition to the idea of an intentional stratification, it must be maintained that our primordial experience of things always approaches them already in the light of practical possibilities *of several levels*—and not just those concerning the use of implements. Perception is not of the order of a *theoria* in which the object would be given as an in-itself, regardless of our interests and capabilities; it is always permeated with meanings that things take on for us in light of our intelligent practices.

Thus, meaning only surfaces in experience as a holistic property of the system formed by a world and a subject endowed with understanding—understanding resting in turn on a variety of practical abilities. In the preceding chapter, I enumerated two kinds of holistic properties: sometimes, holistic properties (as relational properties) are not possessed by the parts of a whole unless other parts possess *the same* properties; sometimes, these properties are only possessed by the parts if other parts possess *other* properties. The characteristic of experience to bear within itself an immanent meaning obeys both these models at once. According to the first model, *a thing only possesses meaning in relation to other things that possess a meaning and to an overall situation.* The overall meaning of the situation determines the meaning of one or another of its aspects, and conversely. What has meaning in the first place is the situation, and only derivatively each of its aspects. Moreover, since a situation always contains many unperceived aspects, a reinterpretation of the meaning of that situation—and hence also of one or another of its aspects—always remains possible in principle. According to the second model, things can only be presented in experience as imbued with meaning relative to a "subject" endowed with understanding, who approaches them in light of his or her practical capabilities—practical abilities that already involve a world—in such a way that *meaning is a holistic property of the system that a subject forms with its world.* An experience only possesses the property of being meaningful if another "part" of the system, the subject, possesses complementary properties: a capacity of understanding and a set of practical capabilities. Being-in-the-world is a relational and holistic structure, and this is why it cannot be conceived of in the terms of a transcendental philosophy, in which the subject, and the subject alone, would play the role of ultimate "condition of possibility."

The capabilities in light of which things take on meaning for us are of several kinds: "natural" capabilities that we share with other living beings, capabilities that depend on a specifically human culture, capabilities-of-being in the Heideggerian sense, that is, capabilities to determine oneself in favor of one or another type of existence, which man alone possesses. This hierarchy of capabilities gives rise, not to different worlds, but to different possible *descriptions* of the world: the natural world of perception, in which what is presented to us is approached in the light of "natural" capabilities, in which a piece of fruit, for example, appears to us as edible and a path easy to follow (here we are situated at the level of Straus's "appetitive vectors" or Gibson's *affordances*); a cultural world, in which a seascape may suddenly bring to mind Cézanne's *L'Estaque* or the fauvists; and finally the existential world, in which things appear invested with a singular historical meaning according to who we have become or aspire to be. To speak of "hierarchy" here is not the same as speaking of "stratification." Far from it being possible to isolate several strata of phenomenality corresponding to so many (natural, psychophysical, or spiritual) "worlds," it is rather one selfsame world, *the* single and shared world, that is understood in light of several capacities, some presenting a continuity with the reign of living beings, others that separate us from them in a radical way. Moreover, against Heidegger, it must be argued that existential possibilities rest on natural ones, and do not replace them; the existential world does not annul the natural world but is the result of the taking into consideration of capabilities and possibilities of a higher level. The natural world is no more derived from the historical and existential one than perception is derived from concern.

These assertions entail another last consequence. By characterizing meaning as a holistic property of the system that a subject endowed with practical capabilities forms with its world, we have acquired a concept of *meaning* sufficiently broad to include both prelinguistic *and* linguistic meaning. For language is also an eminently practical capacity possessed by the human being. It is only if we accept a prelinguistic meaning, that is, a comprehension that is actualized in the very register of our sensibility—and not just in what we do and say—that we can also understand how that spontaneous intelligence is no less at work in our experience of language than in all other domains. Indeed, isn't language experienced? I read this sentence, I hear these words, and I immediately understand their meaning without decipherment or exegesis. Their meaning gives itself to me in the very experience that I have of these characters, of these sounds, without there being any place for a clear-cut dichotomy between sensibility and intellect. Of course, it would be spurious to deny that language is a social acquisition; but our intelligence of language is not only a matter of a special faculty that we develop by means of a specific learning process: it is in direct continuity with our "general" intelligence, and draws on the same resources. Without *that prelinguistic dimension of language itself*, by virtue of which it prolongs perception—for example, the experience we have of a gesture or a face—the properly linguistic aspect of verbal meaning and comprehension would remain ever a dead letter for us.

Only this remark allows us to confer on language its just place and importance—no more, nor less—in the economy of human intelligence as it comes to grips with the world. It allows us to think linguistic understanding, as a socially acquired capability, not as an empire within an empire, but as the prolongation of our bodily being-in-the-world. It does so by avoiding two dangerous extremes: believing that linguistic meaning is the only meaning that can surface in experience, so that experience, if it possesses lineaments of intelligibility, must draw them from language alone—a permanent temptation of an "analytic Kantianism" that we will examine later (see chapter 19); conceiving of language as an "unproductive stratum" of expression,[67] and therefore *reducing* the linguistic meaning to the prelinguistic meaning that it allows to make explicit, and suggest that the appearance of language does not upend our entire being-in-the-world—a temptation that Husserl has not always resisted.

19

The Myths of the Given and the Kantian Framework

> For if you agree to abandon the dogma that "percepts without concepts are blind," as Kant put it, a deep theoretical mess, a genuine quagmire, will dry up.
>
> —James J. Gibson

One of philosophers' sports and pastimes is to trace the genealogy of a theory, to outline a grand narrative at the end of which a trend or a school is placed at the summit of a doctrinal lineage as its crowning achievement. In *The Mirror of Nature*, Rorty presents a history of this kind, according to which the metaphor of mind as mirror of the world and the primacy of the epistemological problematic in philosophy are the result of the Lockean confusion between causes and reasons. Sellars's critique of "the myth of the given" occupies a central place in this account, since the myth denounced by Sellars consists in taking what is only a raw causal impact on our senses for a justification and a basis for knowledge. Dummett, for his part, proposes to define analytic philosophy by the rejection of the primacy of epistemology as it has reigned since Descartes and its eviction in favor of a formal semantics playing the role of first philosophy. As for Ian Hacking, he divides the history of modern philosophy into three periods, which are so many *epistemai* in Foucault's sense: the heyday of ideas (exemplarily, that of classic empiricism), the heyday of meanings (Russell, Wittgenstein, the first Vienna Circle), and the heyday of sentences (Paul Feyerabend and Donald Davidson).[1]

These grand narratives (and others could be added) describe the history of contemporary philosophy by making analytic philosophy, in the form it has been given by Frege, Quine, Sellars, and Davidson, the natural end point of its evolution. But one might wonder whether it would not be just as legitimate to confront these narrations with another, probably quite as mythological as the first, which would go as follows. At the beginning of the twentieth century, three major trends shared the philosophical arena: the heirs of classical empiricism (Mach), the neo-Kantians, and the phenomenologists. The Neo-Kantians, while opposing empiricism, shared the same conceptual framework. Rather than accept an immediate given that would be the starting point of all knowledge, they considered this given as already mediated by concepts, shaped by conceptual schemes or symbolic forms that necessarily involve language. More precisely, in critiquing the given of the empiricists, they ended up rejecting the idea of the given *in general*—and they rejected it because they still conceived of all givenness along the lines of their empiricist opponents, as devoid of immanent meaning and structuration. Thus they rejected the Kantian idea of the two sources of human knowledge (sensibility and understanding, receptivity and spontaneity): they maintained that experience received its meaning and structuration "from on high," thanks to the "logical" functions of thought, science, and culture. By denying to the given the title of knowledge, and by assigning all knowledge to the sphere of judgment, they set up a diametric opposition between facts and values, causality and justification. They are thus the direct precursors of an analytic Neo-Kantianism that will take up on its own behalf—though on the basis of different arguments—their critique of the given and the view that experience is conceptual, that is to say, linguistic "all the way out."[2] Like all neo-Kantianism, that of Sellars and McDowell is also a neo-Hegelianism that refuses the immediate and advances a new version of the critique of sense-certainty. To put it in traditional terms, the rejection of the idea of two sources of knowledge and of the "thing in itself" which is its corollary opens onto a Hegelianism without absolute and dialectic, a Hegelianism of understanding in which the object is nothing but the ideal of a rational and methodological progress of knowledge: the object of knowledge is not given (*gegeben*) but merely posited as a task to be accomplished (*aufgegeben*) in the infinite dynamic process of objectification. One ends up with a "logical idealism," as Natorp calls it, thanks to which it becomes possible to collapse the Kantian transcendental aesthetics in its entirety into the analytics.

Phenomenology developed for the most part outside this constellation of problems: its concepts and fundamental positions cannot be made to enter without violence into the coordinates of the empiricism/Kantianism debate. First of all, phenomenology rejects the mainly epistemological problematic that furnishes to this entire debate its *Cartesian coordinates.* What is given, that is, what is experienced, is not to be understood exclusively, or even mainly, in terms of an epistemological problematic. Secondly, without ever equating fact with norm, causality with justification, experience with judgment, phenomenology rejects the very principle of a transcendental deduction whose aim is to show how experience is shaped from outside by conceptual schemes. As Husserl points out, phenomenology opposes from the outset the idea of "transcendental constructions from above."[3] If it is an idealism, this is not in the sense of an intellectualist idealism that makes all the laws of experience depend on intellectual functions, but in that of an "idealism from below"[4] which vindicates the autonomy of experience with respect to the higher forms of thought and judgment. Thus phenomenology, from its very beginning, found its own way in the margins of the conflict opposing the two other schools. Far from pretending to derive thought from experience, as empiricism would have it, or to derive, by contrast, the order that governs experience from that of thought, phenomenology advances that experience is already meaningful and structured independently of language and discursive thought, that it possesses its own order and an immanent articulation, and in no case comes down to the bare reception of a "given" such as it is assumed by empiricism and only *partially* criticized by Kantianism. Instead of rejecting the very notion of the given and relegating it to mythology under the pretext that such a given is always already informed by concepts and categories, phenomenology attempts to enlarge the concept of the given itself far beyond sense data, in order to be able to think an *experience* of the world—but also of art, of culture, of human interactions and institutions, of history and even of language. On the one hand, phenomenology upends our conception of sensibility, since for it, as Levinas writes, "the sensible is not an *Aufgabe* [task] in the neo-Kantian sense, nor an obscure thought in the Leibnizian sense. The new way of treating sensibility consists in conferring upon it, in its very obtuseness, and in its thickness, a signification and a wisdom of its own and a kind of intentionality. The senses make sense."[5] On the other hand, its reform is not limited to the analysis of *sensibility* alone; it is also necessary to reconsider the concepts of the given and of experience, by opening them up to givens and experiences no longer exclusively "sensible" in kind. This is where phenomenology shows a daring far exceeding that of its rival schools. Without ever equating intuition and thought, it reconsiders their relationships, retaining the autonomy not only of sensibility, but also of a pre-theoretic openness to the world that must be described per se, and to which we must restore its full rights. Phenomenology refuses therefore to follow the neo-Kantian critique of the given, which, in its view, is only valid against an atrophied concept of the given, and not against experience in the broad sense that it seeks to promote. As Scheler writes: "In this context nothing could be more disastrous for epistemology than to set up at the beginning of one's methodical procedure *too narrowly exclusive a concept of 'experience'*—to equate the whole of experience with one particular kind of experience . . . and thus not to recognize as primary data anything which cannot be reduced to *this* one variety."[6]

If this grand narrative is not entirely arbitrary, phenomenology, of the three schools, proves to be the most original and the richest in possibilities for thought. The chances are high that *its* concept of the given will not succumb to the critiques of the "myth of the given" that emerge from the empiricism / neo-Kantianism (and eventually "analytic" neo-Kantianism) divide. This is what we must now examine more closely.

If experience as described by phenomenology is nothing other than the mode of givenness of something (things, processes, events, but also works of art, cultural objects, other individuals), and if all that is given to us is given at the very level of the experience we have of it, that is, before all the *descriptions* we can sketch of that experience, phenomenology does indeed postulate the validity of a certain concept of the given. But what concept? How are we to understand "given," "givenness"—a term that, incidentally, was introduced into philosophy not by the empiricists, but by their main opponent, Kant? Heidegger formulated the problem clearly as early as 1919. "What does 'given' [*gegeben*], 'givenness' [*Gegebenheit*] mean? This magic word of phenomenology and 'stumbling block' for the others?"[7] The given may be considered a stumbling block in the rival schools to phenomenology because they have atrophied or misunderstood it, either because they reduced it, like the empiricists, to amorphous sense data, or because they saw in its acceptance a myth and a prejudice, as did the neo-Kantians. Now what risks being "mythical" is less the given itself than its outright rejection—and this is true because this rejection is the unwitting accomplice of an overly narrow conception of the given borrowed directly from empiricism. Because the neo-Kantians consider the given as *immediate, amorphous, and meaningless,* they in fact continue to subscribe to the "old mythology of an intellect which glues and rigs together the world's matter with its own forms," as Heidegger remarks.[8]

Under these circumstances, should we not reject the alternative itself? This is the question phenomenology is the first to raise. If experience, and perceptual experience in particular, is the mode of givenness of things themselves; if this mode of givenness turns out to be structured by *a priori* laws; if, additionally, experience is a pre-theoretical openness to the world (in the sense that experience does not yet bring into play knowledge in a robust sense, that is conceptual and propositional knowledge, but rather consists in a pre-knowledge, in a realm of certainties prior to all justification, in a bodily "hold" on the world); and finally, if experience possesses a holistic constitution that forbids its being conceived of as a raw causal impact on our senses (a causal relation always being atomistic), which of course should not preclude the possibility of an empirical research on the *causal bases* of experience; does it not follow from this that such an "experience" and such a "given" do not enter into the theoretical framework of the empiricism / neo-Kantianism debate?

That is the question I would like to address in this chapter. In order to do this, I will consider the arguments advanced by more recent (linguistic or analytic) versions of Neo-Kantianism, in the work of Sellars and McDowell. But, it might be objected at the outset, does not this characterization do violence to these authors? After all, McDowell considers philosophical activity to be a form of therapy in Wittgenstein's sense, and not the formulation of substantial theses. Consequently we must begin by showing in what sense these critiques of the given are metaphysically overdetermined, constituting the quasi-literal reworking, in the new vocabulary of the Wittgensteinian "grammar," of a neo-Kantian position about which it is very difficult to see how it could be metaphysically neutral and, what is more, "therapeutic." The confrontation of phenomenology with the thought of Sellars and McDowell has nothing of a stylistic exercise about it. The problem of what it has become customary to call, in the United States, "the non-conceptual content" of experience has awakened a lively increase of interest over the last twenty years, under the impetus of Evans, McDowell, Peacocke, and others.[9] Now, this problem is the very one that preoccupied Husserl when he broadened the experiential meaning beyond the conceptual one. But the confrontation of these two traditions can only have a real philosophical significance if it can be shown first that they share a common background: that of neo-Kantianism.

The most vigorous attack that has been made against the idea of the given in the Marburg school is probably that of Paul Natorp. Following Hermann Cohen, who had already argued that "it is not in the sky that the stars are *given* . . . Sensibility is not in the eye, but in the *reasons of astronomy*,"[10] Natorp denounces "the illusion" (*Täuschung*) of "absolute data,"[11] "the prejudice of the given," "the presupposition of all givenness," that "old *shibboleth* of sensualism."[12] Indeed, from the point of view of the Marburg school, what has become "untenable" in the edifice of the *Critique of Pure Reason*, what must undergo a "radical correction," is the transcendental aesthetic. There is no sensible manifold preceding its shaping by the understanding, conceived of as a legislative function. "There should be no more talk," Natorp writes, "of some given 'multiplicity' that the understanding, bound, moreover, by the given forms of (visual) perception, would merely have to organize, interrelate, and—after the fact—recognize."[13] *Gegebenheit,* here, covers *both* what Kant called "sensuous matter" *and* the *a priori* forms of intuition, space, and time, which, as Kant himself admitted, are given in a "formal intuition."[14] The truth is, for the neo-Kantians, even space and time are only logical constructions, determinations of thought, and not of intuition: as Newtonian theory and more generally physical theory attests, these structures—space and time—"are anything but *given*";[15] they come from a "work of thought," from a determination of the sensibility by the understanding. They are "purely logical formations [*rein logische Gebilde*]."[16] Ruled out as a distinct source of knowledge, the given reappears, so to speak, in Natorp, but only as an object = *x* to be determined, the ideal pole of a rational and methodological progression in the knowledge of the natural sciences and psychology. Thought through to the end, transcendental idealism becomes an "idealism of movement," as in Plato's *The Sophist.*[17] Instead of revolving around the fixed point of a raw given, refractory to constitution, that is, to the (infinite) progress of knowledge, science in movement only recovers the given as a determinable *x* at the end of an intellectual progress: "The supposed *fixed points* of thought must be dissolved, liquefied in the continuity of the thought *process.* Thus, nothing *is* 'given,' but something only *becomes* given . . . but always only 'given' in the process of thinking and through it."[18] Hence Natorp can oppose his genetic theory of knowledge, in his famous review of *Ideas I,* to Husserl's eidetic method, that is, to a static Platonism, and free himself in so doing from the idea of *epochē* according to which subjectivity could be for itself the ultimate given.

Intuition no longer being a factor alien to thought, which would be shaped by thought within the knowledge process, the "given" consequently becomes that which thought determines by means of its intellectual functions, a product of its categories and especially that of reality. "Givenness" (*Gegebenheit*), writes Natorp, "is transformed into a postulate of reality; it acquires a purely *modal* significance."[19] Since nothing can be given to thought that the latter has not already determined, the given becomes merely reality as correlate of the judgments of modality in the infinite judicative constitution of experience, that is to say, in the regulated and methodical process of knowledge—with the result that it is not just the understanding/sensibility duality, but the understanding/reason duality as found in Kant that is dissolved, the categories becoming, like the Kantian ideas, principles whose use is merely regulative. Hence Natorp opposes the idea of a given that would be both *immediate* (not mediated by concepts and judgments) and a form of *knowledge.* His critique strikingly prefigures that of Sellars, since the "myth" that the latter will assail is precisely that of an immediate (in the sense of not requiring the mastery of any concept) given, while at the same time possessing an epistemic status. As Natorp emphasizes, "This immediately given is . . . not also immediately known, but first reveals itself to our knowledge mediately, through the detour of the determination of the object. This is why the word 'given,' however, is immediately a source of error, the moment we take givenness to mean known in advance; it is only through the new, specific point of view of psychology, through which it is for the first time presented and defined as the precondition for the knowledge of the object after the fact, in retrospective (reflective) knowledge, that the immediate becomes the pre-given." [20] Against the "appearance of something falling outside thought,"[21] which triumphs in empiricism, against the prejudice of a given thanks to which one could "construct knowledge starting from something exterior to it" it must be maintained that knowledge as a rational system of judgments is irreducible to any causal fact: "No point of view external to knowledge and on the basis of which it could be engendered in a causal relation, in a manifestly transcendent way, is thinkable."[22] The "logical space of reasons," as Sellars and Davidson will call it, remains heterogeneous to the "logical space" of nature and its causes.

This "logical idealism" moves the Marburg school very close to a Hegelianism, but to a Hegelianism in which the absolute has been replaced by the teleological progress of knowledge, in which the duality of sensibility and understanding, of receptivity and spontaneity, of intuition and thought, of matter and form, is surmounted not by their dialectic identity, but by the ideal of an infinite methodological progress; in which the difference between understanding and reason has disappeared in favor of the first term—a Hegelianism of *understanding*. Thus, as Natorp recognizes, we have "come closer to the great idealists, and especially to Hegel";[23] "we are in agreement with Hegel on many points"; "for us as well, all is thought, and thought is all [*ist Alles Denken, Denken Alles*]."[24] With this formula, we are no longer very far from "the unboundedness of the conceptual" that McDowell will advocate.

But it is probably Cassirer, whose importance was decisive—especially through Carnap[25]—in the emergence of the first Vienna Circle, which constituted the intermediary link between the Marburg school and the nascent analytic philosophy. By his project of enlarging Kant's critique of reason to a critique of culture, which underlies his *Philosophy of Symbolic Forms*, Cassirer undertook to show how at each level of cultural production (language, scientific knowledge, myth, art, religion, and so on) a shaping of experience by the spontaneity of the mind takes place. In doing so, he emphasized more clearly than had Natorp the role of the sign and of language in general. "The process of language formation," he writes, "shows for example how the chaos of immediate impressions takes on order and clarity for us only when we 'name' it and permeate it with the function of linguistic thought and expression. In this new world of linguistic signs the world of impressions itself acquires an entirely new 'permanence,' because it acquires a new intellectual articulation."[26] Henceforth it is the linguistic medium itself that plays the role of a leading thread for the critique of the given, that is to say, of the immediate. Like Cohen and Natorp before him, Cassirer opposes any idea of an aesthetics that might precede logic in principle, and considers the forms of space and time as categories of pure thought. Like them, replaying Hegel's critique of sense-certainty in a minor key, he rejects the starting point of the given as an abstract one. In empiricism, he says, "one posits a concept of the given particular but fails to recognize that any such concept must always, explicitly or implicitly, encompass the *defining* attributes of some universal."[27] In short, the spontaneity of mind is attested in symbolic forms at the very level of what is wrongly called "intuition." "To philosophy, which finds its fulfillment only in the sharpness of the concept, and in the clarity of discursive thought, the paradise of mysticism, the paradise of pure immediacy, is closed."[28]

Consequently, one of Cassirer's major contributions was to inflect Kant's transcendental logic in a linguistic direction—a move foreshadowing that of the post-positivist analytic school: "An essential and necessary connection between the basic function of language and the function of *objective representation* is assumed. 'Objective' representation, as I will attempt to formulate it, is not the *beginning* that this process of the formation of language assumes, but the *goal* to which this process leads: it is not its *terminus a quo,* but its *terminus ad quem* . . . . [Language] is itself the mediation in the formation of objects. Indeed, in a certain sense it is *the* mediation, the most important and the most perfect instrument for the production and the construction of a pure 'object-world.' "[29] Only something linguistically articulated can be *knowledge,* and only knowledge—therefore language—can put us in relation with a domain of *objects.* Hence only language can bring us out of the confined space of our representations and open up for us something like a *world.*

It would hardly be possible to understand the particular mixture of Kantianism and Hegelianism which constitutes the cornerstone of the works of Sellars and McDowell without that neo-Kantian background—even though neo-Kantianism is practically *never* mentioned by the two philosophers. Their critique of the given is elaborated this time no longer against Hume's empiricism, but against that of the Vienna Circle; and their argumentation develops following the leading thread of a Kantianism reinterpreted in light of the linguistic turn, in which Wittgenstein's grammar formally plays the role of Kant's transcendental logic. In my overview of the shifts that take place between these two critiques, I will leave aside the question of the extent to which this reading of Wittgenstein remains faithful to the intentions of the author of *Philosophical Investigations.*

Sellars's "Hegelian Meditations" in his text-manifesto "Empiricism and the Philosophy of Mind" are tributary to a whole context from which they are difficult to extricate. At first reading, the critique of the "myth of the given" is directed both at traditional empiricism, which sees in sense data the starting point for all knowledge, and at one of the branches of logical empiricism, the main representatives of which are Moritz Schlick and Clarence I. Lewis. Counter to the epistemological holism of Neurath, for whom "the ship of science must be reconstructed at sea," science being a permanently self-correcting project, and all of the propositions it advances being subjected to a possible revision, Schlick and Lewis maintain that empirical knowledge is not defined by coherence alone: it has its foundation in elementary observational statements, *Konstatierungen.* These "protocol statements," of the type "here now blue," which are "the unshakable point of contact between knowledge and reality,"[30] possess an absolute validity, Schlick declares, at least at the moment they are formulated, and it makes as little sense to doubt them as in the case of a tautology.[31] The target of Sellars's critique is that idea of protocol statements drawing their authority and justification from self-warranted, nonverbal episodes of consciousness, that is, from a *given* that would at the same time be a form of *knowledge.*

This whole epistemological problematic of the foundation of empirical knowledge, stemming from the debate with the Vienna Circle, will not concern us here—or only tangentially. But the framework of Sellars's critique is broader, and the spectrum of doctrines to which his argumentation can be applied is more widespread. What must be understood by the "given" in this context is everything that claims the rank of knowledge, without requiring any mastery of concepts. On this point, Schlick's and Lewis's Cartesian-like epistemology is not very far from Husserl's. Indeed, if we define phenomenology as "all-embracing science, grounded on an absolute foundation, and absolutely justified,"[32] that is to say, grounded in lived experiences that are evident and reflexively given before any application of concepts, and which as such form ultimate *knowledge,*[33] Husserl's epistemology does in fact belong in the category of what Sellars calls "the framework of the Given," characterized by the following three claims: (1) there is a given that is at the same time indubitable *knowledge*; (2) this given is non-linguistic, non-conceptual, while it does allow for the knowledge of certain facts; (3) its knowledge precedes and grounds all other knowledge. I can leave nevertheless this aspect of the problem aside, since, as I have shown in chapter 12, it is not necessary to adhere to Husserl's Cartesian epistemology to do phenomenology. My problem is not to determine whether phenomenology *in its Husserlian form* is defensible, but whether phenomenology is. I have attempted to show that phenomenology is not a science, and that it cannot be grounded in indubitable instances of evidence—that it would suffice to "see" in order to be able to describe them. If Sellars is right, it is quite possible that some aspects of Husserlian phenomenology are invalidated by his critique, but those are aspects of Husserl's philosophy that I have no intention of defending. Besides, that Cartesian epistemology was dropped very early by nearly all the phenomenologists of the second generation, who tried to remove the problematic of the given and givenness from the still too "gnoseological" ambiance surrounding it in Husserl. Phenomenology "first and foremost must detach the problem [of givenness] from a narrow epistemological problematic,"[34] writes Heidegger—the very problematic that dominates in empiricism and neo-Kantianism. It may be said that the whole phenomenology after Heidegger and Scheler, from Levinas to Merleau-Ponty, from Patočka to Ricoeur and Gadamer, by opening itself up to perception, art, ethics, practical philosophy, and history, has fulfilled this watchword.

But then, where does Sellars's contribution to a (virtual) debate between a post-positivist analytic neo-Kantianism and phenomenology lie? If Sellars only targeted the partisans of sense data and/or the *Konstatierungen* of Schlick and Lewis, the debate would be closed before it began. But Sellars specifies that the critique of the empiricists' given is only "a first step in a general critique of the entire framework of givenness."[35] On his view, his critique is valid, more broadly, against any philosophy that would claim to single out a core of prelinguistic and preconceptual givenness, whether this core is made up of sense data, of the *Gestalten* of Gestalt psychology (which Schlick takes up on his own behalf), or even of the *appearing* of things, processes, or events given to an experience without involving our conceptual abilities. By "concept" Sellars means what the late Wittgenstein meant by the term. As Rorty remarks in his preface to the French edition, "Sellars like the last Wittgenstein, but contrary to Kant, identifies the possession of a concept with the mastery of the use of a word. The mastery of a language is therefore, for him, the necessary precondition for conscious experience."[36] To this non-conceptual nature of the given are added two other important characteristics: its immediacy and its non-inferential character.[37] Let us recall that the neo-Kantians also made immediacy the cornerstone of their critique of the given, which was intended to be, among other things, a critique of phenomenology.[38] How are we to understand this "immediacy"? Sellars clarifies that it must be understood as a chracteristic of what "can occur to human beings (and brutes) without any prior process of learning or concept formation."[39] "Immediate," then, means "requiring no learning," and since the mastery of a concept is the same as the learning of linguistic rules, "immediate" also means "not conceptually elaborated." It may be doubted that the given advanced by phenomenology excludes all learning: according to Husserl, our experience is structured by associative ties pertaining to the sphere of the passive synthesis, which bears witness to the fact that learning transforms the way things appear to us through and through. Nevertheless, if we focus on the specificity of language acquisition, and if we accept the equivalency between the possession of a concept and the mastery of the use of a word, then the experience of the phenomenologists, as preconceptual, does indeed pertain to a form of immediacy in the sense Sellars confers on that term. In the final analysis, the critique of the given, in its most general form, opposes the idea of a givenness that would be at the same time a kind of knowledge while remaining independent of any conceptual acquisition.

However, the main target of this critique remains empiricism, and it might well be that both views share some presuppositions. First of all, if Sellars attacks the idea of sense data as a form of *knowledge*, and therefore as the grounding of empirical science, he never seems to question the philosophical relevance of the concept of sense data to describe our perceptual experience of the world—contrary to Straus, Merleau-Ponty, and others within the phenomenological tradition. Furthermore, Sellars's vocabulary betrays a certain connivance with his opponents. Indeed, his entire reasoning rests on an analysis of "look" statements. The verb "to look," the meaning of which is rather broad and undetermined in English, is translated into French as "sembler." Now, if "sembler" means "avoir l'air de . . ." (without *being* it), that translation is inappropriate. "*You look tired*" may be translated as "tu as l'air fatigué" (implying that you are tired), but in other cases, for example "*you look beautiful*," it is impossible to translate that expression by "tu sembles belle (beau)"—for what could "*sembler* beau" (without *being* beautiful) mean? Beauty is a phenomenal quality: one cannot seem to have it without actually having it. I propose to translate "*to look*" with "paraître"—a verb that, according to the context, in French, may refer either to mere appearance or to appearing. "*On l'attendait, elle parut* [We were waiting for her, she appeared]" means that she showed (in person). The same may be said of "*le bateau parut à la pointe de l'îlot*" [the ship showed at the tip of the island].

These terminological remarks are only apparently off topic. The meaning of Sellars's demonstration is to show that the grammar of "*looks*" excludes the possibility of understanding appearance as a *given* prior to our conceptual resources. We can understand why Sellars chooses to analyze *to look* rather than *to seem*, for example. "*To look*" is in a certain sense neutral with respect to the distinction appearance/mere appearance (*Erscheinung/Schein*), even if it leans slightly toward the second term. Now, the target of Sellars's critique is empiricist and phenomenalist doctrines, that is, doctrines that define the phenomenon, classically, as a mental "entity" for which the distinction between reality and appearance makes no sense: a phenomenon is all it appears to be. Of it, it should be said: "*esse est percipi.*" But as we have begun to show (see chapter 15), this is not the way the phenomenologist defines the phenomenon. Phenomenology is not a phenomenalism.

To follow the argumentation of "Empiricism and the Philosophy of Mind," it will be easier to start with an example. But I will slightly modify the one chosen by Sellars for reasons that will become clear shortly.

Elstir gets back to his studio after dark, carrying a canvas under his arm, after having painted outside all day. When he puts his painting on an easel and starts looking at the result of his efforts by the light of an electric bulb he sees "a sea-wave smashing its lilac froth angrily against the sand."[40] Elstir no longer remembers what color he painted that wave that morning. "Is it really lilac," he wonders, "or is it the effect of the light?" Elstir is an impressionist painter: the goal of his art is to try to restore things as they look or appear [*paraissent ou apparaissent*] to us, and not as our objectifying look (informed by a whole body of knowledge) believes them to be. It is possible that, that morning, he in fact painted that wave lilac because he *saw* it lilac. But he is no longer entirely sure of it. On the other hand, he knows very well that the color seen in electric light doesn't always look the same as outdoors, under normal viewing conditions. Perhaps that wave only looks lilac to him because he is looking at his painting in artificial light.

What is to be learned from such an account? Sellars's response is the following. In order for Elstir to be able to use the word *look* and ask himself the questions he does, he must know a number of facts that have nothing to do with "appearances" considered in themselves: facts concerning the relationship between a color and its viewing conditions across changing lightings or concerning the kind of lighting in which an object must be placed to see its real color. By convention, we say that an object looks the color it really is when it is exposed to daylight. The moral of this little fable is therefore the following: far from "to look lilac" being an original fact that it would suffice to observe, and on the basis of which one might understand the expression "to be lilac" (in such a way that "to be lilac" would mean "to look lilac to a standard observer in standard conditions"), it is rather "to be lilac" that is the more fundamental expression, and the one making it possible to understand "to look lilac." Indeed, to look lilac is to have the appearance of what *is* lilac. It is necessary to be able to say first what things *are* lilac in order to be able to say what things *look* that color, and that priority is of a logical nature. It is only by understanding what is lilac that we can understand what looks lilac, what has the appearance to be that way, that is to say, that we can say what this appearance is the appearance of.

So in order for Elstir to be able to ask himself these questions, it does not suffice for him to observe "phenomena," "appearances" that he might possess privately, nor to give a direct account of his experience in the first person; he must have a whole host of concepts that he acquired at the same time as he acquired language, by "a *public* process which proceeds in a domain of *public* objects and is governed by *public* sanctions,"[41] and he must make a complex judgment, along the following lines: "Things are not always the color they look, for their color varies according to the lighting; the 'normal' lighting in which, by convention, we say things are the color they look, is daylight; my painting is placed in an artificial lighting, it may be, then, that this wave is not the color it looks; since I don't remember how I painted it this morning, I will only say that it 'looks lilac' to me, that is, that it looks to me of the same color that it would look if I placed it in the normal conditions of lighting, and that then it looked lilac to me."

Sellars's objective is to show that all conscious experience of things, all perception as consciousness of particulars, but also all consciousness of similarities or of sorts is "a linguistic affair."[42] He calls this position "psychological nominalism."[43] Let us try to make his argumentation more explicit. He attacks the "framework of the given," that is, the idea of data being the indubitable and non-conceptual knowledge of certain facts, on the basis of three arguments.

(1) The partisans of the given think that primordial knowledge concerns phenomena and that real things are known only on the basis of these phenomena. Against this view, it must be stressed that the language game about phenomena is more complex, and logically derived with respect to the language game about objects, in other words, that the grammar of "to look lilac" is more complex than the grammar of "to be lilac," so that logically there is a primacy of the description of things over the description of appearances.

(2) "To look lilac" expresses no elementary fact, no fact independent of language acquisition: the concept of "looking lilac" is just as much acquired, and as much a linguistic affair, as that of "being lilac." Statements about appearances do not draw their meaning directly from private facts or episodes, but only from a public learning according to public criteria. We are therefore faced with an alternative: either to give up saying that the perception of particulars is a perception of *facts*; or to assert that it is a consciousness of facts—but to draw the consequence that it is no longer "immediate" at all, that is to say, no longer independent of all linguistic mastery.

(3) Not only does "to look red" not express any fact independent of a whole set of other facts, but it does not express any *epistemological* fact, any *knowledge* that would precede de jure other knowledge and could serve as its foundation. In order for this fact to be an epistemic one, it should have been possible to doubt it. Now the perception of particulars is rather characterized by the fact that doubt is logically excluded here, and hence "knowledge" as well. In short, it is only possible to speak legitimately of *knowledge* in cases in which a *statement* can be situated in the logical space of reasons and justifications. "In characterizing an episode or a state as that of *knowing*, we are not giving an empirical description of that episode or state; we are placing it in the logical space of reasons, of justifying and being able to justify what one says."[44]

Sellars's reasoning thus winds up in a double holism: an epistemological holism ("one could not have observational knowledge of *any* fact unless one knew many *other* things as well")[45] and conceptual holism (one cannot possess the concept of looking lilac unless he possesses that of being lilac).

Sellars's arguments are the implicit resumption of those of Wittgenstein, which are centered on the private language problem.

(1) "'It looks red to me.'—'And what is red like?'—'Like *this*.' Here the right paradigm must be pointed to." "Why doesn't one teach a child the language-game 'It looks red to me' from the first? Because it is not yet able to understand the rather fine distinction between seeming and being?"[46]

(2) "Facts cannot be named,"[47] in other words, they can only be identified linguistically.

(3) "'I know . . .' may mean 'I do not doubt . . .' but does not mean that the words 'I doubt . . .' are *senseless*, but that doubt is logically excluded."[48]

Each one of these arguments makes it possible to attack one aspect of the framework of the given: (1) the idea that knowledge must be based on subjective appearances that are prior de jure to all knowledge of objects or facts in the world; (2) the idea that these appearances could be primitive facts independent of language and of any conceptual contribution; (3) lastly, the idea that these elementary and directly perceived "facts" are of a cognitive or epistemic nature, but supply a knowledge that, by contrast with all other knowledge, is absolutely indubitable, that is, is such that there is no room for doubt in it.

But Sellars goes further than Wittgenstein. He proposes a logico-grammatical analysis of "*x* looks green to S" and of "S sees that *x* is green" that makes it possible to definitively dismiss the idea of a given that would be both epistemic and non-conceptual: "Now the suggestion I wish to make is, in its simplest terms, that the statement '*x* looks green to Jones' differs from 'Jones sees that *x* is green' in that whereas the latter both ascribes a propositional claim to Jones's experience *and endorses it,* the former ascribes the claim but does not endorse it. This is the essential difference between the two, for it is clear that the two experiences may be identical *as experiences*."[49] This way of expressing oneself is paradoxical. To attribute a propositional claim to experience: what does this mean? Sellars means it in an utterly literal way: to see that something is green has a propositional content; hence it is something analogous to *judging* that something is green. Sellars expresses this with the utmost clarity: experiences about *seeing that something over there is red,* or about the fact *that it seems to someone that an object over there is red*—"[these experiences] all involve the idea—the proposition, if you please—that the object over there is red."[50] How can an experience "involve" a proposition? It can do so, Sellars says, if the mere consciousness of something is already a "linguistic affair." But why? In the case in which Elstir says he *sees* the wave lilac, he "endorses" the content of this assertion: his statement means that the wave *is* lilac (and that statement is true if and only if the wave in fact has that color). Things are different when Elstir says that the wave *looks* lilac to him. "To look" doesn't express a simple epistemic fact: it means that the wave looks to him the same way a lilac wave would look to him in normal circumstances of observation, that is, in daylight. He does not endorse the content of his assertion. The wave may very well appear lilac to him without being so (this statement may be true although the wave has a different color in standard conditions of observation). Thus, Sellars concludes, the two experiences may be identical as experiences, but the difference between the two statements is a grammatical one.

If Sellars is right in his logico-grammatical explanation of "looks," it follows that to look (whether taken in the sense of seeming or of appearing) is not understandable as a relation: "looks *is not a relation at all*."[51] "To look" does not have the logical structure of a relation at all, whether we are talking about a triadic relation between a physical object, a person, and a quality (red), or about a dyadic relation between an object and a subject.[52] If that analysis is correct, it follows that a description of perception such as the one I proposed in chapters 15 and 16 in terms of relations is not tenable. Perception cannot be the givenness of things themselves with their phenomenal characteristics. Neither can it be maintained that perception is a kind of pre-predicative *certainty* that requires no justification—as opposed to knowledge in the strict sense, which is expressed in propositions, and, as such, can be supported by reasons. On Sellars's view, appearing cannot be knowledge *in any sense whatsoever*, because appearing is not of the nature of a simple epistemic fact, but is rather a complex inference, bringing into play a whole panoply of concepts and requiring the mastery of linguistic skills. One cannot have an appearence of lilac wave without making inferences and without having reached a high degree of sophistication in the mastery of concepts.

It is time to address the problem of the acceptability of Sellars's analysis. First, is his logico-grammatical analysis of "*looks*" conclusive? In this case it is as if the grammarian philosopher was himself unaware of the diversity of uses and tried to make them enter by force into the mold of one single paradigmatic case. Sellars speaks indeed as if "looks" had only one use and meaning. As I noted at the start, this strategy may be explained by the fact that his critique is directed first and foremost against a *phenomenist* doctrine that conceives of "phenomena" as entities located in the mind, and having a being identical with their appearing. But it may very well be that this overlooking of the variety of the uses of "*looks*" reflects a tacit complicity between Sellars and the authors he criticizes—or, to put it differently, the dependency of this critique itself upon the framework of empiricist thought. For, after all, does "*looks*" have the meaning Sellars attributes to it? Elstir, in saying that the wave looks lilac to him, may mean at least two *very different* things: (1) assuming one accepts the idea of "normal" conditions of observation (in fact, there is no such thing, since the light keeps changing from sunrise to sunset),[53] Elstir may mean that the wave looks to him the same way that a wave that *is* lilac would appear to him under normal observation conditions: that is the meaning emphasized by Sellars; (2) but Elstir is an impressionist painter who tries to paint things, places, and the elements in their pure appearance for us, that is to say, such as they present themselves at the pure level of sensing; in saying that the wave looks lilac to him—this time, when he is on the beach, facing his subject—he obviously cannot mean the wave appears to him as it would under normal conditions of observation—since he is in fact in normal conditions of observation! But then, what does he mean? Chisholm has distinguished several senses of "*looks*," and among them, two that interest us more particularly. The comparative sense is the one favored by Sellars. But there is a non-comparative sense[54] in which no logical relation is involved between the way a thing looks and the way it would look in different observational conditions. Perhaps that use of "looks" is rare outside philosophy and painting, but it is attested nonetheless. Elstir might, for example, say to a devoted student: "Be attentive to the way the waves look to you, and forget what you know about them!" How can we characterize his non-comparative sense of "*looks*" more precisely? In "the wave looks lilac to me," "looks" expresses the distinctive and qualitatively unique character of a phenomenon apart from all comparison, the intrinsic distinctive character of the presentation of a thing to someone. It is this sense that is of primary interest to the phenomenologist, although the first sense might also interest him on occasion, for example when he ponders, as does Merleau-Ponty, the problem of the constancy of colors. The question the phenomenologist generally raises is that of what constitutes the intrinsically distinctive character of the phenomena of perception as opposed to those of illusion, imagination, memory, and so on. The meaning of "looks" with which he is involved is the *non-comparative* one.

Nevertheless, Sellars touches on an essential point here: the concepts of semblance [*apparence*] and of appearing [*apparaître*] are not independent of one another; necessary relations hold between them. We cannot have the concept of semblance or of mere appearance, that is, of what a thing *seems* to be, without having the concept of the appearing of that thing as it actually *is*. That is the meaning of Sellars's "conceptual holism." This conceptual holism may be an objection to a phenomenalism committed to the view that the only phenomena are the sense data and that *every* phenomenon is such that its being and its appearing are one and the same; but it certainly cannot be a valid objection to phenomenology. Husserl implicitly, and Heidegger explicitly, have emphasized that the various concepts of phenomenon bear necessary relations to one another. There is no "mere phenomenon" in the sense of a mere appearance (*Schein*) unless there are phenomena in which the thing shows itself *as it is*, and in this case "phenomenon" means *what shows itself in itself* (what Heidegger calls "*Phänomen*" in §7 of *Being and Time*). In other words, the phenomenological concept of phenomenon is infinitely richer and more complex than that current in phenomenalism, and one could reproach Sellars for exactly the same thing as Heidegger did Rickert, when the latter focused his critique of phenomenology on an insufficient understanding of the concept of phenomenon, equating it with the immediately given: "Rickert's critique," Heidegger writes, is expressed as follows: since appearance [*Erscheinung*] "is always appearance of something which is behind it, the immediate cannot be apprehended, so that we are always dealing with something already mediated. Phenomenology is accordingly unsuited to be the basic science of philosophy. It is apparent first that the concept of appearance, phenomenon [*Erscheinung*], is merely taken up without any attempt to see what phenomenon [*Phänomen*] originally means and in phenomenology truly means. Instead, the traditional concept of appearance, an empty verbal concept, is taken as a basis for criticizing the concrete labor of a research effort."[55]

Furthermore, while recognizing the aptness of Sellars's conceptual holism, the phenomenologist could raise the objection that it is impossible to draw the conclusions Sellers draws from his premises. One cannot conclude, from the fact that it is necessary to have the concept of being green to be able to use "to look green,"[56] that it is necessary to possess both these concepts in order to be able to *perceive* green, and that therefore perception is in its very nature conceptual (no more than it follows, from the fact that one must master the concept of atom in order to understand that of electron, that atoms and electrons are of a conceptual nature.) Nor can one draw the conclusion that we must refuse all core of givenness that is not already dependent on a mastery of concepts. Perceptual experience is the givenness of things themselves, prior to the application of concepts, but, *as soon as we apply our concepts* of mere appearance and of appearing-in-person (of the appearing of the thing as it is), we apply them not separately, but as an entire network. Conceptual holism, while justified, has nothing incompatible with the idea of a perceptual givenness that would be preconceptual by its very nature. As Alston remarks, "The holism about concepts does not carry implications for the nature of perceptual experience."[57]

It is not Sellars's grammatical analysis, but his intellectualism, that makes him say not only that perception is conceptual, but that it is propositional in its very nature. "For seeing is a *cognitive* episode which involves the framework of thoughts . . ."[58] In hypostatizing a particular sense of "*looks*" (conceived of as *the* ordinary sense), and in showing that this sense involves various responses to a variety of situations, an entire linguistic acquisition, and, in reality, a complex judgment, Sellars believes himself to be justified to conclude that a mere appearance is nothing but a judgment, a non-endorsed claim, and a perception an endorsed one. But again we have a non sequitur. As long as it has not been explained how an experience can itself be a propositional claim (whether endorsed or not), it will remain possible to retort to Sellars that what we can *say* or *think* about an experience does not entail any consequence as to the nature of that experience itself.

Not only does Sellars not furnish us any element to understand how a perception could be an endorsed propositional claim, but the idea that it is one leads to insurmountable aporias. To have a *belief* about what we see, it is probably necessary—this is a debatable point—to apply concepts to experience. But is it necessary to apply concepts to experience in order to *perceive* something? First, the content of an experience is generally independent of what we judge to be the case. As Stumpf already emphasized in his *Psychology of Sound* (*Tonpsychologie*)—and Husserl followed him on this point—a judgment "exerts no force on the content judged."[59] This is what ensures the autonomy of experience vis-à-vis conceptual thought in general and *a fortiori*, propositional thought. This difference, as Merleau-Ponty remarks, "disappears in intellectualism because judgment is everywhere that pure sensation is not, which is to say that judgment is everywhere."[60] This is what explains the fact that intellectualism needs empiricism (and the concept of sensation) as a permanent foil to justify its thesis of an experience conceptual *all the way out.* Secondly, if experience is already a claim, whether endorsed or not, it is hard to see how that claim can be related to anything other than itself: it is no longer *about* anything. If nothing is given that is not already a judgment, it is not only the concept of the given that is disqualified, but also that of judgment—of judgment *of perception,* at least. Now, seeing is not thinking, it is not having to think. To see the sun as being little is one thing, Aristotle said, but to have the opinion that it is little is another.[61] Lastly, to conceive of perception as a claim leads almost inevitably to conceiving of the perceived content as a mental intermediary, an interface between mind and world, and therefore as different from the perceived thing itself. Characteristic of claims is that they are either true or false depending on whether the state of affairs that they express obtains or not. We are once again drawn into a theory of representation, but instead of these representations being Cartesian ideas, they are now propositional claims.

McDowell, in order to attenuate this difficulty, while remaining faithful to Sellars's general orientation, maintained that "its appearing to me that things are thus and so is not obviously to be equated with my believing something."[62] To McDowell, the content of experience is indeed conceptual, in the sense of being propositional (we perceive *this or that to be the case*) but even though experience has the same "content" as the judgment concerning it, it is not intrinsically a judgment. Thus, we witness a third act of the debate between empiricism and neo-Kantianism—a neo-Kantianism whose progressively weakened claims still remain within the magic circle of formulations and problems from which it cannot extricate itself. After the debate of the original neo-Kantianism with classical empiricism, and after that of Sellars with logical empiricism, McDowell attacks a residuum of givenness that could still tempt philosophers despite Sellars's critiques, and that would bring about the threat of a new division between sensibility and understanding, or, as he likes to say in a Kantian terminology, between receptivity and spontaneity.

In Sellars, as in Davidson, experience continues to be characterized in terms of causal impacts on our sensibility. This experience, conceived of as "made up of impressions,"[63] remains outside "the logical space of reasons"; it can furnish no justification to empirical knowledge. Davidson—the main interlocutor, but behind whom the figure of Sellars is discernible—comes to maintain "a dichotomy of logical spaces,"[64] abandoning the image of experience as a tribunal and with it any form of empiricism, and therefore also the idea that experience could furnish a *justification* for knowledge. A rational constraint is characterized by its normativity: it tells us how we *must* represent things to ourselves, how to *correctly* apply judgments to experience. If experience exerts only a causal action on our senses, it exerts no rational constraint. Davidson concludes from this that "nothing can count as a reason for holding a belief except another belief."[65] Only belief and judgment can occupy the logical space of reasons, as only they depend, for their *correctness* or *incorrectness*, on the way things present themselves. Thus, to escape the "myth" of a preconceptual given that would at the same time be knowledge (or that would constitute a justification for knowledge), Davidson espouses a radical coherentism, in which beliefs are as it were suspended in the air, "frictionless"[66] with reality. In what McDowell compares to a pendular movement or an "interminable oscillation," in order to escape the myth of the given, philosophers abandon any idea of a rational constraint of experience on knowledge and define truth exclusively in terms of coherence; the result is an enclosure or a confinement within the space of beliefs, and this in turn elicits the temptation, in order to reestablish a link with experience, to relapse into the myth of the given. According to McDowell, Evans yielded at least in part to that temptation, in claiming a *non-conceptual* content for experience, while at the same time maintaining that experience can constitute a source of justification for knowledge; he yielded to the idea that the logical space of reasons exceeds that of concepts, which is a version of the myth of the given.

To escape this pendular movement and to reestablish a "minimal empiricism" which, on the one hand, asserts that experience exerts a rational constraint on beliefs, but, on the other hand, avoids falling back into a version of the myth of the given, McDowell proposes that we conceive of experience itself as conceptual "all the way out." He adopts as his leitmotif the famous formula from Kant, according to which "thoughts without content are empty; intuitions without concepts are blind,"[67] but abandons the *heterogeneity* of the two sources of human knowledge. This gambit allows him both to reintegrate receptivity to the logical space of reasons, by asserting that experience can play a normative role for cognitive claims, thus saving the very principle of empiricism, and to abandon what is in his view unacceptable in traditional empiricism, the idea of a "pre-logical" (and mythical) given as a foundation for knowledge. In order to understand how experience can be intrinsically conceptual without thereby rejecting the nature of the moderns, conceived of as the realm of law, McDowell proposes to rehabilitate, in the course of his lectures, the Aristotelian idea of "second nature"; the conceptual capacities passively at work in experience pertain to that second nature which prolongs the first; they are the product of language acquisition. Human animality is a rational one.

Let us insist on the following point. The solution proposed by McDowell does not, in his view, represent the response of a constructive philosophy to a well-formulated problem, but rather a mere "therapy," in the Wittgensteinian sense of the term, applied to a philosophical "worry" that should never have come about. "We should understand what Kant calls 'intuition'—experiential intake—not as a bare getting of an extra-conceptual Given, but as a kind of occurrence or state that already has conceptual content. In experience one takes in, for instance sees, *that things are thus and so.* That is the sort of thing one can also, for instance, judge."[68] McDowell does not ask us to abandon the notion of the given, but to rework it, to adopt "a different notion of givenness."[69] The rejection of an illusion with respect to *what* is given does not entail the rejection of the whole idea of something being given. "In experience," he writes, "one finds oneself saddled with content."[70] According to this third way between Davidson's coherentism and the myth of the given, we should not conceive of the structuration of receptivity by spontaneity—in the Kantian terminology adopted by McDowell—as if there were first an amorphous sensible given, an extra-conceptual intuition, that would only subsequently be shaped by concepts: "We must not suppose that receptivity makes an even notionally separable contribution to its co-operation with spontaneity."[71] Furthermore, *the conceptual and linguistic capacities* that are always already passively at work in experience as such are the same ones that can be actively exercised in judgment. Thus *Mind and World* ends up with the view that only a renewed conception of experience as conceptual through and through can legitimate—for reasons soon to become apparent—the image of an "unproblematic openness to the world"[72] that McDowell discovers in Gadamer, but is originally to be found in Heidegger.

In a very cursory way, and simplifying things a bit, four stages can be distinguished in the line of thought pursued in this work: a neo-Kantian-like reappropriation of Kant, the recourse to the idea of an Aristotelian second nature in order to replace transcendental schematism, the reassertion of Wittgenstein's quietism, and lastly a rediscovery in the land of analytic philosophy of the Heideggerian notion of openness to the world—without, it is true, any mention of Heidegger.

The position of *Mind and World* calls for many comments, and I can only, in the present context, sketch out a few lines of reflection. First, at no point does McDowell discuss the terms themselves in which Sellars characterizes what is allegedly "mythical" in the idea of the given, and in the "framework" of the given as such. McDowell does not seem to be bothered by the doubts I have raised, especially touching the reconstitution of the grammar of "*looks*," the importance of which is pivotal to Sellars's demonstration, so that his contribution to the debate is restricted to the rather narrow parameters of Sellars's dispute against empiricism. His "solution"—therapeutic or otherwise—remains entirely tributary to these initial presuppositions.

In the second place, McDowell asserts that in order for experience to be able to justify a belief, experience itself must be structured like a belief; therefore its contents must be conceptual, and more precisely, propositional. This conclusion rests on the assumption that *what exerts a rational constraint* (the experience) *must have the same characteristics as that on which that constraint is exerted* (the judgment, the belief). But is this necessary? To supply a reason for believing something, must perception be conceptually *articulated*, or does it not suffice that it be conceptually *articulable*? In which case perception would only acquire the status of justification when expressed in judgment, and it would be again a *judgment* that would justify another judgment. In short, *in the thought that expresses experience*, the relation that holds between experience and judgment is a rational (and not a causal) one, but it does not follow from this that experience as such has a conceptual content.

In the third place, contrary to what happens in the phenomenological tradition, the problem of experience is approached here from the exclusive standpoint of an epistemological problematic, and without McDowell giving us the slightest description of what it might mean for an experience to bear concepts within it—for an experience of things, events, works, and so on. For what does it mean, exactly, that experience is "conceptual"—which would be firmly denied by Husserl[73] and his heirs? When we see *that things are such and such*, what happens exactly? Do we pronounce this judgment *in petto*? No, probably not, for although the propositional content of this experience is the same as that of the judgment made *on the basis* of that experience, the experience itself is not a judgment, as McDowell admits. But then does that mean that the experience is itself a *disposition* to apply concepts and formulate propositions? That its distinctive content is potentially all we can correctly state about it? No, because perception cannot be a *disposition* to judge, it is a *state* in which I find myself (and find myself "saturated with content"). Indeed, as McDowell recognizes, "in a picture in which all there is behind the judgement is a disposition to make it, the experience itself goes missing."[74] In other words, there is an unbridgeable gap between experiencing that something is the case and judging it to be so. But then how can we positively characterize the fact that experience *as such* rests on the passive mobilization of conceptual and propositional capacities? The only point that emerges clearly from these analyses is that the concepts that structure experience must not be conceived of solely as general predicates, but also as singular concepts, proper names and indexicals such as "this red" or "that shade of red." Apart from that, we have no other choice but to turn to a metaphor: the conceptual capacities, spontaneity, are at work passively in receptivity. But if these capacities are linguistic, their actualization must also be linguistic. Experience should, in a sense, speak to us. But this is not what McDowell means either.

More precisely, McDowell does not speak about the *exercise* of these capacities (which only occurs in judgment) but rather of their being operative in receptivity. But how are they supposed to be operative? Sometimes McDowell insists on the gap separating perceptual appearing from judgment, and at other times he says that "appearings are just more of the same kind of things beliefs are,"[75] since "spontaneity extends all the way out to the content of experience."[76] We did not make much progress in our understanding of how this logical and propositional articulation of experience can save the specificity of the latter with respect to the judgments we form about it. McDowell's attempt, to be sure, reminds us up to a point the effort made by the phenomenologists to reject both the brute facts of empiricism, which would exert on our sensibility a causal action (and the raw sensible givens that would result from such action), and the hypostatization of judgment leading to the claim that perceiving is nothing other than judging. From the phenomenological standpoint, it must be stressed that experience shelters within itself an immanent meaning because it involves understanding as a capacity that can be actualized *also* in actions, but that remains as such preconceptual and prelinguistic: this capacity concerns our very way of being in the world, of orienting ourselves in it and dwelling in it, and it precedes in principle (if not in fact) all shaping by language. This characterization of experience remains purely descriptive; it concerns the mode of appearing of the "life-world," and does not yet involve an epistemological problematic.

But there is no reason to deny that experience can bring concepts into play up to a point, that it can consist in a diversity of hierarchically ordered modes of apprehension of the world, which become increasingly dependent on language as one moves upward on the scale of the cultural dependency of the objects experienced, and, *a fortiori*, as one moves from naive experience to scientific knowledge. In McDowell's conception, on the contrary, experience is uniformly approached from the point of view of *knowledge*, and in light of the epistemological problematic of justification; and the world experienced is basically the objective, physical world. This world conforms to the definition given in the *Tractatus*: it is the totality of what is the case[77]—the totality of what empirical science can express in true statements.

It will come as no surprise that the apparent similarity between the images of "openness to the world" conceals two radically distinct and even in some respects opposite conceptions. To convince ourselves of this, we may compare the apparently similar critiques McDowell and Taylor address to the thesis of Davidson, that only a belief can justify a belief. According to that thesis, it is not possible to confront our judgments directly at the tribunal of experience. "No such confrontation makes sense," writes Davidson, "for of course we can't get outside our skins to find out what is causing the internal happening of which we are aware."[78] Both authors point out that "coherentist rhetoric suggests images of confinement within the sphere of thinking, as opposed to being in touch with something outside it."[79] Davidson remains the captive of the classic image of knowledge as needing its own medium—not that of ideas, but of beliefs—as distinct from what is known. As Taylor insists, although Davidson refuses to conceive of beliefs as epistemological intermediaries between the world and ourselves, the images of "outside" and "inside" are invoked in an argument whose purpose is to free us from a representationalist view, but whose actual result is to make us lapse back into this view. Why would we have to "get outside our skins" to be able to confront our beliefs with the "outside" world? "Here, paradoxically, we find the picture [of the inside/outside difference] invoked within an argument that is meant to repudiate that very picture. This is what it means to be held captive."[80] Because he remains captive to this picture, Davidson restores some plausibility to the skeptic argument. What prevents us from assuming that our beliefs are mostly or even entirely false? And when, to that concern, he answers that our beliefs must be for the most part true,[81] from the point of view of a radical interpreter, in order for that interpreter to be able to attribute these beliefs rationally, that explanation comes too late to escape skepticism. If Taylor and McDowell agree in denouncing the truism of a confinement in our beliefs as opposed to the "outer" reality, the path they take to escape that dead end is nevertheless different. Taylor argues that we are always already in contact or at grips with a world pervaded by prelinguistic meanings offered to us at the level of perception itself. He chooses to follow Merleau-Ponty when the latter asserts that in perception, in our primary openness to things, "we do not think the object and we do not think the thinking, we are directed toward the object and we merge with this body that knows more than we do about the world."[82] In order to think that experience, Taylor, like Merleau-Ponty or Straus, rejects the notions of "sensation" and "impression," which do not belong to the descriptive content of perception but are nothing more than theoretical constructions. As for McDowell, he follows Wittgenstein,[83] making rather a parallel between thought and perception. If "thinking does not stop short of facts,"[84] and if "the world is made up of the sort of thing one can think,"[85] that must apply to perception as well: "*That things are thus and so* is the conceptual content of an experience, but if the subject of the experience is not misled, that very same thing, *that things are thus and so,* is also a perceptible fact, an aspect of the perceptible world."[86] Far from rejecting impressions and sensations, McDowell maintains that they can put us in contact with the world only if they are structured conceptually, that is, linguistically. As Cassirer insisted, language is "*the mediation* . . . for the production and the construction of a pure 'object-world'"[87]—that is to say, of a *physical world.*

Thus, McDowell does not define truth in terms of correspondence, but of identity: the content of a true judgment is the judged fact itself. The same is true of perception. There is an identity of the true experience with the fact perceived; this is what it means to say that perception is "openness to the layout of reality."[88] As McDowell puts it, "in enjoying an experience one is open to manifest facts, facts that obtain anyway and impress themselves on one's sensibility."[89] But how can facts, which cannot be identified independently of their expression, "impress themselves" on sensibility? The image of "impression" (of the wax seal) refers to a causal impact. But a fact is identical to the content of a true proposition. How can the content of a true proposition impress itself on our sensibility? This image is far from clear. Moreover, it raises other problems. First, if judgment and perception, when they are true, have a content that is *identical to the fact asserted or perceived* (which implies that perception is always propositional), what difference does this leave between experience and judgment? The main difference, McDowell responds, lies in the passivity of perception as opposed to the spontaneity of judgment. But that passivity is mysterious. For Kant, the receptivity of intuition is the indication of the finitude of the human *Gemüt,* and refers to the affection of sensibility by the thing in itself. But McDowell rejects the thing in itself along with Kant's transcendental framework. Then, is that "passivity" a *phenomenological* characteristic of experience? But from a phenomenological point of view, perception is continually subtended with activity; in truth, it is intrinsically neither active nor passive. Does McDowell mean that experience *imposes* a fact upon us that can subsequently be taken up and expressed in a judgment? But a fact is not something that can be conceived of independently of the judgment that expresses it: thus it cannot *impose itself* on us (let alone impress itself on us) independently of the "spontaneity" of our judicative faculty.

In short, what does it mean to say that experience is openness to the world? And if the identity of the content of experience with a fact has nothing specific to experience as such, but *constitutes just as much a characteristic of judgment*, why reserve the image of "openness" for the former, to the exclusion of the latter? More generally, we may wonder whether the image of openness to the world is compatible with the conception of the content of perception as propositional through and through. Facts depend by essence on their linguistic expression; therefore they are not the sort of "thing" we could be *open* to. No doubt, McDowell can defend his image of perceptual openness because he equates facts conceived of in Fregean terms as true propositions and facts understood in a non-Fregean way as constituents of reality. But can facts be understood *in these two ways at the same time*? A contingent proposition is necessarily bipolar: it is susceptible of being true or false. But facts as constituents of the world are not bipolar: the true/false distinction simply doesn't apply to them.[90] Besides, to claim that perception has a propositional content leads inevitably to asserting that it is not *essentially truthful*, which is in contradiction with the disjunctive conception of perception claimed by McDowell in other texts.[91] If the content of perception is propositional *and* contingent, it is bipolar, and therefore a perception can be either true or false. But the disjunctive theory claims that a perception that is not true is not a *perception* at all. There are only two solutions left: either admit that the propositional content of the perception is *necessarily true* (but what could that mean in the case of contingent propositions?), or give up this whole approach to perceptual content on the model of that of a proposition. Since the main virtue of the disjunctive conception was to free us from the skeptical problem, the claim that all perception has a propositional content tends to make us lapse back into a position that is vulnerable to skepticism, into a position analogous to Davidson's, according to which perceptions are nothing more than emissaries of reality that could deliver us messages that are either true or false.[92] Not only does the image of "openness to the world" look more than ever like a rhetorical turn of phrase, and McDowell has only apparently overcome the picture of confinement within the space of thought, but it is hard to see what separates his position from Davidson's coherentism: if the content of perception is bipolar, no perception can justify a belief or a judgment unless the person who has that perception possesses *independently from it* reasons to believe that that perception is not "lying" to him.

So it is as if McDowell, at the same time as he adopts the view—or the metaphor—of our openness to the world, changes its meaning to the point of making it unrecognizable. His openness to the world is not really an openness, and, furthermore, it is not really an openness *to the world* either. Actually, McDowell has no concept of world. Besides the fact that we should take into account the very peculiar proviso of the *Tractatus* according to which most of its propositions are revealed to be nonsense at the end of the work, making it uncertain whether the definition of the world as "everything that is the case" is really taken seriously by Wittgenstein, to determine the world in that way comes down to implying that our only possible transactions with our surroundings are of a judicative and cognitive nature: the world is the content of all true propositions we can state about it, and is nothing beyond this. The only access to what McDowell calls "world" is through language. Before learning a language, therefore, a child has no world. And even after having learned one, the only transactions an adult can have with the world *as world* are of a strictly linguistic kind, even when he is limited to perceiving it. Now we might easily concede that everything from which the world is "made out" is thinkable (and expressible), without thereby conceding that the world is only made out of what is thinkable (and expressible). The latter assertion does not follow from the former.

Although McDowell speaks of "our unproblematic openness to the world,[93] or writes, in a Heideggerian style, that "we find ourselves *always already* engaging in the world in conceptual activity,"[94] he continues to understand the way we are engaged in this world exclusively in terms of an activity of expression and of a propositional shaping. This bespeaks a radical intellectualism that remains very close to Sellars's, and to the view that all awareness is a "linguistic affair." "It is only because experience involves capacities belonging to spontaneity," he says, "that we can understand experience as awareness, or apparent awareness, of aspects of the world."[95] McDowell, like Sellars, does not reject the notion of impression, but only the notion of non-conceptual impressions that are at the same time an (infallible) knowledge. He continues to speak of "the world as it impinges on our senses,"[96] while at the same time pointing out that "the impressions on our senses . . . are already equipped with conceptual content."[97] But what does it mean to say that the impressions are "equipped" with conceptual content if their contribution is not even "notionally separable"[98] from that of our spontaneity? In reality, McDowell would like both to get rid of impressions in order to think our openness to the world (as will post-Husserlian phenomenology) and to retain them. This is because his radical intellectualism needs the foil of traditional empiricism to formulate itself—in an inevitably paradoxical way. "Intellectualism lives on the refutation of empiricism,"[99] wrote Merleau-Ponty. Indeed, on the one hand, "experiences are impressions made by the world on our senses, products of receptivity";[100] on the other hand, "those impressions themselves already have conceptual content."[101] Hence two things must be asserted: (1) that the world is different from the impressions through which it is announced (causally) to us (first concept of world); (2) that the world is what we perceive directly, without intermediaries (second concept of world). The world is both what impinges causally on our senses, and what presents itself to us as a set of facts perceived directly. But in that case, we do not perceive the world itself [*le monde même*], because we do not perceive the same world [*le même monde*] as the one that acts causally on us. We have lapsed back, in a different form, into the dichotomy of logical spaces. The only way, as I see it, to escape this aporia would be to recognize that the one and only world truly worthy of the name is that of our daily experience, and whose descriptive content *nowise* includes "impressions;" and that these impressions are only scientific idealizations, "substructions" built on the life-world (see chapter 23). But if this turned out to be the case, there would no longer be any "myth of the given," not because there would no longer be any myth, but because we would have radically changed our concept of *given*, because the given would be nothing but the world itself—a given that no longer fits into the coordinates of the empiricism-Kantianism debate. We would have abandoned the empiricist concept of experience, instead of being content with flavoring it with neo-Kantianism.

For McDowell's solution is far less Hegelian than he says. In keeping with neo-Kantianism, it unilaterally favors, in its approach to experience, the epistemological problematic. Like the Marburg school, it denies the transcendental aesthetics all autonomy and ends up with a complete "logicization" of the given, to use Heidegger's phrase;[102] like the Marburg school, it finally abolishes the Hegelian distinction between understanding and reason, and in so doing rids itself both of the absolute and of the dialectic. McDowell's watchword "the conceptual is unbounded; there is nothing outside it"[103] echoes Natorp's "*ist Alles Denken, Denken Alles.*" By contrast with Hegel—who thinks the unity of sensibility and understanding, of intuition and concept dialectically, never annulling their difference[104]—and in agreement with neo-Kantianism, McDowell thinks that the contribution of receptivity is not even notionally separable from that of spontaneity. This is why, despite his efforts, he never succeeds in actually moving the front line of the traditional debates.[105] Remaining captive to empiricism, keeping to the notion of impression its full right, he is content to propose a new "logical idealism," in the name of which the only structures of experience are those conferred on it "from on high," those coming from a conceptual contribution and a shaping by spontaneity. In contrast with Husserl, who submits the Kantian opposition between receptivity and spontaneity to a radical critique,[106] McDowell relies on these notions as if they were self-evident.

One is puzzled and even stunned when he says that his "therapy," by proposing a new framework for reflection, "really stands a chance of making traditional philosophy obsolete."[107] *What* traditional philosophy? When we take notice of how much McDowell's thought remains tributary to neo-Kantianism, we may at least have some doubts about this. Under the guise of therapy, *Mind and World* takes us back to a position about which it would be euphemistic to say that it is metaphysically overdetermined. Unless, of course, neo-Kantianism is *the* therapy that frees us from all our philosophical (pseudo-)problems. Never openly referring to this precedent, McDowell often gives the impression—at the risk of sounding disagreeable—of rediscovering America,[108] or rather the Old World of Continental Europe. And he gets to the Continent the way Columbus landed in the Americas: by a navigational error. Therefore, he overlooks necessarily the wealth of alternative possibilities of thought it contains:

> "I miss my native Europe, with its ancient citadels!"[109]

20

Is Experience Subjective?

> Our experiences are *ab initio* encounters with a public world.
> —Hilary Putnam

In Latin, the expressions "to live" and "to be among men" (*inter homines essere*), "to die" and "to cease being among men" (*inter homines esse desinere*), are used as synonyms. All existence in the world is coexistence with other men; all experience of the world is co-experience with them. How should we conceive of this coexistence and this co-experience?

To answer that question, the strategy that has prevailed in linguistic philosophy was developed along the lines of Wittgenstein's remarks called by his exegetes the "private language argument." There is no real agreement on the interpretation to be given of that argument, or, better yet, of that set of arguments taking up §243 through §315 of his *Philosophical Investigations.*[1] There, Wittgenstein considers—only to reject it—the possibility of a logically private language; that is, a language that would be the pure tracing of the inner experiences of a speaker. Such a language would not be learned within a linguistic community, in reference to public objects and according to public criteria; nor would it be derived from the observation of the bodily behavior and expression of other speakers. It would only consist in the association to each sensation or emotion of a word through "private ostensive definition": "The individual words of this language are to refer to what can only be known to the person speaking; to his immediate private sensations. So another person cannot understand the language."[2] Such a language, of course, would be neither a language that I would be the only one to speak for circumstantial reasons, nor a code that, relying on a public, preexistent language, could be decoded. It would be a language that I would be the only one *to be able to speak* just as I am the only one who knows my inner experiences. To show the absurdity of such a language is to show thereby, from a linguistic standpoint, the absurdity of solipsism. A language that I not only would be the only one to speak, but be able to speak, would not be a *language* at all; it is a possibility that self-destructs, since this so-called language lacks any criterion by virtue of which its words could be used correctly or incorrectly. If every word, here, only receives its meaning from a private "ceremony" that associates a term with a sensation, there is no way to decide what are the rules that govern the use of words, because to follow a rule is a social practice. "To *think* one is obeying a rule is not to obey a rule. Hence it is not possible to obey a rule 'privately': otherwise thinking one was obeying a rule would be the same thing as obeying it."[3] In such a "language," any use that would appear correct to the speaker *would be* correct by this very fact, so that there would no longer be criteria nor rules.

Wittgenstein's remarks do not apply to language and meaning alone; they apply equally to our experience of the world and other people. While our experiences are "inner" or "private," Wittgenstein tells us, language is necessarily public; therefore, to the extent that thought is internally related to language, to a language that we can learn only by mastering public rules and on the occasion of processes taking place before our eyes, it is thought that confers on our apparently private world the character of a public one. This is, at any rate, the consequence we can *try* to draw from that set of arguments. It comes down to arguing that *the entrance into a public world logically depends on the mastery of a language that is itself subject to public criteria.* As Davidson puts it, if the problem is "how one person knows the mind of another," the answer can only be the following: to know another person is to interpret what he or she says. "Perhaps it is obvious that if the account I have sketched of our understanding of language, and its connection with the contents of thought, is correct, the accessibility of the minds of others is assured from the start."[4] Can one, should one draw such a radical consequence from Wittgenstein's arguments? I will leave that question open. For the moment it will suffice to emphasize that some philosophers, following—or believing they are following—Wittgenstein, have gone down this path. In their view, intersubjectivity is ensured "from the start" by the public nature of thought and language. That response, incidentally, is not only that of philosophers who have followed the "linguistic turn": it can be found sometimes also in the writings of phenomenologists. Only the intercession of the sign, on this view, opens the dimension of a genuine intersubjectivity.[5]

Are things that simple? To return to Wittgenstein for a moment, what is striking about the "private language argument"—regardless of the *exact* form of that argument—are its unquestioned premises. First of all, experience is assumed to be necessarily internal or private. At least the experiences to which Wittgenstein refers—sensations or emotions—

are taken to be of that nature. Furthermore, to speak of private experiences is allegedly already tautological: "The proposition 'Sensations are private' is comparable to: 'One plays patience by oneself.'"[6] The private language argument rests on an extremely impoverished concept of experience, as a set of private conscious episodes—a concept drawn from the empiricist tradition. But is my experience of a landscape, a monument, or a face "private" in this sense? Is it a tautology to make this assertion? To Wittgenstein, let me remark incidentally, the alleged tautological character of "no one but I can have my experiences" is in no case accompanied by the claim of the incommunicability of those experiences; rather it serves as a starting point for the assertion of their communicability on principle. But then what are we to make of a report of the type: "I am (perceptually) experiencing another person"? Is this still a *private* experience? If so, in what sense? Secondly, the fable of a private language, since it rests on this impoverished concept of experience, reduces to absurdity only a historically determined conception of language, the conception that equates meanings with ideas knowable by the subject alone, and directly associated with words (these words being thereby reduced to *names*): a Lockean picture of language, rather than an Augustinian one. As Locke writes, "*words in their primary or immediate signification, stand for nothing, but the ideas in the mind of him that uses them.*"[7] It is unnecessary to emphasize again that this conception is not that of Husserl, nor of any author in the phenomenologic tradition. Lastly and especially, assuming that the goal of this argument is to help us understand (which Wittgenstein does not explicitly say) how we can live in a single, common world, it comes too late, and takes for granted what it is supposed to establish. If language alone, as social practice based on shared rules and criteria, enables us to enter in a truly *common* world, it remains to be understood how this miracle is accomplished. The learning of language is indeed *already* a social practice. Others are the first interlocutors. Language cannot be a bridge between my ("private") experience and that of others unless others are already given within that experience itself. Actually, one must already have conceded the premise of Cartesian inspiration that our experience of the world is "private" in order to give language the role of the only mediator between us.

In order to make language play the role of intermediary between myself and others, we must presuppose that others exceed my experience or—which amounts to the same thing—that there is no *experience* of others *as such.* But for Wittgenstein—and we will have occasion to return to this point—the existence of others poses no more problems that that of the "outside" world, and for similar reasons. What Wittgenstein does not tell us, however, is how to think a mode of prelinguistic givenness of others at the very heart of our experience of the world. Such a givenness is somehow presupposed by his whole approach to language. It is on this point that the "linguistic way" turns out to be incomplete, to say the least. Not that language doesn't contribute to our experience of others: its role is undoubtedly considerable. But language cannot be substituted for that direct, perceptual experience; it presupposes it. If the only way to "know" others were to interpret what they say, to use Davidson's formulation, we could always wonder whether the sounds being interpreted were words or noises generated by a machine, and the skepticism about the existence of others would remain insurmountable. The problem of intersubjectivity is prior by principle to the problem of two people already possessing language understanding one another, because, without a prior intersubjectivity, I would be unable to acquire language in the first place, and there would be no beginning to speech. On the one hand, language itself is perceived; on the other, it is learned by means of activities taking place at the level of perception and necessarily involving others. Therefore others must be perceptually given even before language is in a position to confer a common character on the world. In sum, the world cannot draw its common character from language. In opposition to an intersubjectivity *from on high,* of which language would be the only operator, we must posit an intersubjectivity *from below,* inscribed at the very heart of our experience. This is the starting point of the phenomenological approach.

Husserl has repeated it almost ad nauseam: our world is a shared one from the start. But it is one thing to say it, and another to conceptualize it. In *Formal and Transcendental Logic,* he writes for example: "*World-experience,* as constitutive, signifies, not just my quite private experience, but *community-experience*: The world itself, according to its sense, is the one identical world, to which all of *us* necessarily have experiential access, and about which all of *us* by 'exchanging' our experiences—that is, by making them common—can reach a common understanding."[8] But as soon as we put this passage back into its original context, things are less clear. We read just before this, separated by a "but": "In the first place, then, it is always I and I again: purely as ego of that life of consciousness by which everything receives being-sense for me."[9] The tension between these two passages summarizes by itself the ambiguity of Husserl's position. On the one hand, the idea of an absolute egological closure of the subject seems to exclude the possibility for his world to harbor already within itself such a thing as an *other*; on the other hand, this presence of the other is necessary, at least if we must be able to speak of a common or public world *ab initio.* How can that tension, and perhaps that contradiction, be solved?

It is not enough to say you have overcome solipsism to have overcome it in fact. As I emphasized, transcendental phenomenology rests on the idea of egological closure. The transcendental ego is "absolute" in a threefold sense: (1) it is a sphere of indubitability or of apodicticity; (2) it is independent vis-à-vis the world, possessing an absolute being, whereas the being of the world is relative; (3) it possesses an essential epistemic priority with respect to all objects, since it constitutes them. According to this transcendental framework, the other subject as transcendental subject must be constituted setting out from the system of lived experience of the pure ego. It is necessary that, in the reduced transcendental sphere, as a sphere of absolute being, a being who necessarily transcends that sphere announces itself. But how is this possible? How, within the being of the ego, could "an existence-meaning that *totally transcends its own being*"[10] announce itself? If all meaning and all validity of being comes from this ego and from it alone, how could this ego be the *constituting principle* of a being that *totally exceeds its being* at the very moment in which the ego constitutes it? This is indeed the problem, and the declarations on transcendental intersubjectivity do nothing to solve it; they remain caught between the horns of the dilemma. How is it possible to maintain at once the absolute egological closure of the ego—of *my* ego—and the transcendental community?

Husserl himself recognized that this difficulty was lodged at the heart of the Cartesian framework orienting the phenomenological description. The reduced transcendental sphere is *mine* because it always belongs to my factual ego, because it is the latter's life. This is why the reduction can only mean, at first sight, a solipsistic reduction. "As for me, I recognize," Husserl writes in *First Philosophy,* "the first intuition I had of the phenomenological reduction was of limited range and such as I have described it above ['a reduction to *my transcendental ego, the one carrying out the reduction, and to my own life*']. For years I saw no possibility of transforming it into an intersubjective reduction. But finally I saw a way opening up before me that was to be of decisive importance."[11] What, then, is this way? It consists in the claim that "the bracketing of the spatial world and therefore of foreign psychophysical bodies and other men does not at all put out of play the pure foreign egos and their *cogitationes.*"[12] In other words, the alleged "discovery" occurring late in Husserl's work lies in the view of the intrinsically intersubjective character of the reduction, which means that the "phenomenological being" to which it leads back is not only that of an isolated phenomenological *I,* my own, but just as much that of other *I*'s constituted by *Einfühlung.*[13] As will be repeated in the Amsterdam lectures, "The concrete, full transcendental subjectivity, from the inside looking out, is the purely transcendentally unified, and only thus concrete, totality of the open community of egos."[14] To be sure, but how can we reconcile this assertion with the one about the absolute closure of my ego? Furthermore, strictly speaking, "*my* ego" is a pleonasm: the ego as phenomenological absolute cannot be put in the plural. Consequently, if what we have here is a "discovery," what kind of discovery is it? Is not this "discovery" rather an entirely verbal way of surmounting an aporia lodged at the heart of Husserlian philosophy?

Reduction is necessarily the reduction to *my* transcendental life of consciousness, for the simple reason that I am the one who performs it.[15] The modification of the look that brings about a change in the appearing of phenomena—by purifying them from any transcendent "positing"—can only be a modification of *my* look, and therefore of the appearing of phenomena *for me*. But then, it is impossible to limit oneself to the *factual* assertion of the co-presence of other transcendental egos in my reduced egological field; that assertion requires justification. Now, its justification can only be supplied by an analysis of the mode of constitution of others on the basis of the constituting performances of the pure ego. Nothing is yet decided as long as it has not been shown how this constitution actually works, and the commentators who take Husserl's declarations at face value overlook that the inclusion of intersubjectivity within transcendental subjectivity is not a *fact* that should be acknowledged, but something whose *right* must be established by showing how the constitution of an *alter* ego is possible.[16]

But *is* it possible? The constitution of the foreign subjectivity is carried out in two stages (the distinction between them being a logical, and not a temporal one): first, the constitution of the other as another lived body (*Leib*), then the constitution by apperception of the other as alter ego on the basis of his or her givenness in the flesh. In some expositions of this complex operation, the classic example of which occurs in *Cartesian Meditations*, in order to explain more thoroughly the concrete modalities of that constitution, Husserl performs an additional reduction, a reduction he himself qualifies as "abstractive," and which consists, for the transcendental ego, in placing oneself deliberately in a solipsistic attitude, that is, in reverting to a "sphere of ownness" (*Eigenheitssphäre*) free from any presence of other egos, and in investigating how the other can be announced there for the first time. Let us start out, then, from the pure ego and its transcendental sphere under reduction. Let us practice, in order to make things more explicit, the abstractive reduction to the sphere of my ownness, that is to say, let us proceed as if no one but myself were given in this "world," and let us ask ourselves how the other can co-appear as such in the absolutely closed sphere of my monadic subjectivity. What do we find in this sphere under reduction? Physical bodies (*Körper*) and my own lived body (*Leib*). This lived body is constituted as *my own* body, an "appendix" of my ego, by virtue of a remarkable phenomenon, the reversibility of my tactile sensations: when my left hand touches my right hand, it appears to me alternately as touching and touched, whereas a physical body can certainly be touched, but it never appears to me as *touching*, that is, is not something in which tactile qualities can be located. Let us take note of the fact that at this stage there can be no question of *objective* physical bodies, nor, consequently, of objects in the strict sense, since only intersubjectivity, once it has been constituted, can confer this meaning on them: "In the case of *our* abstraction the sense 'Objective' . . . vanishes completely."[17] How will the other be able to declare him or herself in and from out of this sphere of ownness? The other is an alter ego, that is, in turn a transcendental ego that defines itself as a closed system of lived experiences and that is primordially embodied or localized in a lived body. Such an ego, as different from mine, is a nexus of lived experiences absolutely autonomous with respect to my own lived experiences, that is, a sphere as closed as my own is, possessing an *absolute* egological closure, so that the foreign consciousness obviously cannot appear immediately within my own world, within the world reduced to the sphere of my ownness; otherwise, I would be purely and simply the other, or the alter ego would be me. The other cannot be given—that is, experienced as such—immediately, but only mediately, by the intermediary of his or her lived body. "It is only to myself that I have access directly by the experience of myself," writes Husserl, "whereas I can have the experience of the *foreign* subjectivity, who, for its part, only exists as experiencing itself directly—only *in the mediate mode of the indication.*"[18] Now the question becomes the following: how can the lived body of the foreign subjectivity be perceived directly in the world that has been reduced to the sphere of ownness?

The idea subtending Husserl's approach, the properly *phenomenological* idea of that approach, is that the foreign subjectivity can be given only mediately by appresentation on the basis of its appearing as a lived body, but that this lived body, for its part, is given directly, that is, perceived as such. Thus, the lived body of the other can refer back like an *indication* (*Anzeige*) to its transcendental ego, but this "indication" is of a very special nature, since what it refers to can never be "given" otherwise than through this indication itself. This is why Husserl will characterize that "'appresentative' indication"[19] as "*originary indication.*"[20] However, this vocabulary is problematic: it still implies that it is not the other him or herself that is perceived, but only its index as lived body. Now, what we are conscious of, what is directly perceived or presented in our experience, is indeed the other in the flesh, and not an external sign of its presence. As Husserl writes, "appresentation as such presupposes a core of presentation."[21] It is this core of presentation, the lived body of the other, that does indeed serve as the starting point for his or her appresentation as foreign transcendental consciousness, alter ego in the strict sense, that is to say, for an intending necessarily empty of intuition, and that must remain so, if we are to avoid reducing the other to a mere appendix to myself. As long as we have not understood how a *foreign* lived body can be given, hence constituted within the sphere of ownness, the entire mediate operation of constitution of the foreign subjectivity will remain a mystery.

Let us therefore read the text that is central to the whole fifth *Cartesian Meditation.* "Let us assume that another man enters our perceptual sphere. Primordially reduced, that signifies: In the perceptual sphere pertaining to my primordial Nature, a physical body [*Körper*] is presented, which, as primordial, is of course only a determining part of myself: an 'immanent transcendency.' "[22] At this stage, no lived body (*Leib*) other than my own has yet appeared, since the lived body is self-constituted as the substrate for the doubled (touching/touched) tactile sensations, and nothing in the body of the other matches that possibility. Now, as long as the other has not appeared as a lived body analogous to my own, all apperceptive constitution of an alter ego will remain excluded on principle. The text continues as follows:

> Since, in this Nature and this world, my lived body is the only body that is or can be constituted originally as a lived body (a functioning organ), the physical body over there, which is nevertheless apprehended as a lived body, must have derived this sense by an *apperceptive transfer from my lived body* and done so in a manner that excludes an actually direct, and hence primordial, showing of the predicates belonging to a lived corporeality [*Leiblichkeit*] specifically, a showing of them in perception proper. It is clear from the very beginning that only a similarity connecting, within my primordial sphere, that physical body over there with my body can serve as the motivational basis for the *'analogizing' apprehension* of that body as another lived body.[23]

Husserl begins by asserting that a lived body [*chair*] other than my own cannot manifest itself in the egological sphere reduced to ownness. But he continues by saying that this lived body *must* nonetheless manifest itself there (in order for a constitution of the other as alter ego to be possible). And he concludes by saying that this lived body *manifests itself* there by virtue of an "apperceptive transfer" or an "analogizing apprehension" on the basis of my own lived body. There is a non sequitur here. As Didier Franck remarks, "indeed, in the primordial sphere, the other comes into view as a physical body [*corps*], or rather, since the meaning *other* is not yet constituted, a physical body comes into view that, like all the others, is a component of myself, a transcendence in immanence. But Husserl should not have the right to say that in the world and nature within the sphere of ownness, from which by definition all living egoic essence is excluded, the physical body 'over there' is grasped as lived body [*chair*]."[24] And of course if the other cannot yet come into view as lived body (and can *never* do so, unless we assume its constitution to have been already realized), he can neither "resemble" my lived body—because he has no reversibility of feeling—nor appear to me in a way that is *analogous* to that of my lived body. The apperceptive transfer of the meaning "lived body" to this body among bodies (a "transfer" that is not based at all on a reasoning, but is a spontaneous association operating passively in the depths of my life of consciousness) must rest on a similarity, but in order for there to be similarity between the body of the other and my own lived body, this transfer must already have taken place. Therefore the apperceptive transfer presupposes itself. And this is the case, even more so because, while Husserl includes, among similarities, the gestures, expressive movements, and facial expressions of foreign subjectivities, these expressions cannot constitute the capstone of empathy (*Einfühlung*), Lipps notwithstanding, because they do not yet allow our assigning to the foreign consciousness a lived body *in the strictly phenomenological sense of the term*, that is, as the substrate of doubled tactile sensations: it is the physical body, not the lived body, that moves and expresses itself.[25]

Of course, if this first stage of constitution fails, the second stage, based on it, in which the lived body presented in perception plays the role of an indication for something not presentable—the pure ego, not only as an other ego, but as the *ego of another*—cannot come to light either. Here we are confronted with a "constitution" that reveals itself to be doubly circular. First, in order for an alter ego to be the object of an appresentation on the basis of a foreign lived body, that foreign lived body must appear in my world reduced to the sphere of ownness, and in order for a foreign lived body to appear in this primordial "world," a lived body (without qualification) must first appear there. But in this sphere of ownness, only my own lived body can appear. A foreign lived body can manifest itself as such only if it *resembles* my own, and it can only resemble my own if it already manifests itself as *lived body*; now, it is the very possibility of that manifestation that is in need of an explanation. Husserl's description, which pretends to exhibit that possibility, actually presupposes it. Secondly, even were we to grant Husserl that first step, even were we to agree that it is indeed a *lived body* that appears "over there" resembling my own and forming a pair with it, according to what Husserl calls a *Paarung*, a coupling by resemblance, it would remain to be explained how that other lived body can become the lived body *of another*, the indication of a transcendental life foreign to my own. The apperception of an alter ego on the basis of its lived body presupposes the appearing of a *foreign* lived body, and the appearing of a foreign lived body (in the required sense of "foreign," that is, in the sense of belonging to an alter ego) presupposes the apperception of an alter ego.[26]

These consequences are not at all surprising; they derive from the primacy and absoluteness of the pure ego. The absoluteness that reigns in the sphere of the subject cannot admit of any sharing: if I bear the absolute within myself, I am *the only* absolute, and the other cannot possess, in my absolute transcendental sphere, any absoluteness comparable to mine; he cannot be constituted as an ego of the same rank or the same nature as my ego. The inconstitutability of the other follows necessarily from the radical monadological closure of transcendental subjectivity. So it is pointless for me to dwell on the complex and technical elaborations of the fifth *Cartesian Meditation.* But there is an additional reason for me to dispense with this detour. I have already had occasion to critique amply and for its own sake—regardless of the problem of the other—the Husserlian transcendental-constitutive framework by virtue of which *all* meaning, including that of a foreign subjectivity, is born in (*in*) and from (*aus*) me, and my objections, if they are well-founded, obviate the necessity of a critique of the transcendentalism that presides over the positing of the problem of the other in terms of the latter's *constitution* by the ego.

It is not pointless, however, to stress a few more general consequences that follow, I believe, for *any* phenomenology of the other. And mainly the following consequence: it does not suffice to adopt an attitude symmetrical to that of Husserl by developing a conception of the other as "the absolutely Other," to get out of the dilemma that I have formulated. Thus, it could be argued that Levinas's entire work consists less in bringing us a positive phenomenological answer to the problem of the mode of appearance of the other than in transforming the aporia of the fifth *Cartesian Meditation* into a paradoxical solution. Given that the other does not succeed in entering a world that has been previously defined as the pure correlate of a constituting system, one is tempted to say that the other does not appear in the world, but elsewhere or beyond it, and that this break from the totality, this Infinity that arises with his face, "cuts across sensibility";[27] in short, that the impossibility for the other to appear in the world is the very modality of its manifestation. The face (*visus*) is no longer, then, what can be seen (*videre*), but what can be neither seen nor stared at, what "breaks with the world"[28] by its refusal to be contained in it. But if "the face is not 'seen,'"[29] perhaps this entails first of all that it is not, in Levinas, what we commonly understand by this term: such a "face" not only contrasts with phenomenality, but it contrasts with phenomenology itself. Levinas himself draws this conclusion explicitly: "I do not know if one can speak of a 'phenomenology' of the face, since phenomenology describes what appears. So, too, I wonder if one can speak of a look turned toward the face, for the look is knowledge, perception. I think rather that access to the face is straightaway ethical."[30] Perhaps Levinas's analysis of the face is *not at all* to be read from a phenomenological *perspective* [*optique*].[31] For, from the point of view of a description of phenomena, it leaves all the problems intact. To escape Cartesian solipsism, Levinas invents a *solipsisme à deux* in which the subjects appear "separated" to the point of no longer being able to share any world. But isn't the world that which is shareable in its very essence?

To sum up, shouldn't the difficulty be approached from an entirely different standpoint? If phenomenology takes appearing as a legitimizing source and describes it in its own right, mustn't it begin necessarily with the givenness of the other *in the world*? Merleau-Ponty and Heidegger have tried to do so. "The perceived world," the former stresses, "is not *my* world alone, for I see the behaviors of others take form there, behaviors that also aim at this world; and the world is the correlate not only of my consciousness, but also of *every consciousness that I might encounter*."[32] The world is not *my* world. I experience the world, but the world I experience is not thereby "subjective"; it is neutral with respect to the I/other distinction—neither "mine" nor "other" since the other announces himself there with the same right as I do. But it is Heidegger, even more so, who has stigmatized the Cartesian starting point in an isolated *I*, qualifying it as an "absurdity."[33] Once the problem has been formulated in the terms of Cartesianism, *Einfühlung* is not a solution, it only aggravates the problem, since, "supposed, as it were, to provide the first ontological bridge from one's own subject, which is given proximally as alone, to the other subject, which is proximally quite closed off,"[34] empathy can never succeed. The phenomenological description, far from being grounded in the phenomena in this case, only develops from prior metaphysical considerations. If "the problem of *empathy* is just as absurd as the question of the reality of the external world,"[35] this is in fact for the same reasons: the Cartesian presuppositions that underlie these two "problems." Heidegger recommends starting out from the exactly opposite assertion:

"the world is always already primarily given as the common world."[36] Phenomenology takes the given as legitimizing source for its descriptions, and the primordial given, here, is the one, shared world, the public world in which I am located with others: "They are there with me in the one world."[37] Instead of envisaging the relation to others on the basis of a situation in which the ego is not only alone, but *alone in being alone*, that is to say, a situation in which I am the only "myself," *solus ipse*, we should rather say that every loneliness and every solitude becomes meaningful solely against the background of a primordial community, of which they are deficient modes. Being with others, which Heidegger calls *Mitsein*, literally "Being-with" or "Being-together," is as originary as being oneself: "Being toward Others [is] . . . an autonomous, irreducible relationship of Being."[38] Moreover, this Being-together is not the result of a contingent encounter with others, but is an ontological characteristic of existence itself. To exist, ontologically speaking, is always already to coexist with others in the one, shared world; it is "Being-with-in-the-world" (*Mit-in-der-Welt-sein*).[39] Existence is intrinsically plural, intrinsically coexistence: "As being-in-the-world it [*Dasein*] is never first merely being among things present-at-hand within the world, then subsequently to uncover other human being as also being among them. Instead, as being-in-the-world it is being-with others, apart from whether and how others are factically there with it themselves."[40]

The question now is whether the new starting point recommended by Heidegger for the formulation of the "problem of the other" is tenable and whether the philosopher has pursued the implications of the revolution he has initiated to their ultimate consequences. One point seems to raise serious difficulties. The Being of *Dasein* is characterized by Heidegger as "in each case mine" (*je meines*), mineness (*Jemeinigkeit*) being the ontological hallmark of all *Dasein*. It is because the Being of *Dasein* is always in each case mine that this mineness can then be declined according to its two fundamental guises: selfhood (*Selbstheit*), in which *Dasein* authentically relates to its existence in the finite project of its potentiality-for-Being, and the lack of selfhood, "the they," in which *Dasein* lets its possibilities be dictated to it by the vox populi and falls short of itself and its ownmost potentiality-for-Being. But how is it possible to maintain both that the Being of *Dasein* understood as Being-in-the-world is in each case mine—which comes down to considering the world, as characteristic of *Dasein's* Being, as also possessing the characteristic of mineness—and that this same world is a public world from the start, a world that I share with others? How can the world, grasped in its phenomenality according to the leading thread of *Dasein's* ontology, be both "mine" and "common"? The difficulty running through *Being and*

Time here comes from the fact that Heidegger, while distancing himself from the Cartesianism of his master, has not in the least abandoned the idealist and transcendental stance of "conditions of possibility." *Dasein*, by the understanding of Being that belongs to its Being itself, is the condition of possibility for the appearing of *all* beings—hence also of a *Mitdasein*; "*Dasein*, seen metaphysically as this Being-in-the-world, is therefore, as factically existent, nothing other than the existent possibility for beings to *gain entry to world* [*des Welteingangs von Seiendem*]."[41] This transcendental—or transcendentally inspired—claim must be true of all beings, or else not true at all. The other can be no exception. Heidegger thus takes back with one hand what he has given away with the other. On the one hand, to exist, for *Dasein*, is always essentially to coexist with others; on the other hand, Being-in-the-world is still conceived of as a structure of the Being of *Dasein* in each case mine, and the world, correlatively, as a transcendental horizon preceding and making possible the ontic manifestation of any other *Dasein*, or of any *Dasein* as another. Thus Heidegger does not hesitate to state that the world, as a structural moment of Being-in-the-world, is "subjective," if what is meant by that is that it belongs to "the well-understood concept of the 'subject' as existing *Dasein*, the *Dasein* as Being-in-the-world."[42] Where *Being and Time* resolutely breaks with Husserlian (and, more broadly, Cartesian) conceptuality is not on the point of whether the world is or is not a characteristic of the "subject" (ontologically well understood), but on that of whether or not it is appropriate to characterize that subjectivity as *interiority*. "World is only, if, and as long as a *Dasein* exists . . . in such a way that the projecting of the world belongs to *Dasein*'s Being. In this projection the *Dasein* has always already *stepped out beyond itself*, it exists [*ex-sistere*], it *is in* a world. Consequently, it is never anything like a subjective inner sphere."[43] *Dasein* has neither interiority nor exteriority; it is its own transcendence as ecstatic openness to the world; but this world remains no less "subjective" as constitutive of that transcendence. And it is indeed in this world, a world understood as an ontological feature of Being-in-the-world *defined by mineness*, that the other, the other *Dasein*, is summoned to appear. In facing the "problem of the other," Heidegger's strategy is, in short, as follows: to maintain a certain sense of the "subjectivity" of the world, while at the same time challenging Husserl's immanence/transcendence division. As a result, Heidegger remains far closer to the Husserlian transcendental system—with all the problems it raises—than he would probably be willing to admit.

Indeed, for Husserl: (1) The problem of the other can only be formulated adequately at the level of a transcendental subjectivity, and therefore authentically intentional, and not at the level of a psychological subjectivity defined by its "interiority." (2) Subjectivity "well understood" plays the transcendental role of condition of possibility for all givenness of the other understood in terms of "constitution" (although Heidegger abandons this last concept). (3) We thus wind up with the paradox that, considered all by itself, that is, leaving aside all contingent encounter with the other, *subjectivity is already transcendental intersubjectivity.* Insofar as he advances that *Mitsein* is an *a priori* formal characteristic of *Dasein,* regardless of whether others are or are not revealed in the world, Heidegger ends up with a position that is very close: *Dasein,* considered formally and in itself, that is, in its Being as determined by *Jemeinigkeit,* is already Being-together (*Mitsein*). "This Being-with-one-another" (*Miteinandersein*), he writes, "is not an additive result of the occurrence of several such others, not an epiphenomenon of a multiplicity of *Daseins,* something supplementary which might come about only on the strength of a certain number. On the contrary, it is because *Dasein* as Being-in-the-world is of itself Being-with [*von sich her Mitsein ist*] that there is something like a Being-with-one-another."[44] This "*von sich her*"[45] is decisive; it is *by itself* that *Dasein* is "plural," that it is relation to others and sharing of existence—this is indeed what remains transcendental here or even, in the broad sense of the term, "*Cartesian,*" even bordering on solipsism. *Dasein* is *Mitsein all by itself,* and it remains so even if it is the only one of its kind, the only *Dasein.* We must find intersubjectivity in "subjectivity" considered formally and in itself, independently of any *encounter* with others, encounter being thereby lowered to the rank of accident and "epiphenomenon."

But shouldn't it be maintained, on the contrary, that the event of the encounter of the other is constitutive of the very "Being" of the one we ourselves are, because the one we are is by essence openness to the event, "*advenant*" as I have called it elsewhere? Because the *advenant* is only *him or herself*—that is, endowed with selfhood—insofar as he responds to, and for, the event that befalls him *as singular,* his encounters, as events, contribute in an essential way to the constitution of his existence or adventure. The phenomenological status of the other is then to be thought on the basis of two connected assertions: first, the other only declares him or herself through the event of a singular encounter, in which, as in all events, I am myself in play as myself; second, although the other only declares him or herself through encounters, there is no first encounter for an adventure: because the *advenant* comes into the world in being born into it, the other is always here in this world in an immemorial way. As far back as I can remember, the other is already present in my own adventure, installed at the heart of it, more innermost to it than it itself is; and this is so because this adventure only befalls the *advenant* through the event of a birth.[46] The problem of the other, because it is inseparable from that of the evential character of all adventure, escapes the formal *a priori* structure of Heidegger's Being-with.

But let us return to the ambiguity of the position of *Being and Time.* Here, it is as if Heidegger, ruling out as an absurdity any starting point in an isolated ego and claiming the necessary "plurality" of existence understood as coexistence, had indicated with insight the only possible anchor point for a phenomenology of the other. But at the same moment, because of his characterization of the Being of *Dasein* as "in each case mine" and his assignment of alterity to a formal ontological structure, he ruined the scope of his own innovation, and ended up with a position—*Dasein* is essentially *Mitsein*—that is neither that much clearer, nor fundamentally different from the one advanced by Husserl: subjectivity is, *all by itself,* transcendental intersubjectivity. And the reason for this move is that rather than denying that the openness to the world—experience itself—is *subjective* (in the sense of the "well-understood" concept of the subject), he maintained that it is so, but according to a new concept of the subject: *Dasein*; and he only rejected the possibility of applying to *Dasein* and its openness the interior/exterior distinction in any sense whatsoever. According to his view, experience, as openness to the world, is indeed subjective, but it escapes all intimacy and all interiority of an ego. Now, another solution to the same problem would have been possible: to *reject the subjectivity of experience, while maintaining the relevance of a* certain *distinction between immanence and transcendence within the—neutral—field of experience itself.*

We are so obsessed with presuppositions of Cartesian origin that this possibility seems excluded to us—it does not even seem to be a *possibility* at all. But what is the truth of the matter? What might it mean to say that experience is not subjective? Am *I* not the one who experiences things and has experiences? "No one but me can have my experiences." Is this not a tautology? It may be that these objections, however obvious they seem at first, are nothing but expressions of a prejudice. In any case, they rest on an insufficient analysis of the meaning of "subjective" in this context. In what sense can it be said of experience that it is "subjective"? In several senses, to be sure. Let us examine some of them.

(1) In qualifying experience as "subjective," we can mean that it is *purely subjective,* that is to say, that it is identical to a mental or psychological state. This use of "subjective" leads almost inevitably to holding experience to be illusory. If color, for example, is *only* subjective in the sense of being a psychological state, it doesn't correspond to any physical state of the world; it is, so to say, projected onto things by us. Phenomenology rejected very early such a concept of subjectivity. The subjectivity of expe-

rience, Husserl clarifies, "should not be confused (as it is so frequently) with the subjectivity of a lived experience, as though the perceived things in their perceptual qualities were themselves lived experiences."[47] (2) By the subjectivity of experience we can mean that experience belongs to a transcendental subject, which is determined in its essence by intentionality. The transcendental ideality of experience is then compatible with its empirical reality. The color I perceive is indeed a property of the world, but of the world considered as the pure correlate of a constituting subjectivity. Taken in this sense, "subjective" is no longer synonymous with "illusory." This word means rather "dependent on its constitution by a transcendental ego." (3) Leaving this distinction between psychological and transcendental subject aside, "subjective" can be interpreted in the sense of *phenomenally subjective*, that is, appearing as a characteristic of myself in the field of experience. An illusion, a daydream, an afterimage, a "physiological" color, according to Goethe's expression—for example a phosphene caused by a pressure on the eyeball—do not correspond to anything in reality. Similarly, in the experience of proprioception, I perceive my body as an island of subjectivity whose mode of appearing is distinct from that of surrounding objects. Of course, for there to be phenomenally subjective entities in the field of perceptual experience there must also be phenomenally objective ones: the lamp, the table, or the wall do not "respond" to my tactile solicitations in the same way as my own body does. The view of an experience being phenomenally subjective *as a whole* is absurd in this respect, since "phenomenally subjective" and "objective" form a pair of opposites that presuppose one another. (4) Experience can be qualified as "subjective," this time in the sense of "*genetically subjective*."[48] Thus, according to neuronal "subjectivism," experiences are produced by complex neuro-physiological processes that take place in the body/brain of an individual.

These first four acceptations are not exclusive from one another. The idea of a genetically subjective experience is compatible either with a materialist perspective, according to which experience is a mental state that is identical to a brain state, or with a transcendental perspective asserting that experience depends both ontologically and epistemologically on the constituting performances of a pure ego. Obviously, these two claims do not have the same consequences as to the status of experience itself: the materialism of brain states is generally accompanied by a psychologism of mental states, while the transcendental problematic attempts to escape this alternative. Incidentally, it is not superfluous to remark that, on a strictly historical level, it is probably the Kantian transcendental perspective that, willy-nilly, has opened the path to the cognitivist and materialist perspective. The duality of sensations, defined by

Kant by their causal impact on the sense organs, and of the intellectual functions whose purpose is to shape sensations by means of the categories, has been replaced, in Schopenhauer, by a theory foreshadowing in many respects the contemporary cognitive sciences, and whose project is to replace the Kantian transcendental subject with the brain. "The understanding . . . , like its underlying forms of space and time, is a function of the brain," Schopenhauer writes, and hence the analytic of pure understanding is destined to become that of "the function of the . . . nerve mass of the brain."[49] Nevertheless, these various meanings of "subjective" do not always intersect. For instance, the transcendental standpoint is compatible both with Kant's view according to which experience is genetically subjective but not phenomenally subjective (since the transcendental subject is not given to itself as phenomenon), and with Husserl's according to which it possesses those two characteristics. In both cases, experience is only *for me* if it is also *from me*—although this "*me*" must be understood in two distinct senses.

Finally, there is a fifth, weaker sense in which it can be said that experience is "subjective." "Subjective" is understood in this case exclusively in the sense of *relative to a subject.* To say that experience is *for me* does not entail in that case that it is *from me.* The transition, apparently so self-evident, from *für mich* (for me) to *aus mir* (from me), which is the mainspring of Husserlian idealism, has no longer any justification. It should be said, then, that experience is "subjective" in that I always occupy its center. All experience appears as self-centered insofar as my body has a privileged place in it: all that I perceive is ordered and distributed according to the perspectives that are born from my situation in the midst of things. This view is compatible with the acceptance of the phenomenally subjective/phenomenally objective distinction. This body that is here, always at the center, reveals itself to me as "mine" or as "my own"; it exhibits a fold of interiority in opposition to which I can say of other things that they are "exterior" to me, or not me. The self-centered experience thus possesses two complementary poles, subjective and objective; it is structured by this very opposition. This body that I touch, that I feel, that can be affected by pain, irritated by loud noises, frozen or sweltered, forms a subjective pole of experience by contrast to which "objectively" hot or cold objects, objectively dull or shrill sounds occupy the objective pole. But these phenomenally objective and subjective poles both enter into the structuration of a single experience, about which one must not say that it is "subjective" *in its very stuff*—in the sense, this time, of *genetically* subjective. The recognition of the centeredness of experience, and hence of its relativity to me as body, implies the acceptance of the polarity between the subjective and the objective *at the phenomenal level*, but it in no way entails that that same experience, with its bipolarity, is "engendered by me" in any sense whatsoever.

This last meaning of "subjective" is by far the least problematic. It is compatible with the conception of experience set forth in chapter 15, and with the following. Experience as such, that is, as openness to the world (in me and outside me), is not genetically subjective, but relational: it is the very modality of my incessant transaction with my surroundings; it is born, so to speak, at this point of juncture where my body projects itself onto things; it is the continuous event of that encounter under the auspices of an agile, acting body. Just as "to meet" is a dyadic predicate—"Peter meets Paul" has the form R(x, y)—similarly, to experience is to encounter something, to confront something. "Perception," as Merleau-Ponty puts it, is "the archetype of the originating encounter."[50] This is why experience is neutral with respect to the distinction between the genetically subjective and the genetically objective: structured according to two complementary poles, experience is always both at the same time *experience of oneself and of the world, experience of oneself in the world, and experience of the world in reference to oneself.* If it has a private dimension, that of sensations that are accessible to me alone—pain, blindness, burning, afterimage, muffling, proprioception in general—and a public dimension that I share from the start with all beings capable of perceiving, these are only the two sides of one selfsame, undivided experience that includes at once things, others, and me. Such an experience is not conceivable as dependent on a transcendental subject—even in the sense, advanced by Heidegger, of a *Dasein* that would be, by its finite understanding of Being, condition for the manifestation of all beings, and hence also the site of such a manifestation, the "there" of the appearing of entities in general. Experience is not an intrinsic property of the subject who is in the world, but rather a property of the *system* formed by the bodily subject and the world, the (pre-subjective and pre-objective) dimension of their dealings. Or rather, experience is not even a *property* of anything at all; it is both something I *have*[51] and something that *takes place* on the occasion of my encounter with things, with others, with myself; it is the continuous form taken on by that encounter.

From this experience that is both centered and polarized, but that is neutral with respect to the differences I/things, I/others, since it includes all that at the same time, should I say that it is mine, that it is inalienable? And if so, in what sense? Here again, it depends on what we mean by "inalienable," as a moment ago it depended on what was meant by "subjective." If by inalienable we mean that I am always located at the center of this experience, that the latter is ordered and distributed around that primary location that I occupy with my body, the answer is undeniably "yes." If by that term we mean that this experience must be conceived of as an intrinsic property of the subject, *engendered* in some way by it—even on the basis of sensory stimulation—the answer is an unambiguous "no." And it is so because this subject only appears (to itself included) as himself situated within that experience itself, lodged in its heart, precisely as one of its poles; and that necessary centeredness of the phenomenal field is something as "objective" as anything else in this field. Experience is inalienable in the sense that it belongs to its essence to unfold outward from our own body [*corps propre*], which is its center and is part of it; but it is not inalienable in the sense of being a property of that body, nor even less of a psyche, an ego, or a consciousness—in short, of a pure subject of perception. It is in fact so far from being inalienable in this second sense that an *alius*, the other, can always in principle declare itself within it and occupy a place in it. Furthermore, if I am the only one to occupy the center of perception, this center is not such that it can be occupied by me alone—on the contrary, it can be occupied by *everybody*. Somebody else can see the world from here, hear a melody from this same point in space, and so on. Experience is neutral with respect to the I/other distinction, since it is the experience of a world in which I and the other both appear, can exchange our places, espouse one another's respective points of view, meet and coexist pacifically. The "conflict of consciousnesses," the rivalry of subjects around the throne of the absolute is, in this respect, no more than a *myth*. Such is, as I have stressed, the only possible starting point for a phenomenology of the other.

What I perceive cannot be the *world* if it is not the same thing as what the other perceives, that totality encompassing and surrounding him or her, in which he or she is caught up and in turn located. If we do not perceive the same world, it is not the world itself that we perceive. Perhaps there is no mystery here, and it is only presuppositions held to be self-evident that make this fact *seem* mysterious to us. The main presupposition, which in a way commands all the others, corresponds to the fourth acceptation of "subjective" analyzed earlier. It resides in the view that experience is genetically subjective "in its very stuff"—assuming that this metaphor makes sense, and thus that there is a sense in attributing to experience a kind of consistency independently from the "objects" it makes present to us, of which it *is* the mode of presence—a view shared by transcendentalism (regardless of whether or not it is formulated in terms of "constitution"), naive psychologism, and cognitivist materialism, all direct or indirect descendants of Cartesian and Lockean metaphysics; more Lockean than Cartesian, probably, since it is Locke who tended to transform Cartesian methodological solipsism into a psychological fact, allowing it to exert its influence for centuries. It is this presupposition that precludes a satisfactory solution to the problem posed by the presence of the other in the flesh *into the world*. If experience is genetically subjective, it is inalienable in the strong sense of the term, and therefore no *alius* can appear in it, unless I infer one from putative premises or constitute one passively as a variant of my ego on the basis of a similitude relationship between us. Therefore it is this presupposition that needs to be examined and discussed in the first place.

What lends credibility to the idea of a subjective experience "in its very stuff"? At first sight, the disparity that we can notice between physical stimulation and the perceived qualities and forms. For example, I listen to a melody, but I do not hear a determinate number of notes, although the musician played a determinate number of them. Is this not because what I perceive is different from what is played—a mere representation, a subjective lived experience different from the acoustic vibrations? But this argument is specious; what we perceive are the played notes, and not a second set of notes, a "subjective" one. But the fact is that we have no need to count the sounds in order to perceive them. Counting and perceiving are two distinct operations, both relating to the same sounds or the same melody. If there is a gestalt quality here that stands out from the totality of the notes, there is no reason to ascribe it to the perceiving subject alone and not to the melody itself. The same goes for some "illusions." We are told that, since we perceive the Müller-Lyer lines as being unequal and they are objectively of an equal length, we do not perceive these lines themselves. The reasoning is only convincing on condition that we bring out its implicit premise: the lines are *either* objective *or* subjective, and if what I perceive differs from the objective lines, it follows that it forms a subjective duplicate of the lines. But why should we grant this premise? Why can't the perceived lines be both "objective" in the sense of phenomenally objective, and relational, that is, dependent on the system that a perceiving body forms with its environment—neither intrinsically objective, nor intrinsically subjective (this time, in the *genetic* sense of the term), but arising from the continuous encounter of an organism with its milieu? The lines perceived as equal and/or unequal according to the attitude I adopt toward them, when I abandon myself to the spontaneous syncretism of perception or attempt to analyze the elements of the figure separately, are indeed the lines of the diagram itself; they belong to the phenomenologically objective pole of experience, as opposed, for example, to purely imagined or hallucinated lines. This notwithstanding, these lines do not possess their properties in the absence of the perceptual relationship that holds between the diagram and my bodily existence. The idea of a perception that would be subjective and would duplicate the perceived, and the idea of lines "in themselves" as *absolutely* objective and without any relation to perception are only the two sides of one single conception and must both be rejected. Visual stimulations do not differ from the perceived world as "in themselves" properties differ from "subjective" properties; they differ from them like *theoretical constructions*, governed by scientific interests regarding the physics and the physiology of vision, differ from the properties of the world in which we are corporally immersed and from the vital interests that underlie perception (see chapter 23).

By this claim, I do not deny the existence of physical stimuli, measurable and knowable independently of the properties of the perceived environment; nor do I deny the existence of physiological causalities, that is, of a factual genesis of experience. These are empirical questions into which phenomenology need not venture. But the difficult conceptual problem is *whether it makes sense to consider this causal-real genesis underlying perception as a* subjective *genesis of experience*, and therefore whether one must consider the perceived qualities of that experience to be properties intrinsic to a subject. A long tradition has persuaded us that colors, warmth, odors, and sounds are nothing but psychic qualities distinct from physical ones—"secondary qualities" as opposed to "primary qualities." On this view, the fact that colors are modified according to the lighting, that they even disappear at night, inform us of the fact that they are merely "ideas in us."[52] At night, the red of porphyry disappears, Locke argues, while its primary qualities, figure, extension, and solidity, are preserved. Red is therefore an ephemeral quality that, since it is not in the object, exists only in the subject—an "idea" or a sensation. But Locke is begging the question. The porphyry would have no color in the dark. But why? From the fact that at night I no longer perceive the red, two opposite consequences may be drawn: either that the porphyry is no longer red, or that it remains red, but this red no longer appears to us—just as porphyry still has figure, size, and weight, even though we do not touch it, measure it, or lift it. In order for this argument to be valid, in order for us to be able to infer the absence of color from the lack of sensation, we must have already admitted that color *is nothing but* a sensation. But that is what the argument was trying to establish.

Let us imagine the case of a color-blind person. Where I perceive an unequivocally green lawn, the color-blind person sees nothing but an almost achromatic expanse, of an indeterminate color and brightness (brown? grayish? it hardly matters). Does this mean that this spring-like green is not a property of the lawn? But then a property of what? Only the disjunction, once it has been accepted, according to which green is either a physical property or a psychological property, can allow us to conclude that, if it is not perceived by everyone, it must be something subjective. But again, the argument is not compelling. We may very well hold that green is a phenomenally objective property of the lawn, just as much as its slope, its size, or the length of the grass, and that this phenomenally objective property, in order to be perceived, calls for the capacities of an observer. If, as a consequence of a cerebral lesion, I am no longer able to see this phenomenally objective property of the lawn, it does not follow that that property never was objective. It is as objective as the lawn itself, which retains its properties even if I turn away and stop looking at it. This phenomenally objective property depends, in order to appear, on its relation to my perceptual capacities; it is an objective property of the lawn *in its relation to me.* In short, why should I say that the color-blind person perceives the lawn as having a different color, and not that he fails to perceive the real color of the lawn? If I see the lawn as blurred, does it follow that it *is* blurred? Of course, by virtue of what physiological processes he fails where I succeed is a completely different problem—one that does not fall within the competence of phenomenology.

A Locke follower might always try to persuade us that the disparity between the physical properties of light and reflective surfaces and the phenomenal properties of colors entails that the latter do not correspond to anything in the world, that they are but well-founded illusions.[53] Indeed, let us suppose that perceived color is a physical property of light as reflected selectively by objects—their surface, by virtue of atomic and nuclear properties, absorbing certain wavelengths. The electromagnetic spectrum is a continuum of wavelengths of which the human eye can detect only a part, approximately the segment between 400 and 700 nanometers. A bee perceives ultraviolet, a diurnal bird, part of the infrared. However, if the light spectrum is a perfect physical continuum, what we perceive is far from being a continuum. Distinct hues are recognizable in it: Newton distinguishes seven, by analogy with the musical scale, Gassendi five, and Leonardo da Vinci six. This is not all: perceived colors are *structured.* There are unitary colors—red, yellow, green, and blue—and binary colors, which are the combination of their adjacent colors within the spectrum. Besides, some of the primary colors are incompatible: green can exist in combination with blue and yellow, but not with red. All these phenomenal properties of colors are without equivalent in the light spectrum. If nothing in the physical properties of light corresponds to the unitary/ binary distinction, to the incompatibility of colors or to the hue / lightness/ saturation differentiation for chromatic colors, must we not conclude that what we perceive are *not* properties of light? But if that is the case, are colors not reducible to psychological states, and perhaps ultimately identical to neurophysiological states? Is color not an illusion? To be sure, an illusion shared by the human kind, and so a “not unfounded" illusion? This consequence does not follow, and for a simple reason: we can very well accept the premises of the argumentation, that is, agree that the phenomenon of color is structured by relations that have no equivalent in the physics of light and its reflection by surfaces, while at the same time denying the conclusion, namely that colors are intrinsic properties of mental or cerebral states. For it might be that colors are not intrinsic properties *of anything at all*, neither of light nor of our mental states, but only relational properties of a complex environment in its relation to a living organism endowed with perceptual capacities. In order for the argument to be convincing, one would have to accept, as I have already said, the disjunction that underlies it: color must be either "outside," as identical to a physical state, or "inside," as identical to a mental state, or even to a neural one.[54]

Perhaps color can be defined only as a relational property of the system that an organism forms with its life environment, that is to say, as an "ecological" property, in the sense that Gibson conferred on this term. If that is the case, we must give up two recurrent ideas that obscure most of the debates about these questions. First, the goal of perception is not to detect physical invariants, that is to say, to represent reality in a physically adequate manner to an observer. An animal is not a budding physicist. The goal of perception is rather to *present* a life environment in such a way that the animal can best carry out its tasks in it. Thus for example, it can be observed that human vision is at its most acute in lighting conditions that are those of the shade beneath leafy boughs. It has also been observed that color vision only confers a selective advantage on an animal, in comparison with achromatic vision, when its action targets are enveloped in a half-light, in changing condition of light and shade. Such considerations invite us to think that color vision is not designed for the detection of physical invariants, but rather for the detection of vital invariants; that is, it tends to present the animal with its environment, not in the most accurate way from a scientific point of view, but in a way that is the best adapted to its tasks, which are life tasks, and not tasks of knowledge.

The second idea to be rejected is the strict correlate of the first. If the animal, it is often argued, fails to detect physical invariants, the perception of color must be a neurophysiological illusion. The same color may correspond to distinct physical realities: the sky derives its blue appearance from a phenomenon of light dispersion, the blue of sapphire from a transference of ions, the blue of Sirius from the average temperature of the atoms and ions that make up the star. Conversely, extremely different colors are due to very close physical causes: the green of the emerald and the red of the ruby both come from an impurity in crystal, chromium, and it is the strength of the crystal field—weaker in the case of the emerald than in that of the ruby—that explains their striking diversity of color.[55] It follows, on this view, that nothing in the world corresponds to color. But of what "world" exactly are we speaking? We must distinguish here between the physical and the phenomenal world. What perception enables us to know is a symbiotic environment as the familiar place of our lives, and not the physical environment which can be reconstructed and inferred through complex procedures of abstraction. *Color is indeed a property of the world*, as "objective" as any other, because belonging to the object-pole of our experience and not to its subject-pole, but it is a property of the world as it forms the surrounding field of our lives, and it is of this "life-world," and of it alone, that it should be said that things in it *are* colored, or that color is *inseparable from things*. Perception is not to be understood as the detection of physical properties by means of *qualia* or sensations by an impartial mind; it is, as Merleau-Ponty says, "this living communication with the world that makes it present to us as the familiar place of our life."[56]

This detour through a classical problem of the phenomenology of perception has taken us away from the problem of the other only in appearance. The question I raised was whether it made sense to qualify experience itself as "subjective." The argument that seemed decisive was that of the absence of a bi-univocal correlation between physical stimuli and perceived qualities. Now, that argument progressively proved to be far weaker than it seemed—in any case burdened with heavy presuppositions. There are certainly colors that are "subjective" from the phenomenal point of view, phosphenes or colored afterimages. These are sensations and not perceptions. The former belong to the awareness of modifications in ourselves, while the latter belong to the awareness of properties in the world. But the fact that some colors are "subjective" does not entail that all are. Nor does it entail that in all perception sensations are necessarily present. Colors are qualities of things as they present themselves to us in *our* world; they are phenomenally objective just as much as other perceived qualities are. The world in which they vibrate and resonate with their outstanding rhythms is the familiar place of our lives, not the environment of the physicist. But, it will probably be objected, when we say that colors emerge as objective phenomenal properties in the life-world—and it alone—are we not once again ascribing to them a form of subjectivity? The life-world—is that not merely the physical world *for us*?

In order to answer this objection, we must return one last time to the distinction between the phenomenally subjective and the genetically subjective. The proponent of the subjectivity of colors, and, more generally, of the subjectivity of our experience, could respond that he accepts to say that colors, grasped at the only relevant level, the phenomenological one, are objective properties of things, because inseparable from them, and that everything I assert about them may well be valid for the "life-world"; but he would add that this life-world is only a creation of our body/brain, that it remains *genetically* subjective, and that this is the only decisive point in the final analysis. To this last salvo, the following response may be given. I do not deny, any more than does my interlocutor, that the perceived world brings a factual-empirical genesis into play—that is, that it is ultimately dependent, in order to be able to appear to us as it does, on physiological processes. I deny only two points: first, that this genesis involves the physical organism alone, regardless of its complex physical environment; secondly, and especially, that it makes sense to qualify that physical organism itself—as opposed to the phenomenal body that occupies the subjective pole of all experience—as "subjective." After all, the body that can play a causal role in the genesis of perceptual experience *has no reason to be qualified as "subjective" in any sense whatsoever,* for the very good reason that the only body that deserves that qualification is the body that appears (and that appears as *mine*), located somewhere in space, always positioned at the center of perception. As for the body causally responsible for my perception, it is *neither mine nor other, neither subjective nor objective.* It is a physical apparatus that remains unnoticed as long as I live, and to which there is no reason to attribute an epithet that has meaning only within the phenomenal field. In other words, nothing obliges us to call "subjective" the physical organism as opposed to our phenomenal body, on the pretext that the physical organism plays a causal role in the genesis of experience. *The genesis of experience is not to be characterized on the basis of one of the poles of what appears in that experience*; it is only understandable in light of the *system* that a body/brain forms with a complex physical environment. Color depends, no doubt, on a body/brain, but that does not make it subjective, because there is no reason to consider this body/brain as subjective—nor, for that matter, as objective: these distinctions are only relevant within the phenomenal world. Color, that gleam of things, is nowise "in us," but, as Cézanne insisted, it is "the place where our brain meets the universe."[57]

My experience does not belong to me. It is neither me, nor in me; it is rather the way the world opens up for me—abrupt, vertical, unexpected, spreading out its horizons and unforeseeable vistas like a flower. If it makes no sense to characterize that experience as "subjective," from the causal-real standpoint; if, furthermore, there is no necessity in assuming that a transcendental genesis is at work here, the problem of the modality of the appearing of the other is less solved than dissolved—by the disappearance of its terms. The conclusion of the argument coincides with the starting point for the description. There is no particular difficulty, once we have abandoned the whole idea of a subjective genesis, in considering that the other is by right one among the possible "contents" of experience. The other is not known and recognized as such through complex operations: inference, similitude-based passive association; he or she is given from the start at the very level of "the sympathetic experience of sensing also possessed by animals."[58] The mystery here lies not in the thing itself, but only in our own prejudices and presuppositions, in the framework first Cartesian and subsequently transcendental which has oriented the whole research. Our relation to the other is already given at the elementary level of perception; *it is less a relation of knowledge than of being.* "The social world," Merleau-Ponty writes, is "a dimension of existence"[59]—precisely the dimension called "*Mitsein*" by Heidegger. The other is not *known* as other, alter ego, on the basis of sensations and private phenomena. He or she coexists always already with us in the world, before any judgment and knowledge, we carry him or her along with us "prior to every objectification." "The social world is already there when we come to know it or when we judge it."[60]

Moreover, it is only if the existence of the other at the perceptual level is as "transparent" as that of things and of myself that the other can also appear mysterious to me in his or her intentions, emotions, and behavior. If my openness to the world were not from the start neutral with respect to the I/other distinction, because permitting us both to appear in the same phenomenal field; if I therefore did not from the outset share the world with the other, with another as manifest and accessible as all the rest, that other could not always remain to me partially unknown, opaque, and even sometimes impenetrable. "My experience must," says Merleau-Ponty, "present others to me in some way, since if it did not do so I would not even speak of solitude, and I would not even declare others to be inaccessible."[61] Therefore skepticism about the existence of the other is as absurd as skepticism about the outside world, and for the same reasons. A specific doubt about another, about his or her thoughts, intentions, or emotions is always possible, but a global doubt about his or her existence is an absurdity. It is because the other is not doubtful in his or her existence, or rather because *it makes no sense to doubt it,* that there can be many reasons to doubt this or that characteristic pertaining to it. Conversely, if the other is doubtful in his very existence, it becomes difficult to say exactly *about what* such a doubt arises, since the expression "other" loses any referent. No more than the existence of the world, the existence of the other calls for no knowledge, opinion, or belief that would require verification or justification. Nor does it depend on an "indubitable" experience, in the sense of infallible and apodictic. The relation to the other, once again, is not a relation of knowledge but of being.

This relation of being is dubbed by Wittgenstein an "attitude" (*Ein-*

stellung), and this attitude, one might say, is the *analogon* of what he will later call in a different context "certainty"—a certainty that is precisely not a knowledge based on reasons. The "belief" in the existence of the other is neither an opinion, nor a conjecture; neither is it a certainty *in the epistemological sense of the term* (which could turn out to be true or false); actually, it is not a *belief* at all. "I could always say of a human that he is an automaton (I could learn it this way in school in physiology) and yet it would not influence my attitude toward someone else. After all, I can also say it about myself. But what is the difference between an attitude and an opinion? I would like to say: the attitude comes *before* the opinion . . . An opinion can be wrong. But what would an error look like here?"[62] The only rational doubt—for doubt needs reasons as much as belief does—is a specific doubt relative to an aspect of the other, and not an overall doubt about his or her existence itself. It is an "ordinary doubt," as Wittgenstein would say, that is raised when the other behaves in a way that is difficult to understand, not a "philosophical" doubt, which ends up in skepticism.[63] Others are open to us, that is, given and available to us especially in their very faces without any reservation—those faces that *are* themselves. A face is not an enigma to be deciphered, that is to say, a sign separated and sundered as it were from what it signifies, but rather an expression, in which the meaning surfaces and comes irrefragably to light—without the detour of any analogy. As Merleau-Ponty writes, "I perceive the other as a behavior, for example, I perceive the other's grief or anger in his behavior, on his face and in his hands, without any borrowing from an 'inner' experience of suffering or of anger and because grief and anger are variations of being in the world, undivided between body and consciousness, which settle upon the other's behavior and are visible in his phenomenal body, as well as upon my own behavior such as it is presented to me."[64] As Wittgenstein, pursuing the same line of thought, emphasized: "In general I do not surmise fear in him—I *see* it. I do not feel that I am deducing the probable existence of something inside from something outside; rather it is as if the human face were in a way translucent and that I were seeing it not in reflected light but rather in its own."[65] That light that only rises with the face is not a halo—the trace of the Infinite—but its full and inescapable phenomenality. The face is not the trace of an absence, the twinkling of an inaccessible beyond, but the attestation of a presence and of an unfailing proximity.

In short, for a genuine description, there is no "problem of the other."

21

The Three Pathways of a Phenomenology of Language

> What is to be elucidated: it is the upheaval that speech introduces into prelinguistic Being.
>
> —Maurice Merleau-Ponty

The deeper our scientific knowledge of language becomes, the more language becomes for us what it has not ceased being for philosophers: a riddle. That riddle that it was already for the Greeks, for instance, since there is no one term in ancient Greek to designate what we call "language." The goal of the following reflections is less to solve that riddle—that would take another book—than to place us back into the heart of it.

What relations does language hold with our being-in-the-world in general and with the understanding that goes along with it? In order to try to answer this question, two investigations that up to this point have been carried out side by side must converge in this chapter: the first bearing upon the limits of Husserlian semantics (see chapters 4 and 5), and the second regarding the necessary transformations that the Husserlian concept of perceptual intentionality must undergo when replaced into the framework of a holistic approach to experience understood as being-in-the-world (see chapters 13 through 18). The main claim underlying the following analyses is that a transformation of semantic intentionality symmetric to that undergone by perceptual intentionality is required in order to account for the structural solidarity and continuity that exist between the pre-discursive understanding of the world and a language-based understanding. If prelinguistic meaning is a holistic property of the system formed by a subject endowed with practical abilities and his world—and we have already stressed that, with the expression "his" world, we must not understand a *subjective* world, but only the world in which he is situated along with others, a world which is ordered around the central "here" of his body—we have thus reached a concept of "meaning" that is entirely de-realized, broad enough to encompass both the linguistic and the prelinguistic, and to allow for a better understanding of their articulation. For language is not an empire within an empire. It is itself *perceived* as meaningful; or rather, its meaning lies in *the very modality of experience* we have of the sounds or characters, without there being any room here for a strict dichotomy between sensibility and understanding. The meaning is not added by consciousness to purely amorphous, phonetic, or graphic givens, it is *given* to us as the correlate of our understanding in the very modality of the experience we have of a read or heard sentence, and *as* this modality of experience itself. The emphasis placed on what forms the hyphen between the general understanding of the world and the language-based understanding constitutes the originality of the phenomenological approach to language. Language being itself an element of the perceived world, our understanding of language and our understanding of the world draw on common resources.

This claim which, in one form or another, and without its always being specifically stated, is at the center of the phenomenological approaches to language, could be called the "thesis of the non-specialization of our linguistic understanding." We should not be misled about the meaning of this "non-specialization." Of course, it is not meant to deny that language is learned and that its learning is rooted, at least in part, in specific exercises. It rather means that even those exercises do not necessarily draw on faculties fundamentally different from those at work in our pre-discursive understanding, although obviously they contribute to deepening that understanding, to enriching and radically transforming it. Even the specialization of our linguistic faculties is rooted in faculties that precede language and that language, in turn, contributes to shape.

What generally keeps us from seeing the problem from this perspective is the Humean and Kantian framework that is perpetuated through a variety of conceptualities, and that sets up a diametrical opposition between language, as a meaningful reality, and experience, as meaningless. On this view, all understanding is already linguistic in nature, bound to language, and even made possible by it. Experience contains no tacit understanding outside its articulation in speech. The problem with this conception is that it sunders our experience of language from our overall experience of the world, with its dumb meanings—some of these being elementary meanings related to our animal constitution, like Gibson's *affordances*, others the product of a long-standing culture, inseparable from a multiplicity of anthropological practices going beyond the domain of speech alone. It is true that language is a highly sophisticated creation, the product of a cultural refinement without precedent in the history of evolution; but not to the point of escaping the modalities of our spontaneous understanding such as it is put into play in *all* experience. There is a native and autochthonous understanding of meaning, already at work in the mere perception of language, which testifies to the fact that the way we perceive signs is already informed and transformed by a whole practical (including gestural, auditory, and visual) memory, which depends on our past transactions with these signs and the afferent linguistic facts. *There is a prelinguistic substructure that operates constantly in language and from which the latter draws its very possibility.* As Merleau-Ponty emphasizes, language is primarily gesture, rhythmic modulation, music that is visible in its spatialization in writing; and all these features, far from being contingent to it, belong to its essence. These perceptual and gestural qualities usually pass unnoticed, except in poetry with the spatialization that belongs to it and contributes directly to the meaning—in an exemplary way in Apollinaire's *Calligrammes.* That is probably the reason why philosophy, even more so since it has taken the turn to "linguistic philosophy," has shown a tendency to insist more on the discontinuity between language and experience than on their continuity. If the main idea of the phenomenological approach to language consists in bringing out that continuity, in putting language back into the domain of our corporeal transactions with others and the world, if language is only one of the forms—indeed an outstanding one—of our practical intelligence engaging with reality, we can attempt to examine, in a manner that will remain necessarily schematic, that continuity made of subtle transitions, insisting on three pathways of phenomenology of language: the intentionalist, the pragmatic, and the hermeneutic pathways, each having its roots in a particular paradigm that I will call, respectively, the paradigm of intention (or intending), the paradigm of the rule or convention, and the paradigm of the event. To move from one paradigm to another will mean at the same time to deepen the holistic character of linguistic meaning and, as a result, to inscribe it in an increasingly systematic way within the conception of experience that I have developed.

There is no need to return at length to Husserl's intentionalist path. Seen from the perspective of an ideal language that might constitute the perfect medium for a theory of knowledge, language was first approached in *Logical Investigations* on the basis of statement, in conformity with a tradition that goes back to Aristotle,[1] insofar as a statement can be true or false and possesses an ideal meaning, freed not only from all ties with the contingent, lived experiences of the interlocutor, but also with the contingent situations of speech. The strict separation between the function of expression, which is essential to linguistic signs, and their function of manifestation or communication, which remains accidental to them, makes it possible to purify the expression, as it can be actualized in soliloquy in an ideal way, from all contamination by contextual elements coming from situations in which, on the other hand, the living speech takes place. This way of posing the problem entails several consequences.

First of all, although dependent on the conventions of a pure, universal grammar, meaning lies primordially in the meaning-conferring act. The *Bedeutung* is always the correlate of a *Bedeuten*, a meaning-intention. Such a meaning-intention is grasped reflectively and adequately in an internal perception. It is given to itself in the self-transparency of a consciousness, so that the expression remains an external vehicle, the neutral and indifferent medium of a thinking that is self-sufficient, "an unproductive layer of meaning," as *Ideas I* will put it.

Secondly, meaning is conceived of as ensuring the mediation between a meaning-act and the object that may eventually fulfill it. Having as its essential function to put us in relation with ideal or sensible, simple or complex objects, meaning is characterized on the basis of the primacy of the referential or designative dimension of language, as is the case in Frege and Russell, but also in contemporary theories that define the meaning of a statement by its truth conditions (Dummett, Davidson). The consequences of this broadly referential conception of language are: (a) a primacy of the name and the statement: the former being the mode of givenness of simple objects, the latter the assertion of a complex state of affairs; (b) the relegation to the background of all the aspects of language that are occasion-sensitive, for example, indexicals and expressions that are neither true nor false, such as prayers, orders, wishes, questions, and promises—which Austin will group under the heading *speech acts.* The pragmatic dimension of language is thus strictly subordinated to a pure semantics. Ideally speaking, the purified language to which Husserl aspires should not contain any "essentially occasional" expression. Here we have the principle of "the unbounded range of objective reason" proclaimed by Husserl, after Bolzano,[2] which entails the principle of the subordination of the various functions of language to the cognitive one.

Indeed, if we are to believe Husserl, the indexicals such as "this," "here," or "I" are closely related to nouns, that is, they should be able to be everywhere and always replaced by nominal expressions in "objective" statements. As for "speech acts," Husserl adopts, in order to analyze them, a path midway between Aristotle and Bolzano. Contrary to Bolzano, he refuses to assimilate them to statements susceptible of being true or false. As opposed to Aristotle, he holds that their objects are the same as those of the corresponding statements, although one cannot ascribe truth or falsity to these acts in the strict sense; except that in addition to referring to states of affairs, these "occasional" expressions communicate or manifest the lived experiences of the speaker—lived experiences that can be known reflectively in an internal perception. For example, the question "Is *S P*?" expresses the same state of affairs as the statement "I desire [one desires] to know whether *S* is *P*," but the meaning of this statement undergoes "circumstantial modifications" here, or yet again, the expression has undergone "contextual ellipsis"[3] in the ordinary contexts of speech, thus manifesting the interrogative lived experience of the one who utters it. Similarly, an order is nothing other than the abbreviation of a complex assertive statement, and it manifests in addition a volitional intention: "Open the door!" is the equivalent of "I order you to open the door." As Husserl writes, "*The expressions of ostensibly non-objectifying acts are really contingent specifications of statements and other expressions, having immense practical and communicative importance, of objectifying acts.*"[4] One must insist, here, on the contingent character of these expressions: in an ideal language, they could be completely removed, for they only serve to facilitate communication "in practice"; they add nothing to the corresponding statement from the point of view of its meaning.

Thus, the primacy of the theoretical attitude in the Husserlian conception of experience has its strict counterpart in the theoreticism that dominates his analysis of linguistic meaning. For the whole of the domain of intentional acts, Husserl maintains that "*each intentional experience is either an objectifying act or has its basis in such an act*,"[5] which is a reformulation of the primacy of representation over the other *intentional* modalities in Brentano.[6] By virtue of this principle, within the sphere of expression, only objectifying acts are authentic bearers of meaning,[7] and the expressions that have undergone "contextual ellipsis," that is, nonobjective ones, are the modification of objective expressions. Since objectifying acts are also called "nominal," it follows that all use of language is referential.[8] A question refers to a state of affairs, to what I want to know about; a wish refers to an object that is wished for, an order to an ordered object, and so on.

Therefore *every* meaning-intention is a modality of the relation to objects; it is either a nominal act or is based on a nominal act. Here we must take care to note that the distinction between a nominal act and, for example, an adjectival one, represent in Husserl's view a purely logical difference, and not an empirical difference bound to a contingent grammar: it is, so to say, analogous to the Fregean difference between function and variable.[9] Of course, in the strict sense it is false to say that a proposition *names* a state of affairs: it *asserts* that that state of affairs obtains or is the case. And yet, in a broad sense, one can consider the act of asserting as a nominal act the objective correlate of which is the state of affairs asserted. Because he approaches all expression in accordance with this referentialist model, Husserl is forced to multiply objects infinitely, since even syncategorematic expressions, the conjunction "and" for example, must possess an objective correlate, the conjunction in itself. Furthermore, he continues to analyze the proposition after the model of the Aristotelian syllogistics, as the synthesis of two "nouns." He thus misses the main reform of Frege's *Begriffsschrift*, the asymmetry of the subject and the predicate. This intentionalist analysis of meaning ends up running into several problems. Since meaning resides in the meaning-intention—in the ideal content of the act and not in its immanent content—the meaning of all expression is entirely *determined* by the meaning-intention that "animates" the contingent expressions of a given language, as a result of which the meaning of what I say can never surprise me. In his desire to free the meaning of an expression as much as possible from its contextual elements, Husserl has made it very difficult to account for all the features of our natural languages that are essentially dependent on the occasion. Language becomes a pure combinatory of elements always ideally isolable from the context of their use and remaining self-identical throughout all their occurrences. The complex meaning of a statement is nothing but the combination of simple meanings. Despite the elaboration of a universal pure grammar, the conception of meaning remains singularly atomistic: not only does Husserl overlook Frege's contextual principle according to which a word only has meaning within a proposition, but he neglects the importance of the nonlinguistic context on which every language act relies and that contribute to its meaning. Since meaning resides in the meaning-intention, understanding can be nothing but the re-actualization of the speaker's meaning-intention.[10] Whence a Platonism that is sustained by a residual psychologism. Since meaning is a self-identical entity coexisting with its expression, every understanding must be a mental act that apprehends that meaning on the occasion of an expression. Even if, in Husserl, "act" generally means "lived experience" and does not refer to an activity in the proper sense of the term, many apparently insoluble questions remain. When I understand a sentence, at what moment does the lived experience of understanding take place? Before the sentence is finished? But then I do not understand it entirely. At the moment it is completed? But in that case I wasn't understanding it during the whole process of its utterance. By what miracle can I recover, behind the signs, the intention that presided in their arrangement? Does understanding amount to the retrieval of an intention, or isn't it the other way round?

Does not the eventual retrieval of an intention presuppose understanding? How many meaning-intentions must be assumed to be at work in a sentence, and how can they be counted?

Despite everything, as is often the case, Husserl goes further than some of his formulations might suggest; he leaves open options in its conceptuality that some of his students will deepen. First, despite his ideal of a pure language that would be a pure vehicle for thought freed from all ties with the contingent situations of speech, not only does Husserl elaborate one of the first theories of "essentially occasional expressions," but he repeatedly emphasizes that language picks up, renews, and carries forward a meaning prior to signs and a broader intelligibility—that of our embodied being-in-the-world—that it prolongs, and to which it constantly leads back. For him, language is only comprehensible when reintegrated into a more primordial relationship to the world: the linguistic *Bedeutung* can never be entirely emancipated from the *Sinn* that infuses our perceptions and gestures before all speech. Then, although his conception of language tends to reduce it to an "algorithm," to use an expression of Merleau-Ponty, that is to say, to make it into a purely external medium of a thought that would be transparent to itself, Husserl breaks radically with the Cartesian conception of thought in another respect. Not only does he refuse to define thought as being everything we are conscious of through reflection (perception, for example, is not a specimen of thought in the strict sense), but he asserts the existence of an *internal* relation between thought and expression: all that is thinkable is expressible and only what is expressible is thinkable. Thus he ventures beyond a purely referentialist conception of linguistic meaning as bi-univocal relation between "ideas" or "lived experiences" given to themselves before their expression and the objects to which they refer. In some texts at least, he maintains the *constitutive* nature of language for all thought, even solitary thought. "In solitary thought in which one expresses oneself, it is surely not the case that we would first have the formation of thought and then seek the suitable words. Thinking is carried out from the very outset as linguistic [*als sprachliches*]."[11]

If it was true that Husserlian semantics subtended all phenomenological conceptions of language, and, furthermore, all conceptions of phenomenology itself, as Tugendhat and his disciples have advanced, phenomenology would have long succumbed to the criticisms of the intentionalist paradigm. But why would Husserl's theory be the only possible one? On the contrary, it must be observed that his theory was criticized very early, on decisive points, within the phenomenological movement. I cannot, in the present framework, take up the entire history of those critiques; I must limit myself to mentioning a few important developments.[12] In doing so, I will follow my guiding question: what is it that makes these competing conceptions authentically *phenomenological*?

Long before Charles Morris and John Austin, the founding act of what will be called after them "pragmatics," dates back—and this is no accident—to the phenomenology of language of Daubert, Marty, and Reinach. Each of these attempted, in his own way, to diminish the primacy devolved by Husserl to the cognitive function in his analysis of an ideal language; they attacked what Austin was to qualify much later as a "descriptivist fallacy."[13] Language cannot aim only at presenting states of affairs in the most accurate possible way, in objective statements. It consists just as much in performing actions: question, prayer, order, promise, wish, praise, blame, and so on. The analysis advanced by Husserl of these "occasionally elliptic statements" raises great difficulties. If a question, for example, expresses an objective state of affairs, and at the same time manifests or communicates an interrogative lived experience, the same type of analysis must be applied to judgment. Judgment must both express the state of affairs judged and manifest a judicative lived experience. But if that is the case, it must be possible to replace *salva veritate* the assertion "*S* is *P*" with "I judge that *S* is *P*," since the former is an occasionally elliptic form of the latter. Now, first, as Husserl himself objects, that would lead to an infinite regression; to judge would always mean to judge that one judges; second, it happens that neither the meaning of these two expressions, nor their truth conditions, are identical.[14] Consequently, must we not assign a different status to occasional and objective expressions, therefore calling into question "the unbounded range of objective reason" defended by Husserl?

This issue is central to Reinach's project in his "pragmatics" (before the term was coined) of "social acts": a promise cannot be the mere manifestation of an intention or a resolution taking place in the speaker's mind, by means of a contingent expression; it is "performed in the very act of speaking" (*im Sprechen selbst*);[15] it is a genuine *social speech act* which is necessarily addressed to an interlocutor and must be heard by him or her. Here it is impossible to separate manifestation and expression. The promise as an act is defined by the type of relation that holds between two people: the first has the right to demand something from the second, and the second has the duty to fulfill that demand by executing the promised action. A promise involves the appearance of a legitimate claim, on the one side, and of an obligation on the other. But for this it must be uttered publicly. A mere declaration of intent is not a promise, for it does not give rise to any claim or obligation. The promise is not an immanent intentional act which, when externalized, would be addressed to another person; it is rather a social act *ab initio*, which, like all social acts, *requires* externalization in order to be performed as such. This is why not only the promise cannot consist in the communication of an inner lived experience, but the very existence of such a lived experience is in that case problematic. As Reinach puts it, "Cannot a claim or an obligation last for years without any change? Are there any such experiences?"[16] Here we are not dealing with a mental act that would subsequently and incidentally be expressed, but with an act that *resides* in that expression itself and is nothing apart from it. Thus, as Reinach emphasizes, the existence of private experiences is "quite irrelevant"[17] to the analysis of the act of promising. It is true that Reinach does not go so far as to deny that there may be internal elements that accompany the promise, in the form of experiences or private intentional acts; he even overtly postulates their existence.[18] His break with an intentionalist semantics is not complete. Still, he does point out that the intentionality *of consciousness* cannot be a good guide in order to understand the nature of those social acts that "are performed in the very act of speaking."

Two aspects of Reinach's conception are properly phenomenological. First, to understand a social act presupposes examining the totality of its context. It is thus necessary to extend the notion of context beyond the intra-linguistic one to the perceived situation (shared with others) in which that social act is performed. The linguistic meaning of the promise is rooted in a prelinguistic meaning that inhabits the other, his gestures, his bearing, the overall situation in which we are both situated, and which alone confers on language its openness to the world. Secondly, although the promise is assuredly a human activity bound to contingent institutions, placed under the jurisdiction of positive law, and therefore tributary to a set of conventions, some of the features of the act of promising are not purely conventional, but are rooted in essences and essential relations. For example, it belongs to *what it is to be* a promise to entail claim and obligation,[19] and this is true regardless of whatever social conventions and positive law may be in vigor. We can easily conceive of societies in which promises would differ as to their object (what it is possible to promise), their duration, their modalities of annulment, the legal sanctions to be applied when the obligation is not met; but we cannot conceive of a society in which the promise would not entail by essence a claim and a corresponding obligation. We have here an "*a priori* structure" (*apriorische Gebilde*) of every promise, from which follow an unconditional necessity and an unrestricted universality. If conventions by essence can always vary, the same is not true of these *a priori* structures on which all convention is grounded, and that are not in turn products of conventions. It belongs to the essence of promise to be a social act, to be addressed to someone, to be realized in the saying itself, to entail claim and obligation, to be able to be canceled on certain conditions, for example when the other frees us from our given word; these features are prior to all contingent conventions and all positive institutions within a given society. In other words, in Reinach's view, *all convention rests on a non-conventional element*, because all convention is essentially variable, and because conversely, the variation of its essential characteristics leads to the destruction of the very idea of promise. Just as the rules of a given language, however conventional they may be, cannot *institute* certain essential properties of language (for example, the essential truth that, in a number of cases, the meaning of an expression is its use in language), the *a priori* laws that govern the promise cannot be *pure* conventions; they are what underlie all possible convention. Reinach conceives of these truths of essence on the Husserlian model of eidetic truths susceptible to be given in self-evident intuition. I will not dwell on the difficulties raised by this last point, which have already been amply discussed.

Of course it could be objected to this approach that the *a priori*—and therefore universal and necessary—character of these "truths" applying to all promises is in no way the character of *truths*, but only of *conventions* of a special kind. On such a view, the conventions that govern the act of promising are not normative rules (like the rules of art), but constitutive rules (like chess rules). They prescribe what counts as a move in this language game. They are, therefore, both *a priori* and "arbitrary." We have adopted constitutive rules according to which certain speech acts, in given circumstances, *count as promises*, engendering obligation and claim; but there is no essence of promise outside of these conventions themselves. But Reinach could answer that to call these necessities "conventions" is necessarily to assume that they can *vary* from one society to another. Now it is possible to conceive of a game similar to chess—let us call it "chess*"—with different chessmen and a chessboard having a greater or lesser number of squares; but is it really possible to conceive of a different language game of promise, a promise* that would not possess the essential features under consideration? If the answer is yes, what could possibly be that language game? If the answer is no, must we not conclude that our conventions are constrained by something, by essential truths belonging to what it is to be a promise—in short, that the alleged conventions are not the last word? This would mean that there are concepts that, though partially conventional, cannot be defined in a non-circular way on the basis of our conventions alone. The concept of *convention* itself would probably be one among them. As Reinach puts it referring to the basic concepts used by positive law, "*they themselves are found, not produced.*"[20]

Karl Bühler, in a book from 1934 that takes place firmly within the phenomenological tradition, even though it is not without other influences, has formulated analogous criticisms directed against Husserl. Bühler, like Reinach, attempts to elucidate the essence of language setting out from an analysis of speech in action, that is of speech as an activity in the world: "All concrete speech is in vital union with the rest of a person's meaningful [*sinnvollen*] behavior; it is *among* actions and is *itself* an action."[21] Speech must not only be approached from the point of view of its "inner field" (*Infeld*), that is, its linguistic *context*, but also from that of its "surrounding field" (*Umfeld*), its situation:[22] both the perceived world and the totality of the practices that take place in it. One cannot start out, in order to analyze it, from a monological consciousness and its immanent acts. Speech comes under the jurisdiction of the *practices* of a community that depends on the "circumstances of life [*Lebensumständen*],"[23] which are not without resemblance to Wittgenstein's "forms of life." Language is an "*implement for orientation in community life,*"[24] and as such, it is not reducible to its semantic aspect, but rather includes an irreducible pragmatic component. Meaning depends on the intentional use of signs in conformity with rules within a community governed by institutions. This is why language in action cannot be reduced to its representational function (*Darstellungsfunktion*), that is, to the ideal coordination that holds between language symbols and states of affairs; additionally, it possesses two other functions that Bühler calls, respectively, the function of manifestation (*Kundgabe*) and the function of triggering (*Auslösung*). For example, the tone of voice manifests the lived experiences and emotions of the speaker; a command has, additionally, a triggering function that may be considered the ancestor of Austin's perlocution—its goal being to produce effects on the listener.[25] Considered from the point of view of these last two functions, language doesn't just aim at presenting states of affairs; it is rather an act, a performance. Orders and acts of baptism are neither true nor false; they *succeed* if they are performed in the appropriate circumstances and *fail* if they are not.

In this respect, Husserl's meaning-conferring acts cannot be a good starting point for a theory of language. "It is not possible to cope with the entirety of the theory of meaning on the basis of the act alone," Bühler writes, "but that is what is attempted in the *Logical Investigations.*"[26] One should insist rather on everything that constrains the meaning-intention, on the employment-rules of expressions that belong to the "*social factor of language,*" which is "of a rank logically prior to or at least . . . of logically equal rank to the subject-based theory of acts."[27] Meaning is intrinsically tied to rules and use in circumstances of life; it cannot be approached in light of meaning-intention alone and from the standpoint of the laws of a pure, universal grammar. This critique of the subjective side of Husserl's theory of meaning is accompanied by a critique of its objective side, that is, of semantic Platonism. Bühler takes a step similar to that of Heidegger, who, during the 1920s, had repeatedly dismissed both psychologism and Platonism, showing their collusion of principle—Platonism being fundamentally nothing but a reaction to psychologism, which perpetuates the same framework of thought:[28] far from breaking with the naturalist idea of psyche as a succession of real events on the model of physical events, Platonism retains its entire legitimacy, since one must after all accept the starting point of psychologism in order to be able to oppose the real processes from which the psyche is allegedly made up with the being "in itself" of the ideal, its validity and atemporality. Like Heidegger, Bühler makes the objection to Husserl that neither the ideal self-identity of meanings identically reproducible and identically comprehensible in all the pragmatic contexts of communication and exchange, nor the polymorphous variability of individual acts conferring meaning make it possible to account for the essentially occasion-sensitive character of meaning. Meaning comes to light only at the point of juncture between signs, with their rules of combination and use, and the surrounding field. It is not something that could subsist on its own, floating in some ether or Fregean "third realm"; it is only the way we understand a sentence on the basis of the concrete situation of interlocution in which it is uttered. Neither "propositions in themselves" nor "meanings in themselves" in Brentano's sense are an adequate guideline for the study of natural languages; they both rest on a methodological operation of abstraction with respect to the pragmatic conditions of the concrete linguistic exchange, on "the release of the sense of the sentence from the speech situation."[29] This operation is indeed legitimate and even necessary when it is a question of understanding the artificial symbolism of logic, but it is prejudicial to the study of natural languages, because it leads to fail to recognize the importance of all the aspects of language that Bühler calls "empractical," such as ellipses, anacolutha, and especially indexicals. It leads to underestimating what is more specific about natural languages, "the surprising capacity for adaptation to the inestimable richness of what, in each concrete case, demands to be grasped linguistically."[30]

From the three functions of language distinguished by Bühler three types of signs are derived: language "is *a symbol* by virtue of its coordination with objects and states of affairs, *a symptom* (index, *indicium*) by virtue of its dependence on an emitter, whose inner world it expresses, and a *signal* by virtue of its appeal to a listener, whose inward and outward behavior it directs, as do other signs of exchange."[31] This typology makes it possible to account for the specific status of indexicals, which are deictic words (*Zeigwörter*), and to distinguish them radically from naming words (*Nennwörter*). Contrary to what Husserl maintained, "here," "I," and "now" are not symbols that could be replaced in all circumstances by names, but mere signals possessing in language a status analogous to that of road signs. Natural languages possess actually two fields: a deictic field (*Zeigfeld*) and a symbolic field (*Symbolfeld*)—this duality of fields being, in Bühler's view, the major contribution of his theory.[32] Thus, what words like "here" or "there" mean depends on the deictic field of language, and not on its symbolic field. The word "here" functions as a "position signal," the word "I" as an "individual signal" of the one who is expressing himself, and the logician who claims he can replace them in all instances with names underestimates "the multiplicity of practical needs that everyday language has to cope with."[33] The deictic field belongs to *the essence of language* just as does its symbolic field; it is not accidental to it. Moreover, Bühler reminds us that the latter field depends in part on the former, since names themselves have to be learned by a learning *deixis*—by what Wittgenstein will call an "ostensive definition." Now, deictics obviously cannot be learned in this way. "This is a pen" has a meaning, but "this is a this" is nonsense, just as is "there is there" or "now is now."[34] Thus, as early as 1909, well before Wittgenstein, Bühler criticizes what he calls "the old conception" of language, the referential paradigm that reduces all words to names. "The old view was based essentially on two assertions that were internally connected. It was believed that the functions of language could all be traced back to the naming function of words: every word is a name for something, its *Bedeutung*, a view most clearly formulated by Hobbes. And it was thought that the sentence contains essentially of an aggregate [*Inbegriff*] of names. And in accordance with this first assertion, the processes of language learning were made out to be a learning to name objects. Both claims are false; the function of naming is only one of several functions of words."[35]

Since the deictics only acquire their meaning by virtue of their insertion in a deictic field, and since their value as signals varies according to the speaker, his or her location in space, and so on, one cannot consider the fluctuations of meaning to be accidental to language, nor can one pretend to eradicate them. "What 'here' and 'there' is changes with the position of the speaker just as the 'I' and 'thou' jumps from one interlocutor to the other with the exchange of the roles of sender and receiver."[36] In Husserl's view, and from the perspective of an ideal language, "all change of meaning must be considered an anomaly,"[37] even though that anomaly is authorized by the grammar of the natural languages. Bühler opposes this view, arguing, on the contrary, that these changes are a necessary characteristic of all language,[38] as opposed to a logical formalism. Not only fluctuation of meaning, but indeterminacy of meaning in general are not the exception, but the rule. "Representation with a language leaves a *latitude* of indeterminacy of meaning open."[39] If this were not the case, Bühler insists, the natural languages would lose what is most specific to them, and most precious: their marvelous adaptability to the circumstances.

It is not necessary to go into all the subtleties of the *Sprachtheorie* here, for example into its remarkable analysis of the ellipsis, which foreshadows, on many points, Wittgenstein's observations.[40] The derealization of meaning and the dependency of the latter both with respect to the act and to the situation of speech lead to no longer conceiving of understanding as the psychological act of grasping an ideal-identical meaning—an act supposed to occur on the occasion of the occurrence of the linguistic act. Understanding is no longer to be thought of as a mental act but as a competency, a practical ability. Language does not signify all by itself: it prolongs an understanding of action and the world that it contributes in deepening.[41] It is true that Bühler does not settle the difficult question of whether the pragmatic dimension of language is prior to its semantic dimension, or the other way round. In his view, the presentative function of language remains preponderant. But in maintaining that meaning is nothing but the counterpart of a comprehension that is itself contextual, understood as a practical human ability, he ends up with a semantic holism. Not only is the meaning of words inseparable from the context of the sentence, but it depends on the circumstances in which that sentence takes place. The understanding of a linguistic act presupposes the understanding of many other uses of language in a situation, and ultimately the understanding of language as a whole, and of the "circumstances of life" underlying it. Such a holism does not contradict the idea that words can *also* signify in isolation. Pragmatics does not cancel out syntax or semantics: it presupposes them. Language remains a combinatorial apparatus that, with a finite number of signs, is able to form an infinite number of significant strings. If one could not give the meaning of a word independently from the sentence in which it appears and from the overall circumstances, the productivity of language would become a mystery. Thus, though never abandoning the contextual principle enlarged beyond the sentence to the circumstances, Bühler nevertheless continues to embrace Husserl's idea of their being "simple meanings" on which complex meanings are built.[42] To maintain that there are simple meanings is not tantamount, however, to maintaining that the meaning of a sentence is merely the combination of such meanings. The whole is greater than the sum of its parts. An assertion "is obviously more than and different from an aggregate of words."[43] Neither the meaning of the words nor that of the sentence can claim absolute priority for linguistic theory, as the words and the sentence are "correlative factors."[44] The meaning of the sentence depends on that of its constitutive parts (which preserves semantics and syntax), but the meaning of a word *in that sentence* depends on the understanding of the entire sentence, that is, on the way it is actually used in that context (and other analogous ones). The meaning of a sentence taken as a whole is something more than the combination of the meanings of its constitutive terms. The same holds for the sentence considered in its spoken context. Of course, to understand a sentence in a given situation is connected to the ability to understand other sentences in other situations, but it does not follow that it is necessary to understand all possible sentences in all possible situations in order to understand the least sentence.

Perhaps we are in a better position to appreciate how this reform of the intentionalist theory of meaning follows a path running parallel to the transformations of the general theory of intentionality that I proposed in chapters 13 through 18. Should this come as a surprise? Our understanding of language is a dimension of our understanding of the world, for language itself must be perceived. Perception, I stressed, is "intentional" if it presents things to us in accordance with a meaning. The analysis of this meaning led me to challenge the primacy of an analysis centered on intentional acts and their fulfillment. Understanding is a practical ability; it is never concerned with things, events, or processes in isolation, but with all these inserted in an overall situation. In contrast to Husserl's intentionality which remains inseparable from an atomism, our comprehensive openness to the world can only be grasped within the framework of a holistic approach. The former, isofar as it postulates intentional states intrinsically evaluable in terms of conformity or lack of it to reality, confers a primacy on the theoretical attitude and leads inevitably to skepticism, since, if my intentional states are evaluable separately (true or false), and if nothing prevents my doubting each one of them, then neither does anything prevent my doubting the totality of them, and therefore my doubting their correlate, the world. The latter, by contrast, leads to dismissing the skeptical argument; it belongs to what it is to be an experience that it does not present itself in the form of isolated parts—that something can only be an experience if it is integrated without hiatus into the whole of experience, which can no longer be reduced to the sum of its parts. The meaning of experience possesses both a relational character (it is related to our practical abilities) and a contextual character (it is dependent on our openness to the world as a whole). The meaning brought to light by understanding depends both on the goals, interests, and background abilities of a subject and on the overall cast of the situation. These different dimensions appear as structurally united within the unitary structure of being-in-the-world.

Language, in turn, presents itself as a dimension of that being-in-the-world. As a speaking being, I possess a capacity to understand linguistic signs that is actualized in the very modality of my experience, and as that experience itself. This understanding of linguistic facts rests on an intelligence both informed and transformed by a practical memory forming its background and permanent resource. I do not deal first with word-things that would only subsequently be invested with meaning, but with agile, vibrant signs that, in their rhythmic spurts, their scansion or spatial arrangement, are perceived as already meaningful—as secreting their own meaning in and by their very springing forth. This is why speech continues, and at the same time transposes, other modalities of expression (gesture, dance, music, etc.); it announces itself as their "natural" prolongation. The fact that understanding is not necessarily a lived experience does not exclude that there is an experience of understanding. The words of a language I am familiar with have a face and a signature that are lacking in the "barbarisms" of a language I have not mastered. The signifying function proper to language is preceded and prepared in the arcana of perception from which signs emerge full-fledged, like Athena from Jupiter's head. Like the *Gestalten* in music, words are forms in formation that address themselves to the listening of our body, and strike us, vibrant arrows stemming from our sensibility, as modulations of space and structurations of time. As Merleau-Ponty stressed, "The 'clarity' of language is of a perceptual order,"[45] and this is why language derives from gesture; it is itself gesture and, as such, like all gesture, it "sketches out its own sense."[46] "Here, then, the sense of words must ultimately be induced by the words themselves, or more precisely their conceptual signification must be formed by drawing from a *gestural signification*, which itself is immanent in speech."[47] In short, language can only be the organon of our discursive intelligence, introducing something new into our experience itself, because it is already foreshadowed in our sensible exposure to things. Here we find no strict dichotomy between sensibility and understanding, nor between nature and culture. "What I maintain," writes Merleau-Ponty, "is that there is an informing of perception by culture, which enables us to say that culture is perceived."[48]

If we tend to neglect this play of subtle transitions and this gestural and perceptual anchorage of speech, it is probably also because our alphabetic writing has not prepared us for it: it is reduced to a signage that highlights only the combinatory aspect of signs. Perhaps we would do well to abandon our Eurocentrism for a while to see language from a different viewpoint. A Chinese character, as Jean-François Billetier writes, "is as much a gesture converting itself into a form as a form turning itself into a gesture."[49] Its learning draws on the resources of a practical, working memory, and Chinese writing needs to be assimilated bodily from the earliest years. "To conceive how it is possible to memorize hundreds and thousands of characters, it must be understood that what is learned is a gesture more than a picture; that it is motorial memory more than visual memory that is called upon. This means that a much larger store of information can be integrated. . . . So it is that Chinese children traditionally begin learning characters by tracing them rhythmically in the air with broad gestures of arm and hand. They name each element as it is traced (a bar, a leg, a dot and so on), and they pronounce the character at the end."[50] Chinese writing is known first by gesture. When two Chinese people fail to agree on a word, homonymy being considerable in that language, they do not hesitate to trace the character out with a quick movement on their open palm. To remember a little-used character, they will not go through their visual memory; they will act "just as we would to recall a forgotten dance step";[51] if the outline escapes them, they will search it with their hand till the gesture forms again spontaneously.

To understand this permanent gestural resource that establishes a continuity between speech and other forms of expression by leading them back to their common basis, to the body as "*primordial expression*,"[52] the whole difficulty lies in the necessity of grasping the prelinguistic basis of language as essential to it, while not overlooking the dramatic changes language introduces in perception as such. We must maintain both that language is anchored in the logos of the sensible world and its silent meanings, in its autonomous order and structure, and that it reconfigures perception in depth—beginning with the perception of language itself. We do not have on the one hand a sensible meaning and on the other language as an intellectual organon. Understanding and sensibility are not two separate realms. The astonishment language produces derives from the fact that meaning springs up within it at the level of sensibility itself, that understanding begins being formed the moment there is perception and overlaps continually with it, that the logos of language comes to inhabit the logos of the world, and a speaking voice to infiltrate its silent voice and unspoken logic. This enigma is well formulated by Merleau-Ponty: "Language as a resumption of the logos of the sensible world in an other architectonic."[53] Language reworks and prolongs perceptual meaning by raising it to the second power in speech. Speech is always the affirmation of a style, that is to say, of a way of being in the world that brings into play our total presence and the infinite declension of our bodily powers. This is why a "linguistic turn" can only constitute a partial view of things: it amounts to imprisoning oneself in language by separating it from the primordial forms of our embodied intelligence, and thus by perpetuating the traditional sensibility/understanding, judgment/perception, and theory/practice divisions. To understand the judgment uttered before me draws on the resources of experience, of intuition (which is never blind), just as to experience something with insight already shows "judgment," even though the latter is never formulated. A good philosophy of language is not necessarily a "philosophy of language." Language is the organon of our sensible reason which is achieved in the higher forms of thought—belief, judgment, inference—but in which these forms in turn have their source and birth. Such is the mystery of language and the fascination it exerts on us. Language invites us to continue Husserl's unfinished project of a "genealogy of logic" starting from the prepredicative—to be sure, by other means.

I have set up an opposition between the paradigm of intention and that of rules and speech as social praxis. A phenomenological pragmatics has brought to the fore what Bühler called "the instrumental model of language" which understands the latter as an instrument of orientation in the life of the community. This paradigm has stressed the preponderant role of the speech situation, beyond the properly linguistic context. It led to a holism of meaning. Nevertheless, this model appears doubly limited. First, it scarcely pursues its inquiry beyond the semantic unit of the sentence, in the text or the conversation. Now can we not say of the text and the conversation what we asserted earlier about the sentence in relation to its constitutive words: the whole is greater than the sum of its parts? A text or a conversation, and even more so a work of language, cannot be characterized as a mere juxtaposition of sentences. Furthermore, if the pragmatics approach insisted on the social dimension of language, it tended to neglect its diachronic and historical dimension. This is the starting point for a third "path toward language," the one that finds its fulfillment in philosophical hermeneutics, and whose paradigm is no longer the rule, but the event of speech insofar as it exceeds conventions and rules. Just as the pragmatics approach did not challenge the validity of syntax and semantics, and just as language as an activity did not cancel the combinatory dimension of signs, similarly, the hermeneutic approach does not abandon the paradigm of the rule: it completes it. This is why it takes one more step in the direction of a semantic holism.

Philosophical hermeneutics' starting point is the problem of understanding. Its originality with respect to the philological hermeneutics of the Enlightenment lies less in the elevation of understanding (*Verstehen*) to the rank of an existential for *Dasein*, in its "ontologization" by Heidegger, than in the broadening of the context that underlies all understanding, in such a way that this context henceforth includes a diachronic dimension. For Schleiermacher, the hermeneutic circle meant the structural referral of the part to the whole and of the whole to the part in the interpretation of a text: in order to understand the overall meaning of a passage, it is necessary to understand its sentences in isolation, but in order to understand the meaning of these sentences *in that context*, the entire passage must be understood. However, when I start reading a text, I already build on meaning anticipations that come from elsewhere than the text itself, for example from its historical reception. A set of presuppositions govern and guide my understanding, from which I can never free myself entirely. This historically conditioned pre-understanding is always already in play in all understanding of a work of language, of thought or of art. The hermeneutic circle, therefore, no longer means the mere back-and-forth movement from the part to the whole and from the whole to the part, but the way a pre-understanding, that is, a set of meaning anticipations, shed light on—and sometimes obscure—my reading of the text, and the way the reading of the text ricochets back on these meaning anticipations, reorienting, modifying, or deepening them. In short, in Heidegger's radicalization of the holistic principle at work in understanding itself, to understand the least text implies to understand many other texts and other things, to be a participant in a culture and a member of a historical community. It is against the background of an *experience broadened to include its historical dimension*, insofar as this experience orients in advance every attempt at understanding, that comprehension as such is carried out. It is not I who freely projects a meaning on neutral cultural objects given in advance, but the latter that *make sense* to me, and contextually acquire a meaning on the basis of my belonging to a historical community.

Of course what applies to large semantic units, such as a text or a work of art, does not necessarily apply to smaller units, such as a sentence. It is only in the first case that interpretation is necessary. Hence the hermeneutic approach does not contradict the one of pragmatics. In ordinary situations of speech, the immediate pragmatic context generally suffices to solve the ambiguities that might arise due to the polyvalence of each term, making interpretation in the strict sense of the term superfluous. If I say "here is a red rose," I generally do not mean that this rose has *one* red petal, or that its stem is painted red, but that the flower is uniformly red—this is how everybody will understand that sentence because this is how it is used in ordinary circumstances. The context and use palliate the residual ambiguities and even act in such a way these are not perceived at all. The situation is different when I start reading a poem. In order to understand this singular poem, I have recourse not only to my knowledge about its form, its situation in literary history, and so on, but to a pre-understanding of the "thing" it is about, and that it attempts to put into words. My understanding, here, is interpretative from the start.

As long as we remain at the level of the sentence, the pragmatics approach in terms of the employment-rules of its constituent expressions suffices to give an account of the phenomenon of understanding. In this context, as Gadamer emphasizes, "understanding is the average case, not misunderstanding."[54] We have no need to *interpret* what is said to us, we *live in the language* that we share with others. "Understanding how to speak is not yet of itself real understanding [in the sense that hermeneutics confers on this term] and does not involve an interpretive process; it is an accomplishment of life. For you understand a language by living in it—a statement that is true, as we know, not only of living but dead languages as well. Thus the hermeneutical problem concerns not the correct mastery of language but coming to a proper understanding about the subject matter, which takes place in the medium of language."[55] As long as we limit ourselves to the sentence, misunderstanding is the exception and understanding the rule, so that most of the time no interpretation is required. As for larger units of meaning, it is the reverse that is true. When we engage in the understanding of a difficult text, separated from us by a historical distance, the spontaneous understanding of the sentences remains, of course, presupposed; but to be understood in its subtleties and nuances, the text *requires* an interpretation. From the exception, interpretation becomes the rule. This is the way we must understand Heidegger's assertion—taken up by Gadamer[56]—that "all interpretation [*Auslegung*] is grounded on understanding"[57] and, correlatively, understanding *is achieved* or completed in interpretation.[58] When we come to grips with a difficult text, we interpret *in order to* understand, but we can only interpret what we already understand, even if in an inchoative manner. Understanding is achieved in interpretation, but the latter is grounded in a prior, spontaneous understanding—an understanding that is exempt from interpretation and inseparable from our linguistic competence—otherwise we would be led into an infinite regression: "A text cannot be reduced to one understandable meaning, but in many respects needs to be interpreted."[59]

Thus hermeneutics suscribes to the extension by pragmatics of the context to the circumstances of use, beyond the semantic context of the sentence, but tries to go a step further. The circumstances that are relevant to grasp the meaning of a speech act from the point of view of pragmatics are archetypal social situations (to pardon, promise, order, baptize, or marry) as referred to customs and institutions. These are not the contingent, unrepeatable circumstances in which the linguistic exchange takes place. Setting out from idealized social situations and from a set of rules governing the use of expressions, pragmatics does not reach down to the historical roots of living speech. In this regard, even the "ordinary language" of Wittgenstein and Austin still remain an *idealized* language. Certain allusions, certain witticisms, for example, only take on their meaning in relation to the absolute particularity of the context and the interlocutors. The insistence on the occasionality of language is common to both approaches, but this occasionality is defined by hermeneutics as a dependency on the speech situation *in its historical singularity and concreteness*, and not only as a dependency on the archetypal social situations envisaged by pragmatics. For an interpretation, the context extends beyond Bühler's "circumstances of life" or Wittgenstein's "forms of life" to the historical world as such. Occasion sensitivity "is not itself occasional," it "constitutes the very essence of speaking."[60] Indeed, even a mere assertive statement is subtended by implicit questions to which it answers, and it is difficult to understand it completely without taking its motivational context into account. Even scientific statements stem from background interests and questions from which they cannot be dissociated. The speech situation is an *open* one, in the sense that even if not all of its aspects are relevant to getting at the meaning of what is said, the fact remains that its relevant aspects cannot be specified *a priori*, so that understanding is always open to rectification by the taking into consideration of aspects of that situation hitherto unnoticed. The understanding of what is said depends on the relevant *circumstances*, but the grasp of the *relevant* circumstances depends on the understanding of what is said. This characteristic becomes more pronounced when, thanks to writing, a text is emancipated from its immediate pragmatic context; in that case, the context must be reconstructed by the interpreter. The reconstitution of a historical context that spreads light on the text, and that the text, in turn, illuminates, is not in the least exclusive of questions we may direct to the text from our present historical situation, that is, of what Gadamer calls the problem of application (*Anwendung*). The text speaks to us from its historical situation, *but also from our own*, and as a function of the distance separating them.

The problem of understanding, therefore, is never reducible to that of the mastery of rules and conventions as defined in reference to idealized situations. Contrary to Wittgenstein's view, "understanding is never just the mere, competent application of a know how."[61] "To be master of a technique"[62] is never sufficient for understanding a particular conversation with its innuendos and implied meanings. We can master rules and conventions as referred to typical situations, but the particular understanding of a word or a text in the concreteness and uniqueness of their contingent historical situation calls for an understanding of the uniqueness of that situation, many aspects of which elude us—a uniqueness which makes the operation of understanding an *adventure* always beyond our control to some extent. "Understanding, like action," Gadamer writes, "always involves a risk and is never just the simple application of a general knowledge of rules . . . Understanding is an adventure and, like any other adventure, is dangerous."[63]

Of course it is not a question here of denying the existence of conventions and rules that underlie understanding. These rules, as Wittgenstein insists, are not precise rules, algorithms, but flexible and largely indeterminate rules; they do not prescribe in advance all their applications to contexts that are always partly unforeseeable. But Wittgenstein, in insisting on the "blind" practice and routine character obtained by simple "training," of the action of following a rule[64] inherent in all mastery of a language, overlooks, at least to some extent, that which transcends, in living understanding, the mere technical application of a competency, calling for the *judgment* of the person applying it. For large linguistic units, understanding bears more resemblance to *phronesis* than to *techne.* The rules underlying it are not rules that it would suffice to apply blindly; they require a *discernment of the particular circumstances* that guides their application and, as such, they resemble rules of experience. Indeed, the rules of experience "require experience in order to [be used] and are basically what they are only in this use."[65] This is why understanding is never only reproductive—the mere mastery of a technique—but productive. It involves originality; it goes beyond all application of rules pertaining to a prior linguistic competency. Understanding, and consequently meaning itself, possess an *evential nature* [*caractère événementiel*]. "The character of event [*Geschehenscharakter*]" as Gadamer points out, "belongs to meaning itself."[66] This evential character of understanding is of a piece with the event-character of speech.[67] Language is not merely made up of reproducible and infinitely combinable expressions and turns of phrase that we have learned to manage and use in paradigmatic situations; it transcends itself in expressive and innovative speech, in the incandescent utterance of the poet or thinker. There is a spoken word, as Merleau-Ponty says, but also a speaking word. The latter finds its fulfillment in the poem in which the word in action surpasses all ability defined in advance by its relation to the circumstances of ordinary discourse, and can go so far as to make itself intelligible precisely in infringing the rules.

This speech, inventing itself if need be against the rules in the singular event of its utterance, is never more manifest than in poetry, and especially in modern poetry, the poetry originating with Rimbaud. Let us pause to consider a stanza from the poem "Eternity."

> Des humains suffrages,
> Des communs élans
> Là tu te dégages
> Et voles selon.[68]
>
> From the voice of the World
> And the striving of Man
> You must set yourself free;
> You must fly as you can.

In the last line "*selon*" ("according to," translated here as "as you can") no longer has the normal prepositional value it has in French; it is used as an adverb, which, strictly speaking, is incorrect. But this incorrect use is not only perfectly intelligible, but strikingly accurate. Any other expression we might be tempted to replace it with would weaken it—and not only metrically. "*Voler selon*" means to fly freely, unconstrainedly, with an imperious freedom, to fly "at random, by chance" without any specific destination. This paraphrase gives probably the meaning, but not better than does that mere apposition of a verb and a preposition. In the verse, "selon" remains suspended, like the flight and, breaking with the verb it completes, echoes "*tu te dégages.*" A flamboyant meteor, the poet's word transgresses the instituted language and may even go so far as to violate the rule in order to place itself at the inaugural moment of speech. "Freedom is taken but not given,"[69] Georges Braque wrote. The same is true of the poet's word. Rimbaud's verse takes on therefore an untranslatable character in the strong sense: it can be transposed, but not translated. We understand this verse although it transgresses French usage, while at the same time that disconcerting turn of phrase leads us to understand/hear [*entendre*] the word "selon," so common in French, differently. The poem is not only "prolonged hesitation between sound and sense" (Paul Valéry), or the putting into relief of the message for its own sake (Roman Jakobson); it is first of all a *regulated transgression of the rules* in order to produce an unprecedented experience of language, and, through it, of the world. Every poem is an experience, as Rilke puts it. The transgression of rules is part of the poetic act, which is a way of keeping constantly on the crest-line of the word [*parole*], in that place in which speech tears itself away from "words [*mots*] of the tribe." The poem perpetuates the act of its birth, and the poet—Rimbaud—with it. "Better than a revolution," Char wrote, "he pierces through and through like a bullet the horizon of poetry and sensibility."[70]

Thus the poem pushes to the extreme the individualizing power of speech [*parole*] as opposed to its conventional traits. It reveals a speech *in statu nascendi*, a language transcending itself as an inherited manifold of rules by its unprecedented use, by the literally never-heard-before [*inouï*] event of the birth of a living word. All language is thus suspended between the generality of rules and the individuality of the living word: "If we consider the tendency toward individuation that is characteristic of living language, we will come to recognize the ultimate form of that tendency in poetic creation."[71] Through other lines of investigation and in an analytic context, Davidson, too, has stressed that constitutive tension of language between convention and individuality.[72] The poet, as the great stylist, is the one who brings to the living word an unsaid, beyond the routines of a language and sometimes in opposition to its best established conventions, while at the same time remaining within the possibilities it affords him. Neologisms, anacolutha, and parataxis are several means for that regulated transgression that is at the inception of a unique style. "The more poetic a poet is, the freer—that is, the more open and prepared to accept the unexpected—is his saying."[73]

These affirmations definitely do not make us relapse into the absurdity of a private language that I would be the only one, not to speak and understand, but to be able to speak and understand. "He who speaks a private language [*Privatsprache*] understood by no one else, does not speak at all. But on the other hand, he who only speaks a language in which conventionality has become total in the choice of words, in syntax, and in style forfeits the power to address and evocation that comes solely with the individualization of a language's vocabulary and of its means of communication."[74] Incidentally, there is an experience that is symmetrical to the one to which the poem initiates us: the experience of the understanding of a language we have not mastered, or that, like a dialect, falls short of the familiar conventions. It occurs frequently that we understand ample portions of a language we are unable to speak. The author of these words understands Spanish rather well, thanks to Latin, French, and Italian, and yet is not able to construct a single correct sentence in that language. To understand is not the same as to master a technique. There is a linguistic competency that is powerless to manifest itself in action, and that probably stems from the memory of similar sonorities and turns of phrase in other languages. Without recognizing an ability to understand that actualizes itself only passively *as sensibility or experience*, it is impossible to account for such a phenomenon.

The mastery of conventions is probably insufficient to account for linguistic competency and understanding. This is what explains the shortcomings of the two analogies proposed by the pragmatics conception of language in both Bühler and Wittgenstein: the instrument and the game. The former implies that language is subordinate to external ends. Now, language is not an auxiliary for thought, but its living accomplishment and its embodiment. It is not an instrument for the communication of preexistent thoughts; it is in it, by it, and through it that we become aware of our thoughts, and thereby of what we can communicate or not. As for the game analogy, it is surely superior to the first one, since according to it, language becomes its own end: its rules are *constitutive* rules *for* the activity it is. Language is no longer *ergon*, but *energeia* (Humboldt). But by contrast with the game of chess favored by Wittgenstein, a language is a system of rules *that never stop evolving as they are applied, and can only be abstracted after the fact from the concrete act of speaking*. This is what confers on language its irreducible *historicity*. As Gadamer emphasizes, "no language is a system of rules that the schoolmaster has in his head and that is the result of the grammarians' abstractions. Every language is always in the process changing. It is probably true that the grammatical structure of our languages is becoming more perfect as their vocabulary becomes richer. But even an in-depth grammar will not prevent the language from keeping something of the rich prosody belonging to all speech."[75] Applied to language, moreover, the very idea of "convention" is problematic; it seems to rest on a vicious circle, since, in order to agree on the meaning to be given to a word, one must already possess language. "The 'conventions' of a language all refer to each other," Merleau-Ponty remarks, "that is, they always presuppose an instituted language."[76] The decisional character of all convention and its subordination to the ends in view of which it is concluded cannot be suitable to the institution of language. And therefore language cannot be an *institution* among others. It will probably be responded that language is not regulated by explicit conventions, but implicit ones. A language "is a convention of custom and not of written law."[77] But besides the fact that the idea of an implicit or purely customary convention sounds very much like a contradiction in terms, the whole problem is to determine whether the paradigm of the rule suffices to account for actual linguistic activity. Without denying that it is possible to extract from every language a set of rules (whether implicit or explicit), a grammar, the question is whether the life of language doesn't always transcend its instituted and sedimented forms; whether the remarkable creativity exhibited by all living language does not extend far beyond all routine, that is, all blind application of rules.

This is why the emergence of meaning in a living, spoken word or in a text is something that eludes all total mastery, and therefore is irreducible to the mere realization of a meaning-intention, of a prior communicative intent. To speak is to experience the emergence of a meaning that depends also on contextual factors that we cannot entirely control, since they always in part escape our vigilance. We are not the masters and possessors of language—not even of the one we have mastered most. Language speaks in us, and speaks to us, rather than our speaking it. Heidegger's inversion has nothing rhetorical about it: "For, strictly, it is language that speaks. Man first speaks when, and only when, he responds to language by listening to its appeal."[78]

To be sure, no one would deny that speaking is an intentional activity, even when we do not "choose" our words; but the linguistic act goes beyond the speaker and reveals his thought to him, rather than his revealing his thought by the intermediary of language. Language is *not at all* an intermediary. It is for this reason that a poem is also an experience. A poem is the estrangement of a thought exiled from its usual borders and only thus delivered unto itself. Behind all attempt to say something there rustles a silence nothing can break and that each word in its own way prolongs and perpetuates. Only what we "have no words to say" is truly worthy of being communicated: such is the fundamentally *poetic* dimension of speech. Always what I try to say goes further than what I say in fact, however carefully and attentively I "choose" my words. The unsaid is inner and essential to the saying; it is as a second potentiality nestled in its power. Quoting Gadamer once again, "What is asserted is not everything. Indeed, it is the unsaid that first makes it, and lets it be, a word that can reach us."[79]

22

Phenomenology as Hermeneutics

> No philosophy can be ignorant of the problem of finitude without thereby being ignorant of itself as a philosophy.
>
> —Maurice Merleau-Ponty

Phenomenology and hermeneutics have often been set in opposition. On such a view, the former is both the science of absolute beginnings and the discipline of ultimate foundations; it is governed by a presupposition-free method and rests on the "principle of principles," self-evident intuition. The latter emphasizes historicity and the finitude of reason, the irremediable historical conditioning of all philosophical activity, the necessity of interpretation and the impossibility of the eidetic method, and the inanity of the ideal of a *fundamentum inconcussum*. Because hermeneutics develops under the auspices of interpretation, it is always in medias res, bogged down in history, never at the beginning or the end. According to Ricoeur, the contrast between these two approaches is so strong that there is a real "gulf" between them.[1]

Such a presentation—at least this is the conviction I would like to defend in this chapter—remains superficial. This is the case for at least two reasons. First, it takes as its exclusive term of comparison phenomenology in Husserl's sense, as if phenomenology had to be Husserlian in its epistemology and method. Second, it rests on a very restrictive view of the tasks and means of hermeneutics. I will advance a strictly opposite view: *genuine hermeneutics is phenomenology and phenomenology is only achieved as hermeneutics.* It could therefore turn out to be the case that the gap and even the "gulf" between the two approaches are quite simply nonexistent—which would make the "graft"[2] of the one onto the other, to borrow one of Ricoeur's famous images, superfluous. Hermeneutics and phenomenology would be blossoms of the same "essence," of the same bud.

Up to this point, hermeneutics has come into our reflections at two crucial moments: (1) In chapter 12, when the issue was to defend both the rootedness of phenomenological descriptions in descriptions of essence and their dependence on history, insofar as essences and relations of essence can only be explicated in light of at least partially inherited conceptual schemes and presuppositions. (2) In chapter 21, in connection with one of the pathways of a phenomenology of language, in which hermeneutics turned out to be a phenomenology attentive to the diachronic dimension of speech, that is, a deepening of the pragmatics paradigm, that eliminates nevertheless some of the latter's residual idealizations and reintegrates the living act of speech and writing into our historical experience as a whole.

It is probably not entirely incidental that hermeneutics presented itself to us at the intersection of language and history. The birth of philosophical hermeneutics in the nineteenth century coincided with the connection drawn between these two problematics. It was Dilthey who, in his concern to give a foundation to the human sciences (*Geisteswissenschaften*) that would make their epistemology as reliable and respectable as that of the natural sciences, responded to the positivist challenge by importing the hermeneutic method, first developed by Schleiermacher in the field of philology, into that of history conceived of as the expression and objectification of life. Historical life interprets itself: such was the watchword of Dilthey, but also the locus of a recurrent problem—that of relativism or historicism. This problem was to become the cumbersome heritage that still haunts philosophical hermeneutics in the twentieth century.

What have we learned from our two incursions in the domain of hermeneutics? (1) First, that Husserl's idea of a *Vorurteilungslosigkeit*, of an absence of presuppositions in phenomenological descriptions, and its corollary, the idea of an eidetic intuition "free from all interpretations" (*hineindeutungen*)[3] are no more than metaphysical dreams. No description aspiring to truth of a philosophical nature can free itself from a conditioning by history as soon as it leaves the terrain of judgments of essence in order to formulate transcendental questions regarding the conditions of possibility of the truths of essence themselves. This is the point in which come in, on the one hand, conceptual schemes borrowed from tradition, according to which, for instance, the pair perception/intellection, when applied to experience, is neither innocent nor devoid of philosophical implications; and, on the other, presuppositions of a theoretical nature, pre-opinions or prejudices that surreptitiously guide the description and can only be called into question and made explicit up to a point. No phenomenology can be a description of essence *through and through.* It must be a constantly renewed interrogation on its own sources and origin. As Heidegger emphasizes, "Even the ontological investigation that we are now conducting is determined by its historical situation and . . . by the preceding philosophical tradition. . . . It is for this reason that all philosophical discussion, even the most radical attempt to begin all over again, is pervaded by traditional concepts and thus by traditional horizons and traditional angles of approach."[4] This is why phenomenology implies a "destruction," that is, a critical de-construction (*Abbau*) of that tradition, which is not in the least its negation, but on the contrary its positive appropriation.[5] Thus hermeneutics has made it possible for us to turn away from any positivist temptation, in the sense in which Husserl asserted of his philosophy that it was the true positivism.[6] But in doing so, hermeneutics exposes us to the risk of a new relativism. (2) Our second incursion revealed to us the constitutive character of language for thought, seen by Husserl up to a point, but almost immediately obfuscated by his thesis that language is an "unproductive layer" of meaning. That language is *constitutive* for thought means not only that we could not have most of our thoughts, beliefs, or opinions if we did not have language, but that we could not have certain feelings, goals, intentions, desires, and so on, either. If an animal cannot feel *an anxiety mixed with anguish that a hope, probably fanciful, will not be realized,* it is not because its sensibility is too coarse, it is first and foremost because it cannot possess *our* concepts. There is no doubt that language goes so far as to deeply transform our *experience* of the world, for example our experience of a colored surface as a painting, or our perception of a melody as a symphony (and even as a Beethoven symphony, the Ninth). At this point, the following question arises: Can we both defend the thesis of the constitutive nature of language for thought (and also for certain feelings, desires, and experiences), and that of a prelinguistic meaning that would permeate our primordial experience of the world? Is the constitutive character of language for thought compatible with the view according to which proto-thoughts are immanent to experience itself, and have no need of linguistic articulation to be the proto-thoughts they are? If we answer in the negative, we run the risk of being forced to conclude that there is no experience—at least for *us,* human beings—that is not already linguistically structured, and even compelled to end up with the idea that without language our experience would present none of the characteristic differences or characteristic structures that we can find in it by an analysis. Language, in that case, would be that which *makes possible* all identity, all difference, and all structure within experience itself. We have already encountered that thesis in chapter 7, and we have called it, after Anscombe, "linguistic idealism." On that view, our linguistic practices create the essential structures of the experienced world from scratch; or rather, this world has no essential structure beyond the rules projected on it by our "grammar." If we push the constitutive nature of language too far, extending it to the totality of experience, we risk ending up with a similar "idealism," which would make *phenomenological* research superfluous.

The two problems I raise are connected. A linguistic idealism almost inevitably leads to a relativism: if experience presents no feature of intelligibility outside its structuration by language, and therefore if the life-world is linguistic and cultural through and through, we must conclude that the depositaries of different cultures do not live in the same world. Conversely, it may be that cultural relativism in its various forms is always connected, whether closely or remotely, to the idea of incommensurable languages, and therefore to the idea of incommensurable worldviews: its implicit premise is that language structures our perception of the world *without remainder*.

Does hermeneutics, as the heir of phenomenology, succumb to these difficulties? In taking a linguistic turn that is not without similarities to the one taken by the analytic tradition, can it still claim to be a phenomenology? And if so, on what conditions?

It might be objected that hermeneutics is far less homogeneous than I make it seem. To speak only of its two major figures (aside from Heidegger), Gadamer and Ricoeur, we may in fact doubt that there is such a thing as the one hermeneutics. Gadamer's hermeneutics is based on a phenomenological description of understanding as it operates in the entire domain of the human sciences, especially in its three principal branches, which are aesthetics, history, and textual criticism. His hermeneutics aspires to be "universal." As for Ricoeur, he sets out with a more restrained concept of hermeneutics: he first conceived of it as an interpretation of symbols forming the complement of a phenomenology of Husserlian inspiration; later, he broadened this concept to "the theory of the operations of understanding in their relation to the interpretation of texts,"[7] but without ceasing to consider hermeneutics as a theory of *symbolic* objectifications and mediations. If for Gadamer, as for Heidegger, hermeneutics and phenomenology have destinies that are intertwined, Ricoeur insisted rather on their heterogeneity of principle: according to him, hermeneutics grafted itself onto a phenomenology of lived experiences and acts of consciousness. While Gadamer saw in conversation the paradigm of the work of understanding the other, which only applies to texts in a derivative way ("being for the text," he says, does not exhaust the problem of hermeneutics),[8] Ricoeur, by contrast, rejected this dialogical model and insisted on the differences separating texts from conversation. His motto is that "writing tears itself free of the limits of face-to-face-dialogue."[9] In the wake of Dilthey and romantic hermeneutics, but also of Heidegger,[10] Gadamer adopted a strong dichotomy between understanding, which belongs to the human sciences, and explanation, which dominates in the natural sciences. As for Ricoeur, he forged the watchword according to which "to explain more is to understand better";[11] he was committed to reintegrate explanation, not in the form it takes in the natural sciences but in the one it has in the sciences of language and in structuralist textual criticism, into the hermeneutic process as a necessary moment, and held that the relations between explaining and understanding are to be approached "dialectically."[12] While Gadamer continues to insist on the necessary deconstruction of the cogito and the philosophy of the subject inspired by Descartes in order to carry out the hermeneutic project, subordinating, after Heidegger, the epistemological problematic of interpretation to an ontology of *Verstehen*, Ricoeur set his entire enterprise in the wake of reflexive philosophy, particularly the post-Kantian (Fichte, Nabert), recommending a reevaluation of the cogito and a "justified repetition of the question of the ego."[13] Contrary to Gadamer, he did not reject a phenomenology of consciousness, but only its idealist version,[14] so that for him, Husserlian phenomenology continues to coexist with hermeneutics in a relation that is also qualified as "dialectic." The *epochē* is no longer primary, but secondary; it remains, nonetheless, confirmed in its rights. As for subjectivity, it "must be lost as radical origin if it is to be recovered in a more modest role." Thus, for example, Ricoeur does not reject Husserlian intersubjectivity, but only a conceptuality that "weakens its scope," namely the subject-object relation.[15]

I am not interested here by all these differences per se. They do not suffice, in any case, to defeat the hypothesis according to which both post-Heideggerian hermeneutics rest on a common basis. Let us limit ourselves for the moment to the minimal definition of hermeneutics furnished by *Being and Time*: "this business of interpreting [*Auslegung*]."[16] There seems to be a point of agreement or at least of a rather strong convergence between the hermeneutics of Gadamer and Ricoeur: their common assertion of the "linguisticality [*Sprachlichkeit*]" of the experience of the world. According to a well-known formulation from *Truth and Method*, "being that can be understood is language [*Sprache*]."[17] But is it not precisely at this point that the peril of a linguistic idealism appears? *All* understanding, according to Gadamer, is a linguistic process, even when it concerns something extra-linguistic: "The idealization of language . . . is already present in any acquisition of experience."[18] *Any* acquisition of experience? But how, under these conditions, can we acquire an experience of language? Must not language be perceived in the first place, that is, precisely, given before any possession of language—especially in order to be learned? Were we not *in-fans* before acceding to speech? And the structural reorganizations that have taken place, thanks to the acquisition of language, even in our very way of perceiving, feeling, and understanding—do they not presuppose a prelinguistic experience with its own principles of organization and structuration on which those "reorganizations" acted? Furthermore, if it is through language that we perceive the world, if our being-in-the-world is linguistic through and through—if, as Gadamer insists, the "presence of the world has a linguistic constitution,"[19] we must conclude that it is never to *the* world that we relate, but always to *a* world, the one to which our language gives us access, and it becomes difficult to understand how we can share that world, or how we can acquire another language.

In short, the risk of a linguistic idealism is never as patent as it is in the transition from the assertion, which is after all rather trivial, that for the human being "the world is only world"[20] by the intermediary of language—which comes down to saying that the grasping of the world *as such* presupposes the possession of a *concept*, that of world—to the one according to which "the world is only world to the extent that it expresses itself in a language."[21] In the first case, the difference between the human world, the *Welt*, and animal environment, the *Umwelt*, is classically related to the possession of language, so that only a being who possesses the concept of world can have an experience of the world *as such*. But Gadamer does not hesitate to go on to say that it is the experience of the world *without qualification* that is made possible by language: there would be an "essentially linguistic character of human being-in-the-world."[22] So it is not because we are in the world that we have language, it is because we have language that we are in the world. This claim goes far beyond the trivial assertion that the possession of language modifies our relation to the world, situates us in the world otherwise than the animal, and gives us access to a world that differs radically from the animal's; it even contradicts this last assertion. Indeed, how could language reshape our experience and modify it, if there is no such thing as an experience prior to language by principle?

On this point, Ricoeur explicitly follows Gadamer.[23] He even goes a step further in the direction of a linguistic idealism. In accordance with the primacy that he gives to the written, and to texts in general, for his definition of hermeneutics, he tends to replace language in its wider extension with a textual model that is deemed to *mediate* all understanding of self and world.[24] Thus, by a kind of transposition of Kantian transcendental idealism, the categories of text and narrative acquire a *constituting* function for experience itself. The central thesis of *Time and the Narrative* is in fact that "there is no human experience that is not already mediated by symbolic systems, and, among them, by narratives."[25] But it is hard to see how narrative could "mediate" an experience about which Ricoeur furthermore asserts that it is "*confused, unformed, and ultimately mute.*"[26] If experience is stripped of all intrinsic intelligibility and all autonomy with respect to thought as it is expressed in the text, *nothing is mediated by anything anymore,* since there is no experience unless by its textual "configuration." It is narration, for example, that is adjudged to overcome the opposition between lived time and cosmic time, that is, to replace not only a missing intuition, but an impossible phenomenology. Time only becomes "human time" to the extent that it is "organized after the manner of a narrative";[27] so much so that there is no legitimacy in describing structures immanent to the experience of time outside of its configuration or its putting-into-a-plot by the narrative mythos. But how can symbolic systems "model"[28] our experience if experience is *confused and unformed,* that is, lacking all true autonomy, all determinable "figure" as opposed to the models that "reconfigure" it? If the narrative is "at the basis of its intelligibility," to speak of a "reconfiguration" of experience is no longer intelligible. Therefore, it should come as no suprise that the event tends, in Ricoeur, to become a mere "narrative component,"[29] time a formation of the narrative—since it is the narrative, and it alone, that "portrays the features of temporal experience"[30]—and the world a projection of the text: "The world is the whole set of references opened by every sort of descriptive or poetic text I have read, interpreted, and loved."[31] In short, it is the text that is invested with the power to transform a mere environment into a world.[32] Gadamer's *In-der-Welt-sein,* with its *Sprachlichkeit,* is henceforth replaced by a "being-in-the-world according to narrativity,"[33] without this hypostatization of the text, and its corollary, the claim of the amorphous character of prelinguistic—or rather, pre-textual—experience, being any more justified. Is it still possible, under these conditions, to *bring together* phenomenology and hermeneutics?

If the world itself is a textual effect, it is also because interpretation, in Ricoeur's view, must run as deep as the roots of perception, including the meaningful perception of a mere *sentence.* Whereas Gadamer maintained an irreducible gap between the spontaneous understanding that is the result of the mastery of a language, and the interpretation of texts or complex works, separated from us by a historical distance, Ricoeur asserts that "to produce a relatively univocal discourse with polysemic words . . . is the first and most elementary work of interpretation,"[34] so that understanding and interpreting become coextensive. This entails the disastrous consequence already stressed that, if interpretation already begins at the most elementary level of understanding, and if interpretation is an activity necessarily expressed in signs, all interpretation must refer back to yet another interpretation, and an infinite regression is inevitable. Nothing can ever be understood, and therefore nothing can ever be interpreted, either: the distinction between understanding and interpreting is destroyed in its very principle.

One might perhaps object, in opposition to this reading of Gadamer and Ricoeur, that each of them seems to have admitted, at least in passing, the existence of a pre-hermeneutic level of experience. Gadamer adds a significant nuance to his thesis of the intrinsically linguistic character of all experience: "Naturally, the fundamental linguisticality of understanding cannot mean that all experiencing of the world can only take place as and in language."[35] But if that is the case, many formulations in *Truth and Method* are no longer valid. We would have to accept a level of understanding that is both prelinguistic and pre-hermeneutic as a condition for the properly hermeneutic fulfillment of understanding. As for Ricoeur, when he endorses the thesis, of Husserlian inspiration, "of the derivative character of linguistic meaning,"[36] a similar problem arises. How is that thesis to be reconciled with the claim that an interpretation is already at work in our very *perception* of things and language, as Husserl, according to Ricoeur, suggested through his idea of intentional *Deutung*?[37] If experience is "unformed" and "confused," how could meanings of the linguistic order be derived from it? Is it possible to maintain both that our experience only "becomes itself" when brought to language[38] and that language is only a moment within a broader experience? "When the latter [hermeneutics] subordinates lingual experience to the whole of our aesthetic and historical experience," writes Ricoeur, "it continues, on the level of the human sciences, the movement initiated by Husserl on the plane of perceptual experience."[39] Can these two assertions be reconciled—that of the linguistic character of *all* experience and that of the subordination of linguistic experience to the whole of historical experience?

This is why the phenomenology/hermeneutics articulation is not an easy one under the aegis of the premise of the linguistic character of experience in general. The difficulties encountered raise a fundamental problem that can be formulated as follows. We have here two requirements that are not necessarily compatible. According to the phenomenological requirement, the primordial experience of the world already bears within itself an immanent order and a pre-conceptual meaning that must be analyzed according to their own necessities; there is an intelligence of sensibility (subjective genitive) that is not a degraded form of thought or judgment: perceiving is neither thinking, nor judging, nor interpreting. According to the hermeneutic requirement, language is constitutive of thought in the strong sense; there is no phenomenological description—which, of course, is a linguistic operation—that does not involve both conceptual schemes and inherited theoretical presuppositions; access to the phenomena to be described is irremediably mediate, requiring the long detour of a historical interpretation.

Are these two requirements contradictory? At first sight, they are not. It is perfectly possible to maintain the existence of an experiential meaning not yet articulated in linguistic form and the constitutive character of language for *thought* in the strong sense. Already in 1913, in "The Doctrine of Judgment in Psychologism," Heidegger made a distinction between a broad and a narrow concept of thought: on the one hand, what I have called proto-thoughts immanent to experience and, on the other, predicative or propositional thoughts.[40] Thus it becomes possible to consider that *the experience* of the world does not involve, generally speaking, any interpretation, but that the *description* of that experience, to the extent that it exceeds by the transcendental questions it formulates a pure description of essence, is only carried out as an interpretation.

For a tension to appear between the two requirements, one must maintain either that all experience in its essence is linguistic (and therefore structured by conceptual schemes), or that it is already an interpretation—or both. The tension that develops between phenomenology and hermeneutics in both Gadamer and Ricoeur comes from the fact that they tend to adhere to these two claims. This problem becomes even more acute if we take into account a point discussed in chapter 12. An interpretation brings into play both linguistic schemes and presuppositions in the strict sense, that is, pre-opinions, prejudices of a theoretical nature that govern and orient understanding. The former belong to the domain of meaning, the latter to that of truth. Meaning and truth are, of course, conceptually distinct: to understand a text, for example, is not necessarily to adhere to what it says. But in fact the question of meaning and that of truth are not independent in the concrete carrying out of the hermeneutic process. As Gadamer insists, "a person trying to understand a text is prepared for it to tell him something."[41] The interpreter's task "*in concreto* is never merely a logical-technical transmission of the sense of some discourse, in which the question of the truth of what it says is completely disregarded."[42] We interpret meaning on the basis of what appears to us as being the truest and most rational beliefs, and beliefs on the basis of what seems to us the most plausible meaning. We understand meaning on the basis of truth and truth on the basis of meaning. But, this being the case, if language and interpretation always already inform our experience of the world, the hermeneutic process has neither beginning nor end, and the beliefs that are amalgamated to the appearance of things resuscitate the specter of relativism.

But let us leave this last problem aside, and return to it later. Does not the tension we discovered in post-Heideggerian hermeneutics originate in Heidegger himself? Granted, *Being and Time* seems to fulfill the phenomenological requirement of a prelinguistic meaning that arises at the very level of our experience (our Being-in-the-world) in light of our practical possibilities. Heidegger breaks away from Husserlian conceptuality by holding that all manifestation of beings in general rests on an understanding of Being, as ontological character of *Dasein*; but he specifies right away, apropos that understanding, that it is both preconceptual[43] and prelinguistic, since meaning, that is, what can be articulated in the explanation-interpretation (*Auslegung*), particularly in the form of statement, precedes its linguistic formulation by principle.[44] There is a "primordial signifying [*Bedeuten*]" belonging to circumspective concern and to its understanding of entities as *zuhanden*, which does not yet draw on linguistic *Bedeutung*. Still, an ambiguity remains, making the position of *Being and Time* unstable, not to say aporetic.[45] Already in §1 of that work, on the occasion of the first formulation of the *Seinsfrage*, Heidegger clearly considers as equivalent the question bearing upon the meaning of Being and that regarding the meaning of "being," the meaning of the *verb "to be"* as it is understood, according to him, in all predication. "Everyone understands 'the sky *is* blue,' 'I *am* merry,' and the like. But here we have an average kind of intelligibility, which merely demonstrates that this is incomprehensible . . . The very fact that we already live in an understanding of Being and that the meaning of Being [*der Sinn von Sein*] is still veiled in darkness proves that it is necessary in principle to raise this question [*dem Sinn von 'Sein'*] again."[46] Here Heidegger moves without any solution of continuity from the question of the meaning of Being to that of the meaning of the expression "being," and that transition is confirmed by many other passages all along his "path of thought."[47] Hence, even if we admit that the understanding of Being, as mere pre-understanding at work in our daily busyness with beings, has a vague, indeterminate, non-thematic character, it becomes difficult, to say the least, to see how this understanding could be prelinguistic and pre-conceptual while at the same time remaining understanding *of Being*. We are faced with the following dilemma: either to maintain the phenomenological requirement, that is, the prelinguistic character of the meaning that comes to light in that understanding, and separate the "question of Being" entirely from all questioning about the meaning of the expression "being" as verb and copula, or to admit that the two questions are inseparable, as we are invited to do by Heidegger's most constant declarations, and thereby make all innerworldly discovery of beings dependent on an already *linguistic* ability.

By subordinating all manifestation of phenomena to an understanding of Being, and by equating phenomenology with fundamental ontology, Heidegger runs the risk of destroying the autonomy of a phenomenological transcendental aesthetics that constituted at least one of the cores of the Husserlian project, and thus of over-intellectualizing perception and making it depend entirely on language. "Any mere prepredicative seeing of the ready-to-hand is, in itself, something which already understands and interprets."[48] But if this is true of *all* perception, it is difficult to maintain the distinction of principle between perceiving and interpreting; it is even difficult to retain a meaning for the concept of interpretation, since interpretation can no longer be about anything, about any *interpretandum* that would precede it. The tension that appears in Heidegger's thought will in a sense be "solved"—but the difficulty itself will be increased—during the second phase of his thought, following what it has been agreed to call the "*Kehre*." Speech (*Sprache*) will henceforth be designated as "the house of Being"; *it will constitute through and through* the very openness of *Dasein* (or man) to beings as beings. "Since language [*Sprache*] is the house of Being, we therefore arrive at beings by constantly going through this house. If we go to the fountain, if we go through the woods, we are already going through the word 'fountain,' through the word 'wood,' even if we are not saying these words aloud or have any thoughts about language."[49] The posterity of this tension, as well as its paradoxical "resolution," probably explain the attraction exerted by linguistic idealism on the thought of both Gadamer and Ricoeur.

This first difficulty brings a second in its wake, which culminates in §7 of *Being and Time*—so decisive for the phenomenology-hermeneutics articulation. Indeed, this paragraph is the locus of an odd short-circuiting between two assertions that are not equivalent: one according to which the *description* of phenomena is hermeneutic and another according to which it is the *giving* of the phenomena themselves that is hermeneutic—in other words, even at the primordial level of our experience of the world, a *hermeneuein* is already at work. In this passage, Heidegger not only defends the idea that "the meaning of phenomenological description as a method lies in *interpretation*"[50] but he declares that it is the phenomena themselves—and, first and foremost, the signal phenomenon of Being—which, in order to be able to *appear* as such, in order to be able to be experienced themselves for their own sake, require the mediation of a *hermeneuein*. Being, this phenomenon par excellence, since it makes possible the phenomenalization of all other phenomena, is defined as "something that does *not* show itself initially and for the most part, something that is *concealed* [*verborgen*] in contrast to what initially and for the most part does show itself. But, at the same time, it is something that essentially belongs to what initially and for the most part shows itself, indeed in such a way that it constitutes its meaning and ground."[51] To Being there belongs an essential concealing, which can only be overcome—though not entirely—by an *Auslegung*. The "phenomenological concept of phenomenon," namely "the Being of beings," can only be conquered in all-out battle and wrested away from its essential concealment, the concealment of its concealment, by phenomenological hermeneutics, and it alone: "What is to become a phenomenon [first and foremost, Being] can be concealed. And it is precisely because phenomena are initially and for the most part *not* given that phenomenology is needed."[52] Here Heidegger disguises in the form of a paradox a real difficulty. How could phenomena be *phenomena* without being given, experienced? Still, this capital passage is perfectly clear: what remains withdrawn, hidden by an inauthentic understanding rooted in tradition, is not the correct *description* of the phenomenon, but the *phenomenon* itself; what is not given initially is once again this phenomenon, and what must be conquered by a phenomenological hermeneutics, torn away from its withdrawal, or rather from the withdrawal of its withdrawal, what can be "given," finally, only by the intermediary of that discipline, is again the phenomenon (of Being); as a consequence, it is phenomenology that, by its interpretation, reveals *for the first time* the phenomenon, which, nonetheless, is qualified as what gives itself of itself [*se donne soi-même à même soi*]. The *Auslegung* does not concern phenomena previously given on which it would exert its elucidative power; it does not enable us to see phenomena better, but purely and simply to see them. But then what does "to *describe* phenomena" mean? If indeed describing can allow us to see better, seeing cannot consist merely in describing. We can only describe better what we already see. We can only make appear by means of a more adequate or "more originary" interpretation what has already appeared prior to that interpretation. If everything that is a phenomenon is not only described, but given through an interpretation, there are no longer phenomena nor interpretation.

What legitimates, in Heidegger's view, this short-circuit between the phenomenon and its description? Probably the desire to meld together his hermeneutic critique of Husserlian phenomenology, by virtue of which all *description* is necessarily bound to historical presuppositions, and his ontological critique of that same phenomenology, according to which all *phenomenon* can only declare itself as such for *Dasein* on the basis of its understanding of Being.[53] Being, Heidegger tells us in substance, is not so much the object as the "subject" of interpretation. As he will specify in *On the Way to Language,* "In *Being and Time,* hermeneutics means neither the theory of the art of interpretation nor interpretation itself, but rather the attempt first of all to characterize the essence of interpretation on the basis of what *is* hermeneutic."[54] What is hermeneutic is Being itself—and its very meaning. Being, the forgotten of metaphysics—the latter living and perpetuating itself by this forgetfulness—can come into view only through an interpretation that uncovers its hidden meaning as it unfolds differently in each era of its history. What Heidegger wants to show by his fusion of ontology and hermeneutics—hermeneutics having to be understood on the basis of ontology, and not the other way round—is, then, that Being, the withdrawn Openness for all manifestation, the condition of possibility for all understanding of beings, is itself declined historically, making the understanding of beings and their manifestation historical through and through. But to maintain that our experience is historical is ambiguous. That might mean that it is *always also* historical or that it is *always only* historical. In the second reading, we have lost all common ground of a trans-historical experience on the basis of which the historical variations themselves would appear. We have abdicated the right to name what undergoes modifications through history, just as we have given up any possibility of speaking of *phenomena* nor previously interpreted historically, for example, phenomena through which history itself declares itself: archives, vestiges, works, monuments. Granted, the interpretation of vestiges is a historical operation; but the vestiges that we can encounter are not what they are *by virtue of* such an interpretation.

The consequence of all this seems to be the following: phenomenological hermeneutics can only formulate itself coherently if it accepts the pre-hermeneutic level of a spontaneous understanding at work in experience itself, a *perceptual* experience not mediated by signs. It is only on this condition that it becomes possible, in a word, to save the hermeneutic character of phenomenology without relegating Merleau-Ponty and his concept of "perception"—regardless of whether or not that *word* seems adequate to us—to the dusty archives[55] of metaphysics. Otherwise, what would be exactly the meaning of this constantly maintained reference to "the things themselves" to which phenomenology's task is to lead us back? Heidegger seems aware of this difficulty when he says that interpretation's "first, last, and constant task is never to allow our fore-having, fore-sight, and fore-conception [*Vorhabe, Vorsicht, und Vorgriff*] to be presented to us by fancies and popular conceptions, but rather to make the scientific theme secure by working out these fore-structures in terms of the things themselves."[56] For how could hermeneutic phenomenology bring phenomena, that is, "what gives itself of itself" to light, by means of the most accurate interpretation, if phenomena, the things or the subject matter of the phenomenologist, are *only* given by means of interpretation? If we reject this distinction, if we maintain that the phenomenon depends, in order to appear (assuming that it appears), on a hermeneutic stage, we inevitably fall into a circle—a *vicious* circle, and not a hermeneutic one: the phenomenon in order to appear needs interpretation, but interpretation must draw its source not in inherited (or "popular") concepts and theories, but in phenomena themselves. There would be a *hermeneutic* circle if understanding-interpretation *shed light on* our experience of phenomena, and the phenomena in turn ricocheted back onto their interpretation, reorienting and enriching it. But the assertion that it is the *access* to phenomena itself that is *made possible* by interpretation contradicts the assertion that interpretation finds in phenomena its starting point. With the phenomenon giving itself only *per via interpretationis,* it seems that we have only two solutions left: either to transform the "thing itself" into a teleological pole, an idea in the Kantian sense, a temptation that Heidegger did not always resist;[57] or to end up with an extreme perspectivism of the Nietzschean variety: "There are no facts [no phenomena], only interpretations. . . . But this is already an interpretation"[58]—perspectivism that is self-contradictory.

We are now in a position to answer the following questions:

(1) Does experience include an understanding?
(2) Does experience include an interpretation?
(3) Does the description of experience include an understanding?
(4) Does the description of experience include an interpretation?

(1) Yes. A prelinguistic meaning, which is not yet articulated as a thought in the strong sense, arises from our understanding of the world in light of our practical possibilities, that is, of a system of capabilities.

(2) That depends. The fact that some experiences already bring an interpretation into play—I saw this gesture as hostile, because I interpreted it that way—actually excludes that all experiences do. We can understand without interpreting, but we cannot interpret without understanding. Interpretation comes in when the first understanding turns out to be defective or partial, when a break occurs in the spontaneous understanding in which we live first and foremost in our daily relationships to the world and other people.

(3) Yes, of course. To describe is a linguistic activity that brings into play both an understanding of what is described and of the words used to describe it.

(4) It depends on the kind of description under consideration. If a sentence as simple as "the sky is blue" is already considered as being a description, then I am not interpreting my perception of the sky in uttering that sentence. I simply rely on my linguistic competency, on my ability to use expressions from ordinary language, and, in the case at hand, to apply the predicate "__ is blue" to the singular term "the sky": I report what I see and nothing more. But phenomenology is interested in complex descriptions, which include theoretical elements and are overdetermined by the history of philosophy. *For those descriptions,* the answer is "yes"; such is the indispensable corrective brought by hermeneutics against the dogmatism of the intuition of essences.

What does this detour through the problem of linguistic idealism teach us about the more classical problem of relativism? The truth is that these two problems are connected, and the same kind of argumentation is applicable in both cases. Not, to be sure, that the philosophical hermeneutics of Ricoeur or Gadamer is *stricto sensu* relativist. Relativism, like solipsism, only has the status of an objection addressed to a philosophical position; it never corresponds to the self-understanding of such a position. In Gadamer the notion of the fusion of horizons tries to preserve both the idea of a horizon belonging to each culture and historical situation, and the view that every horizon *opens onto all the others*; by virtue of the resources inherent in a language and its translation, distinct horizons are not *incommensurable.* If relativism is the philosophically inconsistent position asserting that all truth is truth from one point of view, and therefore that an assertion can be true according to point of view *x* and false according to point of view *y*, such a position is not endorsed by hermeneutics. What makes the difference between the horizons of different interpreters is less the factual truth of this or that statement than the difference of interests, questions, and presuppositions on the basis of which the intelligibility of what is to be interpreted comes to light. The book I am writing could be a good example. To pose the problem of the possibility of a phenomenology at the beginning of the twenty-first century requires the adoption of a different perspective on the subject matter, and an orientation that sets out from different problems than those that would have been privileged in the 1950s, for example. But it does not follow that what is true today wouldn't have been true sixty years ago, and vice versa.

The fact remains that since Dilthey and historicism, the relativist aporia has been a recurrent specter for the hermeneutic tradition. Indeed, as we saw in chapter 12, the *negative* response to the problem of relativism consisting in rejecting both relativism and dogmatism as two symptoms of the same unjustified belief in an absolute method in philosophy (a method that would make it possible to reach absolute truths beyond all revision and all historical conditioning)—that response, as I said, is unsatisfactory. It says what hermeneutics isn't; it doesn't say what it is. Now, the hermeneutic project cannot be formulated in a solely negative way. Hermeneutics claims to bring *truths* to light—but how? Does it suffice to interpret accurately the phenomena to do so? And what does "interpret accurately" mean here? We must not confuse the fact that an interpretation attempts to clarify its own presuppositions and is rooted in its own time with the fact of its being in conformity or not with the thing. Gadamer admits it specifically: "Tradition itself is not a justification."[59] Now, truth is inseparable from its justification. Interpretations cannot lay a legitimate claim to a *truth*—even conditional and fallible—unless we are able to furnish criteria not only for a good interpretation, but for an interpretation in conformity with its object. Such criteria, it seems, do indeed exist. To cite a few of them: (a) the coherence of the interpretation; (b) what might be called its "power," that is, its ability to account for the greatest number of aspects of its object (text, work of art, historical event, etc.); (c) its rootedness in a historical competency allowing it to escape anachronisms, at least involuntary ones; (d) the radicality of the questions it formulates; (e) its originality, which itself rests on the knowledge and taking into account of rival interpretations. But if criteria exist to decide in which cases an interpretation is acceptable, better than another one, and so on, they do not constitute *necessary and sufficient conditions* for a good interpretation. We must not reject, in the field of hermeneutics, the existence of rules and criteria; but neither must we assume that there are more exact criteria than those actually accepted in a given interpretive community; and it is the temptation to raise excessive demands regarding criteria, and thus to subordinate interpretation to an exact methodology like the one that dominates in other disciplines—"Descartes' idea of method"[60]—that ultimately leads to endorsing the relativism/dogmatism dichotomy and, along with it, a misguided epistemological ideal. Hermeneutics does not reject the existence of norms and criteria, but the existence of *exact* norms and criteria that it would suffice to apply mechanically without appealing to discernment, judgment, and experience on the part of the interpreter. The rules of interpretation are *rules of experience.* Hence the diagnosis according to which the attraction exerted by relativism does not come from its coherence—it is clearly incoherent—but from its forgetting of the concrete, historical conditions of philosophical activity, and even from its forgetting of the finitude of *all* reason. As Putnam stresses in a different context, "relativism and the desire for a metaphysical foundation [are] manifestations of the same disease."[61]

But even this line of argument is only convincing up to a point. Indeed, if hermeneutics as philosophical doctrine, and not as a mere practice, aspires to a *truth*, and if the concept of truth is necessarily a normative one, we must try to formulate what justifies hermeneutics' claim to truth still more precisely. Hermeneutics is explicitly presented in Gadamer as a *phenomenology* of understanding. But the moment this phenomenology is formulated positively, the relativist specter returns. If it belongs to *all* understanding to be historically conditioned, and as a result to be fallible or subject to revision, what about the understanding and description of the conditions at work in understanding itself? If understanding what understanding is is *through and through* a conditioned and revisable interpretation, hermeneutics only describes at best the way a certain age grasps the phenomenon of understanding, and not *what understanding is* as such. It becomes a Weltanschauung among others, and its alleged "universality" disappears. If there is such a thing as a phenomenology of understanding, it must *be anchored in truths that are not themselves entirely subordinated to the finite historical conditions of interpretation.*

The only solution seems to be to root the description of understanding in pre-hermeneutic essential truths. Again, hermeneutics can only be formulated consistently if it accepts a pre-hermeneutic level, but in a different sense than just discussed. Indeed, as I have established in chapter 12, essential descriptions cannot themselves be understood as historically conditioned. The historicizing of essences to which *Being and Time* proceeds is untenable, as is its underlying reasoning: essence (*a priori*) is a feature of Being; Being cannot be dissociated from the understanding of Being that belongs to *Dasein*; the Being of *Dasein* and its understanding of Being have a historical (*geschichtlich*) character: therefore essence and the *a priori* are historical, as well as all ontological truths. This argument is untenable because if something is an essence in the relevant sense of the term (leaving aside the possibility of empirical essences or mere "types"), it cannot vary according to the circumstances. It can perhaps be asserted that there are historical, and therefore *a posteriori* essences, for example that what it is to be a painting changes with the invention of non-figurative painting; but it is hard to see what it might mean to say that the finitude of *Dasein*, for example, only characterizes that entity *a priori* under the condition of a particular historical situation. *Dasein* is either essentially mortal or it isn't; it is essentially temporal, or it isn't, and so on. If that were not the case, we would have to go so far as to say the historicality of *Dasein*, this trait of its essence, is historically contingent, *subject to variations*, and belongs essentially to it at one moment and not at another. Essence is what is *necessary* to a thing in order for it to be what it is. The "essential structures"[62] of fundamental ontology can only be ahistorical,[63] which does not mean that the same apply to all the descriptions anchored in those structures. Phenomenological descriptions *set out* from descriptions of essence in order to formulate transcendental questions and justify their own developments by means of transcendental arguments; therefore they are not in their entirety descriptions of essence.

Applied to the problem of hermeneutics, this reasoning leads to the following conclusion: hermeneutics *as* phenomenology sets out from a description of essence of understanding; but as a phenomenological description, it ventures beyond that first step, introducing both transcendental arguments and historically conditioned interpretations. The description of understanding-interpretation is revisable, as is all description, but everything is not revisable in that description, or rather, everything is not ideally revisable if we assume that the arguments through which the initial truths of essence were reached do not prove in turn to be insufficient, and are not defeated by a better argumentation. It can thus be maintained both that this *description of understanding*—hermeneutics—is phenomenological as to its intention and goal, and that phenomenology *in general* is only achieved as hermeneutics.

Up until this point I have shown that the claim of the phenomenological character of hermeneutics does not contradict the claim of the hermeneutic character of phenomenology. But I have not yet shown how the latter can constitute an *achievement* of the former.

In Husserl's view, phenomena prescribe, as it were, the way they should be approached; they are a legitimizing source for their description. Descartes departed from this principle by projecting onto the "things" to be described an axiomatic method inspired by mathematics. It is at this point that hermeneutics deepens Husserl's critique, turning it against Husserl himself. Husserl, because he claimed to gain access to a universal and objective knowledge based on intuition of essences—that intuition remaining identical whether we are men, angels, or gods—and because he tried to make phenomenology a pure analysis of lived experiences sheltered from all historical or cultural relativity, remained much closer to Descartes than he himself admitted. He abandoned what was authentically *phenomenological* about his own method. He replaced the description of our actual understanding, such as it underlies our actual descriptions, and as it is concretely carried out in the sphere of our *Lebenswelt*, with an ideal of knowledge of a still mathematical kind, without any relation to our finitude. Husserl's method remains *idealizing*; it is governed by an epistemic ideal that is not suitable to concrete phenomenology. This is why the hermeneutic critique of phenomenology is also a *radicalization of the phenomenological requirement at work in phenomenology itself*; a radicalization, and consequently, to a certain extent, a fulfillment of phenomenology. Hermeneutics is not only a phenomenology of understanding through which the prejudices inherent in the Cartesian concept of method and its epistemological ideal of absolute foundation are progressively overcome; it is also, and perhaps primarily, a radicalization of the concept of *life-world* thanks to which the residual idealizations that impair the Husserlian project are criticized and surmounted, in the same way that Husserl challenged the idealizations inherent in the philosophy of Descartes, Kant, and empiricism. As Heidegger emphasizes, Husserl's phenomenology is not phenomenological enough *because* it is not hermeneutic enough. "The elaboration of pure consciousness as the thematic field of phenomenology is *not derived phenomenologically by going back to the matters themselves* but by going back to a traditional idea of philosophy."[64] All things considered, "phenomenology is *unphenomenological*," not because of a mere negligence but by virtue of "the force and weight of the tradition."[65]

If I am right, if the hermeneutic approach consists in critiquing the remnants of idealization present in phenomenology itself, thus radicalizing Husserl's move of a return to the life-world on the hither side of scientific "substructions," it would be appropriate to go a step further and to inquire, in conclusion, into that life-world itself.

23

An Anti-Copernican Revolution: The Life-World

> It is a very phenomenological way of proceeding—to discover, in relations of knowledge, foundations that properly speaking lack the structure of knowledge, not because these foundations impose themselves without certainty, but because, being anterior and conditioning, they are more certain than certainty, more rational than reason.
>
> —Emmanuel Levinas

In Kurosawa's masterpiece *Dersu Uzala,* one of the most deeply moving meditations on friendship ever filmed, a captain in the tsarist army, Vladimir Arsenyev, having left on an expedition at the head of a little band in the valley of Ussuri near the Chinese border to perform topographical surveys, meets a Mongolian-born sable hunter, a hermit with a wide experience of the pitfalls of the taiga, who will be their guide and save them on several occasions from death's door. This woodsman, who gives the film its name, is depicted as a simple soul, having had up to that point no contact, or next to none, with the Western world, living on his wisdom alone and on the skin trade, but heir to an ancestral culture he tries unsuccessfully to share with the soldiers. One day, one of the soldiers asks him: "Dersu, do you know what the sun is?" To which he replies: "The sun, everyone knows. You never see sun? If you not know, look!" General peals of laughter.

The soldier is naturally Copernican. To him, it goes without saying that the celestial body visible to all is the central star of the solar system around which Earth and the other planets gravitate, a composite of hydrogen and helium in fusion, obeying the laws of Newtonian mechanics. The hunter does not even understand his question. To him, the sun is the origin of all life: it is this light source that rises and sets at the horizon, that varies in intensity and color in the course of the day cycle, that enables him to find his way in the Siberian forest. The sun—it suffices to *see* what it is to *know*. But the soldier no more understands what Dersu tells him than Dersu understands the soldier. Assured of the superiority conferred on him by scientific knowledge gleaned from handbooks, he is incapable of thinking otherwise than as he has been taught, and he judges the hunter's answer naive, stupid even. Dersu does not know what he is talking about when he says it's enough to look at the sun to know what it is. He is the victim of an *illusion* that only science can dispel.

Kurosawa's parable raises a difficult issue that Husserl is probably the first to have approached philosophically. What are the relations between the world we live in and the one about which science ceaselessly brings us new truths? Is the only true world the one physics speaks to us about, or the one we inhabit, in which we live and act? And does the truth of the former *exclude* that of latter, so that the world of our life is nothing but *an appearance*? These questions make up the background of what is probably one of the most original and fruitful notions phenomenology has elaborated, that of the *Lebenswelt*. The term appears in 1917—possibly earlier—in the appendix to §64 of *Ideas II*, but only receives all the attention it deserves in the texts of the late Husserl, grouped around the *Crisis*.

The question raised by Husserl on the relations between the "life-world" and the truths revealed by science fell mostly on deaf ears in his day and continues to do so to a large extent today. Didn't positivism teach us that science alone can claim to discover *truths* by means of complex experimental protocols—that the task of philosophy is limited to a systematic ordering of these truths, to a synthesis conferring a unity on them, thereby increasing their intelligibility? But the error of positivism is not to place science in too lofty a position—it is to place it too low. If the philosopher is content with generalizing and systematizing the results of science, it is because he does not take science seriously enough. As Bergson noted, we must part ways with positivism "because of the respect and confidence that true science inspires in us. We would be loath to claim to do better, in the domain of science, than science does, or even just something other than what it does . . . And yet that is what would have to be admitted if the philosopher, just by the fact of his invoking philosophy, became capable of going further than the scientist in the same direction."[1] Husserl could endorse this principle unreservedly. If philosophy possesses its own research domain, the phenomenal world, it is because it does not limit itself to consider science as a fact, but inquires into the facticity of this fact starting from a domain of "truths" and "certainties" that is more basic than scientific undertaking. By the "proper return to the naivety of life,"[2] to a *second naïveté* of pre-theoretical life and not not to a first naïveté, philosophy allows us to understand what methodological operations science had to apply in order to free itself from this domain of "innate" certainties and accede to exact truths, inseparable from mathematical formalization. Such are its research domain and the originality of its method. As for positivism, in letting itself be blinded by the success of the positive sciences as sciences of fact, and in conferring upon them the task of answering first and ultimate questions, it has not only "decapitated philosophy,"[3] as Husserl says in a striking expression, but it has deprived science of a part of its meaning. The crisis of Western rationality diagnosed in the *Crisis*—a crisis both of the sciences and of modern culture as a whole—comes precisely from that loss of meaning (*Sinnentleerung*) of science, which, summoned to respond to the fundamental questions of man, is incapable of doing so, and, being also unable by itself to give an account of the methodological meaning of its own activity, becomes the mere organon of a technical transformation of the world. Things would be different if we tried to understand how scientific praxis is connected to prescientific experience in which it is anchored and has its starting point.

Positivism, as I was saying, is deaf to this question, but the same is true of the two main schools dominating the German philosophical scene at the time when Husserl was writing: empiricism and neo-Kantianism. The Kantian concept of *experience*, as attested by the Kantian distinction between judgments of perception and judgments of experience, already brings in the consideration of objects and causal relations that are, in a word, those of Newtonian physics: the idea of a *prescientific experience* remains largely alien to Kant. It is probably even more alien to neo-Kantians. The latter begin with science as a matter of fact and inquire into the conditions of possibility of this fact; they approach the problem of experience from a perspective that is mainly, if not exclusively, gnoseological.[4] Empiricists and neo-empiricists share this same presupposition. For them as well, experience is merely science lying fallow; reduced to atoms of sensation, it contains no other intelligibility than that which is conferred on it by inductions that sketch out and foreshadow the formulation of empirical laws. But is there not a prescientific experience possessing its own rights and its own pre-theoretical logos, a manifold of essential properties and structures that prepare the terrain for science, but without being a part of its domain? That is the question—new, "untimely"—raised by Husserlian phenomenology.

The answer to that question is contained in one word: "*Lebenswelt.*" The life-world "is the spatiotemporal world of things as we experience them in our pre- and extrascientific life and as we know them to be experienceable beyond what is [actually] experienced."[5] It is a world inhabited by *vague essences and types*: trees, houses, bridges, rivers. These sensible types (or these "morphological essences" as Husserl also calls them) are the result of naive anticipations and generalizations that enable us to regulate our behavior, and that have a style and status quite distinct from the exact inductions of science, hence from the field of "objects" to which we accede by means of such inductions: kinetic energy, electromagnetic wave, and so on. The life-world is "this world which precedes knowledge, of which knowledge always *speaks*," writes Merleau-Ponty, "and this world with regard to which every scientific determination is abstract, signitive, and dependent, as is geography in relation to the countryside in which we first learned what a forest, a meadow or a river is."[6] But the fact that the life-world is inhabited by vague essences, regulated by approximate predictions, is not itself a vague or approximate feature of this world; it is one of its *essential structures*, in the strict sense that phenomenology confers on these terms. Thus, on the hither side of the naive inductions and habitual anticipations that have practical value for us, there is a common basis of *strict* essential truths, a domain of material *a priori* (such as the spatiotemporal form of the world or the vague nature of sensible types it comprises), that are not at all dependent on the requirements of life or its naive predictions, but rather fall under the jurisdiction of *phenomenological description.* Thus we are in the presence of three kinds of very different regularities: (1) in our vague experience of the world, prescientific inductive generalizations which are "artless [*Kunstlose*],"[7] and are grounded on the apprehension of sensible types; (2) the "'methodical' inductions, artful [*Kunstvollen*]"[8] of the empirical sciences, physics in particular, whose operational capacity for explaining causal relations and capturing them in mathematical formulae must *idealiter* increase infinitely with the development of that science itself; (3) lastly, a domain of essences *prior to all inductive procedure,* to all hypothesis, a "universal *a priori* of the life-world" that regulates both the world of prescientific experience and the building of science on the ground of this world. The bringing to light of these essences in the strict sense represents the task and the stakes of phenomenological work. Thus, we must avoid confusing "morphological essences," that is, the vague typifying of the life-world, with the essences and relations of essence that are valid *from the point of view of a phenomenology* both for that world and for the construction of the edifice of science on its ground. "Morphological essences" are not essences in the phenomenological sense of the term, that is, material *a priori*; inversely, it is indeed a material *a priori* that "morphological essences" are vague.[9] The possibility of strict descriptions of essence of the life-world is not at all in contradiction with the claim of the vague and indeterminate character of that world.

How can we circumscribe more precisely the difference that exists between naive predictions and inductions, and scientific ones? The latter presuppose the approach to the limit which belongs to idealization, and which brings into play the idea of exactitude. The first measurements that take place in the life-world, for example in the technique of pacing off a parcel of land, are measurements relative to specific practical goals. "In practical life the 'exact' is determined by the [specific] end in view; the 'equal' is that which counts equally for this end, for which there can also be irrelevant differences which do not count."[10] Two lengths may be considered equal from the point of view of our daily activity, even though they are slightly different. But from the practice of pacing off land there arises a first idealization that frees the idea of exactness from all dependency on practical goals and institutes a domain of geometrical idealities. These idealities rest on the idea of the *absolutely equal*, of exactness in the mathematical sense. This idealization in turn leads to the invention of new measurement techniques. Emancipated from its practical limitation, exactness henceforth takes on the meaning of an approximation to the mathematical idealities. This new meaning conferred on the idea of measurement underlies the mathematizing of nature which occurs with Galileo. Geometry applied to the whole of sensible reality produces an *idealization of nature itself*, which subordinates phenomena and their causal relations to the mathematical ideal of exactness, allowing the exclusion from the operation of measurement of all the factors that are not relevant to the bringing to light of physical laws. With the idea of an exact physical law, the operation of measurement is freed from concrete experimental contexts and attains a *constantly increasing* precision tending toward the ideal of an *absolute* precision. Nature itself becomes the teleological pole toward which the formulation of ever more exact hypotheses tends. "In the progression there is growing perfection," Husserl writes, "and for all of natural science taken as a totality this means that it comes more and more to itself, to its 'ultimate' true being. . . . But true nature does not lie in the infinite in the same way that a pure straight line does; even as an infinitely distant 'pole' it is *an infinity of theories* and is thinkable only as verification; thus it is related to *an infinite historical process of approximation*."[11] The physical thing is then no longer what we are dealing with in our daily commerce with our living environment, but rather that which must be approached and understood in the light of physical theory, first and foremost as a mathematical manifold. In this way, the vague inductions of the life-world acquire the status of approximations to the exact predictions of science.

This process of the idealization of nature, in which the increasing precision of measurement and the mathematizing of the sensible world mutually feed back into and reinforce each other, not only results in making nature the telos toward which an infinity of theories tend, but also in *obscuring more and more resolutely the life-world itself,* the very world in which scientific idealization had its starting point. Actually, it is less the scientific idealization alone than the *philosophical interpretation* physics has given of itself since the days of Galileo—of its methodological operations as well as of the status of the truths it brings to light—that has led to that forgetfulness of the infra-scientific world. This is what induced Husserl to maintain that the life-world remains, for philosophy and for science, a terra incognita: "We seek in vain in world literature for investigations that could serve as preparatory studies for us."[12] The modern scientific revolution was characterized by the systematic covering up of the life-world. This world may be characterized, in a preliminary approach, by four main features: (1) it is a pre- or infra-scientific world; (2) that world is given to an *experience,* so that the access afforded us to it is not yet mediated by symbolic systems; (3) it constitutes the "source" or "ground" upon which all elaboration of theories can be carried out; (4) it is "subjective-relative," and by that Husserl means that it is inseparable from our interests, our needs, our practices: it is a realm of *practical certainties*—certainties that as we shall see need not necessarily be conceived of as gnoseological. In characterizing the life-world in this way, I deliberately leave aside some of the most problematic aspects of Husserl's descriptions, especially those connected with the problem of its transcendental constitution by the ego or its status as "foundation" for the sciences. I shall return to this point. In order to understand how this originary world, into which we are plunged before any operation of knowledge, ends up being hidden, disguised under a "garb of ideas [*Ideenkleid*]" by the nascent physics, it will be useful to pause and consider three operations accomplished by that physics, and for which Husserl elaborates three concepts: (1) substruction (*Substruktion*); (2) substitution (*Unterschiebung*); and (3) inversion (*Verkehrung*).

Substruction is the operation through which the vague world of daily experience, with its imprecise typology and its "more-or-less" approximations, is duplicated in the form of an ideal superstructure of precise properties formulated in the language of algebra and geometry. Let us examine the case of the laws of movement discovered by Galileo. Grasped at the level of our daily experience, rest and movement are vague morphological essences belonging to the "more-or-less" of the life-world. When I look out of a train window, for example, I can perceive the vehicle in which I am traveling moving forward through the country-side; but as I give myself over to daydreaming, a gestalt shift takes place, and for a brief moment the appearance of a moving landscape replaces my first perception. This shows that in normal perceptual conditions my body plays the role of an absolute frame of reference—a frame that is "arch-immobile," inseparable from an "earth-ground" that is just as immobile, in relation to which the surrounding bodies may appear to me as being either at rest or moving. "Whether I stand still or walk," Husserl writes, "my lived body [*Leib*] is the center and the bodies at rest and moving are around me and I have a ground that does not move."[13] In abnormal conditions, on the other hand, when I travel in a vehicle that plays the role of "ground" for my apprehension of surrounding movements, the phenomenon of an apparent movement of the land-scape may come to the fore, as the characteristics of absolute frame of reference of my body and the ground supporting it undergo a specific alteration. We have then *relative* "body-grounds" which in turn relativize perceived movement and rest. On this occasion the ambivalent phenom-enon of a movement freed from its anchorage in my corporal centration emerges. But this is only a boundary case that does not contradict the main original phenomenological assertion according to which the Earth, grasped at the level of our normal experience, is "arch-immobile," since "it is first in relation to it that movement and rest take on meaning."[14]

Yet the Copernican revolution and its radicalization by Galileo have taught us that the idea of an absolute frame of reference has no meaning in physics. From the point of view of that science, all motion is relative to a reference point that may be chosen arbitrarily. Motion, Galileo says, "is operative only in the relation that they [mobile bodies] have with other bodies lacking that motion."[15] For example, two bodies that move in the same direction at the same speed are in repose relative to one another, and are only in motion in relation to a third body that does not share *their* movement. There is neither absolute motion nor absolute rest—that is, regardless of any given point of reference. It is only on the condi-tion that movement in its physical definition can be freed from the con-crete conditions of its perception that *laws of movement*, such as the law of the falling bodies, can be formulated. To state this law is to proceed to the abstraction of the ordinary conditions of perception by purify-ing the phenomena of superfluous parameters, such as air resistance, in order to consider the behavior of bodies independently of the environ-ment in which they move. From the point of view of Aristotle's theory, moving bodies of different weights move through the same environment at unequal speeds, their speeds having between them the same proportion as their weights. This assertion is false, retorts Galileo. If we drop two solids of unequal weight from the top of the Tower of Pisa, they will reach the ground *at the same time.*[16] On the face of it, that declaration is counterintuitive. We can make the experiment and drop two lead balls of unequal size, hence of unequal weight, and we will observe that the larger one will hit the ground before the smaller. So, is Aristotle right? He is wrong. Galileo establishes this by means of a "thought experiment" in Mach's sense. If a light stone is attached to a heavier one and their falling speeds are different, as Aristotle would have it, two things would have to be asserted at the same time: that the lighter stone increases the falling speed of the heavier one, since the sum of the two bodies is heavier than each of them taken separately, and that the smaller stone slows down the descent of the larger one, since its falling speed is lesser. Therefore, if Aristotle is right, the fall must be at the same time both faster and slower, which is a contradiction. We can better understand the sort of "idealization" which is at the origin of the advent of modern physics. The experience of which Galileo is speaking is not the one we have in our everyday world when we look at falling bodies; it is an ideal experience, purified of superfluous parameters connected with our ordinary experiential conditions—an experience simplified by a process of *a priori* reasoning. The law of falling bodies can only be formulated under the hypothesis of a vacuum that it was impossible to produce experimentally at the time Galileo elaborated his theory. The experience Galileo speaks of is therefore an *idealized* one, concerning a nature that is reduced to its mathematical structures. Substruction, that is, the operation consisting in clothing the life-world in a "garb of ideas" that expresses its hidden mathematical structure, is an operation legitimate in itself. It is even the only legitimate starting point for the scientific praxis as such. Nevertheless, that operation tends to be self-dissimulating, and to pass itself off as self-evident, so much so that its dependency with respect to the world formerly given to intuition is missed, and soon the intuited world will itself be understood in terms of the substruction it makes possible. This is the second operation, less scientific than philosophical, that Husserl indicates by the term "substitution."

Indeed Galileo, "a discovering and a concealing genius [*entdeckender und verdeckender Genius*]"[17] as Husserl calls him, did not limit himself to conducting thought experiments by which he could abstract from an experiential situation the aspects irrelevant to the calculation of physical laws; he was not content with idealizing experience in order to be able to capture it in mathematical formulae; he furnished an interpretation of his own discoveries whose legitimacy must be examined. Galileo not only asserted that we *can* decipher nature *as if* it were written in mathematical language by applying an adequate formalism to it: he maintained that nature *is* written in mathematical language. What lies hidden behind this assertion? Nothing less than the idea that the mathematical formulae in which nature is expressed enable us to capture "the true being of nature itself."[18] There lies a "substitution of the mathematically substructed world of idealities for the only real world, the one that is actually given through perception, that is ever experienced and experienceable—our everyday life-world."[19] Instead of highlighting the discrepancy that exists between the world that appears and a "world" of pure, mathematized forms, Galileo tends to *replace* the former with the latter, maintaining that the idealized nature of science, as a realm of exact truths, is the truth of the prescientific world given to intuition, that it is even *the one and only reality.* The vocation of science is no longer to "save the phenomena [*sōzein ta phainomena*]," but to reach a *truth in itself,* free from all relation to the concrete and changing conditions of our perception. Thus the ambiguity of Galileo's project and its singular blindness to the life-world are revealed. On the one hand, Galileo institutes a type of idealization that shelters within itself a universal methodological idea playing the role of normative ideal for the whole of modern science; on the other, he fails to recognize the rootedness of mathematical substructions in the life-world in which the man of science also lives, in which he carries out both his thought-experiments and concrete forms of experimentation. Galileo thus tends to *dissimulate* the nature of his methodological operation, and he dismisses the question of the relationships between nature "in itself" and the phenomenal world as being superfluous.

This leads to a third step—less chronological than logical—that Husserl calls "inversion." Since mathematical formulae express the "in itself" of nature itself, since they express its "*truth,*" it follows that the world of everyday appearances can only be, at most, a subjective *appearance,* a well-founded *illusion.* This mathematization of nature considered "not only independent of God, but also independent of man,"[20] as Heisenberg puts it, goes hand in hand with the advent of the distinction between primary and secondary qualities. Secondary qualities exist only in relation to ourselves; they are projected onto the world by the subject. From the fact that science reaches the in-itself of nature independently of all relation to man, it may consequently be concluded that phenomena and the world given to perception "exist only in subjects; they are in them solely as causal results of processes taking place in true nature, which processes exist only in the form of mathematical properties."[21] Thus the world of the senses is basically illusory; and, correlatively, only mathematizable properties that are beyond the reach of sensible perception can be qualified as "true" *in an absolute sense.* Under the impetus of this new image of nature, the life-world is emptied of its meaning, "all the truths of pre- and extrascientific life . . . are deprived of value."[22] The "true" world of science is set in *opposition* to the "apparent" world of perception and life, without the least awareness of the fact that the former can only be understood genetically—but also can only *receive its meaning and validity*—in reference to the latter; not only—and this is a triviality nonetheless worthy of being recalled—because the scientist, in order to be able to go to his laboratory, perform his experiments, make his measurements, get his equipment to work and even discuss his theories, must be an inhabitant of this shared and immediately perceptible world, but also because his theories themselves depend *in their very tenor as theory* on this domain of originary certainties.

This threefold operation, which is both scientific and philosophical, gives rise to what the *Crisis* qualifies as "objectivism." The fundamental postulate of objectivism resides in several internally connected theses: (1) there is a sharp distinction between the properties that things possess "in themselves" and those they possess "for us"—between primary and secondary qualities; (2) a property is either "in itself" or subjective, *tertium non datur*; (3) the subjective properties are the causal consequences of properties in themselves, and the latter are generally conceived of as dispositional properties of bodies, reducible at least ideally to non-dispositional ones (properties about particles, waves, etc.); (4) only fundamental science, that is, physics, can distillate truths about the properties of nature in themselves, insofar as it can confer a mathematical status on them.

Here the originality of the *Crisis* with respect to Husserl's prior works is fully disclosed, an originality of which Husserl himself may not have been entirely aware. Indeed, the idea of "objectivity" *only takes on its "proper" meaning through mathematical idealization* (and its philosophical implications) and, consequently, through the threefold operation of substruction, substitution, and inversion. As Husserl specifies in a key passage, mathematics, "by idealizing the world of bodies in respect to what has spatiotemporal shape in this world . . . created for the first time an objective world in the true sense, out of the undetermined universal form of the life-world . . . i.e., it created an infinite totality of ideal objects which are determinable univocally, methodically, and quite universally for everyone."[23] Therefore, the objective world *is the result of scientific idealization* and not the other way round. This claim calls into question the entire framework of Husserl's philosophy. Indeed as we have seen,

Husserl defined in a first stage of his conception sensible reality and ideality in terms of objectivity: the things of the world and essences are objects of a certain type. Henceforth he defines objectivity in terms of idealization: only an idealized nature can be qualified as "objective" in the proper sense of the term. The objective world is *produced* by scientific idealization.

The consequences of this revolution, on the condition that we take it seriously—against Husserl himself if need be—are far-reaching. They can be best understood if we compare the assertion of the *Crisis* with what may be found in *Ideas I* on the same subject matter. Already in 1913 Husserl criticized the dichotomy between "objective" geometric-physical properties (primary qualities) and "merely subjective" ones (secondary qualities), reduced to the status of mere appearances;[24] he asserted that since physics only determines the given thing (*das gegebene Ding*) through concepts such as *atoms, ions, energy*, and so on, for which "the only characterizations are mathematical expressions," it follows that this given thing is meant as "*something transcendent to the whole physical-thing content standing there 'in person.'*"[25] At that time, however, Husserl refused to conceive of scientific idealizations as mere substructions, that is, as idealizing constructions carried out on the underlying intuited world. The *physical thing* remained for him, at least to some extent, an *object of perception*. It "is nothing foreign to what appears sensuously 'in person'; rather it is something which makes itself known *originaliter* in it and, more particularly, *a priori* (for indefeasible eidetic reasons *only* in it)."[26] In other words, "*even the higher transcendence characterizing the physical thing as determined by physics* does not mean *reaching out beyond the world that exists for consciousness*, or for every ego functioning as a cognizing subject."[27] At this stage, there remains in Husserl's thought an unresolved tension, to say the least, between the assertion that the physical thing is "an empty *x*" whose exact determinations "do not themselves fall within experience proper,"[28] and the assertion that the physical thing is not something of which perception is merely a "sign," but "the *perceived thing itself*."[29] Volume 2 of *Ideas* will confirm this equivalence between "objective thing" and "physical thing"[30]—and consequently the idea of a perception, not of the life-world prior to the substructions of physics, but of the physical world itself: "the true thing" as intuitive object, "is the *physicalistic thing*, determined logico-mathematically."[31]

In the *Crisis*, by contrast, it becomes manifest that the object experienced and experienceable within the life-world *is not, in fact, the physical object*, that *x* of logico-mathematical determinations; rather the physical object comes from a substruction; in short, it *is never* the experienced object. The objectivity of the objective is the product of an idealization and not a phenomenological given. "The objective [in the sense of the correlate of scientific objectification] is precisely never experienceable as itself,"[32] Husserl points out, and consequently must be conceived of as "something metaphysically transcendent."[33] But if that is the case, if scientific objectivity radically transcends our world experience, if it is even beyond the reach of any experienceability, since "experience [yields] a self-evidence taking place purely in the life-world,"[34] *the very idea of a transcendental science concerned with the constitution of objectivity* in general *becomes aporetic*; for, between the transcendence of the thing in our world and the "metaphysical" (inaccessible to intuition) transcendence of the objects of physics, a real gulf has formed. This gulf, it should be added, constantly increases with the development of physics. While it was possible, in Newton's day, to believe that between the object of physics and the one given to our experience there was a certain continuity, in our time the progress in quantum mechanics has undermined the credibility of such a view. What is the intuitive content of the Higgs boson, or of string theory?

We are in a better position to appreciate the critical import of the fully developed concept of the life-world against the original project of Husserl's phenomenology, that of a constitution of the world given in intuition according to the various strata of its objectivity. The physical thing (or the thing of nature) can no longer play the role of fundamental layer for the constitution of higher-level objectivities, belonging either to the psychic or the the spiritual world, as delineated in *Ideas II.* We must say rather that the "world" that is the object of the physicist's concern—if it still deserves to be called a "world"—is situated at a completely different level from the one we can perceive and experience, with its irreducible cultural and historical dimension, since it is nothing other than the product of a set of idealizing symbolic operations outside of which it possesses no consistence of its own. There is neither epistemic nor ontological continuity between the inexact phenomenal world of our lives and the exact truths delivered by physics through its operations of symbolization and measurement. Besides, are the perceived objects and physical ones both "objects" *in the same sense*, if the process of symbolization, which in many cases (for example in quantum mechanics), remains *without any intuitive counterpart*, and the operation of measurement which, partially at least, "constitutes" the physical object, raise that object to the level of a pure correlate of a mathematical formalism? Not only do these two "objects" not seem to fall under the same concept of object, but it is uncertain whether there is a common acceptation of "constitute" according to which one could sustain that a physical object is "constituted" in the same sense as, in Husserl's view, a tree, a forest, or countryside is. Is a substruction, that is, a mediate construction, implemented by activities of symbolization, still a "constitution," in a sense that is even *analogous* to that which prevails in transcendental phenomenology?

Thus there may be an element of truth in the oft-repeated assertion of some of Husserl's disciples (Landgrebe, Fink, Gurwitsch)[35] according to which the concept of *Lebenswelt* leads beyond an idealist phenomenology, or has at least a *critical potential* with respect to the transcendental perspective as such. Not, to be sure, that Husserl abandoned that perspective in *The Crisis*; he is continually reaffirming it without the least ambiguity. The life-world is "a mere transcendental 'phenomenon,'"[36] "a mere 'component' in the concrete transcendental subjectivity, and correlatively its [i.e., the life-world's] *a priori* no longer appears except as a 'stratum' in the universal *a priori* of transcendentality."[37] But the adoption of the concept of *Lebenswelt* leads to highlighting the remnants of objectivism and naturalism inherent in transcendental conceptuality, suggesting a negative answer to the question of whether there can be a constitution of objectivity *in general*. After all, if, as Husserl acknowledges, it is science's operations of substruction that *create for the first time* an *objective world* in the proper sense of the word, the idea of a constitution of objectivity in general (both in its prescientific and its scientific dimension) can hardly appear otherwise than as a residuum of objectivism within phenomenology, *the historically conditioned product of a scientific operation of idealization that is unaware of itself*, and according to which the life-world is ceaselessly infiltrated, at the level of its description, by a manifold of idealizations coming from both modern science and its philosophical interpretation.

That Husserl does not stop projecting—including during the period of the *Crisis*—idealizations coming from the modern scientific revolution into the life-world is relatively easy to show. First, in conceiving of the life-world as the transcendental correlate of constituting subjectivity, does Husserl not legitimate, without admitting it to himself, the *naturalist* ontology? "Naturalism," he points out, "appears in the wake of the discovery of nature in the sense of a unity of spatiotemporal being, a unity that obeys exact laws."[38] Naturalism is therefore, as *Ideas I* repeatedly affirms, nothing but the "philosophical absolutizing" of the natural world and its naive ontology,[39] an absolutizing that confers on objects of nature an independence with respect to their constitution by consciousness. In Husserl's view, this absolutizing of the world is "nonsense"; it is far from being *identical* with the natural attitude. But doesn't a latent naturalism haunt the Husserlian conception of that attitude itself? Doesn't Husserl continue to conceive of the "reality" as being constituted as a domain of objects *in the sense in which physics speaks of them*? Doesn't Husserl's transcendental idealism, in formulating itself as an antithesis to naturalism, remain captive to naturalism? Conversely, if we take seriously what the *Crisis* asserts, namely that *all* objectivity is the product of an idealizing substruction, the starting point of the naturalist attitude, that is, a realm of objects offered to a theoretical grasp, collapses at the same time as does the naturalist ontology: we must set out from a world of *pragmata* and agree, against Husserl, with Merleau-Ponty and Heidegger.

Furthermore, we must consider whether the questionable adhesion to the skeptical argument that weighs on transcendental phenomenology as a whole doesn't also stem from the modern scientific revolution, so that to call into question that revolution in order to investigate into the relationship between idealized nature and the prescientific world would necessarily entail a turning away from transcendental phenomenology as such. As a matter of fact, it is only when the world of our experience is split into a nature "in itself" and subjective appearances, according to a move favored by modern objectivism, that a philosophical doubt with respect to these appearances as a whole takes on a semblance of plausibility. But the life-world, if it is originarily a world of *practical* certainties, is precisely not the sort of "thing" it makes any sense to put in doubt: it forms the background for all doubt and all belief. Nor is the life-world anything it makes any sense to *believe in*. The "certainties" that abound there must not be conceived of as self-evident and self-warranted truths that would supply an absolute grounding for science, but rather, as a system of practical *non-epistemic* certainties, preceeding the very opposition between doubt and belief (see chapter 15). Again, it should be noted that it is the Cartesian epistemology underlying the phenomenological procedure of the *epochē* that imposes on Husserl the idea of the life-world as a realm of evidences, in the epistemological sense of the term, that are valid in the domain of the more-or-less and the inexact, and consequently the idea of a *science of the prescientific* that might supply, for the sciences both exact and inexact, a *fundamentum inconcussum*.

By abandoning the skeptical problem, we thereby abandon the necessity of conceiving the certainties of the life-world otherwise than as certainties *in view of our* praxis, hence we give up the search for something like an absolute foundation for knowledge. The sciences do not have to be based on a first philosophy itself understood as proto-science, and yet the phenomenological description of the life-world does indeed reach a core of certainties, for the most part prelinguistic, which is presupposed by all science and forms its permanent background. Here we must settle the ambiguity of Husserl's vocabulary, which sometimes qualifies the *Lebenswelt* as *Grund*, foundation (of the sciences), and at other times as *Untergrund*, subsoil, base, or background.[40] According to this second concept, it is no longer a question of saying that the life-world supplies a "self-evident grounding"[41] for objective science, but only that it possesses the status of a *presupposition* (*Voraussetzung*) or background for the methodological operations science performs.[42] Now it seems that the first assertion is untenable for at least two reasons. First, if, as Husserl admits, "the scientific world—the systematic theory . . . like all other worlds [determined by specific] ends [*Zweckwelten*], itself 'belongs' to the life-world,"[43] and if, consequently, the scientific idealizations, as cultural contents, are in a sense incorporated into our most everyday practice and into the unquestionable certainties underlying it, the vexing consequence is entailed that the scientific idealizations ground themselves. Husserl sees the difficulty but does not offer a solution: "The concrete life-world, then, is the grounding soil [*der gründende Boden*] of the 'scientifically true' world and at the same time encompasses it in its own universal concreteness. How is this to be understood?"[44] Second, the view that the certainties bound to goals and practical interests must fulfill the function of *ultimate* justifications for science stands in opposition to the view that those certainties can in turn be justified by anything at all—themselves included. As long as these certainties are understood as self-warranted evidences the possibility of doubting them makes sense, because we can always be mistaken about a piece of evidence, and the validity of skeptical doubt is restored at the very level of the life-world, precisely the level that seemed to exclude it. Because he understands the evidences of the life-world as originary *truths*, supplying a grounding for other truths, Husserl remains captive to the skeptic regression: "Prove your proof!" If *some* among the evidences of the life-world are of the nature of beliefs that can be justified, others are prior to all belief, and thereby to all doubt and all possibility of error, to the point that it is hard to see, in their case, *what a justification could mean.* When I study falling bodies, I can probably give reasons that prompt me to believe that my chronometer is working, but what reasons can I give for my "belief" in what my vision tells me when I read the position of the hand on the dial? Perceptual evidence cannot be further justified, neither by other evidences nor by itself. If all truth presupposes at least an ideally possible justification resting on public criteria (for example, on the possibility of verifying that the instruments of measurement are operational), the perceptual certainties that weave the fabric of our lives are not "truths" in this sense. They stand beyond all justification.

Nevertheless, we might wonder whether, in our attempt to free the life-world from both the transcendental standpoint and the foundational

Cartesian epistemology, we still have the means to understand the irreducible *primacy* of the *Lebenswelt* with respect to the "world" of science. Indeed, how are we to conceive of the relation between the truths of science and the certainties of life? Two solutions suggest themselves: ascribe all truth to science and confine the *Lebenswelt* to the domain of *doxa*, or, on the contrary, maintain that the only "true" world is that of our daily experience, and relegate scientific statements to the rank of tools of prediction devoid of all ontological import.

Sellars illustrates the first position well. His famous distinction between "manifest image" and "scientific image of the world" goes hand in hand with the claim that "in the dimension of describing and explaining the world, science is the measure of all things."[45] Of course Sellars admits that the manifest image of the world is useful to our vital purposes; he even recognizes that it is so anchored in ordinary language that it is impossible to extract it therefrom. What is at stake, he declares, is not "a proposal to brain-wash existing populations"[46] and to replace the apparent image with the true one. But that concession is only rhetorical, since the manifest image turns out to be *defective* when the issue is to account for "what there is." In Sellars's view a chair, a table, or an ice cube simply do not belong to what is real, as opposed to the system of imperceptible particles of physics; they are "*mere appearance* in the very radical sense of not existing in the spatiotemporal world at all."[47] As a consequence, "*speaking as a philosopher*, I am quite prepared to say that the common sense world of physical objects in Space and Time is unreal—that is, that there are no such things [tables, chairs, ice cubes]."[48]

According to Husserl's conception, Sellars's position is a variant of objectivism. Not only is it a consequence of the interpretation that the modern scientific revolution has given of itself, but it could quite well turn out to be ultimately incoherent. The goal of science is to furnish an *explanation* of phenomena, but if we hold these phenomena to be entirely unreal, that is, illusory in the strong sense of the term, the risk we face is to destroy the *explanandum* and, along with it, the *explanans*—hence the explanation itself. For there to be an explanation, the phenomena under consideration must possess a reality, an intrinsic consistency independently of their physical explanation; otherwise, what would we have explained? Far from invalidating the reality of the manifest world, science, in order to give an account of it, must begin by recognizing it. As Adolf Reinach remarks, there must be an autonomy of the *essences of the phenomenal world* vis-à-vis the essences postulated by physics, for otherwise the very idea of "reduction" of the former to the latter becomes absurd: "When the physicist reduces colors and tones to waves of determinate kinds, he is dealing with real existence, whose factuality he intends to explain. Leaving the broader sense of reduction undecided, reduction certainly has no application to essences. Or would one perhaps wish to reduce the essence of red, which I can view in any instance of red, to the essence of waves, which nonetheless is an evidently different essence?"[49]

This rejection of objectivism need not necessarily lead to its antithesis, the idea that *all that exists* is the life-world, the statements of physics being no more, in this perspective, than predictive models without any real counterparts. It is true that some passages of the *Crisis* could be interpreted that way. In §9(h) Husserl seems to limit reality (*Wirklichkeit*) to what is or could be given intuitively, when he speaks of "the only real world, the one that is actually given to us through perception, that is ever experienced and experienceable—our everyday life-world."[50] The break from Husserl's original conception of a transcendental constitution of the *physical* reality itself could lead rather naturally to an anti-realism that would consider the objects postulated by physics as fictions, and ultimately to an instrumentalism reducing scientific statements to mere tools for the prediction and mastery of nature. The error of modern science, on this view, was to take what is just a *method* for a *reality*. "It is through the garb of ideas" Husserl writes, "that we take for *true being* what is actually a *method*—a method which is designed for the purpose of progressively improving, *in infinitum*, through 'scientific' predictions, those rough predictions which are the only ones originally possible within the sphere of what is actually experienced and experienceable in the life-world."[51] But it is not certain that the distinction between realism and instrumentalism[52] is the relevant key to understanding the position defended in the *Crisis*. Moreover, such a radical anti-realism leads to paradoxical consequences. Indeed, if the predictive models of science are without any real counterpart, it becomes difficult to maintain that the life-world is *the mode of appearing for a consciousness of the physical reality itself.* Now this is in fact what Husserl maintains throughout his last work. The objects constructed by the symbolic operations of physics, despite their being "substructions," are no less *real*; but they do not possess the same kind of reality as do the objects of our daily experience. Neither more nor less real than the latter, they are *otherwise real.* This is why, contrary to what Sellars affirms, they are not in competition[53] with our perception of the world; they do not contradict it, but complete it. The Galilean revolution contradicts geocentrism as a *physical* theory, but it does not annul the apprehension of the Earth-Ground of our practices as stable and immovable. Thus Husserl can maintain both that "the earth does not move" and that, even with that last assertion, "we do not . . . tamper with physics."[54] It is indeed the reality of our experienced world, for example the solar cycle, which physics seeks to explain by postulating an invisible force, gravity. The primacy of the life-world for us (*proteron pros hemas*) is perfectly compatible with the primacy of the physical universe both in the order of being and in that of explanation (*proteron physei*). As Erwin Straus emphasizes, "physics is proclaimed to be the basic science of psychology. The fact is that we as human beings construct physics in our world of daily experience (Husserl's *Lebenswelt*). Even if it were true that the structure of the universe as conceived by physics were the actual and primary world, for us it is the secondary and mediated one."[55]

Is it possible to approach the life-world *with*, but also *against* Husserl, by tearing it away from some residual idealizations it still incorporates in the *Crisis*? In some passages, Husserl seems very close to recognizing that the *Lebenswelt*, as he thematizes it, remains inseparable from an idealized nature and remains at least in part a theoretical construction. He wonders, specifically, in one manuscript: "When I construct, that is, describe as the starting point, an experience of the world and a meaning of the experience of the world prior to scientific thought, what about that abstraction that I construct?"[56] Doesn't the life-world continue to belong, despite Husserl's break with objectivism, to that "intellectualistic enterprise born of a mania, peculiar to modern life, to theorize everything"?[57] In a sense, my whole book is an attempt to give an affirmative answer to these questions, to propose a conception of being-in-the-world that renounces all anchorage in a naturalism and an objectivism. Nowhere is the latter's shadow cast more insistently than on the concept of hyletic data. Hyletic data—and more broadly the epistemic duality of a sensible given and of a meaning conferred on it by the subject—are nothing other than the transposition to phenomenology of a distinction between a nature "in itself" as a manifold of physical stimuli and its subjective appearances, with all the metaphysical presuppositions it brings with it. The adoption of the idea of hyletic data is merely the unnoticed consequence, on Husserl's part, of the reintroduction into the life-world of the idealizations stemming from the modern scientific revolution and its objectivism.

The same applies to the *apparently* phenomenological distinction, never questioned by Husserl—and hardly more so by his heirs—between the lived body (*Leib*) and the physical body (*Körper*). Is it really relevant to distinguish *at the level of a pure description of our experience* a lived body and an object-body, the one with which the doctor or the anatomist are preoccupied, the one they scrutinize by means of imaging technologies using X-ray or nuclear magnetic resonance? Yes, certainly, on the condition that we do not assert that the object-body is *given to experience* in a sense that is identical or even *comparable* to the one in which the lived body is. Husserl's *Körper* can have only one status, that of a scientific substruction and therefore of a "metaphysical transcendent." But to claim that it is a substruction, an object indissociable from operations of abstraction and measurement, an object *constructed* by physiological theory, amounts to say that it is never an object of experience in the phenomenological sense of the term. The anatomist can probably *consider* a lived body as a cell cluster for his laboratory work; he can probably even *perceive* these cells under a microscope or some other apparatus. But what he perceives at that moment is something that takes on meaning only in light of his theories, something that is not situated on the same level as the lived corporeality (*Leib, Leibkörper*) which reveals itself imperiously and suddenly to him in his daily life-world—a "body" that is not an object, and cannot become one, unless it ceases being the very manner in which other people exist for him and declare themselves to him in their indisputable presence. On a par with the substructions analyzed by the *Crisis*, the *Körper* is an idealization that remains unnoticed as such, to the point of letting us believe that we really *perceive* these "shadows stuffed with organs" of which Descartes speaks, as if they were accessible to us otherwise than through physiological theory. Husserl, too, makes this mistake when he declares that others "can be mere objects [*bloße Objekte*] for us."[58] Even in the case of a corpse, this assertion is open to argument. Only the agile, living body, every gesture of which is fraught with emotive meanings—and which may reveal itself suddenly as "lifeless"—is given to an *experience* in the sense that term takes on for a phenomenology of the life-world. Far from forming two strata of the "constitution" of the world, in daily experience *the mode of being of the object and that of other people are mutually exclusive.*

In the final analysis it is the very idea of a *stratified* experience that turns out to be the product of an unnoticed idealization. Husserl's commentators have long revealed the ambiguity of the *Lebenswelt* concept, which in his writings sometimes designates the natural world (*natürliche Welt*)[59] and sometimes the historical world permeated by culture.[60] This ambiguity raises the problem of "the insoluble unification"[61] of this world. As long as we stick with the idea of intentional stratification, that is, as long as we believe we can discern *in the phenomenon itself* an aesthetic-sensible layer and cultural predicates of several orders that are added or superimposed to it, the unification of the life-world certainly does remain problematic. But a holism of experience disposes of that difficulty. The meaning contained in experience is not conferred from the outside on a raw given (which would come down to understanding phenomena by analogy with the supposed "brute facts" supplied by physics), but manifests itself in light of a system of abilities that form the background for the signal ability called "understanding." It is, then, *the same world, the one and indivisible world,* that, understood in various ways, from the standpoint of different interests, as a function of different capacities and in the light of an overall practical context, can appear now as a purely perceived world, now as exhibiting such and such a cultural characteristic. I can contemplate the landscape of *L'Estaque* as a seascape or try to find within it, by a transposition into the visible spectacle of a pictorial style, the vibrating color of Cézanne or Derain. It is the same landscape, and by extension the same world, that will appear to me in turn according to one or the other of these two way of projecting myself into it, namely, in the light of practical possibilities of several levels, some inherent in my primordial existence in its indefeasible bond with my corporeality, others stemming from my impregnation by the whole history of painting. Hence we must say that the phenomenal world is both natural and cultural throughout. Its historicity does not constitute a "stratum"—furthermore an ideally airtight stratum—in the thick of phenomenality, but a way of apprehending the world in light of practical possibilities of several kinds, and, eventually, a way of describing it through appropriate conceptual schemes. The historicity of the world does not in the least cancel out its experimented character; it is itself experienced as a dimension of our being-in-the-world as subjects of perception and action.

But the holism of the life-world is not only "vertical": it is also "horizontal." Basically, it was the modern scientific revolution and its avatars that made us captive to the false alternative between a nature "in itself" and subjective appearances, primary and secondary qualities, geometric-objective characteristics of objects and lived contents that allegedly have no other location but "inside us." It is that revolution that imposes on us the rigid framework of an "either . . . or . . ." *opposing* objective properties to subjective ones, to which Husserl, even in his transcendental turn, remained tributary. The modern scientific revolution gave plausibility to the idea of an ontological gulf between the physical and the perceived reality, between an objective factor exerting a brute causal impact on our senses, immediately translated into data of sensation, and a subjective factor elaborating this given, "constituting" it as an intentional object. It was that revolution that traced out the entire horizon within which a naturalism and an idealism confront each other. But naturalism and idealism must both be dismissed as opposing variants of the same problem—a problem whose vacuousness will be exposed if we take seriously the concept of *Lebenswelt.* The life-world must not be conceived of in light of a conceptuality stemming from the idealizations of modern science, especially the exact, physical concept of causality. That is the error of naturalism, which tries in vain to persuade us that the phenomenal concept of experience can be described adequately in terms of brute causal impacts that the universe exerts on our sensibility. A causal conception of perception is absurd, for it applies to experience itself a concept, that of causality, which is only valid within the experienced world, and on the condition that a number of methodological operations of abstraction and idealization take place. Though nothing forbids us to study the causal bases of our experience, experience cannot be described in its essential phenomenological content as a mere effect of the physical universe, along the lines of a naive and metaphysical realism. But its antithesis, idealism in its various versions, continues to share with this realism the same frame of thought: it is no longer the mathematizable physical universe, the idealized nature of modern science that causally produces our experience through complex physiological causalities; it is the transcendental subject that constitutes *this same objective world* as a pure vis-à-vis of its active and passive operations. Now, the life-world eludes that distinction, which stems from the modern scientific revolution, of the pure physical objectivity and the pure subjectivity of a consciousness or an ego defined by their interiority. It would be better to pay attention to the term "*Lebenswelt*" and the intertwining presence in it of an apparently "objective" expression, the world, and an apparently "subjective" one, life. Rather than assuming that the "abyss of meaning" between the physical world and consciousness must be filled in by the constituting operations of the pure ego, which make the objective world into a pure intentional product; rather than postulating that being-in-the-world as openness to beings as a whole is a characteristic of *Dasein* considered in itself, regardless of whether or not this *Dasein* exists factually and whether or not there is a world to which it is open, so that "subjectivity, ontologically well understood" still depends on a transcendental framework; we must set out afresh and assert the structural connectedness and the mutual belongingness of the world and a "subject" endowed with practical abilities already involving that world. We are in the world to the extent that we belong to it, and we belong to it to the extent that we are in the world. There is no subject but open to the world and there is no world but containing within itself a subject that essentially belongs to it by its body, and that shares this world from the outset with others; these assertions have nothing empirical or conjectural about them: they belong to an essential characterization of experience as such. The openness to an immediately meaningful world, before all linguistic articulation of that meaning, is a characteristic of the *structural relation* that unites a world and a subject endowed with understanding and practical capabilities of several kinds. The *Lebenswelt* is this world-for-us as the familiar place of our lives, a world prior to the idealizations of science and autonomous with respect to them, a world presupposed by all scientific theory, which is unable to free itself entirely from it, a world escaping the distinction between the pure objectivity of the physical universe and the pure subjectivity of appearances understood as interfaces between the "facts" and us. The "enigma" toward which the life-world beckons is precisely that of this interconnectedness necessary to all description of experience as such between a bodily subject that is always already in the world and a world that is always already open to this subject, before all its alleged constituting and/or possibility-forming operations, the enigma of that mutual belongingness by virtue of which the human being and the world form the two strands of the same phenomenal weave, without the possibility to isolate any of them as an element prior to the other—a transcendental element—without our being able to exit this global configuration in which each part takes on its meaning only in relation to its complementary.

Hence there would be a sense, deeper than the one emphasized by Husserl, in which it may be said that the thematization of the life-world leads to an "anti-Copernican" revolution. This is true, not only because the world in which we move and have our roots is a pre-Copernican world in which the ground is at rest and "the Earth does not move"; but also, because the taking seriously of the *Lebenswelt* culminates in an in-depth questioning of the Kantian "Copernican" revolution, that is to say, *of the transcendental turn in philosophy*. If, as I have emphasized, the skeptical problem is a false one; if, as a disjunctive conception of perception teaches us, there is no element common to perception and illusion, and thus illusion is not a crossed-out perception nor perception a confirmed illusion; if, moreover, experience is not a synthesis of lived experiences that would be evaluable in isolation as being either perceptual or illusory, that is to say, that would remain identical to themselves regardless of whether their object exists or not (thus opening the possibility of a permanent distrust of perception) if, conversely, every experience is only an experience on the condition of being a part of the whole of experience, so that an experience that fails to meet this criterion, possessing no cohesiveness with experience as a whole, is not a misleading experience, but is not an *experience* at all (that which is worthy of the name "experience" being the whole, and only derivatively therefrom this or that part of it); if, in other words, all adequate description of our being-in-the-world must be formulated in holistic terms, it follows that there are only "true" experiences, that is to say, experiences opening to the world itself. The structural connection between life and the world, the latter being understood as the familiar place of that life, is an essential property of the world itself understood as *Lebenswelt*. This is why the task of an elucidation of the life-world is indistinguishable from the project of phenomenology itself as defined in this book.

Epilogue

Let me assume there is still a reader to read these lines.

My effort, throughout these pages, has been to establish the following points. (a) As far as rigor is concerned, the phenomenological method is not inferior to the method that is to be found in linguistic philosophy. (b) The idea of structures of experience as essential structures is worthy of being defended, at least on the condition of an in-depth rethinking of it. (c) The originality of the concept of experience to which phenomenology leads is that it circumvents the alternative of empiricism versus Kantianism, including its contemporary linguistic avatars—what I have called "the Kantian framework," and which dominates analytic philosophy and a part of Continental philosophy to this day. (d) We should replace the *linguistic turn* by an "experiential turn," to take up Bergson's expression, since language has its roots in our prelinguistic openness to the world, as the dimension of our sensible and embodied existence, and draws from it its very possibility. (e) An inquiry into essence cannot leave history behind; it is only possible through a critical deconstruction of the philosophical tradition. Thus phenomenology holds both ends of a chain extending from the second naïveté of our immersion into the world to the refined products of history and culture. It is probably the only philosophical option that is able to embrace and intertwine these two dimensions. If all this makes sense, phenomenology is not a dead possibility—or, as Sartre would have put it, a "dead-possibility [*morte-possibilité*]"—a possibility only belonging to documentary or monumental history, but a living possibility, born of a living investigation. To a large extent, it is true to say that the possibility of phenomenology stands higher than its actuality: this possibility lies before us.

Through the various moments along the way of our journey I have tried to give consistency to what, in my view, is the main claim of phenomenology, and probably the most urgent problem for philosophy in general: to understand the way in which a pre-discursive intelligence incorporated in our initial openness to the world is connected with a verbal intelligence that builds on it, but is often unaware of it; and consequently *to reunite* a reason cut off from its corporeal and experiential roots.

Not only does phenomenology take reason to heart; it strives to reach the heart of reason, to borrow Husserl's Pascalian expression, and it does so, in moving beyond "a narrow-hearted and bad rationality" (*eine engherzige und schlechte Rationalität*)[1] to a different, more generous one. If there is a reason characterized by narrow-heartedness and feebleness, by *Engherzigkeit,* there is also a big-hearted reason, welcoming enough to take back into itself that which only seemingly is its opposite; a reason that, beyond the arid plains of logic with its formalism, mathematics, and, more generally, the exact sciences, rejoins the oasis of sensibility in which being, indefinitely, revitalizes itself.

"All that is 'logical,'" Husserl writes, "comes precisely from a pre-logical sphere, which possesses its own reason [*Vernunft*], its own truth that sustains everything."[2] No longer contrasting reason with sensibility, language with experience, while at the same time maintaining their distinction, phenomenology seeks a *reason of the infra-rational;* it promotes a reason that is "sensible to the heart," because it opens the heart of reason to sensibility.

Notes

Preface

1. Johann Georg Hamann, "Métacritique du purisme de la raison pure," in *Aestetica in nuce: Métacritique du purisme de la raison pure et autres textes,* ed. and trans. Romain Deygout (Paris: Vrin, 2001).

2. Edmund Husserl, *Husserliana* (henceforth abbreviated as Hua), vol. XVII, 297; Eng. trans. Dorion Cairns, *Formal and Transcendental Logic* (The Hague: Martinus Nijhoff, 1969), 292.

3. Hua XXVIII, 68; French trans. Philippe Ducat, Patrick Lang, and Carlos Lobo, *Leçons sur l'éthique et la théorie de la valeur (1908–1914)* (Paris: Presses Universitaires de France, 2009), 146.

4. Hua VI, 14; trans. David Carr, *The Crisis of European Sciences and Transcendental Phenomenology* (Evanston, Ill.: Northwestern University Press, 1970), 16. In reality, Husserl writes "engherzige Rationalität" [literally, "narrow-hearted rationality"—Tr.].

5. Aristotle, *De Anima,* 431a17ff.

6. Martin Heidegger, *Gesamtausgabe* (henceforth abbreviated as GA), vol. 20, 94 (Frankfurt am Main: Vittorio Klostermann Verlag), trans. T. Kisiel, *History of the Concept of Time,* 69. See Edmund Husserl, *Logische Untersuchungen* (henceforth abbreviated as LU), VI, para. 60; Hua XIX, 2, 712; Eng. trans. J. N. Findlay, *Logical Investigations,* vol. 2 (London: Routledge and Kegan Paul, 1977), 306: "thought in the highest sense, without any foundation of sense, is a piece of nonsense."

7. "Edmund Husserl's Letter to Lucien Lévy-Bruhl," March 11, 1935, trans. Lukas Steinacher and Dermot Moran in *The New Yearbook for Phenomenology and Phenomenological Philosophy VIII* (2008): 5.

8. Martin Heidegger, *Sein und Zeit,* 16th ed. (Tübingen: Max Niemayer Verlag, 1988), 27; Eng. trans. John Macquarrie and Edward Robinson, *Being and Time* (New York: Harper and Row, 1962), 50.

9. Emmanuel Levinas, *En découvrant l'existence avec Husserl et Heidegger* (Paris: Vrin, 1982), 127–28; trans. Richard A. Cohen and Michael B. Smith, *Discovering Existence with Husserl* (Evanston, Ill.: Northwestern University Press, 1998), 113.

10. Jean Grondin, *Le Tournant herméneutique de la phénoménologie* (Paris: Presses Universitaires de France, 2003), 99.

11. Ibid., 120.

12. Hua III, 1, §76, p. 161; trans. F. Kersten, *Ideas Pertaining to a Pure Phenom-*

enology and to a Phenomenological Philosophy, First Book (Dordrecht: Kluwer Academic, 1982), 173: "A method, after all, is nothing which is, or which can be, brought in from outside. . . . [A] *determinate* method—determined not with respect to its technical particularity but with respect to the universal type of method 'to which it belongs'—is a norm which arises from the fundamental regional specificity and the universal structures of the province in question, so that a cognitive seizing upon such a method depends essentially on knowledge of these structures." On this point Husserl follows the school of Brentano and specifically his teacher, Carl Stumpf, who writes: "Durchgreifende Unterschiede der Methode wurzeln doch zuletzt immer in Unterschieden der Gegenstände." [Radical differences of method are always rooted, ultimately, in differences in the objects.] (Stumpf, "Zur Einteilung der Wissenschaften," in *Abhandlung der Königlich-Preußischen Akademie der Wissenschaften* [Berlin: Verlag der Königl. Akademie der Wissenschaften, 1906], 4).

13. Heidegger, GA 24, p. 467; trans. Albert Hofstadter, *The Basic Problems of Phenomenology* (Bloomington: Indiana University Press, 1988), 328.

14. Ludwig Wittgenstein, *Bemerkungen über die Farben,* bilingual edition, ed. G. E. M. Anscombe, Eng. *Remarks on Colour,* trans. Linda L. McAlister and Margarete Schäettle (Berkeley: University of California Press, 1977), 4e.

15. "le détour qui vaut le voyage." Michel Deguy, *La Raison poétique* (Paris: Galilée, 2000), 159.

16. J. Conrad, Author's Note to *Chance* (New York: Doubleday, 1950), xi.

Introduction to Part 1

The epigraph to part 1 is from Henri Michaux, *Tent Posts,* trans. Lynn Hoggard (Copenhagen: Green Integer, 1977), 17.

1. Simone de Beauvoir, *The Prime of Life,* trans. Peter Green (Cleveland: World Publishing, 1962), 112.

2. Edmund Husserl, "Tobacco-logishes" (English-German), *The New Yearbook for Phenomenology and Phenomenological Philosophy* 4 (2004): 274–82.

3. A. Chekhov, *The Party & Other Stories,* trans. Constance Garnett (Tallahassee, Fla.: Rowland, 2009), 152.

4. LU IV, §14, "Anmerkungen"; Hua XIX, 1, p. 350; trans. Findlay, *Logical Investigations,* vol. 2, p. 76.

5. For an overview of these several descriptive philosophies, see K. Mulligan, "Descriptions' Objects: Austrian Variations," in *Themes from Wittgenstein,* ed. B. Garrett and K. Mulligan (Canberra: Australian National University, 1993), 62–85.

6. Ludwig Wittgenstein, *Philosophische Untersuchungen,* I, §109; *Philosophical Investigations,* 3rd ed., trans. G. E. M. Anscombe (Malden, Mass.: Blackwell, 2001), 47.

7. Wittgenstein, *Philosophische Untersuchungen,* I, §496; *Philosophical Investigations,* 138. "Grammar . . . only describes and in no way explains the use of signs."

8. Hua III, 1, §24, p. 51; Husserl, *Ideas Pertaining to a Pure Phenomenology, First Book,* 44.

9. Hua, IV, p. 17; Husserl, *The Crisis of European Sciences*, 18.

10. Martin Heidegger, *Les Conférences de Cassel, édition bilingue de Jean-Claude Gens* (Paris: Vrin, 1971), 4ff.

11. Georg Henrik von Wright, *Explanation and Understanding* (Ithaca, N.Y.: Cornell University Press, 1971), 4ff.

12. But we must distinguish, in this last group, between those who in the name of the "unity of science" stand with Neurath, for whom philosophy need not even perform a clarification of scientific statements distinct from their empirical verification—"It is impossible to separate the 'clarification of concepts' from the 'pursuit of science' to which it belongs. Both are inseparably bound together" (Neurath, "Soziologie im Physikalismus," in *Erkenntnis*, 2, 1932; trans. Robert S. Cohen, *Philosophical Papers 1913–1946: With a Bibliography of Neurath in English* [Dordrecht: Reidel, 1983], 59)—and those who, following the example of Schlick and Carnap, defend the position of a sharing of tasks between philosophy and the empirical sciences. (See M. Schlick, "Die Wende der Philosophie" [1930], English trans. P. Heath, "The Turning-Point in Philosophy," in *Philosophical Papers*, 2 (1925–1936) [Dordrecht: Reidel, 1979], 157: "Philosophy elucidates propositions, science verifies them").

13. W. V. Quine, *From Stimulus to Science* (Cambridge, Mass.: Harvard University Press, 1995), 256–57: "Naturalistic philosophy is continuous with natural science."

14. M. Merleau-Ponty, *Phenomenology of Perception*, trans. Donald A. Landes (London: Routledge, 2012), lxxi.

15. H. Putnam, *Realism with a Human Face* (Cambridge, Mass: Harvard University Press, 1992), 51.

16. D. Davidson, "Gadamer and Plato's *Philebus*," in *Truth, Language and History* (Oxford: Clarendon, 2005), 261.

17. Ludwig Wittgenstein, *Zettel*, ed. E. Ascombe and G. H. von Wright (Berkeley: University of California Press, [1970] 2007), 80 (§455). This declaration should be read alongside what von Wright reproaches, and regrets, in Wittgenstein's disciples: "There was a lot of unhealthy sectarianism among his disciples. That caused Wittgenstein much pain. He thought that his influence as a teacher was, all things considered, harmful to the development of his disciples' mental freedom. I am afraid he was right" (G. H. von Wright, *Wittgenstein* [Mauvezin: Trans Europ Repress, 1986), 41).

18. Wittgenstein, *Logische Untersuchungen*, 1, §133; *Philosophical Investigations*, 51.

19. B. Croce, *Ciò che è vivo e ciò che è morto della filosofia di Hegel* (Bari: Laterza, 1907); trans. D. Ainslie. *What Is Living and What Is Dead of the Philosophy of Hegel* (Kitchener, Ont: Batoche, 2001).

Chapter 1

The epigraph is from Edmund Husserl, Hua V, p. 34; trans. Klein and Pohl, *Phenomenology and the Foundations of the Sciences*, in E. Husserl, *Collected Works, Vol. 1* (The Hague: Martinus Nijhoff, 1980), 30.

1. LU, "Einleitung," §2; Hua XIX, 1, p. 10; *Logical Investigations*, trans. Findlay, vol 1, p, 168. Or, in the formulation of *Ideas I*: "To conform *to the things themselves* or to go from words and opinions back to the things themselves, to consult them in their self-givenness and to set aside all prejudices alien to them" (Hua III, 1, p. 41; Husserl, *Ideas I*, 35). See also Reinach, "Über Phänomenologie," in *Sämtliche Werke: Textkritische Ausgabe in 2 Bänden*, vol. I (Munich: Philosophie Verlag, 1989), 538: "durch alle Zeichen und Definitionen und Regeln durchzudringen zu den Sachen selbst"; trans. D. Willard, as "Concerning Phenomenology," *The Personalist*, vol. 50 (1969): 194–221, reprinted in D. Moran, *The Phenomenology Reader* (London: Psychology, 2002), 186: "as philosophers, we must bring ourselves—through all signs, definitions and rules—to the things themselves." According to George Heffernan, it was Heidegger who imposed the shortened form (see *Am Anfang war die Logik: Hermeneutische Abhandlungen zum Ansatz der formalen und transzendentalen Logik von E. Husserl* [Amsterdam: B. R. Grüner, 1988], 13 n18).

2. Hua III, 1, §124, p. 286; Husserl, *Ideas I*, 295: "Anything 'meant as meant,' anything meant in the noematic sense (and, more particularly, as the noematic core) pertaining to any act, no matter which, is *expressible by means of* 'significations.'"

3. Henri Bergson, *An Introduction to Metaphysics*, trans. T. E. Hulme (New York: Putnam's, 1912), 36.

4. In Ernst Mach's view, "it is not bodies that produce sensations, but elementary complexes (complexes of sensations) that constitute bodies" (*The Analysis of Sensations and the Relation of the Physical to the Psychical*, trans. C. M. Williams, revised by Sidney Waterlow [Chicago: Open Court, 1914], 29). This is not limited to the body: "The world consists only of our sensations" (ibid., 12).

5. W. James, *Principles of Psychology, I* (New York: Henry Holt, 1890), 196.

6. W. James, "Does 'Consciousness' Exist?" in *Writings 1902–1910* (New York: Library of America, 1987), 1142.

7. W. Dilthey, *Erfahren und Denken* (1892), in *Gesammelte Schriften*, vol. 5, ed. G. Misch (Berlin: Teubner, 1924), 78–79.

8. Carl Stumpf, *Erscheinungen und Psychische Funktionen* (Berlin: G. Reiner, 1906); French trans. Denis Fisette, *Renaissance de la philosophie: Quatre articles* (Paris: Vrin, 2006), 148. Already in his 1873 study *Über den psychologischen Ursprung der Raumvorstellung*, Stumpf emphasizes that in the contents of perception there are foundational relations, such as in the relation whole/part, or in the dependency of color with respect to extension. These analyses are carried out in the two volumes of Stumpf's *Tonpsychologie* (1883–90) in which he analyzes specifically fusion (*Verschmelzung*) between simultaneous tones, that is, the phenomenon of the chord. This research will have an undeniable influence on the psychology of form (see M. G. Ash, *Gestalt Psychology in German Culture (1890–1967)* [Cambridge University Press, 1998], esp. chapters 2 and 4). Among the first to draw attention to Stumpf's influence on Husserl was Herbert Spiegelberg, in *The Phenomenological Movement: A Historical Introduction*, vol. 1 (The Hague: Martinus Nijhoff, 1976), 58.

9. Stumpf, *Renaissance de la philosophie*, 193.

10. Ibid., 197.

11. C. von Ehrenfels, "Über 'Gestaltqualitäten,'" *Vierteljahrsschrift für wissenschaftliche Philosophie*, t. 14, vol. 3 (1890): 249–92; trans. by D. Fisette, in Husserl, Stumpf, et al., *À l'école de Brentano: De Würzbourg à Vienne* (Paris: Vrin, 2007), 225–59. See also Husserl, Hua XII, p. 210ff.; trans. Dallas Willard, *Philosophy of Arithmetic* (Dordrecht: Kluwer Academic, 2003), 222ff. and LU, III, §4; Hua XIX, 1, pp. 237–38; trans. Findlay, *Logical Investigations*, vol. 2, 7–9.

12. Stumpf, *Renaissance de la philosophie*, 192 (trans. modified).

13. Ibid., 142; see also 295. And see Stumpf, *Über den psychologischen Ursprung der Raumvorstellung* (Leipzig: Hirzel, 1873), 110ff.

14. Alexius Meinong, "Bemerkungen über den Farbenkörper und das Mischungsgesetz," *Zeitschrift für Psychologie und Physiologie der Sinnesorgane* 33, nos. 1 and 2 (1903): 1–80.

15. Stumpf, *Renaissance de la philosophie*, 285.

16. Hua VII, p. 173; trans. A. L. Kelkel, *Philosophie première*, I, *Histoire critique des idées* (Paris: Presses Universitaires de France, 1970), 248.

17. D. Hume, *An Enquiry concerning Human Understanding*, ed. Tom L. Beauchamp (Oxford: Oxford University Press, 1999), 108.

18. Hua, XXIV, p. 350; trans. Laurent Joumier, *Introduction à la logique et à la théorie de la connaissance (1906–1907)* (Paris: Vrin, 1998), 387.

19. Hua VI, p. 117; trans. Carr, *The Crisis*, 115.

20. Kant, *Kritik der reinen Vernunft*, A1; trans. Max Müller, *Critique of Pure Reason* (Garden City, N.Y.: Doubleday, Anchor Books, 1966), 2.

21. Ibid., A126; *Critique*, 115.

22. Ibid., B130; *Critique*, 74.

23. "All connecting [*Verbindung*] is an act of the understanding" (Kant, *Kritik*, B130; *Critique*, 76).

24. Ibid., A125; *Critique*, 114.

25. Russell will make a very similar argument. See *The Problems of Philosophy* (London: Oxford University Press, 1912), 74; "To say [in response to Hume] that logic and arithmetic are contributed by us does not account for this. Our nature is as much a fact of the existing world as anything, and there can be no certainty that it will remain constant."

26. Hua VII, Beilage XIV, p. 354 (my translation of CR's translation—Tr.).

27. In a letter, Husserl declares: "I have learned incomparably more from Hume than from Kant, toward whom I had the deepest antipathy and who, properly speaking (if I judge correctly), has not influenced me at all" (letter of September 4, 1919 to Arnold Metzger, *Philosophisches Jahrbuch des Görres-Gesellschaft* 62, no. 1 [April 1953], 198).

28. At least this is how Husserl reads it. See Hua VII, p. 235; trans. A. L. Kelkel, *Philosophie première*, I, *Histoire critique des idées* (Paris: Presses Universitaires de France, 1970), 294 (modified), where he says one must replace Kant's "still half mythical idea of the *a priori*" with a phenomenological concept "that to tell the truth Hume had already in mind with his *relation of idea*." Many "obscurities" of Kant's thought come from the fact that "he lacked the phenomenologically correct concept of the *a priori*" (LU VI, §66; Hua XIX, 2, p. 733; trans.

J. N. Findlay, *Logical Investigations,* vol. 2 [London: Routledge and Kegan Paul, 1970], 319).

29. Hua XXIV, pp. 234–35; trans. Claire Ortiz Hill, *Introduction to Logic and Theory of Knowledge: Lectures 1906/07* (Dordrecht: Springer, 2008), 230–31. See also Husserl, trans. James S. Churchill and Karl Ameriks, *Experience and Judgment* (Evanston, Ill.: Northwestern University Press, 1973), 374–75.

30. Hua III, 1, §43, p. 89; trans. F. Kersten, *Ideas I,* 92.

31. Although Husserl ventures to use the expression "*mathesis* of experiences [*Mathesis der Erlebnisse*]" in §75 of *Ideas I,* he points out immediately thereafter that "phenomenology . . . belongs however to a *fundamental class of eidetic sciences totally different* from the one to which the mathematical sciences belong" (Hua III, 1, p. 158; trans. F. Kersten, 169–70 [trans. modified—Tr.]).

32. On the connection, in Husserl (who was, we must bear in mind, originally a mathematician), between ideation and mathematics, see Hua IX, p. 87; trans. J. Scanlon, *Phenomenological Psychology: Lectures, Summer Semester 1925* (The Hague: Martinus Nijhoff, 1962), 65: "the seeing of the *a priori,* the inner doing of ideation, is not foreign to us all, insofar as we have all learned at least a little mathematics."

33. Hua VII, p. 235; trans. Ted E. Klein, Jr. and William E. Pohl, "Kant and the Idea of Transcendental Philosophy," *Southwestern Journal of Philosophy* 5 (1974): 13.

34. A. Reinach, "Über Phänomenologie," 544; "Concerning Phenomenology," in *The Phenomenology Reader,* 191.

35. LU III, §6; Hua XIX, 1, p. 242; trans. Findlay, *Logical Investigations,* vol. 2, p. 11.

36. Heidegger, GA 20, p. 101; trans. Theodore Kisiel, *History of the Concept of Time* (Bloomington: Indiana University Press, 1992), 73–74. See also Reinach, "Über Phänomenologie," 545; trans. Willard Dallas, "Concerning Phenomenology," in *The Phenomenology Reader,* 191: "But [*a priori*] 'states of affairs' obtain indifferently of what consciousness apprehends them, and of whether they are apprehended by any consciousness at all. In and for itself, the *a priori* has not even the least thing to do with thinking and knowing."

37. "At the same time, this sense defines the only concept belonging to the multisignificant expression, *a priori,* that I recognize philosophically. That concept alone is meant wherever the locution *a priori* occurs in my writings." (Hua XVII, §98, p. 255, note 1; trans. D. Cairns, *Formal and Transcendental Logic* [The Hague: Martinus Nijhoff, 1969], 248 n1). Here we should add: "*a priori* in the material sense." Indeed, formal idealities (such as "whole" or "part") are in fact referred to by Husserl as "essences" ("formal essences"), but they are not designated as "eide." In his vocabulary, only material *a priori,* that is, *eide,* are "*essences proper*" (*"eigentlichen" Wesen*) (Hua III, 1, §10, p 26; trans. F. Kersten, *Ideas I,* 21).

38. Husserl, *Erfahrung und Urteil* (Hamburg: Glaassen und Goverts, 1954), 321; trans. *Experience and Judgment* (Evanston, Ill.: Northwestern University Press, 1973), 267. To the best of my knowledge, Husserl never really explains what he means by "possible universe." His consideration of possible worlds probably doesn't involve any realism à la Lewis; it envisages possible worlds not as entities

that would have a certain mode of being, but only as thought-possibilities, counterfactual situations. In certain texts, moreover, Husserl deliberately presents possible worlds as "variants" of the real, or factual world: "All possible worlds are variants [*Varianten*] of the world that is valid for us. . . . [namely] our factual world" (Hua VI, Beilage XXV, 500; trans. Gérard Granel, *La Crise des sciences européennes et la phénoménologie transcendantale* [Paris: Gallimard, 1989], 554). To understand this point, we must have a better understanding of the relations between essence and modality (see chapters 10, 11). Necessity (validity in all possible worlds) is rooted in essence, and not the other way round, and essence is always essence *of our world.* See also Husserl, Manuscript E III 4 (1930), p. 62: "There are an infinite number of possible worlds that are modifications [*Abwandlungen*], accessible by intuition, of the world that is valid for us in each case. . . . But ultimately it turns out that there is only one world, the factual world, that is thinkable as the world of the truth" (quoted and translated into French by R. Toulemont, *L'essence de la société selon Husserl* (Paris: Presses Universitaires de France, 1962), 285).

39. Husserl, *Erfahrung und Urteil,* 414; trans. Churchill and Ameriks, *Experience and Judgment,* 343.

40. On eidetic variation, see Husserl, *Erfahrung und Urteil,* 410–12, 417; *Experience and Judgment,* 340–42, 345. See also Hua IX, p. 70–74; trans. J. Scanlon, *Phenomenological Psychology,* 53ff.

41. Hua, XVII, §98, p. 255, n1; trans. D. Cairns, *Formal and Transcendental Logic,* 248 n1.

42. Hua IX, p. 86; trans. J. Scanlon, *Phenomenological Psychology,* 65 (trans. modified—Tr.).

43. Hua, III, 1, p. 19; Husserl, *Ideas I,* 14.

44. Hua XXVIII, p. 403.

45. Hua III, 1, p. 20; *Ideas I,* 15.

46. Hua III, 1, p. 22; *Ideas I,* 17.

47. It is sometimes asserted that spatial and temporal relations are external (see D. M. Armstrong, *Universals* [Boulder, Colo.: Westview, 1989], 43). A relation is internal if, given certain items possessing certain natures, the relation must hold between those items. But here we are not considering the contingent relations that obtain, let us say, between several tones (I can play an E after a D, but also a D after an E) but the temporal relations between the moments these tones occupy: if the note *x* occupies the moment T1 and if the note *y* occupies the moment T2, it is necessary for the note *x* to be prior to the note *y,* because it is necessary for T1 to be prior to T2. The same is true for spatial positions. (We must distinguish necessary relations between spatial positions from contingent relations between the things that happen to occupy these positions.) In the case of moments or of spatial positions, regardless of the objects occupying them, "the terms and their nature dictate a relation" (ibid., 44), which is the specific mark of internal relations.

48. Ludwig Wittgenstein, *Philosophische Bemerkungen* (Oxford: Basil Blackwell, 1964); trans. R. Hargreaves and R. White, *Philosophical Remarks,* Remark no. 26 (Oxford: Basil Blackwell, 1975), 12.

49. Hua XXVIII, p. 403.

50. On the distinction between free / bound idealities, see Husserl, *Erfahrung und Urteil*, 321; trans. Churchill, *Experience and Judgment*, 267.

51. Husserl does point out that "we have all formed the concept of *a priori* science in mathematics," although the domain of psychology is "of a completely different essential type" and calls for a different method (Hua IX, p. 50; trans. John Scanlon, *Phenomenological Psychology: Lectures, Summer Semester, 1925* [The Hague: Martinus Nijhoff, 1977]), 36.

52. Hua I, p. 114; trans. Dorion Cairns, *Cartesian Meditations*, 81. The comparison could be made with what Husserl said in 1911 in "Philosophy as Rigorous Science": "For phenomenology, the singular is eternally the apeiron. Phenomenology can recognize with objective validity only essences and essential relations" (Hua XXV, p. 36; trans. Quentin Lauer, in *Phenomenology and the Crisis of Philosophy* [New York: Harper and Row, 1965], 116).

53. Hua IX, pp. 92–93; Husserl, *Phenomenological Psychology*, trans. John Scanlon (The Hague: Martinus Nijhoff, 1977), 69, 70.

54. A. Reinach, "Über Phänomenologie," 542; "Concerning Phenomenology," 189.

55. Hua III, 1, p. 48; trans. F. Kersten, *Ideas I*, 41.

56. To Natorp, who wrote to him that "experience is itself construction" (*die "Erfahrung" ist selbst Konstruktion*) (letter of September 10, 1901 to Husserl, in *Briefwechsel*, vol. 5, *Die Neukantianer*, ed. Karl Schuhmann with the collaboration of Elisabeth Schuhmann [London: Kluwer Academic, Husserliana Dokumente, III-V, 1994], 88), Husserl responds indirectly: "Die Idealisten aber (gegen die ich mich hier speziell wende) finden ihre Erwartungen auf transzendentale Konstruktionen von oben her enttäuscht" (Husserl, "Entwurf einer 'Vorrede' zu den 'Logischen Untersuchungen,'" ed. E. Fink, *Tijdschrift voor Philosophie* 1 [1939]: 115); trans. P. J. Bossert and C. H. Peters, ed. E. Fink, *Introduction to the Logical Investigations: A Draft of a Preface to the Logical Investigations* (The Hague: Martinus Nijhoff, 1975), 22: "But the idealists (with whom I especially take issue here) find their expectations of transcendental constructions from above disappointed."

57. Hua XVII, p. 90; trans. Cairns, *Formal and Transcendental Logic*, 86.

58. P. Natorp, *Die logischen Grundlagen der exakten Wissenschaften* (1910), §3; See I. Kern, *Husserl und Kant: Eine Untersuchung über Husserls Verhältnis zu Kant und zum Neokantismus* (The Hague: Martinus Nijhoff, 1964), 326–73; Georges Gurvitch, "Phénoménologie et criticisme (E. Lask et N. Hartmann)," *Revue philosophique de la France et de l'Étranger*, vol. 108 [1929]: 235–84; Massimo Ferrari, "Cent ans après Husserl, Natorp et la logique pure," *Philosophie* 74 (2002): 40–57; and Fink's entire debate with the neo-Kantians.

59. Hua V, p. 34; trans. Klein and Pohl, *Phenomenology and the Foundations of the Sciences*, 30.

60. Hua XVII, p. 297; 386. See also V. Costa, *L'estetica trascendentale fenomenologica: Sensibilità e razionalità nella filosofia di E. Husserl* (Milan: Vita e pensiero, 1999).

61. Ibid.

62. Ibid. See Merleau-Ponty, *Phenomenology of Perception*: "a logic of the world that my entire body merges with" (341).

63. Hua XXVII, pp. 166–67; trans. D. Franck, "Phénoménologie et anthropologie," in E. Husserl, *Notes sur Heidegger* (Paris: Minuit, 1993), 59.

64. Husserl, letter of March 11, 1935 to Lévy-Bruhl, published and translated by A. Soulez, *Gradhiva*, no. 4 (Summer 1988): 70.

Chapter 2

The epigraph is from Heidegger, GA 20, p. 108; *History of the Concept of Time: Prolegomena*, trans. Theodore Kisiel (Bloomington: Indiana University Press, 1985), 79.

1. Hua VI, §48, p. 169; trans. Carr, *The Crisis*, 166.

2. Aristotle, *De Anima*, III, 8.431b20.

3. Aristotle, *Metaphysics*, Z, 16.1040b34.

4. R. Brague, *Aristote et la question du monde* (Paris: Presses Universitaires de France, 1988), 347.

5. Aristotle, *De Anima*, III, 8.431b30.

6. The first appearance of a doctrine of object in the "non-technical" sense of what lays across the path, constituting an obstacle, may be found in Augustine's theory of vision, according to which vision is the reverberation of a ray emanating from the eye onto the interposed body: "*irruit radius in corpus obiectum.*" See Augustine, *Sermo CCLXXVII*, P. L. 38, col. 1262 (cap. X, 10): here *obiectum* is synonymous with *ostaculum*. On the genesis of this notion of object, see L. Dewan's classic paper, "'Obiectum': Notes on the Invention of a Word," *Archives d'histoire doctrinale et littéraire du Moyen Âge* 48 (1981): 37–96. See also O. Boulnois, "Être, luire et concevoir: Note sur la genèse et la structure de la conception scotiste de l'*esse objective*," *Collectanea franciscana* 60 (1990): 117–35; and by the same author, *Être et représentation* (Paris: Presses Universitaires de France, 1999).

7. Duns Scotus, *Quodlibet*, XIII, art. 2, §60: "Knowledge in the intellect," writes Duns Scotus, "is not immediately caused by an object qua external, but by something internal . . . For our act of intellection, we have an internal object."

8. Duns Scotus, *Ordinatio*, I, dist. 3, 3, q. 2, §531. See French translation by G. Sondag: Duns Scot, *L'Image* (Paris: Vrin, 1993), 212–13.

9. Duns Scotus, *Quodlibet*, art. 2, §39 (quoted by O. Boulnois, "Être, luire et concevoir," 133).

10. F. Brentano, *Psychologie vom empirischen Standpunkt* (Hamburg: Meiner, 1973), vol. 1, pp. 124–25; *Psychology from an Empirical Standpoint*, trans. Linda L. McAlister (London: Routledge and Kegan Paul, 1973), 68.

11. Several interpreters have gone astray for having failed to grasp the medieval background of Brentano's doctrine—M. Dummett, for example, in his *Origins of Analytical Philosophy* (Cambridge, Mass.: Harvard University Press, 1996), 32. To Brentano, Dummett writes, the intentional object is something external "in the strong sense." Jean-François Courtine brings out this point in *La Cause de la phénoménologie* (Paris: Presses Universitaires de France, 2007), 22. V. Descombes follows Dummett on this point, in *Les Institutions du sens* (Paris: Minuit, 1996), 40 n29.

12. Brentano, *Psychologie vom empirischen Standpunkt,* vol. 2, 133; *Psychology from an Empirical Standpoint,* 211 (appendix prepared for the 1911 edition).

13. Brentano, *Psychology from an Empirical Standpoint,* 212.

14. Ibid., 214.

15. A. Meinong, *Gegenstandtheorie* (1904) in *Gesamtausgabe* (Graz: Akademische Druck- und Verlagsanstalt), vol. 2, p. 490; trans. Isaac Levi, D. B. Terrell, and Roderick M. Chisholm, "The Theory of Objects," in *Realism and the Background of Phenomenology* (New York: Free, 1960), 83.

16. Hua XXII, p. 354; French trans. Jacques English, *Sur les objets intentionnels, 1893–1901* (Paris: Vrin, 1993), 354.

17. Hua XXII, p. 27; French trans. Jacques English, *Sur les objets intentionnels,* 112.

18. This is the point Russell raises against him: one must refuse both to make existence a predicate of any kind (i.e., a property of objects), because existence is a predicate of a propositional function or, by derivation, of a class—and to interpret an expression such as "square circle" as a proper noun, thereby ascribing a reference to it, whereas it is merely a question of a definite description. See Russell's "On Denoting" (1905), in *Mind,* n.s., vol. 14, no. 56. (October 1905): 479–93; and also Meinong, Husserl, and Russell, "Correspondance autour de la théorie de l'objet," trans. B. Gallet, *Philosophie* 72 (2001): 3–35.

19. See the reference to Descartes's theory of the idea as "image" or "picture" which is cited *cum laude* by Twardowski: Hua XXII, pp. 26ff.

20. Hua XXII, p. 305; French trans. Jacques English, *Sur les objets intentionnels,* 282.

21. LU V, "Beilage zu den Paragraphen 11 und 20," Hua, XIX, 1, p. 439; trans. Findlay, *Logical Investigations,* vol. 2, 127.

22. Hua, XIX, 1, p. 437; *Logical Investigations,* vol. 2, p. 126.

23. LU V, §11; Hua XIX, 1, pp. 386–87; *Logical Investigations,* vol. 2, 99.

24. LU V, §21; Hua XIX, 1, p. 432; *Logical Investigations,* vol. 2, 224.

25. Hua XIX, 1, pp. 436ff; *Logical Investigations,* vol. 2, 125. See also Hua III, 1, §90, p. 208; trans. Kersten, *Ideas I,* p. 219. "The main point here is that perception and, then consequently, every mental process, requires a depictive function, unavoidably (as can be seen at once from our critique) leads to an infinite regress"—and, more generally, *Ideas I,* §43, 52 and 90.

26. Hua XIX, 1, p. 436; *Logical Investigations,* vol. 2, 125.

27. LU V, §10; Hua XIX, 1 p. 382; *Logical Investigations,* vol. 2, 96.

28. LU V, §15 (a); Hua XIX, 1, p. 405; *Logical Investigations,* vol. 2, 108–9.

29. LU V, §11; Hua XIX, 1, p. 386; *Logical Investigations,* vol. 2, 98: "We do not experience the object and beside it the intentional experience directed upon it, there are not even two things present in the sense of a part and a whole which contains it: only one thing is present, the intentional experience, whose essential descriptive character is the intention in question." Husserl repeats the same criticism in very similar terms in §36 of *Ideen I* (Hua III, 1, p. 74; trans. Kersten, *Ideas I,* 73.) Now, if it is true that Brentano takes up a naturalist position vis-à-vis the status of the soul, making psychology a part of the natural sciences (*Psychologie vom empirischen Standpunkt* [Hamburg: Meiner, 1973], Second Book, 137; *Psychology from*

an Empirical Standpoint [London: Routledge, 1995], 81), he categorically refuses, on the other hand, to conceptualize the intentional relation (or quasi-relation) peculiar to psychic phenomena, as an external relation of the causal sort; for a causal relation, as opposed to an intentional one, entails the existence of its two *relata,* cause and effect. From this point of view, Husserl is not so far removed from Brentano when he refuses to reduce the intentional relation to a causal one (Hua XIX, 1, p. 40; *Logical Investigations,* vol. 2, 108–9). On the naturalism of Brentano, see also Husserl, *Phänomenologische Psychologie,* Hua IX, p. 36; trans. Scanlon, *Phenomenological Psychology,* 25.

30. Bolzano, *Wissenschaftslehre,* §49, in *Gesamtausgabe,* I, 11/2 (Stuttgart: Friedrich Frommann Verlag, 1947), 78: "One might immediately be tempted to interpret this as if what I understand by 'representation' is nothing but the *object* to which a 'thought' representation refers. But that is not what I mean. My idea is rather to make an across-the-board distinction between the object to which a representation refers, or (to express it in fewer words) the *object of a representation,* and the representation per se—not just a 'thought' representation, but the representation in itself that serves as its foundation, so that if a 'thought' representation has zero, one or several objects, I ask that we also attribute to the objective representation [*objectiven Vorstellung*] that belongs to it zero, one or several objects, and in fact the same ones." See, on this Bolzanian origin of the act/content/object distinction, Paolo Bucci's *Husserl e Bolzano: Alle origini della fenomenologia* (Milan: Edizioni Unicopli, 2000), 77ff.

31. One must always differentiate between "the ideal content of the acts of representation as opposed to their psychological content . . . From the very beginning I have attributed the objective relation of representations to their ideal content" (Hua XXII, p. 311; French trans. Jacques English, *Sur les objets intentionnels,* 289).

32. "In the case of meanings, naturally there can be no question of speaking of a relation between images and things" (Hua XXII, p. 172; French trans. Jacques English, *Sur les objets intentionnels,* 344).

33. Hua XXII, p. 349, note; French trans. Jacques English, *Sur les objets intentionnels,* 350, note.

34. LU V, §20; Hua XIX, 1, p. 429; *Logical Investigations,* vol. 2, 121: "*The matter,* therefore, must be *that element in an act which first gives it reference to an object,* and reference *so wholly definite* that it *not merely fixes the object meant in a general way,* but *also the precise way in which it is meant.*" We should also quote the text from the first edition: "the matter says, in a sense, as what [*als was*] the object is intended in the act, what determinations must be attributed to it" (Hua XIX, 1, p. 520).

35. Hua XXII, p. 166; trans. *Sur les objets intentionnels* (modified), 337–38. See also Hua XXII, p. 336; trans. *Sur les objets intentionnels* (modified), 314: "Meaning, and meaning alone, is the internal and essential determination of representation." J.-F. Courtine has rightly emphasized what he calls "the phenomenologico-semantic theory of intentionality" (*La Cause de la phénoménologie,* 34).

36. Hua XIX/1, p. 439; *Logical Investigations,* vol. 2, 127.

37. Hua XIX/1, p. 386; *Logical Investigations,* vol. 2, 98–99.

38. Brentano, *Psychologie vom empirischen Standpunkt,* 125; *Psychology from an Empirical Standpoint,* 101 (trans. modified—Tr.; my emphasis).

39. LU V, §20; Hua XIX, 1, p. 430; *Logical Investigations,* vol. 2, 122; see also LU V, §10; Hua XIX, 1, pp. 380–81; *Logical Investigations,* vol. 2, 96.

40. Hua III, 1, §52, p. 111; *Ideas I,* 119 (trans. modified—Tr.).

41. LU I, §7; Hua XIX, 1, p. 41; *Logical Investigations,* vol. 1, 190 (trans. modified—Tr.).

42. Hua XIX, 1, p. 387; *Logical Investigations,* vol. 2, 99.

43. Vladimir Nabokov, *Speak, Memory: An Autobiography Revisited* (New York: Vintage International, 1989), 95.

44. Hua III, 1, §111, p. 250; *Ideas I,* 260 (trans. modified—Tr.).

Chapter 3

1. Ludwig, Wittgenstein, *Lectures and Conversations on Aesthetics, Psychology, and Religious Belief,* ed. Cyril Barrett (Berkeley: University of California Press, 2007), 66.

2. E. Tugendhat, *Vorlesungen zur Einführung in die sprachanalytische Philosophie* (Frankfurt am Main: Suhrkamp, 1976), 94; trans. by P. A. Gorner, *Traditional and Analytical Philosophy: Lectures on the Philosophy of Language* (Cambridge, Eng.: Cambridge University Press, 1982), 67.

3. Hua III, 1, §84, p. 188; Husserl, *Ideas I,* 200.

4. Ludwig Wittgenstein, *Zettel,* 78; see also Wittgenstein, *Remarks on the Philosophy of Psychology,* vol. 1, ed. G. E. M. Anscombe and G. H. von Wright, trans. G. E. M. Anscombe (Oxford: Basil Blackwell, 1998 [1980]), §836.

5. See below, Introduction to Part II.

6. Tugendhat, *Traditional and Analytical Philosophy,* 71.

7. Ibid., 73.

8. Ibid., 72.

9. Ibid., 73.

10. Ibid., 74.

11. Ibid., 71

12. Ibid., 66.

13. Husserl, *Erfahrung und Urteil,* §7, p. 23; *Experience and Judgment,* 28–29.

14. Husserl, *Experience and Judgment,* 30 (trans. modified—Tr.).

15. Ibid., 31.

16. Tugendhat, *Traditional and Analytical Philosophy,* 71.

17. Vincent Descombes, "Le Philosophie comme science rigoureusement descriptive," *Critique,* no. 407 (1981): 372. Descombes says in this review that he finds Tugendhat's demonstration "completely convincing" (ibid., 352).

18. R. Chisholm, *Perceiving: A Philosophical Study* (Ithaca, N.Y.: Cornell University Press, 1957), 69–173.

19. F. Dretske, *Seeing and Knowing* (London: Routledge and Kegan Paul, 1969), esp. 18ff.

20. D. Davidson, *Essays on Actions and Events* (Oxford: Clarendon, 1980), 210.

21. LU VI, §40; Hua XIX, 2, p. 658; *Logical Investigations,* vol. 2, 271.

22. Tugendhat, *Traditional and Analytical Philosophy,* 102.

23. Ibid., 103.

24. Correspondence between R. Chisholm and W. Sellars, in F. Cayla, *Routes et déroutes de l'intentionnalité* (Combas: Éditions de l'Éclat, 1991), 30. See "Intentionality and the Mental: Chisholm-Sellars Correspondence on Intentionality," http://www.ditext.com/sellars/sccor-f.html.

25. Tugendhat, *Traditional and Analytical Philosophy,* 32–33.

26. See, for example, Vincent Descombes, *Grammaire d'objets en tous genres* (Paris: Minuit, 1983), 68–69.

27. Paul Ricoeur, *From Text to Action: Essays in Hermeneutics, II,* trans. Kathleen Blamey and John B. Thompson (Evanston, Ill.: Northwestern University Press, 1991), 16.

28. Wilfrid Sellars, "Empiricism and the Philosophy of Mind," in *Science, Perception and Reality,* 4th ed. (London: Routledge and Kegan Paul [1963], 1971), 160.

29. D. Davidson, "Seeing through Language," in *Truth, Language and History,* 135.

30. Daniel C. Dennett, *Consciousness Explained* (Boston: Little, Brown, 1991), 132.

31. J. R. Searle, *Intentionality: An Essay in the Philosophy of Mind* (Cambridge, Eng.: Cambridge University Press, 1983), 40.

32. Ibid., 5.

33. Ibid., 24.

34. Ibid., 52–53.

35. See Pierre Jacob, *L'Intentionnalité* (Paris: Odile Jacob, 2004), 150.

36. "Intentional states are also representations." Searle, *Intentionality,* 5.

37. LU VI, §4; Hua XIX, 2, p. 550; *Logical Investigations,* vol. 2, 195.

38. Merleau-Ponty, *Phenomenology of Perception,* 36.

39. Ibid., 38.

40. Ibid.

41. Ibid., 36.

42. Ibid., 36 (trans. modified—Tr.).

Chapter 4

The epigraph is from *Moby-Dick, or, The Whale* (New York: Penguin Books, 2001), 470.

1. This expression is from Vincent Descombes, *Objects of All Sorts: A Philosophical Grammar,* trans. L. Scott-Fox and J. Harding (Baltimore: Johns Hopkins University Press, 1986), 59 (trans. modified—Tr.).

2. Gilbert Ryle, "Phenomenology versus 'The Concept of Mind,'" in *Critical Essays: Collected Papers,* vol. 1 (New York: Routledge, 2009), chapter 11, 186–204. With a delightful dogmatism, Ryle declares: "In all discussion relating to conceptual research, in philosophy or even more generally, it is important not to

stretch excessively the sense of the term 'meaning' to the point where we include sentences of the type 'the black clouds mean that the rain will fall.' Otherwise the discussion strongly risks losing all philosophical interest." See also *Texts and Dialogues: Maurice Merleau-Ponty,* trans. James Hatley, ed. Hugh J. Silverman and James Barry, Jr. (Atlantic Highlands, N.J., 1992), 69.

3. J. L. Austin, *Philosophical Papers* (New York: Oxford University Press, 1979), 97.

4. Hua I, p. 77; trans. D. Cairns, *Cartesian Meditations,* 38–39 (trans. modified—Tr.).

5. LU I, §29; Hua XIX 1, p. 98; trans. J. N. Findlay, *Logical Investigations,* vol. 1, 225.

6. LU IV, §14; Hua XIX, 1, p. 342; *Logical Investigations,* vol. 2, 74.

7. LU I, "Einleitung"; Hua XIX/1, p. 6; trans. *Logical Investigations,* vol. 2, 166 (slightly altered—Tr.).

8. Hua XIX 1, p. 9; *Logical Investigations,* vol. 1, 168.

9. LU VI, §12; Hua XIX, 2, p. 576; *Logical Investigations,* vol. 2, 213.

10. LU VI, §8; Hua XIX, 2, p. 568; *Logical Investigations,* vol. 2, 207.

11. LU I, "Einleitung"; Hua XIX, 1, p. 10; *Logical Investigations,* vol. 1, 168.

12. LU VI, §63; Hua XIX 2, p. 721; *Logical Investigations,* vol. 2, 312.

13. LU I, §10; Hua XIX, 1, p. 47; *Logical Investigations,* vol. 1, 194.

14. Hua XXVI, p. 15; French trans. Husserl, *Sur la théorie de la signification* (Paris: Vrin, 1995), 36.

15. LU I, §10; Hua XIX, 1, p. 45; *Logical Investigations,* vol. 1, 193 (slightly modified—Tr.).

16. LU I, §3; Hua XIX, 1, p. 34; *Logical Investigations,* vol. 1, 186.

17. LU I, §13; Hua XIX, 1. p. 55; *Logical Investigations,* vol. 1, 199.

18. LU I, §18; Hua XIX, 1, p. 72; *Logical Investigations,* vol. 1, 209.

19. LU I, §12; Hua XIX, 1, p. 52; *Logical Investigations,* vol. 1, 197.

20. M. Dummett, *Origins of Analytic Philosophy* (Cambridge, Mass.: Harvard University Press, 1994), 44.

21. Ibid., 97.

22. LU I, §7; Hua XIX, 1, p. 39; *Logical Investigations,* vol. 1, 189.

23. LU IV, §10ff.

24. LU I, §30; Hua XIX, 1, p. 102; *Logical Investigations,* vol. 1, 228.

25. LU I, §32; Hua XIX, 1, p. 107; *Logical Investigations,* vol. 1, 231.

26. LU I, §35; Hua XIX, 1, p. 110; *Logical Investigations,* vol. 1, 233.

27. See §8 of *Formal and Transcendental Logic,* in which Husserl says of logical meanings, "Thus they can be found in an Objective duration by everyone, can be regeneratively understood in the same sense by everyone, are intersubjectively identifiable, are factually existent even when no one is thinking them" (Hua XVII, §8, p. 30; trans. D. Cairns, *Formal and Transcendental Logic* [The Hague: Martinus Nijhoff, 1969], 34). And Hua XXVI, 3; French trans. Husserl, *Sur la théorie de la signification,* 55: "Acts conferring meaning are fleeting lived experiences; meaning itself is an ideal unity, atemporal, identical to itself like all ideas."

28. Hua XXVI, p. 31; French trans. *Sur la théorie de la signification,* 54 (my emphasis).

29. Gottlob Frege, "Thought," in *The Frege Reader* (Oxford: Blackwell, 2007), 344.

30. See LU I, §31; Hua XIX, 1, p. 105; *Logical Investigations*, vol. 1, 230. "The genuine identity that we here assert is none other than the *identity of the species* [*Spezies*]."

31. Heidegger, GA 21, p. 61; trans. T. Sheehan and R. Lilly, *Logic: The Question of Truth* (Bloomington: Indiana University Press, 2010), 51; see also GA 21, pp. 73–74.

32. Hua XXVI, p. 217; French trans. *Sur la théorie de la signification*, 273 n1.

33. Wittgenstein, *Logische Untersuchungen*, 1, §243.

34. More precisely, *Phantasiebegleitungen*, "imaginary accompaniments," LU I, §17; Hua XIX, 1, p. 68; *Logical Investigations*, vol. 1, 207.

35. LU I, §20; Hua XIX, 1, p. 74; *Logical Investigations*, vol. 1, 210.

36. LU II, §5; Hua XIX, 1, p. 123; *Logical Investigations*, vol. 1, 245. For this relation between the pure laws governing ideal objects and the norms corresponding to them, see Hua XXVIII, pp. 48–49; French trans. *Leçons sur l'éthique et la théorie de la valeur (1908–1914)*, 124.

37. LU IV, §12; Hua XIX, 1, p. 336; *Logical Investigations*, vol. 2, 68.

38. LU VI, §7; Hua XIX, 2, p. 561; *Logical Investigations*, vol. 2, 203.

39. Wittgenstein, *Zettel*, §420 and §422. See below, chapter 19.

40. LU I, §12; Hua XIX, 1, p. 52; *Logical Investigations*, vol. 1, 197.

41. Ibid.

42. Non-declarative acts, such as questions, orders, or requests, are analyzed in §68–70 of the "Fifth Logical Investigation." See below, chapter 21.

43. LU IV, §7; Hua XIX, 1, p. 320; *Logical Investigations*, vol. 2, 59.

44. LU I, title of §34.

45. LU I, §15; Hua XIX, 1, p. 60; *Logical Investigations*, vol. 1, 202.

46. LU IV, §12; Hua XIX, 1, p. 334; *Logical Investigations*, vol. 2, 67.

47. G. Frege, "Über Sinn und Bedeutung," trans. P. T. Geach and M. Black, "Sense and Reference," *The Philosophical Review* 57, no. 3 (May 1948): 210.

48. LU I, §15; Hua XIX, 1, p. 58; *Logical Investigations*, vol. 1, 201: "'Meaning' [*Bedeutung*] is further used by us as synonymous with 'sense' [*Sinn*]."

49. LU I, §13; Hua XIX, 1, pp. 54–55; *Logical Investigations*, vol. 1, 198.

50. See Jitendra Nath Mohanty, "Husserl and Frege: A New Look at Their Relationship," in Hubert L. Dreyfus, *Husserl, Intentionality and Cognitive Science* (Cambridge, Mass.: MIT Press, 1982), 43–52.

51. LU I, §9; Hua XIX, 1, p. 44; *Logical Investigations*, vol. 1, 192.

52. Ibid.

53. LU I, §14; Hua XIX, 1, p. 56; *Logical Investigations*, vol. 1, 199. "Relation to an actually given objective correlate, which fulfills the meaning-intention, is *not* essential to an expression."

54. LU VI, §63; Hua XIX, 2, p. 721; *Logical Investigations*, vol. 2, 312.

55. LU II, §24; Hua XIX, 1, p. 172; *Logical Investigations*, I, 278.

56. LU I, §9; Hua XIX, 1, p. 45; *Logical Investigations*, vol. 1, 321 n4.

57. LU VI, §40; Hua XIX, 2, p. 659; *Logical Investigations*, vol. 2, 272.

58. LU II, §8; Hua XIX, 1, p. 130; *Logical Investigations*, vol. 1, 250.

59. LU VI, §43; Hua XIX, 2, p. 667; *Logical Investigations*, vol. 2, 278.

60. LU VI, §45; Hua XIX, 2, p. 671; *Logical Investigations*, vol. 2, 280.

61. LU VI, §43; Hua XIX, 2, p. 666; *Logical Investigations*, vol. 2, 277.

62. LU V, §28; Hua XIX, 1, p. 46; *Logical Investigations*, vol. 2, 139.

63. LU VI, §44; Hua XIX, 2, p. 669; *Logical Investigations*, vol. 2, 279.

64. See J. L. Austin, "Truth," in *Philosophical Papers*, 132–33.

65. For Reinach, states of affairs exist independently of statements and even of their possibility. See "Zur Theorie des negativen Urteils" (1911), in *Sämtliche Werke*, I, pp. 95–140; French trans. M. de Launay, "Théorie du jugement négatif," *Revue de métaphysique et de morale* 101 (1996): 383–436. See also Barry Smith, "An Essay on Formal Ontology," *Grazer Philosophische Studien* 6, (1978): 39–62, which defends a position close to Reinach's, and, by the same author, "Introduction to A. Reinach: 'On the Theory of Negative Judgements,'" in *Parts and Moments: Studies on Logic and Formal Ontology* (Munich: Philosophia Verlag, 1982), 294.

66. LU V, §34; Hua XIX, 1, p. 484; *Logical Investigations*, vol. 2, 276.

67. LU V, §34; Hua XIX, 1, p. 481; *Logical Investigations*, vol. 2, 150.

68. LU V, §34; Hua XIX, 1, p. 482; *Logical Investigations*, vol. 2, 150.

69. LU VI, §14 (a); Hua XIX, 2, p. 588; *Logical Investigations*, vol. 2, 219–20.

70. LU VI, §38; Hua XIX, 2, p. 651; *Logical Investigations*, vol. 2, 263.

71. LU VI, §38; Hua XIX, 2, p. 651; *Logical Investigations*, vol. 2, 263. See also *Prolegomena*, §6, Hua XVIII, p. 29; *Logical Investigations*, vol. 1, 17.

72. LU IV, §11; Hua XIX, 1, p. 330; *Logical Investigations*, vol. 2, 64.

73. LU VI, §5; Hua XIX, 2, p. 555; *Logical Investigations*, vol. 2, 198.

74. Ludwig Wittgenstein, *The Blue and Brown Books* (Oxford: Basil Blackwell, 1958), 108–9.

75. As Frege points out in a letter of November 1, 1906, to Husserl, predication becomes the subsuming of an object under a concept (Edmund Husserl and Gottlob Frege, *Correspondance*, trans. G. Granel [Mauvezin: Trans Europ Repress, 1987], 43).

76. Whence the famous paradox: when a concept is named, it is no longer a concept: "the concept *horse*" is a saturated expression that, as such, stands in for an object and not a concept. Hence: "the concept *horse* is not a concept" (Gottlob Frege, "On Concept and Object," *Mind* 60, no. 238 [April 1951]: 172).

77. For Frege, sense (or thoughts) are only linguistic in a contingent manner, as Frege suggests it in a letter of November 1906 to Husserl: "The first duty of the logician consists in freeing himself from language [*Sprache*]" (Edmund Husserl and Gottlob Frege, *Correspondance*, 43, trans. modified).

78. Dummett, *Origins of Analytic Philosophy*, 26–27.

79. Hua III, 1, §129, p. 299; trans. F. Kersten, *Ideas I*, 311.

80. Dagfinn Føllesdal, "Husserl's Notion of Noema," *The Journal of Philosophy* 66, no. 20 (October 16, 1969): 681.

81. Hua V, p. 89; trans. Klein and Pohl, *Phenomenology and the Foundations of the Sciences*, 76.

82. Hua III, 1, §124, p. 285; trans. F. Kersten, *Ideas I*, 294 (my emphasis).

83. *Cahiers de Royaumont: La philosophie analytique*, 93; trans. James Hatley, *Texts and Dialogues: Maurice Merleau-Ponty*, 65 (trans. modified—Tr.).

84. LU II, §24; Hua XIX, 1, p. 172; *Logical Investigations,* vol. 1, 278.

85. On the preconceptual nature of perception, which I will revisit for a more ample treatment, see Hua III, 1, §133, p. 305; trans. F. Kersten, *Ideas I,* 317, where Husserl says that the concept of perceptual "sense" contains "nothing pertaining to expression and conceptual signification." See also LU VI, §5; Hua XIX, 2, p. 555; *Logical Investigations,* vol. 2, 198: "perception does not need a "'conceptual' mediation [*'Begriffliche' Vermittlung*]." These assertions have as their counterpart that expression alone confers the form of the conceptual on the noema: "the form of the conceptual [*der Form des Begrifflichen*] . . . is introduced with "the expression" (Hua III, 1, §124, p. 287; *Ideas I,* 296).

86. R. Bernet, *La vie du sujet* (Paris: Presses Universitaires de France, 1994), 86.

87. Hua XVII, "Ergänzender Text IV, " p. 373.

88. Gottlob Frege, "Thought," in *The Frege Reader* (Oxford: Blackwell, 2007), 343.

89. Dummett, *Origins of Analytic Philosophy,* 96–97.

90. On the "*expressibility thesis,*" see David Smith and Ronald McIntyre, *Husserl and Intentionality* (Dordrecht: Reidel, 1982), 182ff.; and "Husserl's Identification of Meaning and Noema," in H. Dreyfus, *Husserl, Intentionality and Cognitive Science* (Cambridge, Mass.: MIT Press, 1982), 87. This is the "reasoning" that gives their paper its title: "We now see that every Sinn is expressible, hence [*sic*] (at least potentially) a *Bedeutung.*" The reader may consult the remarks by François Rivenc, with which I concur: "Husserl avec et contre Frege," *Les Études philosophiques* 1 (1995): 20–22; trans. Elizabeth Davis, "Husserl, With and Against Frege," *The Harvard Review of Philosophy* (Spring 1996): 100–101.

Chapter 5

1. Husserl, LU VI, §40; trans. Findlay, *Logical Investigations,* vol, 2, 272 (trans. modified—Tr.).

2. Tugendhat, *Vorlesung zur Einführung in die sprachanalytische Philosophie,* 77; *Traditional and Analytical Philosophy: Lectures on the Philosophy of Language* (Cambridge, Eng.: Cambridge University Press, 1982), 55.

3. Tugendhat, *Vorlesungen,* 131; *Traditional and Analytical Philosophy,* 97.

4. Tugendhat, *Vorlesungen,* 131; *Traditional and Analytical Philosophy,* 96.

5. Tugendhat, *Vorlesungen,* 87; *Traditional and Analytical Philosophy,* 63.

6. Ludwig Wittgenstein, *Philosophical Investigations,* Part I, §43 (Oxford: Blackwell, 1998), 20e.

7. Tugendhat, *Vorlesungen,* 134–35; *Traditional and Analytical Philosophy,* 99.

8. Tugendhat, *Vorlesungen,* 135; *Traditional and Analytical Philosophy,* 100.

9. Tugendhat, *Vorlesungen,* 139; *Traditional and Analytical Philosophy,* 103.

10. Tugendhat, "Prefazione all'edizione italiana," in *Introduzione alla filosofia analitica* (Genoa: Gasa Editrice Marietti, 1989), 6.

11. Husserl, LU I, §12; Hua XIX, 1, p. 52; *Logical Investigations,* vol. 1, 197.

12. Tugendhat, *Vorlesungen,* 134; *Traditional and Analytical Philosophy,* 99.

13. Ibid.

14. Ludwig Wittgenstein, *Tractatus Logico-Philosophicus* (New Jersey: Humanities, 1974), 5 (proposition 2.01).

15. One might question the way Tugendhat uses "concrete" (*konkrete*) in reference to objects in the *Tractatus*, since Wittgenstein hardly passes judgment on the nature of these objects. Tugendhat relies mainly on proposition 2.03, which asserts that "in a state of affairs objects fit into one another like the links of a chain" (Tugendhat, *Vorlesungen*, 163; *Traditional and Analytical Philosophy*, 123).

16. Tugendhat, *Vorlesungen*, 163; *Traditional and Analytical Philosophy*, 123 (referencing Wittgenstein's *Tractatus*, proposition 2).

17. Tugendhat, *Vorlesungen*, 162ff.; *Traditional and Analytical Philosophy*, 122ff. This difficulty is insoluble in the *Tractatus* for another reason as well. Wittgenstein conceives of objects from which the state of affairs is constituted as "simple" objects, but never says *in what respect* they are simple. Now, nothing is simple *simpliciter*. As the later Wittgenstein will insist, the grammar of "simple" requires that we specify *in what respect* (for what purpose, from the point of view of what interest, in keeping with what need) something is said to be "simple."

18. Tugendhat, *Vorlesungen*, 143; *Traditional and Analytical Philosophy*, 107.

19. Bertrand Russell, "On Denoting," in *Logic and Knowledge: Essays, 1901–1950*, ed. R. C. Marsh (London: Routledge, 2001), 39–56.

20. Wittgenstein, *Tractatus*, 4.0312. Hence there are no logical objects (*Tractatus* 4.441 and 5.4).

21. I will not enter here into the difficult question of what explains this situation. Husserl acknowledges the importance of "the mathematization of the old formal logic" at least in its Boolean version, in opposition to its detractors (Hermann Lotze or Wilhelm Windelband) (Hua XXIV, p. 162); and at the same time, he has always maintained a difference in principle between "the logic of the mathematicians and the logic of the philosophers" (Hua XXIV, p. 163).

22. LU VI §51; *Logical Investigations*, vol. 2, 291.

23. Tugendhat, *Vorlesungen*, 151; *Traditional and Analytical Philosophy*, 114.

24. Actually, Husserl, because he considers that all propositions have the form "S is P," tends to express the state of affairs differently: the state of affairs (obtained through nominalization) corresponding to the proposition "this paper is white" is "the being white of this paper" (see LU, VI, §40; *Logical Investigations*, vol. 2, 273). But Tugendhat's transposition is legitimate. It frees Husserl's doctrine from its initial limitation.

25. Husserl, *Ideen I*, §3, trans. *Ideas I*, 10; quoted by Tugendhat, *Vorlesungen*, 151 (note), trans. *Traditional and Analytical Philosophy*, 114 n9. See also Hua XVII, p. 64; trans. *Formal and Transcendental Logic*, 73: "its concept of an object [that of formal ontology] is the most universal (that of any substrate whatever in possible determining predications)." And Hua XXVIII, p. 9: "all that can become the subject of a true statement" is an object.

26. Tugendhat, *Vorlesungen*, 154; *Traditional and Analytical Philosophy*, 116.

27. Ludwig Wittgenstein, *Tagebücher 1914–1916* (Frankfurt am Main: Suhrkamp, 1984); Eng. trans. G. E. M. Anscombe, *Notebooks 1914–1916* (Oxford: Blackwell, 1979), 107; see *Tractatus*, 3.144.

28. Ludwig Wittgenstein, *The Big Typescript: TS 213*, German-English Scholar's Edition, ed. and trans. C. Grant Luckhardt and M. A. E. Aue (Malden, Mass.: Blackwell, 2005), 142. That Husserl was not sufficiently attentive to this aspect is evinced by his assertion that in the sentence "*That rain has set in at last will delight the farmers*," in which the nominal expression can be replaced by "that," "*that* as it were, points a finger to the state of affairs; it therefore means this same state of affairs" (LU V, §36; Hua XIX, 1, p. 492; *Logical Investigations*, vol. 2, 155–56). At this point the question should be asked: What state of affairs?

29. In the judgment of perception, one manuscript specifies, "a certain explication [*Explikation*] of perception takes place (that is, of the perceptual given as such) in a certain 'articulation and categorial formation'" (Husserl, Ms. K II 2/85a).

30. The pertinent concept of completeness is that of Frege, not Husserl. Indeed, Husserl does not accept Frege's contextual principle (see LU IV, §4; Hua XIX, 1, p. 312; trans. *Logical Investigations* vol. 2, 54–55, in which he proposes a "different interpretation" from the one that asserts that "only the whole expression really has a meaning"). Therefore he would also refuse to say that the expression "that *p*" is incomplete, and "*p*" complete. On his view, a nominal expression is complete (LU V, §34; Hua XIX, 1, p. 481; *Logical Investigations*, vol. 2, 151), or, according to a looser acceptation of "complete," categorematic expressions as a whole are complete (LU IV, §7; Hua XIX, 1, p. 319; *Logical Investigations*, vol. 2, 59). But this argument cannot prevail against Tugendhat, because even for Husserl the expressions "that *p*" and "*p*" have different meanings: the first is nominalized, the second isn't. (Nevertheless, in Husserl one sometimes finds an assertion that anticipates the contextual principle: "the nominal object . . . derives from the corresponding state of affairs, which has an intrinsic priority as regards authenticity"; LU V, §35; Hua XIX, 1, p. 488; *Logical Investigations*, vol. 2, 154.).

31. Tugendhat, *Vorlesungen*, 155; *Traditional and Analytical Philosophy*, 117

32. Tugendhat, *Vorlesungen*, 157; *Traditional and Analytical Philosophy*, 118.

33. LU I, §12; Hua, XIX, 1, p. 52; *Logical Investigations*, vol. 1, 197; quoted in Tugendhat, *Vorlesungen*, 145.

34. Tugendhat, *Vorlesungen*, 155; *Traditional and Analytical Philosophy*, 117.

35. Ibid.

36. Hua XIX, 2, p. 661; *Logical Investigations*, vol. 2, 274–75. Perceived sensible objects can be simple or complex; the simple ideal objects are formal and material essences; the complex ideal objects are states of affairs.

37. Hua XIX, 1, p. 461; *Logical Investigations*, vol. 2, 139.

38. Hua XIX, 2, p. 669; *Logical Investigations*, vol. 2, 279.

39. Hua XIX, 2, pp. 669–70; *Logical Investigations*, vol. 2, 279.

40. Hua XIX, 2, p. 684; *Logical Investigations*, vol. 2, 289.

41. Tugendhat, *Vorlesungen*, 162; *Traditional and Analytical Philosophy*, 122.

42. On this distinction between what is sheer nonsense (*Unsinn*), such as the expression "green is or" and what, while conforming to logical grammar, is a contradiction—either formal (*Widersinn*) or material, see LU IV, §12 to §14; *Logical Investigations*, vol. 2, 67–74.

43. LU I, §15; Hua XIX, 1, p. 61; *Logical Investigations*, vol. 1, 202.

44. LU I, §15; Hua XIX, 1, p. 60; *Logical Investigations*, vol. 1, 202.

45. LU I, §12; Hua XIX, 1, p. 54; *Logical Investigations*, vol. 1, 198 (trans. modified—Tr.).

46. "That the Reichstag has been opened" is a name, he says (LU V, §34; Hua XIX, 1, p. 481; *Logical Investigations*, vol. 2, 150).

47. LU V, §34; Hua XIX, 1, p. 482; *Logical Investigations*, vol. 2, 150.

48. Ibid.

49. LU V, §35; Hua XIX, 1, p. 485; *Logical Investigations*, vol. 2, 152 (trans. modified).

50. LU V, §36; Hua XIX, 1, p. 494; *Logical Investigations*, vol. 2, 156–57.

51. LU V, §36; Hua XIX, 1, pp. 491–92; *Logical Investigations*, vol. 2, 156 (trans. modified—Tr.).

52. LU V, §36; Hua XIX, 1, p. 491; *Logical Investigations*, vol. 2, 156 (trans. modified—Tr.).

53. LU V, §36; Hua XIX, 1, p. 495; *Logical Investigations*, vol. 2, 157 (trans. modified—Tr.).

54. Tugendhat, *Vorlesungen*, 150; *Traditional and Analytical Philosophy*, 112–13.

55. Ibid., 155; trans., 117.

56. Ibid., 158; trans., 120.

57. LU I, §34; Hua XIX, 1, p. 108; *Logical Investigations*, vol. 1, 232 (bracketed material as added by C. Romano).

58. Tugendhat, *Vorlesungen*, 162; *Traditional and Analytical Philosophy*, 122.

59. LU III, §2; Hua XIX, 1, p. 23; *Logical Investigations*, vol. 2, 5.

60. LU VI, §48; Hua XIX, 2, p. 68; *Logical Investigations*, vol. 2, 287.

61. LU VI, §48; Hua XIX, 2, p. 684; *Logical Investigations*, vol. 2, 288.

62. LU VI, §48; Hua XIX, 2, p. 684; *Logical Investigations*, vol. 2, 288–89.

63. LU VI, §48; Hua, XIX, 2, p. 684; *Logical Investigations*, vol. 2, 289.

64. Tugendhat, *Vorlesungen*, 172; *Traditional and Analytical Philosophy*, 130.

65. Tugendhat, *Vorlesungen*, 170; *Traditional and Analytical Philosophy*, 129 (bracketed material as added by CR).

66. Heidegger, "Neue Forschungen über die Logik (1912)," in *Frühe Schriften*, GA 1, p. 17–43; trans. by T. J. Kisiel, ed. T. Sheehan, "Recent Research in Logic," in *Becoming Heidegger: On the Trail of His Early Occasional Writings, 1910–1927* (Evanston, Ill.: Northwestern University Press, 2007), 30–44.

67. Heidegger, *Sein und Zeit*, 160; trans. *Being and Time*, 202.

68. Heidegger, *Einführung in die Metaphysik*, GA 40, p. 197; trans. Gregory Fried and Richard Polt, *Introduction to Metaphysics* (New Haven, Conn.: Yale University Press, 2000), 201.

69. Tugendhat, *Vorlesungen*, 174.

70. LU VI, §47; Hua XIX, 2, p. 679; *Logical Investigations*, vol. 2, 287: "real in the most basic [*ursprünglichsten*] sense of the word" means perceived; for example, "We define the real object directly as being the possible object of a straightforward percept [*Wahrnehmung*]."

71. Hua XII, pp. 203–4; *Philosophy of Arithmetic*, trans. Dallas Willard (Kluwer Academic, 2003), 216.

72. LU IV, §8; Hua XIX, 1, p. 321; *Logical Investigations*, vol. 2, 59.

73. LU VI, §48; Hua XIX, 2, p. 683; *Logical Investigations*, vol. 2, 288.

74. Ibid.

75. LU VI, §48; Hua XIX, 2, p. 684; *Logical Investigations*, vol. 2, 288–89.

76. LU VI, §48; Hua XIX, 2, pp. 684–85; *Logical Investigations*, vol. 2, 289 (trans. modified—Tr.).

Chapter 6

The epigraph is from R. M. Hare, "Philosophical Discoveries," *Mind* 69 (1960): 147.

1. M. Clavelin, "La première doctrine de la signification du Cercle de Vienne," *Les Études philosophiques* 4 (973): 481.

2. P. Jacob, *L'Empirisme logique: ses antécédents, ses critiques* (Paris: Minuit, 1980), 111.

3. Saul Kripke, *Naming and Necessity* (Cambridge, Mass.: Harvard University Press, 1980), 102–3.

4. Kantianism, to the extent that it has tended to limit the scope of the *a priori* by confining it to the human *Gemüt*; hence the accusations of psychologism and anthropologism. See above, chapter 1.

5. Hua IX, p. 86; *Phenomenological Psychology*, trans. Scanlon, 65 (trans. modified—Tr.).

6. Heidegger, *Sein und Zeit*, 50, n1; *Being and Time*, 490, n. x.

7. M. Schlick, "Gibt es ein materiales A priori?" in *Wissenschaftlicher Jahresbericht der Philosophischen Gesellschaft an der Universität zu Wien: Ortsgruppe Wien der Kant-Gesellschaft für das Vereinsjahr 1931/32* (Vienna, 1932), 55–65. I have, like the majority of interpreters, followed the more easily accessible text, in English translation, "Is There a Factual *A Priori?*" in *Readings in Philosophical Analysis*, ed. Feigl and Sellars (New York: Appelton Century Crofts, 1949), 277–85.

8. M. Schlick, "Gibt es intuitive Erkenntnis?"; English trans., "Is There an Intuitive Knowledge?" in *Philosophical Papers*, vol. 1 (Dordrecht: D. Reidel, 1979), 146.

9. LU III, §11; Hua XIX, 1, p. 256; trans. *Logical Investigations*, vol. 2, 19.

10. Hua XVII, §98, p. 255 n1; trans. Cairns, *Formal and Transcendental Logic*, 258 n1.

11. See Bolzano, *Wissenschaftslehre*, §148, in *Gesamtausgabe* (Stuttgart-Bad Canstatt: Frommann-Holzboog Verlag, 1969), I, 12/1, pp. 140ff. Husserl considered Bolzano to be "one of the greatest logicians of all time" (Hua XVIII, p. 227; *Logical Investigations*, vol. 1, 142). On Husserl's ties to Bolzano, see J. Benoist, *L'a priori conceptuel, Bolzano, Husserl, Schlick* (Paris: Vrin, 1999), chapters 6 and 7; Paolo Bucci, *Husserl e Bolzano*.

12. LU III, §12; Hua XIX, 1, p. 259; *Logical Investigations*, vol. 2, 21.

13. LU III, §12; Hua, XIX, 1, p. 260; *Logical Investigations*, vol. 2, 21.

14. LU III, §11; Hua, XIX, 1, p. 257; *Logical Investigations*, vol. 2, 20.

15. LU III, §11; Hua, XIX, 1, p. 258; *Logical Investigations*, vol. 2, 20.

16. LU III, §11; Hua, XIX, 1, p. 257; *Logical Investigations*, vol. 2, 19.

17. LU III, §11; Hua, XIX, 1, p. 257; *Logical Investigations,* vol. 2, 19–20.

18. LU III, §11; Hua, XIX, 1, p. 258; *Logical Investigations,* vol. 2, 20.

19. Kant, *Kritik der reinen Vernunft,* Ak. III, 33; A 6 / B10; trans. F. Max Müller, *Critique of Pure Reason* (Garden City, N.Y.: Doubleday, Anchor Books, 1966), 7.

20. Peter Simons, "Wittgenstein, Schlick and the A Priori," republished in Peter Simons, *Philosophy and Logic in Central Europe from Bolzano to Tarski,* as chapter 15 (The Hague: Martinus Nijhoff, 1992), 374.

21. W. V. O. Quine, "Two Dogmas of Empiricism," in *From a Logical Point of View* (Cambridge, Mass.: Harvard University Press, 1953).

22. M. Schlick, "Form and Content: An Introduction to Philosophical Thinking," in *Gesammelte Aufsätze, 1926–1936* (Vienna: Gerold, 1938), 231.

23. M. Schlick, "Is There a Factual *A Priori?*" in *Philosophical Papers, 1925–1936* (Dordrecht: Reidel, 1979), vol. 2, 164.

24. Ibid.

25. M. Scheler, *Der Formalismus in der Ethik und die materiale Wertethik,* in *Gesammelte Werke,* vol. 2 (Berne: Francke Verlag, 1966), 73; trans. Manfred S. Frings and Ronald L. Funk, *Formalism in Ethics and Non-Formal Ethics of Values: A New Attempt toward the Foundation of an Ethical Personalism* (Evanston, Ill.: Northwestern University Press, 1985), 54.

26. Schlick, "Is There a Factual *A Priori?*" 162.

27. Schlick, "Form and Content," 227.

28. Ibid.

29. Schlick, "Is There a Factual *A Priori?*" 166.

30. Ibid., 162–63.

31. Schlick, "Form and Content," 181.

32. Ibid.

33. Schlick, "Is There a Factual *A Priori?*" 166.

34. Ibid., 162.

35. See C. Romano, "Une phénoménologie du néant est-elle possible?" in *Il y a* (Paris: Presses Universitaires de France, 2003); trans. Michael Smith, "Is a Phenomenology of Nothingness Possible?" in *There Is: The Event and the Finitude of Appearing* (New York: Fordham University Press, 2015). Husserl's annoyance is understandable: he emphasizes concerning the "dismissive criticism" present in Schlick's *Allgemeine Erkenntnistheorie,* "the falsity . . . of his exposition of the meaning of phenomenology" (LU VI, "Vorwort" [1920]; Hua XIX, 2, 535–36; *Logical Investigations,* vol. 2, 179).

36. Ibid., 169.

37. Wittgenstein, *Tractatus,* propositions 6.37 and 6.375, respectively, pp. 70, 71.

38. Ibid., proposition 6.3751; p. 71.

39. David Hume, *An Enquiry concerning Human Understanding,* ed. Tom L. Beauchamp (Oxford: Oxford University Press, 1999), 108.

40. Ibid., 211.

41. Schlick, "Is There a Factual *A Priori?*" 168.

42. Ibid., 169.

43. As opposed to Wittgenstein, Schlick seems to make no distinction

between a senseless (*sinnlos*) proposition, as are the tautologies in the *Tractatus*, and a proposition that is nonsense (*unsinnig*). Hence he also fails to consider the problem of the logical status of the propositions he uses—a problem that had led Wittgenstein to say that he who would understand him must "throw away the ladder after he had climbed up it" (*Tractatus*, 6.54).

44. Schlick, "Is There a Factual *A Priori?*" 170.

45. Ibid., 166.

46. Ibid., 165.

47. Kant, *Kritik der reinen Vernunft*, Ak. III, 142; A 151/B190; *Critique of Pure Reason*, 129.

48. LU VI, §66; Hua XIX, 2, p. 732; *Logical Investigations*, vol. 2, 319: "It was ominous that Kant (to whom we nonetheless feel ourselves quite close) should have thought he had done justice to the domain of pure logic in the narrowest sense, by saying that it fell under the principle of pure contradiction."

49. Ibid.

50. H. Hahn, "Logik, Mathematik und Naturerkennen," *Einheitswissenschaft*, no. 2 (Vienna, 1932); trans. A. J. Ayer, *Logical Positivism* (New York: Free, 1959), 153.

51. Wittgenstein realized this very soon, and it induced him, in his "Some Remarks on Logical Form" (1929) to abandon the thesis in the *Tractatus* (6.3751) according to which "the statement that a point in the visual field has two different colors at the same time is a contradiction." See below, chapter 7.

52. Schlick, "Is There a Factual *A Priori?*" 162.

53. See Barry Smith, "An Essay on Material Necessity," in Philip Hanson and Bruce Hunter, *Return of the A Priori*, in *Canadian Journal of Philosophy, Supplementary Volume 18* (Calgary, Can.: University of Calgary Press, 1992), 314.

54. H. Putnam, "The Analytic and the Synthetic," in *Mind, Language and Reality: Philosophical Papers*, vol. 2, 33–69. See also Putnam's *The Collapse of the Fact/Value Dichotomy* (Cambridge, Mass.: Harvard University Press, 2002), 12–13.

55. Putnam, *The Collapse of the Fact/Value Dichotomy*, 13.

56. Simons, "Wittgenstein, Schlick and the A Priori," 376.

57. Husserl, *Ideen I*, Hua III, 1, §16, pp. 36–37; trans. F. Kersten, *Ideas I*, p. 31. See also §14, for the difference between "full substrates" and "empty substrates," in which there is also an implicit reference to Bolzano.

Chapter 7

The epigraph is from B. Russell, *An Inquiry into Meaning and Truth* (London: Allen and Unwin, 1940), 82.

1. Peter M. S. Hacker, *Insight and Illusion: Wittgenstein on Philosophy and the Metaphysics of Experience* (Oxford: Oxford University Press, 1972), 86.

2. Wilhelm Schapp, *Beiträge zur Phänomenologie der Wahrnehmung*, 2nd ed. (Frankfurt am Main: Klostermann, [1910] 1981).

3. David Katz, *Die Erscheinungen der Farben und ihre Beeinflussung durch die individuelle Erfahrung* (Leipzig: Verlag von Johann Ambrosius Barth, 1911) trans.

R. B. MacLeod and C. W. Fox, *The World of Colour* (London: Routledge, 1999). We should also mention (although it does not belong to phenomenology) Meinong's text, "Bemerkungen über den Farbenkörper und das Mischungsgesetz" (1903) and the precursory works of Hering, *Zur Lehre von Lichtsinn* (Leipzig: Engelmann, 1905).

4. V. Descombes, *Le complément de sujet: Enquête sur le fait d'agir sur soi-même* (Paris: Gallimard, 2004), 12–13.

5. This equivalency is not specifically established in the *Tractatus*, but it follows from the structure of that work. See Wittgenstein, *ProtoTractatus—An Early Version of Tractatus Logico-Philosophicus*, ed. B. F. McGuiness, T. Nyberg, and G. H. von Wright (London: Routledge and Kegan Paul, 1971), proposition 4.44602.

6. Frank Ramsay stressed this point in his critical study of the *Tractatus* that appeared in 1923. It is possible that his critique may have played a role in Wittgenstein's evolution on this point. Ramsay asserts that "there is a great difficulty" in maintaining that "the only necessity is that of tautology, the only impossibility that of contradiction." This is why, Ramsay continues, "he [Wittgenstein] says that 'this is both red and blue' is a contradiction. This implies that the apparently simple concepts red, blue . . . are really complex and formally incompatible. He tries to show how this may be by analyzing them in terms of vibrations. But even assuming that the physicist may produce an analysis of what we mean by 'red' Mr. Wittgenstein is only reducing the difficulty to that of the *necessary* properties of space, time, and matter, or the ether . . . These necessary properties of space and time are hardly capable of a further reduction of this kind"; and, consequently, Ramsay concludes, "it is hard to see how that can be a formal tautology" (F. P. Ramsay, Review of Wittgenstein's *Tractatus Logico-Philosophicus*, in *Mind*, n.s., vol. 32, no. 128 [October 1923]: 473).

7. L. Wittgenstein, "Some Remarks on Logical Form," *Proceedings of the Aristotelian Society*, Suppl. vol. 9, p. 170.

8. Ibid.

9. Ibid.

10. Ibid., 163.

11. Hacker, *Insight and Illusion*, 89.

12. Ibid., 91.

13. Ibid.

14. Ibid., 94–95.

15. *Wittgenstein and the Vienna Circle: Conversations Recorded by Friedrich Waismann*, ed. Brian McGuinness, trans. Joachim Schulte (Oxford: Blackwell, 1983), 67–68.

16. P. Simons, "Wittgenstein, Schlick and the A Priori," 368 (trans. slightly modified—Tr.).

17. Ibid., 369.

18. *Wittgenstein and the Vienna Circle*, 63–64.

19. Ibid., 46.

20. M. Heidegger, "Was ist Metaphysik?" in *Wegmarken*, GA 9, p. 117; trans. "What Is Metaphysics?" in *Existence and Being* (Chicago: Henry Regnery, 1949), 372. Heidegger already insisted in the "Neuere Forschungen über Logik" of 1912

that what Frege says in his writings, particularly *Sinn und Bedeutung*, "cannot be neglected by any philosophy of mathematics" (GA 1, p. 20); but he specified that mathematical logic could not claim to solve properly philosophical problems: "mathematics and the mathematical treatment of logical problems reach their limit at the point where their concepts and methods fail, that is, at the precise point where their conditions of possibility are situated" (GA 1, p. 42).

21. *Wittgenstein and the Vienna Circle*, 46.

22. Wittgenstein, *Wiener Ausgabe*, IV, in *Bermerkungen zur Philosophie*, ed. M. von Nedo (Vienna: Springer-Verlag, 1995), 231. See also *The Big Typescript*, 341.

23. On this point, it is difficult to endorse Élisabeth Rigal's claim in her paper "Y a-t-il une phénoménologie wittgensteinienne?" (in *La Phénoménologie aux confins* [Mauvezin: Trans Europ Repress, 1992], 111), according to which the transition from a 1929 "physics/mathematics-based phenomenology" to a subsequent one "is based on the recognition of a synthetic *a priori*, a recognition that was a complete reversal."

24. G. E. Moore, "Wittgenstein's Lectures in 1930–33" (Part III), in *Mind*, n.s., vol. 64, no. 253 (January 1955): 22.

25. Wittgenstein's *Philosophical Investigations* states clearly what is at stake in the passage from the phenomenological to the grammatical investigation: "We feel as if we had to *penetrate* phenomena: our investigation, however, is directed not towards phenomena, but, as one might say, towards the '*possibilities*' of phenomena. We remind ourselves, that is to say, of the *kind of statement* that we make about phenomena. . . . Our investigation is therefore a grammatical one. . . . This may be called an "analysis" of our forms of expression" (I, §90). Its goal is none other than to understand the logic of our language (I, §93).

26. Wittgenstein, *Philosophical Investigations*, I, §497; Wittgenstein, *The Big Typescript*, 147: "Ohne Grammatik ist es nicht eine schlechte Sprache, sondern keine Sprache" and 185–86; Wittgenstein, *Philosophische Grammatik* in *Werkausgabe*, vol. 4 (Frankfurt am Main: Suhrkamp, 1984), 184; *Philosophical Grammar*, ed. Rush Rhees, trans. Anthony Kenny (Berkeley: University of California Press, 2005), 184–85.

27. "When a sentence is called senseless, it is not as it were its sense that is senseless. But a combination of words is being excluded from the language, withdrawn from circulation." (Wittgenstein, *Philosophical Investigations*, I, §500). See also Husserl, *Logical Investigations*, IV, §12–14.

28. Wittgenstein writes in §27 of his *Cambridge Lectures*, "Of course there isn't a philosophical grammar and ordinary English grammar, the former being more complete since it includes ostensive definitions such as the correlation of 'white' with several of its applications, Russell's theory of descriptions, etc. These are not to be found in ordinary grammar books; but this is not the important difference. The important difference is in the aims for which the study of grammar are pursued by the linguist and the philosopher . . . Our object is to get rid of certain puzzles. The grammarian has no interest in these; his aims and the philosopher's are different. We are pulling ordinary grammar to bits." *Wittgenstein's Lectures, Cambridge, 1932–1935: From the Notes of Alice Ambrose and Margaret Macdonald* (Amherst, N.Y.: Prometheus Books, 2001), 31.

29. Wittgenstein, *Philosophical Grammar,* 184.

30. L. Wittgenstein, *Remarks on Colour,* ed. G. E. M. Anscombe, trans. Linda L. McAlister and Margarete Schättle (Berkeley: University of California Press, [1977] 2007), I, §27, p. 6e.

31. LU III, §7; Hua XIX, 1, pp. 242–43; *Logical Investigations,* vol. 2, 12.

32. LU II, §5; Hua XIX, 1, p. 123; *Logical Investigations,* vol. 1, 245.

33. Wittgenstein, *Remarks on Colours,* I, §16, pp. 2e–3e.

34. Wittgenstein is not a conventionalist in the sense that became current with the Vienna Circle, that is, if conventionalism consists in maintaining that there are *truths* by convention. Grammatical conventions are not in the least to be considered as truths; as we have seen, they are norms of representation.

35. Of course in some texts, for example in §121 of the first part of *Philosophical Investigations,* Wittgenstein seems to reject all meta-philosophy.

36. Wittgenstein, *The Big Typescript,* 187–88.

37. Wittgenstein, *Philosophische Bemerkungen* (Oxford: Basil Blackwell, 1964); *Philosophical Remarks,* ed. Rush Rhees, trans. Raymond Hargreaves and Roger White (Charlottesville, Va.: InteLex, 2000), 53.

38. Wittgenstein, *The Big Typescript,* 188e.

39. Wittgenstein, *Notebooks, 1914–1916,* ed. George H. von Wright, trans. G. E. M. Anscombe (Chicago: University of Chicago Press, 1984), 55e.

40. *Wittgenstein and the Vienna Circle,* 183. And Wittgenstein, *Philosophical Investigations,* I, §128: "If one tried to advance *theses* in philosophy, it would never be possible to debate them, because everyone would agree to them."

41. Hilary Putnam, *Reason, Truth and History* (Cambridge, Eng.: Cambridge University Press, 1981), 110–13.

42. Wittgenstein, *Philosophical Investigations,* I, §133.

43. Hacker, *Insight and Illusion,* 139.

44. Ibid., 166–167.

45. Ibid., 181. Hacker refers here to the famous passage from Wittgenstein's *Remarks on the Foundations of Mathematics* (Cambridge, Mass: MIT Press, 1983), 65: "if you talk about essence—you are merely noting a convention. . . . To the depth that we see in the essence there corresponds the *deep* need for the convention" (I, §74).

46. *Wittgenstein's Lectures, Cambridge 1930–1932,* from the notes of J. King and D. Lee (Oxford: Blackwell, 1980), 8 (quoted by Bouveresse in *Langage, perception et réalité,* vol. 2, *Physique, phénoménologie et grammaire* [Nîmes: Éditions Jacqueline Chambon, 2004], 347).

47. *Wittgenstein's Lectures, Cambridge 1930–1932,* 12 (quoted by Bouveresse, *Langage, perception et réalité,* vol. 2, 374–75).

48. Bouveresse, *Langage, perception et réalité,* vol. 2, 416–17.

49. Ibid., 373.

50. Ibid., 420.

51. Wittgenstein, *The Big Typescript,* 184.

52. Ibid.

53. Bouveresse, *Langage, perception et réalité,* vol. 2, 377.

54. Wittgenstein, *Zettel*, §357–58; *Zettel*, trans. G. E. M. Anscombe (Berkeley: University of California Press, 2007), 64–65.

55. Bouveresse, *Langage, perception et réalité*, vol. 2, 418.

56. This phenomenological (or grammatical) sense of "primary color" differs, of course, from its use in describing the three basic colors of the additive color mixing (mixing of light) or that of the subtractive color mixing (mixing of chemical colors), which can be discovered only empirically.

57. G. E. Moore, "Wittgenstein's lectures in 1930–33," (Part II), *Mind*, n.s., vol. 63, no. 251 (July 1954): 298–99.

58. It seems therefore difficult to maintain, apropos of this same passage from *Zettel*, ("Do the systems reside in *our* nature or in the nature of things?—*Not* in the nature of numbers or colors") that Wittgenstein does not give here a clear-cut answer, and more specifically an answer of a purely anthropological sort. The color system is a manifold of rules belonging to our anthropological "background," which might be otherwise, and which nothing in reality justifies; this is indeed Wittgenstein's claim. As he says consistently in his writings: there is no nature of things, no nature of numbers and of colors; there are no essences, no necessities (in the strong, non-hypothetical sense) in nature or in our experience; they only exist in our linguistic conventions.

59. Wittgenstein, *Philosophical Investigations*, II, xii, p. 321. Another passage from *The Big Typescript*, repeated in *Zettel* (§331), clearly indicates that Wittgenstein doesn't only exclude a type of justification of grammar, built "on the model of justifying a proposition by referring to its verification." Once that idea has been rejected, the text continues as follows: "But still, can't one in some sense say that the grammar of the colour-words characterizes the world as it actually [*tatsächlich*] is?" And Wittgenstein's response is clearly negative: "One is inclined to say: Don't I really search in vain for a fifth primary colour? Don't we group the primary colours together because they are similar, or at least group colours together, as opposed to, say, shapes or tones, because they are similar? Or do I already have a preconceived idea in my head as a paradigm when I posit this classification of the world as the correct one?—An idea about which I can only say, for example: 'Yes, that's the way we look at things' or 'What we want is to create this kind of an image (of reality)'. For if I say: 'But the primary colours do have a certain similarity to each other'—where do I get the concept of this similarity from? Just as the concept of primary colour is nothing more than 'blue or red or green or yellow'—isn't the concept of that similarity also only given via the four colours? Indeed, aren't these concepts the same!—'Well, could one also combine red, green and circular?'—Why not?!" The phenomenologist would protest against such a suggestion, and even more against the idea that the primary colors have nothing more in common than an arbitrary use rule that could be formulated by the disjunction: "blue or red or green or yellow."

60. Wittgenstein, *Philosophical Remarks*, §219, trans. Maximilian A. E. Aue (Chicago: University of Chicago Press, 1975), 274.

61. Wittgenstein, *Philosophical Investigations*, I, §90.

62. David Bloor, in his paper "The Question of linguistic Idealism Revis-

ited," in *The Cambridge Companion to Wittgenstein* (Cambridge, Eng.: Cambridge University Press, 1996) defends the thesis that even Wittgenstein's partial idealism with respect to concepts is in fact complete idealism (361).

63. Wittgenstein, *Philosophical Investigations,* I, §372. See also I, §50.

64. Wittgenstein, *Remarks on Colour,* trans. G. E. M. Anscombe (Berkeley: University of California Press, 1977), III, §41, p. 22e; III, §309, 57e; III, §124, p. 32e.

65. E. Anscombe, "The Question of Linguistic Idealism," in *From Parmenides to Wittgenstein: Collected Philosophical Papers,* vol. 1 (Minneapolis: University of Minnesota Press, 1981), 122.

66. D. Katz, *Die Erscheinungen der Farben und ihre Beeinflussung durch die individuelle Erfahrung* (Leipzig, 1911), I, §4.

67. Wittgenstein, Ms 183, p. 64: "Wenn mein Name fortleben wird dann nur als der Terminus ad quem der grossen abendländlischen Philosophie. Gleichsam wie der Name dessen der die Alexandrinische Bibliothek verbrannt hat."

Chapter 8

The epigraph is from H. Putnam, *The Threefold Cord: Mind, Body, and World* (New York: Columbia University Press, 1999), 9.

1. Hua XVII, p. 333; *Formal and Transcendental Logic,* trans. Dorion Cairns (The Hague: Martinus Nijhoff, 1969), 338. See the entire §4 redacted by Oskar Becker, "Bemerkungen über Tautologie im Sinne der Logistik," in which Becker refers in a note to Wittgenstein's *Tractatus.*

2. Wittgenstein, *Philosophical Investigations,* I, §371.

3. Ibid., I, §383: "We are not analysing a phenomenon (e.g., thought) but a concept (e.g., that of thinking), and therefore the use of a word."

4. Wittgenstein, *Remarks on Colour,* trans. G. E. M. Anscombe (Berkeley: University of California Press, 1977), II §16, p. 16e.

5. Ibid., I, §53, p. 9e.

6. Ibid., II, §3, p. 15e. It is not surprising that certain texts *almost* seem to accredit the idea of a synthetic *a priori,* for example this passage from *Lectures on the Foundations of Mathematics*: "There are propositions regarded as synthetic *a priori,* like 'A patch cannot be at the same time both red and green.' This is not reckoned a proposition of logic. But the impossibility which it expresses is not a matter of experience—It is not a matter of what we have observed . . . People say, 'There is no such thing as reddish green.' There is no reason why we shouldn't call black reddish green. Someone might object that we don't recognize in black the constituents of red and green. And there is something in this, of course" (*Wittgenstein's Lectures on the Foundations of Mathematics,* ed. Cora Diamond [Cambridge, Eng.: Cambridge University Press, 1939], 232–33).

7. Wittgenstein, *Remarks on Colours,* p. 34; III, §133.

8. The same would apply to the opposition between green and red, or between yellow and blue. Wittgenstein, *Remarks on Colours,* III, §46: "Among the colours: Kinship and Contrast. (And that is logic)."

9. Wittgenstein, *Remarks on Colours,* III, §180 (trans. modified—Tr.).

10. Ibid., III, §106.

11. Ibid., III, §62.

12. Ibid., III, §65.

13. R. M. Boynton, "Colour, Hue and Wavelength"; quoted in Jonathan Westphal, *Colour: A Philosophical Introduction* (Basil Blackwell, 1987), 53.

14. Westphal, *Colour: A Philosophical Introduction,* 60.

15. Ibid., 50.

16. Ibid., 68.

17. Marie McGinn, "On Two Recent Accounts of Colour," *The Philosophical Quarterly* 41, no. 164, (1991): 323.

18. Wittgenstein, *Remarks on Colours,* I, §68.

19. Westphal, *Colour: A Philosophical Introduction,* 132.

20. Wittgenstein, *Remarks on Colours,* I, §19.

21. Runge (quoted partially by Wittgenstein, in *Remarks on Colours,* III, §94).

22. Wittgenstein, *Remarks on Colours,* I, §49.

23. Ibid., III, §147.

24. Ibid., I, §45.

25. Ibid., III, §146.

26. Ibid., III, §242.

27. Wittgenstein, *Philosophical Investigations,* I, §372.

28. Wittgenstein, *Wittgenstein's Lectures on the Foundations of Mathematics,* I, §73, p. 60 (trans. modified—Tr.).

29. Ibid., I, §74, p. 61.

30. [In English in the original—Tr.]

31. Westphal, *Colour: A Philosophical Introduction,* 36.

32. Ibid., 22–23.

33. David Katz, *Die Erscheinungsweisen der Farben und ihre Beeinflussung durch die individuelle Erfahrung* (Leipzig, 1911), §45; trans. R. B. MacLeod and C. W. Fox, *The World of Colour* (London: Routledge, 1999), 214.

34. C. L. Hardin, "Could White Be Green?" *Mind* 98, no. 390 (April 1989): 285.

35. Arthur Schopenhauer, *On Vision and Colors,* trans. Georg Stahl (New York: Princeton Architectural Press, 2010), 82–83.

36. See Evan Thompson, *Colour Vision: A Study in Cognitive Science and the Philosophy of Perception* (London: Routledge, 1995), 138.

37. Merleau-Ponty, *Phenomenology of Perception,* 53.

38. Hardin, "Could White Be Green?" 285–86.

39. D. H. Sanford, "The Possibility of Transparent White," *Analysis* 44, no. 4 (October 1986): 214.

40. René Descartes, *Meditationes de Prima Philosophia,* in *Oeuvres de Descartes,* ed. Charles Adam and Paul Tannery (abbreviated henceforth "AT"), (Paris, Vrin, reprint 1996, volume VII), 32.

41. See above, introduction to part 2.

42. *Conversations with Cézanne,* trans. J. L. Cochran, ed. M. Doran (Berkeley: University of California Press, 2001), 120.

43. Putnam, *Realism and Reason*, in *Philosophical Papers*, vol. 3 (Cambridge, Eng.: Cambridge University Press, 1985), 179.

44. Ludwig Wittgenstein, *Philosophische Bemerkungen* (Aus den Nachlaß herausgegeben von Rush Rhees), in *Werkausgabe*, vol. 2, p. 256; Ludwig Wittgenstein and Rush Rhees, *Philosophical Remarks*, trans. R. Hargreaves and R. White, edited from his posthumous writings by Rush Rhees (Oxford: Basil Blackwell, 1975), 256.

Chapter 9

The epigraph is from Edmund Husserl, LU II, §5; Hua XIX, 1, p. 123; *Logical Investigations*, vol. 1, 246.

1. LU II, §42; Hua XIX, 1, p. 223; *Logical Investigations*, vol. 1, 311 (trans. modified—Tr.).

2. Hua I, p. 105; *Cartesian Meditations*, trans. Dorion Cairns (The Hague: Martinus Nijhoff, 1973), 71.

3. John Locke, *An Essay concerning Human Understanding* (London: Penguin Classics, 1997), bk. 3, chap. 3, §6: "All things that exist are . . . particulars"; David Hume, *A Treatise of Human Nature* (London: Penguin Books, 1985), I, I, §7: "Every thing in nature is individual."

4. Locke, *An Essay Concerning Human Understanding*, bk. 3, chap. 3, §11.

5. Locke, *An Essay Concerning Human Understanding*, bk. 3, chap. 3, §7. Those who think of man in general "only leave out of the complex idea they had of Peter and James, Mary and Jane, that which is peculiar to each, and retain only what *is common* to them all" (my emphasis).

6. George Berkeley, *Principles of Human Knowledge and Three Dialogues between Hylas and Philonous* (New York: Penguin Classics, 1988), 42.

7. Hume, *A Treatise of Human Nature*, I, II, §7.

8. LU II, §34; Hua XIX, 1, p. 194; *Logical Investigations*, vol. 1, 292.

9. LU II, §11; Hua XIX, 1, p. 139; *Logical Investigations*, vol. 1, 255.

10. Ibid.

11. LU II, §4; Hua XIX, 1, p. 120; *Logical Investigations*, vol. 1, 243 (trans. modified—Tr.).

12. LU II, §3; Hua XIX, 1, pp. 117–18; *Logical Investigations*, vol. 1, 242.

13. Bertrand Russell, *The Problems of Philosophy* (Oxford University Press, 1912), 49–50.

14. LU II, §3; Hua XIX, 1, p. 118; *Logical Investigations*, vol. 1, 242.

15. LU II, §37; Hua XIX, 1, p. 200; *Logical Investigations*, vol. 1, 296.

16. There are other non-vicious regresses; for example, the regress of the truth: *p*; *p* is true; it is true that *p* is true; it is true that it is true that *p* is true, etc.

17. Locke, *An Essay concerning Human Understanding*, bk. 3, chap. 3, §11 (my emphasis).

18. Ibid., bk. 2, chap. 2, §8 (my emphasis).

19. Hume, *A Treatise of Human Nature*, I, II, §7.

20. John Stuart Mill, *System of Logic, Ratiocinative and Inductive*, ed. John M.

Robson, intro. R. F. McRae (Toronto: University of Toronto Press, London: Routledge and Kegan Paul, 1974), bk. 1, chap. 3, §11.

21. Hume, *A Treatise of Human Nature,* I, I, §7.

22. LU II, §5; Hua XIX, 1, p. 123; *Logical Investigations,* vol. 1, 246.

23. Hua IX, p. 83; trans. John Scanlon, *Phenomenological Psychology: Lectures, Summer Semester, 1925* (The Hague: Martinus Nijhoff, 1977), 62.

24. Hua I, p. 105; trans. Cairns, *Cartesian Meditations,* 71.

25. This presence in the flesh is the highest degree of intuitivity, which does not exclude that a mere re-presentation is already intuitive. The criterion of intuitivity givenness *in person,* which is quite distinct from givenness *in the flesh.* See above, chapter 2.

26. Hua III, 1, §3, p. 15; trans. F. Kersten, *Ideas Pertaining to a Pure Phenomenology, I,* 10.

27. Hua III, 1, p. 14; trans. F. Kersten, *Ideas I,* 9. On the universalization of the notion of object (or of "objecthood") see LU I, §9; Hua XIX, 1, p. 45 (note); *Logical Investigations,* vol. 1, 192. Hua XIX, 1, p. 45 (note) and see above, chapter 4.

28. Hua III, 1, §22, p. 47; trans. Kersten, *Ideas Pertaining to a Pure Phenomenology, I,* 41–41.

29. LU VI, §41; Hua XIX, 2, p. 662; *Logical Investigations,* vol. 2, 274.

30. Hua III, 1, §133, p. 305; trans. Kersten, *Ideas Pertaining to a Pure Phenomenology, I,* 317.

31. Hua XXVI, p. 13; trans. J. English, *Sur la théorie de la signification* (Paris: Vrin, 1995), 34.

32. It is impossible to conceive of Husserl's intuition of essences as an operation that could be accomplished by making abstraction of all linguistic substratums. As Adolf Reinach justly remarks, "When we aspire to essence-analysis, we will naturally set out from words and their significations. . . . Moreover, there is no need of special emphasis on the fact that the essence-analysis which is required is in no wise exhausted by investigations of significations" (Reinach, "Über Phänomenologie," 542; trans. Dallas Willard, "Concerning Phenomenology," *The Personalist,* 50, no. 2 [Spring 1969], 209–10).

33. Hua III, 1, §3, p. 15; *Ideas Pertaining to a Pure Phenomenology, I,* 10.

34. LU VI, §52; Hua XIX, 2, p. 691; *Logical Investigations,* vol. 2, 293: "Our consciousness of the universal has as satisfactory a basis in perception as it has in parallel imagination [*Einbildung*]."

35. E. Fink, "Die phänomenologische Philosophie E. Husserls in der gegenwärtigen Kritik," in E. Fink, *Studien zur Phänomenologie* (The Hague, 1966); trans. R. O. Elveton, "Husserl's Philosophy and Contemporary Criticism," in *The Phenomenology of Husserl: Selected Critical Readings* (Chicago: Quadrangle Books, 1970), 83.

36. The intuition to which Schlick refers, thanks to which "the knower becomes one with the known" ("Is there intuitive knowledge?" in *Philosophical Papers,* I, ed. Henk Mulder and Barbara van de Velde-Schlick, Dordrecht: D. Reidel, 1979,148) and which remains "incommunicable" remains entirely tributary to Bergsonism. It is Bergson, and not Husserl, who defines intuition as "the kind of intellectual sympathy by which one places oneself within an object in order

to coincide with what is unique in it and consequently inexpressible" (Bergson, *La Pensée et le mouvant,* in *Oeuvres* [Paris, Presses Universitaires de France, 1959], 1395; trans. T. E. Hulme [New York: Putnam's, 1912], 7).

37. Hua III, 1, §22, p. 47; *Ideas Pertaining to a Pure Phenomenology, I,* 41.

38. Hua III, 1, §22, p. 48; *Ideas Pertaining to a Pure Phenomenology, I,* 41.

39. Hua III, 1, §24, p. 51; *Ideas Pertaining to a Pure Phenomenology, I,* 44.

40. If intuiting is not thinking, conversely, the thought that is at the basis of knowledge cannot be entirely separated from its linguistic expression: "From the start, thought is accomplished as linguistic" (*Das Denken vollzieht sich von vornherein als sprachliches*) (Hua XVII, Ergänzender Text IV, p. 359).

41. Rudolf Bernet, Iso Kern, and Eduard Marbach, *Edmund Husserl: Darstellung seines Denkens* (Hamburg: Felix Meiner Verlag, 1996), 171; English trans. Rudolf Bernet, Iso Kern, and Eduard Marbach, foreword by Lester Embree, *An Introduction to Husserlian Phenomenology* (Evanston, Ill.: Northwestern University Press, 1993), 185.

42. A. Reinach, *Sämtliche Werke* 1, 542; English trans. by Dallas Willard, "Concerning Phenomenology," 210.

43. LU VI, §41; Hua XIX, 2, p. 661; *Logical Investigations,* vol. 2, 274.

44. Heidegger, GA 20, p. 66; trans. Theodor Kisiel, *History of the Concept of Time: Prolegomena* (Bloomington: Indiana University Press, 1992), 49.

45. LU III, §9; Hua XIX, 1, p. 249; *Logical Investigations,* vol. 2, 15.

46. Husserl, *Experience and Judgment,* §8 and §83.

47. Hua III, 1, §74, p. 155; *Ideas Pertaining to a Pure Phenomenology, I,* 166 (trans. modified—Tr.).

48. Eugenio Montale, "I Limoni," in *Ossi di Seppia* (Milan: Mondadori, 1948), 18.

49. Wittgenstein, *Philosophical Investigations,* I, §43, 20e–21e.

50. P. Geach, *Mental Acts* (London: Routledge and Kegan Paul, 1971), 12.

51. Wittgenstein, *Philosophical Investigations,* I, §208, p. 85e.

52. Ibid., I, §71, p. 34e.

53. LU III, §10; Hua XIX, 1, p. 253: "der Begriff . . . ist ein gegebener"; *Logical Investigations,* vol. 2, p. 17: "the notion . . . is given."

54. E. Anscombe, *Metaphysics and the Philosophy of Mind* (Oxford: Basil Blackwell, 1981), 16.

55. Wittgenstein, *Philosophical Investigations,* I, §155.

56. Richard Rorty, *Philosophy and the Mirror of Nature* (Princeton, N.J.: Princeton University Press, 1979), 34. See also Rorty's entry "Intuition," in *The Encyclopedia of Philosophy,* ed. Paul Edwards, vol. 4 (New York: Macmillan and Free Press, 1967), 204–12.

57. Wittgenstein, *Philosophical Investigations,* I, §213, p. 84e.

58. Ibid., I, §580, p. 155e.

59. On this internal relation between essence and its exemplifications, see Hua, III, 1, §7, p. 20; *Ideas: General Introduction to Pure Phenomenology,* trans. W. R. Boyce Gibson (New York: Collier Books, 1961), 15–16: ". . . the connection (itself eidetic) obtaining between individual object and essence according to which an essential composition [*Wesensbestand*] belongs to each individual object as *its* es-

sence, just as conversely to each essence there corresponds possible individuals which would be its factual singularizations."

60. It might of course be objected, from a Wittgensteinian point of view, that the *eidos* cannot be at once a rule and an object. Indeed, it is hard to see how an object could possess the normative function of a rule, that is, how something to which a word is applied (the object) could simultaneously be what *justifies* the application of the word (see Hacker and Backer, *Meaning and Understanding* [Chicago: University of Chicago Press, 1985], 354). But this type of objection overlooks the specificity of the Husserlian conceptuality. To Husserl, saying that the *eidos* is a rule that prescribes to the imagination's free variation of examples its possibilities and its impossibilities is nowise in contradiction with saying that the *eidos* is an object, that is, the correlate of a possible intuition—an intuition of a particular kind, since it is indissociable from the process of variation itself. The above-mentioned objection is only relevant if "object" is taken in the sense of sensible object, of an *exemplar* to which the word is applied.

61. *Dictées de Wittgenstein à Waismann et pour Schlick*, ed. Anthonia Soulez (Paris, Presses Universitaires de France, 1997), vol. 1, p. 90; Wittgenstein and Waismann, *The Voices of Wittgenstein: The Vienna Circle* ed. Gordon Baker (New York: Routledge, 2003), 173.

62. Ibid.

63. Hacker, *Insight and Illusion*, 283–309.

64. Wittgenstein, *Philosophical Investigations* (I, §66), trans. Anscombe, p. 31e.

65. David Armstrong, *Universals: An Opinionated Introduction* (Boulder, Colo.: Westview, 1989), 84.

66. Wittgenstein, *Philosophische Grammatik*, 75; ed. Rush Rhees, trans. Anthony Kenny, *Philosophical Grammar* (Berkeley: University of California Press, 1978), 75.

67. Ludwig Wittgenstein, *Preliminary Studies for the "Philosophical Investigations": Generally Known as the Blue and Brown Books* (Oxford: Blackwell, 1984), 135.

68. Ludwig Wittgenstein, *Culture and Value* (Chicago: University of Chicago Press, 1980), 54.

69. K. Bühler, *Sprachtheorie: Die Darstellungsfunktion der Sprache* (1934), 3rd ed. (Stuttgart: Lucius & Lucius, 1999), 222: "Ich stimme ihm z. B. nicht bei, wenn er auch die einfachen Farbbegriffe wie 'rot' und 'blau' zu den synchytischen Begriffen rechnet, sondern glaube, dass die Heringsche Analyse sachrichtiger ist. Aber bei 'Haus' oder 'Diebstahl' mag er [von Kries] recht haben."

70. *Wittgenstein and the Vienna Circle*, ed. Friedrich Weismann, trans. Brian McGuinness, Joachim Schulte (Oxford: Basil Blackwell, 1979), 183.

71. P. Geach, *Mental Acts* (London: Routledge and Kegan Paul, 1971; new edition, South Bend, St. Augustine, 2001), 40.

72. The idea that a linguistic analysis may contribute to a phenomenology—the idea of a "linguistic phenomenology," to use Austin's expression—clearly makes no sense unless we are willing to accept that not *all* description of essence is the bringing to light of conventions implicit in our use of words (for otherwise the phenomenological pole of the description would be simply absorbed by its

linguistic or grammatical pole) and therefore unless we abandon the idea of a *complete* arbitrariness of grammar.

73. LU I, §21; Hua XIX, 1, p. 77; *Logical Investigations,* vol. 1, 212.

74. See, on this example, Jonathan Lowe, "Metaphysics as the Science of Essence," 6, http://ontology.buffalo.edu/06/Lowe/Lowe.pdf.

75. E. J. Lowe, "Metaphysics as the Science of Essence," 19, http://ontology.buffalo.edu/06/Lowe/Lowe.pdf.

Chapter 10

1. Hua III, 1, p. 8; trans. F. Kersten, *Ideas Pertaining to a Pure Phenomenology, I,* xxii.

2. Hua III, 1, §2, p. 12; *Ideas Pertaining to a Pure Phenomenology, I,* 7.

3. In the Platonizing language of Husserl, who conceives of properties as general entities, that is, as ideas, this assertion amounts to that of Jean Hering, in his *Bemerkungen über das Wesen, die Wesenheit und die Idee,* in *Jahrbuch für Philosophie und Phänomenologische Forschung,* vol. 4 (1921), 497: "We cannot see why only *individual* objects should have their essence. Indeed, not only does every particular object have its essence, but also every 'idea.'"

4. Hua, III, 1, pp. 12–13; *Ideas Pertaining to a Pure Phenomenology, I,* 7 (trans. modified—Tr.).

5. We know that Aristotle's odd formulation, *to ti ēn einai,* is characterized by the double use of *einai,* the first occurrence of which is in the imperfect.

6. Aristotle, *Métaphysique,* Z, 5.1031a12: *estin ho horismos ho tou ti ēn einai logos*: "the definition is the expression of what it is to be a thing [of the essence]."

7. Aristotle, *Posterior Analytics* II, 7.92b4–11: Aristotle writes of the goat stag that "all one can know is the meaning or name 'goat stag,' but not what the essential nature of a goat stag is."

8. Hua, III 1, §6, p. 19; *Ideas Pertaining to a Pure Phenomenology, I,* 14 (trans. modified—Tr.).

9. Jean Hering, "Bemerkungen über das Wesen," in *Jahrbuch für Philosophie und Phänomenologische Forschung,* vol. 4 (1921): 500. The same remark is made by Ingarden in *Der Streit um die Existenz der Welt II/I: Formalontologie* (Tübingen: Niemeyer), 402: "Wc must not confuse two distinct points of view: that of the essential character [*Wesenhaftigkeit*] of a determination for an object and that of the necessity [*Notwendigkeit*] of something for that object."

10. For example, Alvin Plantinga, in a work that has contributed to a certain reevaluation of essentialism, *The Nature of Necessity* (Oxford: Clarendon, 1974), proposes a modal definition of this kind: "What is it . . . to say that a certain object has a property essentially or necessarily? That, presumably, the object in question could not conceivably have lacked the property in question; that under no possible circumstances could that object have failed to possess that property" (11). See also Penelope Mackie, *How Things Might Have Been: Individuals, Kinds, and Essential Properties* (Oxford University Press, 2006), 2.

11. Hua, XVII, p. 82; trans. D. Cairns, *Formal and Transcendental Logic* (The Hague: Martinus Nijhoff, 1969), 78.

12. Hua, III 1, p. 15; *Ideas Pertaining to a Pure Phenomenology, I,* 10. See also Hua, XVII, p. 77; *Formal and Transcendental Logic,* 73: "eines Substrates überhaupt in möglichen bestimmenden Prädikationen."

13. Hua, III, 1, pp. 26–27: "eidetische Wissenschaft vom Gegenstande überhaupt"; See also Hua, XVII, 111: "Ihr *Gebiet* soll die 'formale Region' des Gegenstandes überhaupt sein."

14. Formal logic deals with concepts, propositions, inferences grasped as pure meanings; formal ontology focuses on formal objects that correspond to these meanings.

15. Hua, III 1, p. 19; *Ideas Pertaining to a Pure Phenomenology, I,* 14 (trans. modified—Tr.).

16. Hua, III 1, p. 20; *Ideas Pertaining to a Pure Phenomenology, I,* 15 (trans. modified—Tr.).

17. Hua, III 1, p. 24; *Ideas Pertaining to a Pure Phenomenology, I,* 19.

18. J. N. Mohanty, "Phenomenology and the Modalities," in *Logic, Truth, and the Modalities* (Dordrecht: Kluwer Academic, 1999), 178. See especially 171: "I think, Husserl held that not only are essential, eidetic modalities (possibility-impossibility, necessity-contingency) irreducible to the logical modalities, but, on the contrary the logical modalities are cases of essential modalities." It must be stressed that Mohanty's text, which first appeared in 1990 in *Acta Philosophica Fennica,* is prior to the works of Kit Fine, to which I will return later, and which insist on the necessity of this "reversal": essence lies at the ground of modalities, not the other way round.

19. LU III, §7 (a), text from the first edition; Hua, XIX, 2, p. 243. [There is no English translation of the first German edition: I have therefore translated Romano's French translation. For purposes of comparison, see Findlay's translation of the corresponding passage of the second German edition, *Logical Investigations,* vol. II, 12—Tr.].

20. LU III, §7; Hua, XIX, 2, p. 243; *Logical Investigations,* vol. 2, 12.

21. Ibid. (trans. modified—Tr.).

22. Kit Fine, "Essence and Modality: The Second Philosophical Perspectives Lecture," *Philosophical Perspectives,* vol. 8, "Logic and Language" (1994): 4.

23. Kit Fine, "Senses of Essence," in *Modality, Morality and Belief,* ed. W. Sinnott-Armstrong (Cambridge, Eng.: Cambridge University Press, 1995), 32.

24. Fine, "Essence and Modality," 3.

25. Ibid., 5.

26. Fine, "Senses of Essence," 56.

27. Fine, "Essence and Modality," 9.

28. Ibid. Other authors have recently followed Fine on this point. See Jonathan Lowe, "Metaphysics as the Science of Essence," http://ontology.buffalo.edu/06/Lowe/Lowe.pdf.

29. LU III, §7; Hua, XIX, 2, p. 243; *Logical Investigations,* vol. 2, 12.

30. K. Fine, "The Varieties of Necessity," in T. Szabo Gendler and J. Haw-

thorne, *Conceivability and Possibility* (Oxford: Clarendon, 2002), 254. On this concept of "logical possibility in the broad sense," see Alvin Plantinga, *The Nature of Necessity* (Oxford: Clarendon, 1974), 2.

31. Fine, "The Varieties of Necessity," 254; and "Essence and Modality," 10: "The metaphysically necessary truths can then be identified with the propositions which are true in virtue of the nature of all objects whatever."

32. Fine, "Essence and Modality," 10.

33. Ibid., 9–10.

34. Ibid., 13.

35. Fine, "Senses of Essence," 56.

36. Fine, "Essence and Modality," 14 n1.

37. Actually, on this point, Fine's position is more subtle: he accepts the difference between several forms of necessity, and in particular a lesser necessity that is valid for the laws of nature, but he asserts that some empirical necessities are nonetheless necessary in an absolute sense: for example, "every electron has a negative charge" (because that belongs to the very definition of what an electron is). See "The Varieties of Necessity," 261. On this problem, see below, chapter 12.

38. Hua, III, 1, p. 17; *Ideas Pertaining to a Pure Phenomenology, I,* 12 (trans. modified—Tr.).

39. Fine, "Senses of Essence," 60.

40. See Fabrice Correia, "Generic Essence, Objectual Essence and Modality," *Noûs* (2006): 762.

41. In this respect it is not necessary, however, to abstain from using "essence" as a substantive, nor, therefore, from referring to essences and quantifying on them, for I do not think it necessary to subscribe to Quine's criterion of ontological commitment according to which "to be is to be the value of a variable."

42. See Correia, "Generic Essence, Objectual Essence and Modality," esp. 763.

43. Fine, "Senses of Essence," 56.

Chapter 11

1. S. Kripke, *Naming and Necessity* (Oxford: Basil Blackwell, 1980), 110.

2. Hering, *Bemerkungen über das Wesen,* §3 (2), p. 500.

3. Hua XVII, p. 255, n1; trans. D. Cairns, *Formal and Transcendental Logic,* 248 n1.

4. LU III, §4; Hua XIX, 2, p. 237; trans. J. N. Findlay, *Logical Investigations,* vol. 2, 8.

5. Hua XVII, p. 255, n1; *Formal and Transcendental Logic,* 248 n1.

6. Hua III, 1, p. 12; trans. F. Kersten, *Ideas Pertaining to a Pure Phenomenology, I,* 7.

7. LU III, §7; Hua XIX/2, p. 243; trans. J. N. Findlay, *Logical Investigations,* 12.

8. Hua III, 1, p. 20; trans. F. Kersten, *Ideas Pertaining to a Pure Phenomenology, I,* §6, p. 15 (trans. modified—Tr.).

9. Hua III, 1, p. 178; *Ideas Pertaining to a Pure Phenomenology, I,* §79, p. 190.

10. Hua III, 1, pp. 12–13; *Ideas Pertaining to a Pure Phenomenology, I,* §2, p. 7–8 (trans. slightly altered, and last emphasis added by CR.—Tr.).

11. Hua III, 1, p. 12; *Ideas Pertaining to a Pure Phenomenology, I,* §2, p. 7.

12. Ibid.

13. Hua III, 1, p. 22; *Ideas Pertaining to a Pure Phenomenology, I,* §8, p. 17.

14. Hua III, 1, p. 23; *Ideas Pertaining to a Pure Phenomenology, I,* §8, p. 18

15. LU III, §7; Hua XIX, 2, pp. 242–43; *Logical Investigations,* vol. 2, 12.

16. Kripke, *Naming and Necessity,* 109.

17. Ibid., 48: "Let's call something a rigid designator if in every possible world it designates the same object."

18. F. Drapeau, Viera Contim, and P. Ludwig, *Kripke: Référence et modalités* (Paris: Presses Universitaires de France, 2005), 122–23.

19. Kripke, *Naming and Necessity,* 34 ("*can*" emphasized by Claude Romano).

20. Ibid., 35.

21. Ibid., 38.

22. Ibid., 53.

23. Locke, *An Essay Concerning Human Understanding,* bk. 3, chap. 3, §15, 374.

24. Ibid.

25. Kripke, *Naming and Necessity,* 118.

26. J. Lowe, *Metaphysics as the Science of Essence,* 13, http://ontology.buffalo.edu/06/Lowe/Lowe.pdf.

27. Husserl, *Experience and Judgment,* trans. J. S. Churchill and L. Eley (Evanston, Ill.: Northwestern University Press, 1973), 333–34.

28. On empirical generalities, see above, chapter 1.

29. On this complexity, see T. Szabo Gendler and J. Hawthorne, eds., *Conceivability and Possibility* (Oxford: Clarendon, 2002), especially the contribution by Kit Fine, "The Varieties of Necessity," which examines (and rejects) Kripke's thesis on the status of natural necessities.

Chapter 12

The epigraph is from Nietzsche, *Fragments posthumes, été 1881–été 1882,* 11 [115] in *Oeuvres philosophiques completes,* vol. 5 (Paris: Gallimard, 1982), 352.

1. Hua XVIII, pp. 124–25; *Logical Investigations,* trans. J. N. Findlay, vol. 1, 79 (translation modified—Tr.).

2. Hua I, p. 52; *Cartesian Meditations,* 11.

3. Hua III/1, p. 42; *Ideas Pertaining to a Pure Phenomenology, I,* 36.

4. Hua III/1, p. 207; *Ideas Pertaining to a Pure Phenomenology, I,* 218.

5. Martin Heidegger, "Die Idee der Philosophie und das Weltanschauungsproblem (Auszug aus der Nachschrift Brecht)," *Heidegger Studies,* vol. 12 (1996): 10.

6. Heidegger, GA 20, pp. 36–37. It is quite surprising to see that, in certain texts, Husserl aknowledges this pluralism of all description; he asserts, for example, that several travelers who would frequent the same country would not return with identical descriptions. In speaking of Meinong, he says: "We are like

two travelers in the very same remote part of the world. Naturally we often see the same thing and describe it, but in keeping with our different characteristics of apperception, in a different way in many respects" (Hua XXIV, p. 444). See also the letter to Meinong of April 7, 1902 (in *Briefwechsel*, I, *Die Brentanoschule* [London: Kluwer, 1994], 139–45; French trans. Bastien Gallet, *Philosophie*, no. 72 [2001]: 16): "When two geographers visit the same countries and travel the same roads to a great extent, the descriptions they then write of these regions never agree entirely."

7. Jean-Paul Sartre, *Situations, I* (Paris: Gallimard, 1947 [reprinted by "folio"]), 227 (My translation. For another trans., see below, "Select Bibiography," Sartre.).

8. "The book got started totally by chance, without any protagonists. The protagonist was The Tree, The Beech. Why? Because at the time I was writing that book I was on my farm. . . . I went for a walk in a spot that is most extraordinary, and where there was a magnificent beech. Looking back on it, I started to write about that beech. And if you look closely at the opening pages of *A King without Diversion*, you can see that at that moment my thoughts are going around in a circle, or perhaps in a spiral, until they get to the center that they imagine—that will, perhaps, give them the beginning. The beginning, suddenly, is the discovery of a crime, a dead body located in the branches of that tree" (J. Giono, *Entretiens avec Jean Amrouche et Taos Amrouche*, presented with notes by Henri Godard [Paris: Gallimard, 1990], conversation no. 14, pp. 192–93).

9. C. Taylor, "The Validity of Transcendental Arguments," in *Philosophical Arguments* (Cambridge, Mass.: Harvard University Press, 1995), 21. The author who originated the contemporary debates on the status of transcendental arguments is Barry Stroud, in a renowned paper ("Transcendental Arguments," *The Journal of Philosophy* 65, no. 9 [1968]: 241–56).

10. Here I take some distance from Taylor. On his view, transcendental arguments are "a string of what one could call indispensability claims" and "*the starting points* [of transcendental arguments] *themselves consist of indispensability claims*" ("The Validity of Transcendental Arguments," 27, my emphasis). It is difficult to see what that means concretely, unless we accept a relevant notion of essence, which Taylor does not do in this article. How is the assertion that every spatial thing is perceived by adumbrations *indispensable* to the account of that experience? Is it only because we express ourselves that way? Because such an assertion is self-evident, in that it states something like a linguistic rule? Or is it rather because it is an essential feature of our perception as such? Taylor does not seem to settle the issue on this crucial point.

11. Taylor, "The Validity of Transcendental Arguments," 32.

12. Heidegger, GA 24, 323; trans., *Basic Problems of Phenomenology*, 228.

13. Heidegger, *Sein und Zeit*, 212; trans., *Being and Time*, 255.

14. GA 24, p. 30; *Basic Problems of Phenomenology*, 22.

15. GA 56/57, p. 101.

16. Gadamer will insist on this in *Truth and Method*: "Understanding is primarily an agreement [*Einverständnis*]" (Gadamer, *Gesammelte Werke* [henceforth

GW], vol. 1: *Hermeneutik I: Wahrheit und Methode: Grundzüge einer philosophischen Hermeneutik* (Tübingen: J. C. B. Mohr [Paul Siebeck], 1985), 183. Of course, this assertion does not in any way contradict the idea that we can understand texts whose assertions seem to us to be erroneous: but the falsity or the truth of what the text tells us must themselves be interpreted according to what appears to us to be that text's most plausible meaning. The understanding of the meaning is indissociable from the aim of truth, because we understand the text not only on the basis of linguistic competence which we share—to some degree—with the author, but in accordance with a preliminary understanding of what the text is telling us, that is, on the basis of presuppositions that govern and subtend the hermeneutic process. Davidson will express an idea close to this one in many passages: "If we know he [our interlocutor] holds the sentence true *and* we know how to interpret it, then we can make a correct attribution of belief. Symmetrically, if we know what belief a sentence held true expresses, we know how to interpret it" (Davidson, *Inquiries into Truth and Interpretation,* 2nd ed. [Oxford: Clarendon, 2001], 162); or yet again, we must "give up the idea that we can clearly distinguish between theory and language" (ibid., 187). Naturally, there are many differences between the theory of interpretation of Heidegger and Gadamer and that of Davidson.

17. Hua III, 1, §90, p. 207; *Ideas I,* 218 (slightly modified—Tr.). See also Hua I, §15, p. 74; trans. D. Cairns, *Cartesian Meditations,* 36.

18. Heidegger, *Sein und Zeit,* 310; *Being and Time,* 358.

19. Ibid., 37; trans., 62.

20. The pre-understandings that guide interpretation, and rest on partly unelucidated presuppositions, must not direct us away from the "things themselves," Heidegger points out, but on the contrary take us back to them. Our goal must be "never to allow our fore-having, fore-sight, and fore-conception be presented to us by fancies and popular conceptions, but rather to make the scientific theme secure by working out these-fore-structures in terms of the things themselves" (*Sein und Zeit,* 153; *Being and Time,* 195).

21. As long as philosophy has not established the existence of truths having an absolute validity within its domain, we have "as a matter of principle, no right to assign philosophy the standard of absolute truth. In other words, there is, as a matter of principle, no justification for characterizing philosophical knowledge in general as skeptical or relativistic" (GA 61, p. 163; trans. R. Rojcewicz, *Phenomenological Interpretations of Aristotle: Initiation into Phenomenological Research* [Bloomington: Indiana University Press, 2001], 123). See also GA 17, p. 99; trans. D. O. Dahlstrom, *Introduction to Phenomenological Research* (Bloomington: Indiana University Press, 2005), 72 (slightly modified—Tr.): "The division between skepticism and absolutism regarding validation rests on a basis that has not been made clear and the division is to be rejected altogether."

22. Heidegger, *Sein und Zeit,* 17; *Being and Time,* 38.

23. GA 24, p. 27; *Basic Problems of Phenomenology,* 20 (trans. modified—Tr.).

24. Heidegger, *Sein und Zeit,* 50, n1; *Being and Time,* 490, note x. (trans. modified—Tr.).

25. *Sein und Zeit*, 42; *Being and Time*, 67.

26. GA 20, p. 207; trans. T. Kisiel, *History of the Concept of Time: Prolegomena* (Bloomington: Indiana University Press, 1985), 154 (trans. modified—Tr.).

27. GA 20, pp. 102–3; *History of the Concept of Time*, 75.

28. Heidegger, *Sein und Zeit*, 227; *Being and Time*, 270 (my emphasis on "all"). It is important to note that Heidegger refuses to speak of eternal truths even with respect to mathematical truths. This point, implicit in §44 (c) of *Sein und Zeit*, is made explicit in *Grundprobleme der Phänomenologie*: "The content intended in the true proposition '2 times 2 = 4' can subsist through all eternity without there existing any truth about it. . . . But that there may be eternal truths will remain an arbitrary assumption . . . The proposition '2 times 2 = 4' as a true assertion is true only as long as *Dasein* exists." (GA 24, p. 315; *Basic Problems of Phenomenology*, 220–21).

29. H.-G. Gadamer, *Wahrheit und Methode*, GW I, p. 280; *Truth and Method*, trans. W. Glen-Doepel, revised by J. Weinsheimer and D. G. Marshall (London: Continuum Impact, 2006), 277.

30. Hua XVIII, 125; *Logical Investigations*, vol. 1, 79.

31. Letter from Heidegger to Richardson (1962), published as preface to the English edition of William J. Richardson, *Heidegger: Through Phenomenology to Thought* (New York: Fordham University Press, 2007), xviii (my emphasis).

32. In *Logik, Die Frage nach der Wahrheit*, his course of 1925–26, Heidegger takes up Husserl's expression as his own: anthropologism is "a specific relativism [*spezifischer Relativismus*]" (GA 21, p. 45; see Hua XVIII, p. 125), and quotes this same passage of "Prolegomena to Pure Logic"; see above, note 30.

33. GA 26, p. 217; *The Metaphysical Foundations of Logic*, trans. Michael Heim (Bloomington: Indiana University Press, 1984), 169.

34. See on this point the analyses in *Metaphysische Anfangsgründe der Logik*, GA 26, especially pp. 171–72; trans. M. Heim, *The Metaphysical Foundations of Logic*, 136–37.

35. Heidegger, *Sein und Zeit*, 25.

36. GA 24, p. 267; *Basic Problems of Phenomenology*, 222.

37. Heidegger, *Sein und Zeit*, 13; *Being and Time*, 34.

38. "The totality of entities can, in accordance with its various domains, become a field for laying bare and delimiting certain definite areas of subject matter. These areas, on their part (for instance, history, Nature, space, life, *Dasein*, language, and the like) can serve as objects which corresponding scientific investigations may take as their respective themes" (Heidegger, *Sein und Zeit*, 9; *Being and Time*, 29). Furthermore, in this same §3, the enumeration of the sciences whose thematic domain has its foundation in fundamental ontology (mathematics, physics, biology, historical sciences, biology) makes no mention of anthropology. Why?

39. See Claude Romano, *Event and World*, trans. S. Mackinlay (New York: Fordham University Press, 2009) and *L'Événement et le temps* (Paris: Presses Universitaires de France, 1999). In these works, I ventured to say that the *advenant* had no essence, because in them I still thought of essence as an ideal, immutable, and atemporal entity. But the *a priori* descriptions of the *advenant* are also anchored

in essential truths, and it is still a truth of essence that the *a priori* characteristics of the *advenant*, his "eventials" in my terminology, are structurally dependent on the fact of his birth, of that event that is at the same time an "arch-fact" and can only be articulated *a posteriori*: an essential *a posteriori* belongs *a priori* to the very content of their apriority. The descriptions of the *advenant* are essential descriptions of man; they are not descriptions of *something else*.

40. [The French punning on the italicized words defies translation: "car l'homme *n'est* homme que s'il *naît* homme."—Tr.]

Introduction to Part 2

The epigraph to part 2 is from Heidegger, *Grundprobleme der Phänomenologie*, GA 58, p. 6.

1. "Sa chose même." Romano's wording recalls Husserl's appeal to return "Zu den Sachen selbst! [to the things themselves]."

2. "jours perdus à la poursuite de cette félicité insaisissable. Je n'ai plus rien à apprendre, j'ai marché plus vite qu'un autre et j'ai fait le tour de la vie." Chateaubriand, *Mémoires d'outre-tombe*, ed. Maurice Levaillant and Georges Moulinier (Paris: Gallimard, Bibliothèque de la pléiade, 1951), vol. 1, p. 76. Translation cited, A. S. Kline, bk. 2, chap. 9: sect. 1, online at http://www.poetryintranslation.com/PITBR/Chateaubriand/Chathome.htm.

3. Wittgenstein, *Philosophical Investigations*, I, §244, p. 89e. See also Wittgenstein's "Notes for Lectures on 'Private Experience' and 'Sense Data,'" *The Philosophical Review* 77, no. 3 (July 1968): 319: "In order to be able to say that I have toothache I don't observe my behavior, say in the mirror. *And this is correct*, but it doesn't follow that you describe an observation of any other kind. Moaning is not the description of an observation."

4. Wittgenstein, *Philosophical Investigations*, I, §246, p. 89e.

5. E. Tugendhat, *Selbstbewusstsein und Selbstbestimmung* (Frankfurt am Main: Suhrkamp, 1979); trans. Paul Stern, *Self-Consciousness and Self-Determination* (Cambridge, Mass.: MIT Press, 1986), 111.

6. Hacker, *Insight and Illusion*, 259–61.

7. I have tried to establish this for verbs of intention. See Claude Romano, "Anscombe et la philosophie herméneutique de l'intention," *Philosophie*, 80, (2003): 60–87.

Chapter 13

The epigraph is from Martin Heidegger, "Editor's Preliminary Remarks" in E. Husserl, Hua X, p. xxv; trans. James S. Churchill, *The Phenomenology of Internal Time-Consciousness* (Bloomington: Indiana University Press, 1964), 15 (trans. modified—Tr.).

1. Hua XVII, p. 288; trans. Dorion Cairns, *Formal and Transcendental Logic* (The Hague: Martinus Nijhoff, 1969), 282 (§106, trans. modified—Tr.).

2. LU, V, §3, Hua XIX, 1, p. 361; trans. Findlay, *Logical Investigations*, vol. 2, 84 (trans. modified—Tr.).

3. [I have modified the parenthetical clause in "que nous *avons* (plutôt que celles que nous *faisons*) [literally "that we *have* (rather than those [experiences] we *make*)": French is able to underline the distinction between the more "objective" *faire une experience*, literally "to make an experience" such as witnessing the wars of 1866 and 1870, and the more subjective turn, "*avoir une experience*," to have an experience.—Tr.].

4. LU, V, §3, Hua XIX, 1, p. 361; *Logical Investigations*, vol. 2, 85 (trans. modified—Tr.).

5. Ibid., Hua XIX, 1, p. 363; *Logical Investigations*, vol. 2, 85 (trans. modified—Tr.).

6. LU V, §2; Hua XIX, 1, p. 359; *Logical Investigations*, vol. 2, 83.

7. LU VI, Beilage; Hua XIX, 2, p. 751ff.; *Logical Investigations*, vol. 2, 335ff.

8. Hua X, p. XV; trans. Churchill, *The Phenomenology of Internal Time-Consciousness*, 15 (trans. modified—Tr.).

9. LU V, "Beilage zu den Paragraphen 11 und 20"; Hua XIX, 1, p. 437; trans. *Logical Investigations*, vol. 2, "Appendix to §11 and §20," 125–27.

10. Hua XIX, 1, p. 382; *Logical Investigations*, vol. 2, p. 96, my emphasis (trans. modified—Tr.).

11. Hua XXIV; trans. P. Alston and George Nakhnikian, *The Idea of Phenomenology* (The Hague: Martinus Nijhoff, 1973).

12. To insist, as we do, on the fusion of two paradigms for the constitution of Husserl's intentionality does not lead to a commitment to the "Fregean readings" of phenomenology—quite to the contrary. These readings limit themselves to conceiving of the relationship between these two models by subordinating the perceptual paradigm to the semantic one, making perceptual intentionality the "generalization" of the semantic model—its extension to the entire domain of acts. I have pointed out some limitations of this reading in chapter 5. Rather, what must be stressed is the *intertwining* formed by these two models, an intertwining in which the perceptual model continues nevertheless to possess a primacy, since it is the general theory of intentionality as relation to objects in general that is primary, and semantic intentionality is a particular instance of this theory. The passage in which this point is made specifically is in the fifth *Logical Investigation*. There, Husserl insists that "any sort of act" possesses necessary characteristics such as an "act quality" and an "intentional matter" and he concludes: "The same may be claimed for expressive acts, for the acts in particular which *lend meaning* to expressions" (Hua XIX, 1, p. 435; *Logical Investigations*, vol. 2, p. 124).

13. E. Levinas, *En découvrant l'existence avec Husserl et Heidegger*, 146; *Discovering Existence with Husserl*, 136.

14. Hua IV, p. 215; trans. Richard Rojcewicz and André Schuwer, *Ideas Pertaining to a Pure Phenomenology and to a Phenomenological Philosophy: Second Book: Studies in the Phenomenology of Constitution* (Dordrecht: Kluwer Academic, 1993), 227. On this distinction between "real [*reell*]" and "real [*real*]," see below, chapter 14.

15. Descartes: *Principes*, I, 9; AT IX, II, 28; English trans. Valentine Rodger Miller and Reese P. Miller, *Principles of Philosophy* (Dordrecht: Reidel, 1983), 5.

16. D. Davidson, "A Coherence Theory of Truth and Belief," in *Subjective, Intersubjective, Objective* (Oxford: Clarendon, 2001), 142.

Chapter 14

The epigraph is from Heidegger, *Seminar in Zähringen* 1973, GA 15, p. 383; Eng. trans. by Andrew Mitchell and Francois Raffoul, *Four Seminars* (Bloomington: Indiana University Press, 2003), 70.

1. Hua I, p. 76; trans. Cairns, *Cartesian Meditations*, 38.

2. Jean-Paul Sartre, *Being and Nothingness*, trans. Hazel E. Barnes (New York: Washington Square, 1992), 329 (trans. modified—Tr.).

3. Emmanuel Levinas, *Time and the Other: And Additional Essays*, trans. Richard A. Cohen (Pittsburgh: Duquesne University Press, 2008), 42.

4. Emmanuel Levinas, *Totality and Infinity*, trans. Alphonso Lingis (Pittsburgh: Duquesne University Press, 1969), 148.

5. Ibid., 54. 46: "The cogito . . . evinces separation."

6. Michel Henry, *The Genealogy of Psychoanalysis*, trans. Douglas Brick (Stanford, Calif.: Stanford University Press, 1993), 11, 12.

7. Hua I, p. 3; trans. Cairns, *Cartesian Meditations*, 1. See also Hua I, p. 43; trans. Peter Koestenbaum, *The Paris Lectures* (Dordrecht: Kluwer Academic, 1998), 3.

8. Hua I, p. 34; *Cartesian Meditations*, 86.

9. For a historical analysis of the stages Husserl went through in elaborating the phenomenological reduction and the constitution of his transcendental idealism, see J.-F. Lavigne, *Husserl et la naissance de la phénoménologie (1900–1913)* (Paris: Presses Universitaires de France, 2005).

10. The "epistemologically confused and psychologically misused distinction of inner and outer perception" should be replaced by the "genuine contrast between *adequate* and *inadequate* perception which has its roots in the *pure* phenomenological essences of such experiences" (LU V, §5; Hua XIX, 1, p. 366; *Logical Investigations*, vol. 2, 87).

11. LU V, §5; Hua XIX, 1, p. 365; *Logical Investigations*, vol. 2, 86 (trans. modified—Tr.).

12. LU VI, Beilage; Hua XIX, 2, p. 753; LU VI, Beilage; *Logical Investigations*, vol. 2, 336. Descartes's entire argument is summarized and approved by Husserl: LU VI, Beilage; Hua XIX, 2, p. 754; *Logical Investigations*, vol. 2, 337.

13. Hua XIX, 1, p. 26; *Logical Investigations*, vol. 1, 178.

14. LU V, §6; Hua XIX, 1, p. 369; *Logical Investigations*, vol. 2, 88 (trans. modified—Tr.).

15. LU V, §16; Hua XIX, 1, p. 412; *Logical Investigations*, vol. 2, 112 (trans. modified—Tr.).

16. LU, V, §2; Hua XIX, 1, p. 359; *Logical Investigations*, vol. 2, 83.

17. LU, V, §2; Hua XIX, 1, pp. 359–160; *Logical Investigations*, vol. 2, 83 (trans. modified—Tr.).

18. LU V, §16; Hua XIX, 1, p. 413; trans. *Logical Investigations*, vol. 2, 113: "If we now oppose *intentional* to real [*reell*] content . . ."

19. Hua XXIV, p. 441; trans. Claire Ortiz Hill, *Introduction to Logic and Theory of Knowledge: Lectures 1906/07* (Dordrecht: Springer, 2009), 451.

20. Hua XXIV, p. 168; *Introduction to Logic and Theory of Knowledge*, 165–66.

21. Hua XXIV, p. 177; *Introduction to Logic and Theory of Knowledge*, 175.

22. Hua XXIV, p. 178; *Introduction to Logic and Theory of Knowledge*, 175.

23. Hua VII, p. 165; French trans. Arion Lothar Kelkel, *Philosophie première I: Histoire critique des idées* (Paris: Presses Universitaires de France, 1970), 237.

24. R. Ingarden, *On the Motives which Led Husserl to Transcendental Idealism*, trans. A. Hannibalsson, (The Hague: Martinus Nijhoff, 1975), 11.

25. D. Davidson, "The Myth of the Subjective," in *Subjective, Intersubjective, Objective* (Oxford: Clarendon, 2001), 46.

26. Hua I, p. 8; trans. Peter Koestenbaum, *The Paris Lectures* (Dordrecht: Kluwer Academic, 1998), 8 (trans. modified—Tr.).

27. Hua I, p. 59; trans. Cairns, *Cartesian Meditations*, 19–20 (trans. modified).

28. The distinction between *epochē* and reduction is made especially in the *Cartesian Meditations*: "The fundamental phenomenological method of the transcendental *epochē*, because it leads back [*zurückleitet*] to that transcendental ground, is therefore called phenomenological reduction" (Hua I, p. 61; trans. Cairns, *Cartesian Meditations*, 21).

29. Hua IX, pp. 443–44: "The idea here is not to carry out the task of a universal critique of experience [*Erfahrung*] from the point of view of its validity, as if to justify, in opposition to the extreme view of skepticism, the conviction of the existence of an objective world. The *epochē*, then, is not that of the skeptics . . . according to which one refrains from pronouncing any judgment concerning objective truth, since they have already demonstrated that man can know nothing objective" (my translation—Tr.).

30. Hua III, 1, §31, p. 63; *Ideas II*, 58–59. See also Hua IX, p. 188; trans. John Scanlon, *Phenomenological Psychology: Lectures, Summer Semester: 1925* (The Hague: Martinus Nijhoff, 1977), 187–88.

31. Alexandre Löwit, "L'épochè de Husserl et le doute de Descartes," *Revue de Métaphysique et de Morale*, no. 4 (1957): 400.

32. Hua VI, p. 100; *Crisis of the European Sciences*, 96–97.

33. Hua I, p. 63; *Cartesian Meditations*, 24

34. Hua I, p. 66; *Cartesian Meditations*, 27.

35. Heidegger, GA 17, §47 (a), p. 267; trans. Daniel O. Dahlstrom, *Introduction to Phenomenological Research* (Bloomington: Indiana University Press, 2005), 205.

36. Given that the "radical subjectivism of the skeptic tradition" harbors "the deepest meaning of modern philosophy" (Hua VII, p. 61; French trans. A. L. Kelkel, *Philosophie première*, I, *Histoire critique des idées* [Paris: Presses Universitaires de France, 1970], 86), and that phenomenology, for its part, expresses "secret

nostalgia of all modern philosophy" (Hua III, 1, p. 118; trans. Kersten, *Ideas I*, 142), one must conclude that Husserl's philosophy is *inseparable* from the taking seriously and the reelaboration of the problem of skepticism.

37. Hua II, p. 5; *The Idea of Phenomenology*, trans. Lee Hardy (Dordrecht: Kluwer Academic, 2010), 63

38. Hua II, p. 4; *Idea of Phenomenology*, 62.

39. Hua II, p. 5; *Idea of Phenomenology*, 62.

40. Husserl, *Erfahrung und Urteil*, 319; *Experience and Judgment*, 265: "We call *real* [*real*] in a specific sense all that which . . . *is, according to its sense, essentially individualized by its spatiotemporal position.*"

41. Hua II, p. 5; *Idea of Phenomenology*, 63.

42. Hua II, p. 6; *Idea of Phenomenology*, 63.

43. Hua II, p. 60; *Idea of Phenomenology*, 45.

44. LU II, §23; Hua XIX, 1, p. 169; *Logical Investigations*, vol. 1, 275.

45. Husserl, Ms AVI 21 (1928 et 1933), p. 25a: "Das transzendentale Ich ist weder in noch ausser der Welt, und auch die Welt ist weder in ihm noch ausser ihm."

46. The ego is not consciousness. But I will use the term "ego," as is often the case with Husserl, metonymically, to designate consciousness, because this distinction will not concern me in these pages.

47. Hua I, p. 65; *Cartesian Meditations*, 26.

48. E. Fink, "The Phenomenological Philosophy of Edmund Husserl and Contemporary Criticism," in R. O. Elveton, *The Phenomenology of Husserl: Selected Critical Readings* (1970 ed.), 119.

49. Hua VIII, p. 166; French trans. A. Kelkel, *Philosophie première, II* (Paris: Presses Universitaires de France, 1972), 231.

50. Hua I, p. 39; trans. Koestenbaum, *The Paris Lectures* (Dordrecht: Kluwer Academic, 1998), 39.

51. Merleau-Ponty, *Phenomenology of Perception*, trans. Landes, lxxviii: "Far from being, as was believed, the formula for an idealist philosophy, the phenomenological reduction is in fact the formula for an existential philosophy: Heidegger's '*In-der-Welt-sein*' [Being-in-the-world] only appears against the background of the phenomenological reduction." Whence the paradox that to complete the reduction would in reality be to discover its limits: "The most important lesson of the reduction is the impossibility of a complete reduction" (ibid., lxxvii).

52. Hua VIII, Beilage XX, p. 432: "To begin with, it would be preferable to avoid speaking of a phenomenological 'residuum,' as well as of the 'switching off [*Ausschaltung*] of the world'. These expressions easily lead to the belief that the world falls henceforth outside the theme of phenomenology, and that in the place of the former, only 'subjective' acts, modes of manifestation, etc., that relate to the world, remain thematic."

53. Hua I, p. 56; *Cartesian Meditations*, 15.

54. Hua, I, p. 56; *Cartesian Meditations*, 15–16.

55. Hua, I, p. 55; *Cartesian Meditations*, 15.

56. Hua II, p. 14; trans. Lee Hardy, *The Idea of Phenomenology*, 69.

57. Hua IX, p. 330; trans. Richard E. Palmer, ed. Thomas Sheehan, *Psychological and Transcendental Phenomenology and the Confrontation with Heidegger (1927–1931): The Encyclopaedia Britannica Article, the Amsterdam Lectures "Phenomenology and Anthropology," and Husserl's Marginal Notes in Being and Time, and Kant and the Problem of Metaphysics* (Dordrecht: Kluwer Academic, 1997), 118 (trans. modified—Tr.).

58. Rudolf Boehm, "Les ambiguïtés des concepts husserliens d' 'immanance' et de 'transcendance,'" *Revue Philosophique* 4 (1959): 486.

59. Hua I, p. 8; *Paris Lectures,* 8.

60. Ibid. (My emphasis on *since.*)

61. Wolfgang Köhler, "Value and Fact," in *The Selected Papers of Wolfgang Köhler* (New York: Liveright, 1971), 363 n.

62. Rudolf Bernet, *La vie du sujet* (Paris: Presses Universitaires de France, 1994), 98.

63. Hua I, p. 60; *Cartesian Meditations,* 21.

64. Hua I, p. 65; *Cartesian Meditations,* 26.

65. Hua III, 1, p. 105; *Ideas I,* 111 (trans. modified—Tr.).

66. R. Ingarden, trans. Limido-Heulot, "Des motifs qui ont conduit Husserl à l'lidéalisme transcendental," in *Roman Ingarden—Husserl, La controverse idéalisme-Réalisme* (Paris: Vrin, 2001), 213–14. (The text of this quotation is not contained in A. Hannibalsson's *On the Motives Which Led Edmund Husserl to Transcendental Idealism,* which is based on a longer, earlier version.—Tr.)

67. Hua III, 1, p. 106; *Ideas I,* 112.

68. Levinas, *Discovering Existence with Husserl,* 102. As for Heidegger, he was already speaking of "an *erroneous subjectivizing* of intentionality" (GA 24, p. 89; *Basic Problems of Phenomenology,* 63–64).

69. LU, VI, §61, Hua XIX, 2, p. 715; *Logical Investigations,* vol. 2, 308, in which Husserl asserts that the object is "grasped . . . by knowledge, . . . but is not thereby distorted"; "Otherwise the original datum of sense-perception would be modified in its own objectivity; relational and connective thought and knowledge would not be of what is, but would be a distorting transformation into something else" (trans. modified).

70. Hua III/1, p. 106; *Ideas I,* 112.

71. "Streichen wir das reine Bewusstsein, so streichen wir die Welt." R. Ingarden, *On the Motives Which Led Husserl to Transcendental Idealism,* 21 (trans. modified—Tr.).

72. Hua XXIV, p. 442; trans. Claire Ortiz Hill, *Introduction to Logic and Theory of Knowledge* (Dordrecht: Springer, 2008), 451.

73. Hua I, p. 33; trans. P. Koestenbaum, *The Paris Lectures,* 33 (trans. modified—Tr.).

74. Ibid.

75. Quoted by W. Biemel, in *Husserl: Cahiers de Royaumont* (Paris: Minuit, 1959), 68–69.

76. Let us not forget that Fink, in his article "Die phänomenologische Philosophie E. Husserl in der gegenwärtigen Kritik," which was approved without reservations by Husserl, qualifies the transcendental constitution as "creation

[*Kreation*]"; see "Husserl's Philosophy and Contemporary Criticism," in R. O. Elveton, *The Phenomenology of Husserl: Selected Critical Readings* (1970 ed.), 134. On the ambiguity of constitution, see also E. Fink "The Operative Concepts in the Phenomenology of Husserl," in *Apriori and World: European Contributions to Husserlian Phenomenology* (The Hague: Martinus Nijhoff, 1981), 67–69.

77. Husserl, Ms D 12 V (circa 1930–31), 9, my emphasis (quoted in E. Holenstein, "L'association en tant que synthèse passive," *Philosophie* 50 [1996], 52). Let me insist that a different line of argument, which is valid not only against transcendental phenomenology, but against *constitutive* phenomenology as a whole, would consist in showing that the very concept of "constitution" is jeopardized the moment we take the temporality of the flow of consciousness into account. In a word, there is no possible *constitution* of time. See Claude Romano, "Les Leçons sur le temps de Husserl dans l'histoire de la métaphysique," in *La Conscience du temps: Autour des leçons sur le temps de Husserl*, ed. J. Benoist (Paris: Vrin, 2008), 95–116, as well as *L'événement et le temps.*

78. Hua III, I, p. 106; *Ideas I*, 113.

79. Here the whole, very complex problematic of the "noema" should be brought in, but I will leave it voluntarily out. Let us say, to get right to the essential, that Husserl uses the word "noema" to refer to the intentional object *under reduction*, that is, the object considered in its phenomenological mode of givenness, the correlate of the intentional act or "noesis." This new terminology, which appears with the transcendental turn, complicates *but in no way modifies* the problem exposed above. And it cannot modify it, for the simple reason that it is the expression of it. The noema must be both, and contradictorily, *one and the same as the intentional object*—otherwise it duplicates it and locks us up once again in a philosophy of representation—and *distinct from that object*—otherwise this intentional object cannot be defined as "an innermost moment of the noema" (*Ideen I*, §129), that is, as what remains identical through a noematic multiplicity. For a presentation of this notion, see Rudolf Bernet, "Le concept de noème," in *La Vie du sujet* (Paris: Presses Universitaires de France, 1994), 65–92.

80. To put this differently, if essences are "objective," independent of subjectivity, and if, as Husserl acknowledges, the constitution of the world takes place, not at random, but in conformity with necessities of essence, the question arises as to whether it still makes sense to speak of constitution as a *subjective operation*, whether the world can still be determined as a "formation" of subjectivity.

Chapter 15

The epigraph is from Wittgenstein, *Philosophical Remarks*, in *Complete Works*, 283.

1. Heidegger, GA 15, p. 382; trans. Andrew Mitchell and François Raffoul, *Four Seminars* (Bloomington: Indiana University Press, 2003), 70.

2. Husserl specifically defended the idea that phenomenology is a "science of trivial [*Wissenschaft von den Trivialitäten*]" (Hua XIX, 1, p. 350; *Logical Investigations*, vol. 2, 76).

3. Husserl, *Erfahrung und Urteil,* §7, p. 23; trans. Churchill and Ameriks, *Experience and Judgment,* 28–29.

4. Hua XVI, p. 15; trans. Richard Rojcewicz, *Thing and Space: Lectures of 1907* (Dordrecht: Kluwer Academic, 1997), 12.

5. Hua XVI, p. 15; *Thing and Space,* 13.

6. Hua XVI, p. 16; *Thing and Space,* 13 (trans. modified).

7. Merleau-Ponty, *Phenomenology of Perception,* trans. Landes, 393.

8. Hua III, 1, p. 320; trans. F. Kersten, *Ideas I,* 332 (trans. modified—Tr.).

9. To speak of "*Deutung,*" of "interpretation" in connection with these data rests on a debatable analogy. Everything, in the conception of intentionality, seems to deflect us from the idea of immanent contents that would just be "signs" of the object; now, it is indeed that analogy with the sign that underlies the introduction of the notion of *Deutung* in *Logical Investigations*: "Here, therefore, we talk of signs and meanings just as we do in the case of expressions and cognate signs [for example of expressions that designate the same object: 'the victor at Jena,' 'the vanquished at Waterloo']" (LU I, §23; Hua XIX, 1, p. 80; *Logical Investigations,* vol. 1, 214).

10. Husserl, Ms B, I, II, p. 8; quoted in Gerd Brand, *Welt, Ich und Zeit* (The Hague: Martinus Nijhoff, 1969), 27, n2: "Ist nicht meine ursprüngliche Auffassung von der immanenten Sphäre mit den immanenten Daten, die am Ende erst durch die passive Leistung der Assoziation zu 'Auffassungen kommen,' noch ein Rest der alten Psychologie und ihres sensualistischen Empirismus?"

11. Hua IX, p. 183; trans. J. Scanlon, *Phenomenological Psychology,* 140–41. (Scanlon's translation does not distinguish between Husserl's "ideell" and his "ideal."—Tr.)

12. Hua III, 1, §143, p. 331; trans. F. Kersten, *Ideas I,* 342.

13. Hua I, p. 57; trans. D. Cairns, *Cartesian Meditations,* 17 (the expression, of course, refers to Leibniz).

14. Hua III, 1, p. 320; *Ideas I,* 333.

15. See Stroud, "Transcendental Arguments."

16. Erwin Straus, *Vom Sinn der Sinne,* 2nd ed. (Berlin: Springer Verlag, 1956), 382 and 379–80; trans. Jacob Needleman, *The Primary World of Senses: A Vindication of Sensory Experience* (London: Collier-Macmillan, 1963), 359 and 357, respectively (trans. modified—Tr.).

17. Quoted by Merleau-Ponty, *Phenomenology of Perception,* trans. Landes, 350.

18. Ibid., 360.

19. Ibid., 354.

20. Ibid., 356–57.

21. Ibid., 356.

22. From *ludus,* "play." This etymology is controversial.

23. Merleau-Ponty, *Phenomenology of Perception,* 311.

24. Ibid., 351.

25. Heidegger, GA 56/57, pp. 93–94; trans. Ted Sadler, *Towards the Definition of Philosophy* (London: Continuum, 208), 73.

26. GA 20, pp. 295–96; trans. Theodore Kisiel, *History of the Concept of Time: Prolegomena* (Bloomington: Indiana University Press, 1985), 215–16.

27. Hua III, 1, p. 263; trans. F. Kersten, *Ideas I,* 273.

28. "Im Erfahren selbst mich bewegend habe ich also immer Reales—aber, wenn ich erfahrend, immerfort gewahrend oder in die mögliche Erfahrung übertragend den gegebenfalls Vorauszusehenden fortschreite, lerne ich zwar die Welt als wirkliche und mögliche kennen; aber ich erkenne nichts" (Husserl, Ms. A VII 14, p. 4 a). See also Husserl, *Erfahrung und Urteil,* §7; trans. J. Churchill and L. Eley, *Experience and Judgment,* 29–31.

29. Straus, *Vom Sinn der Sinne,* 377; *The Primary World of Senses,* 355.

30. Straus, *Vom Sinn der Sinne,* 379; *The Primary World of Senses,* 356–57.

31. Wittgenstein, *Über Gewissheit* (Oxford: Basil Blackwell, 1969), §359: trans. Denis Paul and G. E. M. Anscombe, *On Certainty* (London: Blackwell, 1969), 47. "But that means I want to conceive it [certainty] as something that lies beyond being justified or unjustified; as it were, as something animal."

32. Straus, *Vom Sinn der Sinne,* 365; *The Primary World of Senses,* 344–45; and Merleau-Ponty, *Phenomenology of Perception,* 26.

33. Merleau-Ponty, *Phenomenology of Perception,* 359–60.

34. Heidegger, *Sein und Zeit,* 229; *Being and Time,* 271.

35. Heidegger, *Sein und Zeit,* 202; *Being and Time,* 246–47. In *Zur Bestimmung der Philosophie,* Heidegger already insisted: "The genuine solution to the problem of the reality of the external world consists in the insight that this problem is no problem at all, but rather an absurdity [*Widersinnigkeit*]" (GA 56/57, p. 92; trans. Ted Sadler, *Towards the Definition of Philosophy* [United States: Continuum Books, 2003], 77).

36. Merleau-Ponty, *Phenomenology of Perception,* lxxx.

37. Merleau-Ponty, *Phenomenology of Perception,* 388, 389, 63.

38. See Merleau-Ponty, *Phenomenology of Perception,* 48, 51, 381, 387. "The return of perceptual experience . . . condemns all form of realism" (ibid., 48), because realism goes hand in hand with "causal thinking" (ibid., 51), and because perception "is not primarily presented as an event in the world to which the category of 'causality,' for instance, might be applied" (ibid., 214). This position is foreshadowed by Heidegger in *Sein und Zeit,* §43 (a). It is impossible to understand Being-in-the-world causally: Being cannot be explained through entities (Heidegger, *Being and Time,* trans. Macquarrie and Robinson, 251). Of course, Heidegger specifies, "the external world is really present-at-hand [*real vorhanden*] (ibid.), but "what distinguishes this assertion from realism altogether is the fact that in realism there is a lack of ontological understanding. Indeed realism tries to explain Reality ontically by real connections of interaction between things that are real" (ibid.). To this, the continuation of the text furnishes the following retort: "If what the term 'idealism' says, amount to the understanding that Being can never be explained by entities but is already that which is 'transcendental' for every entity, then idealism affords the only correct possibility for a philosophical problematic" (ibid.).

39. Straus, *Vom Sinn der Sinne,* 372; *The Primary World of Senses,* 351.

40. Straus, *Vom Sinn der Sinne,* 379; *The Primary World of Senses,* 356.

41. This denomination first appeared in the work of J. M. Hinton, *Experiences: An Inquiry into Some Ambiguities* (Oxford: Clarendon, 1973). Austin's concep-

tion is already "disjunctive," as is the one more recently defended by McDowell ("Criteria, Defeasibility and Knowledge," in *Meaning, Knowledge and Reality* [Harvard University Press, 1998], 369ff.) and Putnam (*The Threefold Cord*). As I have already shown, and despite a few residual ambiguities, Merleau-Ponty laid down the main elements of that conception as early as 1945, in *Phenomenology of Perception.*

42. Merleau-Ponty, *Phenomenology of Perception*, 430.

43. Paul Claudel, "La Terre quittée," *Connaissance de l'Est*, in *Oeuvre poétique* (Paris: Gallimard, coll. Bibliothèque de la Pléiade, 1967), 107.

44. Heidegger, *Sein und Zeit*, 28; *Being and Time*, 51.

45. Heidegger, *Sein und Zeit*, 29; *Being and Time*, 52.

46. Heidegger, *Sein und Zeit*, 31; *Being and Time*, 54.

47. Heidegger, *Sein und Zeit*, 28; *Being and Time*, 51.

48. Heidegger, *Sein und Zeit*, 208; *Being and Time*, 251.

49. Heidegger, GA 20, p. 60; *History of the Concept of Time: Prolegomena*, 45.

50. GA 20, p. 52; *History of the Concept of Time: Prolegomena*, 40.

51. Ibid.

52. Ibid.

53. GA 24, p. 66; trans. Albert Hofstadter, *The Basic Problems of Phenomenology* (Bloomington: Indiana University Press, 1982), 49.

54. GA 24, p. 85; *Basic Problems of Phenomenology*, 60. See also GA 24, p. 95; *Basic Problems of Phenomenology*, 68.

55. LU V, §11; Hua XIX, 1, p. 387; *Logical Investigations*, vol. 2, 99.

56. GA 24, pp. 88–89: *Basic Problems of Phenomenology*, 63.

57. Straus, *Vom Sinn der Sinne*, 210; *The Primary World of Senses*, 204.

58. Davidson, "A Coherence Theory of Truth and Belief," 146.

Chapter 16

The epigraph is from William James, *Essays in Radical Empiricism* (New York: Longmans, Green, 1912), 6.

1. Hua IV, p. 215; trans. Richard Rojcewicz, and André Schuwer, *Ideas Pertaining to a Pure Phenomenology and to a Phenomenological Philosophy: Second Book: Studies in the Phenomenology of Constitution* (Dordrecht: Kluwer Academic, 1993), 226–27.

2. Hua IV, p. 215; *Ideas II*, 227; See also Hua III, 1, p. 204; *Ideas I*, 215.

3. Hua III, 1, §90, p. 206; *Ideas I*, 217.

4. Hua III, 1, §124, p. 285; trans. Gibson, 319.

5. LU IV, §14; Hua XIX, 1, p. 399; *Logical Investigations*, vol. 2, 105.

6. Hua I, p. 60; *Cartesian Meditations*, 21.

7. Hua I, §39, p. 113; *Cartesian Meditations*, 81.

8. The circle is *vicious* because it is a matter of "explaining' [*erklären*]" the emergence of meaning, because genetic phenomenology is an "explanatory phenomenology [*'erklärende' Phänomenologie*]" (Hua XI, p. 340; trans. A. Steinbock, *Analyses Concerning Passive and Active Synthesis* [Dordrecht: Kluwer Academic, 2001], 629) and this circle leads us to a true absurdity: in order to know which

past experience to associate with the present experience, the latter must already have a meaning; but in order for it to have a meaning, it must already have been associated with past experiences.

9. We must bear in mind the equivocality of the Latin word *intentio*, which lies at the basis of the whole medieval elaboration of the concept of intentionality. As Duns Scotus insists, this term means at once an act of intending, that is "a way of tending toward the thing [*ratio tendendi in obiectum*]," a relationship (*habitudo*) with the thing, "a formal reason present in the thing [*ratio formalis in re*]," and a notion or concept (*conceptus*) of the latter (*Reportata Parisiensa*, II, 13, art. 1). On the polysemy of *intentio* in the Middle Ages, see Alain de Libera, "Intention," in *Vocabulaire européen des philosophies*, ed. Barbara Cassin (Paris: Seuil-Le Robert, 2004).

10. It might be objected that I am reintroducing here a variant of the referential opacity of the intensional statements referred to in chapter 3. This would entail two problems. (1) How to reconcile my thesis that perception presents things according to a particular apprehension that identifies them at least in some respects with my claim in chapter 3, that "to perceive" in some contexts is referentially transparent? (2) Given that it was (among other things) this referentially transparent use of "to perceive" that entailed that the logical criterion of intensionality *failed* to delimit the class of intentional verbs, in short, that intensionality could not be the (strictly logical) criterion of intentionality, does not my present assertion invalidate my conclusions reached in chapter 3? In order to respond to these objections, I must begin by noting that there are two cases in which "to perceive" is referentially transparent: (a) that of a third-person report: someone different from me can assert that, if I have seen a portrait of Stendhal, I have *ipso facto* seen a portrait of Henri Beyle, whether I am aware of it or not, that is, whether or not I am informed of the fact that the novelist wrote under a pseudonym—because another person can *identify* Stendhal as being Henri Beyle; (b) the case of a report in the first person, but *based on an inference*: only now do I realize that what I had identified perceptually before as a portrait of Stendhal was *ipso facto* a portrait of Henri Beyle. None of these samples of referentially transparent uses of "to perceive" correspond to the one examined here, and consequently they cannot constitute an objection to my *phenomenological* description. In phenomenology, we are interested in descriptions *in the first person* of our experience (perceptual, for example), and in descriptions of that experience as it takes place *at the moment of its taking place*, and not in what we can reconstruct of it later, on an inferential basis.

11. The new nominalism tries to persuade us that *all* individuation should be accomplished by means of predicates or "sortals," given that it is impossible to count individuals unless we know *what* we are counting (see Geach, *Reference and Generality*, 3rd ed. [Ithaca, N.Y.: Cornell University Press, 1980]); or, differently, that all partitioning of reality into physical objects is a linguistic construction drawing on quantification and anaphoric pronominalization (see Quine, *World and Object* [Cambridge, Mass.: MIT Press, 1960]). But many corroborating findings show us that a baby, when he or she is about six months old, can already distinguish objects very accurately, and possesses what has often been called a

"naive physics"—and what should rather be called a structured perception of the life-world. The same is true for most of the higher animals. The discrimination of individuals involves no language, and draws on no logical resources (predication or quantification).

12. Against this, Davidson has contended that "unless we want to attribute concepts to butterflies and olive trees, we should not count mere ability to discriminate between red and green or moist and dry as having a concept, not even if such selective behaviour is learned" (Davidson, "Seeing through Language," in *Thought and Language* [Cambridge, Eng.: Cambridge University Press, 1997], 25). But, first of all, this argument makes the possession of concepts an all-or-nothing affair: such possession would admit of no degrees. Second, the case of the olive tree is not relevant, since we do not attribute to olive trees a perception, and therefore not a *perceptual* capacity to discriminate anything (moist and dry), either. Last, the admission of what Husserl calls "types" does not preclude the recognition of the specificity of the possession of concepts in the strict—that is, linguistic—sense of the term. In this respect, it must be pointed out that the normative character of the possession of concepts properly so called (one may succeed or fail in correctly applying a concept to classify something) has its counterpart in the normative character of the perceptual faculties of discrimination: here as well, one can succeed or fail. Actually, the whole debate turns on the question of whether it suffices to postulate "blind" capacities of discrimination, which might, for example, consist in pure reflex organization, or whether, on the contrary, these capacities for discrimination are the result of what is already an intelligent activity, corresponding to type-specific differences at the level of perception itself—in short, to the possession of "types" or natural concepts. Of course, one can refuse to *call* the correlates of these perceptual faculties of discrimination "concepts"; but one can hardly consider as settled the issue of whether or not these faculties already constitute intelligent modalities of the animal's coping with the world, and whether or not there are degrees in the scale of these abilities, ranging from "automatic" capacities of recognition (those of the butterfly) to more subtle forms in which the typical is apprehended as such (in certain higher animals), and finally to those in which the typical becomes conceptually elaborated. In any case, it is hard to deny that these faculties, whether or not they are considered as "conceptual" in the full sense, are necessary for the acquisition of the mastery of language. Language is neither the first nor the last word.

13. Sartre, *Being and Nothingness*, 627 (trans. modified—Tr.).

14. On this Megarianism, see Claude Romano, "La liberté sartrienne ou le rêve d'Adam," in *Il y a*, trans. Michael Smith, *There Is: The Event and the Finitude of Appearing*.

15. Heidegger, GA 24, p. 85; *The Basic Problems of Phenomenology*, 61. "This relation, which we signify by intentionality, is the *a priori comportmental character* [*der apriorische Verhältnischaracter*] of what we call self-comporting [*Sichverhalten*]."

16. This is further elaborated by M. Okrent (taking his lead from Davidson) in *Rational Animals* (Athens: University of Ohio Press, 2007).

17. Merleau-Ponty, *Phenomenology of Perception*, 140.

18. Merleau-Ponty, *Phenomenology of Perception*, 50 (trans. modified—Tr.).

19. Merleau-Ponty, *Phenomenology of Perception*, 270 (trans. modified—Tr.), 51; see also M. Wrathall, "Motives, Reasons and Causes," in T. Carman and M. Hansen, *The Cambridge Companion to Merleau-Ponty* (Cambridge, Eng.: Cambridge University Press, 2005), 111ff.

20. Merleau-Ponty, *Phenomenology of Perception*, 291.

21. Here we recognize the Stoic conception; see Cicero, *Tusculanes*, IV, XXX, 64.

22. Heidegger, *Sein und Zeit*, 143; *Being and Time*, 183.

23. Heidegger, *Sein und Zeit*, 151; *Being and Time*, 193.

24. Wittgenstein, *Philosophische Grammatik*, II, §32, p. 68; ed. R. Rhees, trans. A. Blackwell, *Philosophical Grammar* (Oxford: Blackwell, 1974), 68.

25. Wittgenstein, *The Blue and Brown Books* (Oxford: Blackwell, 1958), 5.

26. Heidegger, *Sein und Zeit*, 161; *Being and Time*, 204.

27. Wittgenstein, *Philosophische Grammatik*, 71; *Philosophical Grammar*, 71.

28. Heidegger, GA 24, 393; *The Basic Problems of Phenomenology*, 277–78.

29. C. Taylor, "Merleau-Ponty and the Epistemological Picture," in *The Cambridge Companion to Merleau-Ponty*, 30, 33.

30. Heidegger, GA 20, p. 356; trans. Kisiel, *History of the Concept of Time*, 258.

31. Wittgenstein, *Philosophical Investigations*, I, §199, trans. G. E. M. Anscombe (Oxford: Blackwell, 1953), 81e.

32. Heidegger, *Sein und Zeit*, 180–81; *Being and Time*, 224–26.

33. GA 20, p. 211; *History of the Concept of Time*, 15

34. Heidegger has frequently insisted that the logico-formal concept of relation was not suitable to phenomena when the elaboration of the concepts of fundamental ontology was at stake. I cannot follow him on this point. The formality (*Formalität*) of fundamental ontology cannot *replace* that of logic, and fundamental logical concepts like those of intrinsic *versus* relational property (of which Husserl would say that they belong to the domain of a formal ontology) necessarily serve as a basis to *all* conceptual elaboration—including, of course, that of a "fundamental ontology," even if this ontology must elaborate other, more specific concepts.

35. Heidegger, GA 29/30, p. 384; *The Fundamental Concepts of Metaphysics: World, Finitude, Solitude*, trans. William McNeill and Nicholas Walker (Bloomington: Indiana University Press, 1995), 264.

36. Fink formulates an analogous objection in *Das Spiel als Weltsymbol*, French trans. H. Hildenberg and A. Lindenberg, *Le jeu comme symbole du monde*, (Paris: Minuit, 1966), 52–53.

37. [The French expression "avoir conscience"is the normal expression for "to be aware" or "to be conscious." Literally, it translates as "have consciousness." The fact that there is no article before it indicates that "consciousness" is not truly being used as a noun here, but as a verbal phrase. Romano insists on this point to stress the danger of hypostatizing consciousness as an entity—Tr.]

38. Heidegger, *Sein und Zeit*, 14; trans., 34; see also GA 24, p. 155; *The Basic Problems of Phenomenology*, 110.

39. Heidegger, *Sein und Zeit*, 211; *Being and Time*, 254.

40. The world is a structural moment of Being-in-the-world: Heidegger, *Sein*

und Zeit, 64; *Being and Time*, 92–93. See also GA 24, p. 237; *The Basic Problems of Phenomenology*, 18.

Chapter 17

1. Heidegger, GA 56/57, p. 61; trans. Ted Sadler, *Towards the Definition of Philosophy* (London: Athlone, 2000), 51.

2. Heidegger, GA 56/57, p. 52; *Towards the Definition of Philosophy*, 43–44.

3. Quine, "Two Dogmas of Empiricism," 20–46.

4. Hence the tension, in Davidson himself, between a holistic perspective in which what determines the meaning of a belief are its logical relations with other beliefs within a system, and an atomistic perspective in which beliefs could be directly "caused" by objects—the property of being caused not being a holistic property. See S. Evnine, *Donald Davidson* (Cambridge, Eng.: Polity, 1991), 151.

5. A. Gurwitsch, *The Collected Works of Aron Gurwitsch (1901–1973): Phenomenology of Theme, Thematic Field and Marginal Consciousness*, vol. 3, *The Field of Consciousness* (Dordrecht: Springer, 2010), 143.

6. In the following analyses, I draw freely from that of Michael Esfeld, *Holism in Philosophy of Mind and Philosophy of Physics* (Dordrecht: Kluwer, 2001).

7. Esfeld, *Holism in Philosophy of Mind*, 19.

8. Ibid., 23–24.

9. Of course, this remark should not at all be taken to mean that a phenomenology of time would be restricted to envisioning these before/after relations in measurable and objective time.

10. Hua IX, p. 97; trans. John Scanlon, *Phenomenological Psychology* (The Hague: Martinus Nijhoff, 1962), 73.

11. E. Levinas, *En découvrant l'existence*, 132–33; *Discovering Existence with Husserl*, 118 (trans. modified—Tr.).

12. Merleau-Ponty, *Phenomenology of Perception*, 293.

13. Hua I, p. 19; trans. Peter Koestenbaum, *The Paris Lectures*, 19.

14. Hua I, p. 22 and 18; trans. Koestenbaum, *Paris Lectures*, 22 and 18.

15. Hua XI, p. 154; *Analyses Concerning Passive and Active Synthesis*, 202.

16. Hua XI, p. 156; *Analyses Concerning Passive and Active Synthesis*, 204.

17. "To get rid of 'atomism,' one adds the theory that the forms or configurations are founded on these data necessarily and the wholes are therefore prior in themselves to the parts. But, when descriptive theory of consciousness begins radically, it has before it no such data and wholes, except perhaps as prejudices" (Hua I, p. 77; trans. Cairns, *Cartesian Meditations*, 38).

18. Hua IX, p. 96; trans. J. Scanlon, *Phenomenological Psychology*, 72. On this point as well, Husserl's position remains ambiguous, since he appears to deny this position a little earlier: "For us, real single things are experienced, but the world is also experienced; and the two are even inseparable" (Hua IX, p. 95; *Phenomenological Psychology*, 71).

19. Hua IX, p. 98; *Phenomenological Psychology*, 73.

20. Hua I, p. 82; *Cartesian Meditations*, 45.

21. E. Straus, *Vom Sinn der Sinne*, 361; *The Primary World of Senses*, 341.

22. Maurice Merleau-Ponty, *The Visible and the Invisible*, trans. A. Lingis (Evanston, Ill.: Northwestern University Press, 1968), 244 (trans. modified—Tr.).

23. Hua I, p. 84; *Cartesian Meditations*, 46. [For the Levinas-Pfeiffer translation, see *Méditations Cartésiennes* (Paris: Librairie Philosophique J. Vrin, 1947), 40—Tr.]

24. J. Patočka, *Papiers phénoménologiques*, trans. E. Abrams (Grenoble: Millon, 1995), 65.

25. Maurice Merleau-Ponty, *Notes des cours au Collège de France, 1958–1959/1960–1961* (Paris: Gallimard, coll. Bibliothèque de Philosophie, 1996), 112.

26. James J. Gibson, *The Ecological Approach to Visual Perception* (Hillsdale, N.J.: Lawrence Erlbaum Associates, 1986), 160. See also "Perception and Judgement of Aerial Space and Distance . . ." (1947), included in *Reasons for Realism: Selected Essays of James J. Gibson*, ed. Edward Reed and Rebecca Jones (Hillsdale, N.J.: Lawrence Erlbaum Associates, 182), 40.

Chapter 18

1. *Modal*, not in the sense of a theory of modalities, but in that of the *mode of givenness* of something.

2. Hua IV, 186; trans. Richard Rojcewicz and André Schuwer, *Ideas Pertaining to a Pure Phenomenology and to a Phenomenological Philosophy: Second Book: Studies in the Phenomenology of Constitution* (Dordrecht: Kluwer Academic, 1993), 196 (trans. modified—Tr.).

3. Hua IV, p. 9; *Ideas II*, 10. See also Husserl, *Erfahrung und Urteil*, 53; *Ideas II*, 53.

4. Husserl, Ms FI 35, p. 104a, quoted by V. Costa, *La verità del mondo: Giudizio e teoria del significato in Heidegger* (Milan: Vita e Pensiero, 2003), 132.

5. Hua IV, p. 186 and 9, resp.; *Ideas II*, 196 and 11, respectively.

6. Hua IV, p. 187; *Ideas II*, 197.

7. Brentano, *Psychologie vom empirischen Standpunkt*, 113; *Psychology from an Empirical Standpoint*, 61: "presentations are the foundation for the other mental phenomena." Heidegger comments on this passage in GA 20, pp. 27–28.

8. Heidegger, *Sein und Zeit*, 98; *Being and Time*, 131.

9. Heidegger, *Sein und Zeit*, 98–99; *Being and Time*, 131–32.

10. GA 20, p. 247; trans. Kisiel, *History of the Concept of Time*, 183.

11. [Here Romano uses the word "affaire" to convey the sense of personal involvement often conveyed by the German "Sache," and goes on to emphasize this involvement by using the turn of phrase "ces 'affaires' autour desquelles nous nous affairons," that is, "these things with which we busy ourselves."—Tr.]

12. Heidegger, *Sein und Zeit*, 68; *Being and Time*, 97.

13. Ibid., 353; trans. 405.

14. Ibid., 68; trans. 97.

15. Ibid., 70; trans. 99.

16. Ibid., 83; trans. 114.

17. GA 20, p. 259; trans. Kisiel, *History of the Concept of Time*, 191.

18. *Sein und Zeit*, 68–69; *Being and Time*, 97–98 (trans. modified—Tr.).

19. Gadamer, GW 3, *Neue Philosophie I: Hegel, Husserl, Heidegger* (Tübingen: J. C. B. Mohr [Paul Siebeck], 1987), 426. In English, "Martin Heidegger's One Path," trans. P. Christopher Smith, in Kisiel and van Buren, *Reading Heidegger from the Start* (Albany: SUNY Press, 1994), 29. It should be noted that in *History of the Concept of Time: Prolegomena*, Heidegger speaks on several occasions of "closed totality [*geschlossene Ganzheit*]" (GA 20, 252, 255; trans. 187, 188, respectively), which raises a problem. How can an equipmental complex be closed, and what is the meaning of this closure?

20. Heidegger, *Sein und Zeit*, 84; *Being and Time* (modified), 116.

21. GA 20, 258; *History of the Concept of Time*, 190.

22. "In the most natural and the most immediate Being-in-the-world the world in its worldhood is not experienced thematically at all" (GA 20., 250; *History of the Concept of Time*, 185).

23. Heidegger, *Sein und Zeit*, 87; *Being and Time*, 121 (trans. modified).

24. Dilthey is apparently the first to use this expression, and to do so precisely in the framework of a holistic conception of life: "Bedeutsamkeit is die auf der Grundlage des Werkzeugszusammenhangs entstehende Bestimmtheit der Bedeutung eines Teiles für ein Ganzes" (Dilthey, *Gesammelte Schriften*, VII, pp. 238–39).

25. For example, in German *ich kann Deutsch* means I know German; *ich kann chauffieren*: I know how to drive.

26. GA 20, 253–54; *History of the Concept of Time*, 187.

27. Heidegger, *Sein und Zeit*, 67; *Being and Time*, 95.

28. Ibid., 61–62; trans., 89.

29. Heidegger expressly evokes the following of a rule in his course *Prolegomena zur Geschichte des Zeitbegriffs*, GA 20, p. 279, though he never gave the notion of grammar, nor that of institution (*Stiftung*) (see *Sein und Zeit*, 80), their full importance.

30. [The underlying French terms for "thing" in this sentence are "affaire" and "chose," respectively. See above, note 11—Tr.]

31. Heidegger, *Sein und Zeit*, 70; *Being and Time*, 100 (trans. modified).

32. This point is very justly emphasized by Jean-François Courtine ("Vorhanden," in *Vocabulaire européen des philosophies: Dictionnaire des intraduisibles*, ed. Barbara Cassin [Paris: Le Robert, 2004], 1385–86), who proposes distinguishing between two acceptations of *Vorhandenheit*, the first corresponding to what is present there before us as material for . . . , the second pertaining to a deficient mode of concern. See also GA 20, p. 271; *History of the Concept of Time*, 199 (trans. modified—Tr.): "The environmental references, in which nature is present primarily in a worldly way, tell us rather the reverse: *nature as reality can only be understood on the basis of worldhood* . . . . The Presence-at-hand of nature . . . as for its meaning, is uncovered and fundamentally there on the basis of the world of concern."

33. Heidegger, *Sein und Zeit*, 193; *Being and Time*, 238.

34. Ibid., 61; trans. 88.

35. GA 2, p. 83, note a; *Being and Time*, trans. Joan Stambaugh (Albany: SUNY Press, 2010), 61, note *. (The Macquarrie and Robinson translation does not include this note.—Tr.)

36. See Husserl, Ms B I 32, p. 17 (May 1931) titled "Against Heidegger": "Es gehören besondere Motive dazu um theoretische Einstellung möglich zu machen, und gegenüber Heidegger will es mir scheinen, dass ein ursprüngliches Motif liege, für Wissenschaft wie für Kunst, in der Notwendigkeit des Spieles und speziell in der Motivation einer spielerischen, das ist nicht aus Lebensnotdurft, nicht aus Beruf, aus Zweckzusammenhang der Selbsterhaltung entspringenden 'theoretischen Neugier,' die sich die Dinge ansehen, sie kennenlernen will, Dinge, die sie nicht angehen. Und nicht 'defiziente' Praxis soll hier vorliegen." It should be noted that Husserl himself will speak more and more often of a "scientific *praxis*," particularly in the *Crisis*.

37. Jacques Taminiaux, *Heidegger and the Project of Fundamental Ontology*, trans. Michael Gendre (Albany: SUNY Press, 1991), 97.

38. Furthermore, the holism of equipmentality has the inconvenience of raising an impassible barrier between human equipment and the tools used by some higher animals: the twig that enables the chimpanzee to feed on termites is indeed an *isolated* tool. Is there no continuity between these rudimentary tools and those produced by *Homo sapiens*? That is inevitably the consequence to which Heidegger's position leads. Also, Heidegger's claim tends to overlook the difference of levels of complexity and of levels of integration in an instrumental complex of human equipmentality. The hammer is far more isolable from other tools than is a machine tool, not to mention the revolution in the technology of computer science.

39. Heidegger, *Sein und Zeit*, 64; *Being and Time*, 92 (my emphasis). This point has been rightly emphasized by Vincenzo Costa, *La verità del mondo: giudizio e teoria del significato in Heidegger* (Milan: Vita e Pensiero, 2003), 241–42.

40. GA 26, 233; trans. M. Heim, *The Metaphysical Foundations of Logic* (Bloomington: Indiana University Press, 1984), 181 (trans. modified—Tr.).

41. GA 26, p. 248–49; trans. *The Metaphysical Foundations of Logic*, 192.

42. [Here "exist" is used as a transitive verb.—Tr.]

43. Heidegger, *Sein und Zeit*, 143–44; *Being and Time*, 183 (trans. modified—Tr.).

44. Ibid., 145; trans. 186.

45. Tugendhat, *Selbstbewußtsein und Selbstbestimmung* (Frankfurt am Main: Suhrkamp, 1979); trans. *Self-Consciousness and Self-Determination* (Cambridge, Mass: MIT Press, 1986), 165: "We have just seen that Heidegger (incorrectly) thought that if Dasein relates itself to its own being as to-be, its being cannot be understood simultaneously as presence-at-hand."

46. Hua IX, p. 279. [These notes on Heidegger are not included in Scanlon's translation of Hua IX. I therefore quote from Thomas Sheehan's translation, in Edmund Husserl and Martin Heidegger, *Psychological and Transcendental Phenomenology and the Confrontation with Heidegger, 1927–1931* (Dordrecht: Springer, 2011), 274 n87—Tr.].

47. GA 20, p. 288; *History of the Concept of Time*, 210 (trans. modified—Tr.).

48. Here Heidegger is very close to an author like John Dewey: "Mind is primarily a verb. It denotes all the ways in which we deal consciously and expressly with the situations in which we find ourselves. Unfortunately, an influential manner of thinking had changed modes of action into an underlying substance that performs the activities in question. It has treated mind as an independent entity *which* attends, purposes, cares, notices, and remembers" (Dewey, *Art as Experience* [New York: Capricorn Books, G. P. Putnam's Sons, 1958], 263). Heidegger goes further than Dewey on one point: he proposes to do without the word "mind" completely.

49. See above, chapter 12.

50. See Anthony Kenny, *Will, Freedom and Power* (New York: Barnes and Noble, 1976), 136.

51. Ibid., 137.

52. Heidegger, *Sein und Zeit,* 144; *Being and Time* (modified), 183.

53. Heidegger, *Sein und Zeit,* 144; *Being and Time,* 183.

54. GA 24, p. 391; trans. A. Hofstadter, *The Basic Problems of Phenomenology,* 276 (trans. modified—Tr.).

55. Heidegger, *Sein und Zeit,* 145; *Being and Time,* 185.

56. See Charles Taylor, "What Is Human Agency?" in *Human Agency and Language: Philosophical Papers I* (Cambridge, Eng.: Cambridge University Press, 1985).

57. Here the question arises as to whether it is resoluteness that makes a second-order choice possible, as Heidegger asserts, or whether it is not rather the ability to make second-order choices that confers upon death its properly human meaning. I will leave this problem aside.

58. Heidegger, *Sein und Zeit,* 264; *Being and Time,* 308–9 (inserted words in square brackets are those of CR—Tr.).

59. GA 29/30, p. 529; trans. W. McNeill and N. Walker, *The Fundamental Concepts of Metaphysics: World, Finitude, Solitude* (Bloomington: Indiana University Press, 2001), 364.

60. GA 24, p. 241; *Basic Problems of Phenomenology,* 170.

61. GA 24, p. 237; *Basic Problems of Phenomenology,* 166 (trans. modified—Tr.).

62. Heidegger, *Sein und Zeit,* 284; *Being and Time,* 329.

63. GA 24, 308; *Basic Problems of Phenomenology,* 216.

64. GA 26, pp. 218, 232.

65. Heidegger, *Sein und Zeit,* 64; *Being and Time,* 92.

66. See Claude Romano, *Event and World,* trans. Shane Mackinlay (New York: Fordham University Press, 2009), and *L'Événement et le temps* (Paris: Presses Universitaires de France, 1999).

67. Hua I, §124, p. 287; *Ideas I,* trans. Kersten, 296.

Chapter 19

The epigraph is from Gibson, *The Ecological Approach to Visual Perception,* 3.

1. Ian Hacking, *Why Does Language Matter for Philosophy?* (Cambridge, Eng.: Cambridge University Press, 1975).

2. John McDowell, *Mind and World* (Cambridge, Mass.: Harvard University Press, 1994 [8th ed., 2003]), 67.

3. Husserl, "Entwurf einer 'Vorrede' zu den Logischen Untersuchungen," ed. E. Fink, *Tijdschrift voor Philosophie* 1 (1939): 115; "Introduction to the Logical Investigations: A Draft of a *Preface* to the *Logical Investigations*," trans. P. J. Bossert and C. H. Peters, ed. E. Fink (The Hague: Martinus Nijhoff, 1975), 22.

4. Husserl, letter to Natorp of March 18, 1909: "We, at Göttingen, work in a very different state of mind [than the Marburg school] and, though sincere idealists, we are in a sense idealists from below [*Idealisten . . . gewissermaßen von Unter*]" (*Briefwechsel*, V, p. 110).

5. Levinas, "Reflections on Phenomenological 'Technique,'" in *Discovering Existence with Husserl*, trans. and ed. Richard A. Cohen and Michael B. Smith (Evanston, Ill.: Northwestern University Press, 1998), 118.

6. Max M. Scheler, *Von Ewigen im Menschen*, in *Gesammelte Werke*, vol. 5, ed. Maria Scheler (Bayern: Francke Verlag, 1954 [5th ed., 1968]), 250; trans. Bernard Noble, *On the Eternal in Man* (New Brunswick, N.J.: Transaction, 2010), 255–56.

7. Heidegger, GA 58, p. 5; trans. Scott M. Campbell, *Basic Problems of Phenomenology: Winter Semester 1919/1920* (London: Bloomsbury Academic, 2013), 4 (trans. modified—Tr.).

8. Heidegger, GA 20, p. 96; trans. Theodore Kisiel, *History of the Concept of Time* (Bloomington: Indiana University Press, 1985), 70.

9. See Gareth Evans, *Varieties of Reference* (Oxford: Clarendon, 1982); McDowell, *Mind and World* (Cambridge, Mass.: Harvard University Press, 1994): Christopher Peacocke, *Thoughts: An Essay on Content* (Oxford: Basil Blackwell, 1986); for an approach to this entire debate, see the useful collection of York H. Gunther, *Essays on Nonconceptual Content* (Cambridge, Mass.: MIT Press, 2003). Outside the line of these works, Cavell already analyzed in his first publications "Wittgenstein's *Philosophical Investigations* as well as Austin's practice" as being "the first heirs of the task of Kant's transcendental logic"; but he recognizes with lucidity that Austin and Wittgenstein "counting on some intimacy between language and the world . . . were never able satisfactorily to give an account of [this problem]" (Stanley Cavell, *This New Yet Unapproachable America: Lectures After Emerson After Wittgenstein* [Chicago: University of Chicago Press, 2013], 81).

10. ". . . nicht am Himmel sind Sterne gegeben, sondern in der Wissenschaft der Astronomie . . . Nicht im Auge liegt die Sinnlichkeit, sondern in den raisons de l'astronomie." Hermann Cohen, *Das Prinzip der Infinitesimal-Methode und seine Geschichte* (Berlin: Ferd. Dümmlers Verlagsbuchhandlung, Harrwitz u. Grossmann, 1883), 127 (my translation—Tr.).

11. P. Natorp, "Kant und die Marburger Schule," *Kant-Studien*, vol. 17 (1912): 206 (my translation, emphasis by CR—Tr.).

12. P. Natorp, *Allgemeine Psychologie nach kritischer Methode: Erstes Buch: Objekt und Methode der Psychologie* (Tübingen: J.C.B. Mohr, 1912), 278, 40, and 278, respectively (my translation here and in the following quotations—Tr.).

13. Natorp, "Kant und die Marburger Schule," 201 (my translation here and in the following quotations—Tr.).

14. Kant, *Kritik der reinen Vernunft*, B160; trans. F. Max Müller, *Critique of Pure Reason* (Garden City, N.Y.: Doubleday, 1966), 94.

15. Natorp, "Kant und die Marburger Schule," 202 (my translation—Tr.).

16. Ibid., 213.

17. Ibid., 199.

18. Paul Natorp, "Husserl 'Ideen zu einer reinen Phänomenologie," *Logos* 7 (1917–1918): 230 (my translation—Tr.).

19. Natorp, "Kant und die Marburger Schule," 204.

20. Natorp, *Allgemeine Psychologie,* 83.

21. Natorp, "Kant und die Marburger Schule," 206.

22. Ibid., 201–2.

23. Ibid., 211; Heidegger has emphasized this proximity of neo-Kantianism to Hegelianism in Natorp; see GA 56–57, p. 40 and p. 108: "The most radical absolutization of the theoretical, an absolutization that has not been proclaimed since Hegel. (Unmistakable connections with Hegel: everything unmediated is mediated.) An absolutization that radically logicizes the sphere of lived experience [*Erlebnissphäre*] and lets this exist only in the logicized form of the concretion of the *concrete*—which concrete has meaning only in its necessary correlation with the abstract." (English trans. by Ted Sadler, *Towards the Definition of Philosophy: 1. The Idea of Philosophy and the Problem of Worldview; 2. Phenomenology and Transcendental Philosophy of Value; with a Transcript of the Lecture-Course "On the Nature of the University and Academic Study" (Freiburg Lecture-Courses 1919),* London: Continuum, 2008), 91.

24. Natorp, "Kant und die Marburger Schule," 213 and 212.

25. See M. Friedman, *Parting of the Ways: Carnap, Cassirer and Heidegger* (Chicago: Open Court, 2000).

26. Ernst Cassirer, *The Philosophy of Symbolic Forms,* vol. 1, trans. Ralph Manheim (New Haven, Conn.: Yale University Press, 1953), 87.

27. Ibid., 110.

28. Ibid., 113.

29. Ernst Cassirer, *Symbol, Technik, Sprache,* ed. John Michael Krois and Ernst Wolfgang Orth, Philosophische Bibliothek, vol. 372 (Hamburg: Felix Meiner Verlag, 1985), 126.

30. M. Schlick, "Über das Fundament der Erkenntnis," in *Erkenntnis,* 4 (Springer Verlag, 1934), 98; trans. David Rynin, in A. J. Ayer, *Logical Positivism* (New York: Free, 1959), 226.

31. Ibid., 97; trans. 225. Sellars alludes to this point when he stresses that these *Konstatierungen* "resemble analytic statements in that being correctly made is a sufficient and necessary condition of their truth" (Sellars, "Empiricism and The Philosophy of Mind," in *Science, Perception and Reality,* 166). C. I. Lewis will take up this idea in *Mind and the World-Order: Outline of a Theory of Knowledge* (New York: Charles Scribner's Sons, 1929): phenomenal sensible objects (sense data) support the entire edifice of knowledge. As for Schlick, he rejected sense data and accepted the forms of Gestalt psychology.

32. Hua I, §5, p. 52; trans. Dorion Cairns, *Cartesian Meditations,* 11.

33. It may be recalled, however, that Husserl makes an important distinction between knowledge *stricto sensu,* which is of a propositional kind, and simple intuition. Intuition is a "*source of authority for knowledge*" (*Rechtquelle der Erkennt-*

nis) and not knowledge *stricto sensu* (see *Ideen I*, §24; Hua III, 1, p. 51; trans. W. R. Boyce Gibson, *Ideas: General Introduction to Pure Phenomenology* [New York: Collier, 1962], 83). Knowledge is a thought, but "intuiting is not thinking."

34. Heidegger, GA 58, p. 131; trans. Scott M. Campbell, *Basic Problems of Phenomenology: Winter Semester*, 101.

35. Sellars, "Empiricism and the Philosophy of Mind," 128.

36. Richard Rorty, "Preface," in W. Sellars, *Empirisme et philosophie de l'esprit*, trans. Fabien Cayla (Paris: L'éclat, 1992), 9.

37. Sellars, "Empiricism and the Philosophy of Mind," 127.

38. We should add to the texts already mentioned Rickert's "Die Methode der Philosophie und das Unmittelbare," in *Philosophische Aufsätze* (Tubingen: J.C.B. Mohr [Paul Siebeck], 1999), 107–51.

39. Sellars, "Empiricism and the Philosophy of Mind," 132.

40. Marcel Proust, *In Search of Lost Time*, trans. Andreas Mayor and Terence Kilmartin, rev. D. J. Enright (New York: Modern Library, 2003), 565.

41. Sellars, "Empiricism and the Philosophy of Mind," 37.

42. Ibid., 160.

43. Ibid.

44. Ibid., 169.

45. Ibid., 168.

46. Wittgenstein, *Zettel*, ed. Elizabeth Anscombe and Georg Henrik von Wright (Oxford: Blackwell, 1981), 73, 74 (§420, §422).

47. Wittgenstein, *Notebooks 1914–16*, 2nd ed. (Malden, Mass.: Blackwell, 1998), 96.

48. Wittgenstein, *Philosophical Investigations*, trans. G. E. M. Anscombe, 2nd ed. (Oxford: Blackwell, 1958), 221e.

49. Sellars, "Empiricism and the Philosophy of Mind," 145.

50. Ibid., 175.

51. Ibid., 142.

52. Ibid., 141, 142.

53. C. Larry Hardin, *Color for Philosophers: Unweaving the Rainbow* (Indianapolis, Ind.: Hackett, 1988), 67–76.

54. R. M. Chisholm, *Perceiving: A Philosophical Study* (Ithaca, N.Y.: Cornell University Press, 1957), esp. 50–51.

55. Heidegger, GA 20, pp. 121–22; trans. Theodore Kisiel, *History of the Concept of Time: Prolegomena* (Bloomington: Indiana University Press, 1985), 88–89.

56. Sellars, "Empiricism and the Philosophy of Mind," 147.

57. William P. Alston, "Sellars and the 'Myth of the Given,'" *Philosophy and Phenomenological Research* 65, no. 1 (July 2002): 69–86, esp. 80. I am indebted to Alston on several points.

58. Sellars, "Empiricism and the Philosophy of Mind," 191.

59. C. Stumpf, *Tonpsychologie*, vol. 1 (Leipzig: Verlag von S. Hirzel, 1883–1890), 11. As Husserl will restate the point: "experience with its demands precedes conceptual thinking with its demands" (Hua V, p. 34; trans. Ted E. Klein and William. E. Pohl, *Ideas Pertaining to a Pure Phenomenology and to a Phenomenological Philosophy: Third Book: Phenomenology and the Foundations of the Science.* [The Hague:

Martinus Nijhoff, 1980], 30). One doesn't have to wait for G. Evans to discover what he calls the "belief-independence" of perception (*The Varieties of Reference* [Oxford: Clarendon, 1982], 123).

60. Merleau-Ponty, *Phénoménologie de la perception*, 43; trans. Donald A. Landes, *Phenomenology of Perception*, 36. The idea is already present in Max Scheler, precisely in his polemic with neo-Kantianism. See *Die deutsche Philosophie der Gegenwart* (1922) in *Gesammelte Werke*, vol. 7, ed. M. S. Frings (Bern: Francke Verlag, 1973), 310. Scheler denounces the *proton pseudos* of the Kantian doctrine according to which "everything in the given that is not sensuous could only be previously supplied to the object of experience through a hypothetically assumed, synthetically constructed activity of the understanding or the look."

61. Aristotle, *De Anima*, III, 428b2–5.

62. McDowell, *Mind and World*, 140.

63. Ibid., xv.

64. Ibid., xv.

65. Davidson, "A Coherence Theory of Truth and Knowledge," 141.

66. McDowell, *Mind and World*, 14.

67. Kant, *Kritik der reinen Vernunft*, A51/B75.

68. McDowell, *Mind and World*, 9.

69. Ibid., 10.

70. Ibid., 10.

71. Ibid., 41. See also 9 and 51.

72. Ibid., 155. See also 29, 58.

73. Hua III, 1, p. 305; trans. F. Kersten, *Ideas I*, p. 317 (§133).

74. McDowell, *Mind and World*, 61.

75. Ibid., 142

76. Ibid., 13.

77. Wittgenstein, *Tractatus logico-philosophicus*, proposition 1. See McDowell, *Mind and World*, 27.

78. Davidson, "A Coherence Theory of Truth and Knowledge," 144.

79. McDowell, *Mind and World*, 15.

80. Taylor, "Merleau-Ponty and the Epistemological Picture," 29.

81. Davidson, "A Coherence Theory of Truth and Knowledge," 146.

82. Merleau-Ponty, *Phenomenology de la perception*, 275–76; trans. Landes, *Phenomenology of Perception*, 248.

83. Wittgenstein, *Philosophical Investigations*, trans. G. E. M. Anscombe (London: Blackwell, 1958), 44e (I, §95).

84. McDowell, *Mind and World*, 83.

85. Ibid., 27–28.

86. Ibid., 26. In his preface to the French edition (*L'esprit et le monde*, trans. Christophe Alsaleh [Paris: J. Vrin, 2007], 8) McDowell deeply modifies his position in saying that the content of perception is conceptual *and not propositional.* Besides the fact that this "revelation" overturns the entire organization of the work, we may wonder whether it doesn't make McDowell's claim still more obscure, since "concept" here means *linguistic* concept and the conceptual capacities *in that sense* are carried out paradigmatically in judgment. As Davidson stresses, "We

may be inclined to think that the concept formation is more primitive than entering the world of propositional attitudes, the world of particulars, of beliefs. But this is a mistake . . . To have a concept is to *classify* objects or properties or events or situations. . . . Thus there is in fact no distinction between having a concept and having thoughts with propositional content" (Davidson, "Seeing through Language," in *Truth, Language and History* [Oxford: Clarendon, 2005], 139).

87. See above, note 47. Compare with McDowell, *Mind and World*, 47: "It is only because experience involves capacities belonging to spontaneity that we can understand experience as awareness, or apparent awareness, of aspects of the world at all."

88. McDowell, *Mind and World*, 26.

89. Ibid., 29.

90. This point has been emphasized by Lockwood, *Mind, Brain and the Quantum* (Oxford: Blackwell, 1989), 147–48, 300–301 (quoted by Esfeld, *Holism in Philosophy of Mind and Philosophy of Physics*, 149).

91. McDowell, "Criteria, Defeasibility, and Knowledge, in *Meaning, Knowledge, and Reality* (Harvard University Press, 1998), 369–94.

92. Davidson, "A Coherence Theory of Truth and Knowledge," 144.

93. Ibid., 155.

94. Ibid., 34.

95. Ibid., 47.

96. Ibid., 34.

97. Ibid.

98. Ibid., 41.

99. Merleau-Ponty, *Phenomenology of Perception*, 34.

100. McDowell, *Mind and World*, 46.

101. Ibid.

102. Heidegger, GA 56/57, 108; trans. Ted Sadler, *Towards the Definition of Philosophy* (United States: Continuum Books, 2003), 90–91.

103. McDowell, *Mind and World*, 44.

104. See, on this point, the very apt remarks of Robert Pippin, "Concept and Intuition: On Distinguishability and Separability, *Hegel-Studien* 40 (2005): esp. 37.

105. This could again be verified by examining John McDowell's reading of Kant in "Hegel and the Myth of the Given," in *Das Interesse des Denkens: Hegel aus heutiger Sicht*, ed. Wolfgang Welsch (Munich: Fink, 2003), 76–88, in which he goes through the neo-Kantian *topoi* one by one.

106. In opposition to the rigid Kantian duality of activity versus receptivity, see Husserl's *Erfahrung und Urteil*, §23 (a), p. 119; trans. James S. Churchill and Lothar Eley, *Experience and Judgment* (Evanston, Ill.: Northwestern University Press, 1973), 108: "This formulation shows that the distinction between passivity and activity is not inflexible, that it is not a matter here of terms which can be established definitively for all time, but only by means of description and contrast, whose sense must in each case be recreated originally with reference to the concrete situation of the analysis—an observation which holds true for every description of intentional phenomena."

107. McDowell, *Mind and World*, 111.

108. ["redécouvrir l'Amérique" is the French equivalent of reinventing the wheel—Tr.].

109. "Je regrette l'Europe aux anciens parapets!" Arthur Rimbaud, from "Le bateau ivre" (my translation—Tr.).

Chapter 20

The epigraph is from H. Putnam, *The Threefold Cord: Mind, Body, and World* (New York: Columbia University Press, 1999), 40.

1. For an overview of these interpretations, the reader might consult the already old work under the direction of Owen Roger Jones, *The Private Language Argument* (London: Macmillan, St. Martin's, 1971).

2. Wittgenstein, *Philosophical Investigations*, trans. G. E. M. Anscombe, I, §243, 88–89.

3. Ibid., I, §202, 81.

4. Davidson, "The Myth of the Subjective," 46.

5. See, for example, Rudolf Bernet, *Conscience et existence* (Paris: Presses Universitaires de France, 2004), 71: "Only the sign, and, more generally, language, makes it possible for the third person to have a knowledge of the knowledge of a first person and to share it by in turn carrying out a corresponding act of knowledge" (my translation—Tr.).

6. *Philosophical Investigations*, I §248; trans. G. E. M. Anscombe, 90.

7. Locke, *An Essay Concerning Human Understanding* (London: Penguin Classics, 1997), 364 (bk. 3, chap. 2, §2).

8. Hua XVII, §95, p. 243; trans. Dorion Cairns, *Formal and Transcendental Logic* (The Hague: Martinus Nijhoff, 1969), 236.

9. Ibid.

10. Hua I, §48, p. 135; *Cartesian Meditations*, trans. D. Cairns, 105 (trans. modified—Tr.).

11. Hua VIII, p. 174, n2. (Here I translate from the French translation quoted by CR: Edmund Husserl, *Philosophie première, II*, French trans., Arion Lothar Kelkel [Paris: Presses Universitaires de France, 1972], 241, note [and p. 239 for the passage in square brackets]).

12. Hua VIII, p. 177; (my trans. from French trans. quoted by CR: *Philosophie première, II*, 243–44—Tr.).

13. Hua XIII, p. 190; trans. Ingo Farin and James G. Hart, *The Basic Problems of Phenomenology: From the Lectures, Winter Semester, 1910–1911* (Dordrecht: Springer, 2006).

14. Hua IX, p. 344 (my translation—Tr.).

15. Hua VI, §54 (b), p. 187; trans. David Carr, *The Crisis of European Sciences and Transcendental Phenomenology* (Evanston, Ill.: Northwestern University Press, 1970), 187: "I am the one who performs the *epochē*." Thus it is hardly surprising that the reductive method should create "a unique sort of philosophical solitude" (ibid.).

16. It is caricatural, to give only one example, that in a paper by Dan Zahavi dedicated to intersubjectivity in Husserl, "Husserl's Intersubjective Transformation of Transcendental Philosophy" (in Don Welton, ed., *The New Husserl: A Critical Reader* [Indianapolis: Indiana University Press, 2003], 233–51), the author openly decides not to inquire into the only decisive point, the constitution of the Other: "I will not go into a more detailed account of Husserl's analysis of the complex structure of the concrete bodily mediated experience of the Other, but simply assume [*sic*] that it exists one way or the other, and instead go directly to what I take to be the core in Husserl's reflections on intersubjectivity" (235).

17. Hua I, p. 127; trans. Cairns, *Cartesian Meditations*, 96.

18. Hua VIII, p. 175; (my trans. from French trans. quoted by CR: *Philosophie première, II*, 241).

19. Hua VIII, p. 187; (my trans. from French trans. quoted by CR: *Philosophie première, II*, 257).

20. Hua VIII, p. 134–35; (my trans. from French trans. quoted by CR: *Philosophie première, II*, 188).

21. Hua I, p. 150; trans. Cairns, *Cartesian Meditations*, 122.

22. Hua I, p. 140; *Cartesian Meditations*, 110.

23. Hua I, p. 140; *Cartesian Meditations*, 110.

24. Didier Franck, *Chair et corps: Sur la phénoménologie de Husserl* (Paris: Éditions de Minuit, 1981), 124. See also Paul Ricoeur's remarks, "E. Husserl—La cinquième Meditation cartésienne," in *À l'école de la phénoménologie* (Paris: Vrin, 1986), 207–8, and *Du texte à l'action: Essais d'herméneutique II* (Paris: Éditions du Seuil, 1969), 77: "To say that the Other is 'appresented' and never properly speaking 'presented' seems like a way of naming the difficulty rather than of solving it. . . . If the configuration of the ego and the alter ego in a couple is not primal, it will never occur."

25. See Hua XIII, p. 70. "It is a contradiction to tie the whole problem of empathy to simple expressive movements, to bodily expressions, to the externalizing of the psyche, as is usual, and as Lipps also has also done in his commendable studies. The apprehension of the 'externalization,' of the 'expression' of psychic acts and states is already mediated by the apprehension of the lived body as lived body" (my translation—Tr.).

26. To this properly conceptual argument one might add an empirical one. As Merleau-Ponty remarks, and many empirical discoveries have plausibly established since then (see for example Daniel N. Stern, *The Interpersonal World of the Infant* [New York: Basic Books, 1985]; Alain Berthoz and Gérard Jorland, eds., *L'Empathie* [Paris: Odile Jacob, 2004]), a "coupling by resemblance," presupposing an awareness of the similarity of one's own body and of the foreign body, cannot be attributed to an infant, who does, nonetheless, show specific behavior (such as smiling) in the presence of another person. If the foreign consciousness, in order to be recognized, presupposed a resemblance between the other's behavior and my own, the infant would have to "translate" the visual experience of the other person's smile "into a motor language"; "he would have to move his facial muscles in such a way as to reproduce the visible expression called the smile in the other. But how would he do that? He does not naturally possess the

internal motor feeling that the other has of his or her face, and as for himself, he does not have a visual image of himself smiling. Hence, if we want to solve the problem of this transfer of behavior from the other to myself, we absolutely cannot rely on an assumed analogy between the face of the other and that of the child" (Merleau-Ponty, *Parcours, 1935–1951* [Lagrasse: Verdier, 1997], 175). Consequently "the relations observed between my gesticulations and those of others, and between my intentions and my gesticulations, can certainly provide a guide in the methodological knowledge of others and when direct perception fails, *but they do not teach me about the existence of others*" (Merleau-Ponty, *Phenomenology of Perception*, 368 [my emphasis—CR]).

27. Emmanuel Levinas, *Totalité et infini*, (The Hague: Martinus Nijhoff, 1971), reprint Paris, Le livre de Poche, 1990, 210; trans. Alphonso Lingis, *Totality and Infinity*, (Pittsburgh: Duquesne University Press, [1969]), 193.

28. Ibid., 211; 194.

29. Emmanuel Levinas, *Éthique et infini: Dialogues avec Philippe Nemo* (Paris: Fayard, 1982; Livre de Poche, 1984), 81; trans. Richard A. Cohen, *Ethics and Infinity* (Pittsburgh: Duquesne University Press, 1982), 86.

30. Levinas, *Ethique et infini*, 79; *Ethics and Infinity*, 85.

31. [The French plays here on the word *"optique"* which means "perspective," while insisting on the visual aspect of this perspective, on "optiks"—Tr.].

32. Merleau-Ponty, *Phenomenology of Perception*, 354.

33. Heidegger, GA 20, p. 210; trans. Kisiel, *History of the Concept of Time*, 156.

34. Heidegger, *Sein und Zeit*, 124; *Being and Time*, 162.

35. GA 20, p. 335; *History of the Concept of Time*, 243.

36. GA 20, p. 339; *History of the Concept of Time*, 246.

37. GA 20, p. 330; *History of the Concept of Time*, 240

38. Heidegger, *Sein und Zeit*, 125; *Being and Time*, 161.

39. GA 24, p. 394; trans. A. Hofstadter, *The Basic Problems of Phenomenology*, 278.

40. Ibid. (Trans. modified—Tr.)

41. GA 26, p. 249; trans. M. Heim, *The Metaphysical Foundations of Logic* (Bloomington: Indiana University Press, 1984), 193.

42. GA 24, p. 308; *The Basic Problems of Phenomenology*, 216.

43. GA 24, p. 241–42; *The Basic Problems of Phenomenology*, 170 (trans. modified—Tr.).

44. GA 20, pp. 329–30; trans. Kisiel, *History of the Concept of Time*, 239. See also *Sein und Zeit*, 120; *Being and Time*, 156: "Dasein in itself is essentially Being-with [*das Dasein wesenhaft an ihm selbst Mitsein ist*]."

45. This "von sich her" is strongly reminiscent of Husserl's "von innen her": "Die konkret, volle transzendentale Subjectivität ist das von innen her, rein transzendental einige und nur so konkrete All der offenen Ichgemeinschaft" (Hua IX, p. 344).

46. See, on all this, my *Event and World*, trans. Shane Mackinley (New York: Fordham University Press, 2009).

47. Hua III, 1, §52, p. 110; trans. B. Gibson, *Ideas I*, 143.

48. I borrow the distinction phenomenally/genetically subjective from Wolfgang Köhler, who insists on the danger of mixing up these two uses of "subjective." "Quite often the two denotations of the term are confused in the most deplorable manner, as though what is genetically subjective ought also to appear as subjective in experience" (*Gestalt Psychology: An Introduction to New Concepts in Modern Psychology* [New York: Liveright, 1992], 23).

49. Arthur Schopenhauer, *On Vision and Colors*, trans. Georg Stahl (New York: Princeton Architectural Press, 1910), 57.

50. Merleau-Ponty, *The Visible and the Invisible*, trans. A. Lingis, 158.

51. [The text says "something that I *make*," but in French it can be said "je *fais* une expérience"—Tr.]

52. Locke, *An Essay Concerning Human Understanding*, bk. 2, chap. 8, §8.

53. See C. Larry Hardin, *Color for Philosophers: Unweaving the Rainbow* (Indianapolis: Hackett, 1988), 111: "Colored objects are illusions, but not unfounded illusions." Or there would seem to be a "natural illusion of a world of colored objects" (81). In short, "we are to be eliminativists with respect to color as a property of objects, but reductivists with respect to color experiences" (112).

54. See Thompson, *Colour Vision*, 138.

55. See Thompson, *Colour Vision*, 138.

56. Merleau-Ponty, *Phenomenology of Perception*, 53.

57. Paul Cézanne, ed. P. M. Doran. *Conversations with Cézanne* (Berkeley: University of California Press, 2001).

58. Strauss, *Vom Sinn der Sinne*, 324: "Die Erfahrung des fremden Ich vollzieht sich aber in dem von allem Erkennen geschiedenen, auch dem Tier zugehörigen sympathetischen Erleben des Empfindens." (This passage is not included in Jacob Needleman's English trans., *The Primary World of the Senses: A Vindication of Sensory Experience* [New York: Free Press of Glencoe, 1963]—Tr.)

59. Merleau-Ponty, *Phenomenology of Perception*, 379.

60. Ibid.

61. Ibid., 412–13; trans. Landes, 376.

62. Ludwig Wittgenstein, *Last Writings on the Philosophy of Psychology, Vol. II, The Inner and the Outer, 1949–1951*, ed. G. H. Von Wright and Heikki Nyman, trans. C. G. Luckhardt and Maximilian A. E. Aue, MS 169, around 1949 (Malden, Mass: Blackwell, 1999), 38. See also Wittgenstein, *Philosophical Investigations, Part II, iv*, 2nd ed., trans. G. E. M. Anscombe (Malden, Mass: Blackwell, 1999), 178: "'I believe that he is suffering.' Do I also believe that he isn't an automaton? It would go against the grain to use the word in both connexions. (Or is it like this: I believe that he is suffering, but I am certain that he is not an automaton? Nonsense!)"

63. Contrary to Cavell's reading, Wittgenstein never maintained that the existence of another mind is a deep philosophical problem, let alone the only deep philosophical problem. On this point, I refer the reader to the criticisms of Marie McGinn, to which I subscribe: "The Real Problem of Others: Cavell, Merleau-Ponty and Wittgenstein on Scepticism about Other Minds," *European Journal of Philosophy* 6 (1998): 45–58.

64. Merleau-Ponty, *Phenomenology of Perception*, 372.

65. Ludwig Wittgenstein, *Bermerkungen über die Philosophie der Psychologie,* trans. Luckhardt and Aue, *Remarks on the Philosophy of Psychology,* II, §170; (Oxford: Blackwell, 1998), 33.

Chapter 21

The epigraph is from Maurice Merleau-Ponty, *Le Visible et l'invisible,* Paris, Gallimard, 1964, 255; *The Visible and the Invisible,* ed. Claude Lefort, trans. A. Lingis (Evanston, Ill.: Northwestern University Press, 1968), 202 (translation slightly modified—Tr.).

1. Aristotle, *De Interpretatione,* 17a1–5: here the analysis of *logos* concentrates on the statement, which allows the Stagirite to reserve the examination of the other speech acts, such as prayer, for his studies on rhetoric and poetics.

2. LU I §28; Hua XIX, 1, p. 95; trans. J. N. Findlay, *Logical Investigations,* vol. 1 (London: Routledge, 2001), 223.

3. LU VI §69; Hua XIX, 2, respectively, pp. 742, 741 and 740; *Logical Investigations,* vol. 2, 329, 328, 327, respectively.

4. LU VI §70; Hua XIX, 2, p. 749; *Logical Investigations,* vol. 2, 333 (trans. modified—Tr.).

5. LU V, §41; Hua XIX, 1, p. 514; *Logical Investigations,* vol. 2, 167.

6. Brentano, *Psychologie vom empirischen Standpunkte,* I, p. 104 (Leipzig: Duncker und Humblot, 1974); trans. Antos C. Rancurello, D. B. Terrell, and Linda L. McAlister, *Psychology from an Empirical Standpoint* (London: Routledge, 2009), 61.

7. LU VI §70; Hua XIX, 2, p. 749; *Logical Investigations,* vol. 2, 333: "All meaning, whether in intention or fulfilment, [is] of a single kind—the genus of objectifying acts."

8. LU V, §43, Hua XIX, 1, p. 519; *Logical Investigations,* vol. 2, 169: "If every non-objectifying, or not purely objectifying act, is founded on objectifying acts, it is plain that it must ultimately also be founded on nominal acts."

9. LU V, §37; Hua XIX, 1, p. 498–99; *Logical Investigations,* vol. 2, 159: "We need hardly stress, after our whole introduction of the concept of 'normal presentation' in the last chapter, that the expression does not merely cover acts attached to nominal expressions, and conferring or fulfilling their meaning, but also all acts that function analogously, even if not performing the same grammatical role."

10. LU I, §18: Hua XIX, 1, p. 71; *Logical Investigations,* vol. 1, 207–9.

11. Hua XVII, *Ergänzender Text* IV, p. 359; trans. Anthony Steinbock, *Analyses Concerning Passive and Active Synthesis: Lectures on Transcendental Logic* (Dordrecht: Kluwer, 2001), 12.

12. On this subject the reader may consult the excellent paper by Barry Smith, "Towards a History of Speech Act Theory," in *Speech Acts, Meanings and Intentions: Critical Approaches to the Philosophy of John B. Searle,* ed. Armin Burkhardt (Berlin: De Gruyter, 1990), 29–61.

13. [In English in the original—Tr.]

14. LU VI §69; Hua XIX, 2, p. 742; *Logical Investigations*, vol. 2, 328–29. The objection is formulated by Anton Marty, *Untersuchungen zur Grundlegung der allgemeinen Grammatik und Sprachphilosophie*, I (Halle: Niemeyer, 1908), 380. See also Barry Smith, "Towards a History of Speech Act Theory."

15. Adolf Reinach, *Die apriorischen Grundlagen des bürgerlichen Rechts*, in *Sämtliche Werke*, vol. 1, p. 177; trans. John F. Crosby, "The Apriori Foundations of the Civil Law," *Aletheia: An International Journal of Philosophy* 3 (1983): 36.

16. Reinach, *Die apriorischen Grundlagen*, vol. 1, p. 150; trans. Crosby, "The Apriori Foundations of the Civil Law," 9.

17. Ibid., 183; trans. 41.

18. Ibid., 162; trans. p. 22: "As a matter of *a priori* necessity every social act has a foundation in some internal experience of a specific nature, whose intentional content is identical with the intentional content of the social act" (trans. modified—Tr.).

19. Ibid., 167; trans. p. 32.

20. Ibid., p. 143; trans. pp. 5–6.

21. Karl Bühler, *Sprachtheorie: Die Darstellungsfunktion der Sprache*, 3rd ed. (Stuttgart: Lucius & Lucius [1934], 1999), 52; trans. Donald Fraser Goodwin, *Theory of Language: The Representational Function of Language* (Amsterdam: J. Benjamins, 1990), 61. For a more detailed analysis of Bühler's phenomenological pragmatic, see Claude Romano, "Une autre tradition sémantique? Heidegger, Bühler et l'ombre de Wittgenstein," *Po&sie* 122 (2008): 191–225.

22. Bühler, *Sprachtheorie*, 155; *Theory of Language*, 175.

23. Ibid., 24; trans., p. 30.

24. Ibid., 48; trans., p. 56

25. John L. Austin, *How to Do Things with Words* (Oxford: Clarendon, 1962), 101. On the limitations of this parallel, see my study, note 21, above.

26. Bühler, *Sprachtheorie*, 69; *Theory of Language*, 79–80.

27. Ibid.; trans. 80.

28. Heidegger, GA 21, p. 92; trans. Thomas Sheehan, *Logic: The Question of Truth* (Bloomington: Indiana University Press, 2010), 77: "I will say further that this position [Platonism], which thinks itself *so* philosophical in contrast to psychologism, and which believes itself to have surpassed naturalism, in fact harbors an even grosser and more basic form of naturalism, one that is much harder to get a grip on." See also GA 21, p. 63 (trans. Sheehan, *Logic: The Question of Truth*, 3), and Claude Romano, "Une autre tradition sémantique? Heidegger, Bühler et l'ombre de Wittgenstein." (See note 21, above.)

29. Bühler, *Sprachtheorie*, 54; *Theory of Language*, 63.

30. Ibid., 66.

31. Ibid., 28.

32. Ibid., xxiii.

33. Ibid., 105; trans. 120.

34. Here we recognize Wittgenstein's idea: *The Blue and Brown Books*, 108–9.

35. Karl Bühler, "Zur Kritik der Denkexperimente (1909)," *Zeitschrift für Psychologie* (1909): 207; see also Kevin Mulligan, "The Essence of Language: Wittgenstein's Builders and Bühler's Bricks," *Revue de Métaphysique et de Morale* 2 (1997): 3.

36. Bühler, *Sprachtheorie,* 80; *Theory of Language,* 94.

37. LU I, §31; Hua XIX, p. 330; *Logical Investigations,* vol. 1, 229.

38. Bühler, *Sprachtheorie,* 65; *Theory of Language,* 76.

39. Ibid., 66; trans., 76.

40. See Mulligan, "The Essence of Language: Wittgenstein's Builders and Bühler's Bricks"; and Romano, "Une autre tradition sémantique? Heidegger, Bühler et l'ombre de Wittgenstein" (see note 21 above).

41. Bühler, *Sprachtheorie,* 52; *Theory of Language,* 61.

42. Ibid., 292; trans., 331.

43. Ibid., 256; trans., 289–90.

44. Ibid., 74; trans. 86. See also 258; trans., 291–92.

45. Merleau-Ponty, *The Prose of the World,* trans. John O'Neill (Evanston, Ill.: Northwestern University Press, 1973), 29n.

46. Merleau-Ponty, *Phenomenology of Perception,* 192.

47. Ibid., 84.

48. Merleau-Ponty, *The Visible and the Invisible,* 212.

49. Jean-François Billeter, *The Chinese Art of Writing,* trans. Jean-Marie Clarke and Michael Taylor (Geneva: Skira, 1990), 86

50. Ibid., 85.

51. Ibid., 86.

52. Merleau-Ponty, *The Prose of the World,* 78.

53. Merleau-Ponty, *La Nature, notes: Cours du Collège de France* (Paris: Éditions du Seuil, 1995), 282; trans. Dominique Séglard, *Nature: Course Notes from the Collège de France,* trans. Robert Valier (Evanston, Ill.: Northwestern University Press, 2003), 219.

54. Hans-Georg Gadamer, "Writing and the Living Voice," in *Hans-Georg Gadamer on Education, Poetry, and History: Applied Hermeneutics,* ed. Dieter Misgeld and Graeme Nicholson (Albany: SUNY Press, 1992), 71.

55. Gadamer, GW 1, *Wahrheit und Methode,* 341; trans. revised by Joel Weinsheimer and Donald G. Mars, *Truth and Method* (New York: Continuum, 2006), 386–87.

56. Ibid., 401; trans. 399 (modified): interpretation is "the very accomplishment [*Vollzug*] of understanding."

57. Heidegger, *Sein und Zeit,* 153; *Being and Time,* 195.

58. Ibid., 148; trans., 188.

59. Gadamer, GW 1 *Wahrheit und Methode,* 341; trans. (modified), 331.

60. Hans-Georg Gadamer, "Semantik und Hermeneutik" (1968), in GW 2, *Hermeneutik II: Wahrheit und Methode: Ergänzungen, Register* (Tübingen, J.C.B. Mohr [Paul Siebeck], 1986), 179; trans. David E. Linge, "Semantics and Hermeneutics," in *Philosophical Hermeneutics* (Berkeley: University of California Press, 2004), 88.

61. Hans-Georg Gadamer, "Hermeneutics as Practical Philosophy," trans. Frederick G. Lawrence, in *The Gadamer Reader: A Bouquet of the Later Writings,* ed. Richard E. Palmer (Evanston, Ill.: Northwestern University Press, 2007), 243 (trans. modified—Tr.).

62. Wittgenstein, *Philosophical Investigations,* I, §199; trans. G. E. M. Anscombe, 2nd ed. (Oxford: Basil Blackwell, 1967), 81e.

63. Gadamer, "Hermeneutics as Practical Philosophy," 243.

64. Wittgenstein, *Philosophical Investigations*, trans. Anscombe, I, §219, 85e: "When I obey a rule, I do not choose. I obey the rule *blindly*." See also I, §206 and §198.

65. Gadamer, GW 1, *Wahrheit und Methode*, 246; *Truth and Method*, 334. Wittgenstein recognized the existence of rules of this kind, but apparently they only play an accessory role in in his conception of language competency and understanding. See *Philosophical Investigations* II-*xi*, trans. Anscombe, p. 227e: "Can one learn this knowledge [of mankind]? Yes; some can. Not, however, by taking a course in it, but through '*experience*.'—Can someone else be a man's teacher in this? Certainly. From time to time he gives him the right *tip*.—This is what 'learning' and 'teaching' are like here.—What one acquires here is not a technique; one learns correct judgments. There are also rules, but they do not form a system, and *only experienced people can apply them right*. Unlike calculating-rules" (my emphasis).

66. Gadamer, GW 1, *Wahrheit und Methode*, 431; *Truth and Method*, 426 (trans. modified—Tr.). This is why "the significance of an event or the meaning of a text is not a fixed object existing in itself, which we have simply to establish" (*Wahrheit und Methode*, 479; *Truth and Method*, 470); there is no "meaning in itself," but an "event of meaning [*Sinngeschehen*]" (*Wahrheit und Methode*, 476; *Truth and Method*, 468).

67. Ibid., 426; trans. 421.

68. Arthur Rimbaud, *Oeuvres complètes*, ed. Antoine Adam (Paris: Gallimard, 2007), 645; trans. Paul Schmidt and Peter Bauer, *New York Review of Books*, June 1, 1967 (modified—Tr.).

69. Georges Braque, *Le jour et la nuit: Cahiers 1917–1952* (Paris: Gallimard, 1952), 28–29; trans. Stanley Appelbaum, *Georges Braque—Illustrated Notebooks, 1917–1955* (New York: Dover, 1971), 87.

70. "Mieux qu'une révolution, il troue de part en part comme une balle l'horizon de la poésie et de la sensibilité." René Char, "Sous un portrait d'Arthur Rimbaud," in *Dans l'atelier du poète* (Paris: Gallimard, 2007), 645.

71. Gadamer, "Semantik und Hermeneutik," GW 2, 645; trans. P. Christopher Smith, "Semantics and Hermeneutics," in *Philosophical Hermeneutics*, ed. Linge (Berkeley: University of California Press, 2008), 86.

72. Donald Davidson, "A Nice Derangement of Epitaphs," in *Truth, Language and History* (Oxford: Clarendon, 2005), 89–108; and the Davidson-Dummett-Hacking debate in *Truth and Interpretation: Perspectives on the Philosophy of Donald Davidson*, ed. Ernest Lepore (Oxford: Basil Blackwell, 1986), 433–76. Specifically, Davidson writes the following declaration, which is in agreement with Gadamer: "We have discovered no learnable common core of consistent behavior, no shared grammar or rules, no portable interpreting machine set to grind out the meaning of an arbitrary utterance" ("A Nice Derangement of Epitaphs," 107). There is no set of rules that it would suffice to master and apply mechanically—as in the image of a "portable interpreting machine"—to reach a shared intelligence of language. But as McDowell remarks, that idea may not be incompatible with that of belonging to a linguistic community. Davidson, because he insists on the individual aspect of language, ends up devaluing its com-

mon dimension insofar as it contributes to human *Bildung*—a dimension on which Gadamer, by contrast, insists: "[Davidson] proceeds as if shared practice could be philosophically interesting only if it were true that it suffices, of itself, for mutual understanding between parties to it" ("Gadamer and Davidson on Understanding and Relativism," in *Gadamer's Century: Essays in Honor of Hans-Georg Gadamer*, ed. Jeff Malpas, Ulrich Arnswald, and Jens Kertscher [Cambridge, Mass: MIT Press, 2002], 184).

73. Heidegger, GA 7, p. 194; trans. Albert Hofstadter, *Poetry, Language, Thought* (New York: Harper and Row, 1971), 216 (trans. modified—Tr.).

74. Gadamer, "Semantik und Hermeneutik," in GW 2, p. 176; trans. "Semantics and Hermeneutics," 85–86.

75. Gadamer, "Grenzen der Sprache," GW 8, *Ästhetik und Poetik I: Kunst als Aussage* (Tübingen: J. C. B. Mohr [Paul Siebeck], 1993), 357; (my translation from the French of Jean Grondin, in Hans-Georg Gadamer, *La philosophie herméneutique* [Paris: Presses Universitaires de France, 1996], 179—Tr.).

76. Merleau-Ponty, *La Nature, notes: Cours du Collège de France* (Paris: Éditions du Seuil, 1995), 282. This is what will lead Gadamer to understand Aristotle's *syntheke* otherwise than as "convention" and to translate it with "the fact of coming to an agreement" (*Übereinkommen*) in language ("Grenzen der Sprache," GW 8, 353, trans. Grondin, *La philosophie herméneutique*, 174). Language does not create agreement; it is born from agreement. Wittgenstein, too, had suggested that the "conventions" of language are of a very different nature than those established *thanks to* language. See *Philosophical Investigations*, trans. Anscombe, I §241, p. 88e. "It is what human beings *say* that is true and false; and they agree in the *language* they use. That is not agreement in opinions but in form of life."

77. Merleau-Ponty, *La Nature*, 217.

78. GA 7, 194: "Denn eigentlich spricht die Sprache. Der Mensch spricht erst und nur, insofern er der Sprache entspricht, indem er auf ihren Zuspruch hört"; trans. Hofstadter, *Poetry, Language, Thought*, 216.

79. Gadamer, "Selbstdarstellung" (1975), GW 2, 504; trans. Richard E. Palmer, *The Gadamer Reader: A Bouquet of the Later Writings* (Evanston, Ill.: Northwestern University Press, 2007), 33.

Chapter 22

The epigraph is from Merleau-Ponty, *Phénoménologie de la perception*, 48; *Phenomenology of Perception*, 40.

1. Ricoeur, *From Text to Action*, 26.

2. Ibid., 14.

3. Hua I §15, p. 74; trans. Dorian Cairns, *Cartesian Meditations*, 36.

4. GA 24, *Grundprobleme der Phänomenologie*, p. 31; trans. A. Hofstadter, *The Basic Problems of Phenomenology*, 22.

5. The locus classicus of this assertion is found in GA 24, p. 31; trans. *The Basic Problems of Phenomenology*, 22–23. But already in the "Natorp report" of 1922 Heidegger had elaborated the concept of destruction (*Destruktion*). See *Interpré-*

tations phénoménologiques d'Aristote, bilingual edition, French trans. Jean-François Courtine (modified), (Mauverzin: Trans Europ Repress, 1992), 31.

6. Hua III, 1, §20, p. 45; trans. F. Kersten, *Ideas I,* 39.

7. Ricoeur, *From Text to Action,* 53.

8. Hans-Georg Gadamer, *Kleine Schriften* I: *Philosophie, Hermeneutik* (Tübingen: Mohr, 1967); French trans. in *Hermeneutique et philosophie* (Paris: Beauchesne, 1999), 84.

9. Ricoeur, *From Text to Action,* 17.

10. Heidegger, *Sein und Zeit,* 153; *Being and Time,* 195: "Because understanding, in accordance with its existential meaning, is *Dasein's* own potentiality-for-Being, the ontological presuppositions of historiological [*historischer*] knowledge transcend in principle the idea of rigour held in the most exact sciences."

11. Paul Ricoeur, *Time and the Narrative,* vol. 1, trans. Kathleen McLaughlin and David Pellauer (Chicago: University of Chicago Press, 1984), x.

12. Ricoeur, *From Text to Action,* 19. The point is, then, to "situate explanation and understanding along a unique *hermeneutical arc*" (*From Text to Action,* 121).

13. Paul Ricoeur, *The Conflict of Interpretations: Essays in Hermeneutics* (London: Continuum, 2004), 225.

14. Ricoeur, *From Text to Action,* 25.

15. Ibid., 15, 37, and 30 respectively.

16. Heidegger, *Sein und Zeit,* 37; *Being and Time,* 62.

17. Gadamer, *Truth and Method,* 2nd rev. ed. (Continuum), 470.

18. Ibid., 342–43.

19. Ibid., 440 (trans. modified—Tr.).

20. Ibid.

21. Ibid.

22. Ibid.

23. Ricoeur, *From Text to Action,* 38–39. See also 16.

24. Ricoeur, *From Text to Action,* 37: "To understand *oneself* is to understand oneself *in front of the text.*" See also 16, 37, and 110–11.

25. Ricoeur, *Time and Narrative* I, 74.

26. Ibid., xi, my emphasis. See *From Text to Action,* 6 (trans. modified—Tr.).

27. Ricoeur, *Time and Narrative* I, 3.

28. Ibid., 71.

29. Ricoeur, *From Text to Action,* 4.

30. Ricoeur, *Time and Narrative* I, 3.

31. Ibid., 80.

32. Ibid.

33. Ibid., 81.

34. Ricoeur, *From Text to Action,* 55.

35. Gadamer, "Selbstdarstellung," in *Gesammelte Werke,* vol. 2 (Tübingen: J. C. B. Mohr [Paul Siebeck], 1986), 496; *The Gadamer Reader: A Bouquet of the Later Writings,* 25.

36. Ricoeur, *From Text to Action,* 41.

37. This is, in Ricoeur's view, "the hermeneutic presupposition of phenomenology": see *From Text to Action,* 43.

38. Ibid., 39: "To bring it [experience] to language . . . is to make it become itself."

39. Ricoeur, *From Text to Action*, 42.

40. Heidegger, GA 1, 172.

41. Gadamer, GW 1, *Wahrheit und Methode*, 390; *Truth and Method* (2nd ed.), 271.

42. Gadamer, "Rhetorik und Hermeneutik (1976)," in GW 2, p. 285; trans. Joel Weinsheimer, "Rhetoric and Hermeneutics," in *Rhetoric and Hermeneutics in Our Time: A Reader*, ed. Walter Jost and Michael J. Hyde (New Haven, Conn.: Yale University Press, 1997), 53 (trans. slightly modified—Tr.).

43. Heidegger, *Sein und Zeit*, 183; *Being and Time*, 228.

44. Heidegger, *Sein und Zeit*, 161; *Being and Time*, 204: "To significations, words accrue."

45. This ambivalence must not lead us to conclude that the position of *Sein und Zeit* is guilty of linguistic idealism. On this point, I do not subscribe to the thesis of Cristina Lafont in *Sprache und Welterschliessung: Zur linguistischen Wende der Hemeneutik Heideggers* (Frankfurt am Main: Suhrkamp, 1994). I do, on the other hand, agree with several criticisms that have been made of that reading. See the whole controversy surrounding that work, published in *Inquiry* 45 (2002).

46. Heidegger, *Sein und Zeit*, 4; *Being and Time*, 23.

47. See Heidegger, GA 20, pp. 193–94; trans. Theodore Kisiel, *History of the Concept of Time: Prolegomena* (Bloomington: Indiana University Press, 1985), 143–44: "When we thus ask about the sense of Being, then Being, which is to be determined, is in a certain way already understood. . . . There is an understanding of the expression 'being,' even if it borders on a mere understanding of the word. . . . We *always already live in an understanding of the 'is'* without being able to say more precisely what it actually means." See also the whole second edition of *Einführung in die Metaphysik*, and the question asked therein: "How can beings always and in each case be beings for us unless we already understand 'Being' and 'not-Being'?" (GA 40, p. 82; trans. Gregory Fried and Richard Polt, *Introduction to Metaphysics* [New Haven, Conn.: Yale University Press, 2000], 82).

48. Heidegger, *Sein und Zeit*, 149; *Being and Time*, 189.

49. Heidegger, "Wozu Dichter?" (1946), GA 5, p. 310; "Why Poets," ed. and trans. Julian Young and Kenneth Hayes, *Off the Beaten Track* (New York: Cambridge University Press, 2002), 232–33.

50. Heidegger, *Sein und Zeit*, 37; *Being and Time*, 61.

51. Ibid., 35; trans., 33.

52. Ibid., 36; trans., 34.

53. For a more detailed presentation of this ontological critique and its repercussions on the phenomenology/hermeneutics articulation, see also my study "L'Horizon de la phénoménologie," *Iris* 28 (2007): 1–38.

54. Heidegger, GA 12, p. 93; trans. Peter D. Hertz, *On the Way to Language* (New York: Harper and Row, 1989), 11.

55. [In translating CR's "oubliettes" (the term used for those dark places in which the enemies of the French Revoluton were imprisoned and forgotten) as

"dusty archives" I have had to sacrifice an oblique, "co-meant" reference to the Heideggerian doctrine that metaphysics is historically the result of philosophy's forgetting ("oubli") of Being (*Das Sein*).—Tr.]

56. Heidegger, *Sein und Zeit,* 153; *Being and Time,* 195.

57. GA 21, p. 33; trans. Sheehan, *Logik: The Question of Truth,* 28: "So in a certain sense the word 'phenomenon' always implies a task [*Aufgabe*]: negatively, protection against presuppositions [*Vormeinungen*] and prejudgments; positively, to assure that the analysis of so-called phenomena must get clear with itself about which presuppositions it brings to the objects of philosophy. For ultimately we can show that no one can do without such presupposing, and therefore that the critique of the essential act of presupposing is an essential element of philosophical research."

58. Nietzsche, *Fragments posthumes: Automne 1885–automne 1887,* 7 [60], in *Oeuvres philosophiques complètes,* XII, trans. into French by Julien Hervier, éd. Giorgio Colli and Mazzino Montinari (Paris: Gallimard, 1979), 304–5 (my trans. of Julien Hervier's trans.—Tr.).

59. Gadamer, *Kleine Schriften I*; English trans., "Rhetoric, Hermeneutics, and the Critique of Ideology: Metacritical Comments on Truth and Method," in *The Hermeneutics Reader: Texts of the German Tradition from the Enlightenment to the Present,* ed. Kurt Mueller-Vollmer (Oxford: Blackwell, 1985), 286 (trans. modified—Tr.).

60. Indeed, it is the "Cartesian concept of method" (GW 1, p 282; *Truth and Method,* 2nd ed., 279) and not the idea of method in general that is rejected by Gadamer in the domain of hermeneutics.

61. Hilary Putnam, *Renewing Philosophy* (Cambridge, Mass.: Harvard University Press, 1992), 177.

62. Heidegger, *Sein und Zeit,* 17; *Being and Time,* 38.

63. This is what will lead Husserl to say in *The Origin of Geometry* that only the taking into consideration of the "universally essential structures" of history make it possible to give an account of contingent historical changes: "Only the disclosure of the essentially general structure lying in our present and then in every past or future historical present as such . . .—only this disclosure can make possible historical inquiry [*Historie*] which is truly understanding, insightful, and in the genuine sense scientific" (Hua VI, p. 380; trans. David Carr *The Crisis of European Sciences and Transcendental Phenomenology* [Evanston, Ill.: Northwestern University Press, 1970], 371–72).

64. Heidegger, GA 20, 147; trans. Theodore Kisiel, *History of the Concept of Time,* 107.

65. GA 20, p. 178; trans. Kisiel, *History of the Concept of Time,* 128–29.

Chapter 23

The epigraph is from Levinas, *Discovering Existence with Husserl,* trans. Richard A. Cohen and Michael B. Smith (Evanston, Ill.: Northwestern University Press, 1998), 101 (translation modified—Tr.).

1. Henri Bergson, "Philosophie et science" (1911), in *Mélanges* (Paris: Presses Universitaires de France, 1972), 886 (my trans.—Tr.).

2. Hua VI, p. 60; trans. Carr, *The Crisis of European Sciences,* 59.

3. Hua VI, p. 7; *The Crisis of European Sciences,* 9.

4. Certain neo-Kantians are exceptions to this rule: in this connection Cassirer's *Philosophy of Symbolic Forms* may be mentioned.

5. Hua VI, 141; *The Crisis of European Sciences,* 138.

6. Merleau-Ponty, *Phenomenology of Perception,* lxxii (trans. modified—Tr.).

7. Hua VI, 51; trans. Carr, *The Crisis of European Sciences,* 51.

8. Ibid.

9. Hua III, 1, §74, p. 155; trans. F. Kersten, *Ideas I,* 166: "These simple concepts [the morphological concepts of what Husserl does not yet call the 'life-world'] are *essentially, rather than accidentally, inexact* and *consequently* also non-mathematical."

10. Hua VI, pp. 289–90; *The Crisis of European Sciences,* 311.

11. Hua VI, pp. 41–42; *The Crisis of European Sciences,* 42.

12. Hua VI, p. 158; *The Crisis of European Sciences,* 155.

13. Husserl, Ms D17 (1934), included (in German) in *Philosophical Essays in Memory of Edmund Husserl,* ed. Marvin Faber (Cambridge, Mass.: Harvard University Press, 1940), 307–25; trans. Fred Kersten, rev. Leonard Lawlor, "Foundational Investigations of the Phenomenological Origin of the Spatiality of Nature: The Originary Ark, the Earth, Does Not Move," in *Husserl at the Limits of Phenomenology: Including Texts by Edmund Husserl, Maurice Merleau-Ponty,* ed. Leonard Lawlor with Bettina Bergo (Evanston, Ill.: Northwestern University Press, 2002), 123 (trans. modified—Tr.).

14. Husserl, "Foundational Investigations," 118.

15. Galileo, *Dialogue Concerning the Two Chief World Systems, Ptolemaic and Copernican,* trans. Stillman Drake (New York: Modern Library, 2001), 135.

16. Galileo, *Dialogues Concerning Two New Sciences,* trans. H. Crew and A. de Salivo (New York: Macmillan, 1914), 65 (National Ed., 110).

17. Hua VI, p. 53; *The Crisis of European Sciences,* 52.

18. Hua VI, p. 43; *The Crisis of European Sciences,* 44.

19. Hua VI, pp. 48–49; *The Crisis of European Sciences,* 48–49.

20. Werner Heisenberg, "The Representation of Nature in Contemporary Physics," *Daedalus* 87, no. 3 (Summer 1958): 96.

21. Hua VI, p. 54; *The Crisis of European Sciences,* 54 (trans. modified—Tr.).

22. Ibid.

23. Hua VI, 30; *The Crisis of European Sciences,* 32 (trans. modified—Tr.).

24. Hua III, 1, §40, p. 82; trans. Kersten, *Ideas 1,* 40.

25. Hua III, 1, p. 82; *Ideas I,* 84.

26. Hua III, 1, §52, p. 112; *Ideas I,* 120.

27. Hua III, 1, p. 113; *Ideas 1,* 121 (trans. modified—Tr.).

28. Hua III, 1, p. 112; *Ideas 1,* 119.

29. Hua III, 1, p. 111; *Ideas 1,* 119.

30. Hua IV, p. 89; trans. Richard Rojcewicz and André Schuwer, *Ideas . . . Second Book* (Dordrecht: Kluwer Academic, 1989), 94: "There exists already on

the solipsistic level the *possibility of advancing to the constitution of the 'Objective' (physicalistic) thing*."

31. Hua IV, p. 82; *Ideas . . . Second Book*, 87.

32. Hua VI, 131; *The Crisis of European Sciences*, 129.

33. Ibid.

34. Ibid.

35. Ludwig Landgrebe, "Husserls Abschied vom Cartesianismus," *Philosophische Rundschau* 9 (1961): 133–77; Aron Gurwitsch, "The Last Work of Edmund Husserl," *Phenomenology and Philosophical Research* 16 (1956): 380–99 (included in *Studies in Phenomenology and Psychology* [Evanston, Ill.: Northwestern University Press, 1966]).

36. Hua VI, p. 177; *The Crisis of European Sciences*, 174.

37. Ibid.

38. Hua XXV, p. 8; French trans. M. de Launay, *La philosophie comme science rigoureuse* (Paris: Presses Universitaires de France, 1989), 19 (my trans. of de Launay's trans.—Tr.).

39. Hua III, 1, 120; *Ideas 1*, 129.

40. Hua VI, p. 127; *The Crisis of the European Sciences*, 124: "the life-world constantly functions as subsoil [*Untergrund*]."

41. Hua VI, p. 125; *The Crisis of the European Sciences*, 123.

42. Hua VI, p. 123; *The Crisis of the European Sciences*, 121.

43. Hua VI, Beilage XVII, p. 460; *The Crisis of the European Sciences*, 380.

44. Hua VI, p. 134; *The Crisis of the European Sciences*, 130. See also Ms F I 32, "Natur und Geist," 108 b: "Is not science itself a function of life? . . . Is it not itself an element of the world of unitary life? [*Ist den nicht Wissenschaft selbst eine Funktion des Lebens? . . . Ist sie nicht en Stück selbst der einheitlichen Lebenswelt?*]"

45. Sellars, *Science, Perception and Reality*, 137.

46. Ibid.

47. Ibid., 36.

48. Ibid., 173.

49. Reinach, SW I, p. 534; "Concerning Phenomenology," trans. of Adolf Reinach's lecture "Uber Phaenomenologie" by Dallas Willard, http://www.dwillard.org/articles/artview.asp?artID=21.

50. Hua VI, p. 49; *The Crisis of the European Sciences*, 48–49.

51. Hua VI, p. 52; *The Crisis of the European Sciences*, 51–52.

52. On the question of whether Husserl was instrumentalist in his conception of the status of scientific statements, see the remarks of Gail Soffer, "Phenomenology and Scientific Realism: Husserl's Critique of Galileo," *Review of Metaphysics* 44, no. 1 (1990): 67–94.

53. Sellars, *Science, Perception and Reality*, 20: "The scientific image presents itself as a *rival* image."

54. Husserl, Ms D17 (1934); trans. *Husserl at the Limits of Phenomenology*, 122, 129 (trans. modified—Tr.).

55. Straus, *The Primary World of Senses* (New York: Free Press of Glencoe, 1963), 182–83.

56. Husserl, Ms B I 29 p.14 (quoted by Bruce Bégout, *Husserl: L'Enfance du*

monde: Recherches phénoménologiques sur la vie, le monde et le monde de la vie, vol. 1 (Chatou: Éditions de la Transparence, 2007), 71. (My translation of French text by Bruce Bégout—Tr.)

57. Hua VI, p. 135; *The Crisis of the European Sciences*, 132.

58. Hua VI, p. 112; *The Crisis of the European Sciences*, 110.

59. Hua IV, 375; trans. Richard Rojcewicz and André Schuwer, *Collected Works*, vol. 3, *Ideas, Second Book, Studies in the Phenomenology of Constitution* (Dordrecht: Kluwer Academic, 1989), 385.

60. See Iso Kern, "Die Lebenswelt als Grundlagenproblem der objektive Wissenschaften und als universales Wahrheits- und Seinsproblem," in Rudolf Bernet, Iso Kern, and Eduard Marbach, *Edmund Husserl: Darstellung seines Denkens* (Hamburg: Felix Meiner Verlag, 1996), 199–208; see esp. 203.

61. Hua VI, 134; *The Crisis of the European Sciences*, 131 (trans. modified—Tr.).

Epilogue

1. Hua VI, p. 14; *The Crisis of the European Sciences*, 16.
2. Hua XXIX, p. 154.

Select Bibliography

Alston, William P. "Sellars and The 'Myth of the Given.'" Eastern Division Meeting of the American Philosophical Association, 1998. http://www.ditext.com/alston/alston2.html.

Anscombe, Elizabeth. "The Intentionality of Sensation." In *Metaphysics and the Philosophy of Mind (Collected Philosophical Papers, Tome II)*, 3–20. Oxford: Basil Blackwell, 1981.

———. "The Question of Linguistic Idealism." In *From Parmenides to Wittgenstein (Collected Philosophical Papers, Tome I)*, 112–33. Minneapolis: University of Minnesota Press, 1981.

Aristotle. *The Complete Works of Aristotle: The Revised Oxford Translation*, ed. Jonathan Barnes. Princeton, N.J: Princeton University Press, 1984.

Armstrong, David Malet. *Nominalism and Realism: Universals and Scientific Realism, Volume I.* Cambridge, Eng.: Cambridge University Press, 1978.

———. *Universals: An Opinionated Introduction.* Boulder, Colo.: Westview, 1989.

Arnswald, Ulrich, Jens Kertscher, and, Jeff Malpas, eds. *Gadamer's Century: Essays in Honor of Hans-Georg Gadamer.* Cambridge, Mass.: MIT Press, 2002.

Ash, Mitchell G. *Gestalt Psychology in German Culture (1890–1967): Holism and the Quest for Objectivity.* Cambridge, Eng.: Cambridge University Press, 1998.

Austin, John Langshaw. *How to Do Things with Words.* Oxford: Oxford University Press, 1962.

———. *Philosophical Papers.* Oxford: Oxford University Press, 1961.

———. *Sense and Sensibilia.* Oxford: Oxford University Press, 1962.

Baker, Gordon P., and P. M. S. Hacker. *Wittgenstein, Meaning and Understanding: Essays on the Philosophical Investigations.* Chicago: University of Chicago Press, 1985.

———. *Wittgenstein, Rules, Grammar and Necessity.* Oxford: Basil Blackwell, 2000.

Becker, Oskar. "Bemerkungen über Tautologie im Sinne der Logistik." In Hua XVII, pp. 333–35.

Benoist, Jocelyn. *L'A priori conceptuel. Bolzano, Husserl, Schlick.* Paris: Vrin, 1999.

———. *Les limites de l'intentionnalité: Recherches phénoménologiques et analytiques.* Paris: Vrin, 2005.

———. *Phénoménologie, sémantique, ontology: Husserl et la tradition logique autrichienne.* Paris: Presses Universitaires de France, 1997.

Bergson, Henri. *Oeuvres*, éd. of the Centenaire. Paris: Presses Universitaires de France, 1959. 4th ed., 1984.

———. *An Introduction to Metaphysics,* trans. T. E. Hulme. New York: Putnam's, 1912.
———. "Philosophie et science (1911)." In *Mélanges.* Paris: Presses Universitaires de France, 1972.
Berkeley, George. *Principles of Human Knowledge and Three Dialogues Between Hylas and Philonous.* New York: Penguin Classics, 1988.
Bernet, Rudolf. "Le concept de noème," in *La vie du sujet,* pp. 65–92.
———. *La Vie du sujet: Recherches sur l'interprétation de Husserl dans la phénoménologie.* Paris: Presses Universitaires de France, 1994.
Bernet, Rudolf, Iso Kern, and Eduard Marbach. *Edmund Husserl: Darstellung seines Denkens.* Hamburg: Felix Meiner Verlag, 1996.
Berthoz, Alain, and Gérard Jorland, eds. *L'Empathie.* Paris: Odile Jacob, 2004.
Biemel, Walter. "Les phases décisives dans le développement de la philosophie de Husserl." In *Husserl: Cahiers de Royaumont.* Paris: Éditions de Minuit, 1959.
Billeter, Jean-François. *The Chinese Art of Writing,* trans. Jean-Marie Clarke and Michael Taylor. Geneva: Skira, 1990.
Bloor, David. "Linguistic Idealism Revisited," in Hans Sluga and David G. Stern, eds., *The Cambridge Companion to Wittgenstein,* 254–82. Cambridge, Eng.: Cambridge University Press, 1996.
Boehm, Rudolf. "Les ambiguïtés des concepts husserliens d'immanence et de 'transcendance.'" *Revue philosophique,* 4, (1959): 481–526.
———. *Vom Gesichtspunkt der Phänomenologie: Husserl Studien.* The Hague: Martinus Nijhoff, 1968 (Phaenomenologica, no. 26).
Bolzano, Bernard. *Wissenschaftslehre,* critical edition by J. Berg. In *Gesamtausgabe,* I, 11–14. Stuttgart-Bad Canstatt: Frommann-Holzboog Verlag, 1969–.
Boulnois, Olivier. *Être et representation: Une généalogie de la métaphysique moderne à l'époque de Duns Scot.* Paris: Presses Universitaires de France, 1999.
———. " Être, luire et concevoir: Note sur la genèse et la structure de la conception scotiste de l'esse objective." *Collectanea franciscana* 60 (1990): 117–35.
Bouveresse, Jacques. *Langage, perception et réalité, tome II: Physique, phénoménologie et grammaire.* Nîmes: Éditions Jacqueline Chambon, 2004.
Brague, Rémi. *Aristote et la question du monde.* Paris: Presses Universitaires de France, 1988.
Brand, Gerd. *Welt, Ich und Zeit.* The Hague: Martinus Nijhoff, 1969.
Brentano, Franz Clemens. *Psychology from an Empirical Standpoint.* London: Routledge and Kegan Paul, 1973.
Bucci, Paolo. *Husserl e Bolzano: Alle origini della fenomenologia.* Milan: Edizioni Unicopli, 2000.
Bühler, Karl. *Sprachtheorie: Die Darstellungsfunktion der Sprache* (1934). Stuttgart: Lucius & Lucius, 3rd ed., 1999.
Burkhardt, Armin, ed. *Speech Acts: Meanings and Intentions: Critical Approaches to the Philosophy of John R. Searle.* Berlin: De Gruyter, 1990.
Cahiers de l'Herne. *Martin Heidegger.* Paris: Éditions de l'Herne, 1983.
Cahiers de Royaumont. *Husserl.* Paris: Éditions de Minuit, 1959.
Cahiers de Royaumont. *La philosophie analytique.* Paris: Éditions de Minuit, 1962.

Cahiers d'histoire de la philosophie. *Heidegger*, ed. Maxence Caron. Paris: Éditions du Cerf, 2006.

Cahiers d'histoire de la philosophie. *Husserl*, ed. Jocelyn Benoist. Paris: Éditions du Cerf, 2008.

Cairns, Dorion. *Conversations with Husserl and Fink.* The Hague: Martinus Nijhoff, 1976.

Carman, Taylor, and Mark B. N. Hanson, eds. *The Cambridge Companion to Merleau-Ponty.* New York: Cambridge University Press, 2005.

Cassin, Barbara, ed. *Vocabulaire européen des philosophies: Dictionnaire des intraduisibles.* Paris: Seuil-Le Robert, 2004.

Cassirer, Ernst. "Le langage et la construction du monde des objets." *Journal de Psychologie Normale et Pathologique* 30, no. 1 (4) (1933): 18–44; new edition "Die Sprache und der Aufbau der Gegenstandwelt," in *Symbol, Technik, Sprache.* Hamburg: Meiner, 1985.

———. *Philosophie der symbolischen Formen.* New Haven, Conn.: Yale University Press, 1953.

Cassirer, Ernst, Hermann Cohen, and Natorp, Paul. *L'École de Marbourg.* In *Oeuvres, XLVIII,* translated from German and English by Christian Berner, Fabien Capeillères, Marc de Launay, Carole Prompsy, and Isabelle Thomas-Fogiel. Paris: Éditions du Cerf, 1998.

Cavell, Stanley. *This New Yet Unapproachable America. Chicago.* University of Chicago Press, 1989.

Cayla, Fabien. *Routes et déroutes de l'intentionnalité: La correspondence R. Chisholm-W. Sellars.* Combas: Éditions de l'Éclat, 1991. "Intentionality and the Mental: Chisholm-Sellars Correspondence on Intentionality," http://www.ditext.com/sellars/sccor-f.html.

Chisholm, Roderick M. *Perceiving: A Philosophical Study.* Ithaca, N.Y.: Cornell University Press, 1957.

Clavelin, Maurice. " La première doctrine de la signification du Cercle de Vienne." *Les Études Philosophiques* 4 (1973): 475–504.

Cohen, Hermann. *Das Prinzip der Infinitesimal-Methode und seine Geschichte.* Berlin: Ferd. Dümmlers Verlagsbuchhandlung, Harrwitz u. Grossmann, 1883.

Conrad, Joseph. *Chance.* New York: Doubleday, 1950.

Correia, Fabrice. "Generic Essence, Objectual Essence, and Modality." *Noûs* 40, no. 4 (2006): 753–67.

Costa, Vincenzo. *La verità del mondo: Giudizio e teoria del significato in Heidegger.* Milan: Vita e Pensiero, 2003.

———. *L'estetica trascendentale fenomenologica: Sensibilità e razionalità nella filosofia di Edmund Husserl.* Milan: Vita e pensiero, 1999.

Costa, Vincenzo, Elio Franzini, and Paolo Spinicci. *La fenomenologia.* Turin: Einaudi, 2002.

Courtine, Jean-François. *Heidegger et la phénoménologie.* Paris: Vrin, 1990.

———. *La cause de la phénoménologie.* Paris: Presses Universitaires de France, 2007.

———. "Vorhanden." In *Vocabulaire européen des philosophies*, ed. Barbara Cassin. *Dictionnaire des intraduisibles*, 1380–87.

Croce, Benedetto. *Ciò che è vivo e ciò che è morto della filosofia di Hegel.* Bari: Laterza, 1907.

Dastur, Françoise. *Husserl: Des mathématiques à l'histoire.* Paris: Presses Universitaires de France, 1995.

———. *La phénoménologie en questions: Langage, altérité, temporalité, finitude.* Paris: Vrin, 2004.

Davidson, Donald. "A Coherence Theory of Truth and Knowledge." In *Subjective, Intersubjective, Objective,* 137–57.

———. *Essays on Actions and Events.* Oxford: Clarendon, 1980.

———. "Gadamer and Plato's Philebus." In *Truth, Language and History,* 261–76.

———. *Inquiries into Truth and Interpretation,* 2nd ed. Oxford: Clarendon, 2001.

———. "The Myth of the Subjective." In *Subjective, Intersubjective, Objective,* 39–52.

———. "Seeing through Language." In *Truth, Language and History,* 127–42.

———. *Subjective, Intersubjective, Objective.* Oxford: Clarendon, 2001.

———. *Truth, Language and History.* Oxford, Clarendon, 2005.

Dennett, Daniel C. *Consciousness Explained.* Boston: Little, Brown, 1991.

Desanti, Jean-Toussaint. *Introduction à la phénoménologie.* Paris: Gallimard, Coll. Folio, 1994.

Descartes, René. *Meditationes de Prima Philosophia,* in *Oeuvres de Descartes,* ed. Charles Adam and Paul Tannery, Paris, Vrin, reprint 1996, volume VII.

Descombes, Vincent. *Grammaire d'objets en tous genres.* Paris: Minuit, 1983; trans. L. Scott-Fox and J. Harding, *Objects of All Sorts: A Philosophical Grammar,* Baltimore: Johns Hopkins University Press, 1986.

———. "La philosophie comme science rigoureusement descriptive." *Critique,* 407 (1981): 351–75.

———. *Le Complément de sujet: Enquête sur le fait d'agir de soi-même.* Paris: Gallimard, coll. NRF Essais, 2004.

———. *Les institutions du sens.* Paris: Éditions de Minuit, 1996.

Dewan, Lawrence. "'Obiectum': Notes on the Invention of a Word." In *Archives d'histoire doctrinale et littéraire du Moyen Âge* 48 (1981): 37–96.

Dewey, John. *Art as Experience.* New York: Perigee Books, 2005.

Dilthey, Wilhelm. *Erfahren und Denken* (1892). In *Gesammelte Schriften V: Die geistige Welt. Einleitung in die Philosophie des Lebens. Erste Hälfte: Abhandlungen zur Grundlegung der Geisteswissenschaften,* ed. Georg Misch. Berlin: Teubner, 1924.

———. *Gesammelte Schriften, VII: Der Aufbau der geschichtlichen Welt in den Geisteswissenschaften,* ed. Bernhard Groethuysen. Berlin: Teubner, 1927.

Doran, Michael, ed. *Conversations avec Cézanne.* Paris: Éditions Macula, 1978.

Dretske, Frederick. *Seeing and Knowing.* London: Routledge and Kegan Paul, 1969.

Dreyfus, Hubert L., and Harrison Hall. *Husserl, Intentionality, and Cognitive Science.* Cambridge, Mass.: MIT Press, 1982.

Dummett, Michael. *Origins of Analytical Philosophy.* Cambridge, Mass.: Harvard University Press, 199.

Duns Scotus. *L'Image.* French trans. Gérard Sondag. Paris: Vrin, 1993.

Ehrenfels, Christian von. "Über 'Gestaltqualitäten.'" *Vierteljahrsschrift für wissen-*

schaftliche Philosophie, t. 14, vol. 3 (1890): 249–92; French trans. Denis Fisette, "Sur les 'qualités de forme,'" in Ehrenfels, Husserl, Marty, Meinong, Stumpf, and Twardowski, *À l'École de Brentano: De Würzbourg à Vienne.*

Ehrenfels, Christian von, Edmund Husserl, Anton Marty, Alexis Meinong, Carl Stumpf, and Kazimierz Twardowski. *À l'École de Brentano: De Würzbourg à Vienne*, trans. under the direction of Denis Fisette and Guillaume Fréchette. Paris: Vrin, 2007.

Esfeld, Michael. *Holism in Philosophy of Mind and Philosophy of Physics.* Dordrecht: Kluwer, 2001.

Evans, Gareth. *The Varieties of Reference.* Oxford: Clarendon, 1982.

Evnine, Simon. *Donald Davidson.* Cambridge: Polity, 1991.

Farber, Marvin, ed. *Philosophical Essays in Memory of Edmund Husserl.* Cambridge, Mass.: Harvard University Press, 1940.

Feigl, Herbert, and Wilfrid Sellars, eds. *Readings in Philosophical Analysis.* New York: Appleton Century Crofts, 1949.

Ferrari, Massimo. "Cent ans après: Husserl, Natorp et la logique pure." *Philosophie* 74 (2002): 40–57.

Fine, Kit. "Essence and Modality: The Second Philosophical Perspectives Lecture." *Philosophical Perspectives*, vol. 8, "Logic and Language" (1994): 1–16.

———. "Senses of Essence." in *Modality, Morality and Belief*, ed. Walter Sinnott-Armstrong, 53–73. Cambridge, Eng.: Cambridge University Press, 1995.

———. "The Varieties of Necessity." in *Conceivability and Possibility*, ed. Tamar Szabo Gendler and John Hawthorne. Oxford: Clarendon, 2002.

Fink, Eugen. "Die phänomenologische Philosophie E. Husserls in der gegenwärtigen Kritik." In Eugen Fink, *Studien zur Phänomenologie, 1930–1939.* The Hague: Martinus Nijhoff, 1966. Trans. R. O. Elveton, "Husserl's Philosophy and Contemporary Criticism," in *The Phenomenology of Husserl, Selected Critical Readings* (Chicago: Quadrangle Books, 1970).

———. "L'Analyse intentionnelle" (bilingual German-French text). In *Problèmes actuels de la phenomenology: Actes du colloque international de phenomenology: Bruxelles, avril 1951*, 55–87. Paris: Desclée de Brouwer, 1952.

———. *Le jeu comme symbole du monde.* French trans. Hans Hildenberg and Alex Lindenberg. Paris: Éditions de Minuit, 1966.

Fisette, Denis. *Lecture frégéenne de la phénoménologie.* Combas: Éditions de l'Éclat, 1994.

Fitzgerald, F. Scott. *The Crack-Up*, ed. Edmund Wilson. New York: New Directions, 1993.

Føllesdal, Dagfinn. "Husserl's Notion of Noema." *The Journal of Philosophy* 66, no. 20 (October 16, 1969): 680–87.

Franck, Didier. *Chair et corps: Sur la phénoménologie de Husserl.* Paris: Éditions de Minuit, 1981.

Frege, Gottlob. "On Concept and Object." In *Mind*, n.s., vol. 60, no. 238 (April 1951): 168–80.

———. "Sense and Reference," trans. P. T. Geach, M. Black. *The Philosophical Review* 57, no. 3 (May 1948).

———. "Thought." In *The Frege Reader.* Oxford: Blackwell, 2007.

Frege, Gottlob, and Edmund Husserl. *Correspondance,* French trans. Gérard Granel, bilingual edition. Mauvezin: Éditions Trans-Europ-Express, 1987.

Friedman, Michael. *A Parting of the Ways: Carnap, Cassirer and Heidegger.* Chicago: Open Court, 2000.

Gadamer, Hans-Georg. "Autobiographical reflections" (1973), trans. Richard E. Palmer. In *The Gadamer Reader,* 3–38.

———. *The Gadamer Reader: A Bouquet of the Later Writings.* Evanston, Ill.: Northwestern University Press, 2007.

———. *Gesammelte Werke.* Tübingen, J. C. B. Mohr (Paul Siebeck).

———. Vol 1 : *Hermeneutik I: Wahrheit und Methode: Grundzüge einer philosophischen Hermeneutik,* 1986.

———. Vol. 2 : *Hermeneutik II: Wahrheit und Methode: Ergänzungen, Register,* 1986.

———. Vol. 3 : *Neuere Philosophie I: Hegel, Husserl, Heidegger,* 1987.

———. Vol. 8 : *Ästhetik und Poetik I: Kunst als Aussage,* 1993.

———. "Grenzen der Sprache (1985)." In *Gesammelte Werke* 8, 350–61.

———. "Hermeneutics as Practical Philosophy." In *The Gadamer Reader,* 227–45.

———. *Kleine Schriften I. Philosophie, Hermeneutik.* Tübingen: Mohr, 1967.

———. *La philosophie herméneutique.* French trans. Jean Grondin. Paris: Presses Universitaires de France, 1996.

———. *Philosophical Hermeneutics,* ed. D. E. Linge. Berkeley: University of California Press, 2004.

———. *Rhetoric and Hermeneutics in Our Time: A Reader.* New Haven, Conn.: Yale University Press, 1997.

———. "Rhetorik und Hermeneutik" (1976). In *Gesammelte Werke* 2, 276–91. Trans. Joel Weinsheimer, "Rhetoric and Hermeneutics," in *Rhetoric and Hermeneutics in Our Time: A Reader,* ed. Walter Jost and Michael J. Hyde, 45–59. New Haven, Conn.: Yale University Press, 1997.

———. "Semantik und Hermeneutik" (1968). In *Gesammelte Werke* 2, 174–83.

———. "Sprache und Verstehen" (1970). In *Gesammelte Werke* 2, 184–98. Trans. "Language and Understanding," in *The Gadamer Reader,* 89–107.

———. *Truth and Method.* Trans. Joel Weinsheimer and Donald G. Marshall. London: Continuum Impact, 2006.

———. "Writing and the Living Voice." In *Hans-Georg Gadamer on Education, Poetry, and History: Applied Hermeneutics,* ed. Dieter Misgeld and Grame Nicholson, 63–72. Albany: SUNY Press, 1992.

Galileo. *Dialogue Concerning the Two Chief World Systems, Ptolemaic and Copernican,* trans. Stillman Drake. New York: Modern Library, 2001.

———. *Dialogues Concerning Two New Sciences,* trans. H. Crew and A. de Salivo. New York: Macmillan, 1914.

Garrett, B., and Kevin Mulligan, eds. *Themes from Wittgenstein.* Canberra: Australian National University, 1993.

Geach, Peter. *Mental Acts.* London: Routledge and Kegan Paul, 1971; new edition, South Bend, Ind.: St. Augustine, 2001.

———. *Reference and Generality: An Examination of Some Medieval and Modern Theories.* Ithaca, N.Y.: Cornell University Press, 1980.

Gendler, Tamar Szabo, and John Hawthorne, eds. *Conceivability and Possibility.* Oxford: Clarendon, 2002.

Gibson, James Jerome. *The Ecological Approach to Visual Perception.* Hillsdale, N.J.: Lawrence Erlbaum Associates, 1986.

———. "Perception and Judgement of Aerial Space and Distance as Potential Factors in Pilot Selection and Training" (1947). In *Reasons for Realism: Selected Essays of James J. Gibson,* ed. Edward Reed and Rebecca Jones, 29–43. Hillsdale, N.J.: Lawrence Erlbaum Associates, 1982.

Granel, Gérard. *Le Sens du temps et de la perception chez Edmund Husserl.* Paris: Gallimard, Coll. Bibliothèque de Philosophie, 1968.

Greisch, Jean. *Ontologie et temporalité: Esquisse d'une interprétation intégrale de Sein und Zeit.* Paris: Presses Universitaires de France, 1994.

Grondin, Jean. *Le Tournant herméneutique de la phénoménologie.* Paris: Presses Universitaires de France, 2003.

———. *L'Universalité de l'herméneutique.* Paris: Presses Universitaires de France, 1993.

Gunther, York H. *Essays on Nonconceptual Content.* Cambridge, Mass.: MIT Press, 2003.

Gurvitch, Georges. "Phénoménologie et criticisme (E. Lask et N. Hartmann)." *Revue Philosophique de la France et de l'Étranger,* vol. 108 (1929): 235–84.

Gurwitsch, Aron. *The Collected Works of Aron Gurwitsch (1901–1973): Phenomenology of Theme, Thematic Field and Marginal Consciousness, Volume III: The Field of Consciousness.* Dordrecht: Springer, 2010.

———. "The Last Work of Edmund Husserl." *Phenomenology and Philosophical Research* 16 (1956): 380–99. Republished in *Studies in Phenomenology and Psychology,* 397–447. Evanston, Ill.: Northwestern University Press, 1966.

Hacker, Peter M. S. *Insight and Illusion: Wittgenstein on Philosophy and the Metaphysics of Experience.* Oxford: Oxford University Press, 1972.

Hacker, Peter M. S., and Gordon P. Baker. *Wittgenstein, Meaning and Understanding: Essays on the Philosophical Investigations.* Chicago: University of Chicago Press, 1985.

———. *Wittgenstein: Rules, Grammar and Necessity (An Analytical Commentary on the Philosophical Investigations), Volume 2.* 6th ed. Oxford: Basil Blackwell, 2000.

Hacking, Ian. *Why Does Language Matter for Philosophy?* Cambridge, Mass.: Cambridge University Press, 1975.

Hahn, Hans. "Logik, Mathematik und Naturerkennen." *Einheitswissenschaft,* no. 2, Vienna: 1932. English trans. Alfred Jules Ayer, *Logical Positivism.* New York: Free, 1959.

Hall, Harrison, and Hubert Dreyfus, eds. *Husserl, Intentionality, and Cognitive Science.* Cambridge, Mass.: MIT Press, 1982.

Hamann, Johann Georg. "Métacritique du purisme de la raison pure." In *Aestetica in nuce: Métacritique du purisme de la raison pure et autres textes,* ed. and trans. Romain Deygout. Paris: Vrin, 2001.

Hanson, Philip P., and Bruce Hunter, eds. *Return of the A Priori. Canadian Journal of Philosophy. Supplementary Vol. 18.* Calgary: University of Calgary Press, 1992.

Hardin, C. Larry. *Color for Philosophers: Unweaving the Rainbow.* Indianapolis, Ind.: Hackett, 1988.

———. "Could White be Green ?" *Mind* 98, no. 390 (April 1989): 285–88.

Hare, Richard Mervyn. " Philosophical discoveries." *Mind,* 69 (1960): 145–62.

Heffernan, George. *Am Anfang war die Logik: Hermeneutische Abhandlungen zum Ansatz der Formalen und transzendentalen Logik von Edmund Husserl.* Amsterdam: Verlag B. R. Grüner, 1988.

Heidegger, Martin. *The Basic Problems of Phenomenology,* trans. Albert Hofstadter. Bloomington: Indiana University Press, 1988.

———. *Being and Time,* trans. John Macquarrie and Edward Robinson. New York: Harper and Row, 1962.

———. *Les Conférences de Cassel,* French trans. Jean-Claude Gens (bilingual edition). Paris: Vrin, 2003.

———. *Gesamtausgabe.* Frankfurt am Main: Vittorio Klostermann Verlag.

———. Vol. 1: *Frühe Schriften* (1912–1916), ed. F.-W. von Herrmann, 1978.

———. Vol. 2: *Sein und Zeit* (1927), ed. F.-W. von Herrmann, 1977.

———. Vol. 5: *Holzwege* (1935–1946), ed. F.-W. von Herrmann, 1977.

———. Vol. 7: *Vorträge und Aufsätze* (1936–1953), ed. F.-W. von Herrmann, 2000.

———. Vol. 9: *Wegmarken* (1919–1961), ed. F.-W. von Herrmann, 1976.

———. Vol. 12: *Unterwegs zur Sprache* (1950–1959), ed. F.-W. von Herrmann, 1985.

———. Vol. 15: *Seminare* (1951–1973), ed. C. Ochwadt, 1986.

———. Vol. 17: *Einführung in die phänomenologische Forschung* (Winter Semester 1923/24), ed. F.-W. von Herrmann, 1994.

———. Vol. 20: *Prolegomena zur Geschichte des Zeitbegriffs* (Summer Semester 1925), ed. P. Jaeger, 1979.

———. Vol. 21: *Logik: Die Frage nach der Wahrheit* (Winter Semester 1925/26), ed. W. Biemel, 1976.

———. Vol. 24: *Die Grundprobleme der Phänomenologie* (Summer Semester 1927), ed. F.-W. von Herrmann, 1976 (2nd ed. 1989).

———. Vol. 26: *Metaphysische Anfangsgründe der Logik im Ausgang von Leibniz* (Summer Semester 1928), ed. K. Held, 1978 (2nd ed. 1990).

———. Vol. 29/30: *Die Grundbegriffe der Metaphysik: Welt—Endlichkeit—Einsamkeit* (Winter Semester 1929/30), ed. F.-W. von Herrmann, 1983 (2nd. ed. 1992).

———. Vol. 40: *Einführung in die Metaphysik* (Summer Semester 1935), ed. P. Jaeger, 1983.

———. Vol. 56/57: *Zur Bestimmung der Philosophie.* 1. *Die Idee der Philosophie und das Weltanschauungsproblem* (Kriegsnotsemester 1919) / 2. *Phänomenologie und transzendentale Wertphilosophie* (Summer Semester 1919) / 3. *Anhang: Über das Wesen der Universität und des akademischen Studiums* (Summer Semester 1919), ed. B. Heimbüchel, 1987.

———. Vol. 58: *Grundprobleme der Phänomenologie* (Winter Semester 1919/20), ed. H.-H. Gander, 1992.

———. Vol. 61: *Phänomenologische Interpretationen zu Aristoteles: Einführung in die*

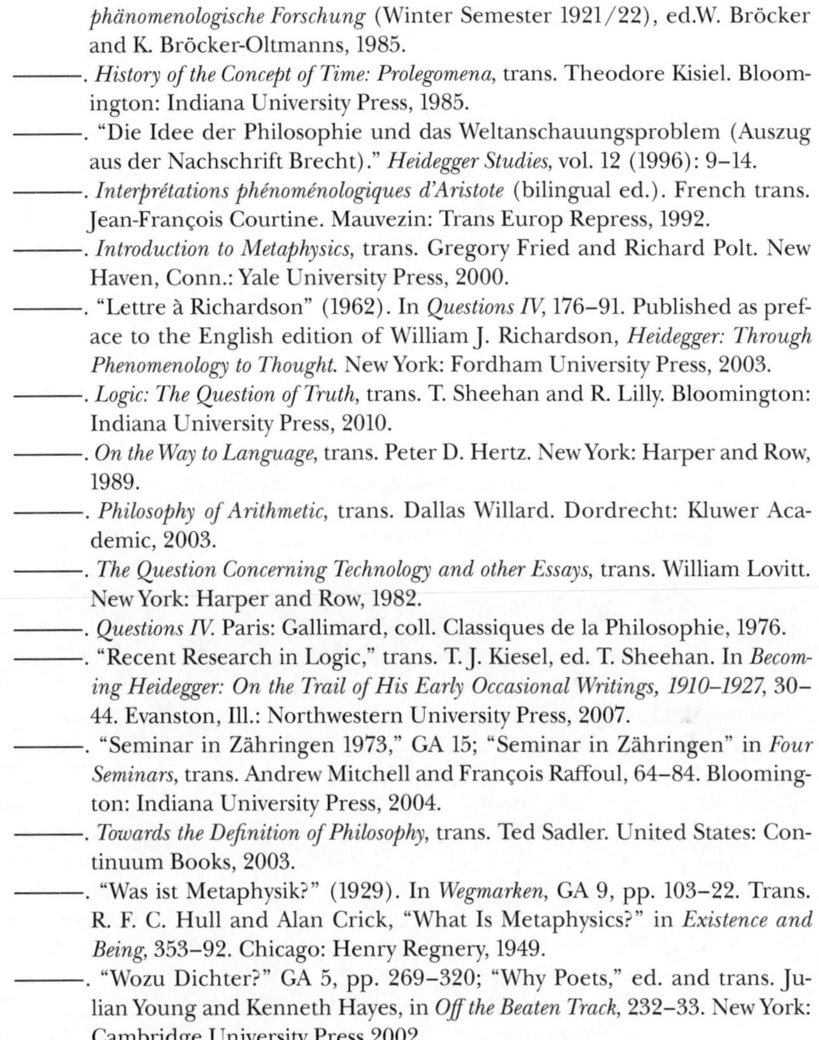

phänomenologische Forschung (Winter Semester 1921/22), ed.W. Bröcker and K. Bröcker-Oltmanns, 1985.

———. *History of the Concept of Time: Prolegomena,* trans. Theodore Kisiel. Bloomington: Indiana University Press, 1985.

———. "Die Idee der Philosophie und das Weltanschauungsproblem (Auszug aus der Nachschrift Brecht)." *Heidegger Studies,* vol. 12 (1996): 9–14.

———. *Interprétations phénoménologiques d'Aristote* (bilingual ed.). French trans. Jean-François Courtine. Mauvezin: Trans Europ Repress, 1992.

———. *Introduction to Metaphysics,* trans. Gregory Fried and Richard Polt. New Haven, Conn.: Yale University Press, 2000.

———. "Lettre à Richardson" (1962). In *Questions IV,* 176–91. Published as preface to the English edition of William J. Richardson, *Heidegger: Through Phenomenology to Thought.* New York: Fordham University Press, 2003.

———. *Logic: The Question of Truth,* trans. T. Sheehan and R. Lilly. Bloomington: Indiana University Press, 2010.

———. *On the Way to Language,* trans. Peter D. Hertz. New York: Harper and Row, 1989.

———. *Philosophy of Arithmetic,* trans. Dallas Willard. Dordrecht: Kluwer Academic, 2003.

———. *The Question Concerning Technology and other Essays,* trans. William Lovitt. New York: Harper and Row, 1982.

———. *Questions IV.* Paris: Gallimard, coll. Classiques de la Philosophie, 1976.

———. "Recent Research in Logic," trans. T. J. Kiesel, ed. T. Sheehan. In *Becoming Heidegger: On the Trail of His Early Occasional Writings, 1910–1927,* 30–44. Evanston, Ill.: Northwestern University Press, 2007.

———. "Seminar in Zähringen 1973," GA 15; "Seminar in Zähringen" in *Four Seminars,* trans. Andrew Mitchell and François Raffoul, 64–84. Bloomington: Indiana University Press, 2004.

———. *Towards the Definition of Philosophy,* trans. Ted Sadler. United States: Continuum Books, 2003.

———. "Was ist Metaphysik?" (1929). In *Wegmarken,* GA 9, pp. 103–22. Trans. R. F. C. Hull and Alan Crick, "What Is Metaphysics?" in *Existence and Being,* 353–92. Chicago: Henry Regnery, 1949.

———. "Wozu Dichter?" GA 5, pp. 269–320; "Why Poets," ed. and trans. Julian Young and Kenneth Hayes, in *Off the Beaten Track,* 232–33. New York: Cambridge University Press 2002.

Heidegger. Cahiers de l'Herne. Paris: Éditions de l'Herne, 1983.

Heidegger. Cahiers d'histoire de la philosophie, ed. Maxence Caron. Paris: Éditions du Cerf, 2006.

Heisenberg, Werner. "The Representation of Nature in Contemporary Physics." *Daedalus* 87, no. 3 (Summer 1958): 95–108.

Henry, Michel. *The Genealogy of Psychoanalysis,* trans. Douglas Brick. Stanford, Calif.: Stanford University Press, 1993.

Hering, Ewald. *Zur Lehre von Lichtsinn.* Leipzig: Engelmann, 1905.

Hering, Jean. "Bemerkungen über das Wesen, die Wesenheit und die Idee." *Jahrbuch für Philosophie und Phänomenologische Forschung,* vol. 4 (1921): 495–543.

Hinton, John Michael. *Experiences: An Inquiry into Some Ambiguities*. Oxford: Clarendon, 1973.

Holenstein, Elmar. "L'Association en tant que synthèse passive." French trans. Bruce Bégout. In *Philosophie*, no. 50 (1996): 30–65.

———. *Phänomenologie der Assoziation*. The Hague: Martinus Nijhoff, 1972 (Phaenomenologica no. 44).

Hume, David. *An Enquiry concerning Human Understanding*, ed. Tom L. Beauchamp. Oxford: Oxford University Press, 1999.

———. *A Treatise of Human Nature*. London: Penguin Books, 1985.

Hunter, Bruce, and Philip P. Hanson. *Return of the A Priori. Canadian Journal of Philosophy. Supplementary Volume 18*. Calgary: University of Calgary Press, 1992.

Husserl, Edmund. *Analyses concerning Passive and Active Synthesis: Lectures on Transcendental Logic*, trans. A. J. Steinbock. Dordrecht: Kluwer Academic, 2001.

———. *Briefwechsel*, Vol. V. *Die Neukantianer*, ed. Karl Schuhmann with the collaboration of Elisabeth Schuhmann. Dordrecht: Kluwer Academic, Husserliana Dokumente, III-V, 1994.

———. *Cartesian Meditations: An Introduction to Phenomenology*, trans. Dorion Cairns. The Hague: Martinus Nijhoff, 1973.

———. *The Crisis of European Sciences and Transcendental Phenomenology*, trans. David Carr. Evanston, Ill.: Northwestern University Press, 1970.

———. "Edmund Husserl's Letter to Lucien Lévy-Bruhl." March 11, 1935. Trans. Lukas Steinacher and Dermot Moran in *The New Yearbook for Phenomenology and Phenomenological Philosophy VIII* (2008): 325–47.

———. " Entwurf einer 'Vorrede' zu den 'Logischen Untersuchungen,'" ed. Eugen Fink. *Tijdschrift voor Philosophie* 1 (1939): 106–33; 319–39.

———. *Erfahrung und Urteil*, Hamburg, Glaassen und Goverts, 1954. Trans. James S. Churchill and Karl Ameriks. *Experience and Judgment*, Evanston, Ill.: Northwestern University Press, 1973.

———. *Formal and Transcendental Logic*, trans. D. Cairns. The Hague: Martinus Nijhoff, 1969.

———. "Foundational Investigations of the Phenomenological Origin of the Spatiality of Nature: The Originary Ark, the Earth, Does Not Move." In *Husserl at the Limits of Phenomenology: Including Texts by Edmund Husserl, Maurice Merleau-Ponty*, ed. Leonard Lawlor with Bettina Bergo, 117–31. Evanston, Ill.: Northwestern University Press, 2002.

———. *Gesammelte Werke* (*Husserliana*), Martinus Nijhoff/Kluwer/Springer Verlag.

———. Bd. I: *Cartesianische Meditationen und Pariser Vorträge*, edited and presented by Stephan Strasser, 1991.

———. Bd. II: *Die Idee der Phänomenologie. Fünf Vorlesungen*, edited and presented by Walter Biemel, 1973.

———. Bd. III: *Ideen zu einer reinen Phänomenologie und phänomenologischen Philosophie. 1. Buch: Allgemeine Einführung in die reine Phänomenologie*, ed. Karl Schuhmann, 1976.
Part One : *Text der 1.-3. Auflage.*
Part Two: *Ergänzende Texte (1912–1929).*

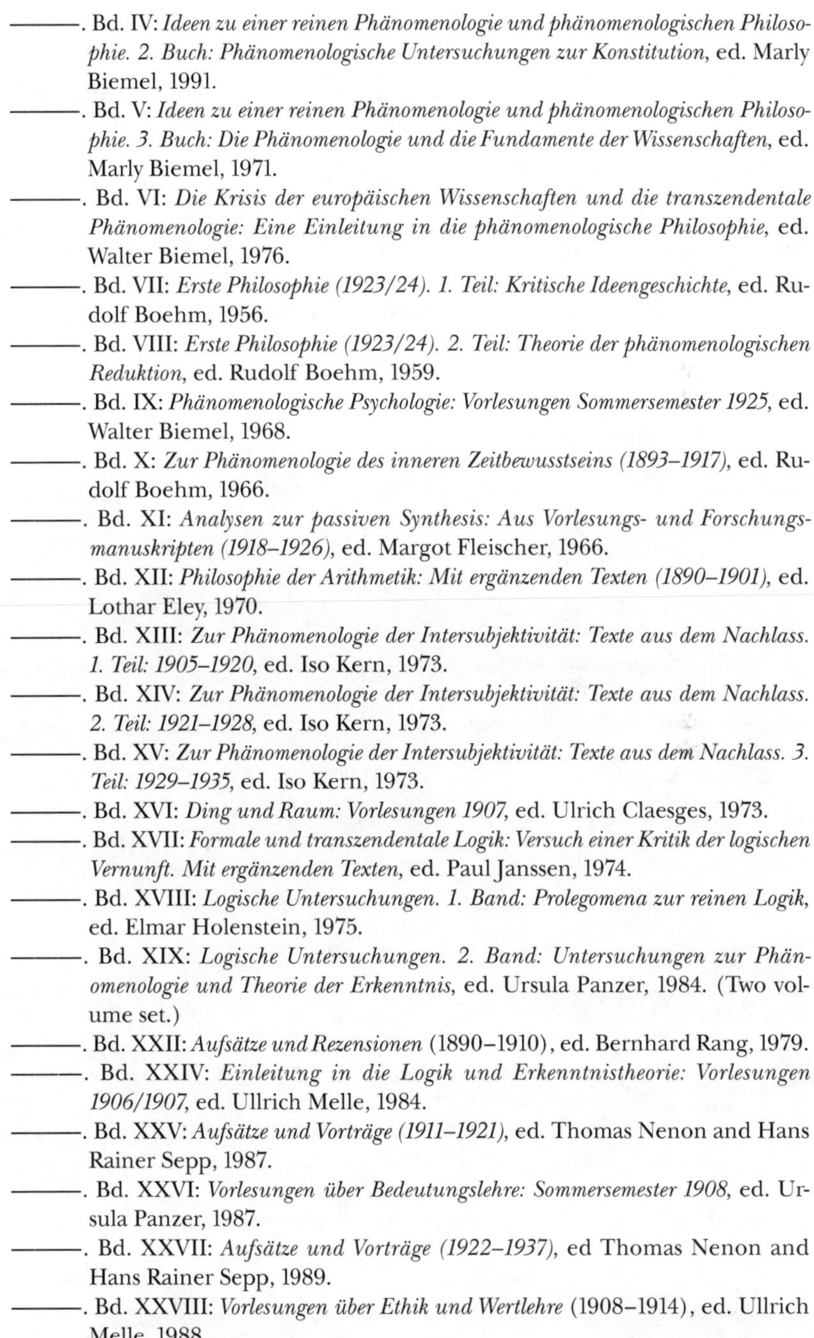

———. Bd. IV: *Ideen zu einer reinen Phänomenologie und phänomenologischen Philosophie. 2. Buch: Phänomenologische Untersuchungen zur Konstitution*, ed. Marly Biemel, 1991.

———. Bd. V: *Ideen zu einer reinen Phänomenologie und phänomenologischen Philosophie. 3. Buch: Die Phänomenologie und die Fundamente der Wissenschaften*, ed. Marly Biemel, 1971.

———. Bd. VI: *Die Krisis der europäischen Wissenschaften und die transzendentale Phänomenologie: Eine Einleitung in die phänomenologische Philosophie*, ed. Walter Biemel, 1976.

———. Bd. VII: *Erste Philosophie (1923/24). 1. Teil: Kritische Ideengeschichte*, ed. Rudolf Boehm, 1956.

———. Bd. VIII: *Erste Philosophie (1923/24). 2. Teil: Theorie der phänomenologischen Reduktion*, ed. Rudolf Boehm, 1959.

———. Bd. IX: *Phänomenologische Psychologie: Vorlesungen Sommersemester 1925*, ed. Walter Biemel, 1968.

———. Bd. X: *Zur Phänomenologie des inneren Zeitbewusstseins (1893–1917)*, ed. Rudolf Boehm, 1966.

———. Bd. XI: *Analysen zur passiven Synthesis: Aus Vorlesungs- und Forschungsmanuskripten (1918–1926)*, ed. Margot Fleischer, 1966.

———. Bd. XII: *Philosophie der Arithmetik: Mit ergänzenden Texten (1890–1901)*, ed. Lothar Eley, 1970.

———. Bd. XIII: *Zur Phänomenologie der Intersubjektivität: Texte aus dem Nachlass. 1. Teil: 1905–1920*, ed. Iso Kern, 1973.

———. Bd. XIV: *Zur Phänomenologie der Intersubjektivität: Texte aus dem Nachlass. 2. Teil: 1921–1928*, ed. Iso Kern, 1973.

———. Bd. XV: *Zur Phänomenologie der Intersubjektivität: Texte aus dem Nachlass. 3. Teil: 1929–1935*, ed. Iso Kern, 1973.

———. Bd. XVI: *Ding und Raum: Vorlesungen 1907*, ed. Ulrich Claesges, 1973.

———. Bd. XVII: *Formale und transzendentale Logik: Versuch einer Kritik der logischen Vernunft. Mit ergänzenden Texten*, ed. Paul Janssen, 1974.

———. Bd. XVIII: *Logische Untersuchungen. 1. Band: Prolegomena zur reinen Logik*, ed. Elmar Holenstein, 1975.

———. Bd. XIX: *Logische Untersuchungen. 2. Band: Untersuchungen zur Phänomenologie und Theorie der Erkenntnis*, ed. Ursula Panzer, 1984. (Two volume set.)

———. Bd. XXII: *Aufsätze und Rezensionen* (1890–1910), ed. Bernhard Rang, 1979.

———. Bd. XXIV: *Einleitung in die Logik und Erkenntnistheorie: Vorlesungen 1906/1907*, ed. Ullrich Melle, 1984.

———. Bd. XXV: *Aufsätze und Vorträge (1911–1921)*, ed. Thomas Nenon and Hans Rainer Sepp, 1987.

———. Bd. XXVI: *Vorlesungen über Bedeutungslehre: Sommersemester 1908*, ed. Ursula Panzer, 1987.

———. Bd. XXVII: *Aufsätze und Vorträge (1922–1937)*, ed Thomas Nenon and Hans Rainer Sepp, 1989.

———. Bd. XXVIII: *Vorlesungen über Ethik und Wertlehre* (1908–1914), ed. Ullrich Melle, 1988.

———. Bd. XXIX: *Die Krisis der europäischen Wissenschaften und die transzendentale Phänomenologie. Ergänzungsband. Texte aus dem Nachlass 1934–1937,* ed. R.N. Smid, 1993.
———. *The Idea of Phenomenology,* trans. Lee Hardy. Dordrecht: Kluwer Academic, 2010.
———. *Ideas Pertaining to a Pure Phenomenology and to a Phenomenological Philosophy, First Book,* trans F. Kersten. Dordrecht: Kluwer Academic, 1982.
———. *Introduction to Logic and Theory of Knowledge: Lectures 1906/07,* trans. Claire Ortiz Hill. Dordrecht: Springer, 2008.
———. "Kant and the Idea of Transcendental Philosophy," trans. Ted E. Klein, Jr. and William E. Pohl. *Southwestern Journal of Philosophy* 5 (1974).
———. *Leçons sur l'éthique et la théorie de la valeur* (1908–1914). French trans. Philippe Ducat, Patrick Lang, and Carlos Lobo. Paris: Presses Universitaires de France, 2008.
———. *Logical Investigations,* 2 vols., trans. J. N. Findlay. London: Routledge and Kegan Paul, 1977.
———. *Notes sur Heidegger.* French trans. Natalie Depraz, Didier Franck, Jean-Luc Fidel, and Jean-François Courtine. Paris: Éditions de Minuit, 1993.
———. *Phenomenological Psychology: Lectures, Summer Semester 1925,* trans. J. Scanlon. The Hague: Martinus Nijhoff, 1962.
———. "Phénoménologie et anthropologie." French trans. Didier Franck, in Husserl, *Notes sur Heidegger,* 57–74.
———. *The Phenomenology of Internal Time-Consciousness,* trans. James S. Churchill. Bloomington: Indiana University Press, 1964.
———. *Phenomenology and the Crisis of Philosophy,* trans. Quentin Lauer. New York: Harper and Row, 1965.
———. *Phenomenology and the Foundations of the Sciences.* In *E. Husserl, Collected Works, Vol. 1,* trans. Klein and Pohl. The Hague: Martinus Nijhoff, 1980.
———. *Philosophie première, I, Histoire critique des idées.* French trans. Arion Lothar Kelkel. Paris: Presses Universitaires de France, 1970.
———. *Philosophie première, II.* French trans. Arion Lothar Kelkel. Paris: Presses Universitaires de France, 1972.
———. "Philosophy as Rigorous Science," trans. Quentin Lauer. In *Phenomenology and the Crisis of Philosophy,* 71–147.
———. *Philosophy of Arithmetic,* trans. Dallas Willard. Dordrecht: Kluwer Academic, 2003.
———. *Psychologie phénoménologique.* French trans. Philippe Cabestan, Natalie Depraz, and Antonino Mazzu. Paris: Vrin, 2001.
———. *Recherches logiques,* vols. I; II, 1; II, 2 and III. French trans. Hubert Élie, Arion Lothar Kelkel, and René Schérer. Paris: Presses Universitaires de France, 1969–1974.
———. *Sur la théorie de la signification.* French trans. Jacques English. Paris: Vrin, 1995.
———. *Sur les objets intentionnels* (1893–1901). French trans. Jacques English. Paris: Vrin, 1993.

———. *Sur l'intersubjectivité, Vol. I.* French trans. Natalie Depraz. Paris: Presses Universitaires de France, 2001.

———. *Sur l'intersubjectivité, Vol. II.* French trans. Natalie Depraz. Paris: Presses Universitaires de France, 2001.

———. *Thing and Space: Lectures of 1907,* trans. Richard Rojcewicz. Dordrecht: Kluwer Academic, 1997.

———. "Tobacco-logisches" (German-English). *The New Yearbook for Phenomenology and Phenomenological Philosophy,* 4 (2004): 274–82.

Husserl, Edmund, Christian von Ehrenfels, Anton Marty, Alexius Meinong, Carl Stumpf, and Kazimierz Twardowski. *À l'École de Brentano: De Würzbourg à Vienne,* French trans. and ed. Denis Fisette and Guillaume Fréchette. Paris: Vrin, 2007.

Husserl, Edmund, and Gottlob Frege. *Correspondance.* French trans. Gérard Granel. Mauvezin: Trans Europ Repress, 1987.

Husserl, Edmund, Alexius Meinong, and Bertrand Russell. "Correspondance autour de la théorie de l'objet." *Philosophie,* no. 72 (2001): 12–35.

Husserl. Cahiers d'histoire de la philosophie, ed. Jocelyn Besnoist. Paris: Éditions du Cerf, 2008.

Husserl: Cahiers de Royaumont. Paris: Éditions de Minuit, 1959.

Ingarden, Roman. *Der Streit um die Existenz der Welt, II/1, Formalontologie.* Tübingen: Max Niemeyer Verlag, 1965.

———. *Husserl: La controverse idéalisme-réalisme.* French trans. Patricia Limido-Heulot. Paris: Vrin, 2001.

Jacob, Pierre, ed. *De Vienne à Cambridge: L'héritage du positivisme logique.* Paris: Gallimard, coll. Bibliothèque des Sciences humaines, 1980; reproduced in coll. Tel, 1996.

———. *L'Empirisme logique, ses antécédents, ses critiques.* Paris: Éditions de Minuit, 1980.

———. *L'intentionnalité.* Paris: Odile Jacob, 2004.

James, William. *Essais d'empirisme radical.* French trans. Guillaume Garreta and Mathias Girel. Marseille: Agone, 2005.

———. *Principles of Psychology.* 2 vols. New York: Henry Holt, 1890.

———. *Writings 1902–1910.* New York: Library of America, 1987.

Jones, Owen Roger, ed. *The Private Language Argument.* London: Macmillan, St. Martin's, 1971.

Kant, Immanuel. *Kritik der reinen Vernunft.* Hamburg: Felix Meiner Verlag, 1956. Trans. Max Müller, *Critique of Pure Reason.* Garden City, N.Y.: Doubleday, Anchor Books, 1966.

———. *Notes and Fragments,* ed. Paul Guyer. Cambridge, Eng.: Cambridge University Press, 2010.

Katz, David. *Die Erscheinungen der Farben und ihre Beeinflussung durch die individuelle Erfahrung.* Leipzig: Verlag von Johann Ambrosius Barth, 1911. trans. R. B. MacLeod and C. W. Fox, *The World of Colour* (London: Routledge, 1999).

Kenny, Anthony. *Will, Freedom and Power.* New York: Barnes and Noble, 1976.

Kern, Iso. "Die Lebenswelt als Grundlagenproblem der objektiven Wissenschaften und als universales Wahrheits- und Seinsproblem." In *Edmund Husserl. Darstellung seines Denkens*, by Rudolf Bernet, Iso Kern, and Eduard Marbach, 199–208. Hamburg: F. Meiner Verlag, 1989.

———. *Husserl und Kant: Eine Untersuchung über Husserls Verhältnis zu Kant und zum Neokantismus*. The Hague: M. Nijhoff, 1964.

Kertscher, Jens, Ulrich Arnswald, and Jeff Malpas, eds. *Gadamer's Century: Essays in Honor of Hans-Georg Gadamer*. Cambridge, Mass.: MIT Press, 2002.

Koffka, Kurt. *Principles of Gestalt Psychology*. New York: Harcourt, Brace and World, 1935; republished as a Harbinger Book, 1963.

Köhler, Wolfgang. *Gestalt Psychology*. New York: Liveright, 1947, revised and expanded ed.

———. *The Selected Papers of Wolfgang Köhler*. New York: Liveright, 1971.

———. "Value and Fact." In *The Selected Papers of Wolfgang Köhler*, 356–75.

Kripke, Saul A. *Naming and Necessity*. Cambridge, Mass: Harvard University Press, 1980.

Lafont, Cristina. *Sprache und Welterschliessung: Zur linguistischen Wende der Hermeneutik Heideggers*. Frankfurt am Main: Suhrkamp, 1994.

Landgrebe, Ludwig. "Husserls Abschied vom Cartesianismus." *Philosophische Rundschau* 9 (1961): 133–77.

———. *Der Weg der Phänomenologie*. Gütersloh: Gerd Mohn, 1963.

Laurent, Jérôme, and Claude Romano, eds. *Le Néant: Contribution à une histoire du non-être dans la philosophie occidentale*. Paris, Presses Universitaires de France, 2006.

Lavigne, Jean-François. *Husserl et la naissance de la phénoménologie (1900–1913)*. Paris: Presses Universitaires de France, 2005.

Lepore, Ernest, ed. *Truth and Interpretation: Perspectives on the Philosophy of Donald Davidson*. Oxford: Basil Blackwell, 1986.

Levinas, Emmanuel. *Discovering Existence with Husserl.* (A partial translation of *En découvrant l'existence avec Husserl et Heidegger.*) Trans. and ed. Richard A. Cohen and Michael B. Smith. Evanston, Ill.: Northwestern University Press, 1998.

———. *Ethics and Infinity: Conversations with Philippe Nemo*. Pittsbugh: Duquesne University Press, 1985.

———. "Reflections on Phenomenological 'Technique.'" In *Discovering Existence with Husserl*, 91–110.

———. *Time and the Other: And Additional Essays*, trans. Richard A. Cohen. Pittsburgh: Duquesne University Press, 2002.

———. *The Theory of Intuition in Husserl's Phenomenology*, trans. André Oriane. Evanston, Ill.: Northwestern University, 1995.

———. *Totalité et infini*, (Den Haag: Martinus Nijhoff, 1971), reprint Paris, Le livre de Poche, 1990.

———. *Totality and Infinity: An Essay on Exteriority*, trans. Alphonso Lingis. Pittsburgh: Duquesne University Press, 1969.

Lewis, Clarence Irving. *Mind and the World-Order: Outline of a Theory of Knowledge.* New York: Charles Scribner's Sons, 1929.

Libera, Alain de. "Intention." In *Vocabulaire européen des philosophies: Dictionnaire des intraduisibles*, ed. Barbara Cassin, 608–19. Paris: Seuil-Le Robert, 2004.

Locke, John. *An Essay Concerning Human Understanding.* London: Penguin Classics, 1997.

Lockwood, Michael. *Mind, Brain and the Quantum.* Oxford: Blackwell, 1989.

Lowe, E. Jonathan. "Metaphysics as the Science of Essence." http://ontology.buffalo.edu/06/Lowe/Lowe.pdf.

Löwit, Alexandre. "L'épochè de Husserl et le doute de Descartes." *Revue de Métaphysique et de Morale*, no. 4 (1957).

Mach, Ernst. *The Analysis of Sensations and the Relation of the Physical to the Psychical*, trans. C. M. Williams, rev. Sidney Waterlow. Chicago: Open Court, 1914.

Mackie, Penelope. *How Things Might Have Been: Individuals, Kinds, and Essential Properties.* Oxford University Press, 2006.

Maldiney, Henry. *Penser l'homme et la folie à la lumière de l'analyse existentielle et de l'analyse du destin.* Grenoble: Éditions Jérôme Millon, 1991.

Malpas, Jeff, Ulrich Arnswald, and Jens Kertscher, eds. *Gadamer's Century: Essays in Honor of Hans-Georg Gadamer.* Cambridge, Mass.: MIT Press, 2002.

Marbach, Eduard, Rudolf Bernet, and Iso Kern. *Edmund Husserl: Darstellung seines Denkens.* Hamburg: Felix Meiner Verlag, 1996.

Marion, Jean-Luc. *Being Given: Toward a Phenomenology of Givenness*, trans. Jeffrey L. Kosky. Stanford, Calif.: Stanford University Press, 2002.

———. *Reduction and Givenness: Investigations of Husserl, Heidegger, and Phenomenology.* Evanston, Ill.: Northwestern University Press, 1998.

Marty, Anton. *Untersuchungen zur Grundlegung der allgemeinen Grammatik und Sprachphilosophie, I.* Halle: Niemeyer, 1908.

McDowell, John Henry. "Criteria, Defeasibility and Knowledge." In *Meaning, Knowledge, and Reality*, 369–94. Cambridge, Mass.: Harvard University Press, 1998.

———. "Gadamer and Davidson on Understanding and Relativism." In *Gadamer's Century: Essays in Honor of Hans-Georg Gadamer*, ed. Jeff Malpas, Ulrich Arnswald, and Jens Kertscher, 173–93. Cambridge, Mass.: MIT Press, 2002.

———. "Hegel et le mythe du donné" ("Hegel and the Myth of the Given"), French trans. Nawal El Yadari, Emmanuel Renault, and Marie Salmon. *Philosophie*, no. 99 (Fall 2008): 46–62.

———. *Mind and World.* Cambridge, Mass: Harvard University Press, 1996.

McGinn, Marie. "On Two Recents Accounts of Colour." *The Philosophical Quarterly* 41, no. 164 (1991): 316–34.

———. "The Real Problem of Others: Cavell, Merleau-Ponty and Wittgenstein on Scepticism about Other Minds." *European Journal of Philosophy* 6, no. 1 (1998): 45–58.

Meinong, Alexius. "Bemerkungen über den Farbenkörper und das Mischungsgesetz" (1903). *Zeitschrift für Psychologie und Physiologie der Sinnesorgane* 32, nos. 1 and 2 (1903): 1–80.

———. *Gegenstandtheorie* (1904). In *Gesamtausgabe.* Graz: Akademische Druck- und Verlagsanstalt, 1968–1978. Vol. II, pp. 483–530. "The Theory of Objects" in *Realism and the Background of Phenomenology,* ed. Roderick M. Chisholm, 76–117. Glencoe, Ill.: Free, 1960; reprint, Atascadero, Calif: Ridgeview, 1981.

Meinong, Alexius, Edmund Husserl, and Bertrand Russell. "Correspondance autour de la théorie de l'objet." French trans. Bastien Gallet, *Philosophie* 72 (2001): 3–35.

Melville, Herman. *Moby-Dick, or, The Whale.* New York: Penguin Books, 2001.

Merleau-Ponty, Maurice. *Nature: Course Notes from the Collège de France: Compiled and with notes by Dominique Séglard,* trans. Robert Vallier. Evanston, Ill.: Northwestern University Press, 2003.

———. *La Nature, Notes: Cours du Collège de France.* Paris: Éditions du Seuil, 1995.

———. *Le Visible et l'invisible,* Paris, Gallimard, 1964.

———. *Notes des cours au Collège de France, 1958–1959/1960–1961.* Paris: Gallimard, coll. Bibliothèque de Philosophie, 1996.

———. *Parcours, 1935–1951.* Lagrasse: Verdier, 1997.

———. *Phenomenology of Perception,* trans. Donald A Landes. London: Routledge, 2012.

———. *The Prose of the World,* ed. Claude Lefort, trans. John O'Neill. Evanston, Ill.: Northwestern University Press, 1973.

———. *The Structure of Behavior,* trans. Alden L. Fischer, with a foreword by John Wild. Boston: Beacon, 1963.

———. *The Visible and the Invisible,* ed. Claude Lefort, trans. Alphonso Lingis. Evanston, Ill.: Northwestern University Press, 1968.

Métaphysique contemporaine: Propriétés, mondes possibles et personnes, ed. Emmanuelle Garcia and Frédéric Nef. Paris: Vrin, 2007.

Michaux, Henri. *Tent Posts,* trans. Lynn Hoggard. Copenhagen: Green Integer, 1997.

Mill, John Stuart. *A System of Logic Ratiocinative and Inductive* [1843]. *Being a Connected View of the Principles of Evidence and the Methods of Scientific Investigation (Books I-III),* ed. John M. Robson, intro. R.F. McRae. Toronto: University of Toronto Press; London: Routledge and Kegan Paul, 1974.

Misgeld, Dieter, and Graeme Nicholson, eds. *Hans-Georg Gadamer on Education, Poetry, and History: Applied Hermeneutics.* Albany: SUNY Press, 1992.

Mohanty, Jitendra Nath. "Husserl and Frege: A New Look at Their Relationship." In *Husserl, Intentionality, and Cognitive Science,* ed. Hubert L. Dreyfus and Harrison Hall, 43–52. Cambridge, Mass.: MIT Press, 1982.

———. "Phenomenology and the Modalities." In *Logic, Truth, and the Modalities: From a Phenomenological Perspective,* 168–79. Dordrecht: Kluwer Academic, 1999.

Moore, George Edward. "Wittgenstein's lectures in 1930–33." In *Philosophical Papers,* 252–324. London: Allen and Unwin, 1959.

Mulligan, Kevin. "Descriptions' Objects: Austrian Variations." In *Themes from Wittgenstein,* ed. B. Garrett and Kevin Mulligan. Canberra: Australian National University, 1993, 62–85.

———. "The Essence of Language: Wittgenstein's Builders and Bühler's Bricks." *Revue de Métaphysique et de Morale,* 2 (1997): 193–216.

Mulligan, Kevin, and B. Garrett, eds. *Themes from Wittgenstein.* Canberra: Australian National University, 1993.

Nabokov, Vladimir. *Speak, Memory: An Autobiography Revisited.* New York: Vintage International, 1989.

Natorp, Paul. *Allgemeine Psychologie nach kritischer Methode, Erstes Buch: Objekt und Methode der Psychologie.* Tübingen: J. C. B. Mohr, 1912. *Psychologie générale selon la méthode critique,* French trans. Éric Dufour and Julien Servois. Paris: Vrin, 2007.

———. "Husserls Ideen zu einer reinen Phänomenologie." *Logos,* 7 (1917–1918): 224–46. French trans. Julien Servois, "Les Idées directrices pour une phénoménologie de Husserl." *Philosophie,* no. 74 (2002): 15–39.

———. "Kant und die Marburger Schule." *Kant-Studien,* vol. 17 (1912): 193–221. French trans. Isabelle Thomas-Fogiel, in Natorp, Cassirer, and Cohen, *L'École de Marbourg,* Paris: Éditions du Cerf, 1998, 39–66.

Neurath, Otto. "Soziologie im Physikalismus." In *Erkenntnis, II, 1931,* 393–431. "Sociology in The Framework of Physicalism," ed. and trans. Robert S. Cohen and Marie Neurath. In *Philosophical Papers 1913–1946,* 58–90. Dordrecht: D. Reidel, 1983.

Nietzsche, Friedrich. *Fragments posthumes: Été 1881–été 1882.* In *Oeuvres philosophiques complètes,* V, French trans. Pierre Klossowski, ed. Giorgio Colli and Mazzino Montinari, rev. Marc B. de Launay. Paris: Gallimard, 1982.

———. *Fragments posthumes: Automne 1885–automne 1887.* In *Oeuvres philosophiques complètes,* XII. French trans. Julien Hervier, ed. Giorgio Colli and Mazzino Montinari. Paris: Gallimard, 1979.

Okrent, Mark. *Rational Animals: The Teleological Roots of Intentionality.* Athens: Ohio University Press, 2007.

Patočka, Jan. *Introduction à la phénoménologie de Husserl,* French trans. Erika Abrams. Grenoble: Éditions Jérôme Millon, 1992.

———. *Papiers phénoménologiques,* French trans. Erika Abrams. Grenoble: Éditions Jérôme Millon, 1995.

Peacocke, Christopher. *Thoughts: An Essay on Content.* Oxford: Basil Blackwell, 1986.

Phénoménologie et logique, ed. Jean-François Courtine. Paris: Presses de l'École Normale Supérieure, 1996.

Phénoménologie et métaphysique, ed. Jean-Luc Marion and Guy Planty-Bonjour. Paris: Presses Universitaires de France, 1984.

Philipse, Herman." Heidegger's Question of Being and the 'Augustinian Picture' of Language." *Philosophy and Phenomenological Research* 52, no. 2 (June, 1992): 251–87.

Pippin, Robert. "Book review: Ernst Tugendhat, "*Traditional and Analytical Philosophy.*" *Independent Journal of Philosophy,* vol. 5/6, (1988): 165–68.

———. "Concept and Intuition. On Distinguishability and Separability." *Hegel-Studien,* 40 (2005): 25–39.

Plantinga, Alvin. *The Nature of Necessity.* Oxford: Clarendon, 1974.

Proust, Joëlle. *Questions de forme: Logique et proposition analytique de Kant à Carnap.* Paris: Fayard, 1986.

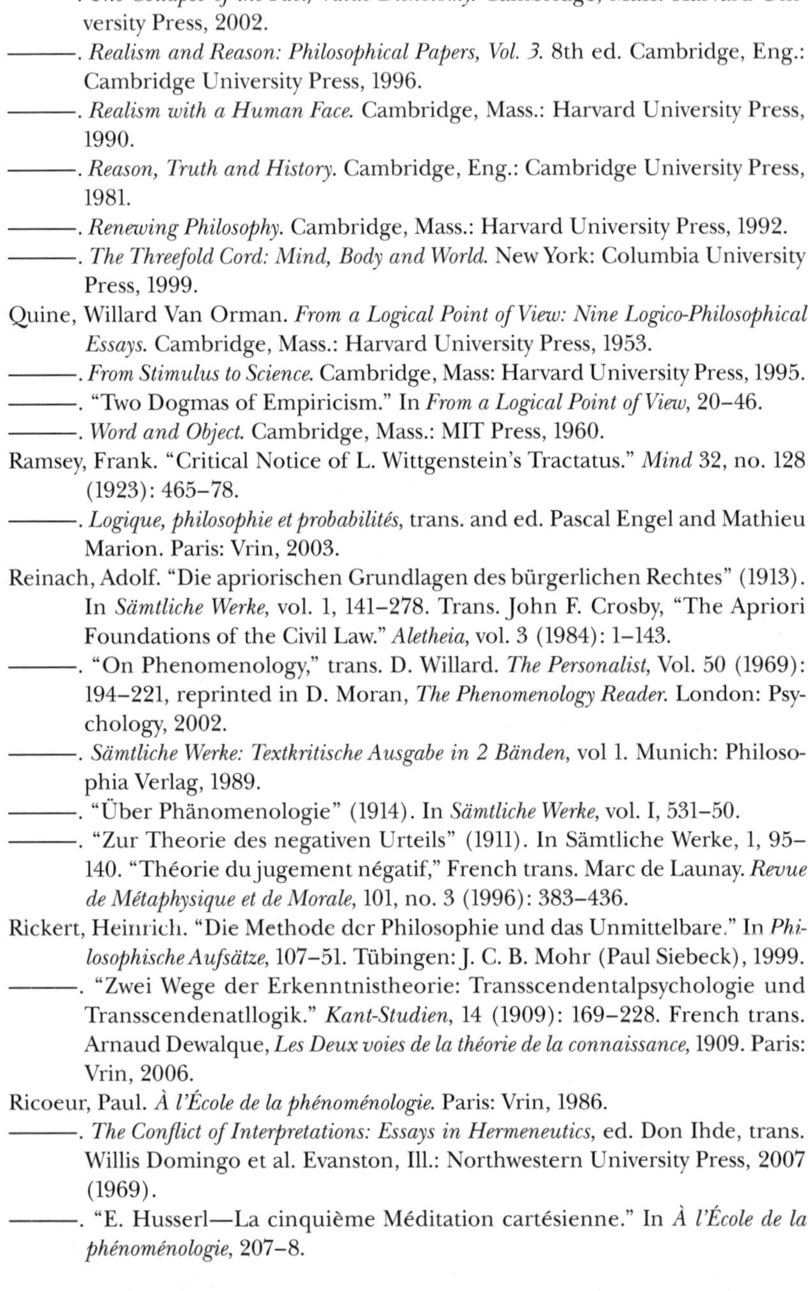

Putnam, Hilary. “The Analytic and the Synthetic.” In *Mind, Language and Reality*, Cambridge, Eng.: Cambridge University Press, 1979, 33–69.

———. *The Collapse of the Fact/Value Dichotomy*. Cambridge, Mass: Harvard University Press, 2002.

———. *Realism and Reason: Philosophical Papers, Vol. 3*. 8th ed. Cambridge, Eng.: Cambridge University Press, 1996.

———. *Realism with a Human Face*. Cambridge, Mass.: Harvard University Press, 1990.

———. *Reason, Truth and History*. Cambridge, Eng.: Cambridge University Press, 1981.

———. *Renewing Philosophy*. Cambridge, Mass.: Harvard University Press, 1992.

———. *The Threefold Cord: Mind, Body and World*. New York: Columbia University Press, 1999.

Quine, Willard Van Orman. *From a Logical Point of View: Nine Logico-Philosophical Essays*. Cambridge, Mass.: Harvard University Press, 1953.

———. *From Stimulus to Science*. Cambridge, Mass: Harvard University Press, 1995.

———. “Two Dogmas of Empiricism.” In *From a Logical Point of View*, 20–46.

———. *Word and Object*. Cambridge, Mass.: MIT Press, 1960.

Ramsey, Frank. “Critical Notice of L. Wittgenstein’s Tractatus.” *Mind* 32, no. 128 (1923): 465–78.

———. *Logique, philosophie et probabilités*, trans. and ed. Pascal Engel and Mathieu Marion. Paris: Vrin, 2003.

Reinach, Adolf. “Die apriorischen Grundlagen des bürgerlichen Rechtes” (1913). In *Sämtliche Werke*, vol. 1, 141–278. Trans. John F. Crosby, “The Apriori Foundations of the Civil Law.” *Aletheia*, vol. 3 (1984): 1–143.

———. “On Phenomenology,” trans. D. Willard. *The Personalist*, Vol. 50 (1969): 194–221, reprinted in D. Moran, *The Phenomenology Reader*. London: Psychology, 2002.

———. *Sämtliche Werke: Textkritische Ausgabe in 2 Bänden*, vol 1. Munich: Philosophia Verlag, 1989.

———. “Über Phänomenologie” (1914). In *Sämtliche Werke*, vol. I, 531–50.

———. “Zur Theorie des negativen Urteils” (1911). In Sämtliche Werke, 1, 95–140. “Théorie du jugement négatif,” French trans. Marc de Launay. *Revue de Métaphysique et de Morale*, 101, no. 3 (1996): 383–436.

Rickert, Heinrich. “Die Methode der Philosophie und das Unmittelbare.” In *Philosophische Aufsätze*, 107–51. Tübingen: J. C. B. Mohr (Paul Siebeck), 1999.

———. “Zwei Wege der Erkenntnistheorie: Transscendentalpsychologie und Transscendenatllogik.” *Kant-Studien*, 14 (1909): 169–228. French trans. Arnaud Dewalque, *Les Deux voies de la théorie de la connaissance*, 1909. Paris: Vrin, 2006.

Ricoeur, Paul. *À l’École de la phénoménologie*. Paris: Vrin, 1986.

———. *The Conflict of Interpretations: Essays in Hermeneutics*, ed. Don Ihde, trans. Willis Domingo et al. Evanston, Ill.: Northwestern University Press, 2007 (1969).

———. “E. Husserl—La cinquième Méditation cartésienne.” In *À l’École de la phénoménologie*, 207–8.

———. *From Text to Action.* Trans. Kathleen Blamey and John B. Thompson. Evanston, Ill.: Northwestern University Press, 1991 (1986).

———. *Time and Narrative,* 3 vols., trans. Kathleen McLaughlin and David Pellauer. Chicago: University of Chicago Press, 1988.

Rigal, Élisabeth. "Y a-t-il une phénoménologie wittgensteinienne?" in Richard Cobb-Stevens, Jacques Taminiaux, Gérard Granel, and Élisabeth Rigal, *La phénoménologie aux confins,* Mauvezin: Trans Europ Repress, 1992, 83–113.

Rivenc, François. "Husserl avec et contre Frege." *Les Études philosophiques,* no. 1 (1995): 13–38.

Romano, Claude. "Anscombe et la philosophie herméneutique de l'intention." *Philosophie,* 80 (2003): 60–87.

———. *Event and Time.* Trans. Stephen E. Lewis. New York: Fordham University Press, 2013.

———. *Event and World.* Trans. Shane Mackinlay. New York: Fordham University Press, 2009.

———. "L'horizon de la phénoménologie." *Iris* (Beirut), vol. 28 (2007): 1–38.

———. *Il y a.* Paris: Presses Universitaires de France, 2003.

———. "Les Leçons sur le temps de Husserl dans l'histoire de la métaphysique," in Jocelyn Benoist ed., *La conscience du temps: Autour des Leçons sur le temps de Husserl,* Paris, Vrin, 2008, 95–116.

———. *There Is: The Event and the Finitude of Appearing,* trans. Michael Smith. New York: Fordham University Press, 2015.

———. " Une autre tradition sémantique? Heidegger, Bühler et l'ombre de Wittgenstein." *Po&sie,* no. 122 (2008): 191–225.

———. "Une phénoménologie du néant est-elle possible ?" *Il y a,* 295–344.

Rorty, Richard. "Book Review: Ernst Tugendhat, *Traditional and Analytical Philosophy,*" *The Journal of Philosophy,* 82 (1985): 720–29.

———. "Intuition." In *The Encyclopedia of Philosophy,* ed. Paul Edwards, vol. 4., 204–12. New York: Macmillan and Free Press, 1967.

———. *Philosophy and the Mirror of Nature.* Princeton, N.J.: Princeton University Press, 1979.

Rosen, Stanley. *The Limits of Analysis.* New York: Basic Books, 1980; reprint, South Bend, Ind.: St. Augustine's, 2000.

Russell, Bertrand. *Écrits de logique philosophique,* foreword and trans. Jean-Michel Roy. Paris: Presses Universitaires de France, 1989.

———. *An Inquiry into Meaning and Truth.* London: Allen and Unwin, 1940.

———. "On Denoting," In *Logic and Knowledge: Essays, 1901–1950,* ed. R. C. Marsh. London: Routledge, 2001.

———. *The Problems of Philosophy.* London: Oxford University Press, 1912.

Russell, Bertrand, Edmund Husserl, and Alexius Meinong. "Correspondance autour de la théorie de l'objet." French trans. Bastien Gallet. *Philosophie* 72 (2001): 3–35.

Ryle, Gilbert. "Phenomenology Versus The Concept of Mind." In *Critical Essays: Collected Papers Vol. 1,* chap. 11, 186–204. New York: Routledge, 2009.

Sanford, David H. "The Possibility of Transparent White." *Analysis* 44, no. 4 (October 1986): 212–15.

Sartre, Jean-Paul. *Being and Nothingness*, trans. Hazel E. Barnes. New York: Washington Square, 1992.

———. *Critical Essays (Situations I)*, trans. Chris Turner. London: Seagull Books, 2010.

———. "Intentionality: A Fundamental Idea of Husserl's Phenomenology," trans. Joseph P. Fell. *Journal of the British Society for Phenomenology* (1970–71): 4–5. Reprint in *Edmund Husserl: Critical Assessments of Leading Philosophers*, ed. R. Bernet, D. Welton, and G. Zavota, 257–59. New York: Routledge, 2005.

Schapp, Wilhelm. *Beiträge zur Phänomenologie der Wahrnehmung*. Frankfurt am Main: Klostermann, 1981.

Scheler, Max. *Der Formalismus in der Ethik und die materiale Wertethik*. In *Gesammelte Werke, Vol. II*. Bern: Francke Verlag, 1966. *Formalism in Ethics and Non-Formal Ethics of Values: A New Attempt Toward the Foundation of an Ethical Personalism*, trans. Manfred. S. Frings and Ronald L. Funk. Evanston, Ill.: Northwestern University Press, 1985.

———. *Die deutsche Philosophie der Gegenwart*. In *Gesammelte Werke, Vol. VII*, ed. M. S. Frings. Bern: Francke Verlag, 1973.

———. *Von Ewigen im Menschen*. In *Gesammelte Werke, Vol. V*, ed. Maria Scheler. Bern: Francke Verlag, 1954, [5th ed.] 1968.

Schlick, Moritz. "Form and Content: An Introduction to Philosophical Thinking." In *Gesammelte Aufsätze, 1926–1936*, 151–249. Vienna: Gerold, 1938.

———. "Gibt es ein materiales Apriori ?" In *Wissenschaftlicher Jahresbericht der Philosophischen Gesellschaft an der Universität zu Wien: Ortsgruppe Wien der Kant-Gesellschaft für das Vereinsjahr 1931/32*, 55–65. Vienna, 1932.

———. "Is There a Factual A Priori ?" In *Readings in Philosophical Analysis*, ed. Herbert Feigland and Wilfrid Sellars, 277–85. New York: Appleton Century Crofts, 1949; reprint, *Philosophical Papers, II, 1925–1936*, 161–70. Dordrecht: Reidel, 1979.

———. "Is There an Intuitive Knowledge?" ["Gibt es intuitive Erkenntnis?"]. Trans. Peter Heath, in *Philosophical Papers*, I, ed. Henk Mulder and Barbara van de Velde-Schlick, 141–52. Dordrecht: D. Reidel, 1979.

———. "On the Foundation of Knowledge," ["Über das Fundament der Erkenntnis"]. Trans. David Rynin, in A. J. Ayer, *Logical Positivism*, 209–27. New York: Free, 1959.

———. "The Turning Point in Philosophy" ["Die Wende der Philosophie"]. Trans. Peter Heath, in *Philosophical Papers, II, 1925–1936*, 154–60. Dordrecht: Reidel, 1979.

Schopenhauer, Arthur. *On Vision and Colors*, trans. Georg Stahl. New York: Princeton Architectural Press, 1910.

Searle, John Rogers. *Intentionality. An Essay in the Philosophy of Mind*. Cambridge, Mass.: Cambridge University Press, 1983.

Sellars, Wilfrid. "Empiricism and The Philosophy of Mind." In *Science, Perception and Reality*. London: Routledge and Kegan Paul, 1963 [4th ed.], 1971.

Sellars, Wilfrid, and Herbert Feigl, eds. *Readings in Philosophical Analysis*. New York: Appleton Century Crofts, 1949.

Simons, Peter. *Philosophy and Logic in Central Europe from Bolzano to Tarski.* The Hague, Martinus Nijhoff, 1992.

———. "Wittgenstein, Schlick and the A Priori." In *Philosophy and Logic in Central Europe from Bolzano to Tarski,* The Hague, Martinus Nijhoff, 1992, 361–76.

Sinnott-Armstrong, Walter, ed. *Modality: Morality and Belief.* Cambridge, Mass.: Cambridge University Press, 1995.

Sluga, Hans, and David G. Stern, eds. *The Cambridge Companion to Wittgenstein.* Cambridge, Mass.: Cambridge University Press, 1996.

Smith, Barry. "An Essay on Formal Ontology." *Grazer Philosophische Studien,* 6 (1978): 39–62.

———. "An Essay on Material Necessity." In Philip P. Hanson and Bruce Hunter, *Return of the A Priori,* Calgary: University of Calgary Press, 1992, 301–22.

———. "Introduction to A. Reinach, "On the Theory of Negative Judgements." In *Parts and Moments: Studies on Logic and Formal Ontology.* Munich: Philosophia Verlag, 1982.

———, ed. *Parts and Moments: Studies in Logic and Formal Ontology.* Munich: Philosophia Verlag, 1982.

———. "Towards a History of Speech Act Theory." In *Speech Acts, Meanings and Intentions: Critical Approaches to the Philosophy of John R. Searle,* ed. Armin Burkhardt, Berlin: New York: De Gruyter, 1990.

Smith, David Woodruff, and Ronald McIntyre. *Husserl and Intentionality.* Dordrecht: Reidel, 1982.

———. "Husserl's Identification of Meaning and Noema." In *Husserl, Intentionality and Cognitive Science,* ed. Hubert L. Dreyfus and Harrison Hall. Cambridge. Mass.: MIT Press, 1982.

Soffer, Gail. "Phenomenology and Scientific Realism: Husserl's Critique of Galileo." *Review of Metaphysics* 44, no. 1 (1990): 67–94.

Spiegelberg, Herbert. *The Phenomenological Movement. A Historical Introduction,* vol. 1. The Hague: Martinus Nijhoff, 1976.

Stern, Daniel N. *The Interpersonal World of the Infant.* New York: Basic Books, 1985.

Straus, Erwin. *The Primary World of the Senses: A Vindication of Sensory Experience,* trans. Jacob Needleman. New York: Free Press of Glencoe, 1963.

Stroud, Barry. "Transcendental Arguments." In *The Journal of Philosophy* 65, no. 9 (1968): 241–56.

Stumpf, Carl. *Renaissance de la philosophie: Quatre articles.* French trans. Denis Fisette. Paris: Vrin, 2006.

———. *Tonpsychologie, Vol. I.* Leipzig: S. Hirzel, 1883; reprint Amsterdam: Bonset, 1965.

———. *Tonpsychologie, Vol. II.* Leipzig: S. Hirzel, 1890; reprint Amsterdam: Bonset, 1965.

———. *Über den psychologischen Ursprung der Raumvorstellung.* Leipzig: S. Hirzel, 1873; reprint Amsterdam: Bonset, 1965.

———. "Zur Einteilung der Wissenschaften." In *Abhandlungen der Königlich-Preußischen Akademie der Wissenschaften,* 1–94. Berlin: Verlag der Königl. Akademie der Wissenschaften, 1906. French trans. Denis Fisette, "De la classification des sciences," in C. Stumpf, *Renaissance de la philosophie: Quatre articles*, 169–254. Paris: Vrin, 2006.

Taminiaux, Jacques. *Heidegger and the Project of Fundamental Ontology*. Trans. Michael Gendre. Albany: SUNY Press, 1991.

Taylor, Charles. *Human Agency and Language: Philosophical Papers I*. Cambridge, Eng.: Cambridge University Press, 1985.

———. *La liberté des modernes*, French trans. Philippe de Lara. Paris: Presses Universitaires de France, 1997.

———. "Merleau-Ponty and the Epistemological Picture." In *The Cambridge Companion to Merleau-Ponty*, ed. Taylor Carman and Mark Hansen.

———. *Philosophical Arguments*. Harvard University Press, 1995.

———. "The Validity of Transcendental Arguments." In *Philosophical Arguments*, 20–33.

———. "What Is Human Agency ?" In *Human Agency and Language*.

Thompson, Evan. *Colour Vision: A Study in Cognitive Science and the Philosophy of Perception*. London: Routledge, 1995.

Toulemont, René. *L'Essence de la société selon Husserl*. Paris: Presses Universitaires de France, 1962.

Tugendhat, Ernst. "Prefazione all'edizione italiana." In *Introduzione alla filosofia analitica*. Genoa: Casa Editrice Marietti, 1989.

———. *Selbstbewusstsein und Selbstbestimmung*. Frankfurt am Main: Suhrkamp, 1979. Trans. Paul Stern, *Self-Consciousness and Self-Determination*. Cambridge, Mass: MIT Press, 1986.

———. *Vorlesungen zur Einführung in die sprachanalytische Philosophie*. Frankfurt am Main: Suhrkamp, 1976. Trans. P. A. Gorner, *Traditional and Analytical Philosophy: Lectures on the Philosophy of Language*. Cambridge, Eng.: Cambridge University Press, 1982.

———. *Der Wahrheitsbegriff bei Husserl und Heidegger*. Berlin: De Gruyter, 1970.

Twardowski, Kazimierz, Christian von Ehrenfels, Edmund Husserl, Anton Marty, Alexius Meinong, and Carl Stumpf. *À l'École de Brentano: De Würzbourg à Vienne*, French trans. and ed. Denis Fisette and Guillaume Fréchette. Paris: Vrin, 2007.

Wagner, Pierre, and Christian Bonnet. *L'Âge d'or de l'empirisme logique: Vienne-Berlin-Prague 1929–1936*. Paris: Gallimard, coll. Bibliothèque de Philosophie, 2006.

Welton, Donn, ed. *The New Husserl: A Critical Reader*. Indianapolis: Indiana University Press, 2003.

Westphal, Jonathan. *Colour: A Philosophical Introduction*. Oxford: Basil Blackwell, 1987.

Wittgenstein, Ludwig. *Bemerkungen über die Farben*. Trans. Linda L. McAlister and Margaret Schättle, *Remarks on Colour*, ed. G. E. M. Anscombe. Oxford: Blackwell, 1998 (1977).

———. *Bemerkungen über die Grundlagen der Mathematik*. In *Werkausgabe*, vol. 6, ed. Elizabeth Anscombe, Rush Rhees, and Georg Henrik von Wright. Frankfurt am Main: Suhrkamp, 1984. *Remarks on the Foundations of Mathe-*

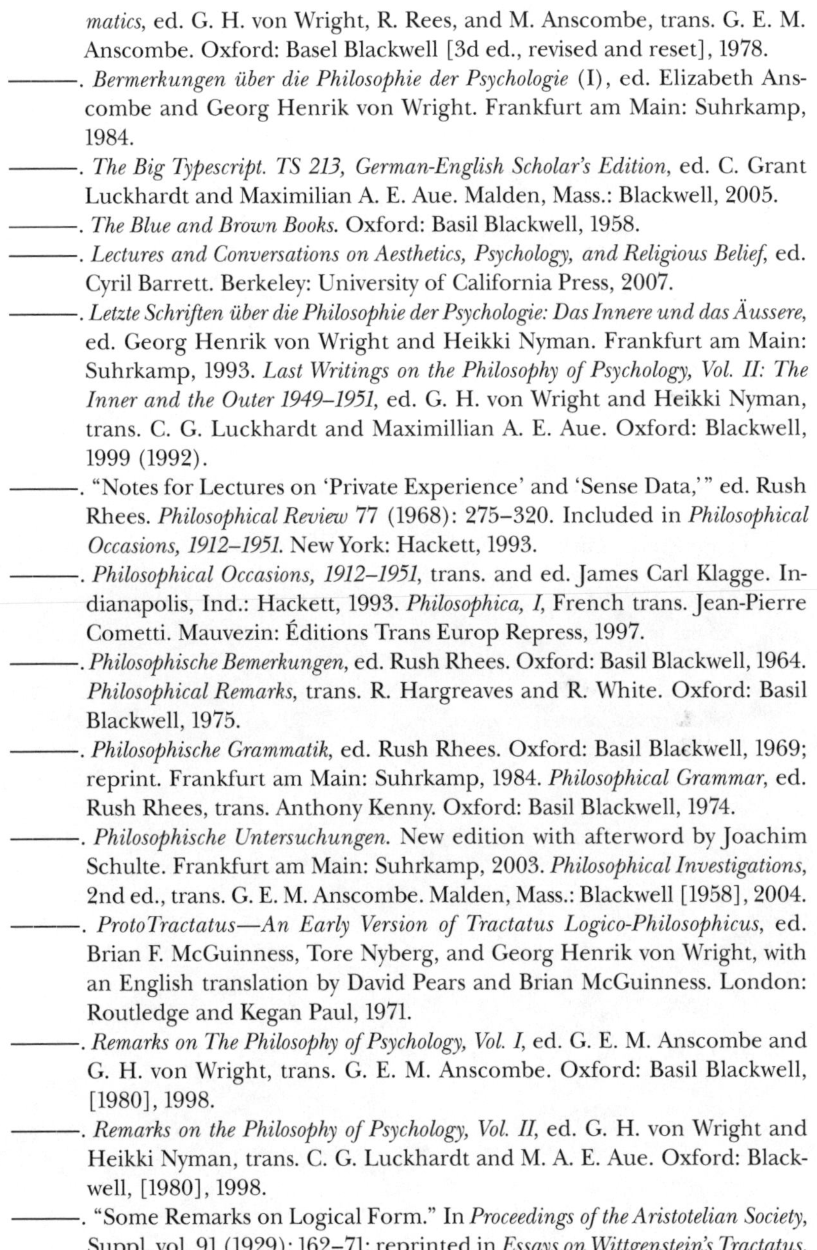

matics, ed. G. H. von Wright, R. Rees, and M. Anscombe, trans. G. E. M. Anscombe. Oxford: Basel Blackwell [3d ed., revised and reset], 1978.

———. *Bermerkungen über die Philosophie der Psychologie* (I), ed. Elizabeth Anscombe and Georg Henrik von Wright. Frankfurt am Main: Suhrkamp, 1984.

———. *The Big Typescript. TS 213, German-English Scholar's Edition*, ed. C. Grant Luckhardt and Maximilian A. E. Aue. Malden, Mass.: Blackwell, 2005.

———. *The Blue and Brown Books*. Oxford: Basil Blackwell, 1958.

———. *Lectures and Conversations on Aesthetics, Psychology, and Religious Belief*, ed. Cyril Barrett. Berkeley: University of California Press, 2007.

———. *Letzte Schriften über die Philosophie der Psychologie: Das Innere und das Äussere*, ed. Georg Henrik von Wright and Heikki Nyman. Frankfurt am Main: Suhrkamp, 1993. *Last Writings on the Philosophy of Psychology, Vol. II: The Inner and the Outer 1949–1951*, ed. G. H. von Wright and Heikki Nyman, trans. C. G. Luckhardt and Maximillian A. E. Aue. Oxford: Blackwell, 1999 (1992).

———. "Notes for Lectures on 'Private Experience' and 'Sense Data,'" ed. Rush Rhees. *Philosophical Review* 77 (1968): 275–320. Included in *Philosophical Occasions, 1912–1951*. New York: Hackett, 1993.

———. *Philosophical Occasions, 1912–1951*, trans. and ed. James Carl Klagge. Indianapolis, Ind.: Hackett, 1993. *Philosophica, I*, French trans. Jean-Pierre Cometti. Mauvezin: Éditions Trans Europ Repress, 1997.

———. *Philosophische Bemerkungen*, ed. Rush Rhees. Oxford: Basil Blackwell, 1964. *Philosophical Remarks*, trans. R. Hargreaves and R. White. Oxford: Basil Blackwell, 1975.

———. *Philosophische Grammatik*, ed. Rush Rhees. Oxford: Basil Blackwell, 1969; reprint. Frankfurt am Main: Suhrkamp, 1984. *Philosophical Grammar*, ed. Rush Rhees, trans. Anthony Kenny. Oxford: Basil Blackwell, 1974.

———. *Philosophische Untersuchungen*. New edition with afterword by Joachim Schulte. Frankfurt am Main: Suhrkamp, 2003. *Philosophical Investigations*, 2nd ed., trans. G. E. M. Anscombe. Malden, Mass.: Blackwell [1958], 2004.

———. *ProtoTractatus—An Early Version of Tractatus Logico-Philosophicus*, ed. Brian F. McGuinness, Tore Nyberg, and Georg Henrik von Wright, with an English translation by David Pears and Brian McGuinness. London: Routledge and Kegan Paul, 1971.

———. *Remarks on The Philosophy of Psychology, Vol. I*, ed. G. E. M. Anscombe and G. H. von Wright, trans. G. E. M. Anscombe. Oxford: Basil Blackwell, [1980], 1998.

———. *Remarks on the Philosophy of Psychology, Vol. II*, ed. G. H. von Wright and Heikki Nyman, trans. C. G. Luckhardt and M. A. E. Aue. Oxford: Blackwell, [1980], 1998.

———. "Some Remarks on Logical Form." In *Proceedings of the Aristotelian Society*, Suppl. vol. 91 (1929): 162–71; reprinted in *Essays on Wittgenstein's Tractatus*, ed. Irving M. Copi and Robert W. Bread. 31–38. London: Routledge and Kegan, 1966.

———. *Tagebücher 1914–1916.* Frankfurt am Main: Suhrkamp, 1984. Trans. G. E. M. Anscombe, *Notebooks 1914–1916.* Oxford: Blackwell, 1979.

———. *Tractatus Logico-Philosophicus.* New Jersey: Humanities, 1974.

———. *Über Gewissheit,* ed. Elizabeth Anscombe and Georg Henrik von Wright. Oxford: Basil Blackwell, 1969. *On Certainty,* ed. G. E. M. Anscombe and G. H. von Wright. London: Blackwell, 1969.

———. *Vermischte Bemerkungen,* ed. Georg Henrik von Wright. Frankfurt am Main: Suhrkamp, 1977. *Culture and Value,* revised 3rd ed. by P. Winch. London: Blackwell, 1998.

———. *The Voices of Wittgenstein: The Vienna Circle,* ed. Gordon Baker with Brian McGuinness. London: Routledge, 2003. *Dictées de Wittgenstein à Waismann et pour Schlick,* ed. Antonia Soulez, vol. I: *Textes inédits,* vol. II: *Études critiques.* Paris: Presses Universitaires de France, 1997

———. *Werkausgabe in 8 Bänden.* Frankfurt am Main: Suhrkamp, 1984–89.

———. *Wiener Ausgabe/Vienna Edition,* volumes 1–5, ed. Michael Nedo. Vienna: Springer Verlag, 1994–96.

———. *Wittgenstein und der Wiener Kreis.* Frankfurt am Main: Suhrkamp, 1984. Friedrich Waismann, *Wittgenstein and the Vienna Circle: Conversations Recorded by Friedrich Waismann,* ed. Brian McGuinness, trans. Joachim Schulte. Oxford: Blackwell, 1983.

———. *Wittgenstein's Lectures, Cambridge 1930–1932: From the Notes of John King and Desmond Lee,* ed. Desmond Lee. Oxford: Blackwell, 1980.

———. *Wittgenstein's Lectures, Cambridge, 1932–35.* Oxford: Basil Blackwell, 1979.

———. *Wittgenstein's Lectures on the Foundations of Mathematics.* Cambridge, 1939. Ed. Cora Diamond, based on the notes of R. G. Bosanquet, N. Malcolm, R. Rhees, and Y. Smythies. Ithaca, N.Y.: Cornell University Press, 1976.

———. *Zettel,* ed. Elizabeth Anscombe and Georg Henrik von Wright. Berkeley: University of California Press, 2007.

Wrathall, Mark A. "Motives, Reasons and Causes." In *The Cambridge Companion to Merleau-Ponty,* ed. Taylor Carman and Mark B. N. Hansen. New York: Cambridge University Press, 2005.

Wright, Georg Henrik von. *Explanation and Understanding.* Ithaca, N.Y.: Cornell University Press, 1971.

Zahavi, Dan. "Husserl's Intersubjective Transformation of Transcendental Philosophy." In *The New Husserl: A Critical Reader,* ed. Donn Welton. Indianapolis: Indiana University Press, 2003.

Index

CLAUDE ROMANO teaches at the University of Paris-Sorbonne and the Australian Catholic University. His publications include *L'Événement et le monde* (1998), translated by Shane Mackinlay as *Event and World* (2009), *L'Événement et le temps* (1999), translated by Stephen E. Lewis as *Event and Time* (2013), *Il y a* (2003), translated by Michael Smith as *There Is: The Event and the Finitude of Appearing* (2015), *Le chant de la vie: Phénoménologie de Faulkner* (2005), and *L'Aventure temporelle* (2010). In 2010 he received the Grand Prix Morton of the Académie Française for his whole work in phenomenology, and in 2011 the Prix Gegner of the Académie des Sciences Morales et Politiques for the present book.

MICHAEL B. SMITH is a professor emeritus of French and philosophy at Berry College in Georgia; he has translated numerous philosophical works into English.